AF655022

R. Gupta's®

Popular Master Guide

SSC

Staff Selection Commission

Constable (GD)

Central Armed Police Forces (CAPFs), NIA, SSF & Rifleman (Assam Rifles)

Recruitment Exam

by

RPH Editorial Board

2027
EDITION

RAMESH PUBLISHING HOUSE, NEW DELHI

USEFUL BOOK FOR THIS EXAM

SSC-Constanble (GD)

CAPFs, NIA & SSF & Rifleman (Assam Fifles)

Previous Years' Papers & Practice Test Papers

(With Answers)

Book Code : R-1909 ❍ Price : ₹ 210 ❍ ISBN : 978-93-87918-43-6

For Online Shopping: www.rameshpublishinghouse.com

Published by

O.P. Gupta *for* Ramesh Publishing House

Admin. Office

12-H, New Daryaganj Road, Opp. Officers' Mess,
New Delhi-110002 ✆ 23275224, 23245124

E-mail: info@rameshpublishinghouse.com
For Online Shopping: www.rameshpublishinghouse.com

Showroom

• Balaji Market, Nai Sarak, Delhi-110006 ✆ 23282525 📱 9354373464
• 4457, Nai Sarak, Delhi-110006

© Reserved with the Publisher

No Part of this book may be reproduced or transmitted in any form or by any means, electronic or mechanical including photocopying, recording or by any transformation storage and retrieval system without written permission from the Publisher.

Indemnification Clause: This book is being sold/distributed subject to the exclusive condition that neither the author nor the publishers, individually or collectively, shall be responsible to indemnify the buyer/user/possessor of this book beyond the selling price of this book for any reason under any circumstances. If you do not agree to it, please do not buy/accept/use/possess this book.

Book Code: R-1394

ISBN: 978-93-5012-093-4

Price: ₹ 410

Printed by : Repro India Ltd.

CONTENTS

Previous Year Paper, 2025 (Exam held on 04 February, 2025) 1-20

Previous Year Paper, 2024 (Exam held on 07 March, 2024) 1-16

Previous Year Paper, 2023 (Exam held on 13 February, 2023) 1-12

Previous Year Paper, 2021 1-12

Previous Year Paper, 2019 1-12

Previous Year Paper, 2015 1-12

Previous Year Paper, 2013 13-23

Previous Year Paper, 2012 24-34

Previous Year Paper, 2011 35-44

- **GENERAL INTELLIGENCE & REASONING** 1-120

  Letter Series; Wrong Letter Series; Repeat Series; Number Series; Wrong Number Series; Word Analogy; Number Analogy; Odd One Out; Coding and Decoding; Statement Analysis; Place Arrangement; Direction Sense; Blood Relationships; Arranging in Order; Calendar, Clock & Time; Rows and Ranks; Common Property; Symbol Substitution; Missing Numbers; Matrices; Alphabet Problems; Logical Diagram; Syllogism; Venn Diagrams; Diagrammatic Puzzle; Non-Verbal Series; Non-Verbal Analogy; Odd Man Out; Completing an Incomplete Pattern; Spotting Hidden Pattern; Components of Figures; Lateral Inversion; Folded or Unfolded Pattern; Mirror Images.

- **ELEMENTARY MATHEMATICS** 1-76

  Numbers; HCF and LCM; Simplification; Surds and Indices; Ratio and Proportion; Partnership; Average; Profit and Loss; Simple and Compound Interest; Time and Work; Area and Perimeter; Volume and Surface Area; Data Interpretation.

- **ENGLISH** 1-48

  Comprehension Passages; English Grammar; Sentence Completion; Spotting Errors; One Word Substitution; Spelling Errors.

- **GENERAL KNOWLEDGE & GENERAL AWARENESS** 1-88

  The Universe; World Geography; Our India; Indian History; Indian Constitution & Polity; Planning In India; National Symbols; General Science; Space Research; Computers; United Nations Organisation; First in India; Cultural Activities; Awards; Sports; National/International Days; Multiple Choice Questions.

MODE OF SELECTION

1. The recruitment process will consist of Computer Based Examination (CBE), Physical Efficiency Test (PET), Physical Standard Test (PST) and Medical Examination.
2. All candidates whose online application are found to be in order will be called to appear in the Computer Based Examination. The Commission will conduct the examination for all candidates in Computer Based Mode only. Admit Cards for Computer Based Examination will be uploaded on the website of the concerned SSC Regional office.
3. Computer Based Examination will be held in English & Hindi only.
4. The number of candidates shortlisted for PET/PST on the basis of merit in the Computer Based Examination will be around 8 (Eight) times of the number of vacancies.

SCHEME OF COMPUTER BASED EXAMINATION

The Computer based examination will consist of one Objective Type Paper containing 80 questions carrying 2 marks each, with the following composition:

	Subject	**Number of Questions**	**Maximum Marks**
Part-A	General Intelligence and Reasoning	20	40
Part-B	General Knowledge and General Awareness	20	40
Part-C	Elementary Mathematics	20	40
Part-D	English/Hindi	20	40

Note:
- All questions will be of Objective Multiple Choice Type.
- The Computer Based Examination will be conducted in English and Hindi only.
- The duration of test will be 60 minutes.

Previous Years' Paper

SSC-CONSTABLE (GD)

CAPF, NIA, SSF and RIFLEMAN, EXAM-2025

(Exam held on 04-02-2025)

PART-A : GENERAL INTELLIGENCE AND REASONING

1. In a certain code language, 'BSGN' is coded as '5-22-10-17' and 'TAUE' is coded as '23-4-24-8'. How is 'PJDQ' coded in the given language?

1. 15-11-5-19
2. 19-13-7-20
3. 16-12-8-18
4. 17-13-6-20

2. Select the Venn diagram that best illustrates the relationship among the following classes.

Female, Cardiologist, Engineer

1. 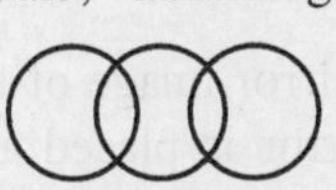   2. 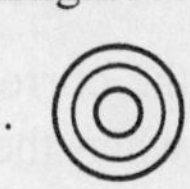

3. 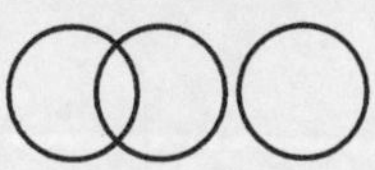   4. 

3. Based on the English alphabetical order, three of the following four letter-clusters are alike in a certain way and thus form a group. Which letter-cluster DOES NOT belong to that group?

(Note: The odd man out is not based on the number of consonants/vowels or their position in the letter-cluster.)

1. HJL   2. SUV
3. FHJ   4. NPR

4. A dice has its faces marked by letters E, R, A, L, O and T. Two positions of the same dice are shown in the given figures. Which face is opposite to face E?

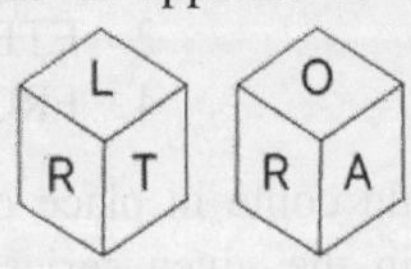

1. L   2. A
3. O   4. R

5. In a certain code language, 'JAMB' is coded as '5139' and 'BALM' is coded as '9521'. What is the code for 'L' in the given code language?

1. 5   2. 9
3. 2   4. 1

6. Based on some logic, 'CLONE' is written as 'BLUKU' and 'BOUND' is written as 'AOAKT'. Following the same logic, 'NICHE' can be written as:

1. NIIET   2. MIIET
3. MIIEU   4. NIIEU

7. What should come in place of the question mark (?) in the given series?

208, 190, 163, 127, 82, ?

1. 28   2. 54
3. 45   4. 12

1. 2	**2.** 1	**3.** 2	**4.** 4	**5.** 3	**6.** 3	**7.** 1

8. Seven people L, M, N, O, P, Q and R are sitting in a straight line facing the north (but not necessarily in the same order). M is sitting to the immediate left of P. O is sitting to the immediate left of Q. R is sitting to the immediate right of P and the immediate left of L. N is sitting to the immediate right of L and the immediate left of O. Who is sitting second to the left of N?

1. P 2. Q
3. R 4. M

9. SBCF is related to RADG in a certain way. In the same way, NVMO is related to MUNP. To which of the following is GUAX related, following the same logic?

1. FTBZ 2. FTBY
3. FTCY 4. FRCY

10. What should come in place of the question mark (?) in the given series based on the English alphabetical order?

EHO, HJP, KLQ, ?, QPS

1. MMR 2. MNR
3. NMR 4. NNR

11. The sequence of folding a piece of paper and the manner in which the folded paper is cut is shown in the following figures. How would this paper look when unfolded?

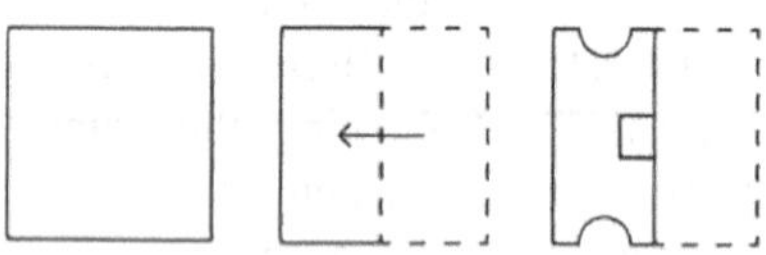

1.  2. 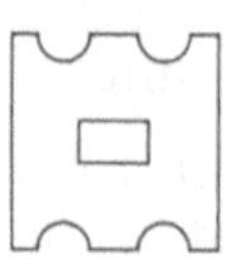

3. 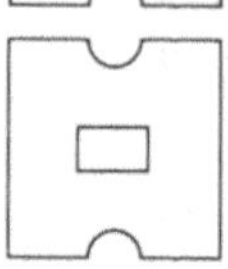 4. 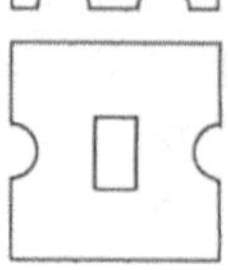

12. The position(s) of how many letters will remain unchanged if each letter in the word GRACEFUL is arranged in the English alphabetical order?

1. Two 2. None
3. One 4. Three

13. Read the given statements and conclusions carefully. Assuming that the information given in the statements is true, even if it appears to be at variance with commonly known facts, decide which of the given conclusions logically follow(s) from the statements.

Statements:

All gabions are walls.
All concretes are walls.
All bridges are walls.

Conclusions:

I. Some bridges are gabions.
II. Some concretes are bridges.

1. Neither conclusion (I) nor (II) follows
2. Only conclusion (I) follows
3. Both conclusions (I) and (II) follow
4. Only conclusion (II) follows

14. Select the correct mirror image of the given figure when the mirror is placed at MN as shown below.

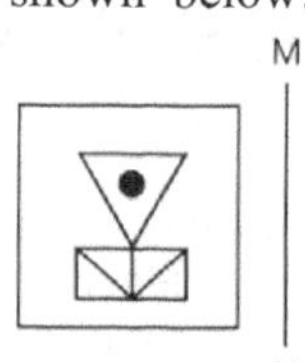

1. 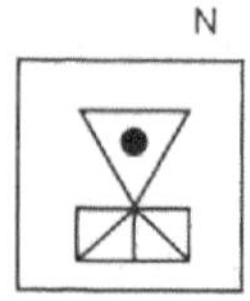 2. 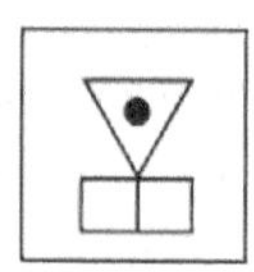

3. 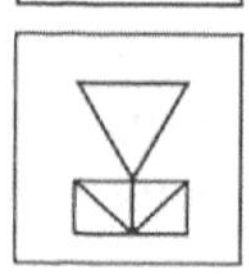 4. 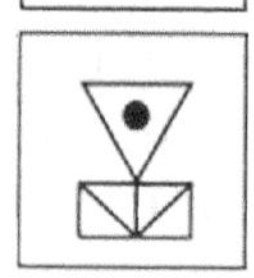

8. 3	**9.** 2	**10.** 4	**11.** 2	**12.** 2	**13.** 1	**14.** 4

15. What will come in the place of the question mark '(?)' in the following equation, if '÷' and '×' are interchanged and '+' and '–' are interchanged?

50 – 9 ÷ 1 + 63 × 7 = ?

1. 53 2. 52
3. 51 4. 50

16. Identify the figure given in the options which when put in place of the question mark (?) will logically complete the series.

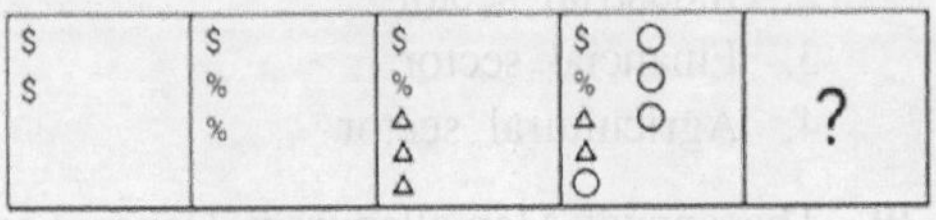

1. 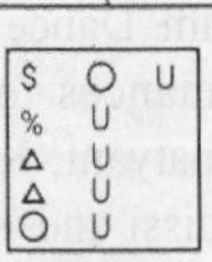 2. 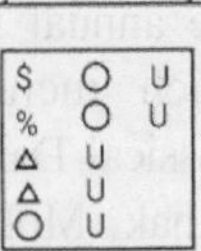

3. 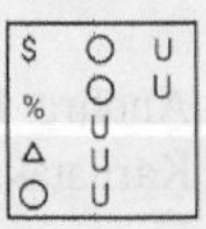 4. 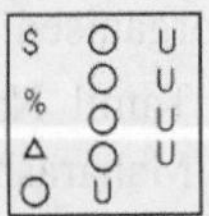

17. Select the combination of letters that when sequentially placed in the blanks of the given series will make the series logically complete.

_HKM O_NP RN_S UQT_ XTW_

1. JKRVX 2. LMQUY
3. LKQVY 4. JMRUX

18. What should come in place of the question mark (?) in the given series?

4, 6, 10, 18, 34, ?

1. 67 2. 65
3. 68 4. 66

19. Eight people are sitting in two parallel rows containing 4 people each in such a way that there is equal distance between adjacent persons.

In row 1, D, E, O and S are seated and all of them are facing south.

In row 2, F, A, R and M are seated and all of them are facing north.

Thus, each person faces another person from the other row.

Only D sits to the left of E. Only R sits to the left of A. Only one person sits between A and F. Only one person sits between D and O.

Which of the following represents both people facing each other?

1. E and A 2. E and R
3. E and M 4. E and F

20. In a certain code language.

'X @ C' means 'X is the daughter of C',

'X $ C' means 'X is the husband of C',

'X = C' means 'X is the mother of C' and

'X * C' means 'X is the father of C'.

Based on the above, how is J related to N if 'N @ E $ J @ S'?

1. Daughter's son
2. Sister's daughter
3. Sister
4. Mother

PART-B : GENERAL KNOWLEDGE AND GENERAL AWARENESS

21. Pradhan Mantri Rojgar Protsahan Yojana is being implemented since ______.

1. 2015 2. 2014
3. 2017 4. 2016

22. Where were the first Asian Games held in India?

1. New Delhi 2. Gwalior
3. Chennai 4. Patiala

15. 4 **16.** 2 **17.** 3 **18.** 4 **19.** 3 **20.** 4 **21.** 4 **22.** 1

23. In August 2024, who bid farewell to the Supreme Court, became the first woman Chief Justice of the High Court for the State of Telangana and was the ninth woman to be elevated to the Supreme Court of India?

1. Aditi Kapoor
2. Hima Kohli
3. Kutti Rameshwaram
4. Usha Iyer

24. Which of the following sports was included as a discipline in the 11th Asian Games Beijing 1990?

1. Wrestling 2. Kabaddi
3. Volleyball 4. Squash

25. Which are the two wettest places on Earth that receive more than 1,080 cm of rainfall in a year?

1. Pasighat and Agumbe
2. Gangtok and Amboli
3. Cherrapunji and Mawsynram
4. Mahabaleshwar and Neriamangalam

26. As per National Multidimentional Poverty Index of India: A Progress Review 2023, which of the following union territories has the highest percentage of multidimensionally poor?

1. Chandigarh
2. Delhi
3. Dadra and Nagar Haveli & Daman and Diu
4. Puducherry

27. What is the penalty amount specified under the Public Examinations (Prevention of Unfair Means) Bill, 2024, for individuals involved in unfair practices or offenses during exams?

1. Up to one lakh rupees
2. Up to twenty lakh rupees
3. Up to eleven lakh rupees
4. Up to ten lakh rupees

28. Which Articles of the Constitution of India deals with the Union Public Service Commission?

1. Articles 300 to 320
2. Articles 330 to 338
3. Articles 210 to 219
4. Articles 315 to 323

29. Which sector of the economy does the Green Revolution belong to?

1. Service sector
2. Industrial sector
3. Financial sector
4. Agricultural sector

30. The annual Mamallapuram Dance Festival, which includes performances of Indian Classical Dances Bharatanatyam, Kuchipudi, Kathak, Mohiniattam, Odissi and Kathakali, is organised in _____.

1. Tamil Nadu 2. Andhra Pradesh
3. Maharashtra 4. Karnataka

31. Which of the following sentences is/are true?

(*i*) The projected growth rate of the Indian agriculture sector for FY 2022-23 was 5.5%.

(*ii*) During the Financial Year 2021-22, agricultural exports of India reached to about US$ 50.2 billion.

(*iii*) During Kharif Marketing Season 2021-22, 581.7 lakh metric tons of rice was procured in India.

1. Only (*i*) and (*ii*) 2. Only (*ii*) and (*iii*)
3. Only (*i*) 4. Only (*ii*)

32. Lakshmi Vishwanathan, who won the prestigious Natya Kalanidhi Award from the Music Academy was famous for which dance form?

1. Kuchipudi 2. Odissi
3. Kathak 4. Bharatanatyam

23. 2 **24.** 2 **25.** 3 **26.** 3 **27.** 4 **28.** 4 **29.** 4 **30.** 1 **31.** 2 **32.** 4

33. What was the major economic challenge addressed in the Third Five-Year Plan (1961-1966)?

1. Liberalisation of the economy
2. Introduction of the service sector
3. Focus on digital technology advancement
4. War-time expenditure and resource allocation

34. 2nd October 2022 marked the ________ birth anniversary of Mahatma Gandhi, celebrated as Gandhi Jayanti.

1. 153rd   2. 150th
3. 152nd   4. 155th

35. The NBPW, which can be considered as the most widespread Iron Age pottery, stands for ________.

1. Northern Blue Polished Ware
2. Northern Brown Polished Ware
3. Northern Black Polished Ware
4. Northern Bronze Polished Ware

36. Part III of the Constitution of India stated about which of the following?

1. Directive Principles of States Policy
2. Fundamental Duties
3. Citizenship
4. Fundamental Rights

37. Which of the following plants can be made to climb walls using special support?

1. Sunflower Plant
2. Lemon plant
3. Rose plant
4. Pumpkin plant

38. Who were the key figures behind the recommendations that formed the basis of the Government of India Act, 1919?

1. Lord Linlithgow and Edwin Montagu
2. Lord Irwin and Edwin Montagu
3. Lord Chelmsford and Edwin Montagu
4. Lord Curzon and Edwin Montagu

39. When did Michael Faraday discover electromagnetic induction, the principle behind the electric transformer and generator?

1. 1853   2. 1820
3. 1875   4. 1831

40. She was a Carnatic legendary singer who sang in Europe, North America and at the United Nations General Assembly. Who was she?

1. Beghum Akhtar
2. Lata Mangeshkar
3. Asha Bhosle
4. Madurai Shanmukhavadivu Subbulakshmi

PART-C : ELEMENTARY MATHEMATICS

41. The LCM of 28, 60, 120 and 135 is:

1. 7626   2. 7560
3. 7608   4. 7569

42. In an examination, there were three papers of Mathematics, two papers of English and one paper of Science. All papers were of 100 marks. S got 60% in Mathematics, 70% in English and 50% in Science. What was his percentage of marks in all papers?

1. 61.33%   2. 60.67%
3. 61.67%   4. 60%

43. A number is first decreased by 15% and then increased by 20%. The number so obtained is 78 more than the original number. The original number is:

1. 3900   2. 2600
3. 4500   4. 5200

44. If at same rate of interest, in 2 years, the simple interest is ₹ 42 and compound interest is ₹ 51, then what is the principal (in ₹)?

1. 44   2. 49
3. 42   4. 53

33. 4 **34.** 1 **35.** 3 **36.** 4 **37.** 4 **38.** 3 **39.** 4 **40.** 4 **41.** 2 **42.** 3 **43.** 1 **44.** 2

45. Mandar has two grandsons Ketan and Tushar. 11 year old Ketan gets some money from Mandar's wealth and 12 year old Tushar gets rest of the money. But Ketan and Tushar will get money only when they turn 22 years old. Till then the money is in a bank getting interest at rate 8% compounded annually. When both turn 22, they receive the same amount. How much had Mandar given Tushar (in ₹) initially, if total money with Mandar was ₹ 24700?

1. 11625 2. 13175
3. 12825 4. 11875

46. What is the cost price of an article which is sold for ₹ 1,566 with 8% profit?

1. ₹ 1,420 2. ₹ 1,390
3. ₹ 1,450 4. ₹ 1,400

47. Two numbers are in the ratio of 4 : 9. If the mean proportional between them is 24, find the positive difference between the two numbers.

1. 30 2. 25
3. 15 4. 20

48. Two trains having lengths of 210 m and 140 m are running at speeds of 80 km/h and 150 km/h, respectively, in the same direction. The time taken (in minutes) by the faster train, coming from behind, to completely cross the other train is:

1. 2 2. 0.3
3. 0.5 4. 1

49. The price (per litre) of petrol increases by 85%. By what percent should its consumption be reduced such that the expenditure on it increases by 48% only?

1. 18% 2. 82%
3. 20% 4. 80%

50. A can do a piece of work in 32 days and B in 48 days. They work together for 8 days and then A goes away. In how much time (in days) will B finish the 60% of the remaining work?

1. $18\frac{2}{5}$ 2. $19\frac{3}{4}$
3. $16\frac{4}{5}$ 4. $17\frac{3}{7}$

51. Find the value of

$$\left[(48 \div 8) \times \left\{\frac{49}{7} + \frac{40}{4} \times (7-3)\right\}\right]$$

1. 282 2. 286
3. 284 4. 273

52. Determine the largest four-digit number that is exactly divisible by 15, 25, 40, and 75.

1. 9600 2. 9975
3. 9999 4. 9960

53. Two cones have their heights in the ratio 4 : 3 and the radii of their bases in the ratio 1 : 2. Find the ratio of their volumes.

1. 4 : 9 2. 1 : 3
3. 2 : 9 4. 2 : 5

54. A dishonest shopkeeper promises to sell his goods at cost price. However, he uses a weight that actually weighs 46% less than what is written on it. Find his profit percentage.

1. $87\frac{10}{27}\%$ 2. $85\frac{5}{27}\%$
3. $84\frac{5}{27}\%$ 4. $86\frac{6}{27}\%$

55. The average weight of Gopal, Akshay and Atul is 46 kg. If the average weight of Gopal and Akshay be 40 kg and that of Akshay and Atul be 45 kg, then the weight of Akshay (in kg) is:

1. 47 2. 42
3. 32 4. 52

45. 3 **46.** 3 **47.** 4 **48.** 2 **49.** 3 **50.** 3 **51.** 1 **52.** 1 **53.** 2 **54.** 2 **55.** 3

56. A student was getting the following four offers on the purchase of a book:

I. Two successive discounts of 20% and 20%
II. Two successive discounts of 25% and 15%
III. Two successive discounts of 30% and 10%
IV. Two successive discounts of 5% and 35%

Which scheme offers the most discount to the student?

1. III 2. II
3. IV 4. I

57. A man goes to Ahmedabad from Kolkata at a speed of 9 km/hr and returns to Kolkata at speed of 18 km/hr, through same route. What is his average speed (in km/hr) of the entire journey?

1. 8 2. 12
3. 17 4. 15

58. Vipul invests a sum of ₹ 5400 and Vijay invests a sum of ₹ 9400 at the same rate of simple interest per annum. If, at the end of 5 years, Vijay gets ₹ 840 more interest than Vipul, then find the rate of interest per annum (in percentage).

1. 6.2 2. 3.2
3. 2.2 4. 4.2

59. The HCF of two numbers is 11 and their sum is 132. If both the numbers are greater than 42, then the difference between the two numbers is:

1. 18 2. 22
3. 26 4. 11

60. What is the third proportional to 16 and 48?

1. 144 2. 121
3. 169 4. 135

PART-D : ENGLISH

61. The following sentence has been split into four segments. Identify the segment that contains a grammatical error.

(A) He spoke passionately about his favourite book, / (B) articulating his thoughts clear / (C) and engaging everyone in a lively discussion / (D) about its themes.

1. C 2. D
3. A 4. B

62. Select the most appropriate option to fill in the blank.

Grey _____ is no sure sign of attaining wisdom.

1. heir 2. air
3. hare 4. hair

63. Select the most appropriate option to fill in the blank.

The dog ran _____ the garden chasing the cat.

1. at 2. on
3. between 4. across

64. Select the most appropriate option to fill in the blank.

It is a sin against God and humanity to _______ places of religious worship.

1. modest 2. desecrate
3. disapprove 4. upright

65. Select the correct collocation to fill in the blank.

The teacher gave the students _____ instructions before the exam.

1. careful 2. great
3. strong 4. clear

66. Select the most appropriate ANTONYM of the given word.

Arrogant

1. Creepy 2. Clumsy
3. Average 4. Humble

56. 3 **57.** 2 **58.** 4 **59.** 2 **60.** 1 **61.** 4 **62.** 4 **63.** 4 **64.** 2 **65.** 4 **66.** 4

67. Select the most appropriate synonym of the given word.

Broad

1. Particular
2. Small
3. Wide
4. Exact

68. Select the most appropriate meaning of the given idiom.

Man of straw

1. A combination of two people that is perfect in every way
2. A child of a celebrity or a famous person
3. A person who is disregarded as lacking character or morality
4. A situation like a close contest

69. Select the most appropriate option to fill in the blank.

We will complete the project ________ without external help.

1. oneself
2. ourselves
3. itself
4. themselves

70. Select the most appropriate ANTONYM of the given word.

Flaunt

1. Parade
2. Hide
3. Wide
4. Open

71. Identify the sentence with the INCORRECTLY spelt word.

1. The film was praised for its stunning cinematography.
2. The scientist presented his findings at the conference.
3. The students wrote an interesting essey on the topic.
4. The bakery makes delicious pastries every day.

72. Select the most appropriate idiom that can substitute the underlined segment in the given sentence.

When it comes to cooking, she can really think <u>creatively and unconventionally</u> to create unique dishes that surprise everyone.

1. outside the wire
2. outside the canvas
3. outside the box
4. outside the law

73. Select the most appropriate ANTONYM of the word in brackets to fill in the blank.

The widespread ____________________ (destruction) of the natural world threatens the food we eat, the water we drink and the air we breathe.

1. contribution
2. creation
3. choice
4. condition

74. The following sentence has been divided into parts. One of them may contain an error. Select the part that contains the error from the given options. If you don't find any error, mark 'No error' as your answer.

Alka had been writing / to her boss until she realises / that he was not interested in resolving her issues.

1. that he was not interested in resolving her issues
2. No error
3. to her boss until she realises
4. Alka had been writing

75. Select the option that rectifies the underlined spelling error.

The students had to write an essay for their <u>asignment.</u>

1. assignmant
2. assignment
3. essignment
4. asignmant

67. 3	**68.** 3	**69.** 2	**70.** 2	**71.** 3	**72.** 3	**73.** 2	**74.** 3	**75.** 2

Directions (Qs. No. 76-80): *In the following passage, some words have been deleted. Read the passage carefully and select the most appropriate option to fill in each blank.*

There is a (1)______ sense of freedom about being alone in a carriage that is jolting noisily through the night. It is liberty unrestrained in a very (2)______ form. You can do anything you like. You can talk to (3)______ as loud as you please and no one will hear you. You can have that argument out with Jones and roll him triumphantly in the dust (4)______ fear of a counterstroke. You can stand on your head and no one will see you. You can sing or dance a two-step or practise a golf stroke, (5)______ play marbles on the floor without let or hindrance.

76. Select the most appropriate option to fill in blank no. 1.

1. pleasant 2. contemptuous
3. tedious 4. baleful

77. Select the most appropriate option to fill in blank no. 2.

1. miserable 2. agreeable
3. humour 4. detestable

78. Select the most appropriate option to fill in blank no. 3.

1. yourself 2. ourselves
3. herself 4. himself

79. Select the most appropriate option to fill in blank no. 4.

1. in 2. with
3. for 4. without

80. Select the most appropriate option to fill in blank no. 5.

1 yet 2. but
3. or 4. because

EXPLANATORY ANSWERS

1. To find the code, observe the letter-position transformation in the given example BSGN → 5-22-10-17. Each alphabetical position increases by +3.

Step 1: Write alphabetical positions

B = 2,
S = 19,
G = 7,
N = 14

Step 2: Apply the rule (+3)

2 + 3 = 5
19 + 3 = 22
7 + 3 = 10
14 + 3 = 17

Thus, the pattern is confirmed.

Step 3: Apply this to PJDQ

P = 16 → 16 + 3 = 19
J = 10 → 10 + 3 = 13
D = 4 → 4 + 3 = 7
Q = 17 → 17 + 3 = 20

Therefore, the correct coded form is 19-13-7-20.

2. Female, Cardiologist and Engineer categories can overlap in all combinations. A woman may be both a cardiologist and an engineer simultaneously, or may belong to any subset of the three.

Thus, the sets must have a region of triple intersection.

Only diagram 1 contains a shared overlapping region among all three circles, representing the full logical relationship where all combinations (single, double and triple membership) are possible.

76. 1 **77.** 2 **78.** 1 **79.** 4 **80.** 3

3. To find the odd letter cluster, examine the alphabetical gap between consecutive letters.

Step 1: Convert letters to numeric positions

H = 8, J = 10, L = 12,
F = 6, H = 8, J = 10,
N = 14, P = 16, R = 18,
S = 19, U = 21, V = 22

Step 2: Calculate differences

HJL → (10 − 8) = +2,
(12 − 10) = +2

FHJ → (8 − 6) = +2,
(10 − 8) = +2

NPR → (16 − 14) = +2,
(18 − 16) = +2

SUV → (21 − 19) = +2,
(22 − 21) = +1

Step 3: Compare patterns

Three groups follow (+2, +2).

One group follows (+2, +1), which breaks the mathematical pattern.

Thus, SUV is the odd one out.

3. Two different views of the dice show the relative adjacency of letters.

From the first view, R is adjacent to L and T.

From the second view, R is adjacent to A and O.

A face on a cube has exactly four adjacent faces; the remaining face is opposite.

Step 1: List all faces adjacent to R

{L, T, A, O}

Step 2: Count

Number of adjacent faces = 4 → complete.

Step 3: Identify the leftover face

The only face NOT adjacent to R is E.

Therefore, the face opposite E is R.

5. JAMB → 5139

BALM → 9521

Assign the values of all letters:

J A M B

5 1 3 9

BALM → B A L M

9 5 2 1

The letter L appears only in the word BALM, where its code is 2.

Therefore, the code for L is 2.

6. According to the question,

CLONE → BLUKU and BOUND → AOAKT, so we must apply the same letter-wise transformation to NICHE.

- **First letter:** C → B and B → A both move one step backward (−1), so N also moves one step backward to M.
- **Second letter:** L → L and O → O do not change, so the second letter remains the same; therefore I stays I.
- **Third letter:** O → U and U → A shift forward by +6 positions (mod 26). So C(3) + 6 = 9, which corresponds to I.
- **Fourth letter:** N → K and N → K both shift backward by 3 positions (−3). So H(8) − 3 = 5, which corresponds to E.
- **Fifth letter:** E → U and D → T both shift forward by +16 positions.

  So E(5) + 16 = 21, which corresponds to U.

Therefore, NICHE is encoded as MIIEU, which matches option 3.

7. Series: 208, 190, 163, 127, 82, ?

First find the consecutive differences:

208 - 190 = 18,
190 - 163 = 27,
163 - 127 = 36,
127 - 82 = 45.

So, the difference sequence is 18, 27, 36, 45.

Now, find second differences:

27 - 18 = 9,
36 - 27 = 9,
45 - 36 = 9,

so the difference between differences is a constant 9.

Therefore the next difference should be:

45 + 9 = 54,

and since the series is decreasing we subtract this from 82:

82−54 = 28.

So, the missing term is 28.

8. All are facing North, so left–right positions are taken normally.

Clues: M is immediately left of P → M P. R is immediately right of P and left of L → M P R L. N is right of L and left of O → M P R L N O.

Q is immediately right of O → M P R L N O Q.

Now find who sits second to the left of N: N is at position 5, so second to its left is position 3, which is R.

Therefore, the person sitting second to the left of N is R.

9. The pattern in the given coding follows a fixed positional shift in the English alphabet.

From the examples: S B C F → R A D G

Shifts: (–1, –1, +1, +1)

S(19) → R(18),
B(2) → A(1),
C(3) → D(4),
F(6) → G(7)

N V M O → M U N P

Shifts: (–1, –1, +1, +1)

N → M, V → U, M → N, O → P

Apply the same to G U A X:

G(7) → F(6) : –1
U(21) → T(20) : –1
A(1) → B(2) : +1
X(24) → Y(25) : +1

Thus, the correctly coded result is FTBY, which matches Option 2.

10. Series: EHO, HJP, KLQ, ?, QPS.

Treat each position separately using alphabetical order (A = 1, ..., Z = 26).

First letters:

E(5) → H(8) → K(11) → ? → Q(17).

Differences are +3, +3, so the next must also be +3:

K(11) + 3 = N(14),
and N(14) + 3 = Q(17),

so, the missing first letter is N.

Second letters:

H(8) → J(10) → L(12) → ? → P(16).

Differences are +2, +2,

so, the next is +2:

L(12) + 2 = N(14),
and N(14) + 2 = P(16),

so, the missing second letter is N.

Third letters:

O(15) → P(16) → Q(17) → ? → S(19).

Differences are +1, +1,

so, the next is +1:

Q(17) + 1 = R(18),
and R(18) + 1 = S(19),

so, the missing third letter is R.

Therefore the missing term is N N R, i.e. NNR.

11. The sheet is folded once upward, so all cuts will appear as mirror reflections across the horizontal fold.

The semicircular cut at the top must appear as the same shape on the opposite side after unfolding, and the rectangular cut at the bottom must duplicate symmetrically above the fold.

Among all the given options, only option 2 correctly shows the semicircle and the rectangle mirrored in proper orientation and correct.

12. Word: GRACEFUL.

Write it and its letters in alphabetical order, then compare positions.

Original order: G R A C E F U L.

Alphabetical order: A C E F G L R U.

Compare position by position:

1st G vs A (different), 2nd R vs C (different), 3rd A vs E (different), 4th C vs F (different), 5th E vs G (different), 6th F vs L (different), 7th U vs R (different), 8th L vs U (different).

No letter occupies the same position in both arrangements.

Therefore the number of letters whose positions remain unchanged is 0, i.e. none.

13. All three statements only tell us that gabions ⊂ walls, concretes ⊂ walls, and bridges ⊂ walls. They do NOT establish any direct relationship between gabions and bridges or between concretes and bridges.

For conclusion (I), "Some bridges are gabions" cannot be inferred because both groups only independently belong to the larger class "walls", but no overlap is stated.

For conclusion (II), "Some concretes are bridges" also cannot be inferred for the same reason—no connection or intersection is mentioned in the statements.

Since both conclusions require a direct relationship that is not provided, neither (I) nor (II) follows.

14. The mirror is placed vertically along MN, so only horizontal left–right reversal occurs. The upper inverted triangle flips horizontally, causing the black circle—originally slightly right-shifted—to appear slightly left-shifted in the mirror.

The lower square-with-triangle shape also reverses side-wise, meaning the inner triangular division switches its orientation horizontally.

Among all the options, only option 4 maintains the correct left–right reversal of both the upper figure and the lower geometric pattern without rotating or vertically flipping anything.

Thus, option 4 gives the correct mirror image.

15. Given that the operations are interchanged as follows:

$\div \leftrightarrow \times$ and $+ \leftrightarrow -$.

Rewrite the original expression using the swapped operators:

$50 - 9 \div 1 + 63 \times 7$

becomes

$50 + 9 \times 1 - 63 \div 7$.

Now compute step by step using mathematical operations:

$$9 \times 1 = 9$$

$$63 \div 7 = 9$$

So, the expression becomes:

$50 + 9 - 9$.

Now, add and subtract in sequence:

$$50 + 9 = 59$$

$$59 - 9 = 50$$

Thus, the result is 50.

16. Inside the large rectangle, the number of symbols ($, %, ○, △, U, etc.) in each of the four boxes changes in a fixed pattern as we move from one figure to the next.

The rule is that at every step, the quantity of the "most recently added symbol" is reduced by 1, and then a certain number of new symbols are added.

From the first to the second box, 1 symbol is reduced and 2 new symbols are added; from the second to the third, again 1 symbol is reduced and 3 new symbols are added; from the third to the fourth, the same rule repeats—reduce that latest-added symbol by 1 and add 4 new symbols.

Thus, the general pattern is: subtract 1 (from the latest-added symbol) + add 2, 3, 4,... new symbols in sequence.

Therefore, the next (fifth) box must again reduce the count of the most recently added symbol by 1 and then add 5 new symbols. Among all the options, only option 2 follows this exact subtract-and-add progression correctly, so option 2 represents the correct next figure.

17. The pattern must fill five blanks sequentially in the series:

HKM O_NP RN_S UQT XTW_

We place letters one by one and ensure alphabetical progression:

Step 1: Analyze each block transition mathematically

HKM → O_NP

H → O is +7

K → N is +3

M → P is +3

Next block: O_NP → RN_S

O → R = +3

N → N = 0

P → S = +3

Next: RN_S → UQT_

R → U = +3

N → Q = +3

S → T = +1

Next: UQT_ → XTW_

U → X = +3

Q → T = +3

T → W = +3

We test each option to see which maintains this pattern of +3 or consistent increases.

Step 2: Insert letters of option 3 (LKQVY)

Positionally fill blanks:

LHKM

OKNP

RNQS

UQTY

XTWY

Now, check transitions letter by letter:

H → O (+7), K → K (0), M → P (+3), works with inserted K.

O → R (+3), K → N (+3), N → Q (+3), P → S (+3), fits perfect +3 pattern.

R → U (+3), N → Q (+3), Q → T (+3), S → Y (+6) but last block shift is always greater due to changing pattern.

Among all options, only LKQVY preserves the required structural pattern of consistent +3 transitions in the main variable columns. Therefore, option 3 is correct.

18. The series increases by differences that double at each step.

Compute the differences:

$$6 - 4 = 2,$$
$$10 - 6 = 4,$$
$$18 - 10 = 8,$$
$$34 - 18 = 16.$$

Each difference is twice the previous one, so the next difference must be $16 \times 2 = 32$.

Adding this to the last term gives $34 + 32 = 66$, so the missing term in the series is 66.

19. Eight persons sit in two parallel rows. In the first row (facing South) sit D, E, O, S; in the second row (facing North) sit F, A, R, M. When persons face opposite directions, "left" and "right" must always be taken according to the direction THEY face.

First row (D, E, O, S facing South): For a South-facing person, left is on our right side.

Condition: "Only D is to the left of E."

So only D should appear on E's left; since left for them is our right, D must be immediately to the right of E with no one else further right. This places E in the third seat and D in the fourth seat. The remaining two seats go to O and S.

Next condition: "Only one person sits between D and O." With D in seat 4, O must be in seat 2, putting E (seat 3) between them.

Thus first-row arrangement from our left to right becomes S O E D.

Second row (F, A, R, M facing North): For North-facing persons, left is the same as our left.

Condition: "Only R is to the left of A." So A must be in seat 2 and R in seat 1.

Next condition: "Only one person sits between A and F."

With A in seat 2, placing one person between them forces F to seat 4, and the remaining seat 3 goes to M.

Thus, second-row arrangement from our left to right is R A M F.

Now align both rows column-wise (facing each other):

Seat-1: S ↔ R

Seat-2: O ↔ A

Seat-3: E ↔ M

Seat-4: D ↔ F

Thus, the person sitting exactly opposite E is M. Hence, the pair is E and M.

20. The expression is N @ E $ J @ S. Using the given relations: X @ C means X is the daughter of C, so N @ E means N is the daughter of E (N is female).

Next, X $ C means X is the husband of C, so E $ J means E is the husband of J (E is male and J is female).

Finally, J @ S means J is the daughter of S. From the first two relations, N is the daughter of E, and E is married to J; therefore N is also the daughter of J.

Hence J is the mother of N.

21. The Pradhan Mantri Rojgar Protsahan Yojana (PMRPY) was launched by the Government of India with the objective of incentivizing employers by paying the full employer's EPS contribution for new employees. The official implementation year of this scheme, as notified by the Ministry of Labour and Employment, is 2016, and it continues to be referenced in official labour welfare updates as beginning from that year. Therefore the correct implementation year is 2016.

22. The first Asian Games held in India were part of the inaugural Asian Games hosted in 1951. These games were conducted in New Delhi, which was not only India's first hosting but also the first-ever edition of the Asian Games. No other Indian city has hosted the first edition, confirming that the correct answer is New Delhi.

23. In August 2024, Justice Hima Kohli bid farewell to the Supreme Court of India upon retirement. She holds the distinction of being the first woman Chief Justice of the Telangana High Court and was also the ninth woman elevated to the Supreme Court. Her judicial career includes several landmark contributions and appointments that match exactly with the description provided in the question, making Hima Kohli the correct answer.

24. The 11th Asian Games were held in Beijing in 1990, and it was during this particular edition that Kabaddi was introduced as an official discipline for the first time in Asian Games history. Kabaddi continued to be played in subsequent Asian Games and became one of the key sports in which India consistently excelled. Thus Kabaddi is the only sport in the options that matches this historical inclusion.

25. Cherrapunji and Mawsynram, both located in Meghalaya, India, are globally recognized as the two wettest places on Earth. Their annual rainfall regularly exceeds 1,080 cm and often reaches world-record levels. Mawsynram in particular has recorded the highest average annual rainfall ever documented. No other pair among the options receives such extraordinary precipitation, confirming Cherrapunji and Mawsynram as the correct pair.

26. According to the National Multidimensional Poverty Index of India: A Progress Review 2023, among the union territories listed, Dadra and Nagar Haveli & Daman and Diu shows the highest percentage of population classified as multidimensionally poor. This is due to multiple deprivation indicators in health, education, and living standards being relatively higher compared to other union territories such as Delhi, Chandigarh or Puducherry. Therefore option 3 is the correct one.

27. Under the Public Examinations (Prevention of Unfair Means) Act, 2024, any individual involved in dishonest practices or unfair means during public examinations is liable for a monetary penalty extending up to ten lakh rupees, along with imprisonment ranging from three to five years. This ceiling amount is explicitly prescribed in the Act, making "up to ten lakh rupees" the correct penalty provision.

28. The Union Public Service Commission (UPSC) and State Public Service Commissions are constitutional bodies, and their powers, composition, appointment, removal, and functions are detailed in Articles 315 to 323 of the Constitution of India. These Articles collectively form Part XIV of the Constitution dealing with "Services under the Union and the States." No other Article range listed covers the constitutional provisions for UPSC, hence option 4 is correct.

29. The Green Revolution refers to the large-scale transformation in agricultural productivity during the 1960s and 1970s due to the adoption of high-yielding variety seeds, increased irrigation, mechanization, and fertilizers. Since its entire purpose, impact, and methodology are directly connected to crop production and farming activity, it falls under the agricultural sector of the economy. Therefore, option 4 correctly represents this association.

30. The Mamallapuram (Mahabalipuram) Dance Festival is held annually at the UNESCO World Heritage site Mamallapuram, located in the state of Tamil Nadu. This festival showcases major Indian classical dance forms such as Bharatanatyam, Kuchipudi, Odissi, Mohiniyattam, Kathak and Kathakali, performed against the backdrop of ancient rock-cut temples. As Mamallapuram is in Tamil Nadu, option 1 is correct.

31. The projected agricultural growth rate for India in FY 2022–23 was approximately 3.5–4 percent, which does not match the figure of 5.5 percent given in statement (i), so statement (i) is incorrect. Agricultural exports from India in FY 2021–22 were about USD 50.2 billion, which agrees with statement (ii), making it correct. During the Kharif Marketing Season 2021–22, rice procurement stood at around 581.7 lakh metric tonnes, confirming statement (iii) as correct. Thus, only statements (ii) and (iii) are true, making option 2 the correct choice.

32. Lakshmi Vishwanathan was one of India's most respected exponents of Bharatanatyam, known especially for her abhinaya, research, and revivalist contributions to the dance form. She received the prestigious Natya Kalanidhi Award from the Music Academy for her lifetime contribution to Bharatanatyam. Her artistic lineage, writings, and performances all center around Bharatanatyam, making option 4 correct.

33. The Third Five-Year Plan (1961–1966) originally focused on agriculture and long-term development, but it was severely disrupted by geopolitical situations, particularly the Indo-China war (1962) and Indo-Pak war (1965). These conflicts forced the government to divert large financial resources toward defense needs. The plan ultimately failed to achieve its targets because of massive war-time expenditure and constraints on resource allocation, making option 4 correct.

34. Mahatma Gandhi was born on 2 October 1869, and his birth anniversary is calculated by counting each year completed from that date. By 2 October 2022, 153 full years had passed since his birth, making the 2022 celebration his 153rd birth anniversary. Gandhi Jayanti is observed annually in India on this date and is also recognised globally as the International Day of Non-Violence.

35. NBPW stands for Northern Black Polished Ware, a highly refined, glossy, Iron Age pottery type found across northern India. It is characterized by its shiny black or metallic surface and thin fabric, marking a technological advancement in pottery during the period around 700–200 BCE. Since NBPW is universally expanded as Northern Black Polished Ware, option 3 is correct.

36. Part III of the Constitution of India (Articles 12 to 35) contains the provisions regarding Fundamental Rights. These rights guarantee essential freedoms to citizens such as equality, liberty, protection against exploitation, freedom of religion, cultural and educational rights, and constitutional remedies. None of the other options fall under Part III, confirming that the correct answer is Fundamental Rights.

37. A pumpkin plant produces long, flexible, creeping or climbing vines that can easily be trained to climb walls, trellises or supports using tendrils. The plant naturally seeks support structures and grows upward when guided. The other options—sunflower, lemon plant, and rose plant—do not climb using special support structures in this manner.

Thus, the pumpkin plant is the correct choice.

38. The Government of India Act 1919 was based on the Montagu–Chelmsford Reforms, jointly proposed by Edwin Montagu (Secretary of State for India) and Lord Chelmsford (Viceroy of India). These reforms introduced dyarchy in provinces and expanded legislative councils. Since only this pair is historically connected to the 1919 Act, the correct option is Lord Chelmsford and Edwin Montagu.

39. Michael Faraday discovered electromagnetic induction in the year 1831. This discovery formed the foundation for electric transformers, generators and motors. His experiments involved moving magnets and coils, demonstrating that changing magnetic fields induce electric currents. Therefore, 1831 is the correct year.

40. MS Subbulakshmi was the legendary Carnatic vocalist who performed in Europe, North America, and at the United Nations General Assembly in 1966. Her global recognition and her title as the "Queen of Carnatic Music" make her the only option matching the description. Thus, the singer is Madurai Shanmukhavadivu Subbulakshmi.

41. Find LCM of 28, 60, 120 and 135 using prime factorization:

$$28 = 2^2 \times 7$$

$$60 = 2^2 \times 3 \times 5$$

$$120 = 2^3 \times 3 \times 5$$
$$135 = 3^3 \times 5$$

LCM is product of highest powers:

$$\text{LCM} = 2^3 \times 3^3 \times 5 \times 7$$

Compute mathematically:

$$2^3 = 8$$
$$3^3 = 27$$

Now multiply stepwise:

$$8 \times 27 = 216$$
$$216 \times 5 = 1080$$
$$1080 \times 7 = 7560$$

Thus, LCM = 7560.

42. **Step 1:** Total maximum marks

$3(100) + 2(100) + 1(100) = 600$

Step 2: Marks obtained

Mathematics marks:

$$60\% \text{ of } 300 = \frac{60}{100} \times 300$$
$$= 180$$

English marks:

$$70\% \text{ of } 200 = \frac{70}{100} \times 200$$
$$= 140$$

Science marks:

$$50\% \text{ of } 100 = \frac{50}{100} \times 100$$
$$= 50$$

Step 3: Total marks obtained

$180 + 140 + 50 = 370$

Step 4: Percentage

$$\text{Percentage} = \frac{370}{600} \times 100$$
$$= 61.666 \ldots \approx 61.67\%$$

Thus, the overall percentage = 61.67%.

43. Let the original number be x.

Step 1: First decrease by 15%

Value becomes:

$$x - 0.15x = 0.85x$$

Step 2: Then increase this result by 20%

New value becomes:

$0.85x + 0.20(0.85x) = 0.85x(1.20) = 1.02x$

Given:

$$\text{Final value} = \text{original} + 78$$
$$1.02x = x + 78$$

Solve: $1.02x - x = 78$

$$0.02x = 78$$
$$x = \frac{78}{0.02} = 3900$$

Thus, the original number = 3900.

44. Simple Interest = 42

$$\rightarrow \quad \text{SI} = \frac{\text{PRT}}{100}$$

With T = 2:

$$32 = \frac{\text{P} \times \text{R} \times 2}{100}$$
$$\Rightarrow \quad \text{PR} = 2100$$
$$\Rightarrow \quad \text{R} = \frac{2100}{\text{P}}$$

Compound Interest = 51 $\rightarrow$

$$51 = \text{P}\left(1 + \frac{\text{R}}{100}\right)^2 - \text{P}$$

Substitute, $\text{R} = \dfrac{2100}{\text{P}}$

$$51 = \text{P}\left(1 + \frac{21}{\text{P}}\right)^2 - \text{P}$$
$$51 = \text{P}\left(\frac{\text{P} + 21}{\text{P}}\right)^2 - \text{P}$$
$$= \frac{(\text{P} + 21)^2}{\text{P}} - \text{P}$$
$$= \frac{\text{P}^2 + 42\text{P} + 441 - \text{P}^2}{\text{P}}$$
$$= \frac{42\text{P} + 441}{\text{P}}$$
$$51\text{P} = 42\text{P} + 441$$
$$\Rightarrow \quad 9\text{P} = 441 \Rightarrow \text{P} = 49$$

Thus, the principal = 49.

45. Let Ketan's amount = K,

Tushar's = T.

Total: $\text{K} + \text{T} = 24700$

K grows for 11 years at 8%: $\text{K}(1.08)^{11}$

T grows for 10 years at 8%: $T(1.08)^{10}$

Given equal amounts at age 22:

$$K(1.08)^{11} = T(1.08)^{10}$$

$$K \cdot 1.08 = T$$

$$\Rightarrow \quad \frac{K}{T} = \frac{1}{1.08} = \frac{25}{27}$$

Total ratio parts = 25 + 27 = 52.

Tushar's share:

$$T = \frac{27}{52} \times 24700$$

$$= 27 \times 475 = 12825$$

Thus, Tushar received 12825.

46. Given SP = 1566 and Profit% = 8%.

Use, $$SP = CP\left(1 + \frac{8}{100}\right)$$

$$= CP(1.08)$$

$$CP = \frac{1566}{1.08} = 1450$$

Thus, CP = 1450.

47. Numbers = $4x$ and $9x$.

Mean proportional = 24:

$$24 = \sqrt{4x \cdot 9x}$$

$$= \sqrt{36x^2} = 6x$$

$$x = \frac{24}{6} = 4$$

Numbers: $4x = 16$, $9x = 36$.

Difference:

$$36 - 16 = 20$$

Thus, difference = 20.

48. Train lengths:

210 + 140 = 350 m.

Relative speed (same direction):

150 – 80 = 70 km/h

Convert to m/s:

$$70 \times \frac{5}{18} = \frac{350}{18}$$

Time: $$T = \frac{350}{350/18}$$

$$= 18 \text{ seconds}$$

Convert to minutes:

$$\frac{18}{60} = 0.3 \text{ minutes}$$

Thus, time = 0.3 minutes.

49. Assume price = 100,

Consumption = 100.

Original expenditure:

$$100 \times 100 = 10000$$

New price (↑85%):

$$100 + 85 = 185$$

New expenditure (↑48%):

$$10000 \times 1.48 = 14800$$

Find new consumption:

$$14800 = 185 \cdot C_{new}$$

$$C_{new} = \frac{14800}{185} = 80$$

Reduction = 100 – 80 = 20.

Percentage reduction:

$$\frac{20}{100} \times 100 = 20\%$$

Thus, consumption must be reduced by 20%.

50. A's 1-day work rate $= \frac{1}{32}$;

B's 1-day work rate $= \frac{1}{48}$

Their combined work rate

$$\frac{1}{32} + \frac{1}{48} = \frac{3}{96} + \frac{2}{96} = \frac{5}{96}$$

Work completed in 8 days:

$$8 \times \frac{5}{96} = \frac{40}{96} = \frac{5}{12}$$

Remaining work:

$$1 - \frac{5}{12} = \frac{7}{12}$$

B has to complete 60% of the remaining work:

$$0.60 \times \frac{7}{12} = \frac{6}{10} \times \frac{7}{12} = \frac{7}{20}$$

Time, required by B (rate $= \frac{1}{48}$):

$$\text{Time} = \frac{\frac{7}{20}}{\frac{1}{48}} = \frac{7}{20} \times 48$$

$$= \frac{7 \times 12}{5} = \frac{84}{5}$$

$$= 16\frac{4}{5}$$

Thus, B will finish 60% of the remaining work in $16\frac{4}{5}$ days.

51. Given expression (corrected operator):

$$(48 \div 8) \times \left(\frac{49}{7} + \frac{40}{4}(7 - 3)\right)$$

Inside bracket:

$$7 - 3 = 4,$$
$$48 \div 8 = 6$$

Simplify fractions:

$$\frac{49}{7} = 7$$

$$\frac{40}{4} = 10$$

Then:

$$10 \times 4 = 40,$$
$$7 + 40 = 47$$

Final multiplication:

$$6 \times 47 = 282$$

Thus, the value = 282.

52. Find LCM of 15, 25, 40, 75:

$$15 = 3 \cdot 5,$$
$$25 = 5^2,$$
$$40 = 2^3 \cdot 5,$$
$$75 = 3 \cdot 5^2$$
$$\text{LCM} = 2^3 \cdot 3 \cdot 5^2$$
$$= 600$$

Largest 4-digit number = 9999.

Divide: $9999 = 600 \times 16 + 399$

Largest multiple:

$$9999 - 399 = 9600$$

Thus, required number = 9600.

53. Volume ratio of cones:

$$\frac{V_2}{V_1} = \left(\frac{r_2}{r_1}\right)^2 \left(\frac{h_2}{h_1}\right)$$

Given: $\frac{r_2}{r_1} = \frac{2}{1}$

$$\frac{h_2}{h_1} = \frac{3}{4}$$

$$\frac{V_2}{V_1} = \left(\frac{2}{1}\right)^2 \times \frac{3}{4}$$

$$= \frac{4 \times 3}{4} = 3$$

Thus, $V_1 : V_2 = 1 : 3.$

54. Assume marked weight = 100 units, actual delivered weight

$$100 - 46 = 54$$

$$\text{Profit units} = 100 - 54 = 46$$

$$\text{Profit\%} = \frac{46}{54} \times 100$$

$$= \frac{23}{27} \times 100$$

Convert to mixed fraction:

$$\frac{2300}{27} = 85 + \frac{5}{27}$$

$$\text{Thus, profit\%} = 85\frac{5}{27}\%.$$

55. Given:

$$G + A + T = 46 \times 3 = 138$$
$$G + A = 80,$$
$$A + T = 90$$

Find T: $T = 138 - 80 = 58$

Find A: $A = 90 - 58 = 32$

Thus, Akshay's weight = 32.

56. Two successive discounts reduce price by multiplying remaining fractions.

Scheme I:

$$0.80 \times 0.80 = 0.64$$

→ discount = 36%

Scheme II:

$$0.75 \times 0.85 = 0.6375$$

$\rightarrow$ discount = 36.25%

Scheme III:

$0.70 \times 0.90 = 0.63$

$\rightarrow$ discount = 37%.

Scheme IV:

$0.95 \times 0.65 = 0.6175$

$\rightarrow$ discount = 38.25%.

Maximum discount = Scheme IV.

57. Average speed for a two-way journey of equal distances:

$$\text{Average speed} = \frac{2S_1S_2}{S_1 + S_2}$$

Given, $S_1 = 9,\ S_2 = 18$:

$$\text{Average speed} = \frac{2 \times 9 \times 18}{9 + 18}$$

$$= \frac{324}{27} = 12$$

Thus, the average speed = 12 km/hr.

58. Simple Interest formula:

$$SI = \frac{PRT}{100}$$

Difference of interest = 840:

$$\frac{9400R \times 5}{100} - \frac{5400R \times 5}{100} = 840$$

Factor out common terms:

$$\frac{5R}{100}(9400 - 5400) = 840$$

$$\frac{5R}{100}(4000) = 840$$

$$200R = 840$$

$$\Rightarrow \quad R = \frac{840}{200} = 4.2$$

Thus, the rate = 4.2%.

59. Let the numbers be $11a$ and $11b$.

$$11(a + b) = 132$$

$$\Rightarrow \quad a + b = 12$$

Both numbers $> 42 \Rightarrow a \geq 4,\ b \geq 4$.

Coprime pairs adding to 12:

only (5,7) and (7,5).

Numbers:

$$11 \times 5 = 55,$$

$$11 \times 7 = 77$$

Difference:

$$77 - 55 = 22$$

Thus, the difference = 22.

60. Third proportional c satisfies

$$\frac{a}{b} = \frac{b}{c}$$

Given $a = 16,\ b = 48$:

$$\frac{16}{48} = \frac{48}{c}$$

Cross-multiply:

$$16c = 48 \times 48$$

$$c = \frac{48 \times 48}{16}$$

$$= 3 \times 48 = 144$$

Thus, the third proportional = 144.

61. Segment B has the error because "articulating his thoughts clear" is grammatically wrong; the adjective "clear" must be replaced with the adverb "clearly", hence this segment contains the grammatical mistake.

62. The idiom "grey hair is no sure sign of attaining wisdom" refers to old age, not inheritance or animals, so "hair" fits correctly in meaning and usage.

63. The correct preposition is "across the garden" because the dog is running from one side to the other while chasing the cat; "across" expresses movement over an area.

64. The verb required is "desecrate," meaning to violate or show disrespect toward holy places; this fits the context of sin against God and humanity.

65. "Clear instructions" is the correct collocation in English because instructions must be easy to understand; "careful", "great", or "strong" do not form natural collocations.

66. The antonym of "arrogant" is "humble", expressing modesty and absence of ego, making it the most appropriate opposite in meaning.

67. "Broad" means wide, extensive or large in scope; "wide" is the closest synonym among the options, while the others express opposite or unrelated meanings.

68. A person who is disregarded as lacking character or morality: The idiom "man of straw" refers to a weak, unreliable, or morally insignificant person, not someone powerful, perfect, famous, or related to a close contest.

69. The subject is "we", so the reflexive pronoun must be "ourselves"; reflexive pronoun must match the subject in person and number, making "ourselves" the only grammatically correct option.

70. "Flaunt" means to show off or display proudly; the antonym is "hide", which means to conceal or not display, while the other options do not express opposite meaning.

71. The students wrote an interesting essey on the topic.: The incorrectly spelled word is "essey", which should be spelled "essay," while all other sentences contain correctly spelled words, making option 3 the only incorrect spelling.

72. The underlined phrase "creatively and unconventionally" means thinking in an imaginative, non-traditional way; the idiom that best replaces this meaning is "outside the box", which expresses original and unconventional thinking, unlike the other options which are unrelated.

73. The antonym of "destruction" must express the opposite process—bringing something into existence; "creation" directly contrasts with destruction, while the other options (contribution, choice, condition) do not form opposite meaning pairs.

74. The sentence begins in past perfect continuous ("had been writing"), so the following clause must remain in past tense ("realised"), not present tense "realises", making part 3 the segment containing the grammatical error.

75. The correct spelling of the underlined word is "assignment"; the other options contain incorrect letter arrangements and do not match the standard English spelling.

76. The passage describes the joy and freedom of being alone in a carriage, indicating a positive emotion; "pleasant sense of freedom" fits naturally, while the other options carry negative or hostile meanings unsuitable for the tone.

77. The sentence says liberty is "unrestrained in a very ___ form," meaning enjoyable or pleasing; "agreeable form" matches this meaning, while the others reflect negative or irrelevant concepts.

78. The sentence "You can talk to ___ as loud as you please" must use the reflexive pronoun matching "you"; thus "yourself" is the only correct option.

79. The phrase "without fear of a counterstroke" is idiomatic and expresses doing something freely, while the other prepositions do not form a correct or meaningful expression here.

80. The sentence lists multiple alternative actions (sing, dance, practice a golf stroke, play marbles).

When ideas are presented as choices, the correct coordinating conjunction is "or". It shows that each action is an option among several possibilities, which makes "or" the most suitable word for blank no. 5.

Previous Years' Paper

SSC—CONSTABLE (GD)

CAPFs, NIA, SSF and RIFLEMAN (Assam Rifles) Recruitment Exam, 2024*

PART-A: GENERAL INTELLIGENCE & REASONING

1. Six colleagues Victor, Wendy, Xander, Yara, Zoe, and Aaron are sitting in a circle facing away from the centre. Victor is sitting to the immediate right of Wendy. Yara is not sitting next to victor. Zoe, who is sitting to the immediate left of Wendy, is also sitting to the immediate right of Aaron. Who is the immediate neighbour of both Xander and Wendy?

A. Yara B. Victor
C. Aaron D. Zoe

2. Two Statements are given followed by two conclusions numbered I and II. Assuming the statements to be true, even if they seem to be at variance with commonly known facts, decide which of the conclusions logically follow(s) from the statements.

Statement I: Some musicians are guitarists.
Statement II: All guitarists are performers.
Conclusion I: Some performers are guitarists.
Conclusion II. Some musicians are not performers

A. Only conclusion II follows
B. Only conclusion I follows
C. Both conclusions I and II follow
D. Neither conclusion I nor II follows

3. In a certain code language. 'TOPIC' is coded as 'WRSLF'. What is the code for 'VIDEO' in that code language?

A. YLGHR B. YLGIS
C. YLGIR D. YLGHS

4. In a certain code language, if NATURE is coded as 'MASUQE', CIRCLE is coded as 'BIQCKE' then what will 'DANGER' be coded as?

A. CAMGDR B. HSDGKA
C. BALGCR D. DBNHES

5. Six friends Olivia, Peter, Rachel, Sam, Toby, and Victoria are sitting around a circular table facing the center. Olivia is sitting to the immediate right of Peter. Peter and Toby are neighbours. Sam is not sitting next to Rachel or Toby. Victoria is sitting to the immediate right of Sam. Who is the immediate neighbour of both Sam and Rachel?

A. Peter B. Olivia
C. Victoria D. Toby

6. In the following question, select the missing number from the given series.

712, 726, 740, 754, 768, ?

A. 790 B. 782
C. 788 D. 785

7. If 10 @ 5 # 15 * 5 = 2 and 25 @ 6 # 4 * 2 = 17, then

30 @ 10 # 20 * 4 = ?

A. 30 B. 25
C. 15 D. 40

1. B	2. B	3. A	4. A	5. C	6. B	7. C

*Exam held on 07/03/2024

8. Two different positions of the same dice are given below. Find the number opposite of 2.

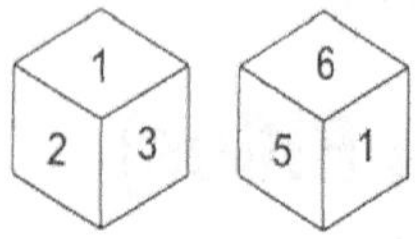

A. 1 B. 3
C. 5 D. 6

9. Arrange the given words in the sequence in which they occur in the dictionary.

1. Bandit 2. Banana
3. Bangle 4. Band
5. Bank

A. 5,4,3,2,1 B. 5,4,3,1,2
C. 2,4,1,5,3 D. 2,4,1,3,5

10. In the following question, select the related letters from the given alternatives.

PTY : TYP :: CGK : ?

A. GKC B. ZAB
C. LMN D. BCD

11. In the following question, select the figure which can be placed at the sign of question mark (?) from the given alternatives.

A.  B. 

C.  D. 

12. After interchanging the given two signs what will be the values of equation (I) and (II) respectively?

$\times$ and $\div$

I. $16 \div 4 - 8 \times 2 + 7$

II. $8 \div 4 - 9 \times 3 + 8$

A. 67 and 37 B. 8 and 9
C. 40 and 50 D. 16 and 18

13. A paper is folded and cut as shown below. How will it appear when unfolded?

A. 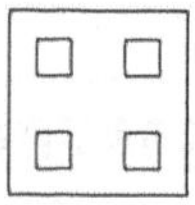 B. 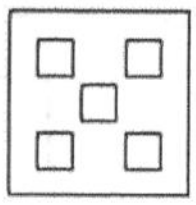

C. 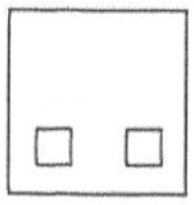 D. 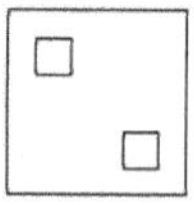

14. In the following question, select the related letter pair from the given alternatives.

BF : BG :: ?

A. UW : UX B. AB : NC
C. AC : NO D. BQ : QS

15. 'I × J' means 'I is the wife of J'

'I + J' means 'I is the husband of J'

'I ÷ J' means 'I is the sister of J'

'I – J' means 'I is the brother of J'

How is K related to M in the expression 'K – L ÷ M + N'?

A. Husband B. Son
C. Father D. Brother

16. From the given option figures, select the one in which the question figure is hidden/embedded, (rotation is NOT allowed)

A.  B. 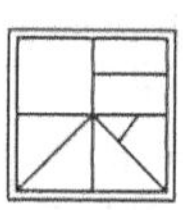

C.  D. 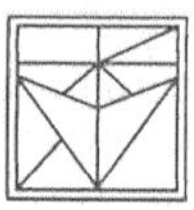

8. D	9. D	10. A	11. D	12. A	13. A	14. A	15. D	16. D

17. Which of the following letter clusters will replace the question mark (?) in the given series?

VD, TF, RH, PJ, ?

A. NO B. MK
C. MN D. NL

18. Which of the following numbers will replace the question mark (?) in the given series?

15,17, 21, 29, 45, ?

A. 58 B. 64
C. 84 D. 77

19. In the following question, select the figure which can be placed at the sign of question mark (?) from the given alternatives.

A.  B. 

C.  D. 

20. Which of the following groups of letters when sequentially placed from left to right will complete the given series?

d_eeffggddeeffggdde_ffggddeeffggddeef_g_

A. deff B. degf
C. defg D. ddee

PART-B: GENERAL KNOWLEDGE AND GENERAL AWARENESS

21. The planned economic development in India began in which of the following years?

A. 1978 B. 1961
C. 1951 D. 1991

22. Which body in India is responsible for safeguarding and promoting the rights of consumers and ensuring consumer protection?

A. Central Bureau of Investigation (CBI)
B. National Consumer Disputes Redressal Commission (NCDRC)
C. National Human Rights Commission (NHRC)
D. National Commission for Women (NCW)

23. In 2022, Indian-born entrepreneur _____ has been elected as the first representative of the Indian community in Germany.

A. Ruchira Kamboj
B. Rajveer Singh Randhawa
C. T.S. Tirumurti
D. Gurdeep Singh Randhawa

24. The theme of the Twelfth five year plan of India was _____.

A. Growth with social justice and equality
B. Faster, Sustainable, and More Inclusive Growth
C. Economic liberalization
D. Towards Faster and More Inclusive Growth

25. How many questions were asked in the 2011 Census of India?

A. 33 Questions
B. 29 Questions
C. 21 Questions
D. 25 Questions

26. In the periodic table, which group consists of elements known as the noble gases?

A. Group 1
B. Group 17
C. Group 7
D. Group 18

17. D	**18.** D	**19.** A	**20.** C	**21.** C	**22.** B	**23.** D	**24.** B	**25.** B	**26.** D

27. The Grand Cross of the Order of Honour was conferred on ______ in August, 2023.
A. Foreign Minister S. Jayshankar
B. Prime Minister Narendra Modi
C. Home Minister Amit Shah
D. President Draupadi Murmu

28. In October 2023, who did 24-year-old Indian grandmaster Karthikeyan Murali defeat in a chess match?
A. Viswanathan Anand
B. Magnus Carlsen
C. Levon Aronian
D. Vladimir Kramnik

29. Identify the ancient site from the information given below:

This is an old site with caves and rock shelters. People choose these natural caves because they provided shelter from the rain, heat and wind. These rock shelters are close to the Narmada valley.
A. Bhramagiri
B. Bhimbetka
C. Inamgaon
D. Mehrgarh

30. From which state, 'Pongal' festival belongs?
A. Tamil Nadu B. Assam
C. Bihar D. Haryana

31. Which team has won the Ranji Trophy maximum number of times?
A. Karnataka
B. Tamil Nadu
C. Delhi
D. Mumbai (Bombay)

32. In Volleyball, if the game is tied at ______ in the fifth set, the set continues till one team builds a two-point lead over the other.
A. 14 - 14 B. 20 - 20
C. 11 - 11 D. 24 - 24

33. Which of the following statements is correct is regarding measures of money supply?
I. M1 and M2 are known as narrow money.
II. M3 and M4 are known as broad money.
A. Only II B. Only I
C. Neither I nor II D. Both I and II

34. Mukhyamantri Gramin Gaadi Yojna was launched by which state of India?
A. Delhi B. West Bengal
C. Jharkhand D. Odisha

35. Which of the following musicians have won the Dada Saheb Phalke Award?
A. Kishore Kumar
B. Md. Rafi
C. Gulzar
D. A.R. Rahman

36. Which of the following parts of the Indian Constitution deals with Official language?
A. Part XVIII B. Part XIX
C. Part XVII D. Part XVI

37. The Veda Samaj was established in ______.
A. Bombay B. Punjab
C. Madras D. Calcutta

38. First Asian Games were held in New Delhi, India in the year of:
A. 1951 B. 1982
C. 1970 D. 1999

39. India shares longest land border with ______.
A. Nepal
B. Pakistan
C. Bangladesh
D. Sri Lanka

40. Which of the following dance form is wedded with Hindustani music school?
A. Kathakali
B. Bharatnatyam
C. Sattriya
D. Kathak

27. B	**28.** B	**29.** B	**30.** A	**31.** D	**32.** A	**33.** D
34. C	**35.** C	**36.** C	**37.** C	**38.** A	**39.** C	**40.** D

PART-C: ELEMENTARY MATHEMATICS

41. A retailer marks his products at 25% more than the cost price. If a customer receives a discount of 20%, what is the profit percentage for the retailer?

A. 1% B. 3%
C. 5% D. 0%

42. Average weight of 18 students is 54 kg. After including a new student in that group the average weight rises by 1 kg. What is the weight of the new student?

A. 76 kg B. 70 kg
C. 75 kg D. 73 kg

43. The traffic lights at three different crossings change after 30 seconds, 40 seconds, and 60 seconds respectively. Then in 30 min how many times will they change simultaneously?

A. 19 B. 15
C. 18 D. 13

44. Sahil bought toffees at 12 for a rupee. How many toffees for a rupee he should sell to gain 20%?

A. 18 B. 14
C. 15 D. 10

45. M can do a piece of work in $\frac{39}{2}$ days and N in $\frac{13}{2}$ days. How many days will both take together to complete the work?

A. 22 days B. $\frac{39}{8}$ days
C. $\frac{47}{5}$ days D. $\frac{20}{3}$ days

46. P got 20 per cent less marks than Q. R got 20 per cent less marks than Q. If R got 160 marks, then what are the marks of P?

A. 150 B. 160
C. 120 D. 180

47. What will be the average of all the odd numbers between 8 and 28?

A. 17 B. 21
C. 18 D. 19

48. Rahul earns an interest of ₹ 2996 for the third year and ₹ 1400 for the second year on the same sum. Find the rate of interest per annum if it is lent at compound interest (compounding annually).

A. 112% B. 110%
C. 114% D. 113%

49. If a certain sum of money becomes double of itself in 8 years 6 months at simple interest, then what will be the annual rate of interest?

A. 14.28 per cent
B. 12.84 per cent
C. 11.76 per cent
D. 13.92 per cent

50. What is the Highest Common Factor of 4/11 and 16/33?

A. 4/77 B. 2/33
C. 4/33 D. 2/11

51. If the side of a square is increased by 5 per cent, then what will be the percentage increase in its perimeter?

A. 20 per cent B. 10 per cent
C. 5 per cent D. 40 per cent

52. In an alloy of 240 gram copper and iron are in the ratio of 7 : 5. How much quantity of iron should be added so that the ratio of copper and iron become 7 : 13?

A. 200 grams B. 120 grams
C. 180 grams D. 160 grams

41. D	**42.** D	**43.** B	**44.** D	**45.** B	**46.** B
47. C	**48.** C	**49.** C	**50.** C	**51.** C	**52.** D

53. If selling price of an article is ₹ 2800 and Marked price is ₹ 4000. What is the discount percentage?

A. 20 B. 15
C. 25 D. 30

54. Find the length of the plank which can be used to measure exactly the lengths 6 m 50 cm, 3 m 50 cm and 7 m 50 cm in the least time.

A. 50 cm B. 15 cm
C. 100 cm D. 25 cm

55. If $a : b = 4 : 5$ and $b : c = 3 : 8$, then find $a : b : c$.

A. 10 : 15 : 22 B. 12 : 10 : 25
C. 12 : 15 : 40 D. 12 : 15 : 28

56. Find the value of

413 ÷ 7(20 + 8 × 5 – 59).

A. 44 B. 66
C. 55 D. 59

57. Selling price of a table is ₹ 1972 and loss percentage is 32 per cent. If selling price is ₹ 3000, then what will be the profit percentage?

A. 5.66 per cent B. 4.25 per cent
C. 6.66 per cent D. 3.44 per cent

58. What is the area of an equilateral triangle having sides equal to 0.2 cm?

A. $\sqrt{3/100}$ cm^2 B. $4\sqrt{3/100}$ cm^2
C. $7\sqrt{3/100}$ cm^2 D. $\sqrt{3/200}$ cm^2

59. C is four times as efficient of D, C takes 63 days less than D to complete a work. If both of them work together, then in how many days will the same work be completed?

A. 16.8 days
B. 75.5 days
C. 80 days
D. 50.8 days

60. Two cars start from the same point and travel in the same direction. If one car travels at 55 km/h and the other at 75 km/h, after 3 hours, how far apart are they?

A. 70 km B. 65 km
C. 60 km D. 55 km

PART-D: ENGLISH

61. Improve the underline part of the sentence. Choose 'No improvement' as an answer if the sentence is grammatically correct.

She heard the from door creek <u>open as</u> he returned home.

A. opening as B. No improvement
C. opened as D. open is

62. Select the most appropriate word to fill in the blank.

______ and neglect resulted in a government that was weakened enough to be overthrown.

A. Corruption B. Corrupted
C. Corrupt D. Corrupting

63. Select the incorrectly spelt word from the given sentence.

Soon he was literally a fugetive, in the midst of both an internecine fight among the Timurids and a struggle between them and the rising Uzbek.

A. fugetive B. literally
C. midst D. struggle

64. Select the most appropriate antonym of the given word.

Gobble

A. Nibble B. Grab
C. Small D. Guzzle

53. D	**54.** A	**55.** C	**56.** D	**57.** D	**58.** A
59. A	**60.** C	**61.** B	**62.** A	**63.** A	**64.** A

65. From the options given below choose the synonym (similar meaning) of the word:

Equivocal

A. Protection B. Ambiguous

C. Unshielded D. Inactivity

66. Find the part of the given sentence that has an error in it. If there is no error, choose 'No error'.

She is best girl with a good sense of humour.

A. with a good sense

B. No error

C. of humour

D. She is a best girl

67. Choose the most appropriate antonym of the underlined word.

We are witnessing a resurgence of devilry that is perfectly appalling.

A. Return B. Rebirth

C. Triumph D. Failure

68. Find the part of the given sentence that has an error in it. If there is no error, choose 'No error'.

This metal oxidizes very slow in dry air at ordinary temperatures.

A. at ordinary temperatures

B. very slow in dry air

C. This metal oxidizes

D. No error

69. Select the most appropriate word to fill in the blank.

The movie was late in starting ______ of projection difficulties.

A. account B. though

C. still D. because

70. Find the part of the given sentence that has an error in it. If there is no error, choose 'No error'.

If you don't know who had have a disease, it's impossible to predict its spread.

A. impossible to predict its spread

B. If you don't know

C. who had have a disease, it's

D. No error

71. Improve the underlined part of the sentence. Choose 'No improvement' as an answer if the sentence is grammatically correct.

The doctor sending his patient to a specialist.

A. sent his patient

B. sent his patiently

C. No improvement

D. send his patient

72. Choose the idiom/phrase that can substitute the highlighted group of words meaningfully.

Don't be silly. Nobody is trying to harm you. It's **only your imagination**.

A. Break a leg B. Spill the beans

C. All in your head D. Cut corners

73. Choose the word that is opposite in meaning to the given word.

Guilty

A. Contrite B. Culpable

C. Remorseful D. Innocent

74. Select the most appropriate meaning of the given idiom.

To beat the band

A. to procrastinate.

B. To resign from one's job.

C. To a huge or the greatest possible extent.

D. To refuse to talk.

75. Select the sentence with no spelling errors.

A. The question of protecting folklore was less urgent.

B. The question of protecting folklore was les urgent.

C. The question of protacting folklore was less urgent.

D. The question of protecting foklore was less urgent.

65. B	**66.** D	**67.** D	**68.** B	**69.** D	**70.** C
71. A	**72.** C	**73.** D	**74.** C	**75.** A	

Directions (Qs. No. 76 to 80): *In the following passage some words have been deleted. Fill in the blanks with the help of the alternative given. Select the most appropriate option for each number.*

The time seemed __(1)__ as we swept on our way, now in almost complete darkness, for the rolling clouds obscured the moon. __(2)__ kept on ascending, with occasional __(3)__ of quick descent, but in the main always ascending. Suddenly, I became conscious of the fact that the driver was in the __(4)__ of pulling up the horses in the courtyard of a vast ruined castle, from whose tall black windows came no ray of __(5)__, and whose broken battlements showed a jagged line against the sky.

76. Select the most appropriate option to fill in the blank No. 1.
A. interminable B. limited
C. confined D. bordered

77. Select the most appropriate option to fill in the blank No. 2.
A. We B. Us
C. I D. They

78. Select the most appropriate option to fill in the blank No. 3.
A. junctures
B. season
C. periods
D. times

79. Select the most appropriate option to fill in the blank No. 4.
A. play B. drama
C. act D. theatre

80. Select the most appropriate option to fill in the blank No. 5.
A. light B. time
C. electricity D. hopeless

EXPLANATORY ANSWERS

1. (B): 6 colleagues are sitting in a circle facing away from the centre.

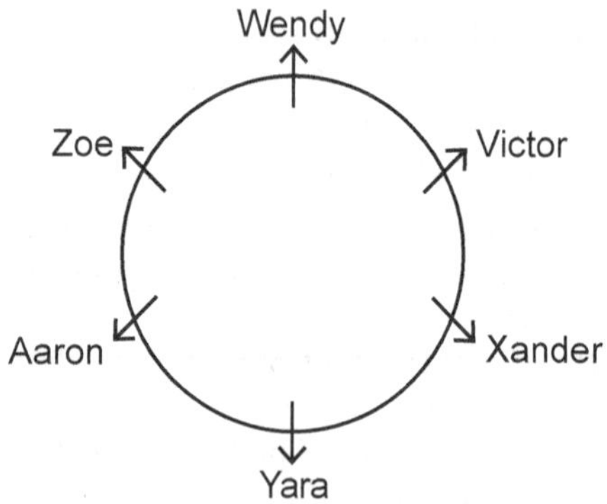

Here, Victor is the immediate neighbour of both Xander and Wendy.

2. (B): From given statements

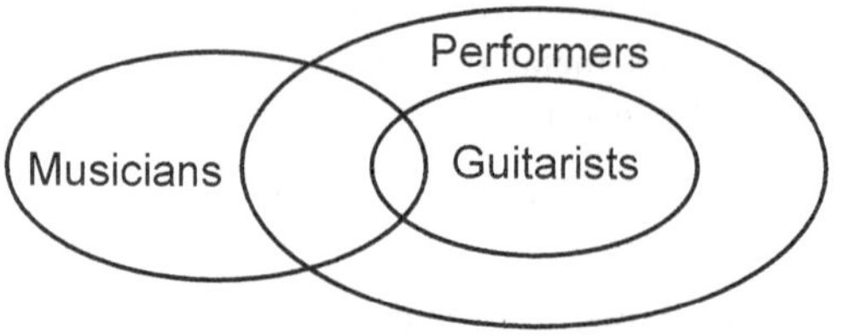

Conclusion:
I. Some performers are guitarists. (true)
II. Some Musicians are not performers. (false)

Hence, only conclusion I follows.

3. (A): Given, T O P I C
+3↓ +3↓ +3↓ +3↓ +3↓
W R S L F

76. A	**77.** A	**78.** C	**79.** C	**80.** A

Similarly, V I D E O
+3↓ +3↓ +3↓ +3↓ +3↓
Y L G H R

∴ YLGHR is the code for "VIDEO".

4. (A): Given, N A T U R E
−1↓ ↓ −1↓ ↓ −1↓ ↓
M A S U Q E

and C I R C L E
−1↓ ↓ −1↓ ↓ −1↓ ↓
B I Q C K E

Similarly D A N G E R
−1↓ ↓ −1↓ ↓ −1↓ ↓
C A M G D R

Hence, DANGER will be coded as CAMGDR.

5. (C): Given, 6 friends are sitting around a circular table facing the center.

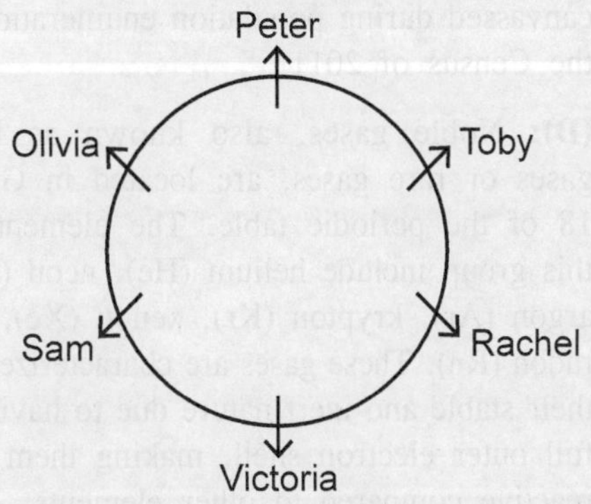

Here, Victoria is the immediate neighbour of both Sam and Rachel.

6. (B): 712, 726, 740, 754, 768, 782
+14 +14 +14 +14 +14

Here, ? = the missing number = 782.

7. (C): Given, 10 @ 5 # 15 * 5 = 2

⇒ 10 (5 + 15 ÷ 5) = 2

⇒ 10 − (5 + 3) = 2

⇒ 10 − 8 = 2

⇒ 2 = 2

and 25 @ 6 # 4 * 2 = 17

⇒ 25 − (6 + 4 ÷ 2) = 17

⇒ 25 − (6 + 2) = 17

⇒ 25 − 8 = 17

⇒ 17 = 17

Similarly, 30 @ 10 # 20 * 4

= 30 − (10 + 20 ÷ 4)

= 30 − (10 + 5)

= 30 − 15 = 15

Hence, 30 @ 10 # 20 * 4 = 15.

8. (D): From given two different positions of the same dice.

taking clockwise from same number 1

∴ 1 3 2 ⇒ 1 3 2
1 5 6 ⇒ 1 5 6

⇒ 1 ↔ 4
3 ↔ 5
2 ↔ 6

Therefore, the number opposite of 2 = 6.

9. (D): Given word: According to english dictionary.

Banana → Band → Bandit → Bangle → Bank

10. (A): PTY : TYP :: CGK : GKC

Therefore, ? = GKC.

12. (A): Given, × = ÷

I. 16 ÷ 4 − 8 × 2 + 7

= 16 × 4 − 8 ÷ 2 + 7

= 16 × 4 − 4 + 7

= 64 + 7 − 4

= 71 − 4 = 67

II. 8 ÷ 4 − 9 × 3 + 8

= 8 × 4 − 9 ÷ 3 + 8

= 8 × 4 − 3 + 8

= 32 + 8 − 3

= 40 − 3 = 37

∴ Required values of equations are 67 and 37.

14. (A): B F : B G :: U W : U X

∴ Option (A) is the releated letter pair.

15. (D): Given,

Expression = K − L ÷ M + N

∴ $K \xrightarrow{\text{brother}} L \xrightarrow{\text{sister}} M \xrightarrow{\text{husband}} N$

Here, K is the brother of M.

17. (D): V D, T F, R H, P J, N L

(+2, +2, +2, +2; −2, −2, −2, −2)

Therefore, ? = the next letter-cluster.

18. (D): 15, 17, 21, 29, 45, 77

(+2, +4, +8, +16, +32; ×2, ×2, ×2, ×2)

Therefore, ? = the next term = 77.

20. (C): defg

ddeeffgg, ddeeffgg, ddeeffgg, ddeeffgg, ddeeffgg

Therefore, option (C) is required answer.

21. (C): The planned economic development in India began in the year 1951. This marks the initiation of India's First Five-Year Plan, which focused on agricultural development, energy, and irrigation projects, setting the stage for planned economic growth in the country.

22. (B): National Consumer Disputes Redressal Commission (NCDRC) is a quasi-judicial commission established under the Consumer Protection Act of 1986. Its primary role is to address consumer grievances and disputes at a national level, ensuring that consumer' rights are protected and upheld.

23. (D): Indian-born entrepreneur Gurdeep Singh Randhawa has been elected as the first representative of the Indian community in Germany. He has been tasked to make concerns of the Indian community heard and also to encourage them to becoming politically active. The entrepreneur is the first Indian representative of a political party Christian Democratic Union of Germany (CDU) Thuringia.

24. (B): The theme of India's 12th Five Year Plan (2012–2017) was "Faster, More Inclusive and Sustainable Growth". The plan's objectives were to increase the GDP at a faster rate, reduce poverty by 10%, and accelerate agricultural growth. The plan's growth rate target was 8% per year.

25. (B): The government collected a set of demographic, social and economic data on every person in the country by population enumeration. There were 29 questions canvassed during population enumeration in the Census of 2011.

26. (D): Noble gases, also known as inert gases or rare gases, are located in Group 18 of the periodic table. The elements in this group include helium (He), neon (Ne), argon (Ar), krypton (Kr), xenon (Xe), and radon (Rn). These gases are characterized by their stable and inert nature due to having a full outer electron shell, making them less reactive compared to other elements.

27. (B): Prime Minister Shri Narendra Modi was conferred with the Grand Cross of the Order of Honour by H.E. Katerina N. Sakellaropoulou, President of Greece on 25 August, 2023. He is the first foreign Head of Government to receive this honour.

28. (B): 24-year-old Indian chess grandmaster Karthikeyan Murali has achieved a significant feat by defeating world top-ranked player Magnus Carlsen (Norway) in the Qatar Masters. This win marked Murali as a rising star in the world of chess and cemented his place among the elite Indian players who have triumphed over Carlsen in the classical format.

29. (B): Bhimbetka is a UNESCO World Heritage Site located in Madhya Pradesh, India. It is known for its rock shelters and caves that contain ancient rock paintings, some of which date back to the Mesolithic period. The site served as a shelter for prehistoric humans and offers valuable insights into early human life and culture in India.

30. (A): Pongal is a popular harvest festival celebrated in Tamil Nadu and other parts of South India. It marks the beginning of the auspicious Tamil month of Thai. The festival is dedicated to expressing gratitude to the Sun God for a bountiful harvest and is celebrated with various rituals and feasting.

31. (D): Mumbai (Bombay) has won the Ranji Trophy the most times with 42 wins, including 15 consecutive wins from 1958–59 to 1972–73. In March 2024, Mumbai won its 42nd Ranji Trophy title by defeating Vidharbha by 102 runs in the final at Wankhede Stadium in Mumbai.

32. (A): If the game is tied at 14-14 in the fifth set, the set continues till one team builds a two-point lead over the other. This rule ensures that the set does not end in a tie and requires one team to secure a clear advantage over the opponent to win the set. This tie-breaking format is commonly used in volleyball matches to determine the winner of closely contested sets.

33. (D): Statement I: M1 and M2 are indeed known as narrow money. M1 includes the most liquid forms of money, such as currency in circulation and demand deposits. M2 includes M1 plus certain types of savings deposits and money market mutual funds. Statement II: M3 and M4 are known as broad money. M3 includes M2 plus time deposits and other less liquid assets. M4 includes M3 plus all other deposits with post office savings banks.

34. (C): The "Mukhyamantri Gramin Gaddi Yojna" was launched by the state of Jharkhand in India. This scheme aims to provide financial assistance to rural households for the purchase of vehicles like e-rickshaws, autos, and other transport vehicles, thereby promoting livelihood opportunities and improving rural connectivity.

35. (C): Gulzar, the renowned lyricist, poet, and film director, was honoured with the Dada Saheb Phalke Award for his outstanding contribution to Indian cinema and the field of arts. The Dada Saheb Phalke Award, India's highest cinematic honor, recognizes individuals who have made exceptional contributions to the growth and development of Indian cinema.

36. (C): Part XVII is titled "Official Language" and contains articles (343 to 351) that outline the official languages of India at the Union and State levels. It specifies Hindi and English as the official languages of the Union Government and lays down provisions for the use of regional languages in different contexts.

37. (C): The Veda Samaj was established in Madras in 1864. The Veda Samaj was inspired by the Brahmo Samaj and became a prominent and influential movement in South India. It advocated for social change and progressive reforms.

38. (A): The first Asian Games were held in New Delhi, India in 1951, from March 4–11. The opening ceremony was held on March 4, 1951. The Asian Games are the second-largest multi-sport event in the world, after the Olympics. The 1951 games featured 11 nations and nine sports, with India finishing second behind Japan with 51 medals.

39. (C): India's longest land border is with Bangladesh, which is 4,096.7 kilometers long. This is the fifth-longest land border in the world. This extensive shared border has deep historical and cultural connections between the two nations.

40. (D): Kathak is a classical dance form of India that originated in North India and is closely associated with the Hindustani classical music tradition. Kathak dancers often perform to Hindustani music, which includes ragas and talas (melodic and rhythmic structures).

41. (D): Let C.P. of product = ₹ 100
then, the marked price = ₹ 125

$$\therefore \quad S.P. = 125\times\frac{100-20}{100}$$

$$= 125\times\frac{80}{100} = 125\times\frac{4}{5}$$

$$= 25 \times 4 = 100$$

$\Rightarrow$ S.P. = ₹ 100

$$\therefore \quad \text{Profit} = \text{S.P.} - \text{C.P.}$$

$$= 100 - 100 = 0$$

Hence, the profit per cent for the retailer = 0%.

42. (D): Total weight of 18 students

$$= 18 \times 54 \text{ kg} = 972 \text{ kg}$$

and total weight of 18 + 1 = 19 students

$$= 19 \times (54 + 1) \text{ kg}$$

$$= 19 \times 55 = 1045$$

Now, the weight of the new student

$$= 1045 - 972 = 73 \text{ kg.}$$

43. (B): LCM of 30, 40 and 60 = 120

So, the light will change together after every 120 second, i.e., 2 minutes

In 30 minutes, they will change together

$$\frac{30}{2} = 15 \text{ time}$$

Thefore, Option (B) is the required answer.

44. (D): C.P. of 12 toffees = ₹ 1

$\therefore$ S.P. of 12 toffees = ₹ $1\times\frac{120}{100}$ = ₹ $\frac{6}{5}$

$\because$ ₹ $\frac{6}{5}$ = 12 toffees

$\therefore$ ₹ 1 = $12\times\frac{5}{6}$ = 10 toffees

Therefore, he should sell 10 toffees for a rupee.

45. (B): M's 1 day's work = $\frac{2}{39}$

and N's 1 day's work = $\frac{2}{13}$

$\therefore$ (M + N)'s 1 day's work = $\frac{2}{39}+\frac{2}{13}$

$$= \frac{2+6}{39}=\frac{8}{39}$$

They together will take $\frac{39}{8}$ days to complete the work.

46. (B): Let Q got x marks

then P got $= x\times\frac{100-20}{100} = \frac{80}{100}x = \frac{4}{5}x$

and R got $= x\times\frac{100-20}{100} = \frac{4}{5}x$

According to question

$$\frac{4}{5}x = 160$$

Therefore, Marks of P = $\frac{4}{5}x$ = 160.

47. (C): The odd numbers between 8 and 28 = 9, 11, 13, 15, 17, 19, 21, 23, 25, 27

Now, Required average

$$= \frac{9+11+13+15+17+19+21+23+25+27}{10}$$

$$= \frac{180}{10} = 18.$$

48. (C): $\because$ $A = P\left(1+\frac{r}{100}\right)^n$

$\therefore$ $₹\ 2996 = P\left(1+\frac{r}{100}\right)^3$ ...(*i*)

and $₹\ 1400 = P\left(1+\frac{r}{100}\right)^2$ ...(*ii*)

From (*i*) is divided by (*ii*), we obtain

$$\left(1+\frac{r}{100}\right) = \frac{2996}{1400} = \frac{14\times214}{14\times100} = \frac{214}{100}$$

$$\Rightarrow 1+\frac{r}{100} = \frac{214}{100} \Rightarrow \frac{r}{100} = \frac{214}{100}-1$$

$$\Rightarrow \frac{r}{100} = \frac{114}{100} \Rightarrow r = 114\%$$

Hence, the rate of interest per annum is 114%.

49. (C): $r = \frac{(n-1)\times100}{t}$

$$= \frac{(2-1)\times100}{8\frac{1}{2}} = \frac{1\times100}{\frac{17}{2}} = \frac{200}{17}$$

$= 11.76\%$

Hence, the annual rate of interest will be 11.76%.

50. (C): HCF of $\frac{4}{11}$ and $\frac{16}{33}$

$$= \frac{\text{HCF of 4 and 16}}{\text{LCM of 11 and 33}} = \frac{4}{33}.$$

51. (C): Let the side of a square $= x$ unit then, its perimeter $= 4x$

given, side is increased by 5%

$\therefore$ New side $= x\times\frac{105}{100} = \frac{21}{20}x$ units

and new perimeter $= 4\times\frac{21}{20}x = \frac{21}{5}x$

Hence percentage increase in its perimeter

$$= \frac{\frac{21}{5}x-4x}{4x}\times100 = \frac{1}{5}\times25 = 5\%.$$

52. (D): Quantity of copper in 240 gm alloy

$$= 240\times\frac{7}{7+5}$$

$$= 240\times\frac{7}{12} = 140 \text{ gm}$$

and quantity of iron in 240 gm alloy

$$= 240\times\frac{5}{12} = 100 \text{ gm}$$

Let x gm of iron should be added

Then, $\frac{140}{100+x} = \frac{7}{13}$

$\Rightarrow 140\times13 = 7(100+x)$

$\Rightarrow 1820 = 700 + 7x$

$\Rightarrow 7x = 1820 - 700$

$\Rightarrow 7x = 1120$

$\Rightarrow x = \frac{1120}{7} = 160$ gm

Hence, $x = 160$ grams.

53. (D): Given, Selling price $=$ ₹ 2800

M.P. $=$ ₹ 4000

Let the discount per cent $= x\%$

Then, $4000\times\frac{(100-x)}{100} = 2800$

$\Rightarrow 100 - x = \frac{2800}{40} = 70$

$\Rightarrow 100 - 70 = 30\%$

Hence, the discount percentage $= 30\%$.

54. (A): HCF of 6 m 50 cm, 3 m 50 cm and 7 m 50 cm

= HCF of 650 cm, 350 cm and 750 cm

= 50 cm.

Hence, the length of the plank = 50 cm.

55. (C): Given, $a : b = 4 : 5$

$= 4 \times 3 : 5 \times 3 = 12 : 15$

and $b : c = 3 : 8$

$= 3 \times 5 : 8 \times 5 = 15 : 40$

$\therefore a : b : c = 12 : 15 : 40.$

56. (D): $413 \div 7(20 + 8 \times 5 - 59)$

$= 413 \div 7(20 + 40 - 59)$

$= 413 \div 7(60 - 59)$

$= 413 \div 7(1)$

$= 413 \div 7 = 59.$

57. (D): Given, S.P. of a table = ₹ 1972,

loss = 32%

$\therefore \quad \text{C.P.} = 1972 \times \frac{100}{100-32}$

$= 1972 \times \frac{100}{68}$

$= 29 \times 100 =$ ₹ 2900

$\Rightarrow$ C.P. = ₹ 2900

and given, S.P. = ₹ 3000

$\therefore$ Profit = S.P. − C.P.

= 3000 − 2900 = ₹ 100

Hence, Profit % $= \frac{\text{Profit} \times 100}{\text{C.P.}}$

$= \frac{100 \times 100}{2900} = 3.44\%.$

58. (A): The area of equilateral triangle

$= \frac{\sqrt{3}}{4} \times (\text{side})^2$

$= \frac{\sqrt{3}}{4} \times (0.2)^2 \text{ cm}^2$

$= \frac{\sqrt{3}}{4} \times 0.04 = \frac{\sqrt{3}}{4} \times \frac{0.04}{1.00}$

$= \frac{\sqrt{3}}{100} \text{ cm}^2.$

59. (A): Given, Ratio of efficiency

C : D = 4 : 1

$\therefore$ Ratio of day

C : D = 1 : 4 = $x : 4x$

According to question

$4x - x = 63$

$\Rightarrow \quad 3x = 63 \Rightarrow x = 21$

$\therefore$ (C + D)'s 1 day's work $= \frac{1}{x} + \frac{1}{4x}$

$= \frac{1}{21} + \frac{1}{4 \times 21} = \frac{1}{21} + \frac{1}{84}$

$= \frac{4+1}{84} = \frac{5}{84}$

Hence, they will take $\frac{84}{5} = 16.8$ days to complete the same work.

60. (C): Two cars start from the same point and travel in same direction

$\therefore$ Relative speed = 75 − 55 = 20 km/h

Hence, after 3 hours distance

= speed × time

= 20 × 3 = 60 km.

61. (B): No improvement. The original sentence "She heard the from door creek open as he returned home" is already grammatically correct.

62. (A): The correct word to fill in the blank is 'Corruption'. "Corruption" is a noun that refers to dishonest or fraudulent conduct by those in power, typically involving bribery or misuse of public funds.

63. (A): The correct spelling of the word should be fugitive, which refers to a person who is fleeing from custody, especially avoiding arrest or detention.

64. (A): The most appropriate antonym of the word "gobble" is: Nibble. Gobble means to eat quickly and noisily, often in large mouthfuls. Nibble refers to eating something slowly, taking very small bites.

65. (B): The most appropriate synonym for "equivocal" is: Ambiguous. Equivocal means open to multiple interpretations, unclear, or deliberately misleading. Ambiguous also signifies a lack of clarity and having multiple possible meanings.

66. (D): The phrase "a best girl" is grammatically incorrect. When comparing a superlative degree is used. We can use "the best girl" in a superlative sense or simply "a good girl."

67. (D): The most appropriate antonym of the underlined word is: Failure. Resurgence means a revival or comeback, indicating something becoming active or popular again after a period of dormancy or decline. Among the options provided, "Failure" is the most suitable antonym for "resurgence," as it represents the opposite concept of success or revival.

68. (B): The error is in the phrase very slow in dry air. The correct adverb for speed is "slowly," not "very slow." "Very" modifies adjectives, while "slowly" is an adverb modifying the verb "oxidizes."

69. (D): Because indicates a cause-and-effect relationship. It is used to introduce the reason for a particular situation or action. In this context, "because" explains why the movie was late in starting (due to projection difficulties).

70. (C): The phrase "who had have a disease" is incorrect grammatically. The correct form should use the past perfect tense to indicate an action that occurred before a certain point in the past. The corrected phrase "who has had a disease" uses the present perfect tense, which is appropriate for describing an action that started in the past and has relevance to the present (such as someone having had a disease).

71. (A): The original sentence is incomplete and lacks proper structure. "Sent his patient" corrects the sentence by using the past tense of the verb "send" to create a complete verb tense that connects the doctor to the action.

72. (C): All in your head perfectly captures the idea that something is just a product of one's imagination and not real. The phrase "It's only your imagination" suggests that the perceived threat or harm exists only in the person's mind and is not real.

73. (D): "Guilty" refers to being responsible for committing a crime or offense; deserving blame or punishment. "Innocent" means not guilty of a crime or wrongdoing; free from blame or guilt.

74. (C): To a huge or the greatest possible extent captures the essence of doing something with great energy, force, or amount, which is the typical meaning of "to beat the band."

75. (A): The question of protecting folklore was less urgent is the correct sentence with correct spelling and no errors.

76. (A): This word perfectly captures the feeling of endlessness and the passage describes the time as seeming "interminable."

77. (A): The passage describes a shared experience of the people travelling, so "we" is the most suitable pronoun.

78. (C): "Periods" refers to intervals of time, which best fits the context of occasional moments of descent.

79. (C): "Act" signifies an ongoing process, and here it describes the driver's action of pulling up the horses.

80. (A): The darkness is a key element described in the passage, so "light" is the most contrasting and relevant missing word.

R. Gupta's®

INTELLIGENCE / REASONING TEST / QUIZ Books

Book Name	Code	Price (₹)
• All About Reasoning (Verbal & Non-Verbal)	R-768	620
• रीजनिंग टेस्ट (भाषिक एवं अभाषिक)	R-807	620
• All About Reasoning (Verbal)	R-296	380
• रीजनिंग टेस्ट (भाषिक)	R-785	295
• All About Reasoning (Non-Verbal)	R-767	280
• रीजनिंग टेस्ट (अभाषिक)	R-805	210
• Test of Reasoning Ability	R-835	130
• Logical and Analytical Reasoning	R-273	160
• बौद्धिक एवं तर्कशक्ति परीक्षा (भाषिक एवं अभाषिक)	R-181	145
• General Intelligence Test/Mental Ability Test	R-42	170
• सामान्य बुद्धिमत्ता परीक्षण/मानसिक योग्यता परीक्षा	R-513	160
• World Quiz Book	R-555	160
• India Quiz Book	R-556	160
• Intelligence Quiz Book-1	R-646	70
• Intelligence Quiz Book-2	R-647	75
• Religion, Mythology & Culture Quiz Book	R-700	60
• Geography Quiz Book	R-723	60
• Junior English Quiz Book	R-764	60

Ramesh Publishing House

12-H, New Daryaganj Road, Opp. Officers' Mess, Delhi-110002

For Online Shopping: www.rameshpublishinghouse.com

2405

Previous Paper (Solved)

SSC—Constable (GD)

CAPFs, NIA, SSF and Rifleman (Assam Rifles)

Recruitment Exam, 2023*

Part-A : General Intelligence & Reasoning

1. Six students Melanie, Sucheta, Martin, Suzanne, Danish and Jacob are sitting around a circular table facing the centre. Melanie is sitting second to the right of Sucheta. Suzanne is an immediate neighbour of Melanie and Sucheta. Danish is sitting third to the right of Suzanne. Martin is an immediate neighbour of Sucheta and Danish. Jacob is sitting third to the right of Sucheta. Who is sitting between Martin and Suzanne?

A. Jacob B. Melanie
C. Sucheta D. Danish

2. Which of the following numbers will replace the question marks (?) in the given series?

99, 110, 132, ? , 209, ? , 330

A. 165, 264 B. 188, 294
C. 168, 268 D. 169, 288

3. In a certain code language, 'FOREST' is written as 'SPGVUG' and 'FRENCH' is written as 'FSGJEP'. How will 'FRIEND' be written as in that language?

A. IRFDNE B. IRFFPG
C. JSGDNE D. JSGFPG

4. There are six members of a family- A, B, C, D, E and F. D has 3 sons A, B and C. D is not the father of the children. B has one son E. C has one daughter F. How is B related to F?

A. Father's brother
B. Son
C. Father's father
D. Father

5. Select the option that is related to the third term in the same way as the second term is related to the first term.

ELECTRIC : GNGEVTKE :: NUCLEAR : ?

A. PWENGCT B. MTBKDZQ
C. PDZQDBS D. OVDMDBS

6. Three statements are given followed by three conclusions numbered I, II and III. Assuming the statements to be true, even if they seem to be at variance with commonly known facts, decide which of the conclusions logically follow(s) from the statements.

Statements:

All hands are fingers.
All legs are fingers.
All fingers are toes.

Conclusions:

I. All legs are toes.
II. All toes are hands.
III. Some toes are legs.

A. Only conclusions I and II follow
B. Only conclusions II and III follow
C. Only conclusions I and III follow
D. All conclusions follow

7. Select the correct combination of mathematical signs to sequentially replace the * signs and to balance the given equation.

420 * 42 * 10 * 2 * 102

A. =, +, ×, ÷ B. ÷, ×, +, =
C. ÷, +, =, × D. ×, ÷, =, +

* *Exam held on 13-02-2023.*

8. Select the option that is related to the third word in the same way as the second word is related to the first word.

(The words must be considered as meaningful English words and must not be related to each other based on the number of letters/number of consonants/vowels in the word)

Tiger : India :: Giant Panda : ?

A. Taiwan B. Vietnam
C. China D. Russia

9. Select the correct mirror image of the given figure when the mirror is placed at MN as shown below.

A.  B. 
C.  D. 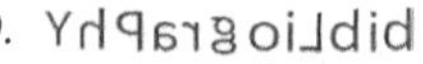

10. Select the option that is related to the third term in the same way as the second term is related to the first term and the sixth term is related to the fifth term.

13 : 196 :: 16 : ? :: 17 : 324

A. 289 B. 298
C. 258 D. 292

11. Which of the following terms will replace the question mark (?) in the given series?

MDVG, NFYK, OHBO, PJES, ?

A. QIGQ B. QKGU
C. QLFU D. QLHW

12. Seven people, A, B, C, D, E, F and G are sitting in a straight row, facing north. A sits second from the left. Only two people sit between A and C. Only three people sit between D and F and D is an immediate neighbour of A. B is an immediate neighbour of D and E is not an immediate neighbour of C. Who sits to the immediate left of F?

A. E B. B
C. C D. G

13. Select the figure from among the given options that can replace the question mark (?) in the following series.

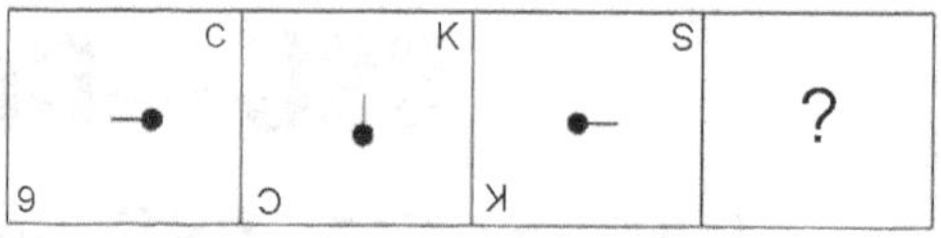

A. 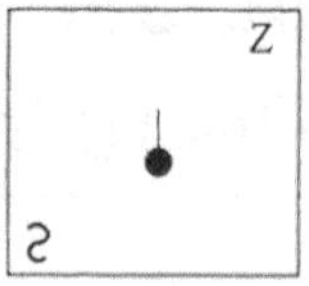 B. 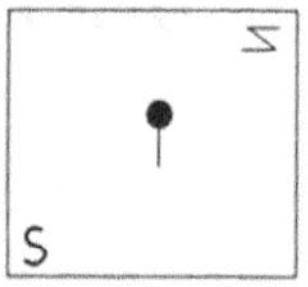

C. 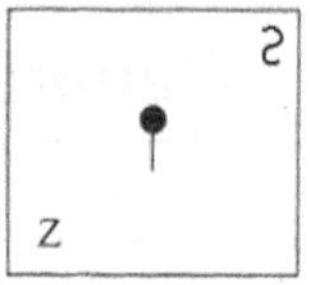 D. 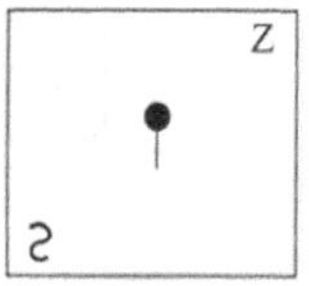

14. Which of the following numbers will replace the question mark (?) in the given series?

2, 5, 18, 41, ?

A. 74 B. 43
C. 31 D. 67

15. Which of the following letter-clusters will replace the question mark (?) in the given series?

PDYI, MGVL, ?, GMPR, DPMU

A. KJRO B. JJTP
C. IJSO D. JJSO

16. In a certain code language, 'COGENT' is written as 'FMJCQR' and 'BRINK' is written as 'EPLLN'. How will 'RANKED' be written in that language?

A. UZRJGA B. NVLOZA
C. UYQIHB D. MXCHVI

17. Which two signs should be interchanged to make the below equation mathematically correct?

$24 + 72 \div 12 \times 36 - 12 = 168$

A. ÷ and − B. × and +
C. × and ÷ D. + and −

18. Select the option that represents the correct order of the given words as they would appear in an English dictionary.

1. PRISM 2. PRINT
3. PRIOR 4. PRISE
5. PROBE 6. PRIZE

A. 5, 6, 4, 1, 2, 3 B. 1, 3, 2, 4, 6, 5
C. 2, 3, 4, 1, 6, 5 D. 3, 2, 4, 1, 6, 5

19. Select the option figure in which the given figure is embedded as its part (rotation is not allowed).

A. 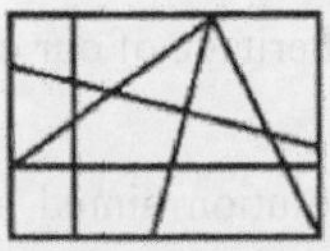 B. 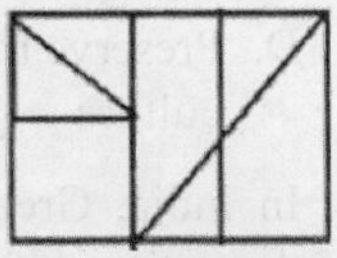

C. 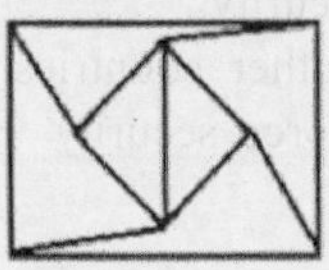 D. 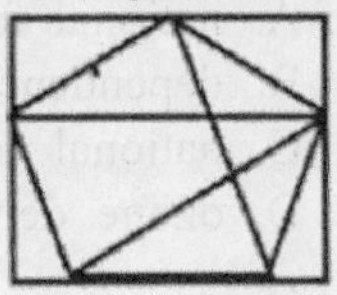

20. A paper is folded and cut as shown below. How will it appear when unfolded?

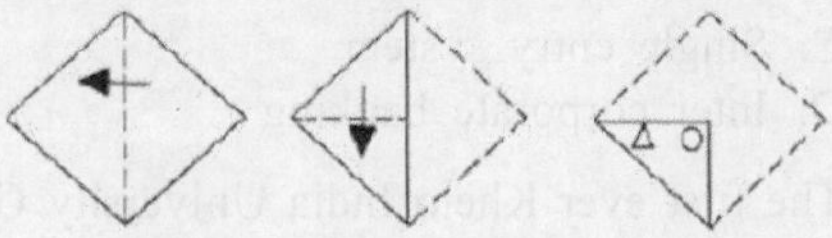

A. 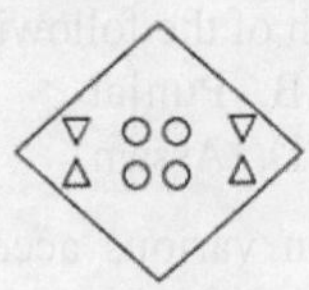 B. 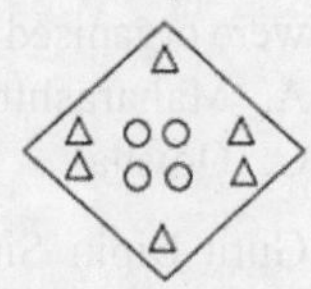

C. 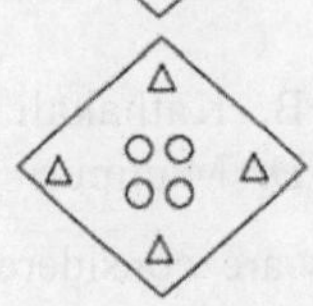 D. 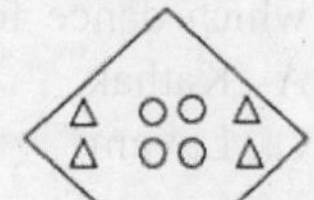

Part-B : General Knowledge & General Awareness

21. Who became Punjab's Chief Minister after election in 2022?
A. Amarinder Singh
B. Charanjit Singh Channi
C. Bhagwant Mann
D. Parkash Singh Badal

22. The Narmada river rises in which of the following place?
A. Satpura B. Nasik
C. Amarkantak hills D. Mahabaleshwar

23. Which of the following Indian states does not share its border with China?
A. Sikkim B. Arunachal Pradesh
C. Himachal Pradesh D. Uttar Pradesh

24. The five-day long Ganga Mahotsav is celebrated in which city of Uttar Pradesh?
A. Varanasi B. Lucknow
C. Noida D. Kanpur

25. Wangala is the famous folk dance of ______.
A. Mizoram B. Bihar
C. West Bengal D. Meghalaya

26. The Code of Criminal Procedure was enacted in year ______ in India.
A. 1971 B. 1975
C. 1973 D. 1977

27. The term 'shooting guard' is used in which of the following games/sports?
A. Basketball B. Tennis
C. Volleyball D. Table tennis

28. In the Tamil region, landless labourers, including slaves, were known as ______ during Sangam age.
A. kadaisiyar and adimai
B. vellalar and adimai
C. kadaisiyar and uzhavar
D. vellalar and uzhavar

29. As of November 2022, who is the Union Minister for Law and Justice in India?
A. Devendra Fadnavis
B. Kiren Rijiju
C. Ashwini Vaishnav
D. Piyush Goyal

30. Who was responsible for the Jallianwala Bagh massacre?
A. General Dawson B. General Dyer
C. General Haunters D. General Panters

31. ______ is an electronic payment system that enables customers of a bank or other financial institution to conduct a range of financial transactions through the financial institution's website.

A. Internet banking
B. Interstate banking
C. Single entry system
D. Inter corporate banking

32. The first ever Khelo India University Games were organised in which of the following state?
A. Maharashtra B. Punjab
C. Odisha D. Assam

33. Guru Bipin Singh won various accolades in which dance form?
A. Kathak B. Kathakali
C. Lavani D. Manipuri

34. Manufacturing sectors are considered as the ______ of general and economic development.
A. hand B. foot
C. knee D. backbone

35. Which of the following equations is correct for one mole of gas?
A. $V_1/V_2 = T_1^2/T_2^2$ (at constant pressure)
B. $V_1/V_2 = \sqrt{T_1}/\sqrt{T_2}$ (at constant pressure)
C. $V_1/V_2 = T_1/T_2$ (at constant pressure)
D. $p_1/V_1 = p_1/V_2$ (at constant temperature)

36. Cell is the ______ living part of an organism.
A. longest B. smallest
C. finest D. thinnest

37. What does Sub-Section (g) of the list of Fundamental Duties deal with?
A. Education of Child
B. Protect and improve the natural environment
C. Safeguarding public property
D. Preserve the rich heritage of our composite culture

38. In India, Green Revolution aimed at:
A. national food security
B. dependency on other countries
C. national armed force security
D. ozone depletion

39. Quorum in a parliamentary procedure can be understood as the ______.
A. total number of strength of the house
B. minimum number of strength to run the business of the house
C. total members of Lok Sabha
D. total number of ministers present in Rajya Sabha

40. IPR-1956 laid the foundation of the ______ Five-Year Plan.
A. Second
B. Sixth
C. Fourth
D. Tenth

Part-C : Elementary Mathematics

41. Two boats A and B start moving towards each other from two places, 272 km apart. The speed of the boat A and B in still water are 32 km/h and 36 km/h, respectively. If A moves in downstream and B moves in upstream, then in how much time they will meet each other?
A. 4 hours
B. 3 hours
C. 5 hours
D. 6 hours

42. What is the value of 10% of 20% of 1750?
A. 30 B. 35
C. 28 D. 32

43. A shopkeeper allows a discount of 20% on an article. What will be the selling price of the article marked for ₹ 600?
A. ₹ 400 B. ₹ 480
C. ₹ 450 D. ₹ 420

44. A boat can travel at a speed of 10 km/h in still water. If the speed of the stream is 2 km/h, find the time taken by the boat to go 72 km downstream.
A. 4 hours
B. 7 hours
C. 5 hours
D. 6 hours

45. A solid metallic cylinder of base radius 3 cm and height 4 cm is melted to form cones, each of height 2 cm and radius 1 cm. The number of cones is:

A. 58 B. 64
C. 56 D. 54

46. Simplify $\left[3\frac{1}{2} \div \left\{1\frac{1}{4} - \left(\frac{1}{2} + \frac{1}{3}\right)\right\} + \frac{7}{5}\right]$.

A. 5 B. 7
C. $9\frac{4}{5}$ D. $8\frac{5}{6}$

47. Find the compound interest, compounding annually on ₹ 75,000 for 3 years, if the rate of interest is 5% for the first year, 6% for the second year and 8% for the third year.

A. ₹ 15,150 B. ₹ 15,153
C. ₹ 15,160 D. ₹ 15,260

48. The average of 3, 5, 10 and x is 5. The average of 8, 12, 15, x and y is 9. x and y, respectively, are:

A. 3 and 8 B. 3 and 9
C. 2 and 3 D. 2 and 8

49. A carton of mango juice contains 500 ml. A special offer carton contains an extra 15 per cent. How much mango juice is there in the special offer carton?

A. 575 ml
B. 640 ml
C. 590 ml
D. 545 ml

50. A dishonest seller sells rice at ₹ 24/kg, which he has bought at ₹ 20/kg, and he gives 800 g instead of 1 kg. His actual profit percentage is:

A. 43.75% B. 40%
C. 50% D. 56.25%

51. The greatest common divisor of 2.16, 2.44 and 3.36 is:

A. 0.05 B. 0.02
C. 0.03 D. 0.04

52. A and B can do a piece of work in 60 days and 75 days respectively. How many days are required to complete the task if they work together?

A. 35 B. 35.5
C. $33\frac{1}{3}$ D. 36

53. Rakesh has to fill water in a cylindrical container of height 10 cm and radius 10 cm with a hemispherical bowl of radius 5 cm. How many times does he have to pour water into the cylindrical container with the hemispherical bowl to fill the tank completely with water?

A. 16 B. 19
C. 12 D. 15

54. What will be the amount on a sum of ₹ 1,000 for 3 years at 10% compound interest per annum compounding annually?

A. ₹ 1,331 B. ₹ 2,311
C. ₹ 4,121 D. ₹ 3,122

55. A dealer professes to sell his articles at cost price but he uses a false weight of 735 grams for a kilogram. The gain per cent of the dealer is: (correct to 2 decimal places)

A. 38.15% B. 36.05%
C. 35.25% D. 40.05%

56. Aman, Raman and Yash together can complete a piece of work in 29 days. Raman and Yash together can complete the same work in 58 days. Aman, Raman and Yash started working together but Aman left the work after 15 days from starting. Find the number of days in which Raman and Yash completed the remaining work.

A. 21 days B. 50 days
C. 28 days D. 54 days

57. Determine the list price of an item if a 10% discount on the item amounts to ₹ 100.

A. ₹ 800 B. ₹ 1,000
C. ₹ 1,500 D. ₹ 1,200

58. 20 kg of rice priced at ₹ 9 per kg has been mixed with 25 kg of rice priced at ₹ 10 per kg. What is the average price of 1 kg of the mixed rice? (Rounded off to one decimal place)

A. ₹ 7.2 B. ₹ 6.3
C. ₹ 8.5 D. ₹ 9.5

59. Two numbers are in the ratio 2 : 3. If 7 is subtracted from each number, the new numbers are in the ratio 7 : 11. The smaller number is:

A. 65 B. 54

C. 56 D. 45

60. If 48, x^2 and 27 are in proportion, then the value of x is:

A. 4

B. 36

C. 6

D. 16

Part-D : English

61. Select the correctly spelt word.

A. Entrepreneur B. Entreprineyour

C. Enterpreneur D. Entripreiniur

62. Select the most appropriate option that can substitute the underlined segment in the given sentence.

The marksheets of many students have been <u>withheld</u> by the university.

A. kept back B. gone through

C. handed out D. given away

63. Parts of the following sentence have been given as options. One of them may contain an error. Select the part that contains the error from the given options. If you don't find any error, mark 'No error' as your answer.

How foolish I was to have believe that young woman!

A. to have believe

B. No error

C. How foolish I was

D. that young woman

64. Select the most appropriate ANTONYM of the underlined word in the given sentence.

She is found to pass <u>derogatory</u> remarks to others.

A. cunning B. appreciative

C. critical D. sarcastic

65. Select the INCORRECTLY spelt word.

A. Hapily B. Quickly

C. Bravely D. Slowly

66. Select the most appropriate synonym of the word given in brackets to fill in the blank.

Some women have reached the ______ (peak) in their profession.

A. zenith B. finale

C. sky D. crossroads

67. Select the most appropriate ANTONYM of the given word.

Smart

A. Elegant B. Shabby

C. Speedy D. Leisurely

68. Select the most appropriate option that can substitute the underlined segment in the given sentence. If there is no need to substitute it, select 'No substitution'.

You cannot walk <u>throughout deserts by</u> bare feet or they'll get burned.

A. through deserts on

B. through deserts by

C. No substitution

D. though deserts on

69. Select the most appropriate meaning of the underlined idiom in the given sentence.

<u>An ox on their tongue</u> was the only way officers would have allowed him to carry on the unlawful activities he was involved in.

A. Bribed to remain silent

B. Being frank

C. Telling lies

D. Getting no appreciation

70. Select the most appropriate synonym of the given word.

Hypocrisy

A. Trickery
B. Honesty
C. Inaccuracy
D. Sincerity

71. Select the most appropriate ANTONYM of the given word.

Flexible

A. Obstinate
B. Snobbish
C. Hysterical
D. Staunch

72. Select the most appropriate synonym of the given word.

Obliterate

A. Erase
B. Assist
C. Construct
D. Create

73. Select the most appropriate option that can substitute the underlined segment in the given sentence.

His wife has a bad <u>habit for accusing him</u> for others' mistakes too.

A. habit of accusing him
B. habit at accusing him
C. habit on accusing him
D. habit in accusing him

74. Select the most appropriate meaning of the given idiom.

Up a creek without a paddle

A. In an unfinished mission
B. In a partially complete construction work
C. In a satisfied and calm atmosphere
D. In a troublesome and serious situation

75. Select the most appropriate synonym of the word given in brackets to fill in the blank.

I suppose it is a ______ (fair) solution to the problem at hand.

A. pale B. reasonable
C. bright D. exhibition

Directions (Qs. No. 76-80): *In the following passage, some words have been deleted. Read the passage carefully and select the most appropriate option to fill in each blank.*

Road rage is a common __(1)__ in most parts of the world. Although there are a few countries where the drivers involved just stay stationed __(2)__ the police arrive, without getting into any argument, it is not the case in many other countries. There have been instances where people __(3)__ killed due to road rage because of the collision or even a minor scratch to one or two of the vehicles involved. Although the insurance companies are doing their best to __(4)__ for the losses, the number of instances of road rage continues to __(5)__.

76. Select the most appropriate option to fill in blank number 1.

A. dominion
B. structure
C. phenomenon
D. pavilion

77. Select the most appropriate option to fill in blank number 2.

A. besides B. for
C. along D. till

78. Select the most appropriate option to fill in blank number 3.

A. were B. where
C. would D. are

79. Select the most appropriate option to fill in blank number 4.

A. compensate
B. infiltrate
C. compete
D. hesitate

80. Select the most appropriate option to fill in blank number 5.

A. oscillate
B. weaken
C. ruminate
D. escalate

ANSWERS

1. (C): According to information

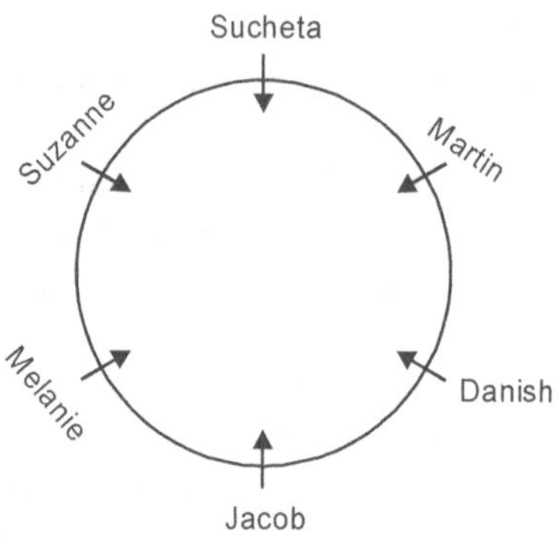

Here, Sucheta is sitting between Martin and Suzanne.

2. (A):

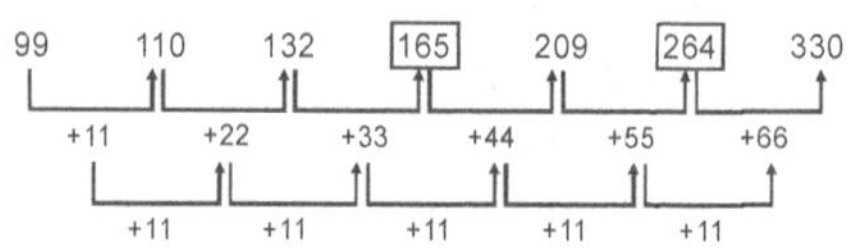

Here, missing number are ? = 165 and ? = 264.

3. (D): Given,

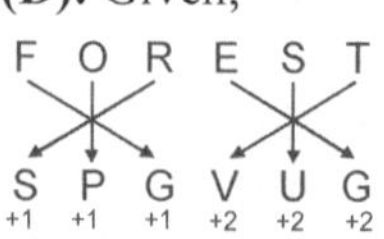

and,

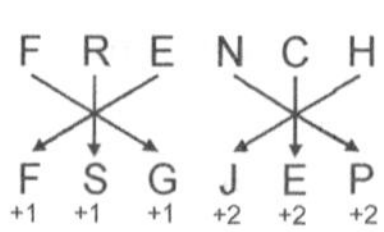

Similarly,

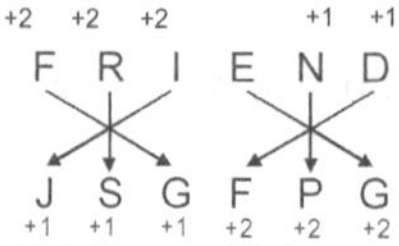

Hence, 'FRIEND' will be written as JSGFPG.

4. (A):

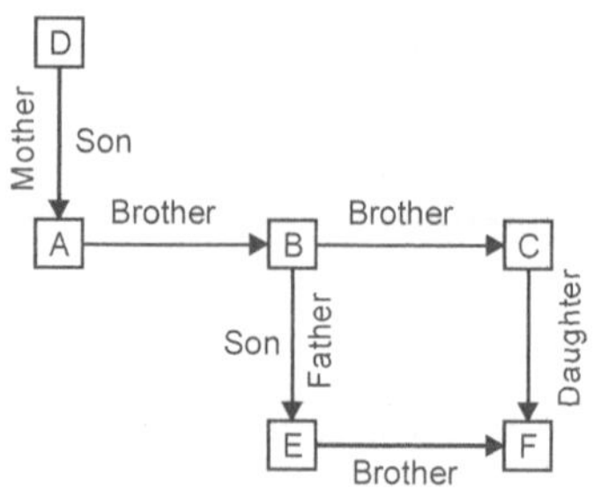

Here, B is the Father's brother.

5. (A):

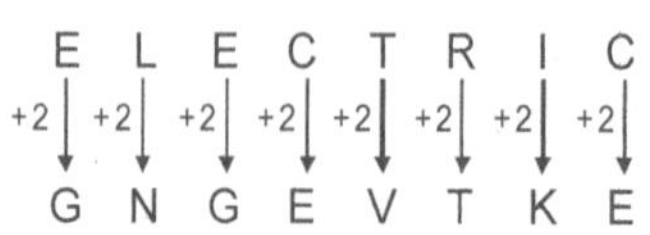

Similarly,

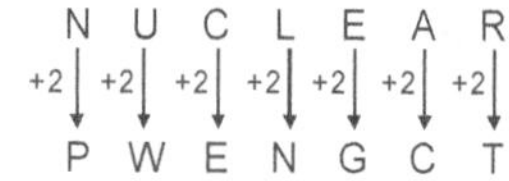

∴ ELECTRIC : GNGEVTKE

:: NUCLEAR : PWENGCT.

6. (C): According to given statement:

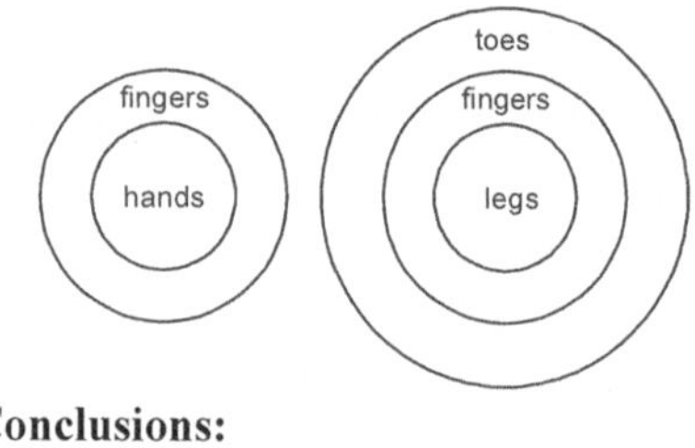

Conclusions:

I. All legs are toes. (True)

II. All toes are hands (False)

III. Some toes are legs (True).

Hence, only conclusions I and III follow.

7. (B): $\div, \times, +, =$

$420 * 42 * 10 * 2 * 102$

$\Rightarrow \quad 420 \div 42 \times 10 + 2 = 102$

$\Rightarrow \quad 10 \times 10 + 2 = 102$

$\Rightarrow \quad 100 + 2 = 102$

$\Rightarrow \quad 102 = 102.$

8. (C) **9. (A)**

10. (A): $13 : 196 \Rightarrow (13 + 1)^2 = (14)^2 = 196$

$16 : ? \Rightarrow (16 + 1)^2 = (17)^2 = 289$

$17 : 324 \Rightarrow (17 + 1)^2 = (18)^2 = 324$

∴ 13 : 196 :: 16 : 289 :: 17 : 324.

11. (D):

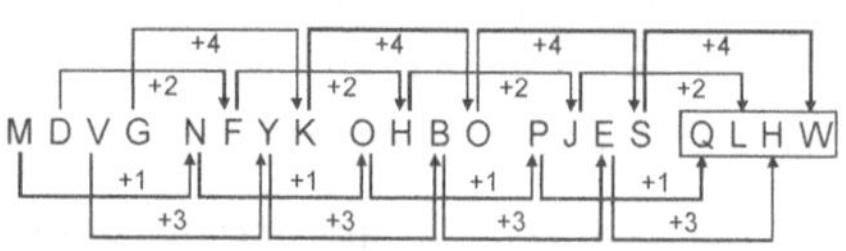

Here, ? = the next term = QLHW.

12. (D): 7 people are sitting in a straight row.

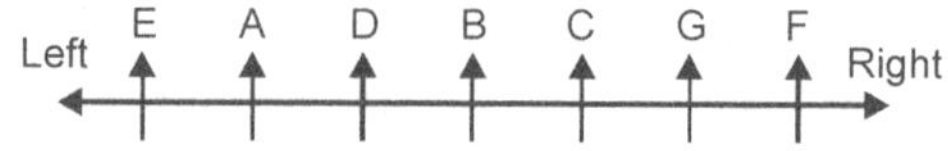

Here, G sits to the immediate left of F.

13. (D)

14. (A): 2 5 18 41 [74]

+3 +13 +23 +33

+10 +10 +10

Here, ? = The next number = 74.

15. (D): P D Y I M G V L [J J S O] G M P R D P M U

+3 +3 +3 +3 / +3 +3 +3 +3

−3 −3 −3 −3 / −3 −3 −3 −3

Here, ? = the missing letter cluster = JJSO.

16. (C): Given,

C O G E N T

+3 −2 +3 −2 +3 −2

F M J C Q R

and

B R I N K

+3 −2 +3 −2 +3

E P L L N

Similarly,

R A N K E D

+3 −2 +3 −2 +3 −2

U Y Q I H B

∴ RANKED will be written as UYQIHB

17. (B): × and +

$\therefore$ $24 + 72 \div 12 \times 36 - 12 = 168$

$\Rightarrow 24 \times 72 \div 12 + 36 - 12 = 168$

$\Rightarrow 24 \times 6 + 36 - 12 = 168$

$\Rightarrow 144 + 24 = 168$

$\Rightarrow 168 = 168.$

18. (C): According to English dictionary.
PRINT → PRIOR → PRISE → PRISM → PRIZE → PROBE.

19. (A) **20. (A)** **21. (C)**
22. (C) **23. (D)** **24. (A)**
25. (D) **26. (C)** **27. (A)**
28. (A) **29. (B)** **30. (B)**
31. (A) **32. (C)** **33. (D)**
34. (D) **35. (C)** **36. (B)**
37. (B) **38. (A)** **39. (B)**
40. (A)

41. (A): Let the speed of the stream is x km/hr.
Then, downstream speed of A = $(32 + x)$ km/h
Upstream speed of B = $(36 - x)$ km/h
Two boats A and B start moving towards each other

∴ Relative speed = $32 + x + 36 - x = 68$ km/hr

Now, time = $\frac{\text{distance}}{\text{speed}} = \frac{272}{68} = 4$ hours

Hence, they will meet each other in 4 hours.

42. (B): 10% of 20% of 1750

$= 1750 \times \frac{20}{100} \times \frac{10}{100}$

$= 1750 \times \frac{2}{100} = 35 \times \frac{2}{2} = 35.$

43. (B): Selling price of the article

$= ₹\ 600 \times \frac{100 - 20}{100}$

$= 600 \times \frac{80}{100} = 600 \times \frac{4}{5}$

$= 120 \times 4 = ₹\ 480.$

44. (D): Speed downstream of boat

$= 10 + 2 = 12$ km/h

∴ Time taken by the boat to go 72 km downstream

$= \frac{72}{12} = 6$ hours.

45. (D): Volume of a metallic cylinder $= \pi r^2 h$

$= \pi(3)^2 \times 4 \text{ cm}^3$

and volume of a cone $= \frac{1}{3}\pi r^2 h$

$= \frac{1}{3}\pi(1)^2 \times 2 \text{ cm}^3$

Hence, the number of cones

$= \frac{\pi(3)^2 \times 4}{\frac{1}{3}\pi(1)^2 \times 2}$

$= \frac{3 \times 9 \times 4}{1 \times 2}$

$= 3 \times 9 \times 2 = 54.$

46. (C): $\left[3\frac{1}{2} \div \left\{1\frac{1}{4} - \left(\frac{1}{2} + \frac{1}{3}\right)\right\} + \frac{7}{5}\right]$

$$= \left[\frac{7}{2} \div \left\{\frac{5}{4} - \frac{5}{6}\right\} + \frac{7}{5}\right]$$

$$= \left[\frac{7}{2} \div \left\{\frac{15-10}{12}\right\} + \frac{7}{5}\right]$$

$$= \left[\frac{7}{2} \div \frac{5}{12} + \frac{7}{5}\right] = \frac{7}{2} \times \frac{12}{5} + \frac{7}{5}$$

$$= \frac{42}{5} + \frac{7}{5} = \frac{49}{5} = 9\frac{4}{5}.$$

47. (B): Given, P = ₹ 75000, t = 3 years

$r_1 = 5\%$, $r_2 = 6\%$ and $r_3 = 8\%$

$$\therefore \text{ A} = \text{P}\left(1 + \frac{r_1}{100}\right)\left(1 + \frac{r_2}{100}\right)\left(1 + \frac{r_3}{100}\right)$$

$$= 75000\left(1 + \frac{5}{100}\right)\left(1 + \frac{6}{100}\right)\left(1 + \frac{8}{100}\right)$$

$$= 75000 \times \frac{105}{100} \times \frac{106}{100} \times \frac{108}{100}$$

$$= 15 \times 105 \times \frac{106}{2} \times \frac{27}{25}$$

$$= 3 \times 105 \times 53 \times \frac{27}{5}$$

= 3 × 21 × 53 × 27 = ₹ 90153

∴ Compound interest = A – P

= 90153 – 75000 = ₹ 15,153.

48. (D): Here, $3 + 5 + 10 + x = 5 \times 4$

$\Rightarrow \quad 18 + x = 20 \Rightarrow x = 2 \quad ...(i)$

and $8 + 12 + 15 + x + y = 9 \times 5$

$\Rightarrow \quad 35 + x + y = 45$

$\Rightarrow \quad x + y = 45 - 35$

$\Rightarrow \quad x + y = 10 \quad ...(ii)$

from (i) and (ii)

$$2 + y = 10 \Rightarrow y = 8.$$

49. (A): Quantity of mango juice in the special offer carton

$$= 500 \times \frac{115}{100} = 575 \text{ ml.}$$

50. (C): S.P. of 1 kg rice = ₹ 24

C.P. of 800 g rice = $\frac{20}{1000} \times 800$ = ₹ 16

∴ Profit = S.P. – C.P. = 24 – 16 = ₹ 8

$$\therefore \text{ Profit\%} = \frac{\text{Profit} \times 100}{\text{C.P.}} = \frac{8 \times 100}{16} = 50\%.$$

51. (D): The greatest common divisor of 2.16, 2.44 and 3.36

⇒ g.c.d. of 216, 244 and 336 = 4

⇒ g.c.d. of 2.16, 2.44 and 3.36

$$= \frac{4}{100} = 0.04.$$

52. (C): (A + B)'s 1 day's work = $\frac{1}{60} + \frac{1}{75}$

$$= \frac{5+4}{300} = \frac{9}{300} = \frac{3}{100}$$

∴ They can work together in $\frac{100}{3}$ days

$$= 33\frac{1}{3} \text{ days.}$$

53. (C): Volume of water in a cylindrical container

$= \pi r^2 h = \pi(10)^2 \times 10$

$= 1000\ \pi \text{ cm}^3$

and volume of water in a hemisphere bowl

$$= \frac{2}{3}\pi r^3 = \frac{2}{3}\pi(5)^3 \text{ cm}^3$$

∴ The pour water $\frac{1000\pi}{2/3\pi\,(5)^3}$ times to fill the tank = 12.

54. (A): Amount = $\text{P}\left(1 + \frac{r}{100}\right)^n$

$$= 1000\left(1 + \frac{10}{100}\right)^3 = 1000\left(\frac{11}{10}\right)^3$$

$$= 1000 \times \frac{1331}{1000} = ₹\ 1331.$$

55. (B): Gain % = $\left[\frac{\text{Error}}{\text{True Value} - \text{Error}} \times 100\right]\%$

$$= \frac{265}{1000 - 265} \times 100 = \frac{26500}{735} = 36.05\%.$$

56. (C) **57. (B)**

58. (D): Total price of 20 + 25 = 45 kg rice

$= 20 \times 9 + 25 \times 10 = 180 + 250 = ₹\ 430$

$\therefore$ The average price of 1 kg of the mixed rice

$$= \frac{430}{45} = ₹\ 9.5.$$

59. (C): Let two numbers are $2x$ and $3x$

Then, $\frac{2x-7}{3x-7} = \frac{7}{11}$

$\Rightarrow \quad 11(2x - 7) = 7(3x - 7)$

$\Rightarrow \quad 22x - 77 = 21x - 49$

$\Rightarrow \quad 22x - 21x = 77 - 49$

$\Rightarrow \quad x = 28$

$\therefore$ The smaller number $= 2x = 2 \times 28 = 56.$

60. (C): Given, 48, x^2 and 27 are in proportion

$\therefore\ 48 : x^2 :: x^2 : 27$

$\Rightarrow \quad 48 \times 27 = x^2 \times x^2$

$\Rightarrow \quad x^4 = 48 \times 27$

$\Rightarrow \quad x^4 = 16 \times 3 \times 3^3$

$\Rightarrow \quad x^4 = 2^4 \times 3^4$

$\Rightarrow \quad x^4 = (2 \times 3)^4$

$\Rightarrow \quad x = 6.$

61. (A)	**62. (A)**	**63. (A)**
64. (B)	**65. (A)**	**66. (A)**
67. (B)	**68. (A)**	**69. (A)**
70. (A)	**71. (A)**	**72. (A)**
73. (A)	**74. (D)**	**75. (B)**
76. (C)	**77. (D)**	**78. (A)**
79. (A)	**80. (D)**	

R. Gupta's® USEFUL BOOKS ON MATHEMATICS/REASONING

- All About Reasoning (Verbal & Non-Verbal) *(R-768)* 580
- All About Reasoning (Verbal) *(R-296)* 370
- All About Reasoning (Non-Verbal) *(R-767)* 260
- Test of Reasoning Ability *(R-835)* 110
- Logical and Analytical Reasoning *(R-273)* 160
- Mental Ability Test *(R-784)* 240
- General Intelligence Test/Mental Ability Test *(R-42)* 170
- World Quiz Book *(R-555)* 160
- India Quiz Book *(R-556)* 140
- Religion, Mythology & Culture Quiz Book *(R-700)* 40
- Geography Quiz Book *(R-723)* 60
- Junior English Quiz Book *(R-764)* 50
- Senior English Quiz Book *(R-765)* 70
- Tricky Mathematics *(R-1781)* 320
- Mathematics (10+2 Level) Competitive Examinations *(R-1297)* 410
- Mathematics (PG Level) Competitive Examinations *(R-1296)* 595
- Quantitative Aptitude *(R-1121)* 640
- Mathematics Formulae & Definitions (Pocket Book) *(R-1009)* 70
- Objective Arithmetic for Practice *(R-195)* 160
- All About Arithmetic *(R-703)* 290
- Super Quicker Arithmetic *(R-197)* 340
- Objective Mathematics *(R-662)* 220
- A Guide to Mathematics *(R-187)* 160
- NDA Mathematics *(R-447)* 620
- Popular Arithmetic *(R-382)* 45
- Pocket Book—Mathematics Dictionary *(R-517)* 70

Ramesh Publishing House 2306

12-H, New Daryaganj Road, Opp. Officers' Mess, Delhi-110002

For Online Shopping: www.rameshpublishinghouse.com

Previous Paper (Solved)

SSC—Constable (GD)

CAPFs, NIA, SSF and Rifleman (Assam Rifles)

Recruitment Exam, 2021*

Part-A : General Intelligence & Reasoning

1. Four letter-clusters have been given, out of which three are alike in some manner and one is different. Select the letter-cluster that is different.

A. FDB B. OMK
C. JHF D. USP

2. In a certain code language, 'MANGO' is written as 'QERKS' and 'APPLE' is written as 'ETTPI'. How will 'GUAVA' be written in that language?

A. KYFXF B. KYGZE
C. KYEZE D. KXEZE

3. In a certain code language, GAME is written as TUZANOVW, and CAR is written as XYZAIJ. How will POST be written in that language?

A. OQNPRTSV B. QRPQTUUV
C. KLLMHIGH D. KLMNJKGH

4. Select the option that is related to the third number in the same way as the second number is related to the first number.

20 : 480 :: 25 : ?

A. 700 B. 725
C. 655 D. 625

5. Select the option that is related to the third term in the same way as the second term is related to the first term.

ZYGOTE : ZYTOGE :: SEQUENCE : ?

A. USQNEEEC B. USQENCEE
C. SUQNEEEC D. USNQEEEC

6. Select the dice that can be formed by folding the given sheet along the lines.

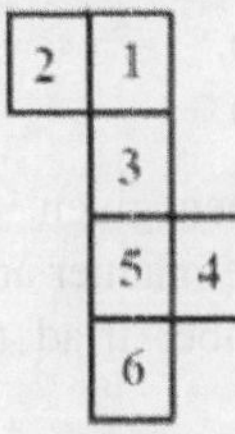

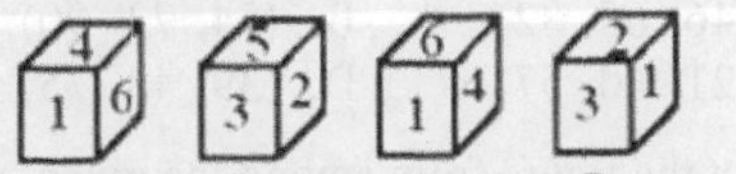

A. Only B and D B. Only B, C and D
C. Only B D. Only A and C

7. Aditi is the daughter of Sanket. Vritti is the daughter of Ankit. Kriti is the mother of Mahi. Neeta is Sanket's wife. Neeta is the mother-in-law of Vritti's mother Kriti. Which of the following statements is NOT correct?

A. Ankit is the father of Mahi.
B. Vritti is the sister of Mahi.
C. Aditi is the daughter of Neeta.
D. Kriti is the daughter of Sanket.

8. If 'A' denotes 'addition', 'B' denotes 'multiplication', 'C' denotes 'subtraction', and 'D' denotes 'division', then what will be the value of the following expression?

100 D (1 B 4) A 2 B (13 A 11) C 3 B (17 C 12)

A. 52 B. 58
C. 49 D. 60

---

* *Exam held on 16-11-2021.*

9. Select the Venn diagram that best represents the relationship between the following classes.

School, Teacher, Employee

A.  B. 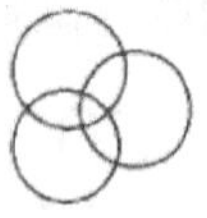

C. 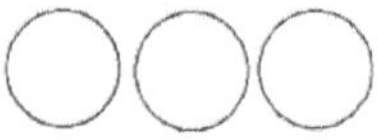 D. 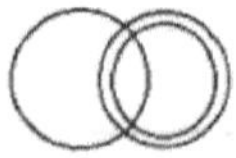

10. Select the number from among the given options that can replace the question mark (?) in the following series.

5, 9, 18, 34, ?, 95

A. 65 B. 69
C. 63 D. 59

11. Four number triads have been given, out of which three are alike in some manner and one is different. Select the number triad that is different.

A. (46, 65, 82) B. (54, 73, 90)
C. (21, 40, 57) D. (39, 48, 75)

12. Select the figure from among the given options that can replace the question mark (?) in the following series.

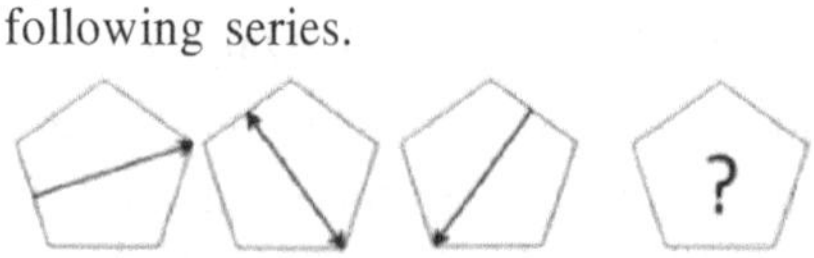

A. 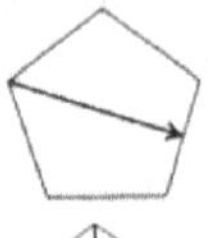 B. 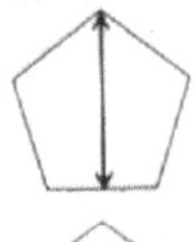

C. 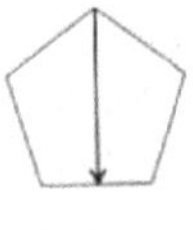 D. 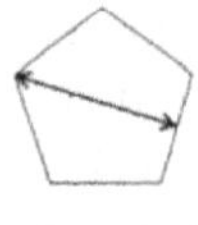

13. Select the correct option that indicates the arrangement of the given words in the order in which they appear in an English dictionary.

1. Dermatitis
2. Desistance
3. Derogation
4. Descendant
5. Dereliction

A. 5, 4, 1, 3, 2 B. 5, 1, 3, 2, 4
C. 5, 2, 1, 3, 4 D. 5, 1, 3, 4, 2

14. Select the combination of letters that when sequentially placed in the blanks of the given series will complete the series.

A _ _ B _ _ A B _ C A _ B B C

A. B, C, A, A, A, B
B. B, A, B, A, C, B
C. A, B, C, A, B, A
D. B, B, C, C, A, B

15. O, P, Q, R, S, T and U are sitting in a row facing north. U is sitting to the immediate right of T. Q is sitting in between R and O. P, who is on the extreme right, is sitting to the immediate right of O. S is sitting to the immediate left of R. Who is sitting in the middle of the row?

A. S B. R
C. T D. Q

16. Read the given statements and conclusions carefully. Assuming that the information given in the statements is true, even if it appears to be at variance with commonly known facts, decide which of the given conclusions logically follow(s) from the statements.

Statements : Some cats are animals.
All animals are plants.

Conclusions : I. All cats are plants.
II. Some plants are cats.
III. Some plants are animals.
IV. All animals are cats.

A. Only conclusion I follows
B. All the conclusions follow
C. Only conclusions I, II and III follow
D. Only conclusions II and III follow

17. Six friends are sitting in a straight line. E is 4th from the right. E is between B and D. A is adjacent to B. D is adjacent to C. D is between E and C. F is adjacent to C. Who is sitting between F and D?

A. A B. E
C. C D. B

18. Select the number from among the given options that can replace the question mark (?) in the following series.

153, 149, 143, 135, ?

A. 131　B. 125
C. 129　D. 127

19. If the diagonal of a square is increased by 4 cm, its area increases by 56 cm^2. Find the ratio of the new area of the square to the initial area of the square.
A. 16 : 9　B. 13 : 8
C. 18 : 11　D. 12 : 5

20. Select the letter-cluster from among the given options that can replace the question mark (?) in the following series.
IOM, NTR, SYW, ?
A. XDB　B. JPN
C. NSX　D. OTZ

21. Select the correct mirror image of the given combination when the mirror is placed at 'PQ' as shown.

A. 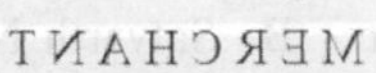　B. 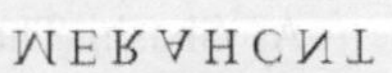
C. 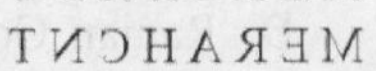　D. 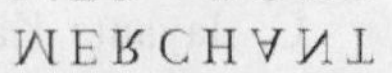

22. The sequence of folding a piece of paper and the manner in which the folded paper has been cut is shown in the following figures. How would this paper look when unfolded?

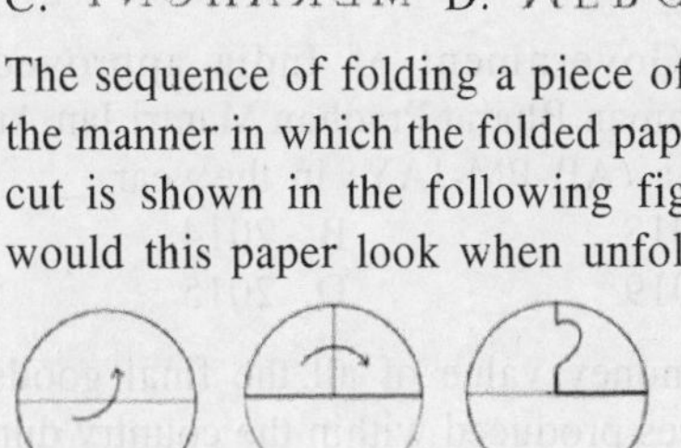

(i)　(ii)　(iii)

A. 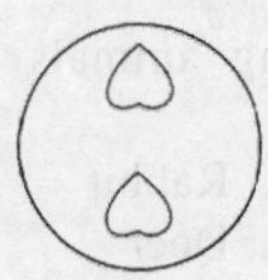　B. 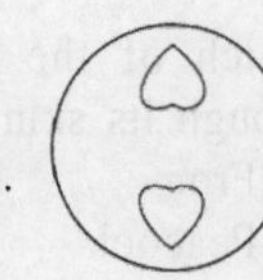
C. 　D. 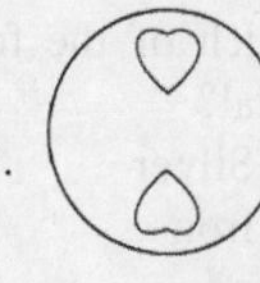

23. In a certain code language, 'PHENYL' is coded as '9-11-17-8-5-13' and 'COLONY' is coded as '6-12-13-12-8-5'. How will 'COLONEL' be coded in that language?
A. 6-12-12-13-8-17-13
B. 6-12-13-12-8-17-13
C. 6-12-12-13-8-11-13
D. 6-17-12-13-8-13-11

24. Select the option in which the given figure is embedded (rotation is NOT allowed).

A. 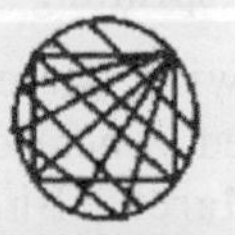　B. 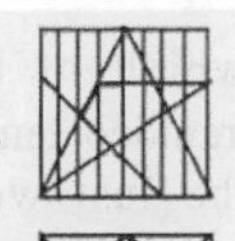
C. 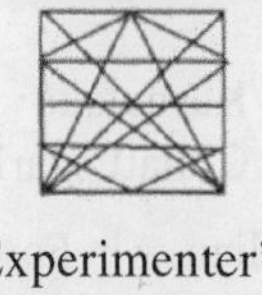　D. 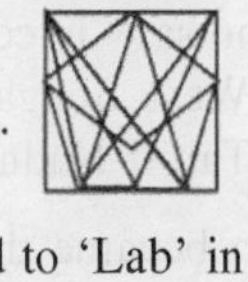

25. 'Experimenter' is related to 'Lab' in the same way as 'Chef' is related to '________'.
A. Cooking　B. Food
C. Dishes　D. Kitchen

Part-B : General Knowledge & General Awareness

26. ______ launched the Fit India Mobile App at an event at Major Dhyan Chand National Stadium, New Delhi in August, 2021.
A. Anurag Singh Thakur
B. Nisith Pramanik
C. Ravi Mittal
D. Usha Sharma

27. The acceleration of an object is said to be ______ when an object travels in a straight line and its velocity increases or decreases by equal amount in equal intervals of time.
A. negative　B. non-uniform
C. uniform　D. positive

28. Who was appointed as the State Election Commissioner of Jammu and Kashmir on October 30, 2020?
A. Kewal Kumar Sharma
B. V Bhaskaran
C. Shatrunjay Kumar Singh
D. Manoj Kumar

29. Which of the following animals breathes through its skin?
A. Frog B. Rabbit
C. Peacock D. Deer

30. Which of the following is the most reactive metal?
A. Silver B. Aluminium
C. Iron D. Potassium

31. Which non-metal among the following is poly-atomic?
A. Sulphur B. Argon
C. Oxygen D. Helium

32. Who among the following was appointed as the first Municipal Commissioner of Bombay in 1865?
A. William Hunter B. Charles Atkinson
C. H Fowler D. Arthur Crawford

33. 'La Liga' title is associated with _______.
A. tennis B. football
C. cricket D. sprinting

34. In which of the following states is the Bhoramdeo temple located, where each year in the last week of March 'Bhoramdeo Mahotsav' is celebrated?
A. West Bengal B. Karnataka
C. Tamil Nadu D. Chhattisgarh

35. Who became the first Indian Air Force pilot to perform a wingsuit skydive jump? S/he achieved this feat in July, 2019.
A. Shital Mahajan Rane
B. Archana Sardana
C. Rachel Thomas
D. Tarun Chaudhri

36. ______ was the son of a Chief of the Jnatrika (or Jhatrika) Kshatriya clan.
A. Gautama Buddha
B. Rishabhanath
C. Vardhamana Mahavira
D. Parshvanath

37. ________ was the residence of the Mughal emperors of India for nearly 200 years until 1857.
A. Jehangir Mahal B. Red Fort
C. Agra Fort D. Pari Mahal

38. Which of the following states won the 'Best Tableau' award at the 71st Republic Day parade in January, 2020?
A. Assam B. Goa
C. Odisha D. Uttar Pradesh

39. The Uttar Pradesh cabinet approved a proposal to name a zoological garden at ________ after the freedom fighter and revolutionary Ashfaqullah Khan.
A. Gorakhpur B. Faizabad
C. Shahjahanpur D. Ghaziabad

40. Which of the following statements about the Mahanadi river is INCORRECT?
A. It rises in the highlands of Chhattisgarh.
B. It drains into the Arabian Sea.
C. A part of its river basin lies in Maharashtra.
D. It is about 860 km long.

41. Who is the author of the book 'Courts of India: Past to Present'?
A. Shashi Tharoor B. Satyarth Nayak
C. Jayanta Kalita D. Ranjan Gogoi

42. The Government of India approved the Ayushman Bharat Pradhan Mantri Jan Arogya Yojana (AB-PM-JAY) in the year ______.
A. 2018 B. 2014
C. 2019 D. 2015

43. The money value of all the final goods and services produced within the country during a particular year is called _________.
A. per capita income
B. Net Domestic Product
C. National Income
D. Gross Domestic Product

44. Which of the following options gives the correct chronological order of rulers of the Mauryan Empire?
A. Brihadratha - Chandragupta - Bindusara - Ashoka
B. Ashoka - Brihadratha - Chandragupta - Bindusara
C. Chandragupta - Bindusara - Ashoka - Brihadratha
D. Bindusara - Chandragupta - Ashoka - Brihadratha

45. Which of the following is NOT a fundamental right under the 44th Amendment Act, 1978 of Indian constitution?

A. Right to property
B. Right to equality
C. Right against exploitation
D. Right to religion

46. Which of the following countries hosted the 13th edition of the 2020 ICC Under 19 Cricket World Cup?

A. England B. South Africa
C. Australia D. India

47. In which state is the Hogenakkal Falls located?

A. Andhra Pradesh B. Kerala
C. Maharashtra D. Tamil Nadu

48. The Life Insurance Corporation of India Act was passed by the Parliament in the year ______.

A. 1956 B. 1948
C. 1971 D. 1965

49. Which of the following is a biometric enabled digital service for pensioners launched by the Government of India?

A. Pradhan Mantri Jeevan Jyoti Beema Yojna
B. Pradhan Mantri Mudra Yojna
C. Pradhan Mantri Jan Dhan Yojna
D. Jeevan Pramaan

50. Tvesa Malik is an Indian ______ player.

A. volleyball B. golf
C. chess D. basketball

Part-C : Elementary Mathematics

51. The value of $42 \div 9$ of $6 - [64 \div 48 \times 3 - 15 \div 8 \times (11 - 17) \div 9] \div 14$ is:

A. $\frac{19}{36}$ B. $\frac{7}{18}$
C. $\frac{29}{72}$ D. $\frac{5}{12}$

52. A can do $\frac{2}{5}$ of a work in 6 days and B can do 30% of the same work in 3 days. They worked together for 4 days. The remaining work was completed by C alone in 6 days. B and C together can complete 70% of the original work in:

A. $5\frac{1}{2}$ days B. 4 days
C. 5 days D. $4\frac{1}{2}$ days

53. The amount of a certain sum in 3 years at simple interest at $x\%$ p.a. is ₹ 5,472 and the amount of the same sum in $7\frac{1}{2}$ years at the same rate, at simple interest is ₹ 6,930. The value of x is:

A. 7.2 B. 8.5
C. 8 D. 6.5

54. There are two sections A and B of a class, consisting of 38 and 42 students, respectively. If the average weight of the students of section A is 55 kg and that of section B is 32 kg, find the average weight of all the students in the class:

A. 42 kg B. 42.925 kg
C. 44.925 kg D. 40.925 kg

55. A dealer sold an article at a loss of 4%. Had he sold it for ₹ 120 more, he would have gained 8%. To gain 11%, he should sell the article for?

A. ₹ 1,110 B. ₹ 1,200
C. ₹ 1,320 D. ₹ 1,210

56. A sum fetched a simple interest of ₹ 3,040 at the rate of 8% p.a. in 5 years. What is the sum?

A. ₹ 8,600 B. ₹ 7,600
C. ₹ 7,700 D. ₹ 6,600

57. The greatest number that on dividing 2675 and 2320 leaves the reminders 5 and 6, respectively, is:

A. 168 B. 170
C. 187 D. 178

58. Speed of an aircraft is 120 km/min. This speed in m/sec is:

A. 120000 B. 12000
C. 1200 D. 2000

59. A and B can complete a piece of work in 120 days, B and C can complete it in 150 days, and A and C can complete it in 200 days. In how many days can B alone complete two-fifths of the same work?

A. 200 B. 100
C. 80 D. 175

60. If the sides of a triangle measure 21 cm, 35 cm and 28 cm, what is the measure of its in radius? (in cm)

A. 8 cm B. 7 cm
C. 21 cm D. 9 cm

61. After giving a discount of 20% on the marked price of an article, it is sold for ₹ 120. Had the discount not been given, the profit would have been 20%. What is the cost price of the article?

A. ₹ 120 B. ₹ 130
C. ₹ 100 D. ₹ 125

62. A discount of 20% on the price of an article is the same as a discount of 25% on the price of another article. The prices of the two articles will be, respectively:

A. ₹ 40 and ₹ 50 B. ₹ 60 and ₹ 50
C. ₹ 50 and ₹ 40 D. ₹ 50 and ₹ 60

63. The sides of a triangular park are 96 m, 110 m and 146 m. Its area is equal to the area of a field in the shape of a rhombus, one of whose diagonals is 60 m. The length (in m) of its other diagonal is:

A. 176 B. 132
C. 218 D. 88

64. What is the third proportional to 9 and 36?

A. 72 B. 288
C. 144 D. 122

65. Solve the following:

$523 + 523 \times 523 \div 523$

A. 1005 B. 1235
C. 1542 D. 1046

66. A shopkeeper has some toys. He sells two-third of the toys at a profit of 35% and the remaining toys at 10% loss. What is his overall percentage of profit?

A. 16% B. 20%
C. 18% D. 25%

67. Two trains start from places A and B, respectively, and travel towards each other at the speeds of 60 km/h and 50 km/h, respectively. By the time they meet, the faster train has travelled 110 km more than the slower train. What is the distance between A and B?

A. 1100 km B. 1200 km
C. 1150 km D. 1210 km

68. The ratio of two numbers is 9 : 5. If S is added to the larger number and 4 is subtracted from the smaller number, the greater number becomes twice the smaller number. The larger number is:

A. 110 B. 104
C. 144 D. 114

69. Vignesh spends 42% of his monthly salary on food, 16% on house rent, 11% on entertainment and 7% on conveyance. But due to some family function, he has to borrow ₹ 12,000 from a money lender to meet the expenses of ₹ 18,000. What is his monthly salary?

A. 20,000 B. 24,000
C. 30,000 D. 25,000

70. The average of 4, 6, 8, 12 and x is 7 and the average of x, 9, 13, 15 and y is 9. What is the value of $2x - 3y$?

A. 5 B. 3
C. 19 D. 1

71. If the compound interest on a certain sum of money for two years at 9% p.a. is ₹ 3,762, then the sum is:

A. ₹ 20,000 B. ₹ 18,000
C. ₹ 25,000 D. ₹ 24,000

72. The ratio of the ages of A, B and C, 5 years ago, was 4 : 5 : 7. The sum of their present ages is 135 years. What will be the sum of the ages (in years) of B and C, 3 years from now?

A. 100 B. 96
C. 106 D. 112

73. Three numbers are in the ratio 4 : 9 : 13 and their LCM is 2340. Then HCF is:

A. 7 B. 3
C. 4 D. 5

74. A man sells two articles at ₹ 9,180 each. He gains 8% on one article and loses 15% on the other. His overall profit or loss is:
A. Profit ₹ 840 B. Loss ₹ 840
C. Loss ₹ 940 D. Profit ₹ 940

75. The price of a car increased by 5% while its sales decreased by 16%. What is the percentage change in the total revenue?
A. 5% decrease B. 9% increase
C. 9% decrease D. 5% increase

Part-D : English

76. Select the most appropriate meaning of the given idiom.

To be on the same page
A. To be published together
B. To read a book together
C. To understand what the other says
D. To agree on something

77. Select the option that can be used as a one-word substitute for the given group of words.

One who collects coins
A. Fatalist B. Philatelist
C. Numismatist D. Anthropologist

78. Select the most appropriate ANTONYM of the given word.

Spellbound
A. Amazed B. Captivated
C. Enthralled D. Disenchanted

79. The following sentence has been split into four segments. Identify the segment that contains a grammatical error.

We'll look at / your pet / when you go / on a vacation.
A. We'll look at B. on a vacation
C. when you go D. your pet

80. Select the most appropriate option that can substitute the underlined word in the given sentence.

Besides generating revenue, tourism brings a break from the <u>ceremony</u> of daily life.
A. scrutiny B. symphony
C. monotony D. company

81. Select the correctly spelt word.
A. Asassisnation B. Bureaucracy
C. Philianthropist D. Peadeatrician

82. Select the most appropriate meaning of the given idiom.

Tickled pink
A. Fond of pink B. Very sensitive
C. Very pleased D. Easily teased

83. Select the most appropriate option to fill in the blank.

My sister bought the _____ watch.
A. antipathy B. colloquial
C. antilocal D. antique

84. Select the most appropriate SYNONYM of the given word.

Ample
A. Sparse B. Sufficient
C. Limited D. Scarce

85. Select the option that can be used as a one-word substitute for the given group of words.

Many fish swimming together
A. Shoal B. Bevy
C. Brood D. Flock

86. Select the option that can be used as a one-word substitute for the given group of words.

A person who supervises during an examination
A. Invigilator B. Examinee
C. Principal D. Administrator

87. The following sentence has been split into four segments. Identify the segment that contains a grammatical error.

The most important / of all my goals / are to/ learn English.
A. of all my goals B. The most important
C. are to D. learn English

88. Select the most appropriate option that can substitute the underlined segment in the given sentence. If there is no need to substitute it, select 'No substitution required'.

The condition of the house <u>had been so deteriorated</u> from lack of maintenance that nobody wanted to purchase it.
A. No substitution required
B. was deteriorating
C. was so deteriorated
D. had so deteriorated

89. Select the most appropriate synonym of the given word.

Submissive
A. Adamant B. Obdurate
C. Obedient D. Obstinate

90. Select the option that will improve the underlined part of the given sentence. In case no improvement is needed, select 'No improvement required'.

The new President has <u>bring in</u> many reforms.
A. No improvement required
B. brought about
C. bring up
D. brought out

91. Select the most appropriate ANTONYM of the given word.

Fictitious
A. False B. Factual
C. Imaginative D. Subjective

92. Select the most appropriate option to fill in the blank.

She ________ why I had not sent her an invitation.
A. granted B. enquired
C. desired D. denied

93. Select the most appropriate option to fill in the blank.

The government should take steps to _____ pollution.
A. control B. convey
C. conduct D. consume

94. Select the INCORRECTLY spelt word.
A. Wistle B. Cereal
C. Tunnel D. Rustle

95. The following sentence has been split into four segments. Identify the segment that contains a grammatical error.

I wish / I am / the Principal / of the school!
A. I wish B. of the school
C. I am D. the Principal

Directions (Qs. No. 96-100): *In the following passage, some words have been deleted. Read the passage carefully and select the most appropriate option to fill in each blank.*

Writing is a form (1) _____, and neat handwriting is important when writing (2) _____ that will be read by someone else. We (3) _____ by the quality of our handwriting, and (4) _____ our handwriting is poor, we (5) _____ to be lazy or incompetent.

96. Select the most appropriate option to fill in blank no. 1.
A. in expression
B. to expressing
C. for expression
D. of expression

97. Select the most appropriate option to fill in blank no. 2.
A. nothing B. everything
C. anything D. each thing

98. Select the most appropriate option to fill in blank no. 3.
A. should be often judged
B. are often judged
C. have been often judged
D. judged often

99. Select the most appropriate option to fill in blank no. 4.
A. as B. while
C. where D. when

100. Select the most appropriate option to fill in blank no. 5.
A. appear B. see
C. expose D. look

ANSWERS

1. (D): F D B O M K J H F U S P (−2, −2; −2, −2; −2, −2; −2, −2)

Hence, USP is different.

2. (C): In a certain code language,

M A N G O is written as (+4 each) Q E R K S

and A P P L E is written as (+4 each) E T T P I

G U A V A is written as (+4 each) K Y E Z E

3. (C)

4. (B): 20 : 480 :: 25 : 725

20 × 20 + 20 × 4 = 400 + 80 = 480

25 × 25 + 25 × 4 = 625 + 100 = 725

Hence, 725 will come at the place of question mark.

5. (A) **6. (B)** **7. (D)**

8. (B): 100 ÷ (1 × 4) + 2 × (13 + 11) − 3 × (17 − 12) = 25 + 48 − 15 = 73 − 15 = 58.

9. (B):

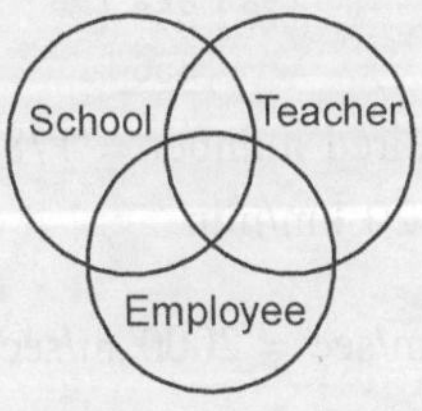

The Venn diagram is the best represents the given relationship.

10. (D): 5 9 18 34 59 95

+4 +9 +16 +25 +36

2^2 3^2 4^2 5^2 6^2

Hence, 59 will come at the place of question mark.

11. (D): 46 65 82 (+19, +17); 54 73 90 (+19, +17)

21 40 57 (+19, +17); 39 48 75 (+9, +27)

Hence, 39, 48, 75 is different.

12. (D) **13. (D)** **14. (C)**

15. (B): T U S R Q O P

Hence, R is sitting in the middle of the row.

16. (D)

17. (C): Six friends are sitting in a straight line.

B A E D C F

Clearly, C is sitting between F and D.

18. (B): 153 149 143 135 125

−4 −6 −8 −10

Hence, 125 will come at the place of question mark.

19. (A) **20. (A)** **21. (A)**

22. (D) **23. (B)** **24. (B)**

25. (D): Experiment is related to 'Lab' in the same way as 'Chef' is related to 'Kitchen'.

26. (A) **27. (C)** **28. (A)**

29. (A) **30. (D)** **31. (A)**

32. (D) **33. (B)** **34. (D)**

35. (D) **36. (C)** **37. (B)**

38. (A) **39. (A)** **40. (B)**

41. (D) **42. (A)** **43. (D)**

44. (C) **45. (A)** **46. (B)**

47. (D) **48. (A)** **49. (D)**

50. (B)

51. (C): 42 ÷ 9 of 6 − [64 ÷ 48 × 3 − 15 ÷ 8 × (11 − 17) ÷ 9] ÷ 14

$$= 42 \div 54 - \left[\frac{64}{48} \times 3 - \frac{15}{8} \times \frac{(-6)}{9}\right] \div 14$$

$$= \frac{42}{54} - \left[4 + \frac{5}{4}\right] \div 14 = \frac{7}{9} - \frac{21}{4} \times \frac{1}{14} = \frac{7}{9} - \frac{3}{8}$$

$$= \frac{56 - 27}{72} = \frac{29}{72}.$$

52. (D): Whole work will be done by A in

$$\frac{5}{2} \times 6 = 15 \text{ days}$$

Whole work will be done by B in

$$\frac{10}{3} \times 3 = 10 \text{ days}$$

4 days work done by A and B

$$= 4\left(\frac{1}{15} + \frac{1}{10}\right) = 4\left(\frac{2+3}{30}\right) = 4 \times \frac{1}{6} = \frac{2}{3}$$

$$\text{Remaining work} = 1 - \frac{2}{3} = \frac{1}{3}$$

Whole work will be done by C in 3 × 6

= 18 days

(B and C)'s 1 day work

$$= \frac{1}{10} + \frac{1}{18} = \frac{9+5}{90} = \frac{14}{90}$$

(B + C) $\frac{14}{90}$ part can do in 1 day

$\therefore$ (B + C) $\frac{7}{10}$ part can do in $\frac{90}{14} \times \frac{7}{10}$ days

$$= \frac{9}{2} \text{ days} = 4\frac{1}{2} \text{ days.}$$

53. (A): Simple interest in $4\frac{1}{2}$ years

= 6930 – 5472 = ₹ 1458

Simple interest in 1 year

$$= \frac{2 \times 1458}{9} = 2 \times 162 = ₹\ 324$$

Simple interest in 3 years = ₹ 972

Principal = 5472 – 972 = ₹ 4500

$$x = \frac{972 \times 100}{4500 \times 3} = \frac{36}{5} = 7.2\%$$

Hence, the value of x = 7.2.

54. (B): Total weight of 38 students of section A

= 38 × 55 = 2090 kg

Total weight of 42 students of section B

= 42 × 32 = 1344 kg

Total weight of section A and B students

= 2090 + 1344 = 3434 kg

$$\text{Average} = \frac{3434}{80} = 42.925 \text{ kg}$$

Hence, Average weight of all the students in the class = 42.925 kg.

55. (A): Let C.P. be ₹ x, then

108% of x – 96% of x = 120

$\Rightarrow$ 12% of x = 120

$$\Rightarrow \quad x = \frac{100 \times 120}{12} = 1000$$

For 11% gain, S.P. = $\text{C.P.} + \frac{11}{100} \times 1000$

= 1000 + 110 = ₹ 1110.

56. (B):

$$P = \frac{SI \times 100}{r \times t} = \frac{3040 \times 100}{8 \times 5}$$

= 1520 × 5 = ₹ 7600.

57. (D): 2675 – 5 = 2670

and 2320 – 6 = 2314

```
2314 ) 2670 (
       2314
       356 ) 2314 ( 6
             2136
             178 ) 356 ( 2
                   356
```

Hence, the required number = 178.

58. (D): Speed = 120 km/min

$$= \frac{120 \times 1000}{60} \text{ m/sec} = 2000 \text{ m/sec.}$$

59. (C): (A + B)'s 1 day work = $\frac{1}{120}$

(B + C)'s 1 day work = $\frac{1}{150}$

(A + C)'s 1 day work = $\frac{1}{200}$

[(A + B) + (B + C) + (C + A)]'s 1 day work

$\Rightarrow$ 2[A + B + C]'s 1 day work

$= \frac{1}{120} + \frac{1}{150} + \frac{1}{200} = \frac{5+4+3}{600} = \frac{12}{600} = \frac{1}{50}$

$\therefore$ (A + B + C)'s 1 day work

$$= \frac{1}{2 \times 50} = \frac{1}{100}$$

$\therefore$ B's 1 day work $= \frac{1}{100} - \frac{1}{200} = \frac{1}{200}$

$\frac{1}{200}$ part B can do in 1 day

$\therefore$ $\frac{2}{5}$ part B can do in $200 \times \frac{2}{5}$ days

$= 40 \times 2$ days $= 80$ days.

60. (B): $S = \frac{a+b+c}{2} = \frac{21+28+35}{2} = \frac{84}{2}$

$= 42$ cm

Area of the triangle $= \sqrt{S(S-a)(S-b)(S-c)}$

$= \sqrt{42(42-21)(42-28)(42-35)}$

$= \sqrt{42 \times 21 \times 14 \times 7} = \sqrt{2 \times 21 \times 21 \times 2 \times 7 \times 7}$

$= 21 \times 2 \times 7 = 294$ cm^2

Radius of in circle of a triangle

$= \frac{A}{S} = \frac{294}{42} = 7$ cm.

61. (D): Let CP = 100, SP = ₹ 120

Let MP = ₹ x

Then, 80% of $x = 120$

$\Rightarrow \frac{80}{100} \times x = 120$

$\Rightarrow x = \frac{100 \times 120}{80} =$ ₹ 150

When SP ₹ 120, then CP = ₹ 100

When SP ₹ 150, then CP $= \frac{100}{120} \times 150 =$ ₹ 125

Hence, the cost price of the article = ₹ 125.

62. (C): Required prices of the two articles will be ₹ 50 and ₹ 40 respectively

Because, $\frac{20}{100} \times 50 =$ ₹ 10

and $\frac{20}{100} \times 40 =$ ₹ 10.

63. (A): Area of the triangle $= \frac{1}{2} \times 96 \times 110$

$= 48 \times 110 = 5280$ m^2

Area of rhombus $= \frac{1}{2} \times d_1 \times d_2$

$\Rightarrow 5280 = \frac{1}{2} \times 60 \times d_2$

$\Rightarrow 5280 = 30d_2$

Other diagonal $= \frac{5280}{30} = 176$ m.

64. (C): 9, 36, x are in proportional

$\therefore \frac{9}{36} = \frac{36}{x}$

$\Rightarrow 9x = 36 \times 36$

$\Rightarrow x = \frac{36 \times 36}{9} = 4 \times 36 = 144$

Hence, third proportional = 144.

65. (D): $523 + 523 \times 523 \div 523$

$= 523 + 523 \times 1 = 523 + 523 = 1046$.

66. (B): Let C.P. of the toys = ₹ x

C.P. of the $\frac{2}{3}$ part = ₹ $\frac{2x}{3}$

and C.P. of $\frac{1}{3}$ part = ₹ $\frac{x}{3}$

Total SP $= \left(\frac{2x}{3} \times 135\%\right) + \left(\frac{x}{3} \times 90\%\right)$

$= \left(\frac{2x}{3} \times \frac{135}{100} + \frac{x}{3} \times \frac{90}{100}\right)$

$= \frac{9x}{10} + \frac{3x}{10} = \frac{12x}{10} = \frac{6x}{5}$

Profit $= \frac{6x}{5} - x = \frac{x}{5}$

Profit% $= \frac{\frac{x}{5}}{x} \times 100 = \frac{x}{5x} \times 100 = 20\%$.

67. (D): Let distance travelled by slower train

$= x$ km

Distance travelled by faster train

$= (x + 110)$ km

$$\therefore \quad \frac{x}{50} = \frac{x+110}{60}$$

$$\Rightarrow \quad 60x = 50x + 5500 \Rightarrow x = 550$$

Distance between A and B

$= (x + x + 110)$ km

$= (550 + 550 + 110)$ km $= 1210$ km.

68. (D): Let numbers are $9x$ and $5x$

$$9x + 8 = 2(5x - 4)$$

$$\Rightarrow \quad 9x + 8 = 10x - 8$$

$$\Rightarrow \quad -x = -16 \Rightarrow x = 16$$

$\therefore$ Numbers are $9 \times 16 = 144$

and $5 \times 16 = 80$

Hence, the larger number = 144.

69. (D): Let monthly salary = ₹ x

According to the question,

24% of $x = 6000$

$$\Rightarrow \quad \frac{24}{100} \times x = 6000 \Rightarrow x = \frac{100 \times 6000}{24}$$

= ₹ 25000.

70. (D): $4 + 6 + 8 + 12 + x = 35$

$$\Rightarrow \quad x = 35 - 30 \Rightarrow x = 5$$

and $x + 9 + 13 + 15 + y = 45$

$$\Rightarrow \quad x + y + 37 = 45$$

$$\Rightarrow \quad x + y = 8, y = 3$$

Value of $2x - 3y = 2 \times 5 - 3 \times 3$

$= 10 - 9 = 1.$

71. (A): Let P = ₹ 100,

$$A = P\left(1+\frac{r}{100}\right)^2 = 100\left(1+\frac{9}{100}\right)^2$$

$$= \frac{100 \times 109 \times 109}{100 \times 100} = 118.81$$

C.I. = A − P = 118.81 − 100 = ₹ 18.81

When CI ₹ 18.81, then P = ₹ 100

When C.I. ₹ 3762, then $P = \frac{100}{18.81} \times 3762$

$$\Rightarrow \quad P = \frac{100 \times 100 \times 3762}{1881}$$

$$\Rightarrow \quad P = 20000.$$

72. (C): According to the question,

$4x + 5 + 5x + 5 + 7x + 5 = 135$

$$\Rightarrow \quad 16x + 15 = 135$$

$$\Rightarrow \quad 16x = 120$$

$$\Rightarrow \quad x = \frac{120}{16} = \frac{15}{2}$$

Now, After 3 years sum of B and C age

$= 5x + 5 + 3 + 7x + 5 + 3$

$= 12x + 16 = 12\left(\frac{15}{2}\right) + 16$

$= 6 \times 15 + 16 = 90 + 16 = 106$ years.

73. (D): Let numbers are $4x$, $9x$ and $13x$

LCM of $4x$, $9x$ and $13x = 468x$

$$468x = 2340$$

$$\Rightarrow \quad x = \frac{2340}{468} = 5$$

$\therefore$ Numbers are 20, 45 and 65

HCF of 20, 45 and 65 = 5.

74. (C): First article

S.P. = ₹ 9180; Gain = 8%

C.P. = $\frac{100}{108} \times 9180$ = ₹ 8500

2nd article, S.P. = ₹ 9180; Loss = 15%

C.P. = $\frac{100}{85} \times 9180$ = 10800

Total C.P. = 8500 + 10800 = ₹ 19300

Total S.P. = 9180 + 9180 = ₹ 18360

Loss = 19300 − 18360 = ₹ 940.

75. (D)	**76. (D)**	**77. (C)**
78. (D)	**79. (A)**	**80. (C)**
81. (D)	**82. (C)**	**83. (D)**
84. (B)	**85. (A)**	**86. (A)**
87. (C)	**88. (D)**	**89. (C)**
90. (B)	**91. (B)**	**92. (B)**
93. (A)	**94. (A)**	**95. (C)**
96. (D)	**97. (C)**	**98. (B)**
99. (D)	**100. (A)**	

Previous Paper (Solved)

SSC—Constable (GD)

CAPFs, NIA, SSF and Rifleman (Assam Rifles)

Recruitment Exam, 2019*

Part-A : General Intelligence & Reasoning

1. Identify the correct option to complete the following series:

5, 8, 13, 20, 29, ____, 53, 68, 85

A. 40 B. 39

C. 35 D. 36

2. Identify the number that is different from the rest.

A. 625 B. 115

C. 125 D. 25

3. Select the Venn diagram that best illustrates the relationship between the three given classes.

Languages, Hindi, Malayalam

A.  B. 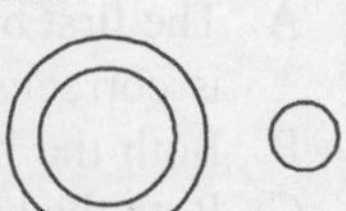

C.  D. 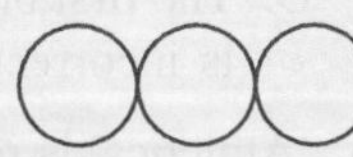

4. A medical representative plans to visit each of six hospitals—A, B, C, D, E and F—exactly once during the course of one day. He is setting up his schedule for the day according to the following conditions.

(*i*) He must visit A before B and E.

(*ii*) He must visit B before D.

(*iii*) The third hospital he visits must be C.

Which of the following could be the order in which the medical representative visits the six hospitals?

A. A, F, C, D, E, B

B. C, E, A, B, D, F

C. C, F, A, E, D, B

D. A, B, C, D, E, F

5. Read the given statements and conclusions carefully. Assuming that the information given in the statements is true, even if they appear to be at variance with commonly known facts, decide which of the conclusions logically follow(s) from the statements beyond reasonable doubt.

Statement : No cat is a monkey.
No monkey is a cow.

Conclusions : I. No cat is a cow.
II. Some cows are monkeys.

A. Only conclusion I follows.

B. Only conclusion II follows.

C. Neither conclusion I nor conclusion II follows.

D. Both conclusions I and II follow.

6. Select the option that is related to the third term in the same way as the second term is related to the first term.

ACE : EIM : : DFH : ?

A. PLH B. HPL

C. PHL D. HLP

7. Select the option in which the given figure is embedded.

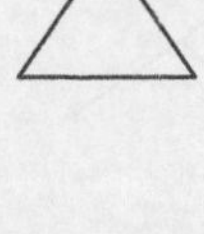

* *Exam held on 11-02-2019.*

A. 

B. 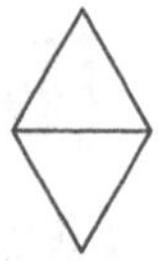

C. 

D. 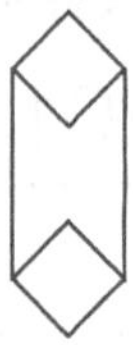

8. Identify the correct option to complete the following series.

50, 49, 47, 44, 40, 35, _____, 22

A. 30 B. 27
C. 29 D. 25

9. Select a figure from amongst the four alternatives, that when placed in the blank space (?) of figure X will complete the pattern. (Rotation is not allowed).

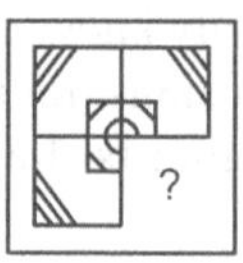

A. 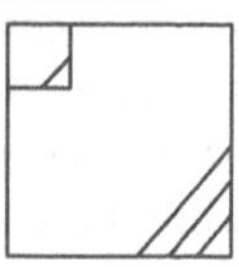

B. 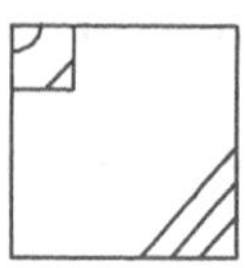

C. 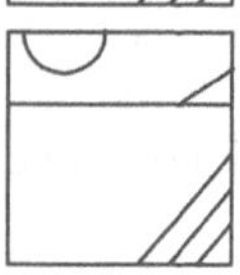

D. 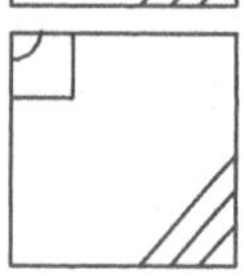

10. Choose the alternative which most closely resembles the mirror image of the given figure when mirror is placed at right side:

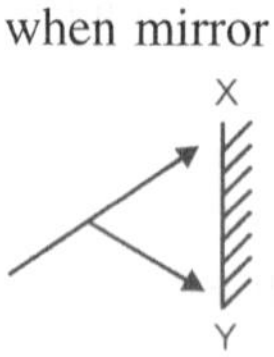

A. 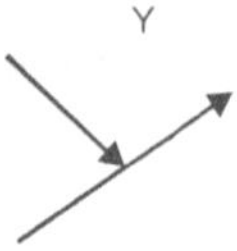

B. 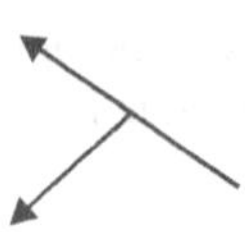

C. 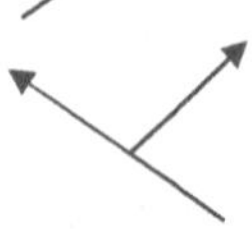

D. 

11. If KITCHEN is coded as LKWGMKU, then SHAMPOO will be coded as _____ .

A. TJDQUUV B. TJDQTUU
C. TJDQTUV D. TJEQUUV

12. Identify the odd pair from the following.

A. Eagle : Swoop B. Pig : Sty
C. King : Palace D. Bird : Nest

13. Select the figure that will come next in the following series.

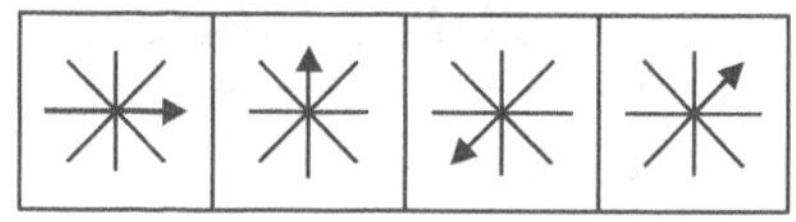

A. 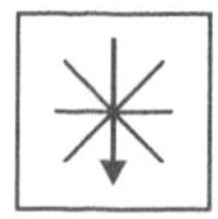

B. 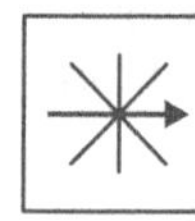

C. 

D. 

14. In the following number series, two numbers have been put within brackets. Study the series carefully and select the correct alternative with respect to the series.

3, 9, (27), 81, (243), 729, 2187

A. The first bracketed number (from the left) is correct and the second is incorrect.
B. Both the bracketed numbers are correct.
C. Both the bracketed numbers are incorrect.
D. The first bracketed number (from the left) is incorrect and the second is correct.

15. 'Athletics' is related to 'Stadium' in the same way as 'Skating' is related to '_____'.

A. Ground B. Track
C. Rink D. Court

16. Seven employees, T, U, V, W, X, Y and Z reach their factory in a particular sequence. Y reaches immediately before T but does not immediately follow W. V is the last one to reach. X immediately follows T and is subsequently followed by Z. W reaches before T. Who is the second to reach the factory?

A. U B. X
C. W D. Z

17. If B = 3 and H = 9, then SCHOOL = ______.
A. 78 B. 76
C. 69 D. 96

18. Identify the odd one from the following.
A. Volume B. Small
C. Height D. Weight

19. A square transparent sheet with a pattern is given. How will the pattern appear when the transparent sheet is folded along the dotted line?

A.  B. 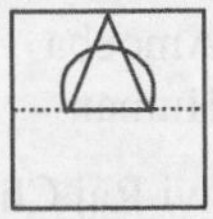

C.  D. 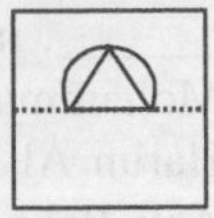

20. Identify the odd one from the following.
A. EV B. KP
C. DX D. HS

21. Five students are sitting in a row. Akbar is to the left of the person sitting in the middle, but to the right of Sekar. Prakash is to the right of Deva, and Ram is to the right of Prakash. Ram is second from the person sitting in the middle. Who is the person sitting in the middle?
A. Sekar B. Akbar
C. Deva D. Ram

22. The statements below are followed by two conclusions labelled I and II. Assuming that the information in the statements is true, even if it appears at variance with generally established facts, decide which conclusion(s) logically and definitely follow(s) from the information given in the statements.

Statements : All papers are books.
All books are papaya.

Conclusions : I. All papers are papaya.
II. Some papayas are papers.

A. Only conclusion I follows.
B. Neither conclusion I nor conclusion II follows.
C. Only conclusion II follows.
D. Both conclusions I and II follow.

23. Which two signs need to be interchanged to make the given equation correct?
$20 \div 20 + 20 - 20 \times 20 = 20$
A. + and ÷ B. + and −
C. ÷ and × D. + and ×

24. Select the term that will come next in the following series.
a, cd, fgh, jklm, opqrs, ______
A. uvwxyz B. vwxyza
C. uvwxy D. tuvwxy

25. Select the option that is related to the third term in the same way as the second term is related to the first term.
$\frac{5}{6} : 121 :: \frac{8}{9} :$ ______
A. 145 B. 300
C. 289 D. 356

Part-B : General Knowledge & General Awareness

26. The directional growth movement in plants due to touch is called ______.
A. thigmonasty B. geotropism
C. phototropism D. chemotropism

27. The deltas of the Mahanadi and the Godavari are rich in ______ soil.
A. black B. arid
C. forest D. alluvial

28. A person with the blood group ______ is considered to be a universal donor.
A. O negative B. AB positive
C. AB negative D. O positive

29. When was the Planning Commission set up?
A. 2019 B. 2000
C. 1947 D. 1950

30. The three-tier system of local government does NOT include the ______.
A. Panchayat Samiti B. Village Committee
C. Gram Panchayat D. Zila Parishad

31. The United States of America adopted a democratic constitution in ______ .
A. 1932 B. 1787
C. 1877 D. 2000

32. In which battle Napoleon was defeated?
A. Ligny B. Jena
C. Waterloo D. Arcole

33. Which of the following is the hardest substance?
A. Coal B. Diamond
C. Silver D. Iron

34. The Statue of Unity in India is the world's tallest statue of _____ .
A. M.K. Gandhi
B. Sardar Vallabhbhai Patel
C. Vinoba Bhave
D. Dr. B.R. Ambedkar

35. Begum Hazrat Mahal is associated to which of the following revolts of India?
A. Moplah Revolt 1921
B. Paik Revolt 1817
C. Gond Revolt 1941
D. Sepoy Mutiny 1857

36. The National Rural Employment Guarantee Act was passed in ______ .
A. 2005 B. 1900
C. 2019 D. 2000

37. Name the famous Indian cricketer who wrote the book 'A Century Is Not Enough'.
A. Virender Sehwag B. Virat Kohli
C. Sachin Tendulkar D. Sourav Ganguly

38. ______ won the Miss World 2017 pageant.
A. Lara Dutta B. Anukreethy
C. Manushi Chillar D. Yukta Mukhi

39. ______ is a dance form which represents a unique synthesis of Hindu and Muslim genius in art.
A. Kathak B. Manipuri
C. Odissi D. Kathkali

40. The smallest living bird is the ______ .
A. hummingbird B. canary
C. house sparrow D. dove

41. The largest backwater lake in Odisha is _____.
A. Dal lake B. Wular lake
C. Chilika lake D. Pulicat lake

42. In India, currency notes of ₹ 500 and ₹ 1,000 were declared invalid in the year?
A. 1998 B. 2019
C. 2016 D. 2001

43. The first lady Indian Air Force officer to fly MIG 21 is ______ .
A. Khusboo Mehta B. Bhavna Sharma
C. Anjali Gupta D. Avani Chaturvedi

44. Which of the following is NOT a multicellular animal?
A. Amoeba B. Cat
C. Human D. Horse

45. Prithvi Raj Chauhan was defeated at the hands of _______, in the battle of Tarain, 1192.
A. Mohammad Ghori
B. Harun Al Rashid
C. Abu Bakr
D. Umar II

46. Which state has the largest coast line?
A. Karnataka B. Kerala
C. Tamil Nadu D. Gujarat

47. The All-India War Memorial, built in the memory of the Indian soldiers who laid down their lives in the First World War, is known today as ______ .
A. Char Minar B. Lal Qila
C. Jama Masjid D. India Gate

48. Which Hindi movie is based on the Indian hockey team on their first Olympic gold since India became independent?
A. Lagaan B. MS Dhoni
C. Gold D. Chak De

49. Identify the author of the book "Straight from the heart".
A. Sachin Tendulkar B. Kapil Dev
C. M.S. Dhoni D. Saurav Ganguly

50. Which country gave universal suffrage since the 19th century?
A. Sri Lanka B. India
C. Pakistan D. New Zealand

Part-C : Elementary Mathematics

51. A person purchased 12 bags of sugar at the rate of ₹ 1200 per bag, 8 bags at the rate of ₹ 1500 per bag and 10 bags at the rate of ₹ 2100 per bags. What will be the average cost of all the bags together?

A. ₹ 1420 B. ₹ 1680
C. ₹ 1580 D. ₹ 1640

52. The line chart given below shows the profit percentage of a company on 5 different products P1, P2, P3, P4 and P5.

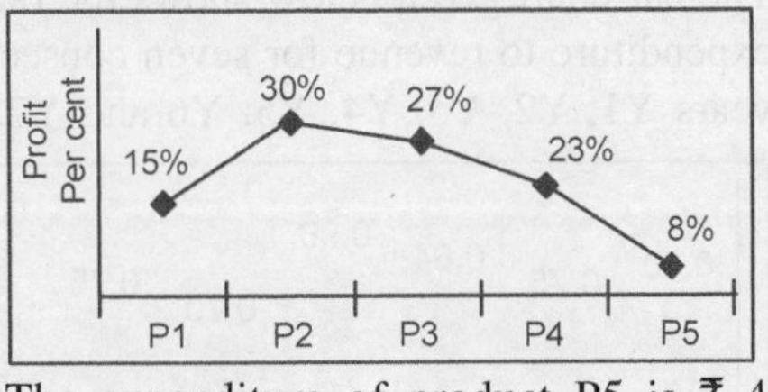

The expenditure of product P5 is ₹ 46000. What is revenue of product P5?

A. ₹ 52780 B. ₹ 49680
C. ₹ 47360 D. ₹ 4600

53. A bowler has taken 0, 3, 2, 1, 5, 3, 4, 5, 5, 2, 2, 0, 0, 1 and 2 wickets in 15 consecutive matches.
What is the median of the given data?

A. 1 B. 3
C. 0 D. 2

54. A sum of ₹ 9800 gives simple interest of ₹ 4704 in 6 years. What will be the rate of interest per annum?

A. 9% B. 8.5%
C. 8% D. 7.5%

55. What is the value of $7\frac{1}{4}+[6+(5-8\div 4)-1]$?

A. $\frac{61}{4}$ B. $\frac{29}{2}$
C. $\frac{23}{2}$ D. $\frac{57}{4}$

56. If Rohit can cover a distance of 1188 km in 22 hours, then what is the speed of Rohit?

A. 54 m/s B. 25 m/s
C. 15 m/s D. 48 m/s

57. The average weight of a group of 24 students increases by 2 kg when the weight of teacher is also included. If the initial average weight of the group of 24 students was 30 kg, then what is the weight of teacher?

A. 32 kg B. 82 kg
C. 80 kg D. 92 kg

58. Selling price and cost price of an article are ₹ 1333 and ₹ 2150. What will be the loss percentage?

A. 38% B. 61.30%
C. 48% D. 54.4%

59. If the diameter of a circle increases by 15%, then what will be the percentage increase in its area?

A. 35.75% B. 30.3%
C. 25% D. 32.25%

60. Mohit goes to his office at the speed of 10 m/s and returns to his home at the speed of x km/hr. If average speed of Mohit for the whole journey is 12 m/s, then what is the value of x?

A. 25 km/hr B. 15 km/hr
C. 36 km/hr D. 54 km/hr

61. If A : B = 7 : 8 and B : C = 7 : 9, then what is the ratio of A : B : C?

A. 56 : 49 : 72 B. 49 : 56 : 72
C. 56 : 72 : 49 D. 52 : 56 : 49

62. Rohit multiplies a number by 2 instead of dividing the number by 2. Resultant number is what percentage of the correct value?

A. 200% B. 300%
C. 50% D. 400%

63. The perimeter of a square and a circle are same. If the area of the circle is 1386 cm^2, then what will be the area of the square?

A. 1089 cm^2 B. 841 cm^2
C. 1024 cm^2 D. 1225 cm^2

64. Rohan purchased tables at the rate of ₹ 275 per table. If he sells 16 tables for ₹ 5060, then what will be the profit percentage?

A. 13.04% B. 16%
C. 15% D. 12.5%

65. If Highest Common Factor of two numbers is 8, then which of the following cannot be their Least Common Multiple?
A. 72 B. 24
C. 68 D. 48

66. P and Q together can complete a work in 105 days. Q and R together can complete the same work in 90 days, P and R together can complete the same work in 126 days. In how many days P, Q and R together can complete the same work?
A. 70 days B. 74 days
C. 76 days D. 72 days

67. A alone can complete a work in 14 days and B alone can complete the same work in 21 days. A and B start the work together but A leaves the work after 4 days of the starting of work. In how many days B will complete the remaining work?
A. 9 days B. 16 days
C. 12 days D. 11 days

68. The bar chart given below shows the amount of sugar used in making 7 different varieties of sweets S1, S2, S3, S4, S5, S6 and S7 has been shown as a percentage of total weight of the sweet.

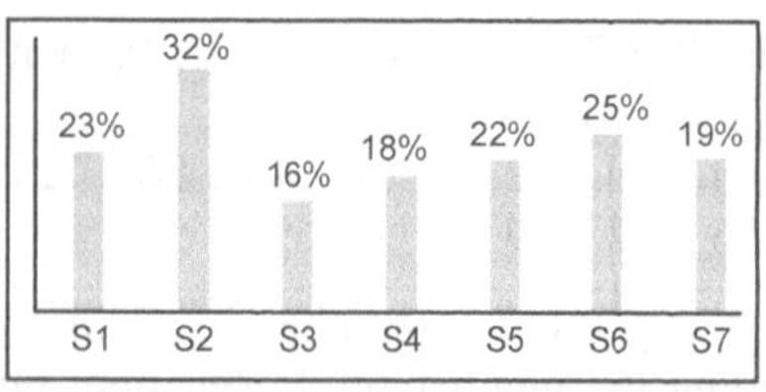

The combined weight of sweet S5 and S3 is 300 kg. What is the total amount of sugar used in these two sweets together?
A. Cannot be determined
B. 54 kg
C. 57 kg
D. 60 kg

69. The marked price of a chair and a table are in the ratio 2 : 3 respectively. The shopkeeper gives 20% discount on the chair. If the combined discount on both the chair and the table is 26%, then what will be the discount given on the table?
A. 34% B. 32%
C. 30% D. 28%

70. In a Company, number of engineers doubles itself in every 2 years. In how much time will the number of engineers become 1024 times of its original number?
A. 12 years B. 20 years
C. 15 years D. 24 years

71. A : B = 5 : 8 and B : C = 11 : 13. If A = 110, then what is the value of C?
A. 176 B. 104
C. 208 D. 88

72. The bar chart given below shows the ratio of expenditure to revenue for seven consecutive years Y1, Y2, Y3, Y4, Y5, Y6 and Y7.

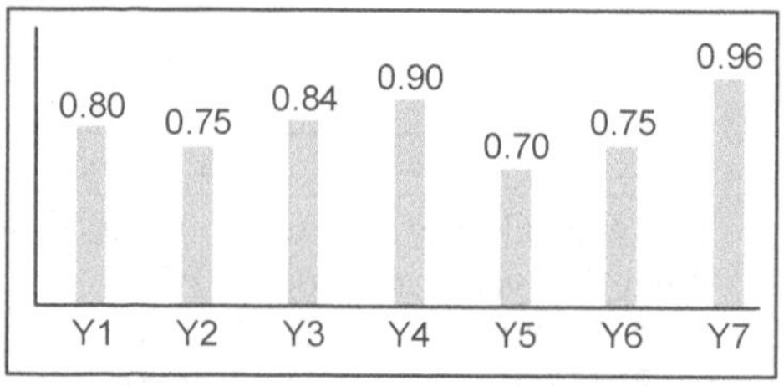

In which year is the profit-highest?
A. Y5
B. Y6
C. Cannot be determined
D. Y2

73. If the side of a square increases by 20%, then what will be per cent increase in its perimeter?
A. 44% B. 20%
C. 80% D. 40%

74. If P : Q : R = 5 : 3 : 6, then what will be the ratio of (P/Q) : (Q/R) : (R/P)?
A. 50 : 15 : 36 B. 50 : 45 : 36
C. 75 : 15 : 36 D. 40 : 12 : 27

75. What is the value of

$$\left(\frac{5}{2} \text{ of } 5 \div 4 - 2 \text{ of } \frac{1}{7} \div \frac{1}{7}\right)?$$

A. $\frac{13}{8}$ B. $\frac{23}{18}$

C. $\frac{17}{16}$ D. $\frac{9}{8}$

Part-D : English

76. Select the word which means the same as the group of words given.

A disease that is prevalent in a particular area.

A. Genetic B. Contagious
C. Endemic D. Viral

77. Select the correctly spelt word.

A. Changeble B. Changable
C. Chageable D. Changeable

78. Select the word which means the same as the group of words given.

One who studies and cares about environment.

A. Archeologist B. Ecologist
C. Anthropologist D. Biologist

79. Select the most appropriate word to fill in the blank.

The Prime Minister was as good as his _____.

A. word B. office
C. sword D. dress

80. Select the most appropriate word to fill in the blank.

While in Rome we must do as Romans _____.

A. is doing B. was doing
C. had done D. do

81. Select the most appropriate word to fill in the blank.

They never _____ those who have done wrong.

A. condemn B. outcast
C. blame D. forgive

Directions (Qs. No. 82-86): *In the following passage some words have been deleted. Fill in the blanks with the help of the alternatives given.*

Every day for a whole year, all kinds of holy men, hermits, scholars and nobles came, and related to the priests their deeds of ___**(82)**___, and the priests in solemn council heard their claims. At last, they decided that the one who seemed to be the greatest lover of ___**(83)**___ was a rich man who had that very year given all his ___**(84)**___ to the poor. So they gave him the plate of gold, but when he took it in his hand, it turned into ___**(85)**___ lead; though, when he dropped it on the floor, to his ___**(86)**___, it became gold again.

82. A. charity B. kindness
C. happiness D. sympathy

83. A. destitute B. moneyless
C. mankind D. women

84. A. wealth B. energy
C. time D. life

85. A. gold B. worthy
C. worthless D. valuable

86. A. confusion B. happiness
C. admiration D. amazement

87. Select the antonym of the given word.

HORIZONTAL

A. Parallel B. Financial
C. Official D. Vertical

88. From the given options, identify the segment in the sentence which contains the grammatical error.

Does he like to go for sightseeing when he is in holiday?

A. when he is
B. Does he like
C. in holiday?
D. to go for sightseeing

89. Select the option that means the same as the given idiom.

In a nutshell

A. In discussion B. In writing
C. In detail D. In brief

90. Select the most appropriate word to fill in the blank.

I make friends ____ I go.

A. moreover B. wherever
C. however D. whenever

91. Select the synonym of the given word.

APPARENT

A. Considerable B. Doubtful
C. Obvious D. Questionable

92. From the given options, identify the segment in the sentence which contains the grammatical error.

She was known for her skills in dance and music; she is equal proficient in the allied art of painting.

A. skills in dance
B. allied art of painting
C. was known
D. is equal proficient

93. Select the antonym of the given word.

ABOLISH

A. Build
B. Affirm
C. Cancel
D. Finish

94. From the given options, identify the segment in the sentence which contains the grammatical error.

The population of Sri Lanka are less than that of India.

A. than that
B. Sri Lanka are
C. of India
D. The population

95. Select the correctly spelt word.

A. Milennium
B. Millenium
C. Millenniumm
D. Millennium

96. Select the most appropriate option to substitute the underlined segment in the given sentence. If there is no need to substitute it, select No Improvement.

The football coach urged the team **were give its best** to the final match.

A. No Improvement
B. That it give its best
C. Try to give it best
D. To give its best

97. Select the synonym of the given word.

CURATIVE

A. Trembling
B. Damaging
C. Feeding
D. Healing

98. Select the most appropriate option to substitute the underlined segment in the given sentence. If there is no need to substitute it, select No Improvement.

She **give me everything** I asked for.

A. Is giving me everything
B. gave me everything
C. No Improvement
D. gave myself everything

99. Select the most appropriate option to substitute the underlined segment in the given sentence. If there is no need to substitute it, select No Improvement.

A Study has shown that the use of mobile data in India **have increased 50 times** over the last three years.

A. No improvement
B. has increased 50 times
C. Has been increased to 50 times
D. Is increasing 50 times

100. Select the option that means the same as the given idiom.

To keep an eye on

A. To keep a watch
B. To be cautious
C. To follow
D. To stare

ANSWERS

1	2	3	4	5	6	7	8	9	10
A	B	C	D	C	D	D	C	B	B
11	**12**	**13**	**14**	**15**	**16**	**17**	**18**	**19**	**20**
A	A	A	B	C	A	A	B	D	C
21	**22**	**23**	**24**	**25**	**26**	**27**	**28**	**29**	**30**
C	D	D	A	C	A	D	A	D	B
31	**32**	**33**	**34**	**35**	**36**	**37**	**38**	**39**	**40**
B	C	B	B	D	A	D	C	A	A

41	42	43	44	45	46	47	48	49	50
C	C	D	A	D	D	D	C	B	D
51	**52**	**53**	**54**	**55**	**56**	**57**	**58**	**59**	**60**
C	B	D	C	A	C	C	A	D	D
61	**62**	**63**	**64**	**65**	**66**	**67**	**68**	**69**	**70**
B	D	A	C	C	A	D	A	C	B
71	**72**	**73**	**74**	**75**	**76**	**77**	**78**	**79**	**80**
C	C	B	A	D	C	D	B	A	D
81	**82**	**83**	**84**	**85**	**86**	**87**	**88**	**89**	**90**
D	A	C	A	C	D	D	C	D	B
91	**92**	**93**	**94**	**95**	**96**	**97**	**98**	**99**	**100**
C	D	B	B	D	D	D	B	B	A

EXPLANATORY ANSWERS

1. 5 8 13 20 29 [40] 53 68 85

+3 +5 +7 +9 +11 +13 +15 +17

2. Except (B), 115, all others are perfect square of a number.

3.

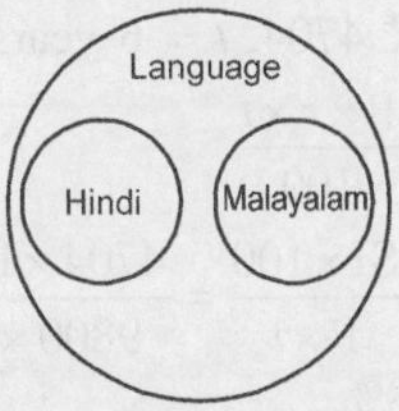

4. Required order in which the medical representative visits the six hospitals A, B, C, D, E, F.

5.

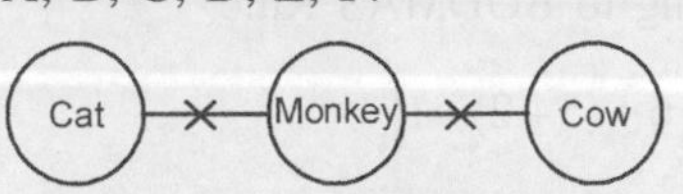

∴ No cat is a cow. (False)

Some cows are monkeys. (False)

So, Neither conclusion I nor II follows.

6. A C E : E I M :: D F H : [H L P]

+4 +6 +8 +4 +6 +8

7.

8. 50 49 47 44 40 35 [29] 22

–1 –2 –3 –4 –5 –6 –7

10. In mirror image

Left → Right

Right → Left

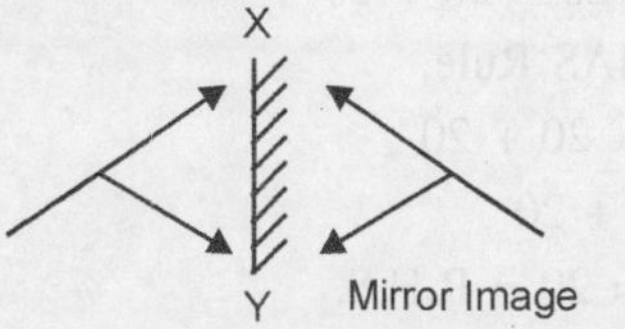

11. As, K I T C H E N

+1 +2 +3 +4 +5 +6 +7

L K W G M K U

Similarly, S H A M P O O

+1 +2 +3 +4 +5 +6 +7

[T J D Q U U V]

12. Eagle dwelling place name is Eyrie.

14. 3 9 (27) 81 (243) 729 2187

3^1 3^2 3^3 3^4 3^5 3^6 3^7

Hence, both the bracketed numbers are correct.

16. The sequence of reaching the factory W, U, Y, T, X, Z, V

∴ U is the second to reach the factory.

17. As, B = 2 + 1 (No. of letters) = 3

H = 8 + 1 = 9

SCHOOL = (19 + 3 + 8 + 15 + 15 + 12) + 6 (No. of letters)

= 72 + 6 = 78.

20. Except DX, in all other groups both the letters are opposite in the english alphabet series.

21.

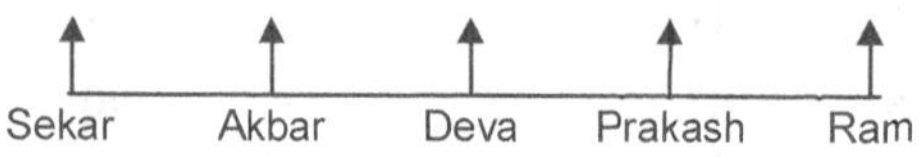

∴ Deva is sitting in the middle.

22.

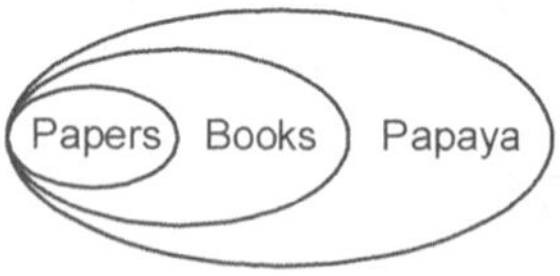

∴ All papers are papaya.

Some papayas are papers.

Both conclusions I and II follow.

23. 20 ÷ 20 + 20 − 20 × 20 = 20

(D) Interchange + and ×

20 ÷ 20 × 20 − 20 + 20

By BODMAS Rule,

= 1 × 20 − 20 + 20

= 20 − 20 + 20

= 20 − 0 = 20 = R.H.S.

Hence, option (D) is the correct.

24.

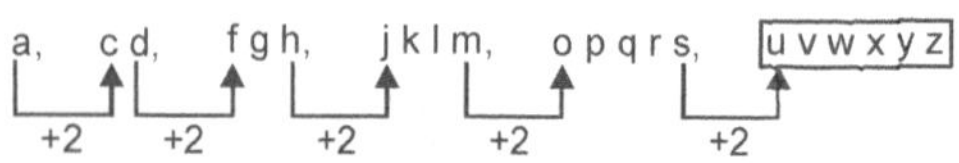

25.

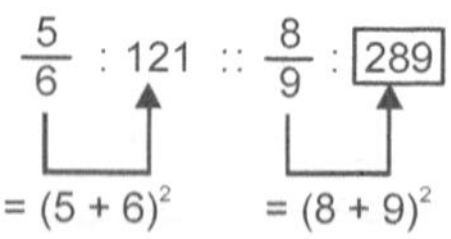

51. Average cost of the bag

$$= \frac{12 \times 1200 + 8 \times 1500 + 10 \times 2100}{12 + 8 + 10}$$

$$= \frac{14400 + 12000 + 21000}{30}$$

$$= \frac{47400}{30}$$

= ₹ 1580.

52. Let Revenue = ₹ x

$$\%P = \frac{\text{Revenue} - \text{Expenditure}}{\text{Expenditure}} \times 100$$

$$8 = \frac{x - 46000}{46000} \times 100$$

$x - 46000 = 3680$

So, Revenue, x = ₹ 49680.

53. Arrange the data in Ascending order

0, 0, 0, 1, 1, 2, 2, 2, 2, 3, 3, 5, 5, 5

↑ 8th

∵ $n = 15$ (odd)

∵ Median $= \left(\frac{n+1}{2}\right)$ th term

$= \left(\frac{15+1}{2}\right)$ th term

= 8th term *i.e.*, 2

∴ Median = 2.

54. Given sum (P) = ₹ 9800

SI = ₹ 4704, t = 6 years

∵ $SI = \frac{P \times r \times t}{100}$

$r = \frac{SI \times 100}{P \times t} = \frac{4704 \times 100}{9800 \times 6}$

r = 8%.

55. $7\frac{1}{4} + [6 + (5 - 8 \div 4) - 1]$

According to BODMAS Rule

$= \frac{29}{4} + [6 + (5 - 2) - 1]$

$= \frac{29}{4} + [6 + 3 - 1] = \frac{29}{4} + [9 - 1]$

$= \frac{29}{4} + 8 = \frac{61}{4}.$

56. Speed of Rohit

$= \frac{\text{Distance}}{\text{Time}} = \frac{1188 \text{ km}}{22 \text{ hours}} = 54$ km/h

$= 54 \times \frac{5}{18}$ [∵ 1 km/h $= \frac{5}{18}$ m/s]

= 15 m/s.

57. Let the weight of teacher = x kg

$$24 \times 30 + x = 25\ (30 + 2)$$
$$720 + x = 800$$
$$x = 80 \text{ km}$$

Hence, the weight of teacher = 80 kg.

58. Selling Price = ₹ 1333

Cost Price = ₹ 2150

$$\% \text{ Loss} = \frac{\text{Cost Price} - \text{Selling Price}}{\text{Cost Price}} \times 100$$
$$= \frac{2150 - 1333}{2150} \times 100$$
$$= \frac{817}{2150} \times 100 = 38\%.$$

59. $\because$ A $\propto r^2$

A $\propto d^2$

$\therefore$ Let, Initial diameter Final diameter

100 $\xrightarrow{15\%\uparrow}$ 115

$\therefore$ Initial Area Final Area

$(100)^2 \longrightarrow (115)^2$

10000 13225

% increase in the Area

$$= \frac{13,225 - 10,000}{10,000} \times 100 = \frac{3225}{100} = 32.25\%.$$

60. Average speed $= \dfrac{2x_1 x_2}{x_1 + x_2}$

$$\frac{2 \times 10 \times x}{10 + x} = 12$$
$$\frac{20x}{10 + x} = 12$$
$$20x = 120 + 12x$$
$$8x = 120$$
$$x = 15 \text{ m/s} = 15 \times \frac{18}{5} \text{ km/h}$$
$$[\because 1 \text{ m/s} = \frac{18}{5} \text{ km/h}]$$
$$= 54 \text{ km/h}.$$

61. A : B = (7 : 8) × 7 = 49 : 56

B : C = (7 : 9) × 8 = 56 : 72

$\therefore$ A : B : C = 49 : 56 : 72.

62. Let Number = x

$\therefore$ Resulting Number = $2x$

Correct value $= \dfrac{x}{2}$

Required percentage

$$= \frac{2x}{x/2} \times 100 = \frac{4x}{x} \times 100 = 400\%.$$

63. Given that, Area of circle = 1386 cm^2

$$\pi r^2 = 1386$$
$$\frac{22}{7} \times r^2 = 1386$$
$$r^2 = \frac{1386 \times 7}{22}$$
$$r^2 = 63 \times 7$$
$$r = 7 \times 3 \Rightarrow r = 21$$

Perimeter of circle = $2\pi r$

$$= 2 \times \frac{22}{7} \times 21 = 132 \text{ cm}$$

$\therefore$ Perimeter of square = Perimeter of circle

$$4a = 132 \Rightarrow a = 33 \text{ cm}$$

$\therefore$ Area of square = $(a)^2 = (33)^2 = 1089$ cm^2.

64. Cost price of one table = ₹ 275

Selling price of 16 tables = ₹ 5060

Selling price of one table

$$= \frac{5060}{16} = ₹\ 316.25$$

$$\% \text{ Profit} = \frac{\text{SP} - \text{CP}}{\text{CP}} \times 100$$
$$= \frac{316.25 - 275}{275} \times 100$$
$$= \frac{41.25}{275} \times 100 = \frac{4125}{275} = 15\%.$$

65. $\because$ Least common multiple, should be the multiple of Highest common factor. 68 is not divisible by 8. Hence 68 can not be their LCM.

66. (P + Q), together complete the work in one day $= \dfrac{1}{105}$ part

(Q + R), together complete the work in one day $= \dfrac{1}{90}$ part

(R + P), together complete the work in one day = $\frac{1}{126}$ part

$\therefore$ 2(P + Q + R), together complete the work in one day = $\frac{1}{105}+\frac{1}{90}+\frac{1}{126}$ part

$= \frac{6+7+5}{630} = \frac{18}{630} = \frac{1}{35}$

So, (P + Q + R), together can complete the work in one day = $\frac{1}{35\times 2} = \frac{1}{70}$ part

(P + Q + R) together complete the work = 70 days.

67. (A + B) complete the work together in 4 days

$= 4\left(\frac{1}{14}+\frac{1}{21}\right) = 4\left(\frac{3+2}{42}\right) = \frac{20}{42} = \frac{10}{21}$ part

Remaining work = $1-\frac{10}{21} = \frac{11}{21}$ part

$\because$ B complete $\frac{1}{21}$ part of work = 1 day

B complete $\frac{11}{21}$ part of work

$= \frac{1}{\left(\frac{1}{21}\right)}\times\frac{11}{21} = \frac{21}{1}\times\frac{11}{21}$ = 11 days.

68. Let total weight of sweet S5 and S3 are x kg and y kg respectively

Then, $x \times 55\% + y \times 16\% = 300$

$55x + 16y = 30000$

$\because$ We have only one equation of two variable, So we can not determine.

69. Let Marked price of a chair and a table are ₹ $2x$ and ₹ $3x$ respectively

Discount on a chair = $2x \times 20\% = \frac{2x}{5}$

Discount on a chair and a table

$= (2x + 3x) \times 26\%$

$= 5x\times\frac{26}{100} = \frac{13}{10}x$

Discount on a table = $\frac{13x}{10}-\frac{2x}{5} = \frac{9x}{10}$

% Discount on a table = $\frac{\frac{9x}{10}}{3x}\times 100 = 30\%.$

70. $\because$ No. of engineers doubles itself in every 2 years

Then, 1024 = 2^{10} times itself in 2 × 10 = 20 years.

71.

A : B = 5 : 8

B : C = 11 : 13

A : B : C = 5 × 11 : 11 × 8 : 8 × 13

= 55 : 88 : 104

Let A, B and C are $55x$, $88x$ and $104x$ respectively

$\therefore$ $55x = 110$

$x = 2$

$\therefore$ C = $104x$ = 104 × 2 = 208.

73. Let Initial side = 100 unit

then, perimeter = 4 × side = 400 unit

New side = 120 unit (20% ↑)

New perimeter = 4 × side

= 4 × 120 = 480 unit

$\therefore$ Percent increase in perimeter

$= \frac{480-400}{400}\times 100 = \frac{80}{4} = 20\%.$

74. Let P, Q and R are $5x$, $3x$ and $6x$ respectively

then, $\frac{P}{Q}:\frac{Q}{R}:\frac{R}{P} = \frac{5x}{3x}:\frac{3x}{6x}:\frac{6x}{5x}$

$= 50x : 15x : 36x$

= 50 : 15 : 36.

75. $\left(\frac{5}{2}\text{ of } 5\div 4-2\text{ of }\frac{1}{7}\div\frac{1}{7}\right)$

According to BODMAS rule,

$= \left(\frac{25}{2}\div 4-\frac{2}{7}\div\frac{1}{7}\right)$

$= \left(\frac{25}{8}-\frac{2}{7}\times\frac{7}{1}\right) = \frac{25}{8}-2 = \frac{9}{8}.$

Previous Paper (Solved)

SSC – Constable (GD) Exam, 2015*

ITBPF/CISF/CRPF/BSF/SSB

Rifleman (Assam Rifles)

PART-I : GENERAL INTELLIGENCE & REASONING

Directions (Qs. 1-3): *Find the odd word/letters/number from the given alternatives.*

1. (*a*) JG (*b*) RN
(*c*) NJ (*d*) UQ

2. (*a*) 22 (*b*) 12
(*c*) 15 (*d*) 18

3. (*a*) Speed post (*b*) SMS
(*c*) Letter (*d*) Money order

4. Observing the Trend find the missing number.

5	4	3
6	7	8
4	2	?
34	30	30

(*a*) 5 (*b*) 3
(*c*) 6 (*d*) 10

Directions (Qs. 5-8): *Select the related word/letters/number from the given alternatives.*

5. DIMO : DMIO : : JUVR : ?
(*a*) JUVR (*b*) JVRU
(*c*) JVUR (*d*) JRVU

6. FRENCH : FRANCE : : DUTCH : ?
(*a*) HOLLAND (*b*) FIJI
(*c*) NORWAY (*d*) SWEDAN

7. 4 : 19 : : 7 : ?
(*a*) 52 (*b*) 28
(*c*) 49 (*d*) 68

8. BOOK : LIBRARY : : TREE : ?
(*a*) FRUIT (*b*) FURNITURE
(*c*) SHADE (*d*) FOREST

9. If STOVE is coded as EVOTS and CANDLE is coded as ELDNAC, then REPORT is coded as?
(*a*) PORTRE (*b*) SFQPSU
(*c*) QDONQS (*d*) TROPER

10. A word is represented by only one set of numbers as given in any one of the alternatives. The sets of numbers given in the alternatives are represented by two classes of alphabets as in two matrices given below. The columns and rows of matrix I are numbered from 0 to 4 and that of matrix II are numbered from 5 to 9. A letter from these matrices can be represented first by its row and next by its column, *e.g.*, 'D' can be represented by 00, 12 etc., and 'P' can be represented by 56, 68 etc. Similarly, you have to identify the set for the word 'FIRE'.

MATRIX – I

	0	1	2	3	4
0	D	E	F	I	N
1	I	N	D	E	F
2	E	F	I	N	D
3	N	D	E	F	I
4	F	I	N	D	E

MATRIX – II

	5	6	7	8	9
5	O	P	R	S	T
6	S	T	O	P	R
7	P	R	S	T	O
8	T	O	P	R	S
9	R	S	T	O	P

(*a*) 33, 34, 76, 22 (*b*) 21, 22, 88, 33
(*c*) 02, 03, 57, 01 (*d*) 14, 10, 69, 14

* Held on 04/10/2015 (Morning Session)

11. Which of the answer figures can be formed using the question figure:

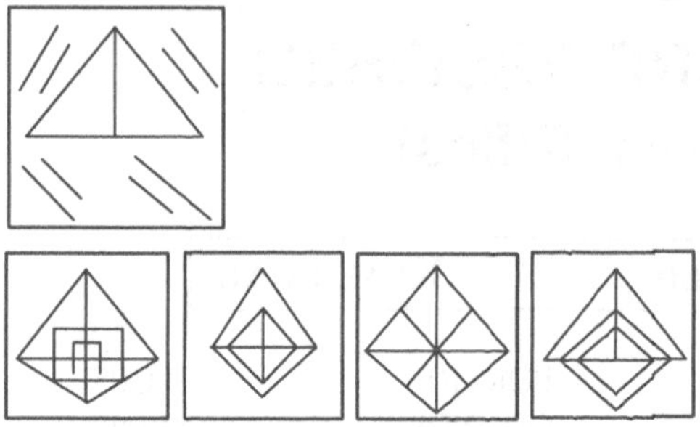

(*a*) (*b*) (*c*) (*d*)

12. Five friends are sitting in a row facing South. Here Mohan is between Balu and Raju and Raju is to the immediate right of Praveen and Amit is to the right of Balu. Who is in extreme right end?

(*a*) Amit (*b*) Balu
(*c*) Praveen (*d*) Mohan

13. IF 2 = 0, 3 = 3, 4 = 6, 5 = 9 then 7 = ?

(*a*) 16 (*b*) 15
(*c*) 18 (*d*) 12

14. If
÷ stands for ×
× stands for –
– stands for + and
+ stands for ÷, then
48 + 6 – 12 ÷ 2 + 10 = ?
(Do chronologically and not according to BODMAS rule)

(*a*) 9 (*b*) 16
(*c*) 4 (*d*) 14

15. A piece of paper is folded and cut as shown below in the question figures. From the given answer figures, indicate how it will appear when opened.

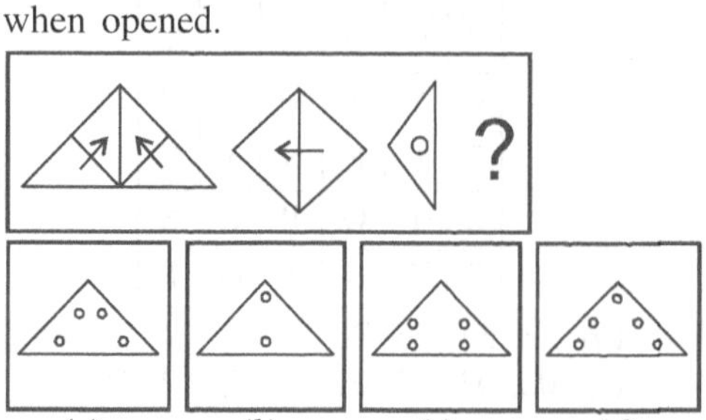

(*a*) (*b*) (*c*) (*d*)

16. Which answer figure will complete the pattern in the question figure?

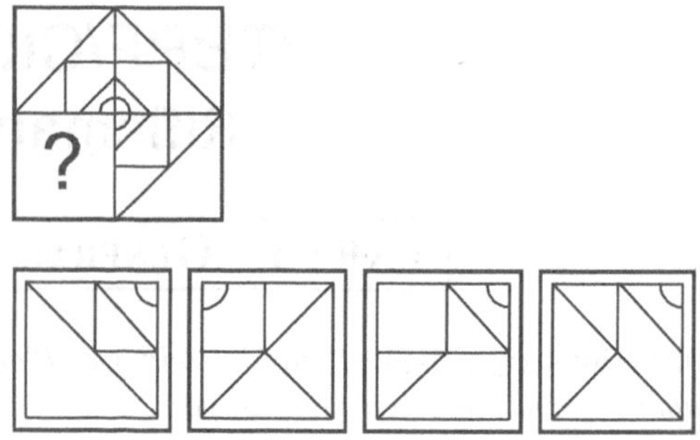

(*a*) (*b*) (*c*) (*d*)

Directions (Qs. 17 & 18): *A series is given, with one-term missing. Choose the correct alternative from the given ones that will complete the series.*

17. 0.15, 0.3, __?__, 1.2, 2.4

(*a*) 4.8 (*b*) 0.9
(*c*) 0.6 (*d*) 0.06

18. BCD, DBC, EFG, __?__, HIJ

(*a*) GEF (*b*) EGF
(*c*) IJH (*d*) FEG

19. Which of the answer figure indicates the best relationship between Milk, Goat, Cow, Hen?

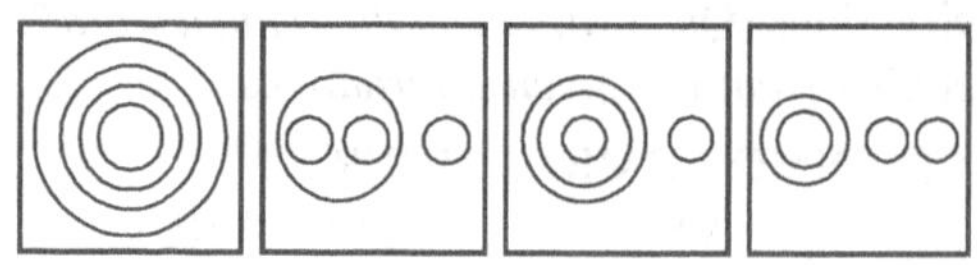

(*a*) (*b*) (*c*) (*d*)

20. A florist had 133 roses, she sold $\frac{5}{7}$ of them.

How many roses had she left?

(*a*) 57 (*b*) 38
(*c*) 58 (*d*) 19

21. Which of the answer figure is exactly the mirror image of the given figure?

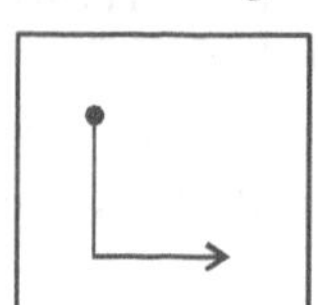

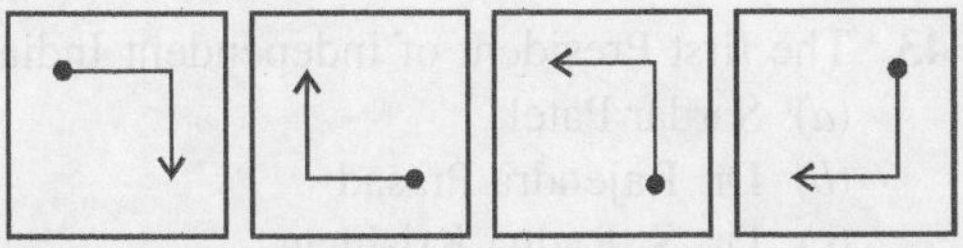

(a) (b) (c) (d)

22. From the given alternative words, select the word which cannot be formed using the letters of the given word.

INTERDEPENDENT

(a) RETREAT (b) DEEPEN
(c) DEPEND (d) REPENT

23. Directions: *Two statements are given followed by two Conclusions/Assumptions, I and II. You have to consider the statement to be true, even if it seems to be at variance from commonly known facts. You are to decide which of the given conclusions/assumptions can definitely be drawn from the given statement. Indicate your answer.*

Statements: 1. All children are students.
2. All students are players.

Conclusions: I. All cricketers are students.
II. All children are players.

(a) Neither conclusion I nor II follows
(b) Only conclusion I follows
(c) Only conclusion II follows
(d) Both conclusion I and II follow

24. Select the answer figure in which the question figure is hidden.

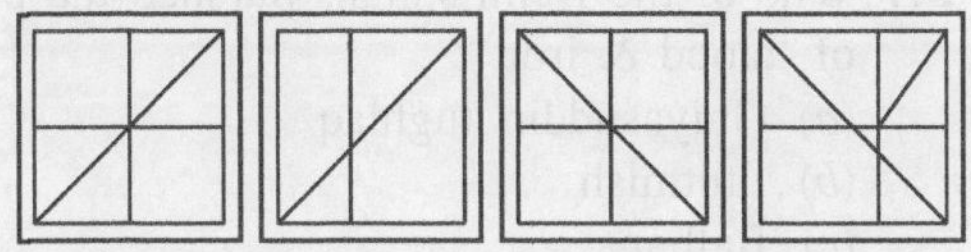

(a) (b) (c) (d)

25. Which one of the given responses would be a meaningful order of the following:

1. Child 2. Profession
3. Marriage 4. Infant
5. Education

(a) 1, 3, 5, 2, 4 (b) 2, 1, 4, 3, 5
(c) 5, 4, 1, 3, 2 (d) 4, 1, 5, 2, 3

PART-II : GENERAL KNOWLEDGE & GENERAL AWARENESS

26. The smallest ocean is:
(a) Pacific (b) Arctic
(c) Atlantic (d) Indian

27. The Head quarters of World Trade Organisation (WTO) is situated in:
(a) London, UK
(b) Geneva, Switzerland
(c) New Delhi
(d) Washington, USA

28. When water freezes its density ....
(a) Remains constant (b) Increases
(c) Decreases (d) Becomes Zero

29. The headquarters of United Nations Organization is located at:
(a) Geneva (b) New York
(c) Washington (d) Rome

30. The acid which fails to liberate carbon dioxide from sodium bicarbonate is:
(a) Sulphuric acid (b) Formic acid
(c) Carbonic acid (d) Acetic acid

31. Name the first Indian to be banned for using anabolic steroid in Olympic games:
(a) Sumita Laha
(b) T. Sanmancha Chanu
(c) Aswini Akunji
(d) Pratima Kumari

32. When was the office of District Collector created?
(a) 1771 (b) 1773
(c) 1772 (d) 1786

33. In B.C.G. Vaccine the word 'C' stands for:
(a) Calmette (b) Cough
(c) Chlorine (d) Cadmium

34. Oxide of sulphur present in the atmosphere are washed down by rains to cause:

(*a*) Industrial smog formation
(*b*) Depletion of fossil fuel reserves
(*c*) Eutrophication in lakes
(*d*) Lowering of pH of soil

35. Chemical composition of heavy water is:
(*a*) H_2O (*b*) HDO
(*c*) H_2O_2 (*d*) D_2O

36. Which one of the following is an autotroph?
(*a*) Algae (*b*) Butterfly
(*c*) Mushroom (*d*) Grasshopper

37. Who of the Delhi sultans pursued the policy of 'blood & iron'?
(*a*) Ghiyasuddin tughlaq
(*b*) Iltutmish
(*c*) Balban
(*d*) Alauddin Khilji

38. Dadabhai Naroji has described his theory of 'Drain of Wealth' in the book ....
(*a*) British Rule and its Consequences
(*b*) Poverty and Un-British Rule in India
(*c*) Nature of British Colonial Rule
(*d*) Exploitative Nature of British Rule in India

39. Which one of the following is a non-dimensional quantity?
(*a*) Co-efficient of viscocity
(*b*) Plank's constant
(*c*) Strain
(*d*) Gas constant

40. Who was the author of Telugu Work Amuktamalyada?
(*a*) Harihara (*b*) Bukka
(*c*) Krishnadevaraya (*d*) Devaraya

41. The presence of pollutants in the environment is usually expressed in ppm, where ppm stands for:
(*a*) pollutant prevent measures
(*b*) parts per million
(*c*) purity per microgram
(*d*) particles per mole

42. Economics classifies the man-made instrument of production as:
(*a*) capital (*b*) organization
(*c*) equipment (*d*) labour

43. The first President of independent India was:
(*a*) Sardar Patel
(*b*) Dr. Rajendra Prasad
(*c*) Dr. S. Radha Krishnan
(*d*) J.L. Nehru

44. Who established the 'Sharda Sadan', a school for Indian Widows in colonial India?
(*a*) Sarojini Naidu
(*b*) Pandita Ramabai
(*c*) Mahadev Govind Ranade
(*d*) Dayanand Saraswati

45. Democracy is a government in which everyone has a share was the opinion of:
(*a*) Seeley (*b*) Abraham Lincoln
(*c*) Plato (*d*) Jeovans

46. The Cash Reserve Ratio is a tool of:
(*a*) Fiscal policy
(*b*) Monetary policy
(*c*) Tax policy
(*d*) Agricultural policy

47. The greatness of Shershah lies in his:
(*a*) Secular attitude
(*b*) Administrative reforms
(*c*) Superior generalship
(*d*) Victories against Humayun

48. The term 'URL' used in Internet technology stands for:
(*a*) Uniform Remote Locater
(*b*) Unique Resource Locater
(*c*) Uniform Resource Locater
(*d*) Unique Remote Locater

49. Which of the following countries has brought out a stamp on Mother Teresa to celebrate her birth anniversary?
(*a*) Pakistan (*b*) India
(*c*) USA (*d*) UK

50. How does agriculture promote the Indian industrial development?
(*a*) By providing food and clothing to labourers
(*b*) By opening up market for industrial products
(*c*) All of the given options
(*d*) By supplying raw materials

PART-III : ELEMENTARY MATHEMATICS

51. 16 men are able to complete a piece of work in 12 days working 14 hours a day. How long will 28 men, working 12 hours a day, take to complete the work?

(*a*) 7 days (*b*) 10 days
(*c*) 8 days (*d*) 6 days

52. A certain sum amounts to ₹ 1725 at 15% per annum at simple interest and ₹ 1800 in the same time at 20% per annum at simple interest. Find the sum.

(*a*) ₹ 1700 (*b*) ₹ 1500
(*c*) ₹ 1650 (*d*) ₹ 1200

53. A dealer marks his goods 20% above cost price and allows a discount of 10% to his customers. His gain percentage is:

(*a*) 6% (*b*) 7%
(*c*) 8% (*d*) 9%

54. Raja can do a piece of work in 20 days while Ramesh can finish it in 25 days. Ramesh started working and Raja joined him after 10 days. The whole work is completed in:

(*a*) 20 days (*b*) $16\frac{2}{3}$ days
(*c*) 15 days (*d*) 18 days

55. 1008 divided by which single digit number gives a perfect square?

(*a*) 7 (*b*) 8
(*c*) 9 (*d*) 4

56. A right circular cone of height 20 cm and base radius 15 cm is melted and casted into smaller cones of equal sizes of height 5 cm and base radius 1.5 cm. The number of casted cones are:

(*a*) 100 (*b*) 300
(*c*) 150 (*d*) 400

57. A student starting from his house walks at a speed of $2\frac{1}{2}$ km/hour and reaches his school 6 minutes late. Next day starting at the same time he increases his speed by 1 km/hour and reaches 6 minutes early. The distance between the school and his house is:

(*a*) 4 km (*b*) 6 km
(*c*) $3\frac{1}{2}$ km (*d*) $1\frac{3}{4}$ km

58. The mean proportion of 1.21 and 0.09 is:

(*a*) 3.03 (*b*) 0.033
(*c*) 0.33 (*d*) 3.3

59. The value of $\sqrt{.000441}$ is equal to:

(*a*) 0.21 (*b*) 0.021
(*c*) 0.0021 (*d*) 0.00021

60. A batsman makes a score of 87 runs in the 17th inning and thus increased his average by 3. Find his average after 17th inning.

(*a*) 90 (*b*) 84
(*c*) 39 (*d*) 87

61. A fruit merchant makes a profit of 25% by selling mangoes at a certain price. If he charges ₹ 1 more on each mango, he would gain 50%. At first the price of one mango was:

(*a*) ₹ 6 (*b*) ₹ 4
(*c*) ₹ 7 (*d*) ₹ 5

62. A seller increases the cost price of an article by 30% and fixed the marked price as ₹ 286. But during sale he gave 10% discount to the purchaser. Percentage of Profit will be:

(*a*) 15 (*b*) 20
(*c*) 17 (*d*) 10

63. An item was sold for ₹ 3600 at 25% discount. Its marked price was:

(*a*) ₹ 4500 (*b*) ₹ 4800
(*c*) ₹ 2700 (*d*) ₹ 2880

64. If the cost of an article is ₹ P after two successive reductions of 20% and 25%, the original price of the article was:

(*a*) ₹$\frac{4}{5}$P (*b*) ₹$\frac{3}{5}$P
(*c*) ₹$\frac{5}{3}$P (*d*) ₹$\frac{5}{4}$P

65. A plane can cover 6000 km in 8 hours. If the speed is increased by 250 kmph, then the time taken by the plane to cover 9000 km is:
(*a*) 5 hours (*b*) 8 hours
(*c*) 6 hours (*d*) 9 hours

66. A solid right prism made of iron has cross section of a triangle of sides 5 cm, 10 cm, 13 cm and of height 10 cm. If one cubic cm of iron weighs 7g, then the weight of the prism is (approximately):
(*a*) 1371.32 gram (*b*) 1100.68 gram
(*c*) 1570.8 gram (*d*) 1470.8 gram

67. A sum of ₹ 800 becomes ₹ 956 in 3 years at a certain rate of simple interest. If the rate of interest is increased by 4%, what amount will the same sum become in 3 years?
(*a*) ₹ 1052 (*b*) ₹ 1042
(*c*) ₹ 1024 (*d*) ₹ 1025

68. A shopkeeper, in order to clear his old stock of T.V. sets, offers 12% discount on the T.V. sets. If the marked price of a T.V. set is ₹ 6500, the selling price of the T.V. set is:
(*a*) ₹ 5700 (*b*) ₹ 6000
(*c*) ₹ 5720 (*d*) ₹ 5400

69. Average income of 'A' and 'B' is ₹ 200 and average income of 'C' and 'D' is ₹ 250. The average income of A, B, C and D is:
(*a*) ₹ 200 (*b*) ₹ 225
(*c*) ₹ 125 (*d*) ₹ 106.25

70. The average of 1, 3, 5, 7, 9, 11, ... 25 terms is:
(*a*) 125 (*b*) 13
(*c*) 625 (*d*) 50

71. The ratio of ages of two persons is 5 : 9 and the age of one of them is greater than the other by 40 years. The sum of their ages in year is:
(*a*) 140 (*b*) 180
(*c*) 150 (*d*) 160

Directions (Qs. 72 & 73): *Study the data and answer the questions.*

The score of students of a class are given as follows:

IQ Score	80-90	90-100	100-110	110-120	120-130	130-140
No. of Students	6	9	16	13	4	2

72. The number of students whose IQ score is 100 and more is:
(*a*) 36 (*b*) 29
(*c*) 46 (*d*) 35

73. Number of students whose IQ score is 140 is:
(*a*) 1
(*b*) 2
(*c*) 0
(*d*) undeterminable from given data

74. The smallest number by which 243000 be divided so that the quotient is a perfect cube is:
(*a*) 9 (*b*) 27
(*c*) 3 (*d*) 1

75. In a college election a candidate secured 62% of the votes and is elected by a margin of 144 votes. The total number of votes polled is:
(*a*) 800 (*b*) 925
(*c*) 1200 (*d*) 600

PART-IV : ENGLISH

Directions (Qs. 76-78) : *Some parts of the sentences have errors and some are correct. Find out which part of a sentence has an error and mark the appropriate correct option. If a sentence is free from error, mark to "No Error" option in the Answer Sheet.*

76. He finds fault at everything I do.
(*a*) He finds fault (*b*) at everything
(*c*) I do (*d*) No error

77. The kitchen need painting badly and I must get it done.
(*a*) need painting badly
(*b*) The kitchen
(*c*) and I must get it done
(*d*) No error

78. If I will play my best I can win any day against anybody.
(*a*) If I will play my best
(*b*) I can win any day

(*c*) against anybody
(*d*) No error

Directions (Qs. 79-81) : *A part of the sentence is underlined. Below are given alternatives to the underlined part which may improve the sentence. Choose the correct alternative. In case no improvement is needed choose* ***"No Improvement."***

79. Years ago, I met a man which was President and Chairman of the board of a company.
(*a*) No improvement (*b*) Who
(*c*) Whom (*d*) Whose

80. Covering thirty kilometers in thirty minutes are not a great distance using a brand new car
(*a*) aren't a great distance
(*b*) No imprevement
(*c*) is no distance
(*d*) is not a great distance

81. Where are you coming from?
(*a*) do you come from
(*b*) were you from
(*c*) No improvement
(*d*) you are coming from

Directions (Qs. 82-85): *Sentences given with blanks to be filled in with an appropriate word(s). Four alternatives are suggested for each question. Choose the correct alternative out of the four and indicate it in the Answer Sheet.*

82. She had to .... illness in order to avoid going to the party meeting.
(*a*) feint (*b*) fain
(*c*) faint (*d*) feign

83. Your .... nature will aid you in attaining success in every venture you undertake.
(*a*) persevering (*b*) catalytic
(*c*) rotund (*d*) lackadaisical

84. The publisher is bringing .... a revised edition of this book.
(*a*) about (*b*) up
(*c*) round (*d*) out

85. This is our house and that is ....
(*a*) them (*b*) their
(*c*) theirs (*d*) their's

Directions (Qs. 86-88): *Out of the four alternatives, choose the one which can be substituted for the given word/sentences and indicate it in the Answer Sheet.*

86. One who can not be corrected:
(*a*) Indefatigable (*b*) indolent
(*c*) ineligible (*d*) incorrigible

87. Put side by side:
(*a*) Propose (*b*) Depose
(*c*) Juxtapose (*d*) Impose

88. Chief of commander of army:
(*a*) Colonel (*b*) Lieutenant
(*c*) Major (*d*) General

Directions (Qs. 89-91): *Choose the word opposite in meaning to the given word and mark it in the Aswer Sheet.*

89. superficial
(*a*) Natural (*b*) Amicable
(*c*) Artificial (*d*) Genuine

90. fragile
(*a*) weak (*b*) strong
(*c*) discard (*d*) brittle

91. harmonious
(*a*) Discordant (*b*) Balanced
(*c*) Concordant (*d*) Sonorous

Directions (Qs. 92-94): *Out of the four alternatives, choose the one which best expresses the meaning of the given word and mark it in the Answer Sheet.*

92. felicitated
(*a*) adored (*b*) encouraged
(*c*) admired (*d*) congratulated

93. honour
(*a*) discipline (*b*) courage
(*c*) respect (*d*) determination

94. rectify
(*a*) regularise (*b*) condone
(*c*) clarify (*d*) correct

Directions (Qs. 95-97): *Four alternatives are given for the Idiom/Phrase underlined in the sentence. Choose the alternative which best expresses the meaning of the Idiom/Phrase and mark it in the Answer Sheet.*

95. He <u>beats about the bush.</u>
(*a*) talks continuously
(*b*) does not talk specifically
(*c*) talks sensibly
(*d*) speak well

96. I have <u>taken fancy to</u> this car.
(*a*) improved
(*b*) developed liking for
(*c*) given imaginative touches
(*d*) revised

97. <u>carry out</u>
(*a*) continue
(*b*) complete something
(*c*) bring
(*d*) to take in

Directions (Qs. 98-100): *Four words are given in each question, out of which only one word is correctly spelt. Find the correctly spelt word and mark your answer in the Answer Sheet.*

98. (*a*) juvinnile (*b*) juvenile
(*c*) juvinile (*d*) juvenille

99. (*a*) deteriorate (*b*) deterriorate
(*c*) deteriorrate (*d*) detariorate

100. (*a*) knoledgeable (*b*) knowledgable
(*c*) knowledgeble (*d*) knowledgeable

ANSWERS

1	2	3	4	5	6	7	8	9	10
(*a*)	(*a*)	(*b*)	(*c*)	(*c*)	(*a*)	(*a*)	(*d*)	(*d*)	(*c*)
11	**12**	**13**	**14**	**15**	**16**	**17**	**18**	**19**	**20**
(*d*)	(*a*)	(*b*)	(*c*)	(*a*)	(*a*)	(*c*)	(*a*)	(*b*)	(*b*)
21	**22**	**23**	**24**	**25**	**26**	**27**	**28**	**29**	**30**
(*d*)	(*a*)	(*c*)	(*a*)	(*d*)	(*b*)	(*b*)	(*c*)	(*b*)	(*c*)
31	**32**	**33**	**34**	**35**	**36**	**37**	**38**	**39**	**40**
(*d*)	(*c*)	(*a*)	(*d*)	(*d*)	(*a*)	(*c*)	(*b*)	(*c*)	(*c*)
41	**42**	**43**	**44**	**45**	**46**	**47**	**48**	**49**	**50**
(*b*)	(*a*)	(*b*)	(*b*)	(*a*)	(*b*)	(*b*)	(*c*)	(*c*)	(*c*)
51	**52**	**53**	**54**	**55**	**56**	**57**	**58**	**59**	**60**
(*c*)	(*b*)	(*c*)	(*b*)	(*a*)	(*d*)	(*d*)	(*c*)	(*b*)	(*c*)
61	**62**	**63**	**64**	**65**	**66**	**67**	**68**	**69**	**70**
(*d*)	(*c*)	(*b*)	(*c*)	(*d*)	(*c*)	(*a*)	(*c*)	(*b*)	(*b*)
71	**72**	**73**	**74**	**75**	**76**	**77**	**78**	**79**	**80**
(*a*)	(*d*)	(*d*)	(*a*)	(*d*)	(*b*)	(*a*)	(*a*)	(*b*)	(*d*)
81	**82**	**83**	**84**	**85**	**86**	**87**	**88**	**89**	**90**
(*a*)	(*d*)	(*a*)	(*d*)	(*c*)	(*d*)	(*c*)	(*d*)	(*d*)	(*b*)
91	**92**	**93**	**94**	**95**	**96**	**97**	**98**	**99**	**100**
(*a*)	(*d*)	(*c*)	(*d*)	(*b*)	(*b*)	(*b*)	(*b*)	(*a*)	(*d*)

EXPLANATORY ANSWERS

1. Odd letter is JG because the difference between the letters is 3 but rest of the word's, difference is 4.

2. All alternatives except 22 are divisible of 3. Hence, the odd number is 22.

3. SMS is an electronic service but rest are delivered by a postman which is a person. Then, the odd is SMS.

4. $6 \times 5 + 4 = 30 + 4 = 34$

$4 \times 7 + 2 = 28 + 2 = 30$

Same as

$3 \times 8 + ? = 24 + ? = 30$

$\Rightarrow \quad ? = 6$

5. As in DIMO : DMIO, the middle two letters are reversed. So following the same pattern, JUVR : JVUR.

6. French is the language of France. Dutch is language of Holland.

7. 4 : 19 : : 7 : ?

$\Rightarrow \quad 4 = 4^2 + 3 = 16 + 3 = 19$

and $\quad 7 = 7^2 + 3 = 49 + 3 = 52$

8. As BOOK is found in LIBRARY, Similarly TREE is found in FOREST.

9. Here,

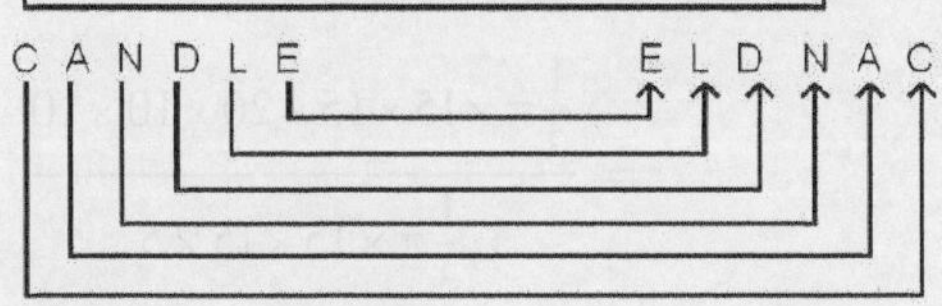

Similarly,

All the three follow the same pattern. Pattern is: letters are reversed from last.

10. F = 02, 14, 21 ....

I = 03, 10, 22 ....

R = 57, 69, 76 ....

E = 01, 13, 20 ....

12. According to the question

Amit Balu Mohan Raju Praveen

Then, Amit is in extreme right end.

Hence, the answer is Amit.

13. $2 + 0 = 0 \times 3 = 2 = 0$

$2 + 1 = 1 \times 3 = 3 = 3$

$3 + 1 = 2 \times 3 = 4 = 6$

$4 + 1 = 3 \times 3 = 5 = 9$

$5 + 1 = 4 \times 3 = 6 = 12$

Same as

$6 + 1 = 5 \times 3 = 7 = 15$

Hence, the answer is 15.

14. $48 + 6 - 12 \div 2 + 10$

From question

$\Rightarrow 48 \div 6 + 12 \times 2 \div 10$

$\Rightarrow 8 + 12 \times 2 \div 10$

$\Rightarrow 20 \times 2 \div 10$

$\Rightarrow 40 \div 10$

$\Rightarrow 4.$

17.

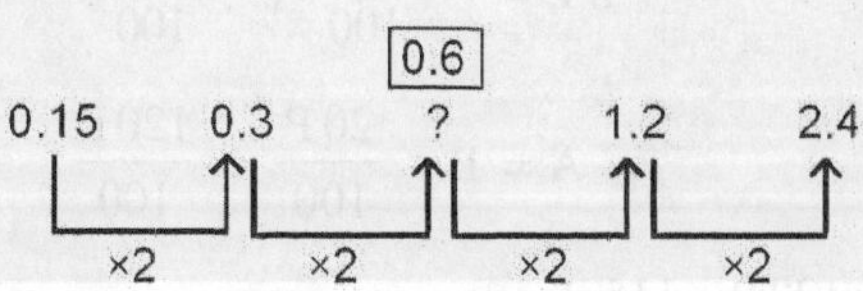

Hence, 0.6 will come at the place of question mark.

18. Since,

Similarly,

19. Cow & Goat give milk and Hen gives eggs.

20. Remaining no. of roses $= 133 - \left(133 \times \frac{5}{7}\right)$

$= 133 - 95 = 38.$

21. Figure in option '(*d*)' is exactly the mirror image of the given figure.

22. The letter 'A' of the word 'RETREAT' is not available in the word 'INTERDEPENDENT'.

23.

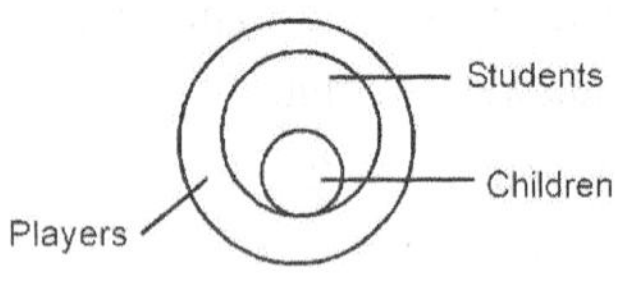

From above fig. it is clear that all children are players.

51. $\because \ M_1 \times D_1 \times T_1 = M_2 \times D_2 \times T_2$

$\Rightarrow \ 16 \times 12 \times 14 = 28 \times 12 \times D_2$

$\Rightarrow \qquad D_2 = \frac{16 \times 12 \times 14}{28 \times 12} = 8$ days.

52.

$$\text{S.I.} = \frac{P \times 15 \times T}{100} = \frac{15P}{100}$$

$$A = P + \frac{15P}{100} = \frac{115P}{100}$$

$$\text{S.I.} = \frac{P \times 20 \times T}{100} = \frac{20P}{100}$$

$$A = P + \frac{20P}{100} = \frac{120P}{100}$$

$$\frac{120P}{100} - \frac{115P}{100} = 75$$

$\Rightarrow \qquad 5P = 75 \times 100$

$\Rightarrow \qquad P = \frac{75 \times 100}{5} =$ ₹ 1500

53. Let, cost price = ₹ 100

Marked price = ₹ 120

Discount $= \frac{10}{100} \times 120 =$ ₹ 12

Selling price = 120 − 12 = ₹ 108

Profit = 108 − 100 = 8

Profit % $= \frac{8}{100} \times 100 = 8\%$.

54. Raja's 1 day work $= \frac{1}{20}$

Ramesh's 1 day work $= \frac{1}{25}$

(Raja + Ramesh)'s 1 day work $= \frac{1}{20} + \frac{1}{25}$

$= \frac{9}{100}$

Ramesh's 10 days work $= \frac{1}{25} \times 10 = \frac{2}{5}$

Remaining work $= 1 - \frac{2}{5} = \frac{3}{5}$

$\frac{9}{100}$ part (Raja + Ramesh) can do in 1 day

$\frac{3}{5}$ part they can do in $\frac{100}{9} \times \frac{3}{5} = \frac{20}{3}$ days

$= 6\frac{2}{3}$ days

Whole work done $= 10 + 6\frac{2}{3} = 16\frac{2}{3}$ days.

55. 1008 ÷ 7 = 144 which is perfect square.

144 = 12 × 12

Hence, required number = 7.

56. Required number of casted cones

$$= \frac{\frac{1}{3}\pi \times 15 \times 15 \times 20 \times 10 \times 10}{\frac{1}{3}\pi \times 15 \times 15 \times 5}$$

$= 400.$

57. Let, distance between school and house = x km

According to the question,

$$\frac{x}{\frac{5}{2}} - \frac{x}{\frac{7}{2}} = \frac{6}{60} + \frac{6}{60} = \frac{12}{60} = \frac{1}{5}$$

$$\Rightarrow \quad \frac{2x}{5}-\frac{2x}{7} = \frac{1}{5}$$

$$\Rightarrow \quad \frac{14x-10x}{35} = \frac{1}{5}$$

$$\Rightarrow \quad \frac{4x}{35} = \frac{1}{5} \quad \Rightarrow \quad 20x = 35$$

$$x = \frac{35}{20} = \frac{7}{4} = 1\frac{3}{4} \text{ km}$$

Hence, required distance = $1\frac{3}{4}$ km.

58. Let, mean proportion of 1.21 and 0.09 = x

$\therefore \quad x^2 = 1.21 \times 0.09$

$$\Rightarrow \quad x^2 = \frac{121}{100}\times\frac{9}{100}$$

$$\therefore \quad x = \sqrt{\frac{121\times 9}{100\times 100}} = \frac{11\times 3}{100} = \frac{33}{100}$$

$= 0.33.$

59. $$\sqrt{.000441} = \sqrt{\frac{441}{1000000}}$$

$$= \sqrt{\frac{21\times 21}{10\times 10\times 10\times 10\times 10\times 10}}$$

$$= \frac{21}{1000} = 0.021.$$

60. Let, the average after 17th inning = x

Then, average after 16th inning = $(x - 3)$

$\therefore \quad 16(x - 3) + 87 = 17x$

$\Rightarrow \quad 16x - 48 + 87 = 17x$

$\Rightarrow \quad x = 39$

Hence, the average after 17th inning = 39.

61. Initial S.P. of the each mango

$$= \frac{(100+25)\times 1}{50-25} = \frac{125}{25} = ₹\ 5.$$

62. Let, C.P. of the article = ₹ 100

$\therefore$ Marked price = ₹ 130

When M.P. ₹ 130, then C.P. = ₹ 100

When M.P. ₹ 286, then C.P. = $\frac{100}{130}\times 286$

= ₹ 220

Discount = $\frac{10}{100}\times 286$ = ₹ 28.60

S.P. = 286 − 28.60 = ₹ 257.40

Profit = 257.40 − 220 = ₹ 37.40

Profit % = $\frac{37.40}{220}\times 100$ = 17%.

63. Let, marked price = ₹ 100

Discount = $\frac{25}{100}\times 100$ = ₹ 25

S.P. = 100 − 25 = ₹ 75

When S.P. ₹ 75, then M.P. = ₹ 100

When S.P. ₹ 3600, then M.P. = $\frac{100}{75}\times 3600$

= 4 × 1200 = ₹ 4800.

64. Let, original price of the article = ₹ 100

Value after first discount = $100-\frac{20}{100}\times 100$

= ₹ 80

Value after 2nd discount = $80-\frac{25}{100}\times 80$

= ₹ 60

When cost of an article ₹ 60, then original price = 100

When cost of an article ₹ P, then original price

$$= \frac{100}{60}\times P = \frac{5P}{3}.$$

65. Speed of the plane = $\frac{6000}{8}$ km/hr

= 750 km/hr

Now, Speed = 750 + 250

= 1000 km/hr

$$\text{Time taken} = \frac{\text{Distance}}{\text{Speed}}$$

$$= \frac{9000}{1000} = 9 \text{ hrs.}$$

67. S.I = A – P = 956 – 800 = ₹ 156

$$\text{Rate of interest} = \frac{\text{SI} \times 100}{p \times t}$$

$$= \frac{156 \times 100}{800 \times 3}$$

$$= \frac{13}{2}\% = 6.5\%$$

$$\text{Now, rate of interest} = \frac{13}{2}\% + 4\% = \frac{21}{2}\%$$

$$\text{S.I.} = \frac{800 \times 21 \times 3}{2 \times 100} = 252$$

Amount = P + SI = 800 + 252
= ₹ 1052.

68. M.P. of the T.V. = ₹ 6500

$$\text{Discount} = \frac{12}{100} \times 6500 = 780$$

S.P. = 6500 – 780 = 5720

Hence, S.P. of the T.V. = ₹ 5720.

69. Total income of A and B = 2 × 200 = 400
Total income of C and D = 2 × 250 = 500
Total income of A, B, C, D = 900

$$\therefore \text{ Required average} = \frac{900}{4} = 225.$$

70. $$\text{Average} = \frac{1+3+5+7+9+11+......+25}{n}$$

$$\text{No. of odd terms} = \frac{25+1}{2} = 13$$

$$\left[\text{Sum of odd no.} = \frac{\text{Last odd no.} + 1}{2}\right]$$

Sum of odd nos. = $(13)^2$ = 169

$$\therefore \quad \text{Average} = \frac{169}{13} = 13.$$

71. Let, their ages be $5x$ and $9x$ years
According to the question,

$9x - 5x = 40$

$\Rightarrow \quad 4x = 40 \Rightarrow x = 10$

$5x = 5 \times 10 = 50$ years

$9x = 9 \times 10 = 90$ years

Sum of their ages = 50 + 90 = 140 years.

74. 243000 ÷ 9 = 27000
= 3 × 3 × 3 × 10 × 10 × 10
which is perfect cube.
Hence, required number = 9.

75. Let, the total number of votes
Polled = x
According to the question,

$(62 - 38)\%$ of $x = 144$

$\Rightarrow \quad 24\%$ of $x = 144$

$$\Rightarrow \quad \frac{24}{100} \times x = 144$$

$$\Rightarrow \quad x = \frac{144 \times 100}{24} = 600$$

Hence, total number of votes polled = 600.

Previous Paper (Solved)

SSC – Constable (GD) Exam, 2013

ITBPF/CISF/CRPF/BSF/SSB

Rifleman (Assam Rifles)

PART-I : GENERAL INTELLIGENCE & REASONING

Directions (Q. 1-5): *Select the related word/number for the given alternatives.*

1. Psychology : Mind : : Arithmetic : ?
(*a*) Knowledge (*b*) Number
(*c*) Height (*d*) Formulas

2. Ice : Coldness : : Earth : ?
(*a*) Weight (*b*) Jungle
(*c*) Gravitation (*d*) Sea

3. Teacher : School : : Nurse : ?
(*a*) Doctors (*b*) Patients
(*c*) Medicine (*d*) Hospitals

4. 11 : 1331 : : 9 : ?
(*a*) 979 (*b*) 991
(*c*) 729 (*d*) 829

5. Window : Carpenter : : Statue : ?
(*a*) Sculptor (*b*) Mason
(*c*) Blacksmith (*d*) Goldsmith

Directions (Q. 6 and 7): *Find the odd number/letter from the given alternatives.*

6. (*a*) XWVU (*b*) SRQP
(*c*) NMLK (*d*) EDCA

7. (*a*) 24 (*b*) 56
(*c*) 84 (*d*) 94

8. Which of the given responses would be a meaningful order of the following in ascending order?
1. 0640 hr 2. 1930 hr
3. 1335 hr 4. 2000 hr
(*a*) 4, 2, 3, 1 (*b*) 1, 4, 3, 2
(*c*) 1, 2, 3, 4 (*d*) 1, 3, 2, 4

9. Which one set of letter when sequentially placed at the gaps in the given letters series shall complete it?
b _ f _ _ _ d f g _
(*a*) dgggb (*b*) dggbg
(*c*) dgdgg (*d*) gdggb

Directions (Q. 10 and 11): *A series is given, with on term mission. Choose the correct alternatives from the given ones that will complete the series.*

10.
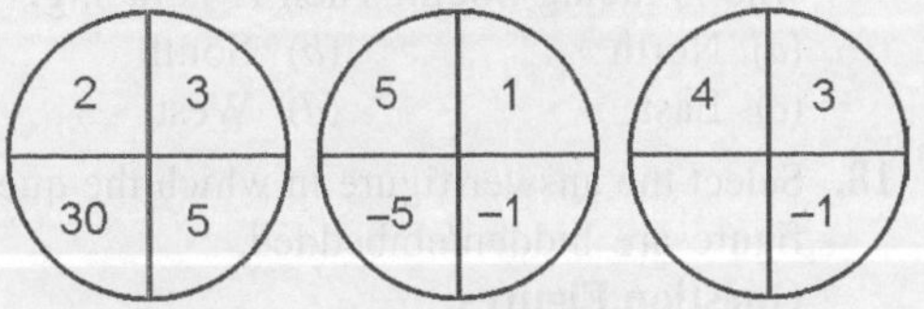

(*a*) 7 (*b*) –12
(*c*) 12 (*d*) 9

11. 50, 65, 82, ...?..., 122
(*a*) 101 (*b*) 97
(*c*) 105 (*d*) 100

12. In a group of 20 people, 8 read Hindi, 11 read English while 5 of them read none of these two. How many of them read Hindi and English both?
(*a*) 8 (*b*) 6
(*c*) 4 (*d*) 2

13. Unscramble the following letters to frame a meaningful word and find out the correct value of the letters.

E S R T A R U N A T

1 2 3 4 5 6 7 8 9 10

(*a*) 10 2 3 5 1 6 4 7 8 9
(*b*) 3 1 2 4 5 7 6 9 8 10
(*c*) 1 3 5 2 9 4 8 6 7 10
(*d*) 9 1 3 6 2 7 5 4 8 10

14. If 'DICTIONARY' is coded as 5479482361 then 'YARD' can be coded as:

(*a*) 1653 (*b*) 1635
(*c*) 1536 (*d*) 1365

15. In a row of students Ganesh is 7th from one extreme and 11th from the other. Find the total number of students in the row

(*a*) 17 (*b*) 18
(*c*) 19 (*d*) 20

16. Find the correct answer for the unsolved equation:

$5 \times 6 \times 3 = 356$, $1 \times 0 \times 5 = 510$, $5 \times 6 \times 7 = ?$

(*a*) 567 (*b*) 657
(*c*) 210 (*d*) 756

17. A, B, C and D are playing a game of carom. A, C and B, D are partners. C is to the left of D who is facing South. Then A is facing:

(*a*) North (*b*) South
(*c*) East (*d*) West

18. Select the answer figure in which the question figure are hidden/embedded.

Question Figures:

Answer Figures:

(*a*) (*b*) (*c*) (*d*)

19. Which of the following diagram best depicts the relationship between student, college and school?

(*a*)

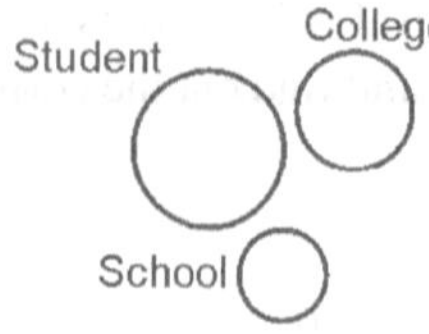

(*b*)

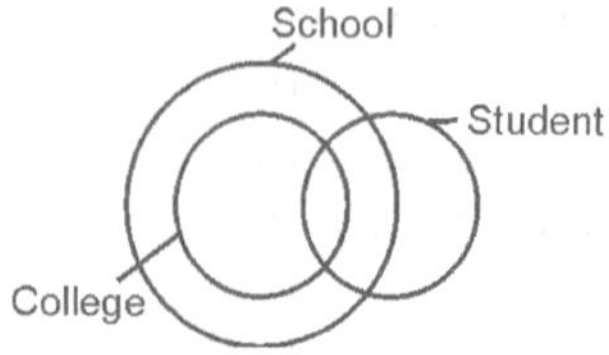

(*c*)

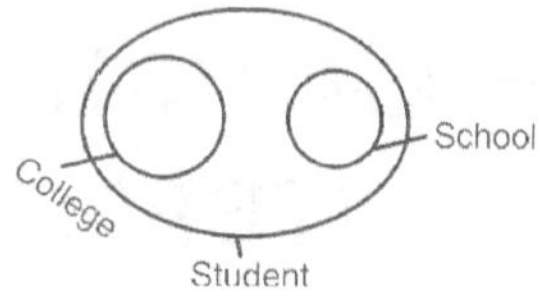

(*d*)

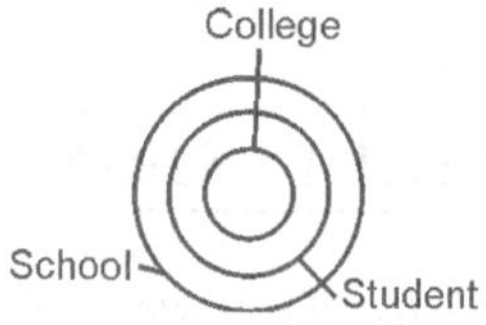

20. Statement is given followed by three conclusions, I, II and III. You have to consider the statement to be true even they seem to be at variance from commonly known facts. You have to decide which of the given conclusions, if and, follows from the given statement.

Statement: Comic books contain pictures.

Conclusions:

(*i*) All books contain pictures.
(*ii*) Books may or may not contain pictures.
(*iii*) Books other than the comic books do not contain pictures.

(*a*) Only Conclusion I follows
(*b*) Both Conclusions I and II follow
(*c*) Only Conclusion II follows
(*d*) Neither Conclusion follows

21. Which one of the answer figures shall complete the given question figure?

Question Figure:

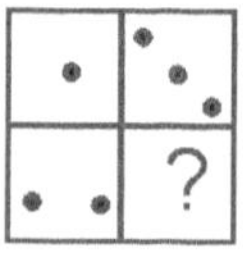

Answer Figures:

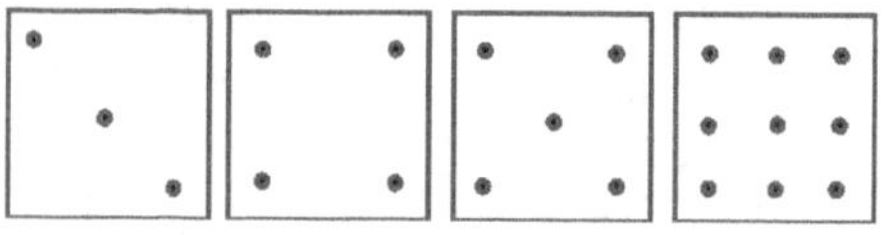

(*a*) (*b*) (*c*) (*d*)

22. From the given answer figures, select the one in which the question figure is hidden/ embedded.

Question Figure:

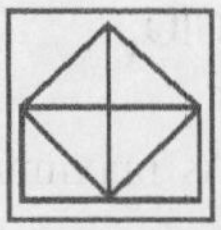

Answer Figures:

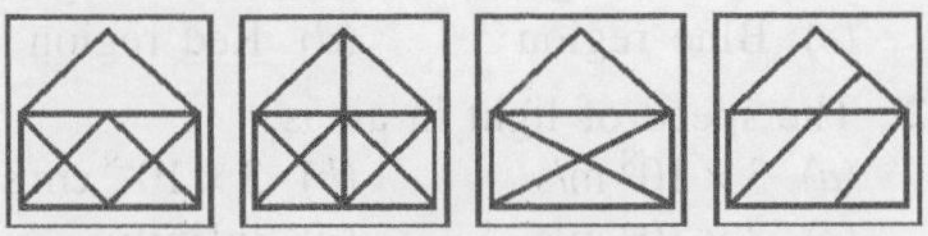

(*a*) (*b*) (*c*) (*d*)

23. A piece of paper is fold and cut as shown below in the question figures. From the given answer figures, indicate how it will appear when opened.

Question Figures:

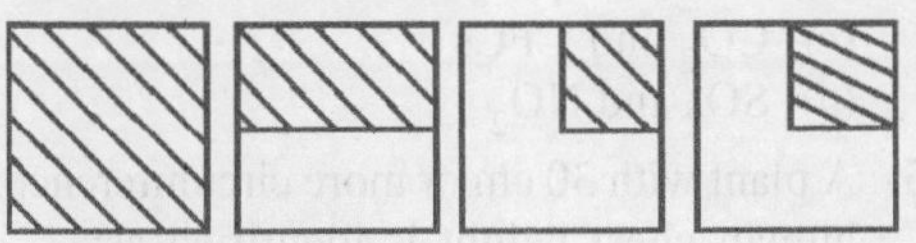

Answer Figures:

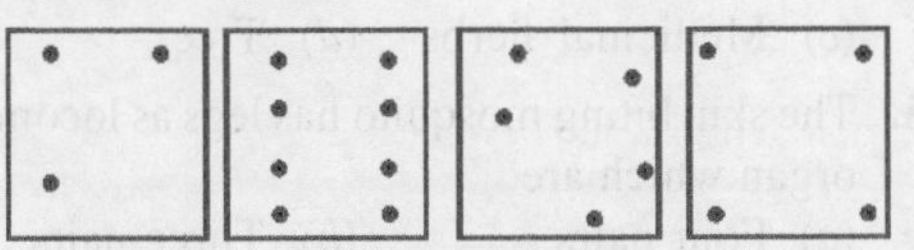

(*a*) (*b*) (*c*) (*d*)

24. Which of the answer figure is the right image of the given figure?

PRAYER

(*a*) ᑫᴚAYƎᴚ (*b*) ᴚƎᑫAƎY

(*c*) ᴚƎYAᴚᑫ (*d*) ᑫᴚAYƎᴚ

25. A word is represented by only one set of numbers as given in any one of the alternatives. The sets of numbers given in the alternatives are represented by two classes of alphabets as in two matrices given below. The columns and rows of Matrix I are numbered from 0 to 4 and that of Matrix II are numbered from 5 to 9. A letter from these matrices can be represented first by its row and next by its column, e.g., 'A' can be represented by 01, 13 etc., and 'S' can be represented by 55, 67 etc. Similarly, you have identify the set for the letters given.

Matrix–I

	0	1	2	3	4
0	P	A	I	V	R
1	I	P	R	A	V
2	A	R	V	P	I
3	V	I	P	R	A
4	R	V	A	I	P

Matrix–II

	5	6	7	8	9
5	S	L	K	M	E
6	K	M	S	E	L
7	M	E	L	K	S
8	L	K	E	S	M
9	E	S	M	L	K

(*a*) 65, 23, 14, 55

(*b*) 86, 34, 42, 69

(*c*) 78, 41, 23, 86

(*d*) 57, 11, 33, 96

PART-II : General Knowledge & General Awareness

26. Deflation is a situation in which:
(*a*) The value of money is falling
(*b*) The price of goods is increasing
(*c*) The value of money is increasing
(*d*) The price level is stagnant

27. Who presented the Union Budget in 1970?
(*a*) T.T. Krishnamachari (*b*) C. Subramaniam
(*c*) Indira Gandhi (*d*) R. Venkatraman

28. Which is the most important system in Democracy?
(*a*) Social (*b*) Political
(*c*) Economic (*d*) Governmental

29. What is the system of Local Self-Government in the Panchayati Raj set-up?
(*a*) Four tier system at the village, block, district and state level
(*b*) Three tier structure at village, block and district level
(*c*) Two tier system at village and block level
(*d*) Single tier set-up at village level

30. Gandhiji withdraw the Non-cooperation Movement due to:
(*a*) Chauri-Chaura Incident
(*b*) Champaran Movement
(*c*) Kakori Conspiracy
(*d*) Bardoli Movement

31. "The word impossible is found in the dictionary of fools" was the famous quote of:
(*a*) Hitler
(*b*) Alexander the Great
(*c*) Julius Caesar
(*d*) Napoleon

32. Which one of the following is not include the 'Eight Fold Path' of Buddhism?
(*a*) Right Speech
(*b*) Right Contemplation
(*c*) Right Desire
(*d*) Right Conduct

33. Which of the following dynasty succeeded the Mauryas?
(*a*) Satavahanas (*b*) Sungas
(*c*) Yavanas (*d*) Pandya

34. The important metal used with iron to product stainless steel is:
(*a*) Aluminum (*b*) Chromium
(*c*) Tin (*d*) Carbon

35. The name of uncreative gas is:
(*a*) Carbon dioxide (*b*) Hydrogen
(*c*) Nitrogen (*d*) Oxygen

36. Approximate life span of parrot is:
(*a*) 20 years (*b*) 40 years
(*c*) 70 years (*d*) 140 years

37. Tendons and ligaments are:
(*a*) Connective tissue (*b*) Muscular tissue
(*c*) Epithelial tissue (*d*) Skeletal tissue

38. What is a compound microscope?
(*a*) A microscope that has one lens
(*b*) A microscope that has two sets of lenses: and ocular lens and eyepiece
(*c*) A microscope whose lenses are concave
(*d*) A microscope whose lenses are convex

39. Heavy water is so called because it contains:
(*a*) Heavy isotope of hydrogen
(*b*) Heavy isotope of oxygen
(*c*) Mole number of hydrogen atoms
(*d*) Mole number of oxygen atoms

40. Glass is soluble in:
(*a*) H_2SO_4 (*b*) $HClO_4$
(*c*) HNO_3 (*d*) HF

41. Sensitivity of the human eye is maximum in the:
(*a*) Violet region (*b*) Green region
(*c*) Blue region (*d*) Red region

42. The speed of light in air is:
(*a*) 3×10^8 m/s (*b*) 3×10^{-8} cm/s
(*c*) 8×10^3 m/s (*d*) infinity

43. A collection of HTML page makes up the:
(*a*) Hyperlinks (*b*) Hypertext
(*c*) World Wide Web (*d*) Hypermedia

44. Acid rain caused by:
(*a*) SO_2 and particulates
(*b*) NO_2 and particulates
(*c*) CO_2 and CFCs
(*d*) SO_2 and NO_2

45. A plant with 30 cm or more circumference from human chest height is identified as:
(*a*) Herb (*b*) Shrub
(*c*) Medicinal herbs (*d*) Tree

46. The skin biting mosquito has legs as locomotors organ which are:
(*a*) Four pairs (*b*) Three pairs
(*c*) Two pairs (*d*) One pair

47. For the first time Commonwealth Games were played during 1930 in:
(*a*) London (*b*) Canada
(*c*) Brazil (*d*) Pakistan

48. Tidal forests comprising mainly the mangrove vegetation are found in:
(*a*) Nagarjuna Sagar
(*b*) Narmada Basin
(*c*) Sundarban Delta
(*d*) Ranganthitto Bird Sanctuary

49. The river known as Padma in Bangladesh is:
(*a*) Jamuna (*b*) Ganga
(*c*) Tista (*d*) Brahmaputra

50. Which one of the following is ***not*** correctly matched?
(*a*) Chipko Movement—S.L. Bahuguna
(*b*) Save Narmada Movement— Medha Patkar
(*c*) Appico Movement—P. Hegde
(*d*) Silent Movement—Baba Amte

PART-III : ELEMENTARY MATHEMATICS

51. $3\frac{3}{5}\times3\frac{3}{5}+2\times3\frac{3}{5}\times\frac{2}{5}+\frac{2}{5}\times\frac{2}{5}=$

(*a*) 15 (*b*) 16
(*c*) 17 (*d*) 18

52. Five bells begin to toll together and toll respectively at intervals of 6, 7, 8, 9, 12 seconds. After how many seconds will they toll together again?

(*a*) 72 (*b*) 612
(*c*) 504 (*d*) 318

53. Find the value of:

$\sqrt{156.25}+\sqrt{0.0081}-\sqrt{0.0361}$

(*a*) 13.4 (*b*) 15.4
(*c*) 12.4 (*d*) 17.4

54. A can do a piece of work in 20 days and B can do the same piece of work in 30 days. Find how many days both can do the work?

(*a*) 16 days (*b*) 14 days
(*c*) 10 days (*d*) 12 days

55. A, B, C together earn ₹ 150 per day while A and C together earn ₹ 94 and B and C together earn ₹ 76. The daily earning of C is:

(*a*) ₹ 56 (*b*) ₹ 20
(*c*) ₹ 34 (*d*) ₹ 75

56. A solid sphere is melted and recast into a right circular cone with a base radius equal to the radius of sphere. What is the ratio of the height and radius of the cone so formed?

(*a*) 4 : 3 (*b*) 2 : 3
(*c*) 3 : 4 (*d*) 4 : 1

57. If the triangle ABC is right angled at B. Find its circumradius if the side AB and BC are 15 cm and 20 cm respectively.

(*a*) 25 cm (*b*) 20 cm
(*c*) 15 cm (*d*) 12.5 cm

58. A radio set, marked ₹ 750 is sold at ₹ 570. The rate of discount offered is:

(*a*) 14% (*b*) 34%
(*c*) 24% (*d*) 20%

59. If a shirt cost ₹ 64, after 20% discount is allowed, what was its original price in ₹?

(*a*) 76.8 (*b*) 80
(*c*) 88 (*d*) 86.80

60. A trader allows a discount of 10% on the marked price. He still has a profit of 17% on the cost price. Find the profit % if he sells at the marked price.

(*a*) 27% (*b*) 33%
(*c*) 30% (*d*) 19%

61. In a factory one out of every 9 is a female worker. If the number of female workers is 125, the total number of workers is

(*a*) 1250 (*b*) 1125
(*c*) 1025 (*d*) 1000

62. If A = 2/3 of B and B = 4/5 of C, then A : B : C is:

(*a*) 12 : 8 : 10 (*b*) 15 : 10 : 8
(*c*) 10 : 15 : 12 (*d*) 8 : 12 : 15

63. The average of first ten prime number is:

(*a*) 10.1 (*b*) 10
(*c*) 12.9 (*d*) 13

64. Two years ago the average age of a family of 8 members was 18 years. After the addition of baby, the average age of the family remain the same today. What is the age of the baby?

(*a*) 2 years (*b*) 1.5 years
(*c*) 1 year (*d*) 2.5 years

65. The average of 9 integers is found to be 11. But after the calculation, it was detected that, by mistake, the integer 23 was copied as 32, while calculating the average. After the due correction is made, the new average will be:

(*a*) 10 (*b*) 9
(*c*) 10.1 (*d*) 9.5

66. By selling 90 ball pens for ₹ 160 a person loss 20%. The number of ball pens, which should be sold for ₹ 96 so as to have a profit 20% is:

(*a*) 36 (*b*) 37
(*c*) 46 (*d*) 47

67. A dealer buys a wrist watch for ₹ 225 and spend ₹ 15 on its repairs. If he sells the same for ₹ 300, his profit per cent is:

(*a*) 15% (*b*) 20%
(*c*) 25% (*d*) 30%

68. Raman's salary is increased by 5% this year. If his present salary is ₹ 1806, the last year's salary was:

(*a*) ₹ 1720 (*b*) ₹ 1620
(*c*) ₹ 1520 (*d*) ₹ 1801

69. In an examination 80% of the boys passed in English and 85% passed in Mathematics, while 75% passed in both. If 45 boys failed in both, the number of boys who sat for the examination was:

(*a*) 400 (*b*) 450
(*c*) 200 (*d*) 150

70. A speed of 30.6 km/hr is the same as:

(*a*) 8.5 m/sec (*b*) 10 m/sec
(*c*) 12 m/sec (*d*) 15.5 m/sec

71. A train 200 m long running at 36 kmph takes 55 sec to cross a bridge. The length of the bridge is:

(*a*) 375 m (*b*) 300 m
(*c*) 350 m (*d*) 325 m

72. Two equal sums were lent out 7% and 5% S.I. respectively. The interest earned on the two loans add up to ₹ 960 for 4 years. The total sum lent out is:

(*a*) ₹ 3500 (*b*) ₹ 2500
(*c*) ₹ 4000 (*d*) ₹ 3000

73. ₹ 800 at 5% per annum compounded annually will amount to ₹ 882 in:

(*a*) 1 year (*b*) 2 years
(*c*) 3 years (*d*) 4 years

Directions (Q. 74-75): *The following is a graphical representation of income and expenditure of 5 persons during the month of January. Read the graph and indicate the correct alternative of the questions given below.*

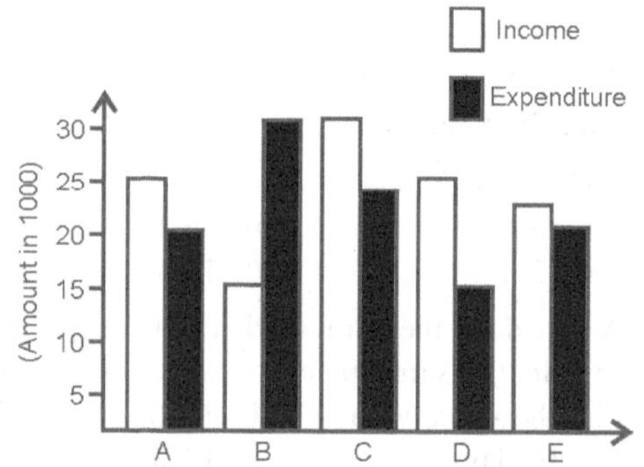

74. What is the average income of five persons per months?

(*a*) ₹ 57750 (*b*) ₹ 24600
(*c*) ₹ 61500 (*d*) ₹ 62500

75. Who save maximum amount?

(*a*) A (*b*) C
(*c*) D (*d*) E

PART-IV : ENGLISH

Directions (Q. 76-78) : *In the following questions, some part of the sentences have errors and some are correct. Find out which part of a sentence has an error and indicate the alternative corresponding to appropriate letter (a), (b), (c). If a sentence is free from errors, indicate the alternative corresponding to letter (d).*

76. (*a*) The director along with his assistant/ (*b*) have thoroughly examined/ (*c*) the new proposals. (*d*) No error

77. (*a*) I bought/ (*b*) tow/ (*c*) slippers. (*d*) No error

78. (*a*) You are very lovable person/ (*b*) but I/ (*c*) am not loving you./ (*d*) No error

Directions (Q. 79-82) : *In the following questions, sentences are given with blanks to be filled with appropriate word(s). Four alternatives are suggested for each question. Choose the correct alternative out of the four and indicate it by choosing the appropriate alternative.*

79. Arun has .... his work.

(*a*) completely (*b*) completing
(*c*) complete (*d*) completed

80. Rather than .... other, why don't you look for your own mistakes?
(*a*) helping (*b*) pointing
(*c*) blaming (*d*) watching

81. We have been living in this house .... 1965.
(*a*) when (*b*) for
(*c*) before (*d*) since

82. Since Amit was an .... photographer, he did not charge any money for taking our picture.
(*a*) amateur (*b*) professional
(*c*) useless (*d*) unknown

Directions (Q. 83-85) : *In the following questions, choose the word opposite in meaning to the given bold word and indicate the correct alternative.*

83. Flood
(*a*) Drought (*b*) Dry
(*c*) Cyclone (*d*) Desert

84. Liberal
(*a*) Irrelevant (*b*) Free
(*c*) Sensitive (*d*) Intolerant

85. Bane
(*a*) curse (*b*) boon
(*c*) base (*d*) violent

Directions (Q. 86-88) : *In the following questions, four alternatives are given for the Idiom/Phrase* ***bold*** *in the sentence. Choose the alternative which best expresses the meaning of the Idiom/Phrase and indicate the correct alternative.*

86. It **poured cats and dogs**
(*a*) rained heavily
(*b*) rained lightly
(*c*) dazzled
(*d*) hail storm

87. The manager was **above board in** all his dealings with his employees.
(*a*) dishonest (*b*) rude
(*c*) honest (*d*) charitable

88. Whenever I **feel blue** I like to listen to slow music.
(*a*) happy (*b*) gleeful
(*c*) troubled (*d*) gloomy

Directions (Q. 89-91) : *In the following questions a sentence/part of sentence is* ***bold****. Below are given alternatives bold sentence/part of the sentence at (a), (b) and (c) which may improve the sentence. Choose the correct alternative. In case no improvement is letter needed, your answer is (d).*

89. He had hardly gone when his friend came.
(*a*) Hardly he had gone
(*b*) He had gone hardly
(*c*) Hardly had he gone
(*d*) No improvement

90. Neither Ted nor Johan **are going**.
(*a*) have been going
(*b*) were going
(*c*) is going
(*d*) No improvement

91. You are played instead of **worked.**
(*a*) working
(*b*) having worked
(*c*) being worked
(*d*) No improvement

Directions (Q. 92-94) : *In the following questions, out of the four alternatives, choose the one which can be substituted for the given words/sentences and indicate it by choosing the appropriate alternative.*

92. A from of government in which the supreme power rests with people is:
(*a*) Monarchy (*b*) Oligarchy
(*c*) Democracy (*d*) Bureaucracy

93. Animals that live in a particular region:
(*a*) fauna (*b*) wildlife
(*c*) native (*d*) beast

94. Send or bring somebody back to his own country:
(*a*) asylum (*b*) refuge
(*c*) repatriate (*d*) emigrate

Directions (Q. 95-97) : *In the following questions, four words are given in each question, out of which only one word is correctly spelt. Find the correctly spelt word and mark your correct answer.*

95. (*a*) omission (*b*) ocassion
(*c*) commission (*d*) posesion

96. (*a*) comemmorate (*b*) commemmorate
(*c*) comemmorate (*d*) commemorate

97. (*a*) Indigenious (*b*) Indigenous
(*c*) Indiginous (*d*) Indeginous

Directions (Q. 98-100) : *In the following questions, you have one brief passage with 3 questions following the passage. Read the passage carefully and choose the best answer to each question out of the four alternatives.*

In the evening we decided to pitch camp as the weather was not encouraging. The wind was high and gathering storm clouds predicted a wild wet night. Moreover, we had arrived at a spot which looked promising for a camp. A level expanse in the lee of a high hill afforded some shelter from the wind; fresh water was near at hand in a stream which flowed across the plain; a copse of trees provided adequate supplies of fuel; and the dry grasses which abounded on the hillside would enhance the comfort of our beds.

Each member of the party was allotted a task. Some erected the tents; others prepared a scanty meal; yet others attended to the needs of the ponies that were now exhausted after a very strenuous day. As the angry sun sank, the bustle of activity was hushed into silence and each man settled down to sleep.

98. As the weather was not encouraging we decided to:
(*a*) set up the camp (*b*) pack up the camp
(*c*) extend the camp (*d*) shift the camp

99. The camp site looked encouraging because:
(*a*) it was sheltered by some trees
(*b*) the dry grass would provide fuel
(*c*) we had been promised that spot
(*d*) it was level and sheltered

100. The day had been very:
(*a*) exciting (*b*) tiring
(*c*) boring (*d*) comfortable

ANSWERS

1	2	3	4	5	6	7	8	9	10
(*b*)	(*c*)	(*d*)	(*c*)	(*a*)	(*d*)	(*d*)	(*d*)	(*b*)	(*b*)
11	**12**	**13**	**14**	**15**	**16**	**17**	**18**	**19**	**20**
(*a*)	(*c*)	(*b*)	(*d*)	(*a*)	(*d*)	(*c*)	(*a*)	(*c*)	(*c*)
21	**22**	**23**	**24**	**25**	**26**	**27**	**28**	**29**	**30**
(*b*)	(*b*)	(*b*)	(*c*)	(*d*)	(*a*)	(*c*)	(*b*)	(*b*)	(*a*)
31	**32**	**33**	**34**	**35**	**36**	**37**	**38**	**39**	**40**
(*d*)	(*c*)	(*b*)	(*b*)	(*c*)	(*a*)	(*a*)	(*b*)	(*a*)	(*d*)
41	**42**	**43**	**44**	**45**	**46**	**47**	**48**	**49**	**50**
(*b*)	(*a*)	(*a*)	(*d*)	(*b*)	(*d*)	(*b*)	(*c*)	(*b*)	(*d*)
51	**52**	**53**	**54**	**55**	**56**	**57**	**58**	**59**	**60**
(*b*)	(*c*)	(*c*)	(*d*)	(*b*)	(*d*)	(*d*)	(*c*)	(*b*)	(*c*)
61	**62**	**63**	**64**	**65**	**66**	**67**	**68**	**69**	**70**
(*b*)	(*d*)	(*c*)	(*a*)	(*a*)	(*a*)	(*c*)	(*a*)	(*b*)	(*a*)
71	**72**	**73**	**74**	**75**	**76**	**77**	**78**	**79**	**80**
(*c*)	(*c*)	(*b*)	(*b*)	(*c*)	(*b*)	(*b*)	(*c*)	(*d*)	(*c*)
81	**82**	**83**	**84**	**85**	**86**	**87**	**88**	**89**	**90**
(*d*)	(*a*)	(*a*)	(*d*)	(*b*)	(*a*)	(*c*)	(*d*)	(*c*)	(*c*)
91	**92**	**93**	**94**	**95**	**96**	**97**	**98**	**99**	**100**
(*d*)	(*c*)	(*c*)	(*c*)	(*c*)	(*d*)	(*b*)	(*a*)	(*d*)	(*b*)

SOME SELECTED EXPLANATORY ANSWERS

5. One who makes window, door and all wooden items is called Carpenter. In same way statue is made by one who called Sculptor.

6. X W V U $\xrightarrow{\text{Arrange in reverse order}}$, S R Q P $\xrightarrow{\text{Arrange in reverse order}}$, N M L K $\xrightarrow{\text{Arrange in reverse order}}$, E D C A

7. Except '94' all three are divisible by '4'.

8. Ascending order is
0640 hr, 1335 hr, 1930 hr, 2000 hr.

9. The sequence is bdfgg, bdfgg.

10.

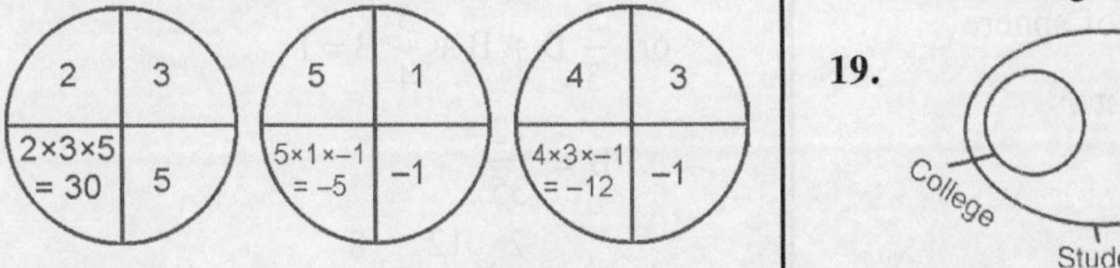

11. 50 → 7^2+1, 65 → 8^2+1, 82 → 9^2+1, 101 → 10^2+1, 122 → 11^2+1

12. $n(A)$ = Number of people read Hindi = 8
$n(B)$ = Number of people read English = 11
$n(A \cap B)'$ = Neither Hindi nor English = 5.

$\therefore\ n(A \cup B) = n(U) - n(A \cap B)'$
$= 20 - 5 = 15$

$\therefore\ n(A \cap B) = -1\{n(A \cup B) - n(A) - n(B)\}$
$= -1\{15 - 8 - 11\} = 4$

13. Meaningful word :

R	E	S	T	A	U	R	A	N	T
3	1	2	4	5	7	6	9	8	10

14.

D	I	C	T	I	O	N	A	R	Y
↓	↓	↓	↓	↓	↓	↓	↓	↓	↓
5	4	7	9	4	8	2	3	6	1

Similary,

Y	A	R	D
↓	↓	↓	↓
1	3	6	5

15. Total number of students in a row
$= 11 + 7 - 1 = 17$

16. $5 \times 6 \times 3 = 356,\ 1 \times 0 \times 5 = 510$
Similarly, $5 \times 6 \times 7 = 756$

17. Position of four players

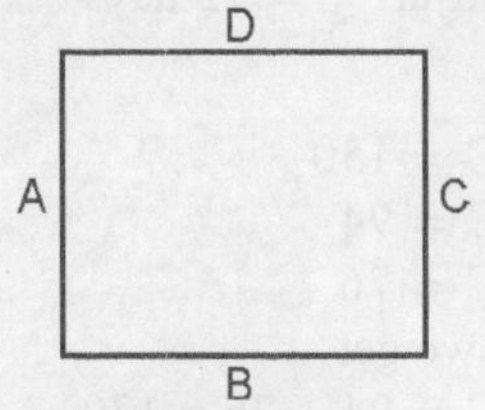

A is facing East
B is facing North
C is facing West and
D is facing South.

19.

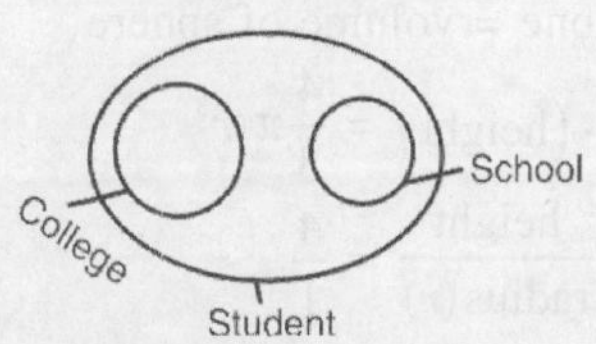

Correct answer is (*c*). As all student either study in school or college.

25. Given word is K P R S

K : (57), 65, 78, 86, 99
P : 00, (11), 23, 32, 44
R : 04, 12, 21, (33), 40
S : 55, 67, 79, 88, (96)

51. $3\frac{3}{5} \times 3\frac{3}{5} + 2 \times 3\frac{3}{5} \times \frac{2}{5} + \frac{2}{5} \times \frac{2}{5}$

$= \left(3\frac{3}{5} + \frac{2}{5}\right)^2 = (4)^2 = 16$

52. L.C.M. of 6, 7, 8, 9, 12

2	6, 7, 8, 9, 12
3	3, 7, 4, 9, 6
2	1, 7, 4, 3, 2
	1, 7, 2, 3, 1

L.C.M. $= 2 \times 3 \times 2 \times 7 \times 2 \times 3 = 504$

53. $\sqrt{(12.5)^2} + \sqrt{(0.09)^2} - \sqrt{(0.19)^2}$
$= 12.5 + 0.09 - 0.19 = 12.4$

54. Work done by them together in 1 day

$$= \frac{1}{20} + \frac{1}{30} = \frac{5}{60} \text{ work}$$

$\therefore$ Work completed in $\frac{60}{5} = 12$ days

55. Given that

$$A + B + C = 150 \quad ...(i)$$
$$A + C = 94 \quad ...(ii)$$
$$B + C = 76 \quad ...(iii)$$

from (*ii*) and (*iii*), we get

$$A + B + 2C = 94 + 76 = 170$$

$\therefore$ $C = 170 - 150 = 20$

56. Let radius of sphere = radius of base of cone $= r$.

Volume of cone = volume of sphere

$$\frac{1}{3}\pi\left(r^2\right)\cdot\left(\text{height}\right) = \frac{4}{3}\pi\cdot r^3$$

$$\therefore \quad \frac{\text{height}}{\text{radius}(r)} = \frac{4}{1}$$

$\therefore$ 4 : 1

57.

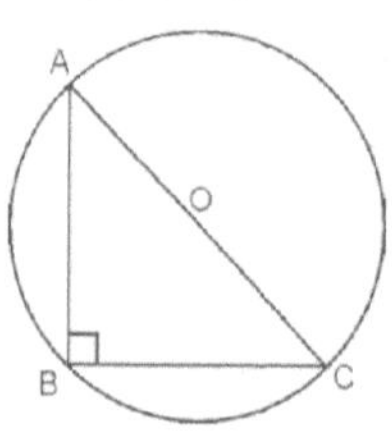

As $\angle B = 90^o$

$\therefore$ AC is the diameter of the circumcircle.

$$AC = \sqrt{(AB)^2 + (BC)^2}$$
$$= \sqrt{(15)^2 + (20)^2}$$
$$= \sqrt{625} = 25$$

$\therefore$ Circumradius (r) = $\frac{25}{2} = 12.5$ cm

58. Discount % = $\left(\frac{750 - 570}{750}\right) \times 100$

$$= \frac{180}{750} \times 100 = 24\%$$

59. Original Price = $64 \times \frac{100}{(100 - 20)}$

$$= \frac{64 \times 100}{80} = ₹\ 80$$

60. Let marked price = 100

Price after discount = 90

$$\text{Cost price} = 90 \times \frac{100}{117} = 77$$

$$\text{Profit \%} = \frac{(100 - 77)}{77} \times 100 = 30\%$$

61. Total number of workers

$= 9 \times 125 = 1125$

62. $A = \frac{2}{3}B$ and $B = \frac{4}{5}C$

$\therefore$ $C = \frac{5}{4}B$

Now, A + B + C = 1

or, $\frac{2}{3}B + B + \frac{5}{4}B = 1$

$\therefore$ $B = \frac{12}{35}$

$\therefore$ $A = \frac{2}{3} \times \frac{12}{35} = \frac{8}{35}$

$C = \frac{5}{4} \times \frac{12}{35} = \frac{15}{35}$

$$A : B : C = \frac{8}{35} : \frac{12}{35} : \frac{15}{35} = 8 : 12 : 15$$

63. First ten prime number:

2, 3, 5, 7, 11, 13, 17, 19, 23, 29

$$\text{Average} = \frac{\text{Sum of all numbers}}{\text{Number of Numbers}} = \frac{129}{10} = 12.9$$

64. Let Age of baby = x yr.

Two years ago,

Average age, 18

$$= \frac{\text{Sum of age's of all members}}{8}$$

Sum of age's of all 8 members = 144

Today average age is unchanged

so, $18 = \frac{144 + 2 \times 8 + x}{9}$

or, $162 = 144 + 16 + x$

$x = 162 - 160 = 2$ yrs.

65. Sum of all 9 integers = $11 \times 9 = 99$

When 32 is corrected and written as 23 then change in sum of integer

$= 99 - (32 - 23) = 90$

New average = $\dfrac{90}{9} = 10$

66. Cost price of 90 ball pens

$= 160 \times \dfrac{100}{(100-20)} = 200$

Selling price, when profit is 20%

$= 200 \times \dfrac{120}{100} = 240$

Number of pen he sold in ₹ 96

$= \dfrac{96}{\left(\dfrac{240}{90}\right)} = 36 = \dfrac{96 \times 90}{240} = 36$

67. Cost price = 225 + 15 = ₹ 240

Profit = 300 – 240 = 60

Profit % = $\dfrac{60}{240} \times 100 = 25\%$

68. Last year salary = $1806 \times \dfrac{100}{(100+5)} = 1720$

69. Number of boys passed in English $n(E) = 0.8$

Number of boys passed in Math $n(M) = 0.85$

Number of boys passed in both subjects $n(E \cap M) = 0.75$

$\therefore\ n(E \cup M) = 0.8 + 0.85 - 0.75$

$= 0.9 = 90\%$

∴ Number of boys who fail in both subjects

= 100 – 90 = 10%

According to the question,

Total number of boys sit for the exam

$= \dfrac{45 \times 100}{10} = 450$

70. Speed in $\dfrac{\text{m}}{\text{sec}}$

$\dfrac{\text{km}}{\text{hr}} = \dfrac{1000\ \text{m}}{3600\ \text{sec}}$

$\dfrac{\text{km}}{\text{hr}} = \dfrac{5\ \text{m}}{18\ \text{sec}}$

$= 30.6 \times \dfrac{5}{18}$

$\cong 8.5$ m/sec

71. Let length of bridge = l m.

Speed of train = 36 km/h

$36 \times \dfrac{5}{18} = 10$m/sec

Distance travelled in 55 sec.

55 × 10 = 550 m.

$\therefore\ l + 200 = 550$

$\therefore\ l = 350$ m.

72. Let total sum lent out = 2P

$960 = \dfrac{P \times 7 \times 4}{100} + \dfrac{P \times 5 \times 4}{100}$

48P = 96000

∴ P = 2000

total sum lent out = 2 × 2000 = 4000

73. From compound interest formula

$A = P\left(1 + \dfrac{r}{100}\right)^t$

$\dfrac{882}{800} = \left(1 + \dfrac{5}{100}\right)^t$

$\dfrac{441}{400} = \left(\dfrac{105}{100}\right)^t$

or, $\left(\dfrac{21}{20}\right)^2 = \left(\dfrac{21}{20}\right)^t$

∴ $t = 2$ years

74-75.

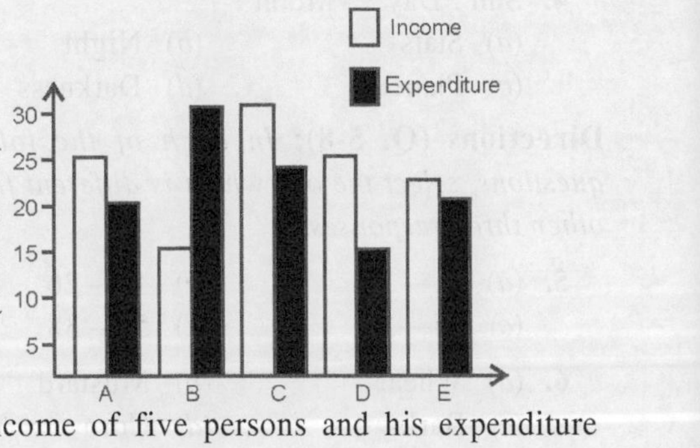

Income of five persons and his expenditure in month January.

74. Average income of five persons

$= \dfrac{25000 + 15000 + 30000 + 28000 + 25000}{5}$

= ₹ 24600

75. Saving of A = 25000 – 20000 = 5000

Saving of B = 15000 – 30000 = 15000

Saving of C = 30000 – 25000 = 5000

Saving of D = 28000 – 15000 = 13000

Saving of E = 25000 – 18000 = 7000

∴ Maximum saving is done by D.

Previous Paper (Solved)

SSC – Constable (GD) Exam, 2012*

ITBPF/CISF/CRPF/BSF/SSB

Rifleman (Assam Rifles)

PART-I : GENERAL INTELLIGENCE & REASONING

Directions (Q. 1-4): *In each of the following questions, select the related word/letters/number from the given alternatives.*

1. Wood : Paper : : Steel : ?
(*a*) Metal (*b*) Nail
(*c*) Glass (*d*) Iron

2. 7 : 28 : : 2 : ?
(*a*) 8 (*b*) 12
(*c*) 16 (*d*) 24

3. RAT : TAR : : PIT : ?
(*a*) BIT (*b*) CAT
(*c*) TIP (*d*) TOP

4. Sun : Day : : Moon : ?
(*a*) Stars (*b*) Night
(*c*) Planets (*d*) Darkness

Directions (Q. 5-8): *In each of the following questions, select the one which is different from the other three responses.*

5. (*a*) 21—37 (*b*) 42—26
(*c*) 35—51 (*d*) 56—38

6. (*a*) Wheat (*b*) Mustard
(*c*) Barley (*d*) Corn

7. (*a*) Bus (*b*) Scooter
(*c*) Car (*d*) Cycle

8. (*a*) ACE (*b*) GIK
(*c*) JLM (*d*) SUW

9. Find the correct alternative from the given responses that will complete the series.

2, 5, 9, <u>?</u>, 20, 27
(*a*) 14 (*b*) 16
(*c*) 18 (*d*) 24

10. How many 9 are followed by an even number and preceded by an odd number in the following series?

469259339467924894
(*a*) 4 (*b*) 3
(*c*) 2 (*d*) 1

11. From the given alternatives, select the word which **cannot be formed** using the letters of the given word.

CELEBRATION
(*a*) TAILOR (*b*) ACTION
(*c*) CREATE (*d*) BREATH

12. Which one of the given responses would be a meaningful order of the following words?
1. Word 2. Paragraph
3. Sentence 4. Letter
(*a*) 1, 3, 4, 2 (*b*) 3, 4, 1, 2
(*c*) 4, 1, 2, 3 (*d*) 4, 1, 3, 2

13. Which one set of letters when sequentially placed at the gaps in the given letter series shall complete it?

b _ y _ _ by _ b _ yt
(*a*) *bgtbt* (*b*) *btbtb*
(*c*) *atbbt* (*d*) *cbbtc*

14. In a platform, train 'A' 225 m long is stopped to allow train 'B' 375 m long to pass. Speed of 'B' is 90 km per hour time taken by train 'B' to cross train 'A' completely will be
(*a*) 6.67 sec (*b*) 9 sec
(*c*) 2.5 sec (*d*) 24 sec

15. Some equations are solved on the basis of a certain system. On the same basis, find out the correct answer for the unsolved equation.

* Exam held on 22-04-2012

$5 \times 6 \times 9 = 659$
$4 \times 7 \times 3 = 743$
$9 \times 2 \times 8 = ?$

(*a*) 928 (*b*) 298
(*c*) 982 (*d*) 829

16. If in a certain code language NOITCELES represents SELECTION, then what will AIDNI represent?

(*a*) AIDS (*b*) INDIA
(*c*) HINDI (*d*) HANDI

17. A man goes 5 km East, then he turns right and goes 4 km, then he turns left and goes 5 km. Which direction is he facing now?

(*a*) North (*b*) South
(*c*) East (*d*) West

18. Umesh is taller than Satish, Suresh is shorter than Neeraj but taller than Umesh. Who is the tallest among them?

(*a*) Umesh (*b*) Suresh
(*c*) Satish (*d*) Neeraj

19. Two statements are given followed by two inferences I and II. You have to consider the statements to be true even if they seem to be at variance from commonly known facts. You are to decide which of the given inferences, if any, follow from the given statements. Indicate your answer.

Statements:

1. All players are educated.
2. All educated are cultured.

Inferences:

I. All players are cultured.
II. All cultured persons are players.

(*a*) Only inference I follows
(*b*) Only inference II follows
(*c*) Both inferences I and II follow
(*d*) Neither inference I nor II follows

20. Which answer figure will complete the pattern in the question figure?

Question Figure:

Answer Figures:

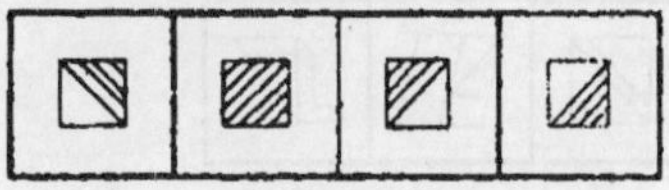

(*a*) (*b*) (*c*) (*d*)

21. Find the missing number from the given responses.

16	12	13
32	24	26
48	?	39

(*a*) 28 (*b*) 36
(*c*) 42 (*d*) 32

22. Which of the answer figure is exactly the mirror image of the given figure, when the mirror is held on the line MN?

Question Figure:

Answer Figures:

(*a*) (*b*) (*c*) (*d*)

23. In the following figure, the triangle represents teachers, the circle represents students and the rectangle represents actors. Which number represents teachers who are also students and actors?

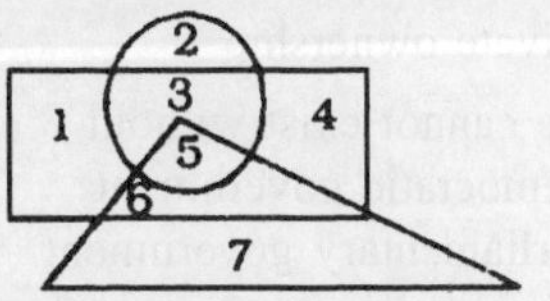

(*a*) 3 (*b*) 6
(*c*) 5 (*d*) 2

24. Select the answer figure in which the question figure is hidden/embedded.

Question Figure:

Answer Figures:

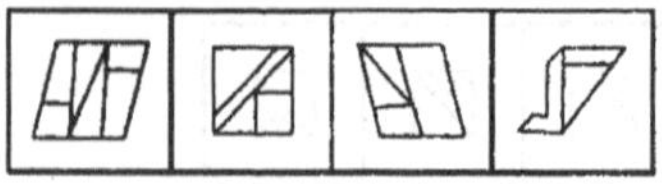

(*a*) (*b*) (*c*) (*d*)

25. A piece of paper is folded and punched as shown below in the question figures. From the given answer figures, indicate how it will appear when opened?

Question Figures:

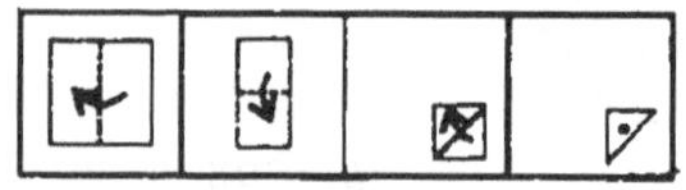

Answer Figures:

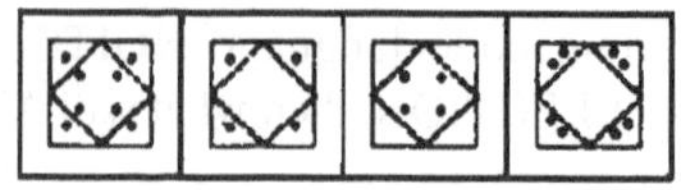

(*a*) (*b*) (*c*) (*d*)

PART-II : GENERAL KNOWLEDGE & GENERAL AWARENESS

26. The oldest era is
(*a*) Saka era (*b*) Buddhist era
(*c*) Mohammadan era (*d*) Vikrama era

27. The most accessible medium in India is
(*a*) Television (*b*) Radio
(*c*) Cinema (*d*) Newspapers

28. Name the curve which shows the quantity of products a seller wishes to sell at a given price level.
(*a*) Demand curve (*b*) Cost curve
(*c*) Supply curve (*d*) None of these

29. The supply of labour in the economy depends on
(*a*) Population (*b*) National income
(*c*) Per capita income (*d*) Natural resources

30. The main feature of a capitalist economy is
(*a*) Administered prices
(*b*) Public ownership
(*c*) Economic planning
(*d*) Private ownership

31. A State cannot exist without
(*a*) Democratic government
(*b*) Parliamentary government
(*c*) Presidential government
(*d*) Some kind of government

32. The second largest producer of cotton textiles in India is
(*a*) Maharashtra (*b*) Tamil Nadu
(*c*) Andhra Pradesh (*d*) Gujarat

33. An instrument that records earthquakes is
(*a*) Ergograph (*b*) Ediograph
(*c*) Thermograph (*d*) Seismograph

34. A matured mammalian cell without nucleus is
(*a*) Lymphocyte (*b*) Erythrocyte
(*c*) Spermatozoan (*d*) Oocyte

35. Haemoglobin contains the metal
(*a*) Copper (*b*) Molybdenum
(*c*) Iron (*d*) Magnesium

36. Whom do we call "The Iron Man of India"?
(*a*) Gopal Krishna Gokhale
(*b*) B.G. Tilak
(*c*) M.K. Gandhi
(*d*) Sardar Patel

37. Sikh army was called
(*a*) Akali (*b*) Singh Dal
(*c*) Khalsa (*d*) Gurudwara

38. The most common cause of pollution of air is
(*a*) Carbon dioxide (*b*) Carbon monoxide
(*c*) Sulphur dioxide (*d*) Smoke

39. The Industrial Revolution has led to
(*a*) Conservation of forests
(*b*) Increased pollution
(*c*) Conservation of wildlife
(*d*) Ecological balance

40. The process by which milk is converted to curd is called
(*a*) Pasteurization (*b*) Vernalization
(*c*) Fermentation (*d*) Retting

41. The historic Ellora Caves are located near
(*a*) Delhi (*b*) Agra
(*c*) Ahmedabad (*d*) Aurangabad

42. Citizens of India can vote at the age of

(*a*) 18 years (*b*) 21 years
(*c*) 22 years (*d*) 25 years

43. The author of 'The Satanic Verses' is

(*a*) Kushal Das (*b*) Salman Rushdie
(*c*) Rammurthy (*d*) John Grisham

44. The technique of calculating the age of fossil organisms is

(*a*) Radiocarbon dating
(*b*) Electroporation
(*c*) Counting the annual rings
(*d*) Micromanipulation

45. 'Comose' seeds are seeds with

(*a*) Long hairs (*b*) Wings
(*c*) Bristles (*d*) Hooks

46. Velocity of sound in air does not depend on

(*a*) Density of air (*b*) Temperature of air
(*c*) Pressure of air (*d*) Humidity of air

47. A dynamo is used to convert

(*a*) mechanical energy into electrical energy
(*b*) electrical energy into mechanical energy
(*c*) electrical energy into magnetic energy
(*d*) magnetic energy into mechanical energy

48. .... allows users to access accounts and pay bills.

(*a*) Distance Learning (*b*) Online Banking
(*c*) E-Commerce (*d*) Multimedia

49. Nitrogen forms a variety of compounds in all oxidation states ranging from

(*a*) – 3 to + 5 (*b*) – 3 to + 3
(*c*) – 3 to + 4 (*d*) – 3 to + 6

50. The next higher homologue of C_6H_{14} is

(*a*) C_7H_{14} (*b*) C_7H_{12}
(*c*) C_6H_{12} (*d*) C_7H_{16}

PART-III : ELEMENTARY MATHEMATICS

51. The sum of all those prime numbers which are not greater than 17 is

(*a*) 59 (*b*) 58
(*c*) 41 (*d*) 42

52. A can do $\frac{1}{6}$ of a work in 5 days and B can do $\frac{2}{5}$ of the work in 8 days. In how many days, can both A and B together do the work?

(*a*) 12 days (*b*) 18 days
(*c*) 15 days (*d*) 20 days

53. The simplified value of $\sqrt{0.25 \times 2.25}$ is

(*a*) 0.075 (*b*) 0.705
(*c*) 0.750 (*d*) 7.500

54. The decimal fraction $2.3\overline{49}$ is equal to

(*a*) 2326/999 (*b*) 2326/990
(*c*) 2347/999 (*d*) 2347/990

55. A milk vendor has 21 litres of cow milk, 42 litres of toned milk and 63 litres of double toned milk. If he wants to pack them in cans so that each can contains same number of litres of milk and does not want to mix any two kinds of milk in a can, then the least number of cans required is

(*a*) 3 (*b*) 6
(*c*) 9 (*d*) 12

56. The number of integers between 100 and 600, which are divisible by 4 and 6 both, is

(*a*) 40 (*b*) 42
(*c*) 41 (*d*) 50

57. From a solid cylinder whose height is 12 cm and diameter 10 cm, a conical cavity of same height and same diameter of the base is hollowed out. The volume of the remaining solid is approximately $\left(\pi = \frac{22}{7}\right)$.

(*a*) 942.86 cm^3
(*b*) 314.29 cm^3
(*c*) 628.57 cm^3
(*d*) 450.76 cm^3

58. After allowing a discount of 12% on the marked price of an article, it is sold for ₹ 880. Find its marked price.

(*a*) ₹ 1,100 (*b*) ₹ 2,000
(*c*) ₹ 1,000 (*d*) ₹ 2,100

59. A trader marks his goods at 20% above the cost price. If he allows a discount of 5% for cash down payment, his profit per cent for such a transaction is

(*a*) 15 (*b*) 12
(*c*) 14 (*d*) 17

60. A, B and C individually can do a work in 10 days, 12 days and 15 days respectively. If they start working together, then the number of days required to finish the work is

(*a*) 16 days (*b*) 8 days
(*c*) 4 days (*d*) 2 days

61. The length of the three sides of a right angled triangle are $(x - 2)$ cm, x cm and $(x + 2)$ cm respectively. Then the value of x is

(*a*) 10 (*b*) 8
(*c*) 4 (*d*) 0

62. Dinesh bought two radios for ₹ 1,920. He sold one at a profit of 20% and the other at a loss $6\frac{2}{3}$%. If the selling price of both radios are same, the cost prices of the two radios are

(*b*) ₹ 800 and ₹ 1,120
(*b*) ₹ 840 and ₹ 1,080
(*b*) ₹ 860 and ₹ 1,060
(*b*) ₹ 900 and ₹ 1,020

63. If Y% of one hour is 1 minute 12 seconds, then Y is equal to

(*a*) 2 (*b*) 1
(*c*) $\frac{1}{2}$ (*d*) $\frac{1}{4}$

64. A number, on subtracting 15 from it, reduces to its 80%. What is 40% of the number?

(*a*) 75 (*b*) 60
(*c*) 30 (*d*) 90

65. In covering a distance of 30 km, Abhay takes 2 hours more than Sameer. If Abhay doubles his speed, then he would take 1 hour less than Sameer. Abhay's speed (in km/hr) is

(*a*) 5 (*b*) 6
(*c*) 6.25 (*d*) 7.5

66. In what time will ₹ 1,860 amount to 2,641.20 at simple interest 12% per annum?

(*a*) 3 years (*b*) $3\frac{1}{2}$ years
(*c*) 4 years (*d*) $4\frac{1}{2}$ years

67. If the annual income of A, B and C are in the ratio 1 : 3 : 7 and the total annual income of A and C is ₹ 8,00,000, then the monthly salary of B (in ₹) is

(*a*) 20,000
(*b*) 25,000
(*c*) 30,000
(*d*) 15,000

68. The ratio of successful and unsuccessful examinees in an examination in a school is 6 : 1. The ratio would have been 9 : 1 if 6 more examinees had been successful. The total number of examinees is

(*a*) 140 (*b*) 120
(*b*) 200 (*d*) 160

69. Out of four numbers, the average of the first three is 18 and that of the last three is 16. If the last number is 19, the first is

(*a*) 19 (*b*) 18
(*c*) 20 (*d*) 25

70. B was born when A was 4 years 7 months old and C was born when B was 3 years 4 months old. When C was 5 years 2 months old, then their average age was

(*a*) 8 years 9 months
(*b*) 7 years 3 months
(*c*) 8 years 7 months
(*d*) 8 years 11 months

71. Peter buys a table for ₹ 450 and spends ₹ 30 on its transportation. If he sells the table for ₹ 600 his gain per cent will be

(*a*) 30% (*b*) 25%
(*c*) 28% (*d*) 24%

Directions (Q. 72-75): *The following diagram shows the percentage of population of Hindus, Sikhs and Muslims with respect to total population in a town during 2005 to 2008. Study the diagram and answer the questions :*

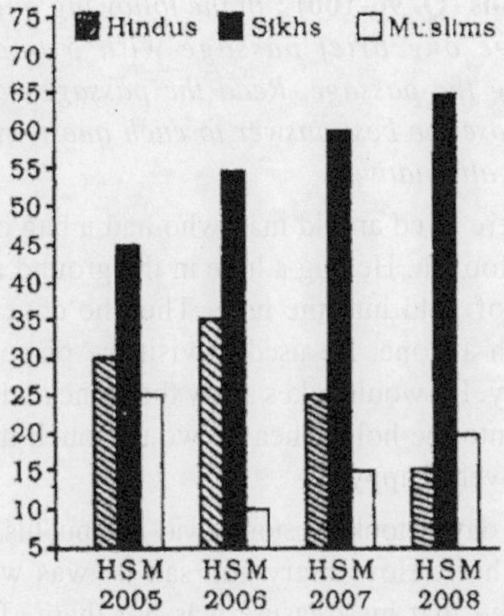

72. If the total population in 2007 was 80 lakh, then the number of Hindus in 2007 was (in lakh)

(*a*) 25 (*b*) 16
(*c*) 18 (*d*) 20

73. Percentage decrease in Hindu population from 2005 to 2008 is

(*a*) 50 (*b*) 40
(*c*) 25 (*d*) 15

74. Difference of percentage of population of Hindus in 2005 and 2008 is

(*a*) 20 (*b*) 15
(*c*) 25 (*d*) 30

75. If the total number of Hindus in 2008 was 12 lakh, the number of Muslims in 2008 was (in lakh)

(*a*) 18 (*b*) 12
(*c*) 24 (*d*) 16

PART-IV : ENGLISH

Directions (Q. 76-81) : *In the following questions, sentences are given with blanks to be filled in with an appropriate word(s). Four alternatives are suggested for each question. Choose the correct alternative out of the four.*

76. I haven't .... butter but I have a lot of bread.

(*a*) a lot of (*b*) little
(*c*) much (*d*) some

77. People from .... and near came to see the final match of the tournament yesterday.

(*a*) distance (*b*) long
(*c*) above (*d*) far

78. The student .... book I still have, can take it from me.

(*a*) that (*b*) whose
(*c*) which (*d*) his

79. Corruption should be .... out with the utmost vigour.

(*a*) talked (*b*) left
(*c*) rooted (*d*) brought

80. Books are a great source .... happiness.

(*a*) of (*b*) for
(*c*) into (*d*) with

81. He spoke .... his travels.

(*a*) of (*b*) on
(*c*) about (*d*) along

Directions (Q. 82-84) : *In the following questions, out of the four alternatives, choose the one which best, expresses the meaning of the given word.*

82. Conceal

(*a*) show (*b*) hide
(*c*) cancel (*d*) excuse

83. Efficient

(*a*) clever (*b*) smart
(*c*) known (*d*) capable

84. Disease

(*a*) fall (*b*) damage
(*c*) illness (*d*) injury

Directions (Q. 85-87) : *In the following questions, choose the word opposite in meaning to the given word.*

85. Destructive

(*a*) structural (*b*) constructive
(*c*) wind speed (*d*) static

86. Corrupt

(*a*) honest (*b*) unclean
(*c*) heartless (*d*) hateful

87. Prominent
(*a*) notorious (*b*) obscure
(*c*) wicked (*d*) hostile

Directions (Q. 88-89) : *In the following questions, four alternatives are given for the idiom/phrase. Choose the alternative which best expresses the meaning of the idiom/phrase.*

88. Not my cup of tea
(*a*) A refreshing drink (*b*) A routine work
(*c*) Not what I like (*d*) Not liked by me

89. To have second thoughts
(*a*) To change decision
(*b*) To plan carefully
(*c*) To take someone
(*d*) To reconsider

Directions (Q. 90 and 91) : *In the following questions, a part of the sentence is underlined. Below are given alternatives to the underlined part at (a), (b), (c) and (d) which may improve the sentence. Choose the correct alternative.*

90. The teacher <u>told</u> that Monday would be a holiday.
(*a*) is telling (*b*) has told
(*c*) said (*d*) might tell

91. We <u>have to</u> respect our elders.
(*a*) should (*b*) may
(*c*) can (*d*) better

Directions (Q. 92 and 93) : *In the following questions, out of the four alternatives, choose the one which can be substituted for the given words/sentence.*

92. Work for which one does not take salary or payment
(*a*) remunerated (*b*) charge-sheet
(*c*) complementary (*d*) honorary

93. No longer in use
(*a*) absolute (*b*) obsolete
(*c*) contemporary (*d*) remote

Directions (Q. 94 and 95) : *In the following questions, groups of four words are given. In each group, one word is correctly spelt. Find the correctly spelt word.*

94. (*a*) Misterious (*b*) Mistereous
(*c*) Mysterious (*d*) Mystereous

95. (*a*) Dictionery (*b*) Dectionary
(*c*) Dictionary (*d*) Dictienary

Directions (Q. 96-100) : *In the following questions, you have one brief passage with 5 questions following the passage. Read the passage carefully and choose the best answer to each question out of the four alternatives.*

Once there lived an old man who had a bag of gold. He was foolish. He dug a hole in the ground and put the bag of gold into the hole. Then he covered the hole with a stone. He used to visit the place nearly every day. He would takes away the stone and put his fingers into the hole. Then he would touch the gold and feel very happy.

One day he took the stone away and put his fingers into the hole. How angry and sad he was when he discovered that his treasure was not there. The old man went to a friend and sadly told him the story. His friend said. There is no reason for you to be sad. Your gold was useless to you. You still have the hole. You can visit it whenever you like. All you have to do is to imagine that your treasure is still there.

96. The old man hid the gold
(*a*) in a secret chamber
(*b*) in a bank locker
(*c*) underground
(*d*) in an unknown place

97. The old man was pleased when he
(*a*) used the gold
(*b*) touched the gold
(*c*) added to the gold
(*d*) gave away the gold

98. The old man visited the place where he had kept the gold hidden
(*a*) everyday
(*b*) once a week
(*c*) almost everyday
(*d*) as often as possible

99. The friend's words possibly made the old man
(*a*) happy (*b*) angry
(*c*) relieved (*d*) excited

100. The friend told the old man that
(*a*) he had not lost anything
(*b*) he would get back his gold
(*c*) he should complain to the police
(*d*) he should not have hidden it in a hole

ANSWERS

1	2	3	4	5	6	7	8	9	10
(*b*)	(*a*)	(*c*)	(*b*)	(*d*)	(*b*)	(*d*)	(*c*)	(*a*)	(*c*)
11	**12**	**13**	**14**	**15**	**16**	**17**	**18**	**19**	**20**
(*d*)	(*d*)	(*b*)	(*d*)	(*b*)	(*b*)	(*c*)	(*d*)	(*a*)	(*c*)
21	**22**	**23**	**24**	**25**	**26**	**27**	**28**	**29**	**30**
(*b*)	(*a*)	(*c*)	(*d*)	(*a*)	(*b*)	(*d*)	(*b*)	(*a*)	(*d*)
31	**32**	**33**	**34**	**35**	**36**	**37**	**38**	**39**	**40**
(*d*)	(*d*)	(*d*)	(*b*)	(*c*)	(*d*)	(*c*)	(*b*)	(*b*)	(*c*)
41	**42**	**43**	**44**	**45**	**46**	**47**	**48**	**49**	**50**
(*d*)	(*a*)	(*b*)	(*a*)	(*a*)	(*d*)	(*a*)	(*c*)	(*b*)	(*d*)
51	**52**	**53**	**54**	**55**	**56**	**57**	**58**	**59**	**60**
(*b*)	(*a*)	(*c*)	(*b*)	(*b*)	(*c*)	(*c*)	(*c*)	(*c*)	(*c*)
61	**62**	**63**	**64**	**65**	**66**	**67**	**68**	**69**	**70**
(*b*)	(*b*)	(*a*)	(*c*)	(*a*)	(*b*)	(*b*)	(*a*)	(*d*)	(*d*)
71	**72**	**73**	**74**	**75**	**76**	**77**	**78**	**79**	**80**
(*b*)	(*d*)	(*a*)	(*b*)	(*d*)	(*c*)	(*d*)	(*b*)	(*c*)	(*a*)
81	**82**	**83**	**84**	**85**	**86**	**87**	**88**	**89**	**90**
(*a*)	(*b*)	(*d*)	(*c*)	(*b*)	(*a*)	(*b*)	(*c*)	(*a*)	(*c*)
91	**92**	**93**	**94**	**95**	**96**	**97**	**98**	**99**	**100**
(*a*)	(*d*)	(*b*)	(*c*)	(*c*)	(*c*)	(*b*)	(*c*)	(*c*)	(*a*)

SOME SELECTED EXPLANATORY ANSWERS

1. Wood is used in the production of paper. Similarly, steel is used to make nail.

2. $7 \times 4 = 28$; $2 \times 4 = 8$

3.

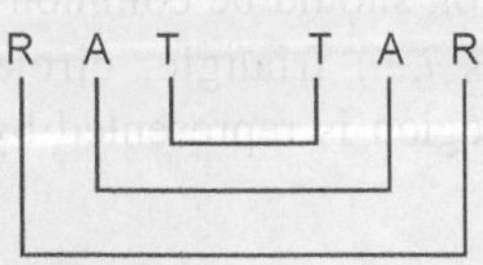

Similarly,

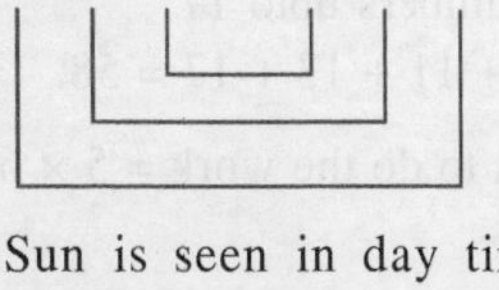

4. Sun is seen in day time. Similarly, moon appears in night.

5. $31 - 21 = 16$

$42 - 26 = 16$

$51 - 35 = 16$

But,

$56 - 38 = 18.$

6. Wheat, barley and corn are grains. While mustard is an oilseed.

7. Bus, scooter and car are automobiles and need fuel. Cycle does not need fuel.

8. $A \xrightarrow{+2} C \xrightarrow{+2} E$

$G \xrightarrow{+2} I \xrightarrow{+2} K$

$J \xrightarrow{+2} L \xrightarrow{+1} M$

$S \xrightarrow{+2} U \xrightarrow{+2} W$

9. 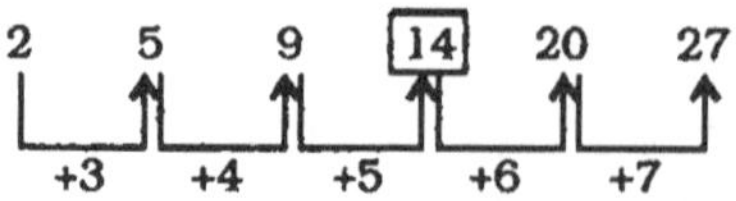

10.

Odd Number	9	Even Number

469259 [394] 6 [792] 4894.

11. 'H' is not given in the keyword.

12. Meaningful order of words is :
4 Letter → 1 Word → 3 Sentence → 2 Paragraph.

13. *b* [*b*] *y* [*t*] / [*b*] *by* [*t*] / *b* [*b*] *yt*.

14. Speed of train 'B'

$= 90 \times \frac{5}{18} = 25$ m per second

Time taken by train 'B' to cross the train 'A'

$= \frac{225 + 375}{V} = \frac{600}{25} = 24$ seconds.

15. 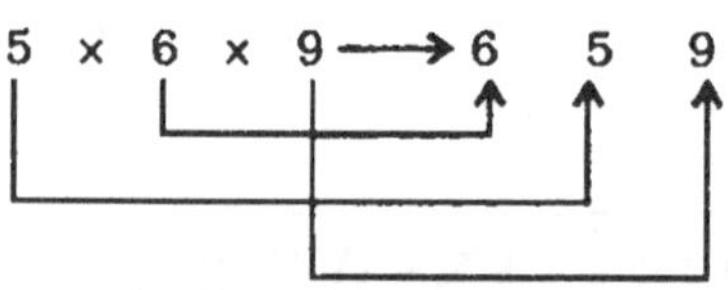

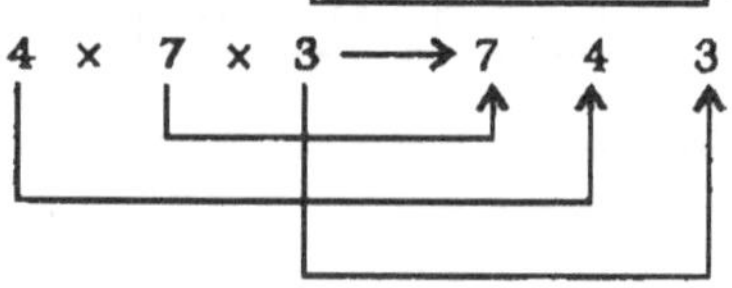

Similarly,

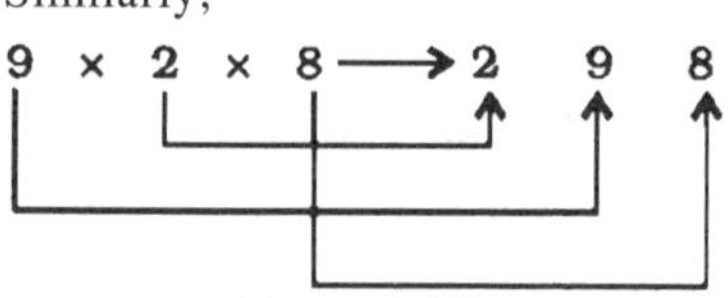

16.

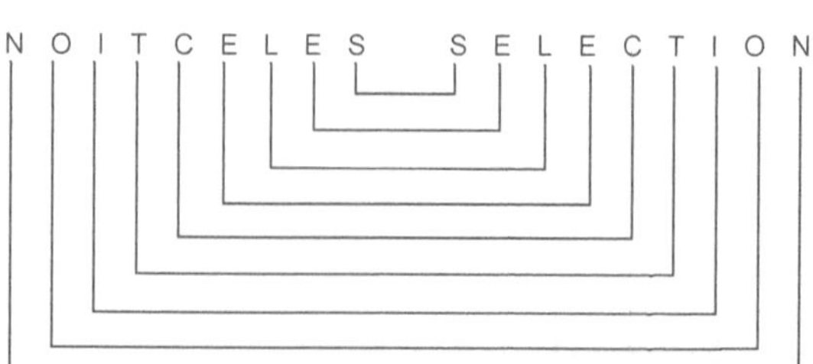

Similarly,

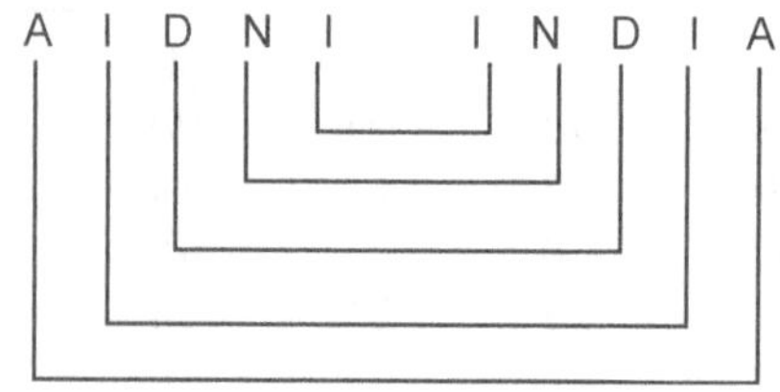

17.

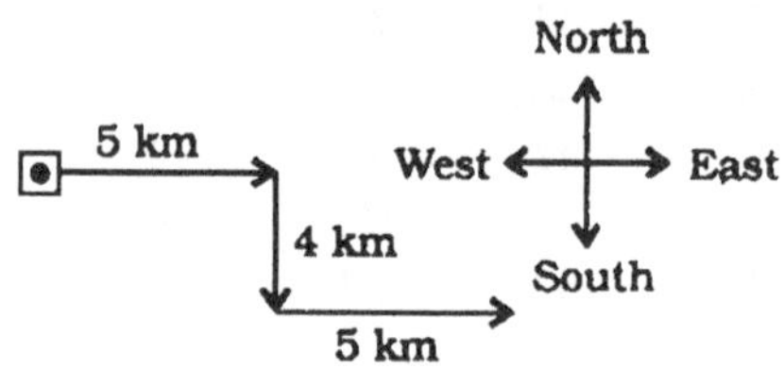

18. Umesh > Satish
Neeraj > Suresh > Umesh
Neeraj > Suresh > Umesh > Satish.

19.

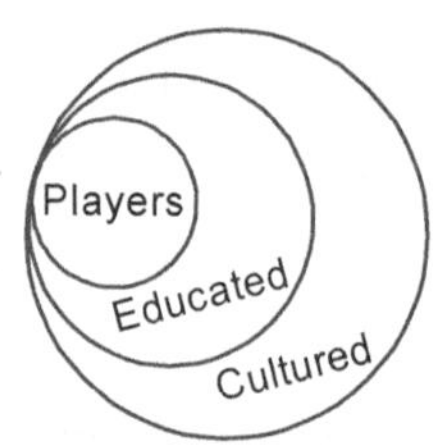

Hence, only inference I follows.

21. 16 + 32 = 48

12 + 24 = [36]

13 + 26 = 39.

23. The required region should be common in all the three figures *i.e.*, triangle, circle and rectangle. Such region is represented by 5.

24. 

51. Sum of prime numbers upto 17
= 2 + 3 + 5 + 7 + 11 + 13 + 17 = 58.

52. Time taken by A to do the work = 5 × 6 = 30 days

Time taken by B to do the work = $\frac{8 \times 5}{2}$
= 20 days

$\therefore$ (A + B)'s 1 day's work = $\frac{1}{30}+\frac{1}{20}=\frac{2+3}{60}$

$= \frac{1}{12}$

$\therefore$ Required time to do the work = 12 days.

53. $\sqrt{0.25\times 2.25} = 0.5 \times 1.5 = 0.75$

54. $2.3\overline{49} = \frac{2349-23}{990} = \frac{2326}{990}$.

55. Maximum quantity in each can
= HCF of 21, 42 and 63 litres = 21 litres
Hence, least number of cans

$= \frac{21}{21}+\frac{42}{21}+\frac{63}{21} = 1 + 2 + 3 = 6.$

56. Such numbers which are divisible by 12 (LCM of 4 and 6).
Number of numbers divisible by 12 from 1 to 600

$= \frac{600}{12} - 1 = 49$

Number of numbers divisible by 12 from 1 to 100 = $\frac{100}{12} = 8$

$\therefore$ Required number = 49 – 8 = 41.

57. Volume of solid cylinder = $\pi r^2 h$

Volume of cone = $\frac{1}{3}\pi r^2 h$

Difference = $\pi r^2 h - \frac{1}{3}\pi r^2 h$

$= \frac{2}{3}\pi r^2 h = \frac{2}{3}\times\frac{22}{7}\times 5\times 5\times 12$

= 628.57 cu.cm.
Hence,
Volume of remaining solid = 628.57 cu.cm.

58. Marked price = $\frac{100}{100-12}\times 880$ = ₹ 1000.

59. Let C.P. be ₹ 100

Marked price = ₹ 120

Selling price = $\frac{120\times 95}{100}$ = ₹ 114

Hence, gain per cent = 14.

60. Work finished by A, B and C in 1 day

$= \frac{1}{10}+\frac{1}{12}+\frac{1}{15} = \frac{6+5+4}{60}$

$= \frac{15}{60} = \frac{1}{4}$

$\therefore$ Required time = 4 days.

61. Since, $(\text{Hypotenuse})^2 = (\text{Perpendicular})^2 + (\text{Base})^2$

$\Rightarrow \quad (x+2)^2 = (x-2)^2 + x^2$

$\Rightarrow \quad x^2 + 4x + 4 = x^2 - 4x + 4 + x^2$

$\Rightarrow \quad x^2 - 8x = 0$

$\Rightarrow \quad x(x-8) = 0$

$\Rightarrow \quad x = 8.$

62. Cost price of radio sold on profit = ₹ x
Cost price of radio sold on loss = ₹ $(1920 - x)$

$\therefore \quad x\times\frac{120}{100} = (1920-x)\times\frac{\left(100-\frac{20}{3}\right)}{100}$

$\Rightarrow \quad x\times 120 = (1920-x)\times\frac{280}{3}$

$\Rightarrow \quad 3x = (1920-x)\times\frac{7}{3}$

$\Rightarrow \quad 9x + 7x = 1920\times 7$

$\Rightarrow \quad 16x = 1920\times 7$

$\Rightarrow \quad x =$ ₹ 840

$\therefore$ Cost price of second radio = ₹ 1080.

63. $60\times 60\times\frac{y}{100}$ = 1 minute 12 seconds

$\Rightarrow 36y = 72 \Rightarrow y = 2.$

64. Let the number be x, then

$x - 15 = \frac{4x}{5}$

$\Rightarrow \quad 5x - 75 = 4x \Rightarrow x = 75$

$\therefore \quad 40\%$ of $75 = \frac{75\times 40}{100} = 30.$

65. Let Abhay's speed = x kmph and Sameer's speed = y kmph
from question,

$$\therefore \quad \frac{30}{x} - \frac{30}{y} = 2 \quad ...(i)$$

$$\text{and,} \quad \frac{30}{y} - \frac{30}{2x} = 1 \quad ...(ii)$$

On adding,

$$\frac{30}{x} - \frac{30}{2x} = 3$$

$$\Rightarrow \quad \frac{60-30}{2x} = 3$$

$$\Rightarrow \quad \frac{30}{2x} = 3$$

$$\Rightarrow \quad 6x = 30$$

$$\Rightarrow \quad x = 5.$$

66. S.I. = Amount – Principal
= 2641.20 – 1860 = ₹ 781.2

$$\text{Time} = \frac{\text{S.I.} \times 100}{\text{Principal} \times \text{Rate}}$$

$$= \frac{781.2 \times 100}{1860 \times 12} = 3.5 \text{ years.}$$

67. Let annual incomes of A, B and C are x, $3x$ and $7x$ respectively.
from question,

$$x + 7x = 800000$$

$$\Rightarrow \quad 8x = 800000$$

$$\Rightarrow \quad x = 100000$$

∴ B's monthly income

$$= \frac{100000 \times 3}{12} = ₹\ 25000.$$

68. Let successful student = $6x$
and unsuccessful student = x
Total students = $6x + x = 7x$

$$\therefore \quad \frac{6x+6}{x-6} = \frac{9}{1}$$

$$\Rightarrow \quad 6x + 6 = 9x - 54$$

$$\Rightarrow \quad 9x - 6x = 54 + 6 = 60$$

$$\Rightarrow \quad 3x = 60$$

$$\Rightarrow \quad x = 20$$

∴ Total number of students = 7 × 20 = 140.

69. $a + b + c = 18 \times 3 = 54$
and, $b + c + d = 16 \times 3 = 48$
$\therefore a + b + c - b - c - d = 54 - 48 = 6$

$$a - d = 6$$

$$a - 19 = 6$$

$$a = 19 + 6 = 25.$$

70. From question, C = 5 years 2 months
B = 8 years 6 months
A = 13 years 1 month

$$\therefore \text{Required average} = \frac{\text{26 years 9 months}}{3}$$

= 8 years 11 months.

71. Actual cost price of the table = 450 + 30 = ₹ 480

$$\therefore \text{Gain per cent} = \frac{600-480}{480} \times 100 = 25\%.$$

72. Number of Hindus = $80 \times \frac{25}{100}$ = 20 lakhs.

73. Percentage decrease = $\frac{30-15}{30} \times 100 = 50.$

74. Required difference = 15.

75. Number of Muslims = 16 lakhs.

Previous Paper (Solved)

SSC – Constable (GD) Exam, 2011

ITBPF/CISF/CRPF/BSF/SSB

Rifleman (Assam Rifles)

PART-I : GENERAL INTELLIGENCE & REASONING

***Directions:** From the given alternative words, select the word which **cannot** be formed using the letters of the given word.*

1. ARCHITECTURE
(*a*) TACT (*b*) CHAT
(*c*) TORCH (*d*) RICH

2. If 'P' stands for '–', 'Q' stands for '×', 'R' for '÷' and 'S' for '+', then what is the value of the given equation?
14 Q 3 P 12 S 4 R 2 = ?
(*a*) 17 (*b*) 32
(*c*) 28 (*d*) 6

3. Find the number of triangles in the given figure.

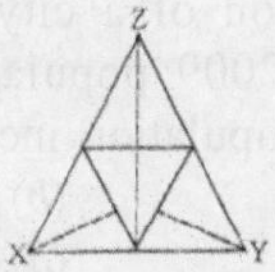

(*a*) 17 (*b*) 15
(*c*) 13 (*d*) 9

***Directions:** Here are given the name of a town and a date followed by four alternatives. Of these, only one matches while the others have some mistakes. You are to choose exactly the same as the given one as your answer.*

4. TRIVANDRUM, AUGUST, 31,2008
(*a*) TRIVANDRUM, 31 AUGUST, 2008
(*b*) Trivandrum, August 31, 2008
(*c*) TRIVANDRUM, AUGUST, 31, 2008
(*d*) TRIVANDRUM, August, 31, 2008

5. Suhas travelled 15 km. towards East, then turned towards North and travelled 15 km and turned towards West and travelled 15 km. How far is he from the starting point?
(*a*) 15 km (*b*) 30 km
(*c*) 45 km (*d*) 0 km

***Directions:** Select the missing number from the given responses.*

6.

3	15	5
5	35	7
9	–	5

(*a*) 54 (*b*) 50
(*c*) 49 (*d*) 45

***Directions (7-10) :** Select the related letters/word/number/figure from the given alternatives.*

7. 5 : 30 : : 7 : ?
(*a*) 54 (*b*) 50
(*c*) 49 (*d*) 56

8. Saw : Carpenter : : Scissors : ?
(*a*) Farmer (*b*) Tailor
(*c*) Painter (*d*) Artist

9. ACDF : MOPR : : TVWY : ?
(*a*) LNPR (*b*) PRSU
(*c*) STVW (*d*) RUWZ

10. ***Question Figures:***

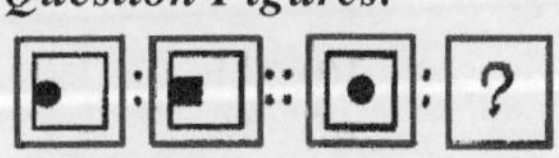

Answer Figures:

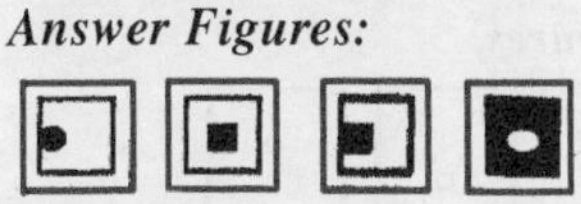

(*a*) (*b*) (*c*) (*d*)

***Directions (11-14) :** Find the odd number/word/figure from the given alternatives.*

11. 18, 34, 36, 48
(*a*) 48 (*b*) 36
(*c*) 18 (*d*) 34

12. (*a*) Iron (*b*) Aluminium
(*c*) Wood (*d*) Copper

13. (*a*) KJML (*b*) GFIH
(*c*) TSVU (*d*) ZABY

14. (*a*)  (*b*) 
(*c*)  (*d*) 

Directions : *Which one set of letters when sequentially placed at the gaps in the given letter series shall complete it?*

15. *a – yz – xy – ax – zax – z*
(*a*) *xayzy* (*b*) *xayyz*
(*c*) *xazyy* (*d*) *axzyy*

Directions : *Which one of the given responses would be a meaningful order of the following?*

16. A. Evaporation B. Rain
C. Sea D. Clouds
(*a*) A, B, C, D (*b*) D, A, B, C
(*c*) C, A, D, B (*d*) B, D, A, C

Directions: *Arrange the following words as per order in the dictionary.*

17. A. Critical B. Criterion
C. Crisis D. Crisp
(*a*) C, D, B, A (*b*) A, C, D, B
(*c*) C, D, A, B (*d*) D, C, A, B

Directions (18-19) : *A series is given with one term missing. Choose the correct alternative from the given ones that will complete the series.*

18. 6, 12, 20, 30, ?
(*a*) 40 (*b*) 41
(*c*) 42 (*d*) 48

19. ***Question Figures:***

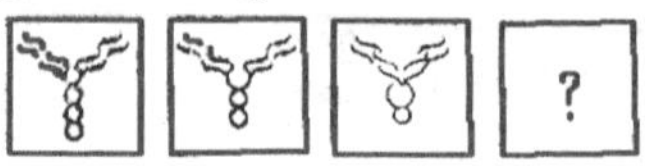

Answer Figures:

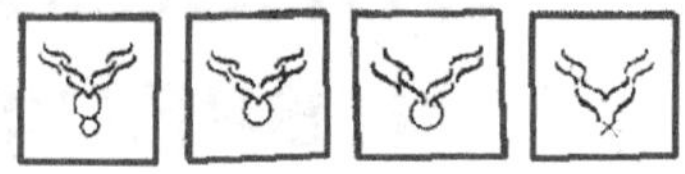

(*a*) (*b*) (*c*) (*d*)

20. Ramesh walked 3 km. towards West and turned to his left and walked 2 km. He, then turned to his right and walked 3 km. Finally, he turned to his right again and walked another 2 km. In which direction is Ramesh from his starting point now?
(*a*) East (*b*) West
(*c*) North (*d*) South

21. If in certain code PATTERN is written as NRETTAP, then how MENTION can be written in that code?
(*a*) NOITMEN (*b*) NMOEINT
(*c*) NOITNEM (*d*) NOTIMEN

22. Vijay says "Ananda's mother is the only daughter of my mother". How is Ananda related to Vijay?
(*a*) Brother (*b*) Father
(*c*) Nephew (*d*) Grand Father

23. The population of a city doubles every 7 years. If in 2009 population is 12483, by which year population increases by 49932?
(*a*) 2016 (*b*) 2023
(*c*) 2030 (*d*) 2037

24. P, Q, R and S are four friends. P, is shorter than Q but taller than R who is shorter than S. Who is the shortest among all?
(*a*) P (*b*) Q
(*c*) R (*d*) S

25. If in certain code 'EDITION' is written as 3891965, then how 'TIDE' will be written in that code?
(*a*) 3819 (*b*) 1983
(*c*) 1839 (*d*) 1586

PART-II : General Knowledge & General Awareness

26. The dance Kathakali is associated with the State of
(*a*) Andhra Pradesh (*b*) Kerala
(*c*) Tamil Nadu (*d*) Orissa

27. Who of the following is not a recipient of 'Bharat Ratna'?
(*a*) Morarji Desai

(*b*) Gulzari Lal Nanda
(*c*) Rajiv Gandhi
(*d*) Atal Bihari Vajpayee

28. Srinagar is located on the bank of the river
(*a*) Indus (*b*) Jhelum
(*c*) Chenab (*d*) Ravi

29. What causes common cold?
(*a*) Bacteria (*b*) Fungi
(*c*) Virus (*d*) Protozoa

30. The element used for making solar cells is
(*a*) Magnesium (*b*) Sodium
(*c*) Calcium (*d*) Silicon

31. Chief of the Indian Navy has the rank of
(*a*) General of Indian Navy
(*b*) Chief of Indian Navy
(*c*) Naval Chief
(*d*) Admiral

32. Meningitis is a disease which affects the
(*a*) Kidneys (*b*) Liver
(*c*) Heart (*d*) Brain

33. The concurrent list in the Indian Constitution is adopted from the Constitution of
(*a*) U.S.A. (*b*) Canada
(*c*) Germany (*d*) Australia

34. Who among the following was the pioneer of Yoga?
(*a*) Patanjali (*b*) Vagbhata
(*c*) Atreya (*d*) Vrudukanta

35. The sea which existed in the place of the Himalayas was
(*a*) Red Sea (*b*) Arabian Sea
(*c*) Tethys Sea (*d*) Dead Sea

36. Who discovered Solar System?
(*a*) Newton (*b*) John Hadley
(*c*) Copernicus (*d*) Galileo

37. Number of teeth which are replaced in man are
(*a*) 12 (*b*) 20
(*c*) 32 (*d*) 16

38. Who is the director of the film 'Lagaan'?
(*a*) B.R. Chopra
(*b*) Govind Nehlani
(*c*) Ashutosh Gowarikar
(*d*) Anil Sharma

39. India has the monopoly in the International market in the supply of
(*a*) Iron (*b*) Mica
(*c*) Bauxite (*d*) Copper

40. "Not to destroy the Government property" is a
(*a*) Positive duty (*b*) Legal duty
(*c*) Civil duty (*d*) Negative duty

41. Who proposed the Preamble before the drafting committee of the Constitution?
(*a*) Jawaharlal Nehru (*b*) B.R. Ambedkar
(*c*) B.N. Rao (*d*) Mahatma Gandhi

42. Which of the following is not the "Tri Ratna" of Jainism?
(*a*) Right faith (*b*) Right knowledge
(*c*) Right view (*d*) Right conduct

43. The National Tree of India is
(*a*) Neem (*b*) Peepal
(*c*) Banyan (*d*) Mango

44. In the 2010 Commonwealth Games held in Delhi from October 3 to October 14, Deepika Kumari won gold medal in the
(*a*) Women's Free Style Wrestling (67 kg)
(*b*) Women's Archery (Individual Recurve)
(*c*) Women's 25m Pistol
(*d*) Women's Weightlifting (58 kg)

45. When was the First Gerneral Election to the Lok Sabha held?
(*a*) 1950-51 (*b*) 1951-52
(*c*) 1952-53 (*d*) 1956-57

46. Which one of the following is a water borne disease?
(*a*) Diabetes (*b*) Cholera
(*c*) Small Pox (*d*) Malaria

47. Shaving mirror is
(*a*) Convex (*b*) Concave
(*c*) Plane (*d*) Parabolic

48. Teachers Day is observed every year on
(*a*) 5th September (*b*) 15th September
(*c*) 20th September (*d*) 25th September

49. As we go from Equator to North pole the value of 'g', the acceleration due to gravity
(*a*) remains the same (*b*) decreases
(*c*) increases (*d*) None of the above

50. Which of the following is used for wrapping of fractured bones?
(*a*) White cement (*b*) White lead
(*c*) Zinc oxide (*d*) Plaster of Paris

PART-III : ELEMENTARY MATHEMATICS

51. The compound interest on ₹ 6,400 for 2 years at $7\frac{1}{2}\%$ per annum is (in₹)
(*a*) ₹ 1,016 (*b*) ₹ 996
(*c*) ₹ 976 (*d*) ₹ 966

52. John invested a sum of money at an annual simple interest rate of 10%. At the end of four years the amount invested plus interest earned was ₹ 770. The amount invested was
(*a*) ₹ 650 (*b*) ₹ 350
(*c*) ₹ 550 (*d*) ₹ 500

53. By selling an article for ₹ 960 a man incurs a loss of 4%; what was the cost price?
(*a*) ₹ 1000 (*b*) ₹ 784
(*c*) ₹ 498.4 (*d*) ₹ 300

54. One-third of 1206 is what per cent of 134?
(*a*) 100 (*b*) 150
(*c*) 200 (*d*) 300

55. If population of women in a village is 90% of population of men, what is the population of men as a percentage of population of women?
(*a*) 100% (*b*) 105%
(*c*) 108% (*d*) 111%

Directions (56-57) : *Given here is a graph showing the number of workers with their daily payment by a workshop. Study the graph and answer questions based on this graph.*

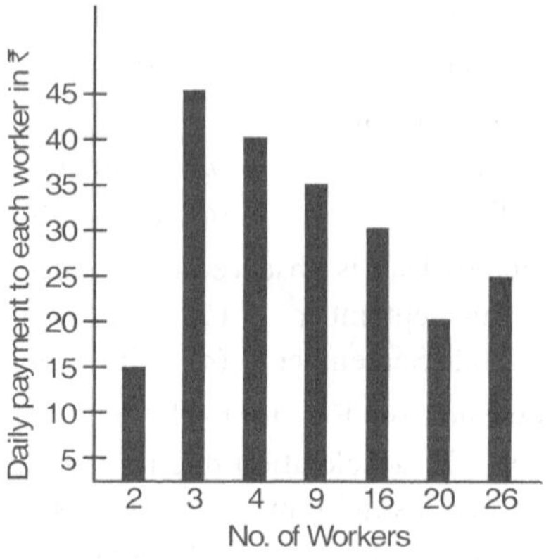

56. The number of workers whose daily payment is ₹ 20 is
(*a*) 9 (*b*) 16
(*c*) 20 (*d*) 4

57. The total daily payment made to the group which contains 9 workers is (in₹)
(*a*) ₹ 400 (*b*) ₹ 315
(*c*) ₹ 480 (*d*) ₹ 135

58. A stock of foodgrain lasts for 21 days for village A. The same stock would last for 28 days for village B. If the foodgrains are used for both the villages together, the stock would last for
(*a*) 14 days (*b*) 12 days
(*c*) 7 days (*d*) 49 days

59. A train of length 500 feet crosses a platform of length 700 feet in 10 seconds. The speed of the train is
(*a*) 70 ft/second (*b*) 85 ft/second
(*c*) 100 ft/second (*d*) 120 ft/second

60. Working 8 hours a day, Anu can copy a book in 18 days. How many hours a day should she work so as to finish the work in 12 days?
(*a*) 12 hours (*b*) 10 hours
(*c*) 11 hours (*d*) 13 hours

61. The lengths of two sides of an isosceles triangle are 15 and 22 respectively. What are the possible values of perimeter?
(*a*) 52 or 59 (*b*) 52 or 60
(*c*) 15 or 37 (*d*) 37 or 29

62. The speed of two cars are in the ratio 5 : 4. The ratio between the time taken by them to travel the same distance is
(*b*) 5 : 4 (*b*) 6 : 4
(*b*) 6 : 5 (*b*) 4 : 5

63. $1+\frac{1}{1+\frac{1}{5}}=?$
(*a*) 11/6 (*b*) 13/6
(*c*) 15/6 (*d*) None of the above

64. Marks of two candidates P and Q are in the ratio of 2 : 5. If the marks of P are 120, marks of Q are

(*a*) 120 (*b*) 240
(*c*) 300 (*d*) 360

65. The LCM of two numbers is 520 and their HCF is 4. If one of the numbers is 52, then the other number is

(*a*) 40 (*b*) 42
(*c*) 50 (*d*) 52

66. A discount of 24% on the marked price of an article is allowed and then the article is sold for ₹ 342. The marked price of the article is

(*a*) ₹ 500 (*b*) ₹ 490
(*c*) ₹ 450 (*d*) ₹ 430

67. If $0.42 \times 100^k = 42$, then the value of k is

(*a*) 4 (*b*) 2
(*c*) 1 (*d*) 3

68. $1 + 2 + 3 + ... + 100 = x$, then x is

(*a*) 5,050 (*b*) 5,000
(*b*) 10,100 (*d*) 10,000

69. $\sqrt{64} - \sqrt{36}$ is equal to

(*a*) –2 (*b*) 2
(*c*) 0 (*d*) 1

70. Find out the wrong number in the sequence

169, 144, 121, 100, 82, 64, 49

(*a*) 144 (*b*) 49
(*c*) 64 (*d*) 82

71. A semicircular shaped window has diameter of 63 cm. Its perimeter equals $\left(\pi = \frac{22}{7}\right)$

(*a*) 126 cm (*b*) 162 cm
(*c*) 198 cm (*d*) 251 cm

72. The length of longest pole that can be placed in a 12 m long, 8 m broad and 9 m high room, is

(*a*) 12 m (*b*) 17 m
(*c*) 19 m (*d*) 21 m

73. A milkman bought 70 litres of milk for ₹ 630 and added 5 litres of water. If he sells it at ₹ 9.00 per litre, his profit percentage is

(*a*) $8\frac{1}{5}\%$ (*b*) 7%
(*c*) $8\frac{2}{5}\%$ (*d*) $7\frac{1}{7}\%$

74. If average of 20 observations $x_1, x_2, ..., x_{20}$ is y, then the average of $x_1 - 101, x_2 - 101, x_3 - 101, ..., x_{20} - 101$ is

(*a*) $y - 20$ (*b*) $y - 101$
(*c*) $20y$ (*d*) $101y$

75. The average of 27 numbers is 60. If one number is changed from 28 to 82, the average is

(*a*) 56 (*b*) 58
(*c*) 62 (*d*) 64

PART-IV : ENGLISH

Directions (76-80) : In the following questions out of the four alternatives, choose the one which best expresses the meaning of the given word.

76. Speculate

(*a*) think (*b*) guess
(*c*) argue (*d*) speak

77. Obscene

(*a*) beautiful (*b*) unhealthy
(*c*) unwanted (*d*) indecent

78. Tame (N)

(*a*) wild (*b*) savage
(*c*) domesticated (*d*) silent

79. Mercy

(*a*) merit (*b*) sympathy
(*c*) loss (*d*) pain

80. Effect

(*a*) result (*b*) warning
(*c*) chance (*d*) purpose

Directions (81-85) : *In the following questions choose the word opposite in meaning to the given word.*

81. Honest
(*a*) infect (*b*) cleanse
(*c*) corrupt (*d*) pollute

82. Tentative
(*a*) definite (*b*) insufficient
(*c*) plentiful (*d*) active

83. Compulsory
(*a*) easy (*b*) optional
(*c*) unnecessary (*d*) mandatory

84. Adamant
(*a*) satisfied (*b*) comfortable
(*c*) yielding (*d*) luxurious

85. Oral
(*a*) written (*b*) correct
(*c*) mental (*d*) verbal

Directions (86-90) : *In the following passage some of the words have been left out. First read the passage over and try to understand what it is about. Then fill in the blanks with the help of the alternatives given.*

There **86** in the city of Ujjain a poor tailor **87** Ramphal. As he was very poor, he **88** to live and work in one little room with his wife and **89** three small children. The children fought **90** each other and made so much noise.

86. (*a*) lived (*b*) stayed
(*c*) inhabited (*d*) existed

87. (*a*) famous (*b*) named
(*c*) known (*d*) titled

88. (*a*) wished (*b*) liked
(*c*) had (*d*) wanted

89. (*a*) few (*b*) a few
(*c*) their (*d*) some

90. (*a*) to (*b*) upon
(*c*) for (*d*) with

Directions (91-95) : *In the following questions sentences are given with blanks to the filled in with an appropriate word(s). Four alternatives are suggested for each question. Choose the correct alternative out of the four.*

91. I prevailed .... him to contest the election.
(*a*) on (*b*) off
(*c*) over (*d*) of

92. Poets have compared this world .... a stage.
(*a*) with (*b*) to
(*c*) by (*d*) on

93. The telephone kept .... ringing, but no one attended.
(*a*) off (*b*) on
(*c*) up (*d*) up with

94. She is sad, because her father turned .... her request.
(*a*) up (*b*) off
(*c*) out (*d*) down

95. You should not confide .... a stranger.
(*a*) in (*b*) to
(*c*) with (*d*) by

Directions (96-100) : *In the following questions some of the sentences have errors and some are correct. Find out which part of a sentence has an error the number of that part is your answer. If a sentence is free from errors, then your answer is (d) i.e. No error.*

96. He walks (*a*) / as if the earth (*b*) belonged to him. (*c*) / No error (*d*)

97. Beside Hindi, (*a*) / she knew (*b*) / Bengali well. (*c*) / No error (*d*)

98. Pacific Ocean is (*a*) / the deepest ocean (*b*) / in the world. (*c*) / No error (*d*)

99. You will come (*a*) / to my sister's wedding tomorrow, (*b*) / isn't it? (*c*) / No error (*d*)

100. I am (*a*) / your's (*b*) / affectionate son. (*c*) / No error (*d*)

ANSWERS

1	**2**	**3**	**4**	**5**	**6**	**7**	**8**	**9**	**10**
(*c*)	(*b*)	(*a*)	(*c*)	(*a*)	(*d*)	(*d*)	(*b*)	(*b*)	(*b*)
11	**12**	**13**	**14**	**15**	**16**	**17**	**18**	**19**	**20**
(*b*)	(*c*)	(*d*)	(*a*)	(*c*)	(*c*)	(*a*)	(*c*)	(*b*)	(*b*)

21	22	23	24	25	26	27	28	29	30
(*c*)	(*c*)	(*c*)	(*c*)	(*b*)	(*b*)	(*d*)	(*b*)	(*c*)	(*d*)
31	**32**	**33**	**34**	**35**	**36**	**37**	**38**	**39**	**40**
(*d*)	(*d*)	(*d*)	(*a*)	(*c*)	(*c*)	(*a*)	(*c*)	(*b*)	(*c*)
41	**42**	**43**	**44**	**45**	**46**	**47**	**48**	**49**	**50**
(*a*)	(*a*)	(*c*)	(*b*)	(*b*)	(*b*)	(*b*)	(*a*)	(*c*)	(*d*)
51	**52**	**53**	**54**	**55**	**56**	**57**	**58**	**59**	**60**
(*b*)	(*c*)	(*a*)	(*d*)	(*d*)	(*c*)	(*b*)	(*b*)	(*d*)	(*a*)
61	**62**	**63**	**64**	**65**	**66**	**67**	**68**	**69**	**70**
(*a*)	(*d*)	(*a*)	(*c*)	(*a*)	(*c*)	(*c*)	(*a*)	(*b*)	(*d*)
71	**72**	**73**	**74**	**75**	**76**	**77**	**78**	**79**	**80**
(*b*)	(*b*)	(*d*)	(*b*)	(*c*)	(*b*)	(*d*)	(*c*)	(*b*)	(*a*)
81	**82**	**83**	**84**	**85**	**86**	**87**	**88**	**89**	**90**
(*c*)	(*a*)	(*b*)	(*c*)	(*a*)	(*a*)	(*b*)	(*c*)	(*c*)	(*d*)
91	**92**	**93**	**94**	**95**	**96**	**97**	**98**	**99**	**100**
(*c*)	(*a*)	(*b*)	(*d*)	(*b*)	(*d*)	(*a*)	(*a*)	(*c*)	(*b*)

SOME SELECTED EXPLANATORY ANSWERS

2. $14 \times 3 - 12 + 4 \div 2$

$\Rightarrow 42 - 12 + 2$

$\Rightarrow 44 - 12 = \boxed{32}$

3.

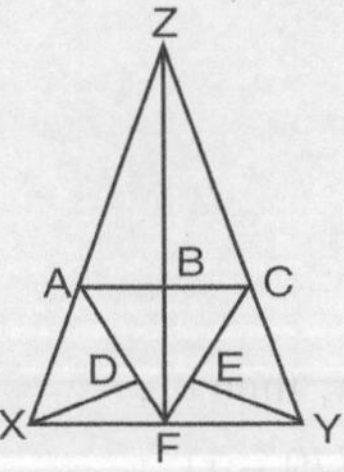

The triangles are:

Δ ZAB ; Δ ZBC ; Δ XAD ; Δ XDF ;
Δ FAB ; Δ FBC ; Δ YEC ; Δ FEY ;
Δ ZAC ; Δ XAF ; Δ YFC ; Δ FAC ;
Δ ZFX ; Δ ZFY ; Δ AFZ ; Δ CFZ ;
Δ ZXY

5.

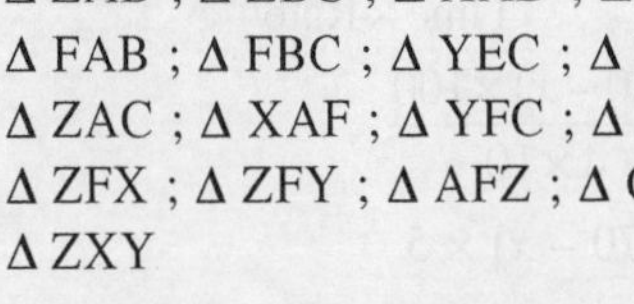

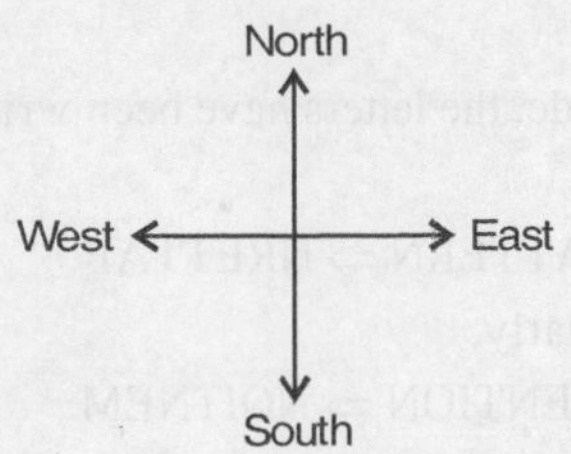

Required distance = AD = 15 km.

6. First Row $\Rightarrow 3 \times 5 = 15$

Second Row $\Rightarrow 5 \times 7 = 35$

Third Row $\Rightarrow 9 \times 5 = \boxed{45}$

9. $A \xrightarrow{+2} C \xrightarrow{+1} D \xrightarrow{+2} F$

$M \xrightarrow{+2} O \xrightarrow{+1} P \xrightarrow{+2} R$

$T \xrightarrow{+2} V \xrightarrow{+1} W \xrightarrow{+2} Y$

Similarly,

$P \xrightarrow{+2} R \xrightarrow{+1} S \xrightarrow{+2} U$

13. $K \xrightarrow{-1} J \xrightarrow{+3} M \xrightarrow{-1} L$

$G \xrightarrow{-1} F \xrightarrow{+3} I \xrightarrow{-1} H$

$T \xrightarrow{-1} S \xrightarrow{+3} V \xrightarrow{-1} U$

$Z \xrightarrow{+1} A \xrightarrow{+1} B \xrightarrow{-3} Y$

18. 6 12 20 30 [42]

+6 +8 +10 +12

+2 +2 +2

19. In each subsequent figure one circle from the lower side is deleted and the first circle is in same word in size.

20.

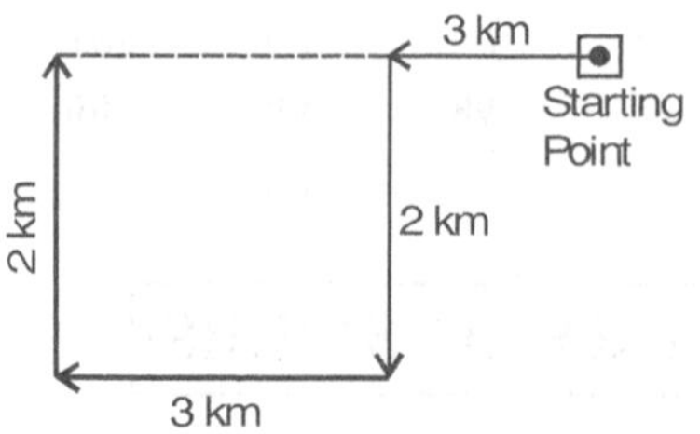

Ramesh is towards West from the starting point.

21. In code, the letters have been written is reverse order.

PATTERN ⇒ NRETTAP

Similarly,

MENTION ⇒ NOITNEM

22. Only daughter of Vijay's mother means sister of Vijay.

Sister of Vijay is mother of Anand. Therefore, Anand is nephew of Vijay.

23. In 2016, the population would be

= 12483 × 2 = 24966

In 2023, the population would be

= 24966 × 2 = 49932

In 2030, the population would be

= 49932 × 2 = 99864

Therefore, increase in population by 2030

= 99864 – 12483 = 87381

Increase in population by 2023

= 49932 – 12483 = 37449

Thus, the required year would be after 2023 and before 2030.

24. Q > P > R < S

Clearly, R is the shortest.

25.

E	D	I	T	I	O	N
↓	↓	↓	↓	↓	↓	↓
3	8	9	1	9	6	5

Therefore,

T	I	D	E
↓	↓	↓	↓
1	9	8	3

51. $CI = P\left[\left(1+\frac{R}{100}\right)^T - 1\right]$

$$= 6400\left[\left(1+\frac{15}{200}\right)^2 - 1\right]$$

$$= 6400\left[\left(\frac{43}{40}\right)^2 - 1\right]$$

$$= 6400\left(\frac{1849}{1600} - 1\right)$$

$$= \frac{6400 \times 249}{1600} = 996.$$

52. If the principal be Rs. x, then

Simple interest = Rs. $(770 - x)$

$$\therefore \text{Principal} = \frac{\text{S.I.} \times 100}{\text{Time} \times \text{Rate}}$$

$$\Rightarrow x = \frac{(770 - x) \times 100}{4 \times 10}$$

$\Rightarrow 2x = (770 - x) \times 5$

$\Rightarrow 2x + 5x = 770 \times 5$

$\Rightarrow 7x = 770 \times 5$

$$\therefore x = \frac{770 \times 5}{7} = \text{Rs. } 550.$$

53. C.P. of article

$= \frac{100}{100 - \text{loss per cent}} \times \text{S.P.}$

$= \frac{100}{96} \times 960 = \text{Rs. } 1000$.

54. $\frac{1}{3}$ of $1206 = 1206 \times \frac{1}{3} = 402$

$\therefore$ Required per cent $= \frac{402}{134} \times 100 = 300$.

55. If the number of men be 100, then

Number of women = 90

$\therefore$ Required per cent $= \frac{100}{90} \times 100 \approx 111$.

56. It is obvious from the graph.

57. Required total daily payment = 35 × 9 = Rs. 315.

58. Amount of foodgrains used by both the villages in 1 day

$= \frac{1}{21} + \frac{1}{28} = \frac{4+3}{84} = \frac{7}{84} = \frac{1}{12}$

Hence, the stock will last for 12 days.

59. Speed of train

$= \frac{\text{Length of (train + platform)}}{\text{Time taken to cross}}$

$= \left(\frac{500+700}{10}\right)$ feet/second

= 120 feet/second.

60. Days working hours/day

$\begin{matrix}12\\18\end{matrix}\uparrow \qquad \begin{matrix}8\\x\end{matrix}\downarrow$

$\Rightarrow \frac{12}{18} = \frac{8}{x}$

$\Rightarrow 12x = 18 \times 8$

$\Rightarrow x = \frac{18 \times 8}{12}$ = 12 hours.

61. Perimeter of isosceles triangle
= 15 + 15 + 22 or 15 + 22 + 22
= 52 or 59 units.

62. Time and speed are inversely proportional
$\therefore$ Required ratio = 4 : 5.

63. Expression $= 1 + \frac{1}{1 + \frac{1}{5}}$

$= 1 + \frac{1}{\frac{5+1}{5}}$

$= 1 + \frac{5}{6} = \frac{6+5}{6} = \frac{11}{6}$.

64. Marks of Q $= \frac{5}{2} \times 120 = 300$.

65. First number × second number
= HCF × LCM

$\Rightarrow 52 \times$ second number $= 4 \times 520$

$\Rightarrow$ Second number $= \frac{4 \times 520}{52} = 40$.

66. If the marked price of article be Rs. x, then

$\frac{x \times 76}{100} = 342$

$\Rightarrow x = \frac{342 \times 100}{76} = \text{Rs. } 450$.

67. $0.42 \times 100^k = 42$

$\Rightarrow \frac{42}{100} \times 100^k = 42$

$\Rightarrow 100^k = \frac{42 \times 100}{42} = 100^1$

$\Rightarrow k = 1$.

68. 1+ 2 + 3 + 4 + ... + 100

$= \frac{n(n+1)}{2}$

$\Rightarrow \frac{100(100+1)}{2} = x$

$\Rightarrow x = 50 \times 101 = 5050$.

69. $\sqrt{64}-\sqrt{36}=8-6=2$.

70. The pattern of the sequence is:

$169 = 13^2$

$144 = 12^2$

$121 = 11^2$

$100 = 10^2$

$81 = 9^2 \neq \boxed{82}$

71. Perimeter of semi-circular shaped window

$= (\pi r + 2r)$ cm $= r(p + 2)$ cm

$= \frac{63}{2}\left(\frac{22}{7}+2\right)$ cm

$= \frac{63}{2}\times\frac{36}{7}=162$ cm.

72. Length of the longest pole

$= \sqrt{12^2+8^2+9^2}$

$= \sqrt{144+64+81}=\sqrt{289}=17$ metre.

73. CP of 75 litres of mixture of milk and water

= Rs. 630

SP of 75 litres of mixture of milk and water

= 9 × 75 = Rs. 675

Gain = 675 – 630 = Rs. 45

$\therefore$ Gain per cent $= \frac{45}{630}\times 100$

$= \frac{50}{7}=7\frac{1}{7}\%$.

74. Required average

$= \frac{x_1+x_2+...+x_{20}}{20}-\frac{101\times 20}{20}$

$= y - 101$.

75. Difference of numbers = 82 – 28 = 54

$\therefore$ Required average $= 60+\frac{54}{27}=62$.

General Intelligence & Reasoning

1 Letter Series

In letter series, the letters follow a definite order. The given series of letters can be in natural order or in reverse order or combination of both. The letters may be skipped or repeated or consecutive. The given series may be single or may even comprise of two different series merged at alternate positions. While attempting questions on letter series one should note the pattern of alphabet series.

Alphabets in natural series are :

A B C D E F G H I J K L M N O P Q R S T U V W X Y Z

A ↓ 1st, E ↓ 5th, J ↓ 10th, O ↓ 15th, T ↓ 20th, Y ↓ 25th

Alphabets in reverse series are :

Z Y X W V U T S R Q P O N M L K J I H G F E D C B A

Z ↓ 1st, V ↓ 5th, Q ↓ 10th, L ↓ 15th, G ↓ 20th, B ↓ 25th

Note : On reaching Z, the series restarts from A and on reaching A, it restarts from Z.

EXERCISE

Directions : *In each of the following series determine the order of the letters. Then from the given options select the one which will complete the given series.*

1. B Y C X D W E ?
(*a*) S (*b*) T
(*c*) U (*d*) V

2. B A F E J I P O ? U
(*a*) V (*b*) T
(*c*) S (*d*) Q

3. B A D C ? H G J I
(*a*) E F (*b*) F E
(*c*) F G (*d*) D F

4. ADG, XVT, BEH, WUS, ?
(*a*) VTR (*b*) CFI
(*c*) DFJ (*d*) STU

5. GMSY, IOUA, KQWC, ?
(*a*) MSYE (*b*) NSYE
(*c*) MTYE (*d*) MSYF

6. ADG, GJM, ?, SVY
(*a*) MPS (*b*) MQR
(*c*) MQS (*d*) SPM

7. XYZ, UVW, ?, OPQ
(*a*) RST (*b*) STU
(*c*) QRS (*d*) TUV

8. JOBS, KMEO, LKHK, ?, NGNC
(*a*) MJLH (*b*) LIKG
(*c*) MIKG (*d*) MNGM

9. AZ, GT, MN, ?, YB
(*a*) KF (*b*) TS
(*c*) RX (*d*) SH

10. BMY, DNW, FOU, ?
(*a*) HPT (*b*) HPS
(*c*) HQS (*d*) GPS

11. AZ, CX, EV, ?
(*a*) HU (*b*) GS
(*c*) GT (*d*) HT

12. DMP, FLN, HKL, JJJ, ?
(*a*) MIH (*b*) III
(*c*) LIH (*d*) MII

13. ECA, JHF, OMK, ?, YWU
(*a*) TRP (*b*) LNP
(*c*) QPN (*d*) RPT

14. ABP, CDQ, EFR, ?
(*a*) GHS (*b*) HGS
(*c*) GHR (*d*) GHT

15. BEH, KNQ, TWZ, ?
(*a*) IJL (*b*) BDF
(*c*) CFI (*d*) ADG

16. EJO, TYD, INS, XCH, ?
(*a*) MRW (*b*) NRV
(*c*) MRV (*d*) NRW

17. ABP, CDQ, EFR,?
(*a*) GHS (*b*) GIS
(*c*) GGS (*d*) GJS

18. NRA, PRC, RRE, TRG, ?
(*a*) USI (*b*) VRI
(*c*) WRJ (*d*) TRI

19. FJKP, ILMQ, LNOR, OPQS, ?
(*a*) RQTV (*b*) RQSS
(*c*) RRST (*d*) RTTU

20. DQCP, EPEN, FOGL, GNIJ, ?
(*a*) HNLG (*b*) HLJG
(*c*) HOMI (*d*) HMKH

21. DFST, FSTD, STDF, ?
(*a*) TSFD (*b*) FDTS
(*c*) TDFS (*d*) SFDT

22. IXT, MAV, QDX, ?
(*a*) WGX (*b*) VHY
(*c*) UGZ (*d*) YHZ

23. QYK, ?, ISG, EPE
(*a*) NWJ (*b*) MVI
(*c*) NVI (*d*) MVJ

24. JMC, CLT, KND, ?, LOE, GPX
(*a*) ENV (*b*) DMX
(*c*) EOU (*d*) DRX

25. ZDV, XGS, VJP, ?
(*a*) SNM (*b*) TMM
(*c*) TNR (*d*) SNT

EXPLANATORY ANSWERS

1. (*d*) : There are two alternate series.

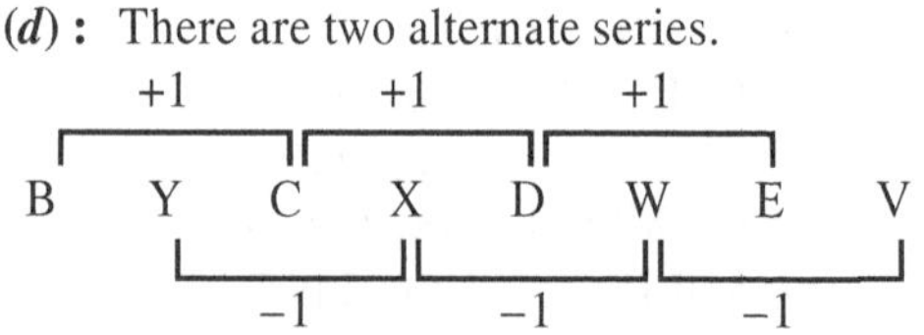

Series I : BCDE (natural order)
Series II : YXWV (reverse order)

2. (*a*) : Each vowel (AEIOU) is preceded by the letter that comes next to it in the natural alphabetical series.

B A F E J I P O V U

3. (*b*) : The letters in natural series are divided into sections of two letters each. The letters in each section are written backward.

BA DC FE HG JI

4. (*b*) : There are two alternate series.

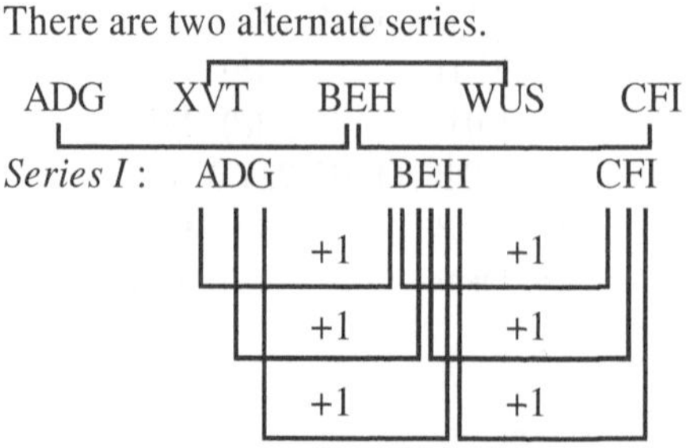

Series II :
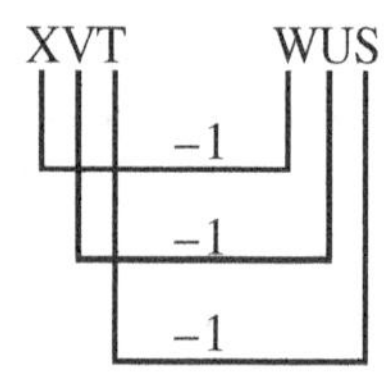

5. (*a*) : The series is formed by moving each letter two steps forward from one group to the next.

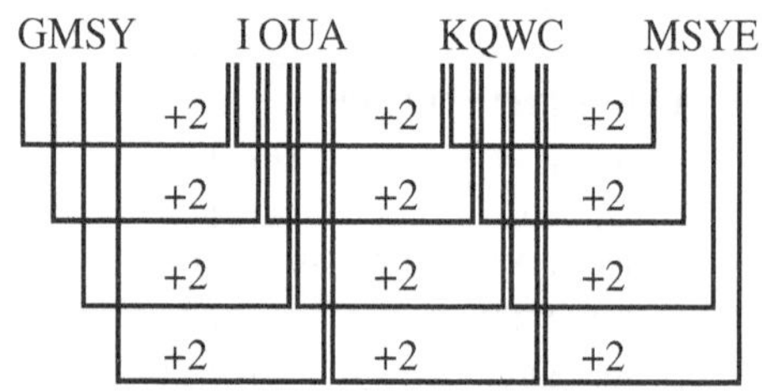

(The series restarts from A on reaching Z)

6. (*a*) : In each group of three letters the alphabet is in the succession of +3. The next group begins with the last alphabet of the previous group.

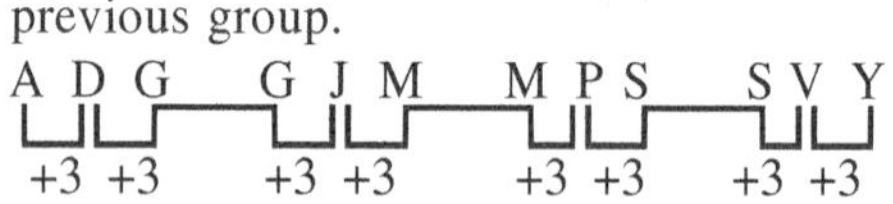

7. (*a*) : The alphabet from one group to the next are in recession of –3, *i.e.,*

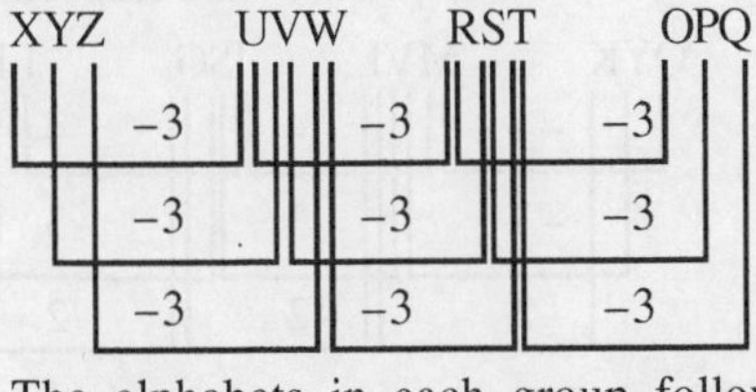

8. (*c*) : The alphabets in each group follow the pattern +1, –2, +3 and –4 respectively from one group to the next group.

9. (*d*) : The letters in one group correspond to the letters in the next group in the manner +6, –6 respectively, *i.e.,*

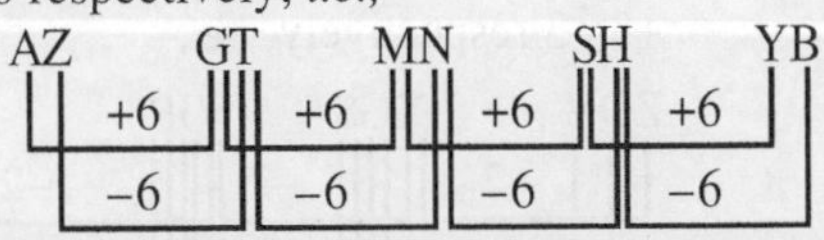

10. (*b*) : The letters in one group correspond to the letters in the next group in the manner +2, +1, -2 respectively, *i.e.,*

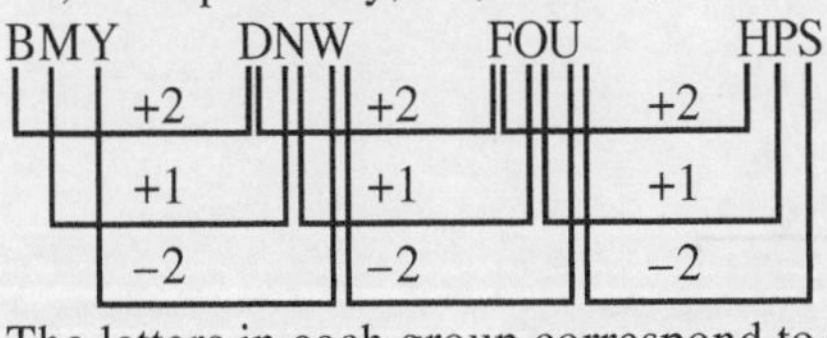

11. (*c*) : The letters in each group correspond to the letters in the next group in the manner +2, –2 respectively, *i.e.,*

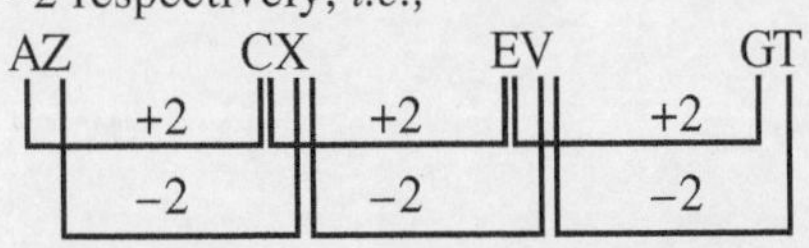

12. (*c*) : The alphabets in each group correspond to the alphabets in the next group in the manner +2, –1, –2 respectively, *i.e.,*

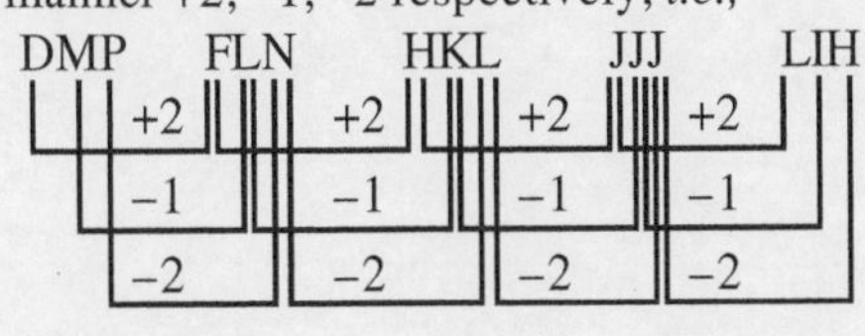

13. (*a*) : The alphabets in each group are moved five steps forward, *i.e.,*

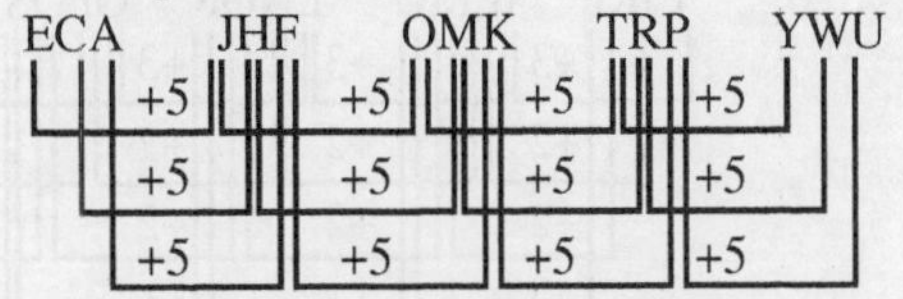

14. (*a*) : The letters in one group correspond to the letters in the next group in the manner +2, +2, +1 respectively, *i.e.,*

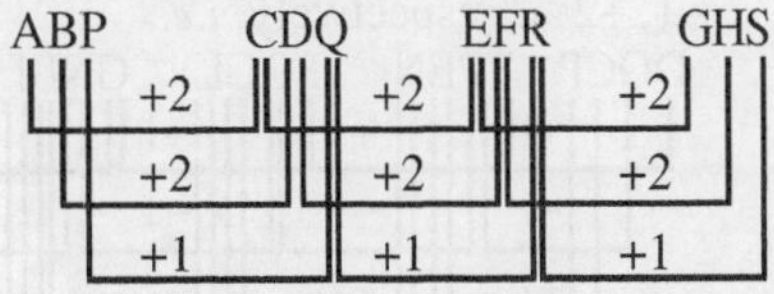

15. (*c*) : All the letters in each group are moved nine steps forward.

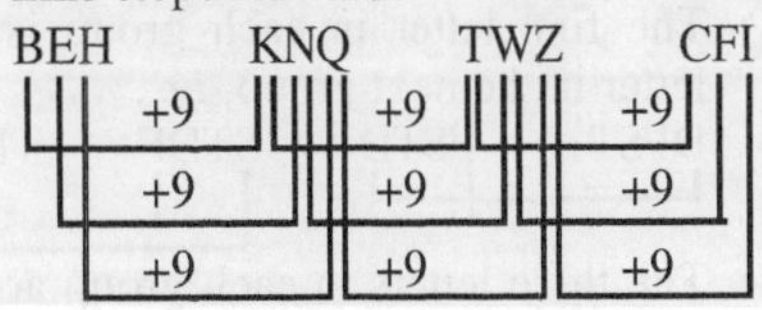

16. (*a*) : There are two alternate series :

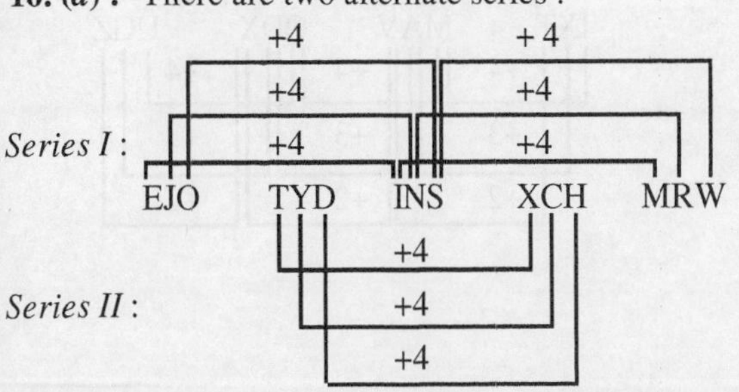

17. (*a*) : The letters in one group correspond to the letters in the next group in the manner +2, +2, +1 respectively, *i.e.,*

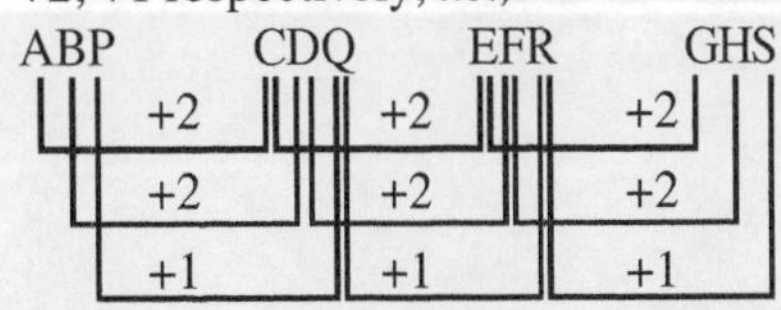

18. (*b*) : The first and third letters are moved two steps forwards while the middle letter remains unchanged, *i.e.,*

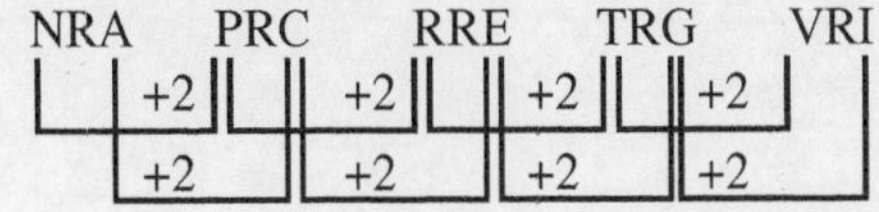

19. (*c*) : The four letters are moved 3, 2, 2, 1 steps forward respectively, *i.e.,*

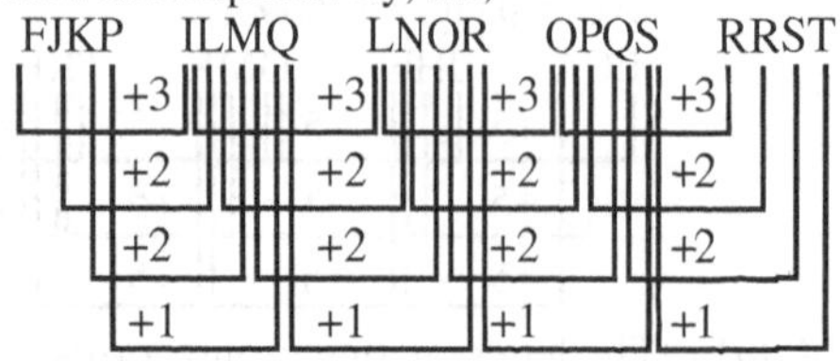

20. (*d*) : The letters in one group correspond to the letters in the next group in the manner, +1, –1, +2 –2 respectively, *i.e.,*

21. (*c*) : The first letter in each group is the last letter in the next group, *i.e.,*

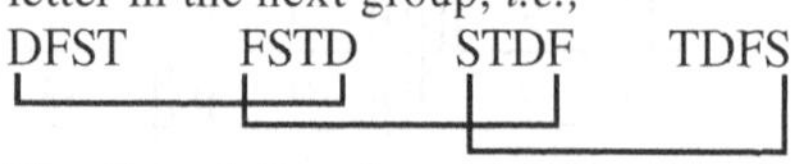

22. (*c*) : The three letters in each group are moved 4, 3 and 2 steps forward respectively, *i.e.,*

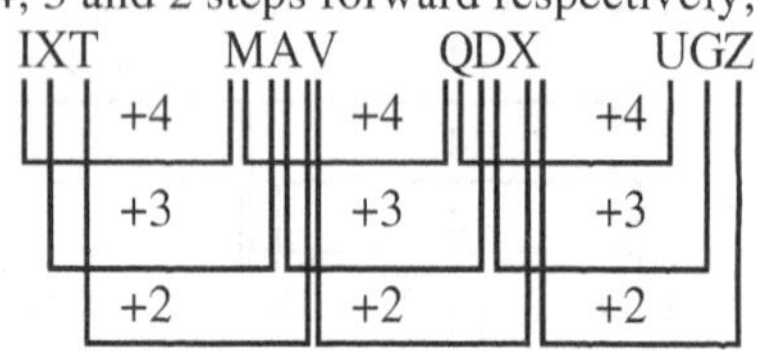

23. (*b*) : The three letters in each group are moved 4, 3 and 2 steps backward respectively, *i.e.,*

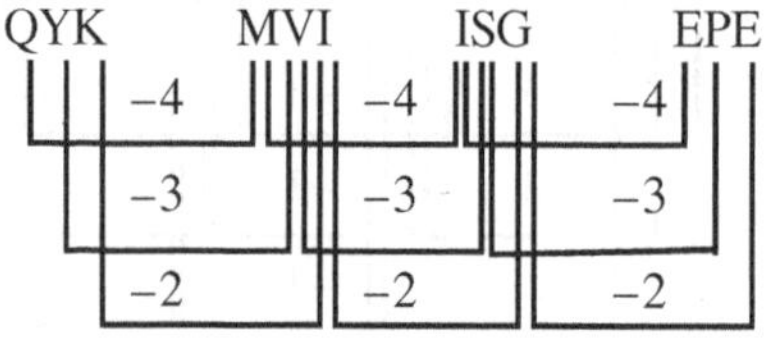

24. (*a*) : There are two alternate series :

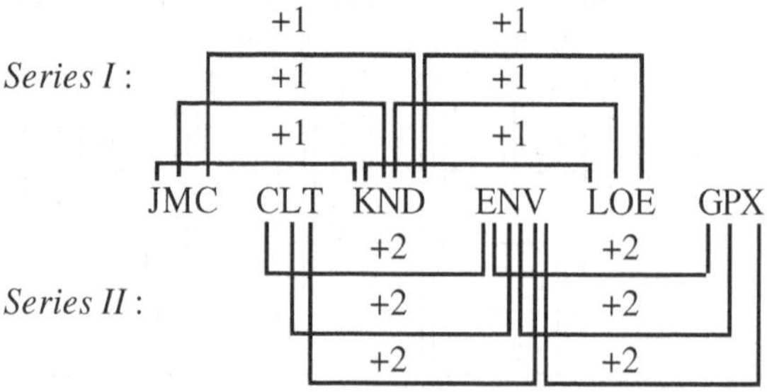

25. (*b*) : The letters in one group correspond to the letters in the next group in the manner –2, +3 –3 respectively, *i.e.,*

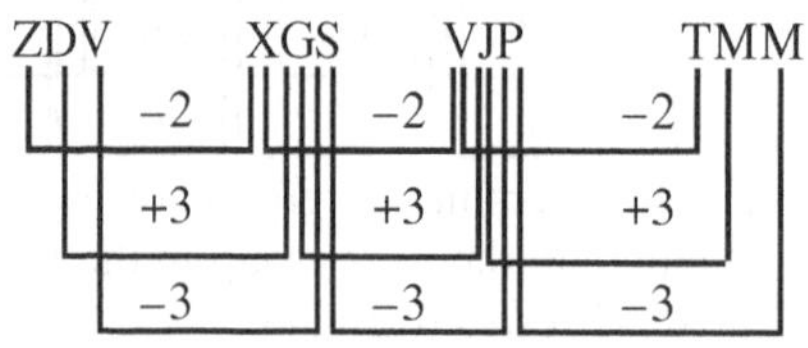

2 Wrong Letter Series

In this type of series, the candidates are not required to find the letter or group of letters which will complete the given series but, they have to identify the letter or number which is wrong or misfit in the given series.

SOLVED EXAMPLE

1. Which of the following letters in the given series is wrong?

J M P T V Y

(*a*) J (*b*) P (*c*) T (*d*) Y

Ans. (*c*) : The letters in this series are moved three steps forward, *i.e.*,

J M P S V Y
+3 +3 +3 +3 +3

Letter 'T' should have been 'S'.

EXERCISE

Directions : *Which letter(s) in each of the following series is wrong or is misfit in the series?*

1. A E H O U
(*a*) U (*b*) O
(*c*) H (*d*) E

2. C H M S W B
(*a*) C (*b*) S
(*c*) B (*d*) W

3. X S N I C Y
(*a*) Y (*b*) C
(*c*) S (*d*) I

4. Z A W B X C
(*a*) D (*b*) C
(*c*) X (*d*) W

5. M L O N Q P R
(*a*) R (*b*) O
(*c*) Q (*d*) L

6. D K R Y F L
(*a*) L (*b*) D
(*c*) R (*d*) Y

7. L N Q T W Z C F
(*a*) C (*b*) Q
(*c*) L (*d*) F

8. XW, DC, CB, NM, PQ
(*a*) NM (*b*) CB
(*c*) PQ (*d*) XW

9. B E I N S A I
(*a*) A (*b*) E
(*c*) S (*d*) I

10. Z T P K H F
(*a*) Z (*b*) P
(*c*) T (*d*) F

EXPLANATORY ANSWERS

1. (*c*) : The series is made with vowels only. AEIOU. I should be in place of H.

2. (*b*) : The letters in the series are moved five steps forward.

C H M R W B
+5 +5 +5 +5 +5

R should be in place of S
(The series restarts from A on reaching Z)

3. (*b*) : The pattern in the series is –5, *i.e.*,

X S N I D Y
–5 –5 –5 –5 –5

D should be in place of C.

4. (*d*) : There are two alternate series

+1 +1

Z A Y B X C

−1 −1

Series I : ZYX (reverse series)
Series II : ABC (natural series)
Y should be in place of W.

5. (*a*) : Two consecutive letters are written backwards.

ML ON QP SR

S should be in place of R.

6. (*a*) : The pattern in this series in moving the letters seven steps forward.

D K R Y F M

+7 +7 +7 +7 +7

M should be in place of L.

7. (*c*) : The pattern in the series is +3

K N Q T W Z C F

+3 +3 +3 +3 +3 +3 +3

K should be in place of L.

8. (*c*) : The series is made with any two consecutive letters written backwards.

XW DC CB NM QP
← ← ← ← ←

Q should come before P in the series.

9. (*c*) : The difference between the letters is increased by one at each step.

B E I N T A I

+3 +4 +5 +6 +7 +8

T should be in place of S.

10. (*b*) : The difference between the letters is decreased by one at each step.

Z T O K H F

−6 −5 −4 −3 −2

O should be in place of P.

3 Repeat Series

In this type of series, small letters of the alphabet are used to make a set of letters which are repeated. The candidate has to find the set of letters which will fit the blanks left in the given series in such a manner that one section of the series is further repeated in the same manner.

SOLVED EXAMPLE

1. Which of the following groups of letters will complete the given series?
ba-b-aab-a-b
(*a*) baab (*b*) abba (*c*) abaa (*d*) babb

Ans. (*b*) : The series is baab, baab, baab. Here the section 'baab' is repeated in the series.

Solving steps : The candidate has to look for clues to solve such series pattern. 'aab' in the Series indicates that 'b' in this series is preceded by two 'a' so, the first blank and the last blank will be filled by 'a'. Now the first set is formed, *i.e.*, 'baab' in the beginning. This set is repeated, so the second and third blanks will have 'b' filling them. Now, solve the exercise given below to know the different ways in which these series are formed.

EXERCISE

Directions : *Which of the following groups of letters will complete the given series?*

1. ab---b-bbaa-
(*a*) babba (*b*) abaab
(*c*) abbab (*d*) baaab

2. aa-ab--aaa-a
(*a*) baaa (*b*) abab
(*c*) aaab (*d*) aabb

3. -baa-aab-a-a
(*a*) baab (*b*) abab
(*c*) aaba (*d*) aabb

4. -a cca-ccca-acccc-aaa
(*a*) ccaa (*b*) acca
(*c*) caac (*d*) caaa

5. c-bbb--abbbb-abbb-
(*a*) abccb (*b*) bacbb
(*c*) aabcb (*d*) abacb

6. ac-cab-baca-aba-acac
(*a*) bcbb (*b*) aacb
(*c*) babb (*d*) acbc

7. --aba--ba-ab
(*a*) abbab (*b*) bbaba
(*c*) baabb (*d*) abbba

8. --babbba-a--
(*a*) bbaba (*b*) babbb
(*c*) baaab (*d*) ababb

9. k-mk-lmkkl-kk-mk
(*a*) lklm (*b*) lkmk
(*c*) lkmm (*d*) lkml

10. abc-d-bc-d-b-dd
(*a*) decdb (*b*) dadac
(*c*) cdabe (*d*) bacde

11. b-abbc-bbca-bcabb-ab
(*a*) acba (*b*) acaa
(*c*) cacc (*d*) cabc

12. aca-ac--a-ac
(*a*) babc (*b*) aaac
(*c*) cacc (*d*) caca

13. ba-cb-b-bab-?
(*a*) acbb (*b*) bcaa
(*c*) cabb (*d*) bacc

14. ab-aa-caab-aab-a
(*a*) bcbc (*b*) bbca
(*c*) cbcc (*d*) caba

15. -bbcaa-bcaa-bc-a-bca
(*a*) bacab (*b*) abbab
(*c*) abcba (*d*) bcaab

16. a-bccb-ca-cca-baab-c
(*a*) accab (*b*) abcaa
(*c*) bacaa (*d*) ababc

17. b-dabbcd-b-c-ab
(*a*) cabd (*b*) bcad
(*c*) dcba (*d*) acbd

18. a-ba-caacb-bc-
(*a*) acbb (*b*) cbab
(*c*) cbaa (*d*) cbba

19. c-baa-aca-cacab-acac-bca
(*a*) acbaa (*b*) cbaac
(*c*) bccab (*d*) bbcaa

20. -bcc-ac-aabb-ab-cc
(*a*) bacab (*b*) abaca
(*c*) aabca (*d*) bcaca

21. ab-ccca-bccc-bbcc-
(*a*) abbc (*b*) bbac
(*c*) bbca (*d*) cabc

22. -cbc-a-bcaac-ca
(*a*) aaba (*b*) caab
(*c*) bcab (*d*) aacb

23. ab-ba--ba-
(*a*) abba (*b*) baab
(*c*) baba (*d*) abab

24. yx-yx-yxz-xz-y-zyxz
(*a*) zzyx (*b*) xxzy
(*c*) yyzx (*d*) yzxz

25. xxxy-y-xxy-yxx-
(*a*) xyxy (*b*) yxyx
(*c*) yyxx (*d*) xxyy

EXPLANATORY ANSWERS

1. (*d*) : The series is abbaab, abbaab.
2. (*c*) : The series is aaaaba, aaaaba.
3. (*b*) : The series is aba, aba, aba, aba.
4. (*d*) : The series is c,a,cc,aa, ccc, aaa, cccc, aaaa.
5. (*a*) : The series is cabbbb, cabbbb, cabbbb.
6. (*b*) : The series is acac, abab, acac, abab, acac.
7. (*a*) : The series is ab, ab, ab, ab, ab, ab.
8. (*b*) : The series is bababb, bababb.
9. (*d*) : The series is klmk, klmk, klmk, klmk.
10. (*b*) : The series is abcdd, abcdd, abcdd.
11. (*d*) : The series is bcab, bcab, bcab, bcab, bcab.
12. (*c*) : The series is ac, ac, ac, ac, ac, ac.
13. (*d*) : The series is babc, babc, babc.
14. (*c*) : The series is abca, abca, abca, abca.
15. (*b*) : The series is abbca, abbca, abbca, abbca.
16. (*d*) : The series is aabcc, bbcaa, ccabb, aabcc.
17. (*a*) : The series is bcdab, bcdab, bcdab.
18. (*c*) : The series is acbabca, acbabca.
19. (*a*) : The series is cabaac, acabca, cabaac, acabca.
20. (*a*) : The series is bbccaa, ccaabb, aabbcc.
21. (*b*) : The series is abbccc abbccc.
22. (*d*) : The series is acbca acbca acbca.
23. (*d*) : The series is ab ab ab ab ab.
24. (*a*) : The series is yxz yxz yxz yxz yxz yxz.
25. (*b*) : The series is xxx yyy xxx yyy xxx.

4 Number Series

In this type of series, the set of given numbers in a series are related to one another in a particular pattern or manner. The relationship between the numbers may be (i) consecutive odd/even numbers; (ii) consecutive prime numbers; (iii) squares/cubes of some numbers with/without variation of addition or subtraction of some number; (iv) sum/product/difference of preceding numbers; (v) addition/subtraction/multiplication/division by some number; and (vi) many more combinations of the relationships given above.

EXERCISE

Directions : *In the following questions, select the number(s) from the given options for completing the given series.*

1. 7776, 1296, 216, 36, 6, ?
(*a*) 6 (*b*) 0
(*c*) 3 (*d*) 1

2. 29282, 2662, 242, 22, ?
(*a*) 1 (*b*) 2
(*c*) 0 (*d*) 11

3. 1, 2, 2, 4, 16, ?, 65536
(*a*) 276 (*b*) 64
(*c*) 256 (*d*) 198

4. 3, 5, 9, 15, 23, ?, 45
(*a*) 37 (*b*) 35
(*c*) 31 (*d*) 33

5. 7, 21, 35, 49, 63, ?
(*a*) 70 (*b*) 77
(*c*) 81 (*d*) 108

6. 10, 14, 23, 39, 64, ?, 149
(*a*) 78 (*b*) 128
(*c*) 103 (*d*) 100

7. 6, 24, 29, 116, 121, ?, 489
(*a*) 468 (*b*) 484
(*c*) 243 (*d*) 363

8. 5, 50, 45, 450, 445, ?, 4445
(*a*) 4450 (*b*) 4600
(*c*) 4550 (*d*) 4500

9. 6.25, 9, 12.25, 16, 20.25, 25, 30.25?
(*a*) 36 (*b*) 32
(*c*) 28.25 (*d*) 40.25

10. 243, 5, 81, 15, 27, 45, 9, ?
(*a*) 5 (*b*) 15
(*c*) 135 (*d*) 27

11. 2, 7, 14, 23, ?, 47
(*a*) 31 (*b*) 38
(*c*) 28 (*d*) 34

12. 0, 1, 8, 27, 64, ?
(*a*) 125 (*b*) 128
(*c*) 256 (*d*) 121

13. 37, 47, 58, ?, 79, 95
(*a*) 71 (*b*) 69
(*c*) 68 (*d*) 67

14. 4, –8, 14, –22, 32, ?
(*a*) –44 (*b*) 42
(*c*) –42 (*d*) 44

15. 6, 7, 9, 11, 15, 15, 24, 19, ?
(*a*) 32 (*b*) 34
(*c*) 36 (*d*) 37

16. 2, 6, 12, 20, 30, ?
(*a*) 42 (*b*) 36
(*c*) 41 (*d*) 40

17. 1, 4, 5, 11, 9, 18, ?, 25
(*a*) 12 (*b*) 13
(*c*) 19 (*d*) 23

18. 27, 45, 9, 15, 3, 5, ?
(*a*) 1 (*b*) 1/3
(*c*) 1/5 (*d*) 1/9

19. 3, 1/3, 14, 1/14, 25, 1/25, ?
(*a*) 1/36 (*b*) 34
(*c*) 35 (*d*) 36

20. 1/2, 3/4, 5/8, 7/16, ?
(*a*) 10/17 (*b*) 9/32
(*c*) 11/34 (*d*) 12/35

21. 4, 8, 7, 14, 12, 22, 19, ?, 28
(*a*) 12 (*b*) 24
(*c*) 28 (*d*) 32

22. 96, 90, 78, ?, 36, 6
(*a*) 60 (*b*) 72
(*c*) 48 (*d*) 54

23. 6, 3, 11, 8, 18, 15, 27, 24, ?, ?
(*a*) 36, 33 (*b*) 36, 35
(*c*) 38, 35 (*d*) 38, 34

24. 1, 6, 15, ?, 45, 66, 91
(*a*) 25 (*b*) 26
(*c*) 27 (*d*) 28

25. 1, 2, 5, 12, 27, 58, 121, ?
(*a*) 246 (*b*) 247
(*c*) 248 (*d*) 249

26. (2,1), (1,5), (5,7), (7,11), (11,13), ?
(*a*) (13, 15) (*b*) (13,17)
(*c*) (13, 19) (*d*) (15,16)

27. 2, 7, 4, 9, 6, 11, 8, 13, 10, 15, 12, ?
(*a*) 16 (*b*) 17
(*c*) 19 (*d*) 21

28. 1, 1, 3, 9, 6, 36, 10, 100, ?, 225
(*a*) 15 (*b*) 16
(*c*) 20 (*d*) 22

29. 2, 11, 7, 16, 12, ?, 17, 26
(*a*) 21 (*b*) 8
(*c*) 11 (*d*) 76

30. 54, 45, 38, 33, ?
(*a*) 32 (*b*) 31
(*c*) 30 (*d*) 29

EXPLANATORY ANSWERS

1. (*d*) : The numbers in this sequence are divided by 6 each time.

2. (*b*) : The numbers in the series are divided by 11 at each step.

3. (*c*) : The number in the series is product of all the numbers preceding it.

1 2 2 4 16 256 65536

(1×2) (1×2×2) (1×2×2×4) (1×2×2×4×16) (1×2×2×4×16×256)

4. (*d*) : The difference between consecutive numbers increases by 2 at each step.

3 5 9 15 23 33 45

+2 +4 +6 +8 +10 +12

5. (*b*) : The series is multiplication of 7 by odd numbers starting from 3.

7 21 35 49 63 77

× 3 × 5 × 7 × 9 × 11

6. (*d*) : The number plus the square of numbers in natural order starting from 2 gives the next number in the series.

10 14 23 39 64 100 149

$+2^2$ $+3^2$ $+4^2$ $+5^2$ $+6^2$ $+7^2$

7. (*b*) : The sequence in the series is ×4, +5, which is repeated.

8. (*a*) : The sequence in the series is ×10, –5, which is repeated.

9. (*a*) : There are two alternate series :

+6 +8 +10

6.25 9 12.25 16 20.25 25 30.25 36

+7 +9 +11

Series I : 6.25, 12.25, 20.25, 30.25 (sequence is +6, +8, +10)

Series II : 9, 16, 25, 36 (sequence is +7, +9, +11)

10. (*c*) : There are two alternate series :

÷ 3 ÷ 3 ÷ 3

243 5 81 15 27 45 9 135

×3 ×3 ×3

Series I : 243, 81, 27, 9 (division by 3)

Series II : 5, 15, 45, 135 (multiplication by 3)

11. (d) : The difference between two consecutive numbers is increasing by 2 starting from 5.

2 7 14 23 34 47

+5 +7 +9 +11 +13

12. (a) : The numbers are cubes of numbers in natural order.

13. (a) : The sum of the digits of the number is added to the number to obtain the next number in the series.

37 47 58 71 79 95

+(3+7) +(4+7) +(5+8) +(7+1) +(7+9)

14. (a) : Alternate numbers are marked positive and negative, but the difference between their magnitude increases by 2 at each step.

4 – 8 14 – 22 32 – 44

4 6 8 10 12

15. (c) : There are two alternate series :

+3 +6 +9 +12

6 7 9 11 15 15 24 19 36

+4 +4 +4

Series I : 6, 9, 15, 24, 36 (sequence is +3, +6, +9, +12)

Series II : 7, 11, 15, 19 (addition of 4 at each step)

16. (a) : The difference between the consecutive numbers in the series increases by 2 at each step.

2 6 12 20 30 42

+4 +6 +8 +10 +12

17. (b) : There are two alternate series :

+4 +4 +4

1 4 5 11 9 18 13 25

+7 +7 +7

Series I : 1, 5, 9, 13 (addition of 4)

Series II : 4, 11, 18, 25 (addition of 7)

18. (a) : There are two alternate series :

÷ 3 ÷ 3 ÷ 3

27 45 9 15 3 5 1

÷ 3 ÷ 3

Series I : 27, 9, 3, 1 (division by 3)

Series II : 45, 15, 5 (division by 3)

19. (d) : Two consecutive numbers form a pair. The difference between the numbers placed at odd places increases by 11 and the second number is the fraction part of the number.

$3 \quad \frac{1}{3} \quad 14 \quad \frac{1}{14} \quad 25 \quad \frac{1}{25} \quad 36$

+11 +11 +11

20. (b) : In this fraction series the numbers on the top are increased by 2 and at the bottom, multiplied by 2.

21. (d) : There are two alternate series :

+3 +5 +7 +9

4 8 7 14 12 22 19 32 28

+6 +8 +10

Series I : 4, 7, 12, 19, 28 (sequence is +3, +5, +7, +9)

Series II : 8, 14, 22, 32 (sequence is +6, +8, +10)

22. (a) : The series is formed by multiples of 6 in this manner :

6 × 16 = 96		
6 × 15 = 90	(16 – 1)	= 15
6 × 13 = 78	(15 – 2)	= 13
6 × 10 = 60	(13 – 3)	= 10
6 × 6 = 36	(10 – 4)	= 6
6 × 1 = 6	(6 – 5)	= 1

23. (c) : There are two alternate series :

+5 +7 +9 +11

6 3 11 8 18 15 27 24 38 35

+5 +7 +9 +11

Series I : 6, 11, 18, 27, 38

Series II : 3, 8, 15, 24, 35

(Both series follow the pattern +5, +7, +9, +11)

24. (d) : The difference between the numbers in this series is increased by 4 at each step.

1 6 15 28 45 66 91

+5 +9 +13 +17 +21 +25

25. ***(c)*** **:** The sequence in this series is number into 2 plus the numbers in natural order starting from 0.

1   2   5   12   27   58   121   248

(1×2)+0 (2×2) +1 (5×2)+2 (12×2) +3 (27×2)+4 (58×2)+5 (121×2)+6

26. (b) : The second number in one section is the first number in the next section and the sequence of the second numbers in the sections is +4, +2 which is repeated.

27. ***(b)*** **:** The sequence followed in the series is +5, –3 which is repeated.

28. ***(a)*** **:** Two consecutive numbers form a pair. The difference between the first number increases in the manner +2, +3, +4, +5 and the second number is the square of the number.

1^2 3^2 6^2 10^2 15^2

1 1   3 9   6 36   10 100   15 225

+2   +3   +4   +5

29. ***(a)*** **:** The sequence in the series is +9, – 4 which is repeated.

30. ***(c)*** **:** The difference between the numbers in the series is decreased by 2 at each step.

54   45   38   33   30

–9   –7   –5   –3

5 Wrong Number Series

In this type of series, the given series may be complete but what needs to be identified is the number in the given completed series which is disturbing the sequential pattern of that series and does not fit in with the relationship shared between the other numbers.

EXERCISE

Directions : *In the given series find the number which is wrong.*

1. 5, 25, 120, 625, 3125, 15625
(*a*) 15625 (*b*) 625
(*c*) 120 (*d*) 5

2. 4, 8, 11, 22, 18, 36, 24, 50
(*a*) 8 (*b*) 22
(*c*) 36 (*d*) 24

3. 2, 4, 12, 24, 72, 142, 432
(*a*) 432 (*b*) 12
(*c*) 142 (*d*) 72

4. 2, 3, 4, 4, 6, 8, 9, 12, 16
(*a*) 3 (*b*) 9
(*c*) 6 (*d*) 12

5. 97, 91, 86, 83, 79, 77, 76, 76
(*a*) 86 (*b*) 76
(*c*) 91 (*d*) 83

6. 7, 11, 11, 9, 15, 7, 19, 5, 23, 1
(*a*) 5 (*b*) 7
(*c*) 1 (*d*) 9

7. 3, 7, 12, 28, 48, 118, 192, 448
(*a*) 12 (*b*) 118
(*c*) 28 (*d*) 7

8. 10, 100, 1100, 11000, 111000, 1210000
(*a*) 1210000 (*b*) 11000
(*c*) 100 (*d*) 111000

9. 24576, 6144, 1536, 386, 96, 24
(*a*) 386 (*b*) 6144
(*c*) 96 (*d*) 1536

10. 11, 13, 15, 17, 19, 23, 29, 31, 37
(*a*) 13 (*b*) 23
(*c*) 15 (*d*) 31

11. 36, 43, 49, 54, 60, 61, 63, 64
(*a*) 60 (*b*) 63
(*c*) 54 (*d*) 43

12. 3, 10, 41, 206, 1236, 8660
(*a*) 10 (*b*) 41
(*c*) 206 (*d*) 1236

13. 17, 25, 37, 50, 65, 82, 101
(*a*) 25 (*b*) 17
(*c*) 101 (*d*) 65

14. 12, 20, 38, 42, 56, 72
(*a*) 20 (*b*) 38
(*c*) 56 (*d*) 72

15. 5, 6, 11, 22, 42, 88, 176
(*a*) 5 (*b*) 42
(*c*) 176 (*d*) 11

16. 905, 180, 175, 35, 30, 6, 1
(*a*) 6 (*b*) 1
(*c*) 175 (*d*) 905

17. 5040, 840, 160, 42, 14, 7
(*a*) 7 (*b*) 160
(*c*) 14 (*d*) 840

18. 3, 32, 363, 3993, 43923
(*a*) 363 (*b*) 3
(*c*) 32 (*d*) 43923

19. 3, 18, 38, 78, 123, 178, 243
(*a*) 78 (*b*) 3
(*c*) 123 (*d*) 18

20. 0, 1, 2, 2, 4, 4, 6, 8, 8, 10
(*a*) 6 (*b*) 0
(*c*) 1 (*d*) 10

21. 5, 12, 16, 24, 27
(*a*) 12 (*b*) 16
(*c*) 24 (*d*) 27

22. 27, 36, 45, 60, 71, 99
(*a*) 27 (*b*) 45
(*c*) 60 (*d*) 71

23. 81, 64, 49, 35, 25, 16
(*a*) 64 (*b*) 35
(*c*) 25 (*d*) 16

24. 625, 125, 25, 5, 0
(*a*) 0 (*b*) 125
(*c*) 5 (*d*) 625

25. 25, 19, 17, 13, 11, 7
(*a*) 25 (*b*) 17
(*c*) 13 (*d*) 7

EXPLANATORY ANSWERS

1. (*c*) : The numbers in the series are multiplied by 5 to get the next number.
∴ 125 should be in place of 120.

2. (*d*) : Two numbers form a pair. The first number increases by 7 for the next pair and the second number is the double of first number.

4 8 11 22 18 36 25 50
(×2 within each pair; +7 between pairs)

∴ 25 should be in place of 24.

3. (*c*) : There are two alternate series and in each series, the numbers are multiplied by 6 to get the next number.

2 4 12 24 72 144 432
(×6 ×6 ×6 above; ×6 ×6 below)

∴ 144 should be in place of 142.

4. (*b*) : There are three alternate series and in each series, the numbers are multiplied by 2 to get the next number.

2 3 4 4 6 8 8 12 16
(×2 ×2; ×2 ×2; ×2 ×2)

Series I : 2, 4, 8
Series II : 3, 6, 12
Series III : 4, 8, 16
∴ 8 should be in place of 9.

5. (*d*) : The difference between the consecutive numbers in the series decreases by 1 at each step.

97 91 86 82 79 77 76 76
−6 −5 −4 −3 −2 −1 −0

∴ 82 should be in place of 83.

6. (*c*) : There are two alternate series :

7 11 11 9 15 7 19 5 21 3
(+4 +4 +4 +4 above; −2 −2 −2 −2 below)

Series I : 7, 11, 15, 19, 23 (addition of 4)
Series II : 11, 9, 7, 5, 3 (subtraction of 2)
∴ 3 should be in place of 1.

7. (*b*) : There are two alternate series and in each series, the numbers are multiplied by 4 to get the next number.

3 7 12 28 48 112 192 448
(×4 ×4 ×4 above; ×4 ×4 ×4 below)

∴ 112 should be in place of 118.

8. (*d*) : The numbers in this series are multiplied by 10 and 11 alternately is, *i.e.*, × 10, × 11.

10 100 1100 11000 121000 1210000
× 10 × 11 × 10 × 11 × 10

∴ 121000 should be in place of 111000.

9. (*a*) : The numbers in this series are divided by 4 to get the next number.

24576 6144 1536 384 96 24
÷ 4 ÷ 4 ÷ 4 ÷ 4 ÷ 4

∴ 384 should be in place of 386.

10. (*c*) : The series comprises of prime numbers in increasing order. Only 15 is an exception.

11. (*a*) : The difference between two consecutive numbers is decreasing by 1 at each step.

36 43 49 54 58 61 63 64

+7 +6 +5 +4 +3 +2 +1

∴ 58 should be in place of 60.

12. (*d*) : The sequence followed in this series is :

$3 \times 3 + 1 = 10$

$10 \times 4 + 1 = 41$

$41 \times 5 + 1 = 206$

$206 \times 6 + 1 = 1237$; and

$1237 \times 7 + 1 = 8660$

∴ 1237 should be in place of 1236.

13. (*a*) : The numbers in the series are 1 plus the squares of numbers in natural order starting from 4.

17 26 37 50 65 82 101

↓ ↓ ↓ ↓ ↓ ↓ ↓

$4^2 + 1$ $5^2 + 1$ $6^2 + 1$ $7^2 + 1$ $8^2 + 1$ $9^2 + 1$ $10^2 + 1$

∴ 26 should be in place of 25.

14. (*b*) : The sequence followed in this series is :

$3 \times 4 = 12$

$4 \times 5 = 20$

$5 \times 6 = 30$

$6 \times 7 = 42$

$7 \times 8 = 56$

$8 \times 9 = 72$

∴ 30 should be in place of 38.

15. (*b*) : The numbers in the series are the sum of all the numbers preceding them.

5 6 11 22 44 88 176

(5 + 6)

(5 + 6 + 11)

(5 + 6 + 11 + 22)

(5 + 6 + 11 + 22 + 44)

(5 + 6 + 11 + 22 + 44 + 88)

∴ 44 should be in place of 42.

16. (*d*) : The sequence followed in the series is ÷ 5, – 5 which is repeated.

900 180 175 35 30 6 1

÷ 5 – 5 ÷ 5 – 5 ÷ 5 – 5

∴ 900 should be in place of 905.

17. (*b*) : The numbers in the series are divided by numbers in reverse order starting from 6 to get the next number.

5040 840 168 42 14 7

÷ 6 ÷ 5 ÷ 4 ÷ 3 ÷ 2

∴ 168 should be in place of 160.

18. (*c*) : The numbers in this series are multiplied by 11 to get the next number.

3 33 363 3993 43923

× 11 × 11 × 11 × 11

∴ 33 should be in place of 32.

19. (*b*) : 3 is the only prime number in the series.

20. (*d*) : There are two alternate series :

+2 +2 +2 +2

0 1 2 2 4 4 6 8 8 16

× 2 × 2 × 2 × 2

Series I : 0, 2, 4, 6, 8, (addition of 2)

Series II : 1, 2, 4, 8, 16 (multiplication by 2)

∴ 16 should be in place of 10.

21. (*c*) : The sequence in the series is +7, +4 which is repeated, *i.e.*,

5 12 16 23 27

+7 +4 +7 +4

∴ 23 should be in place of 24.

22. (*d*) : All other numbers are divisible by 3.

23. (*b*) : The sequence is the square of the number in decreasing order starting from 9, *i.e.*,

$9^2 = 9 \times 9 = 81$

$8^2 = 8 \times 8 = 64$

$7^2 = 7 \times 7 = 49$

$6^2 = 6 \times 6 = 36$

$5^2 = 5 \times 5 = 25$

$4^2 = 4 \times 4 = 16$

∴ 36 should be in place of 35.

24. (*a*) : The number in the series are divided by 5 to get the next number

625 125 25 5 1

÷ 5 ÷ 5 ÷ 5 ÷ 5

∴ 1 should be in place of 0 digit.

25. (*a*) : Other numbers are prime numbers.

6 Word Analogy

In Analogy Tests, the relationship between two given words is established and then applied to the other words. The type of relationship may vary, so while attempting such questions the first step is to identify the type of relationship, which can be any one of the following.

EXERCISE

Directions : *In the questions given below one term is missing. Based on the relationship of the two given words find the missing term from the given options.*

1. HUNGER : FOOD : : THIRST : ?
(*a*) Water (*b*) Drink
(*c*) Tea (*d*) Coffee

2. HUNTER : GUN : : WRITER : ?
(*a*) Book (*b*) Pen
(*c*) Poem (*d*) Page

3. WOOL : SHEEP : : SILK : ?
(*a*) Saree (*b*) String
(*c*) Silkworm (*d*) Moth

4. FOOD : STOMACH : : FUEL : ?
(*a*) Engine (*b*) Automobile
(*c*) Rail (*d*) Aeroplane

5. WATER : SAND : : OCEAN : ?
(*a*) Island (*b*) River
(*c*) Desert (*d*) Waves

6. ADULT : BABY : : FLOWER : ?
(*a*) Seed (*b*) Bud
(*c*) Fruit (*d*) Butterfly

7. WRITER : READER : : PRODUCER : ?
(*a*) Creator (*b*) Contractor
(*c*) Creature (*d*) Consumer

8. ENTRANCE : EXIT : : LOYALTY : ?
(*a*) Treachery (*b*) Patriotism
(*c*) Fidelity (*d*) Reward

9. MOTHER : MATERNAL : : FATHER : ?
(*a*) Eternal (*b*) Detrimental
(*c*) Paternal (*d*) Formidable

10. PEARL : NECKLACE : : FLOWER : ?
(*a*) Plant (*b*) Garden
(*c*) Petal (*d*) Bouquet

11. ALPHABET : WORD : : WORD : ?
(*a*) Sound (*b*) Music
(*c*) Sentence (*d*) Dictionary

12. LIFE : DEATH : : HOPE : ?
(*a*) Cry (*b*) Pain
(*c*) Despair (*d*) Sad

13. GOOD : BAD : : VIRTUE : ?
(*a*) Blame (*b*) Sin
(*c*) Despair (*d*) Vice

14. BIRD : FLY : : SNAKE : ?
(*a*) Timid (*b*) Clatter
(*c*) Crawl (*d*) Hole

15. CAT : MOUSE : : BIRD : ?
(*a*) Cage (*b*) Trap
(*c*) Eagle (*d*) Worm

16. STATE : EXILE
(*a*) Police : Arrest
(*b*) Judge : Convict
(*c*) Constitution : Amendment
(*d*) Church : Excommunicate

17. CAPRICIOUSNESS : RELIABILITY
(*a*) Extemporaneous : Predictability
(*b*) Unreliable : Inhuman
(*c*) Tenacious : Practicality
(*d*) Arbitrary : Whimsical

18. LOATH : COERCION
(*a*) Detest : Caressing
(*b*) Irritate : Caressing
(*c*) Irate : Antagonism
(*d*) Reluctant : Persuasion

19. SCALES : FISH
(*a*) Lady : Dress (*b*) Tree : Leaves
(*c*) Bird : Feather (*d*) Skin : Man

20. TREE : SAPLING
(*a*) Hut : Mansion
(*b*) Giant : Dwarf
(*c*) Horse : Foal
(*d*) Ant : Elephant

21. CHALK : BLACKBOARD
(*a*) Door : Handle
(*b*) Table : Chair
(*c*) Ink : Paper
(*d*) Type : Paint

22. PRIMEVAL : MEDIEVAL
(*a*) Dinosaur : Dragon
(*b*) Gorilla : Soldier
(*c*) Evolution : Revelation
(*d*) Thorn : Rose

23. TRILOGY : NOVEL
(*a*) Rice : Husk
(*b*) Milk : Cream
(*c*) Fabric : Weaving
(*d*) Serial : Episode

24. PEDANT : ERUDITION
(*a*) Prude : Modesty
(*b*) Blunt : Politician
(*c*) Diplomats : Tactless
(*d*) Enemy : Friendly

25. FURY : IRE
(*a*) Convulsion : Spasm
(*b*) Amusement : Happiness
(*c*) Joke : Laugh
(*d*) Dispassion : Emotion

26. BaBy : TaTa : : LiLy : ?
(*a*) PooL (*b*) ROse
(*c*) HaNd (*d*) DoWN

27. BCDA : STUR : : KLMJ : ?
(*a*) VWXU (*b*) EFHG
(*c*) SRTU (*d*) QSRP

28. AEI : LPT : : CGK : ?
(*a*) OSV (*b*) RUY
(*c*) TXC (*d*) FJN

29. RUX : TRP : : BEH : ?
(*a*) SQN (*b*) QON
(*c*) QOM (*d*) QNL

30. CART : ART : : FOUR : ?
(*a*) RUN (*b*) TWO
(*c*) QUE (*d*) OUR

31. FIK : JGO : : DFR : ?
(*a*) BIO (*b*) HDV
(*c*) GCU (*d*) FLP

32. LJH : KKI : : CIA : ?
(*a*) BJB (*b*) DHB
(*c*) BJC (*d*) BBJ

33. ACE : HIL : : MOQ : ?
(*a*) SVW (*b*) TUX
(*c*) RTW (*d*) WUS

34. BCDE : WVUT : : QRST : ?
(*a*) EFHG (*b*) JIHG
(*c*) POML (*d*) GEDC

35. PNLJ : IGEC : : USQO : ?
(*a*) HJLN (*b*) LNJH
(*c*) NLJH (*d*) JHNL

36. DIMO : DMIO : : JUVR : ?
(*a*) JVRU (*b*) JRVU
(*c*) JVUR (*d*) JUVR

EXPLANATORY ANSWERS

1. **(*a*) :** Hunger is satiated by food, thirst by water.
2. **(*b*) :** Weapon of a hunter is a gun, weapon of a writer is a pen.
3. **(*c*) :** Wool is obtained from sheep, silk is obtained from silkworm.
4. **(*a*) :** Food is consumed in stomach, fuel is consumed in engine.
5. **(*c*) :** The related words are near opposites.
6. **(*b*) :** The youngone of an adult is a baby and that of a flower is a bud.
7. **(*d*) :** A writer aims to please the readers by his writings, a producer aims to please the consumers by his products.
8. **(*a*) :** The related words are opposites.
9. **(*c*) :** Relations on the mother's side are maternal and on the father's side paternal.

10. *(d)* : Many pearls make a necklace, many flowers make a bouquet.

11. *(c)* : More than one alphabet make a word, more than one word make a sentence.

12. *(c)* : The related words are opposites.

13. *(d)* : The related words are opposites.

14. *(c)* : Birds fly, snakes crawl.

15. *(d)* : Cat chases the mouse, bird chases the worm.

16. *(d)* : Punishment of leaving the State is exile, punishment of leaving the Church is excommunication.

17. *(c)* : The related words are antonyms.

18. *(d)* : Loathing is the result of constant coersion, reluctance is the result of constant persuasion.

19. *(d)* : Covering of the fish is scales, covering of man is skin.

20. *(c)* : Young tree is a sapling, young horse is a foal.

21. *(c)* : Chalk is used to write on blackboard, ink is used to write on paper.

22. *(a)* : The related words represent almost the same time period and answer option represents almost the same sized creatures.

23. *(d)* : Trilogy is section of a novel, episode is a section of a serial.

24. *(a)* : The related words are synonyms.

25. *(b)* : Fury causes ire, amusement causes happiness.

26. *(c)* : In each group the alternate letters are capitals.

27. *(a)* : In each group the first three letters are consecutive and they follow the fourth letter.

ABCD : RSTU : : JKLM : UVWX

28. *(d)* : In each group the letters jump three letters between them, *i.e.*, they are moving to the fourth letter.

AEI : LPT : : CGK : FJN

+4 +4   +4 +4   +4 +4   +4 +4

29. *(c)* : The letters in first set are jumping two letters, *i.e.*, moving three steps forward and in the second they are jumping one letter, *i.e.* moving two steps backward.

RUX : TRP : : BEH : QOM

+3 +3   −2 −2   +3+3   −2 −2

30. *(d)* : The first set of letters drop the first letter to get the second set.

CART : ART : : FOUR : OUR

31. *(b)* : The three letters in first set are moved +4, −2, and +4 steps respectively.

FIK : JGO : : DFR : HDV

+4, −2, +4   +4, −2, +4

32. *(a)* : The letters in the first set are moved −1, +1 and +1 steps respectively.

LJH : KKI : : CIA : BJB

−1, +1, +1   −1, +1, +1

33. *(b)* : The three letters are moved +7, +6 and +7 steps forward respectively.

ACE : HIL : : MOQ : TUX

+7, +6, +7   +7, +6, +7

34. *(b)* : The consecutive letters in the first set are in natural order and in the second set, they are in reverse order.

BCDE : WVUT : : QRST : JIHG

→ ← → ←

35. *(c)* : The letters are moved seven steps backwards.

PNLJ : IGEC : : USQO : NLJH

−7, −7, −7, −7   −7, −7, −7, −7

36. *(c)* : Only the middle letters are reversed to obtain the second set of letters.

DIMO : DMIO : : JUVR : JVUR

7 Number Analogy

In number analogy also, the relationship between the given numbers is detected and then applied to the second part to find the missing numbers. This relationship between the numbers can be based on any of the following patterns : *(i)* numbers can be odd/even/prime numbers; *(ii)* numbers can be multiples of one number; *(iii)* numbers can be squares/cubes of different numbers; *(iv)* some numbers can be added to/ subtracted from/multiplied to/divided into the first number to get the second number; *(v)* the second number can be the sum/product/difference of the digits of first number; and *(vi)* combinations of any mathematical calculations given above can apply to the relationship between the two given numbers.

EXERCISE

Directions : *In the following questions, select the number from the given options which follows the same relationship as shared between the first two numbers.*

1. 1 : 11 : : 2 : ?
(*a*) 20 (*b*) 22
(*c*) 24 (*d*) 44

2. $\frac{1}{7} : \frac{1}{14} :: \frac{1}{9} : ?$
(*a*) $\frac{1}{88}$ (*b*) $\frac{1}{80}$
(*c*) $\frac{1}{81}$ (*d*) $\frac{1}{18}$

3. 0.16 : 0.0016 : : 1.02 : ?
(*a*) 10.20 (*b*) 0.102
(*c*) 0.0102 (*d*) 1.020

4. 663 : 884 : : 221 : ?
(*a*) 332 (*b*) 554
(*c*) 773 (*d*) 442

5. 16 : 0.16 : : ?
(*a*) 2 : 0.02 (*b*) 7 : 0.007
(*c*) 1.3 : 0.13 (*d*) 0.01 : 0.001

6. $3 \frac{1}{3}$: : ?
(*a*) 6 : 12 (*b*) 5 : 2/15
(*c*) 8 : 1/8 (*d*) 9 : 27

7. 65 : 13 : : 180 : ?
(*a*) 93 (*b*) 36
(*c*) 133 (*d*) 102

8. 125 : 27 : : 343 : ?
(*a*) 729 (*b*) 64
(*c*) 216 (*d*) 512

9. 357 : 73 : : ?
(*a*) 429 : 94 (*b*) 201 : 21
(*c*) 138 : 38 (*d*) 93 : 39

10. 731 : 902 : : 655 : ?
(*a*) 646 (*b*) 800
(*c*) 793 (*d*) 556

11. 162 : 9 : : 310 : ?
(*a*) 33 (*b*) 27
(*c*) 16 (*d*) 4

12. 13 : 17 : : 15 : ?
(*a*) 19 (*b*) 11
(*c*) 21 (*d*) 16

13. 225 : 15 : : 256 : ?
(*a*) 26 (*b*) 16
(*c*) 20 (*d*) 28

14. 46 48 : : 54 : ?
(*a*) 59 (*b*) 40
(*c*) 67 (*d*) 62

15. 33 : 36 : : 21 : ?
(*a*) 9 (*b*) 18
(*c*) 25 (*d*) 32

16. 123 : 149 : : 201 : ?
(*a*) 202 (*b*) 404
(*c*) 401 (*d*) 227

17. 7 : 105 : : 5 : ?
(*a*) 97 (*b*) 83
(*c*) 75 (*d*) 61

18. 11 : 101 : : 73 : ?
(*a*) 153 (*b*) 330
(*c*) 543 (*d*) 703

19. 4 : 32 : : 8 : ?
(*a*) 34 (*b*) 68
(*c*) 92 (*d*) 128

20. 94 : 26 : : 62 : ?
(*a*) 16 (*b*) 22
(*c*) 39 (*d*) 48

EXPLANATORY ANSWERS

1. (*b*) : The first number is repeated to obtain the second number.

2. (*d*) : The first fraction is multiplied by half to obtain the second fraction.

$\frac{1}{7} : \frac{1}{14} :: \frac{1}{9} : \frac{1}{18}$ ($\times \frac{1}{2}$, $\times \frac{1}{2}$)

3. (*c*) : The decimals are divided by 100.

0.16 : 0.0016 : : 1.02 : 0.0102 (÷ 100, ÷ 100)

4. (*d*) : The digits at tens and hundreds place is same but the digit at the units place is half the other identical digits.

66 3 : 88 4 : : 22 1 : 44 2

5. (*a*) : Of the two related numbers, the second number is the result of first number divided by 100.

16 : 0.16 : : 2 : 0.02 (÷ 100, ÷ 100)

6. (*c*) : Of the two related numbers, the second number is the part fraction of the first number, *i.e.* 3 is related to one-third $\left(\frac{1}{3}\right)$. Similarly, 8 will be related to one-eighth $\left(\frac{1}{8}\right)$.

7. (*b*) : The first number is divided by 5 to get the second number.

65 : 13 : : 180 : 36 (÷ 5, ÷ 5)

8. (*a*) : The numbers are cubes of different odd numbers.

125 : 27 : : 343 : 729
↓ ↓ ↓ ↓
5^3 3^3 7^3 9^3

9. (*a*) : The central digit of the first number is left out and the corner digits written in reverse order to get the second number.

357 : 73 : : 429 : 94

10. (*a*) : The sum of the digits of both the numbers is same.

731 : 902 → 7 + 3 + 1 = 9 + 0 + 2 *i.e.* 11 = 11
655 : 646 → 6 + 5 + 5 = 6 + 4 + 6 *i.e.* 16 = 16

11. (*d*) : The sum of the digits of the first number is the second number.

162 : 9 : : 310 : 4 (1 + 6 + 2, 3 + 1 + 0)

12. (*a*) : First number plus 4 gives the second number.

13 : 17 : : 15 : 19 (+4, +4)

13. (*b*) : The root of first number is the second number.

225 : 15 : : 256 : 16 ($\sqrt{225}$, $\sqrt{256}$)

14. (*b*) : The product of the digits of first number is multiplied by 2 to get the second number.

46 : 48 : : 54 : 40 ((4 × 6) 2, (5 × 4) 2)

15. (a) : The square of the sum of the digits of the first number is the second number.

33 : 36 :: 21 : 9

$(3 + 3)^2$ $(2 + 1)^2$

16. (c) : Each digit of the first number are squared to get the digits of the second number.

123 : 149 :: 201 : 401

1^2, 2^2, 3^2 2^2, 0^2, 1^2

17. (c) : The first number is multiplied by 15 to get the second number.

7 : 105 :: 5 : 75

× 15 × 15

18. (d) : Zero is inserted in between the digits of the first number to get the second number.

11 : 1<u>0</u>1 :: 73 : 7<u>0</u>3

19. (d) : Double the first number multiplied by the number itself gives the second number.

4 : 32 :: 8 : 128

(4 × 2) 4 (8 × 2) 8

20. (a) : The sum of the digits of the first number multiplied by two gives the second number.

94 : 26 :: 62 : 16

(9 + 4) × 2 (6 + 2) × 2

8 Odd One Out

In this type of classification, four words are given out of which three are almost same in matter or meaning and only one word is different from the common three. One has to find out the word which is different from the rest.

EXERCISE

Directions : *In each of the following questions, three words are alike in some manner. Spot the odd one out.*

1. (*a*) Green (*b*) Red (*c*) Colour (*d*) Orange

2. (*a*) Stable (*b*) Hole (*c*) Canoe (*d*) Sty

3. (*a*) Nose (*b*) Eyes (*c*) Skin (*d*) Teeth

4. (*a*) Venus (*b*) Moon (*c*) Pluto (*d*) Mars

5. (*a*) Happy (*b*) Gloomy (*c*) Lively (*d*) Cheerful

6. (*a*) Cone (*b*) Circle (*c*) Triangle (*d*) Rectangle

7. (*a*) Lead (*b*) Mercury (*c*) Copper (*d*) Iron

8. (*a*) Kite (*b*) Bird (*c*) Radar (*d*) Jet

9. (*a*) Knee (*b*) Shoulder (*c*) Ankle (*d*) Palm

10. (*a*) Deluge (*b*) Calamity (*c*) Catastrophe (*d*) War

11. (*a*) Cub (*b*) Chicken (*c*) Pig (*d*) Pup

12. (*a*) Rabbit (*b*) Crocodile (*c*) Earthworm (*d*) Snail

13. (*a*) Tree (*b*) Leaf (*c*) Bush (*d*) Herb

14. (*a*) Doctor (*b*) Teacher (*c*) Engineer (*d*) Diver

15. (*a*) Trot (*b*) Equestrian (*c*) Derby (*d*) Grunt

16. (*a*) Ornate (*b*) Pleasant (*c*) Decorate (*d*) Beautify

17. (*a*) Polo (*b*) Chess (*c*) Ludo (*d*) Squash

18. (*a*) Tutor (*b*) Principal (*c*) Pupil (*d*) Professor

19. (*a*) Pond (*b*) River (*c*) Stream (*d*) Brook

20. (*a*) Quotation (*b*) Duty (*c*) Tax (*d*) Octroi

21. (*a*) Root (*b*) Tree (*c*) Branch (*d*) Flower

22. (*a*) Mumbai (*b*) Chandigarh (*c*) Lucknow (*d*) Hyderabad

23. (*a*) Immortal (*b*) Eminence (*c*) Perpetual (*d*) Everlasting

24. (*a*) Spinach (*b*) Potato (*c*) Carrot (*d*) Ginger

25. (*a*) Van (*b*) Aeroplane (*c*) Helicopter (*d*) Transport

Directions : *Three of the following four in each question are alike in a certain way and so form a group. Select the group of letters that does not belong to that group.*

26. (*a*) ACE (*b*) LOR (*c*) GIK (*d*) VXZ

27. (*a*) TSR (*b*) LKJ (*c*) PQO (*d*) HGF

28. (*a*) EF LM (*b*) KJ SR (*c*) XW HG (*d*) ED YX

29. (*a*) JOPK (*b*) BOPC (*c*) QOPR (*d*) TOPS

30. (*a*) DfH (*b*) MoQ (*c*) UwY (*d*) lnO

31. (*a*) JKkL (*b*) OPpQ
(*c*) DEEf (*d*) VWwX

32. (*a*) BdfH (*b*) FHJL
(*c*) RTvX (*d*) uVwX

33. (*a*) DFHEG (*b*) TWXUV
(*c*) OQSPR (*d*) JLNKM

34. (*a*) FEUV (*b*) DCXW
(*c*) BAZY (*d*) HGTS

35. (*a*) UTSR (*b*) XYZW
(*c*) ONML (*d*) IHGF

Directions : *In each of the following questions, there are four options. Three numbers, in these options, are alike in certain manner. Only one number does not fit in. Choose the one which is different from the rest.*

36. (*a*) 1948 (*b*) 2401
(*c*) 966 (*d*) 1449

37. (*a*) 182 (*b*) 169
(*c*) 130 (*d*) 158

38. (*a*) 129 (*b*) 130
(*c*) 131 (*d*) 132

39. (*a*) 3215 (*b*) 9309
(*c*) 4721 (*d*) 2850

40. (*a*) 1776 (*b*) 2364
(*c*) 1976 (*d*) 3776

41. (*a*) 64 (*b*) 84
(*c*) 16 (*d*) 36

42. (*a*) 24 (*b*) 90
(*c*) 54 (*d*) 36

43. (*a*) 7658 (*b*) 1234
(*c*) 9876 (*d*) 6543

44. (*a*) 3 (*b*) 9
(*c*) 5 (*d*) 7

45. (*a*) 6450 (*b*) 1776
(*c*) 2392 (*d*) 3815

Directions : *In the following questions select the pair which is different from the other three.*

46. (*a*) Chair - Furniture
(*b*) Shirt - Garment
(*c*) Necklace - Jewellery
(*d*) Bogie - Engine

47. (*a*) Crayon - Paper
(*b*) Pencil - Lead
(*c*) Pen - Ink
(*d*) Brush - Paint

48. (*a*) War - Peace
(*b*) Real - Natural
(*c*) Premiere - First
(*d*) Wrath - Anger

49. (*a*) Finger - Thimble
(*b*) Head - Cap
(*c*) Waist - Tiara
(*d*) Foot - Shoe

50. (*a*) Day - Night
(*b*) Clever - Foolish
(*c*) Clear - Blurred
(*d*) Arrive - Come

Directions : *In the following questions, which of the following pair of letters is different from the other three?*

51. (*a*) FGH - HIJ (*b*) PQR - RST
(*c*) MNO - OPQ (*d*) CDE - DEF

52. (*a*) JuM - jUm (*b*) iLo - Ilo
(*c*) PSa - psA (*d*) ZeX - zEx

53. (*a*) NQT - JMP (*b*) CFI - RUX
(*c*) ADG - FGH (*d*) SVY - ORU

54. (*a*) DXD - XDX (*b*) KUK - UKU
(*c*) FHF - EHE (*d*) RSR - SRS

55. (*a*) AYT - BZU (*b*) FNG - EMF
(*c*) RWO - QVN (*d*) HJD - GIC

56. (*a*) POT - TOP (*b*) TAN - ANT
(*c*) BIN - NIB (*d*) DUB - BUD

57. (*a*) LT - HF (*b*) IN - VA
(*c*) ZE - XM (*d*) RB - SC

58. (*a*) MQU - CGK (*b*) BGL - TYD
(*c*) RWB - FKP (*d*) JOT - DIN

59. (*a*) JLN - KMO (*b*) GIK - HJL
(*c*) DFJ - EGI (*d*) OQS - PRT

60. (*a*) URS - UrS (*b*) JPL - JpL
(*c*) PQM - PqM (*d*) MoN - MON

Directions : *Which of the following pair of numbers is different from the other three pairs?*

61. (*a*) 28, 4 (*b*) 63, 7
(*c*) 56, 8 (*d*) 35, 5

62. (*a*) 3, 11 (*b*) 8, 16
(*c*) 5, 13 (*d*) 14, 24

63. (*a*) 13, 156 (*b*) 12, 144
(*c*) 15, 180 (*d*) 16, 176

64. (*a*) 32, 13 (*b*) 46, 20
(*c*) 51, 24 (*d*) 72, 45

65. (*a*) 5, 25 (*b*) 9, 81
(*c*) 4, 64 (*d*) 6, 36

66. (*a*) 91, 10 (*b*) 57, 12
(*c*) 69, 15 (*d*) 72, 13

67. (*a*) 20, 10 (*b*) 45, 27
(*c*) 15, 12 (*d*) 30, 18

68. (*a*) 7, 3 (*b*) 13, 9
(*c*) 11, 7 (*d*) 17, 8

69. (*a*) 10, 20 (*b*) 40, 50
(*c*) 30, 40 (*d*) 50, 60

70. (*a*) 16, 26 (*b*) 3, 4
(*c*) 26, 24 (*d*) 27, 25

EXPLANATORY ANSWERS

1. ***(c)* :** All others are types of colour.

2. ***(c)* :** Canoe is a boat. Others are resting places of birds/animals.

3. ***(d)* :** All others are sense organs.

4. ***(b)* :** All others are planets.

5. ***(b)* :** All others are expressions of joy.

6. ***(a)* :** All others are geometrical figures.

7. ***(b)* :** All others are solid metals.

8. ***(c)* :** All others are flying objects. Radar traces the objects in sky.

9. ***(d)* :** All others are joints in human body.

10. ***(d)* :** All others are nature-bound. Only war is man-made.

11. ***(c)* :** All others are young ones of animals.

12. ***(a)* :** All others are crawling animals.

13. ***(b)* :** All others are types of vegetation.

14. ***(d)* :** All others are professions, but only Diver's profession comprises of diving under water.

15. ***(d)* :** All other terms are related with activities of a horse.

16. ***(b)* :** All other words have the same meaning.

17. ***(a)* :** All others are indoor games.

18. ***(c)* :** All others are instructors. Pupil learns from the instructor.

19. ***(a)* :** All others are running forms of water.

20. ***(a)* :** All others are forms of taxes.

21. ***(a)* :** All others are parts of tree which are above the ground.

22. ***(b)* :** All are capitals but Chandigarh is the capital of two states.

23. ***(b)* :** All others have the same meaning.

24. ***(a)* :** All others are underground vegetables.

25. ***(d)* :** All others are means of transport.

26. ***(b)* :** The sequence in each group is +2. Only option B has sequence in +3, *i.e.*,

A B C D E (+2 +2) L M N O P Q R (+3 +3)

G H I J K (+2 +2) V W X Y Z (+2 +2)

27. ***(c)* :** The sequence of alphabet in each group is in reverse order. Only option (*c*) has sequence in disturbed order.

28. ***(a)* :** Two consecutive alphabet in each group are in reverse sequence (–1), *i.e.*,

KJ (–1) SR (–1); XW (–1) HG (–1); ED (–1) YX (–1)

Only in option (*a*) the sequence is in natural order (+1), *i.e.*,

E F (+1) L M (+1)

29. ***(d)* :** In each group, letters 'OP' are common. The two corner alphabet are in natural order (+1); *i.e.*,

JOPK (+1); BOPC (+1); QOPR (+1)

Only in option (*d*) they are in reverse order (–1); *i.e.*,

TOPS (–1)

30. ***(d)* :** In other groups, only the alphabet in the centre is of lower case. In this option letter 'L' on the left is also in lower case.

31. ***(c)* :** In other groups, the third letter which is a repeat of the second alphabet is in lower case.

32. ***(d)* :** In each group, the sequence of the alphabet, irrespective of the case, is +2; *i.e.*,

B D f H ; F H J L ; R T v X

+2 +2 +2 ; +2 +2 +2 ; +2 +2 +2

Only in option (*d*) the sequence is in natural order (+1), *i.e.*,

u V w X

+1 +1 +1

33. *(b)* : In each group; the alphabet at positions-first, fourth, second, fifth and third, form a natural sequence.

In option (*b*), the alphabet at positions first, fourth, fifth, second and third, form the natural sequence.

34. *(a)* : In each group, two alphabets in the corner and two alphabets in the centre correspond to their reverse order positioned alphabet.

i.e.,

natural order → A B C D E F G H I J K L M
reverse order → Z Y X W V U T S R Q P O N
natural order → N O P Q R S T U V W X Y Z
reverse order → M L K J I H G F E D C B A

As such—

D corresponds with W and
C corresponds with X.
B corresponds with Y and
A corresponds with Z.
H corresponds with S and
G corresponds with T.

Similarly,

F should correspond with U and
E should correspond with V;
i.e. letters 'UV' should be written as 'VU'

35. *(b)* : In each group, the alphabet are in reverse order.

36. *(a)* : Other numbers are divisible by 7.

37. *(d)* : Other numbers are multiples of 13.

38. *(c)* : 131 is a prime number.

39. *(b)* : In other numbers, no digit is repeated.

40. *(b)* : In other numbers, the last two digits are same.

41. *(b)* : All other numbers are perfect squares.

42. *(a)* : In other numbers, the sum of both the digits is 9.

43. *(a)* : In others, the digits are consecutive in natural or reverse series.

44. *(b)* : All others are prime numbers.

45. *(d)* : All other numbers are divisible by 2.

46. *(d)* : Bogie is a part of train which is a type of conveyance. Chair, Shirt and Necklace are types of furniture, garment and jewellery respectively.

47. *(a)* : The medium used for writing with pencil is lead, with pen it is ink and with brush, it is paint. With crayon it should be wax.

48. *(a)* : The pair of words are opposite. Other pairs are synonyms.

49. *(c)* : Tiara is worn on the head.

50. *(d)* : Other words are opposite to each other.

51. *(d)* : In all other groups, the letters are in natural series and the last letter of first part is the first letter of the second part.

52. *(b)* : In all other groups, only the vowel is in lower case in the first part and in second part the case is reversed.

53. *(c)* : In all other groups, the letters jump two letters in between them.

54. *(c)* : In all other groups, the single letter in first part is repeated in the second and vice versa.

55. *(a)* : In all other groups, the letters in the first part are one step forward than the corresponding letters in the second part.

56. *(b)* : In all other groups, the letters in the first part are written backwards in the second part.

57. *(d)* : All other groups have letters made by straight lines only.

58. *(a)* : In all other groups, the letters jump four letters in between then.

59. *(c)* : In all others groups, the letters jump one letter between them.

60. *(d)* : In all other groups, the second part is same as first except that the middle letter is changed to small letter.

61. ***(b)*** **:** In all other pairs 7 times the second number is the first number. In this option 9 times 7 is the first number.

62. ***(d)*** **:** In all other groups, the difference between the two numbers is 8.

63. ***(d)*** **:** In other groups 12 times, the first number is the second number. In this option 11 times the first number is the second number.

64. ***(a)*** **:** 13 is a prime number.

65. ***(c)*** **:** In all other pairs, the second number is a perfect square of the first.

66. ***(d)*** **:** In all other pairs, the second number is the sum of the digits of the first number.

67. ***(a)*** **:** In all other pairs, the numbers are divisible by 3.

68. ***(d)*** **:** In other groups, the difference between the numbers is 4.

69. ***(a)*** **:** In this option, the second number is double the first number. In other groups the difference between the two numbers is 10.

70. ***(a)*** **:** In other groups, the first digits of the two numbers are same (consider 3 and 4 as 03 and 04).

9 Coding and Decoding

Coding is a secretive language which is used to change the representation of the actual term/word/value. This coded language can be framed by *(i)* moving the letters one or more steps forward or backward; *(ii)* substituting numbers for letters and vice–versa; *(iii)* writing the letters of the given word in reverse order in part or in whole; and *(iv)* replacing the letters in their natural series by the same positioned letters in their reverse series.

There is variety in ways of coding. Coding language is not only for words and numbers but also for hiding a group of words, statements or even sentences. This form of coding pattern may appear to be confusing but after solving only a few questions it is very easy to understand. Questions based on this coding pattern require no moving of steps or straining efforts of calculations, but only quick tallying or comparing ability. The codes can be letters or numbers.

EXERCISE

Directions : *In the following questions select the right option which indicates the correct code for the word or letter given in the question.*

1. If MUSK is coded as 146816, then ZERO will be coded as :

(*a*) 113811 (*b*) 122912
(*c*) 15915 (*d*) 2651815

2. If BAD is coded as 7, HIS as 9, LOW will be coded as :

(*a*) 50 (*b*) 8
(*c*) 23 (*d*) 5

3. In a certain code LIBERATE is written as 56403170, TRIBAL will be written in the same code as :

(*a*) 734615 (*b*) 736415
(*c*) 136475 (*d*) 034615

4. In certain military code, SYSTEM is written as SYSMET, and NEARER as AENRER, what will be the code for FRACTION?

(*a*) CRAFNOIT (*b*) FRCAITNO
(*c*) CARFNOIT (*d*) FRACNOIT

5. If CRUDE is written as BSTED, then MOIST will be coded as :

(*a*) NNJRU (*b*) LNHRS
(*c*) NPJTU (*d*) LPHTS

6. In a certain code ALPACA is written as ACAPLA. How will ANIMAL be written in that code?

(*a*) LAMINA (*b*) ALAMIN
(*c*) LAMNIA (*d*) AAMLIN

7. In a certain code FINGER is written as DGLECP. What will be the code for KIDNEY?

(*a*) IGBLCW (*b*) IGCLBW
(*c*) IBCGLE (*d*) IGBKCV

8. In a certain code QUESTION is written as NXBVQLLQ. How will REPLY be coded?

(*a*) YHMOV (*b*) OBMVI
(*c*) VHSOB (*d*) OHMOV

9. If in a certain code SKEW is coded as PNCY, then what will JXQV will stand for?

(*a*) MUTS (*b*) MUST
(*c*) MTSU (*d*) STUM

10. In a certain code LONDON is written as MPOEPO. What will IVOHSZ mean in the same code?

(*a*) HUNGRY (*b*) HUNDRY
(*c*) GRUNHY (*d*) HONDUS

11. In a certain code language 8514 is a code for HEAD, 3945 for RIDE and 057 for BEG. What will be the code for GRADE?

(*a*) 71345 (*b*) 73415
(*c*) 74135 (*d*) 73145

12. If MOTHERLAND is coded as 9501623748, how will DREAM be coded?
(*a*) 82697 (*b*) 86297
(*c*) 82769 (*d*) 82679

13. If OATH is coded in a certain language as TEYL, then how will WORD be coded?
(*a*) BWRH (*b*) HRWB
(*c*) BSWH (*d*) CSXI

14. If FINANCE is coded as GKQESIL, then how will BANK be coded in the same manner?
(*a*) CBOL (*b*) CDRP
(*c*) CCQO (*d*) CCPN

15. PLANNING is coded in a certain language as UFFHSCSA. How will AUTHORITY be coded in the same language?
(*a*) FOYBTLNND
(*b*) FYOTBNNLT
(*c*) FBOYTLNTN
(*d*) FBOYTNLTN

Directions : *In the following questions study the coded patterns and then select the right option from the given alternatives.*

16. In a certain language, (a) 'go ju mi' stands for 'plenty of money'; (b) pao ju go nei vu' for 'money creates lots of problems'; (c) 'kol vu nei' for 'problems create tension'; and (d) 'sol tun ju haw' for 'still money is needed'. Which of the following words stand for 'money'?
(*a*) nei (*b*) ju
(*c*) haw (*d*) go

17. In a certain language, (a) 'FOR' stands for 'old is gold'; (b) 'ROT' stands for 'gold is pure'; (c) 'ROM' stands for 'gold is costly'. How will 'pure old gold is costly' be written?
(*a*) TFROM (*b*) FOTRM
(*c*) FTORM (*d*) TOMRF

18. In a certain code '415' means 'milk is hot'; '18' means 'hot soup'; and '895' means 'soup is tasty'. What number will indicate the word 'tasty'?
(*a*) 9 (*b*) 8
(*c*) 5 (*d*) 4

19. In a certain code '643' means 'she is beautiful', '593' means 'he is handsome', and '567' means 'handsome meets beautiful'. What number will indicate the word 'meets'?
(*a*) 5 (*b*) 3
(*c*) 7 (*d*) 6

20. In a certain code language, (a) 'dugo hui mul zo' stands for 'work is very hard'; (b) 'hui dugo ba ki' for 'Bingo is very smart'; (c) 'nano mul dugo' for 'cake is hard', and (d) 'mul ki qu' for 'smart and hard'. Which of the following words stand for 'Bingo'?
(*a*) jalu (*b*) dugo
(*c*) ki (*d*) ba

Directions : *Read the given coded information and choose the correct answer from the given options.*

21. If 'water' is called 'blue', 'blue' is called 'red', 'red' is called 'white', 'white' is called 'sky', 'sky' is called 'rain', 'rain' is called 'green', 'green' is called 'air' and 'air' is called 'table', which of the following is the colour of milk?
(*a*) white (*b*) rain
(*c*) sky (*d*) green

22. If 'light' is called 'dark', 'dark' is called 'green', 'green' is called 'blue', 'blue' is called 'red', 'red' is called 'white' and 'white' is called 'yellow', what is the colour of blood?
(*a*) red (*b*) dark
(*c*) white (*d*) yellow

23. If 'sky' is called 'sea', 'sea' is called 'water', 'water' is called 'air', 'air' is called 'cloud' and 'cloud' is called 'river', then what do we drink when thirsty?
(*a*) sky (*b*) air
(*c*) water (*d*) sea

24. If 'yellow' means 'red', 'white' means 'green', 'red' means 'orange', 'blue' means 'white' and 'green' means 'blue', then the colour of sky is :
(*a*) white (*b*) green
(*c*) blue (*d*) yellow

25. If 'land' is called 'sky', 'sky' is called 'air', 'air' is called 'water', 'water' is called 'sand' and 'sand' is called 'solid', where do fishes swim?
(*a*) air (*b*) sky
(*c*) water (*d*) sand

EXPLANATORY ANSWERS

1. *(b)* **:** The coded number signifies the position of the alphabet in its reverse order of the alphabetical series (ZYXW...)

M U S K → MUSK
↓ ↓ ↓ ↓
14th 6th 8th 16th → 146816

Similarly,

Z E R O → ZERO
↓ ↓ ↓ ↓
1st 22nd 9th 12th → 122912

2. *(d)* **:** The coded number is the sum of number digits signifying the position of the alphabet in the natural order.

B A D
↓ ↓ ↓
2nd 1st 4th *i.e.,* 2 + 1 + 4 = 7

Similarly,

H I S
↓ ↓ ↓
8th 9th 19th *i.e.,* 8 + 9 + 19 = 36
further, 3 + 6 = 9

Also,

L O W
↓ ↓ ↓
12th 15th 23rd *i.e.,* 12 + 15 + 23 = 50
further, 5 + 0 = 0

3. *(b)* **:** The letters of the word TRIBAL are picked from LIBERATE. So will be the coded numbers.

L I B E R A T E → given word
5 6 4 0 3 1 7 0 → codes

Similarly,

T R I B A L → word to be coded
7 3 6 4 1 5 → answer codes

4. *(c)* **:** The word is divided into two equal parts and the letters of each part are written in reverse order.

SYS TEM SYS MET NEA RER AEN RER

Similarly,

FRAC TION CARF NOIT

5. *(d)* **:** The code is formed by moving the letters one step backwards and one step forward alternately.

CRUDE BSTED
−1
+1
−1
+1
−1

Similarly,

MOIST LPHTS
−1
+1
−1
+1
−1

6. *(a)* **:** The letters of the word are written backwards.

ALPACA ACAPLA

Similarly,

ANIMAL LAMINA

7. *(a)* **:** The word is coded by moving the letters two steps backwards.

FINGER DGLECP
−2
−2
−2
−2
−2
−2

Similarly,

KIDNEY IGBLCW
−2
−2
−2
−2
−2
−2

8. ***(d)*** **:** The letters of the word are coded by moving three steps backward and three steps forward alternately.

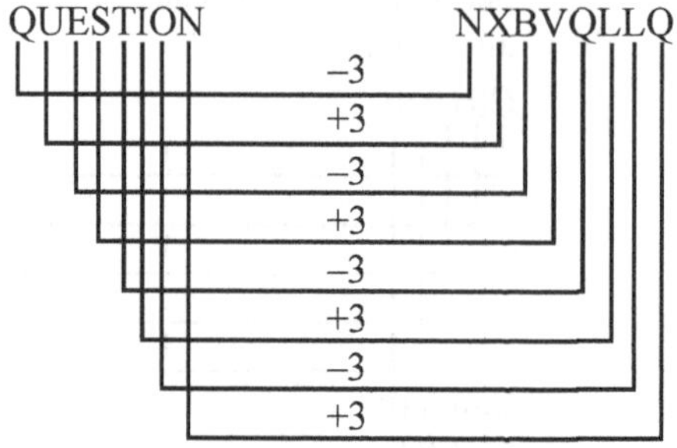

Similarly,

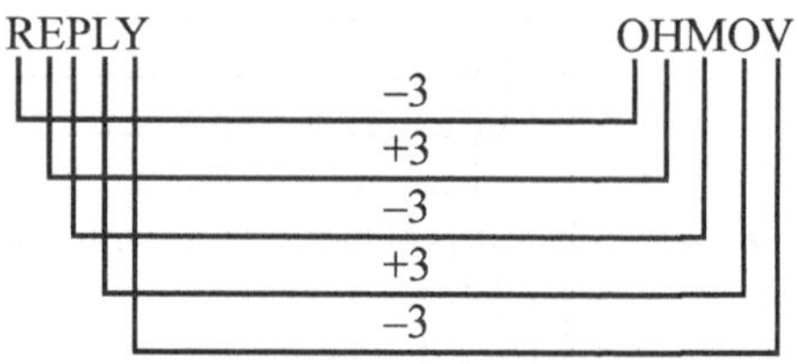

9. ***(b)*** **:** The letters are decoded by moving the letters +3, –3, +2 and –2 steps respectively.

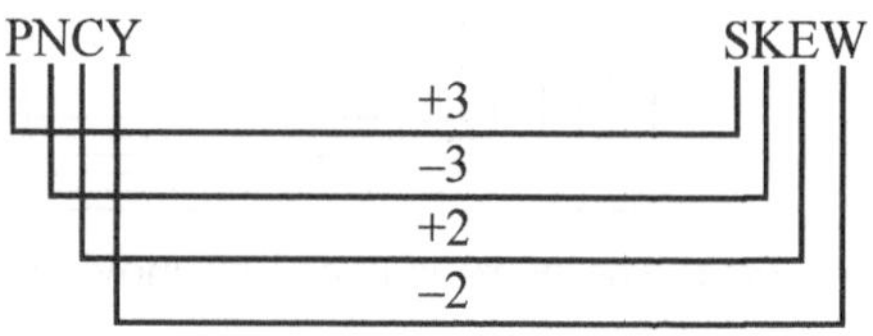

Similarly,

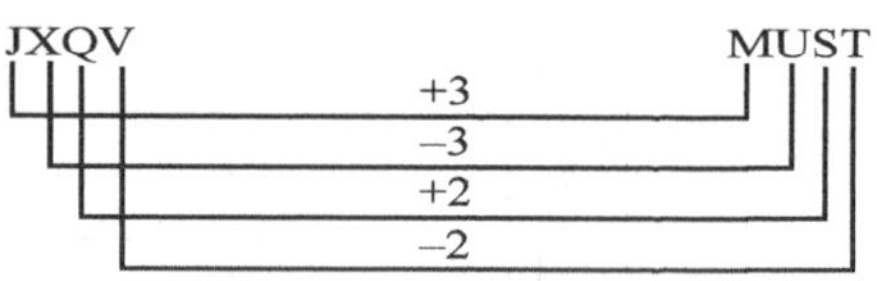

10. ***(a)*** **:** The letters of the coded word are moved one step backward.

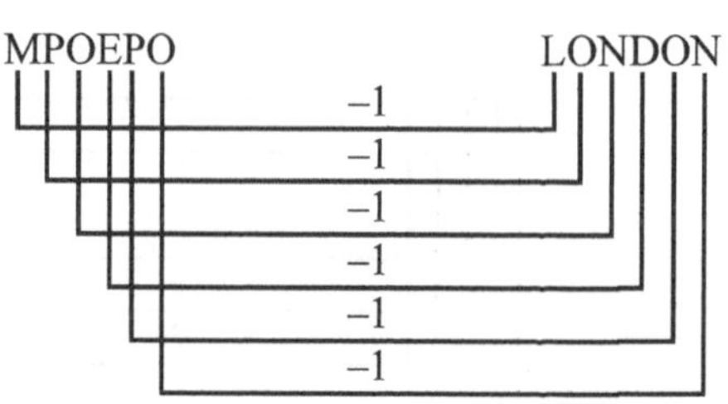

Similarly,

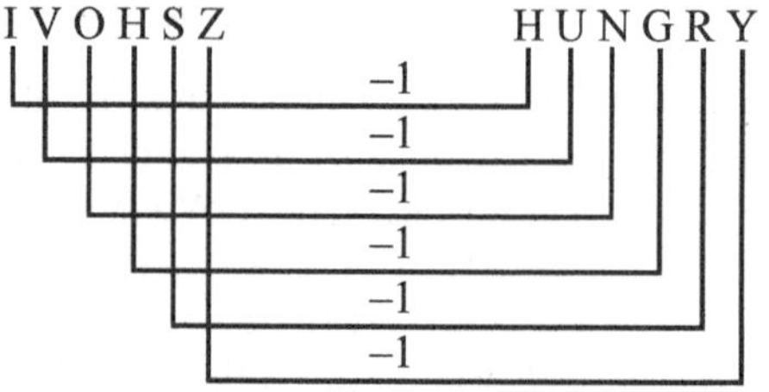

11. ***(d)*** **:** The word GRADE is framed by letters in the given words. So, in order to find the code for GRADE select the respective number codes.

H E A D   R I D E   B E G → letters
8 5 1 4   3 9 4 5   0 5 7 → codes

So,

G R A D E →letters
7 3 1 4 5 →answer codes

12. ***(d)*** **:** The letters of the word are coded by numbers. So to find the code for DREAM select the respective numbers.

M O T H E R L A N D → letters
9 5 0 1 6 2 3 7 4 8 → codes

So, D R E A M → letters
8 2 6 7 9 → answer codes

13. ***(c)*** **:** The letters are coded by moving five and four steps forward alternately.

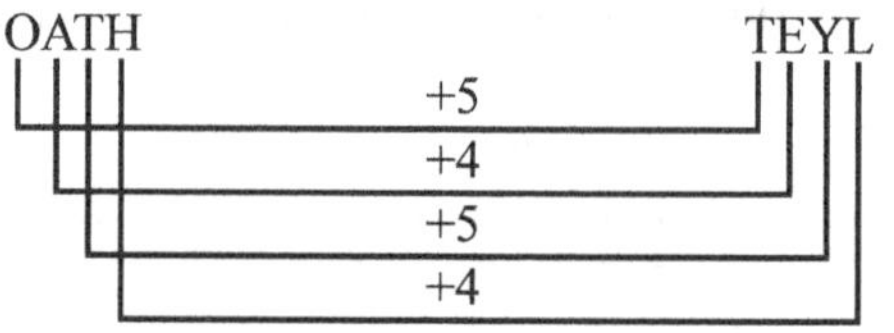

Similarly,

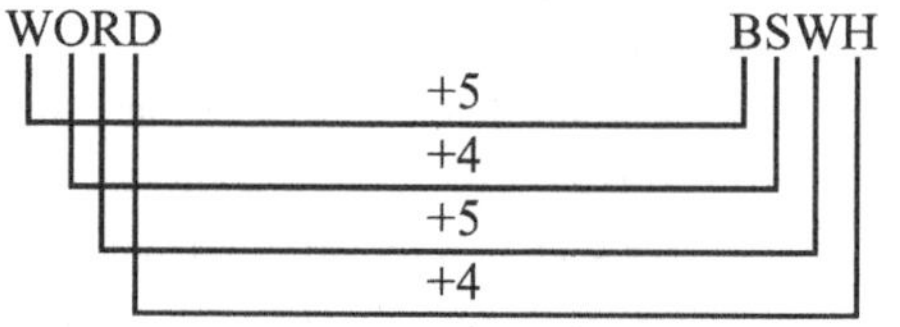

14. ***(c)*** **:** The letters of the word are coded by moving one step ahead and increasing the difference by one.

FINANCE GKQESIL

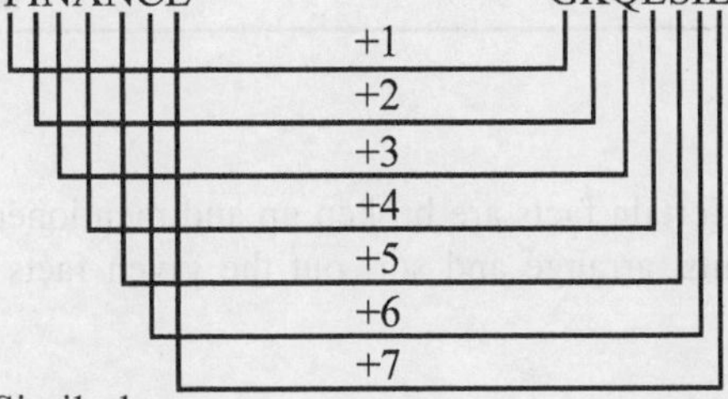

Similarly,

BANK CCQO

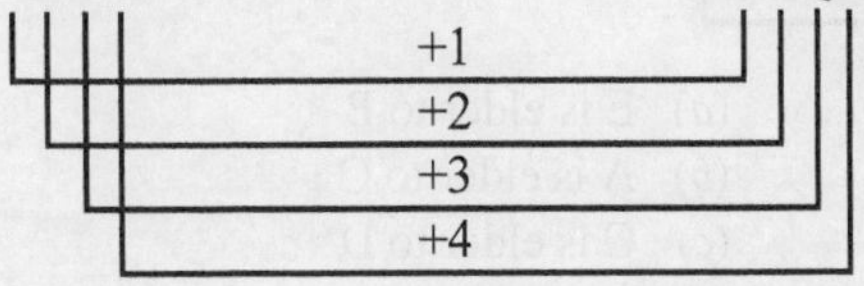

15. (a) : The letters of the word are coded by moving five steps forward and six steps backward alternately.

PLANNING UFFHSCSA

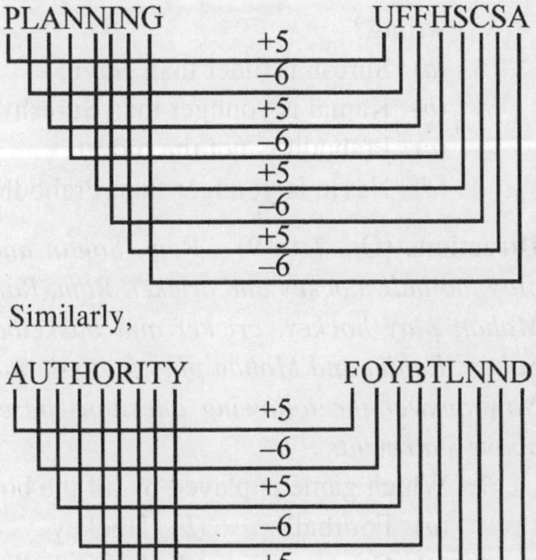

Similarly,

AUTHORITY FOYBTLNND

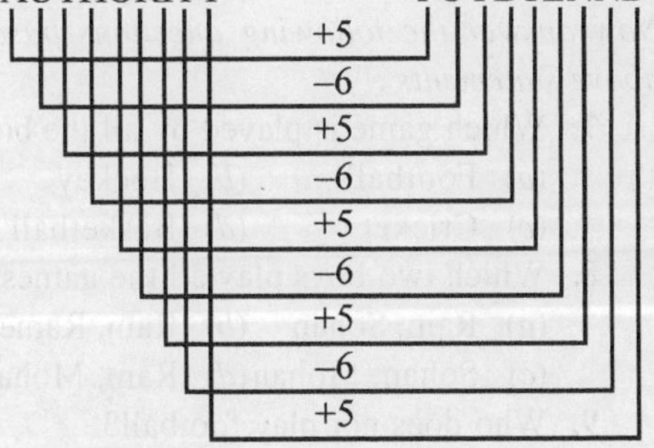

16. (b) :

	Code	*Sentence*
1.	go *ju* mi	plenty of *money*
2.	pao *ju* go nei vu	*money* creates lots of problems
3.	kol vu nei	problems create tension
4.	sol tun *ju* haw	still *money* is needed

In 1st, 2nd and 4th codes and their sentences the word 'ju' is repeated and so is 'money'.

17. (a) :

	Code	*Sentence*
1.	FOR	old is gold

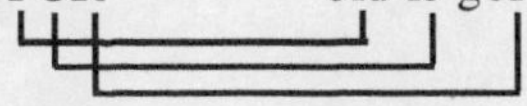

2.	ROT	gold is pure

3.	ROM	gold is costly

Therefore,

F	stands	for	old
O	stands	for	is
R	stands	for	gold
T	stands	for	pure
M	stands	for	costly

So, 'pure old gold is costly' will be written as 'TFROM'.

18. (a) :

	Code	*Sentence*
1.	415	milk is hot
2.	18	hot soup
3.	895	soup is *tasty*

From 3rd code and its sentence neither number '9' is repeated nor the word 'tasty'.

19. (c) :

	Code	*Sentence*
1.	643	she is beautiful
2.	593	he is handsome
3.	567	handsome *meets* beautiful

From 3rd code and its sentence, neither number '7' nor the word 'meets' is repeated.

20. (d) :

	Code	*Sentence*
1.	*dugo hui* mul zo	work *is very* hard
2.	*hui dugo* **ba** *ki*	**Bingo** *is very smart*
3.	nano mul *dugo*	cake is *hard*
4.	mul *ki* qu	*smart* and hard

From 2nd code and its sentence, neither 'ba' nor 'Bingo' is repeated.
(Words repeated are in italics)

21. (c) : Colour of milk is 'white' and 'white' is called 'sky'.

22. (c) : Colour of blood is 'red' and 'red' is called 'white'.

23. (b) : We drink 'water' when we are thirsty and 'water' is called 'air'.

24. (a) : Colour of sky is 'blue' and 'blue' means 'white'.

25. (d) : Fishes swim in 'water' and 'water' is called 'sand'.

10 Statement Analysis

In these type of questions, a few statements are given. Certain facts are broken up and mentioned in these statements. What is required is to analyse the statements, arrange and sort out the given facts and then answer the questions related to the given statements.

EXERCISE

1. Among five friends, A is heavier than B; C is lighter than D; B is lighter than D but heavier than E. Who among them is the heaviest?

(*a*) B (*b*) C
(*c*) A (*d*) Can't say

2. Pune is bigger than Jhansi, Sitapur is bigger than Chittor. Raigarh is not as big as Jhansi, but is bigger than Sitapur. Chittor is not as big as Sitapur. Which is the smallest?

(*a*) Jhansi (*b*) Pune
(*c*) Chittor (*d*) Sitapur

3. Ajay works more than Ram. Alok works as much as Raju. Pankaj works less than Alok. Ram works more than Alok. Who works the most of all?

(*a*) Ajay (*b*) Ram
(*c*) Alok (*d*) Raju

4. Among five friends P, Q, R, S and T, who is the youngest? To arrive at the answer which of the following information given in the statements (A) and (B) is sufficient?

(A) R is younger than P and T.
(B) S is younger than Q.

(*a*) Only A alone is sufficient
(*b*) Either A or B is sufficient
(*c*) Both A and B together are needed
(*d*) Both A and B together are not sufficient

5. A is elder to B while C and D are elder to E who lies between A and B. If C be elder to B, which one of the following statements is necessarily true?

(*a*) E is elder to B
(*b*) A is elder to C
(*c*) C is elder to D
(*d*) D is elder to C

6. Suresh is as much older than Kamal as he is younger than Prabodh. Navin is as old as Kamal. Which of the following statements is wrong?

(*a*) Suresh is older than Navin
(*b*) Kamal is younger than Suresh
(*c*) Prabodh is not the oldest
(*d*) Navin is younger than Prabodh

Directions (Qs. 7 to 9) : *Ram, Sohan and Mohan play football, hockey and cricket. Ram, Ramesh and Mohan play hockey, cricket and basketball. Ram, Sohan, Rahim and Mohan play football and cricket. Now answer the following questions based on the above statements :*

7. Which game is played by all the boys?

(*a*) Football (*b*) Hockey
(*c*) Cricket (*d*) Basketball

8. Which two boys play all the games?

(*a*) Ram, Sohan (*b*) Ram, Ramesh
(*c*) Sohan, Mohan (*d*) Ram, Mohan

9. Who does not play football?

(*a*) Ramesh (*b*) Sohan
(*c*) Rahim (*d*) Mohan

Directions (Qs. 10 to 12) : *Read the following directions and answer the questions given below :*

There are five persons in a group. Out of these two are men. Only three persons know swimming, of which one is a man. There is a couple, of which the husband knows swimming. A is the younger sister of D and B is the husband of E. C is a swimming champion.

10. Who is the other man in the group?

(*a*) C (*b*) B
(*c*) A (*d*) D

11. The two women who know how to swim are:

(*a*) A and C (*b*) C and D
(*c*) D and E (*d*) A and E

12. The two persons who do not know how to swim are :

(*a*) B and D (*b*) D and E
(*c*) A and E (*d*) A and D

Directions (Qs. 13 to 15) : *Read the following statements and answer the questions given below :*

Rajat, Sushil and Nagesh play football, hockey and cricket. Rajat, Ramu and Nagesh play hockey, cricket and basketball. Rajat, Sushil, Mayank and Nagesh play football and cricket.

13. Which game is played by all the boys?

(*a*) Hockey (*b*) Basketball
(*c*) Football (*d*) Cricket

14. Who does not play football?

(*a*) Rajat (*b*) Nagesh
(*c*) Sushil (*d*) Ramu

15. Which of the following two boys play all the games?

(*a*) Nagesh, Rajat
(*b*) Mayank, Ramu
(*c*) Ramu, Nagesh
(*d*) Sushil, Mayank

Directions (Qs. 16 to 20) : *Read the following information and answer the questions given below:*

(*i*) P, Q, R, S, T and U are six members in a family in which there are two married couples.
(*ii*) T a teacher is married to the doctor who is mother of R and U.
(*iii*) Q the lawyer is married to P.
(*iv*) P has one son and one grandson.
(*v*) Of the two married ladies one is a housewife.
(*vi*) There is also one student and one male engineer in the family.

16. Who among the following is the housewife?

(*a*) Q (*b*) P
(*c*) S (*d*) T

17. Which of the following represents the group of females in the family?

(*a*) QTR (*b*) PSR
(*c*) PSU (*d*) Data inadequate

18. Which of the following is true about the granddaughter in the family?

(*a*) She is a student
(*b*) She is an engineer
(*c*) She is a lawyer
(*d*) Data Inadequate

19. How R is related to U?

(*a*) Brother
(*b*) Sister
(*c*) Brother or Sister
(*d*) Data inadequate

20. How is P related to R?

(*a*) Grandfather (*b*) Mother
(*c*) Sister (*d*) Grandmother

EXPLANATORY ANSWERS

1. (*d*) **:** The five friends in descending order of weight are : A/D, B/C, E or A/D, B, C/E. Either A or D is the heaviest.

2. (*c*) **:** The order of cities in descending order of size is : Pune, Jhansi, Raigarh, Sitapur, Chittor.

3. (*a*) **:** On the basis of doing work, the descending order will be : Ajay, Ram, Alok/Raju, Pankaj.

4. (*d*) **:** Statements are not inter-related.

5. (*a*) **:** The order in descending seniority will be : A/C/D, E, B.

6. (*c*) **:** On the basis of age the descending order will be : Prabodh, Suresh, Kamal/Navin.

Chart for Answers 7 to 9

Boy	*Games Played*
Ram	Football, Hocky, Cricket, Basketball
Sohan	Football, Hockey, Cricket
Mohan	Football, Hockey, Cricket, Basketball
Ramesh	Hockey, Cricket, Basketball
Rahim	Football, Cricket.

7. *(c)* **8.** *(d)* **9.** *(a)*

For Answers 10 to 12 the information chart will be :

A. Woman ((younger sister of D); knows swimming.

B. Man (husband of E); knows swimming

C. Woman; Swimming champion

D. Man (brother of A)

E. Woman (wife of B)

From the couple B & E, B (husband) knows swimming. C is a swimming champion. Three persons know how to swim of which only B is a man. So, the two women who know how to swim are C and A (the younger sister of D). There are two men in the group of five. One is B and the other will be D.

10. *(d)* **11.** *(a)* **12.** *(b)*

Chart for Answers 13 to 15

Boy	*Games Played*
Rajat	— Football, Hockey, Cricket, Basketball
Sushil	— Football, Hockey, Cricket, Basketball
Nagesh	— Football, Hockey, Cricket, Basketball
Ramu	— Hockey, Cricket, Basketball
Mayank	— Football, Cricket

13. *(d)* **14.** *(d)* **15.** *(a)*

Chart for Answers 16 to 20

P (female/housewife) — Q (male/lawyer) *Grandparents*

T (male/teacher) — S (female/doctor) *Parents*

R, U Children

(of R and U, one is a male engineer and one is a student)

16. *(b)* **:** One married lady S who is mother of R and U is a doctor. Q the lawyer is married to P. Of the two married ladies one is a house-wife. As Q is a lawyer the other married lady who is a housewife should be P.

17. *(d)* **:** Sex of R and U is not given.

18. *(a)* **:** P has one son T and one grandson either R or U one of whom is an engineer. So, the granddaughter is a student.

19. *(c)* **:** Sex of R and U is not given, but as both are children of S and one is a male engineer, the relationship between the two is of brother and sister.

20. *(d)*

11 Place Arrangement

Place arrangement generally refers to the positioning of persons or objects in a manner indicated by set of information given. One has to understand the order of placement and then attempt questions following the given information.

EXERCISE

Directions : *In the following questions, understand the arrangement pattern and then select the right answer from the given options :*

1. Five boys are sitting in a row. Raghu is not adjacent to Shyam or Amit. Ajay is not adjacent to Shyam. Raghu is adjacent to Mayank. If Mayank is at the middle in the row, then Ajay is adjacent to whom out of the following?

(*a*) Amit (*b*) Raghu
(*c*) Mayank (*d*) Shyam

2. Mini is to the right of Rajni but to the left of Ananta. Saya is to the right of Mini but to the left of Jaya. Who is on the extreme left if all the girls are facing North?

(*a*) Jaya (*b*) Mini
(*c*) Rajni (*d*) Saya

3. O, P, Q, R, S and T are standing on a bench according to their height. P is taller than O but shorter than S. Only S is taller than T. R is shorter than P but taller than Q. Who is the shortest?

(*a*) O (*b*) Q
(*c*) P (*d*) Cannot be said

4. Five personalities are living in a multistoried building. Mr. Effortless lives in a flat above Mr. Active, Mr. Charge lives in a flat below Mr. Diligent, Mr. Active lives in a flat above Mr. Diligent and Mr. Behaved lives in a flat below Mr. Charge. Who lives in the topmost flat?

(*a*) Mr. Charge (*b*) Mr. Diligent
(*c*) Mr. Effortless (*d*) Mr. Behaved

5. Six friends are sitting in a circle and playing cards. Kenny is to the left of Danny. Michael is in-between Bob and John. Roger is in between Kenny and Bob. Who is sitting to the right of Michael?

(*a*) Danny (*b*) John
(*c*) Kenny (*d*) Bob

6. Four girls A, B, C and D are sitting in a circle. B and C are facing each other. Which of the following is definitely true?

(*a*) A is to the left of C
(*b*) D is to the left of C
(*c*) A and D are facing each other
(*d*) A is not between B and C

7. Brijesh, Jayesh, Amar and Praveer are playing a game of cards. Amar is to the right of Jayesh who is to the right of Brijesh. Who is to the right of Amar?

(*a*) Brijesh
(*b*) Praveer
(*c*) Brijesh or Praveer
(*d*) Jayesh

8. In a pile of 10 books there are 3 of History, 3 of Hindi, 2 of Maths, and 2 of English. Taking from above there is an English book between a History and Maths book, a History book between a Maths and an English book, a Hindi book between an English and a Maths book, a Maths book between two Hindi books, and two Hindi books between a Maths and a History book. Book of which subject is at the sixth position from the top?

(*a*) English (*b*) Hindi
(*c*) History (*d*) Maths

9. Five persons A, B, C, D and E are sitting in a row facing you such that D is on the left of C and B is on the right of E. A is on the right of C and B is on the left of D. If E occupies a corner position, then who is sitting in the centre?
(*a*) A (*b*) B
(*c*) C (*d*) D

10. Six friends A, B, C, D, E and F are standing in a circle. B is between F and C; A is between E and D; F is to the left of D. Who is between A and F?
(*a*) C (*b*) B
(*c*) D (*d*) E

EXPLANATORY ANSWERS

1. ***(b)*** **:** The order of sitting is :
Amit, Shyam, Mayank, Ajay, Raghu
or
Ajay, Raghu, Mayank, Amit, Shyam

2. ***(c)*** **:** The order in which the girls are positioned is :
Rajni, Mini, Ananta, Saya, Jaya
or
Saya, Jaya, Ananta
or
Saya, Ananta, Jaya

3. ***(d)*** **:** In descending order of height, the standing positions are :

S		S
T		T
P	*or*	P
R		R
O		Q
Q		O

Either O or Q is the shortest. The information given is not enough to clarify the answer.

4. ***(c)*** **:** The personalities living in flats in multi-storied building are in order given below :
Mr. Effortless
Mr. Active
Mr. Diligent
Mr. Charge
Mr. Behaved

5. ***(d)*** **:** The order in which the friends are sitting is :

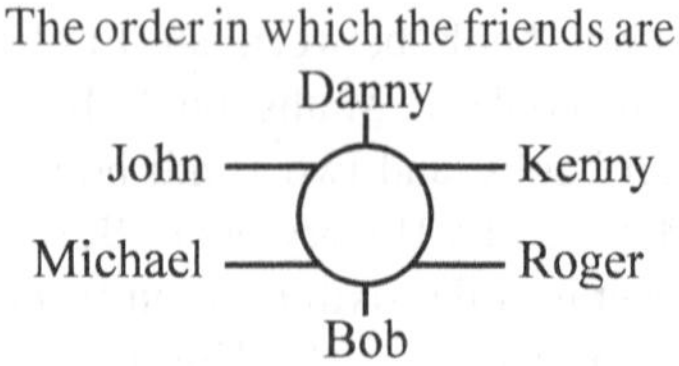

6. ***(c)*** **:** The sitting positions are :

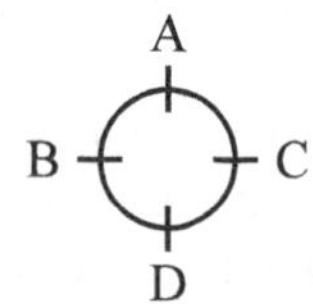

or

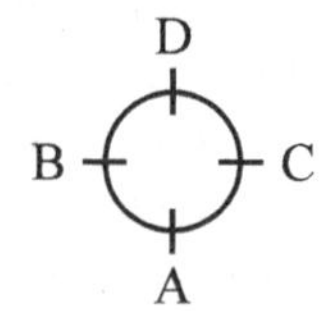

7. ***(b)*** **:** The order from left to light is :
Brijesh, Jayesh, Amar, Praveer

8. ***(b)*** **:** The pile of books is in the order :

1st — History
English
Maths
History
English
6th — Hindi
Maths
Hindi
Hind
10th — History

9. ***(d)*** **:** Sitting order while facing us is :
A, C, D, B, E

10. ***(c)*** **:** The pattern of standing is :

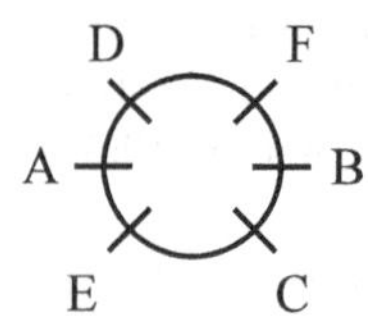

12 Direction Sense

In these type of tests, the directions in questions needs to be perceived. Such questions are based on the direction chart.

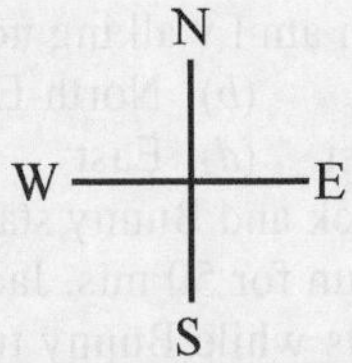

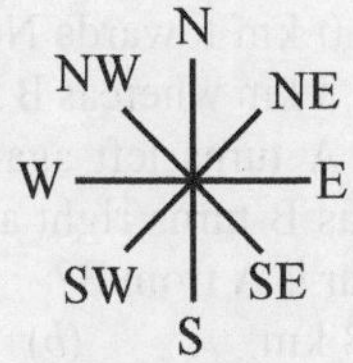

N = North S = South E = East W = West

The sense of the different directions are guided by the left and right turns or angular turns.

EXERCISE

Directions : *In the following questions, select the right answer from the given options to depict the correct direction/distance.*

1. Kittu walks towards East and then towards South. After walking some distance he turns towards West and then turns to his left. In which direction is he walking now?

(*a*) North (*b*) South
(*c*) East (*d*) West

2. A person is driving towards West. What sequence of directions should he follow so that he is driving towards South?

(*a*) left, right, right
(*b*) right, right, left
(*c*) left, left, left
(*d*) right, right, right

3. Richa drives 8 km to the South, turns left and drives 5 km. Again, she turns left and drives 8 km. How far is she from her starting point?

(*a*) 3 km (*b*) 5 km
(*c*) 8 km (*d*) 13 km

4. Dingi runs 40 km towards North then turns right and runs 50 km. He turns right and runs 30 km, and once again turns right and runs 50 km. How far is he from his starting point?

(*a*) 90 km (*b*) 50 km
(*c*) 10 km (*d*) 5 km

5. If North is called North-West, North-West is called West, West is called South-West and so on. What will South-East be called?

(*a*) East (*b*) West
(*c*) North-East (*d*) South-East

6. A man travels 100 km towards South. From there he turns right and travels 100 km and again turns right to travel 50 km. Which direction is he in from his starting point?

(*a*) North (*b*) North-East
(*c*) East (*d*) South-West

7. A train runs 120 km in West direction, 30 km in South direction and then 80 km in east direction before reaching the station. In which direction is the station from the train's starting point?

(*a*) South-West (*b*) North-West
(*c*) South-East (*d*) South

8. Facing the West direction, Priya jogs for 20 m, turns left and goes further 40 m. She turns left again and jogs for 20 m. Then she turns right to go 20 m to reach the park. How far is the park from her starting point and in which direction?

(*a*) 20 m South (*b*) 40 m West
(*c*) 60 m South (*d*) 100 m East

9. If all the directions are rotated, *i.e.,* if North is changed to West and East to North and so on, then what will come in place of North-West?

(*a*) South-West (*b*) North-East
(*c*) East-North (*d*) East-West

10. A and B start together from one point. They walk 10 km towards North. A turns left and covers 5 km whereas B turns right and covers 3 km. A turns left again and covers 15 km whereas B turns right and covers his 15 km. How far is A from B?

(*a*) 18 km (*b*) 10 km
(*c*) 5 km (*d*) 8 km

11. Tarun is walking towards East. What direction he should not follow if he should walk towards North?

(*a*) right, right, left, right, right
(*b*) right, right, left, left, left
(*c*) right, right, right
(*d*) right, left, right, left

12. Sony and Moni start walking from a point. Sony walks in West direction and Moni in South direction. After covering 20 km, Soni turns left and walks 15 km. Moni walks 10 km, turns left and walks 5 km. Soni, then turns left again and walks 25 km, whereas Moni turns right and walks 5 km. How far are Sony and Moni from each other?

(*a*) 5 km
(*b*) They are back at the starting point
(*c*) They are at same place at the finishing point
(*d*) Data is insufficient

13. I was walking in South-East direction. After a while I turned 90° to the right and walked ahead. Later I turned 45° to the right. In which direction am I walking now?

(*a*) North (*b*) North-East
(*c*) South-West (*d*) East

14. Two friends Jack and Bunny start a race, and together they run for 50 mts. Jack turns right and runs 60 mts while Bunny turns left and runs 40 mts. Then Jack turns left and runs 50 mts while Bunny turns right and runs 50 mts. How far are the two friends now from each other?

(*a*) 60 mts (*b*) 100 mts
(*c*) 20 mts (*d*) 150 mts

15. A policeman left his police post and proceeded south 4 km, after hearing a loud sound from point A. On reaching the place he heard another sound and proceeded 4 km to his left to the point B, only to find that the sound was coming from left of B. From B he proceeded left to reach that place 4 km away. In which direction he has to go to reach his police post?

(*a*) North (*b*) South
(*c*) East (*d*) West

EXPLANATORY ANSWERS

1. (*b*) :

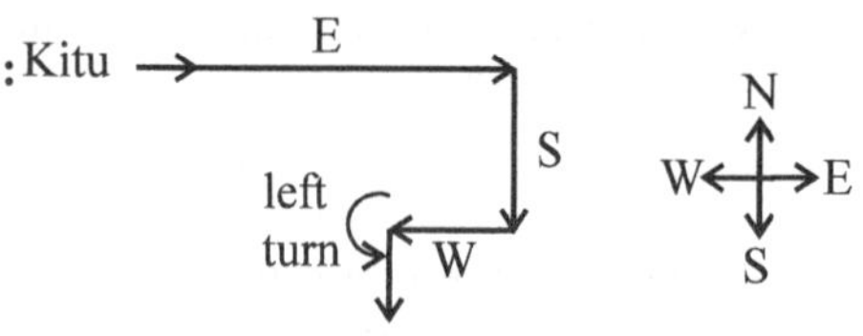

2. (*d*) :

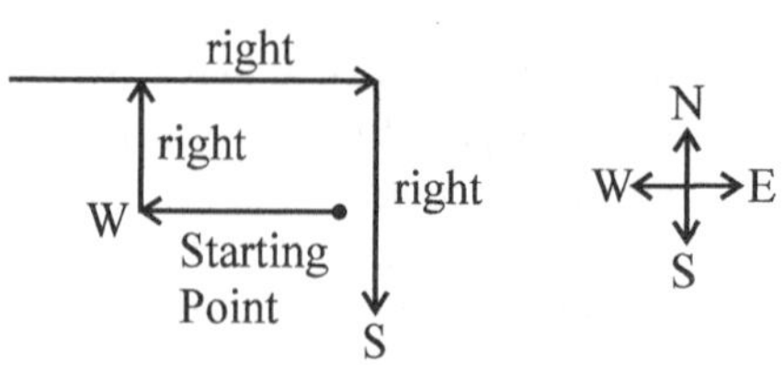

3. (*b*) :

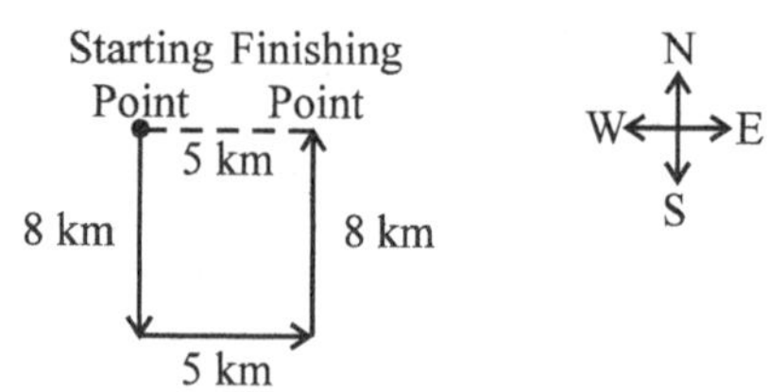

4. (*c*) :

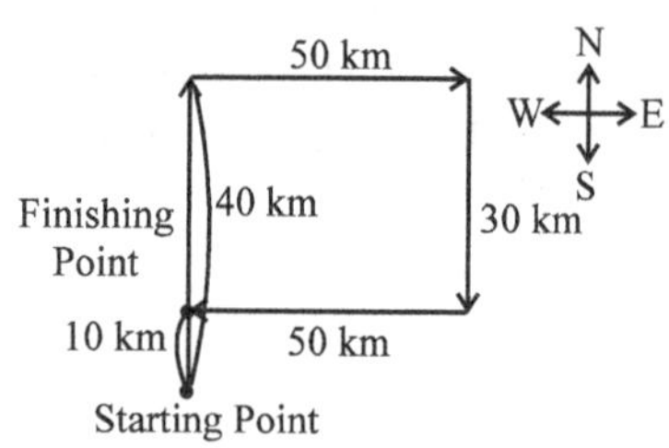

5. (a) : **Original Directions**

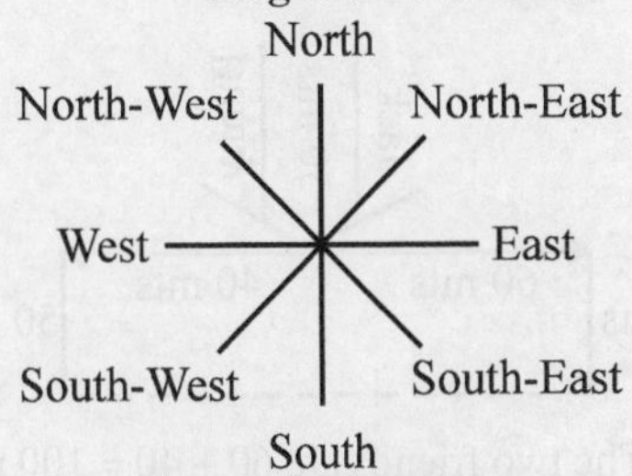

Changed Directions

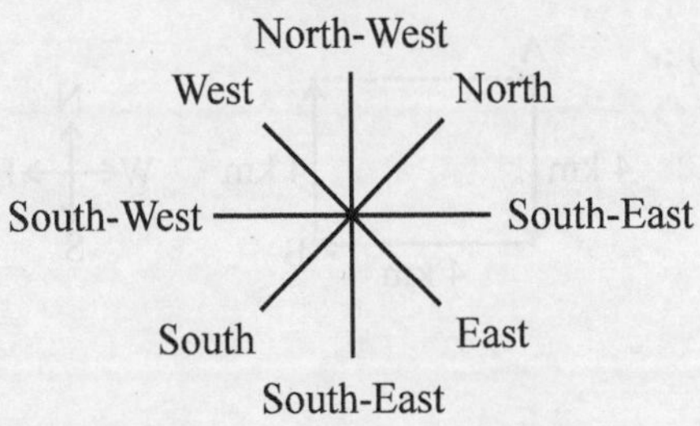

6. (d) :

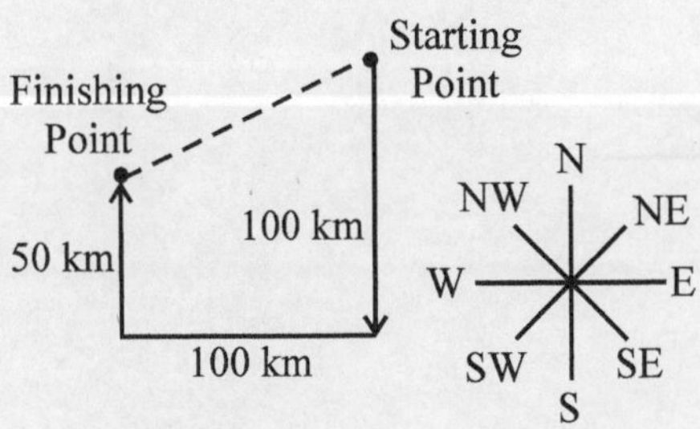

7. (a) :

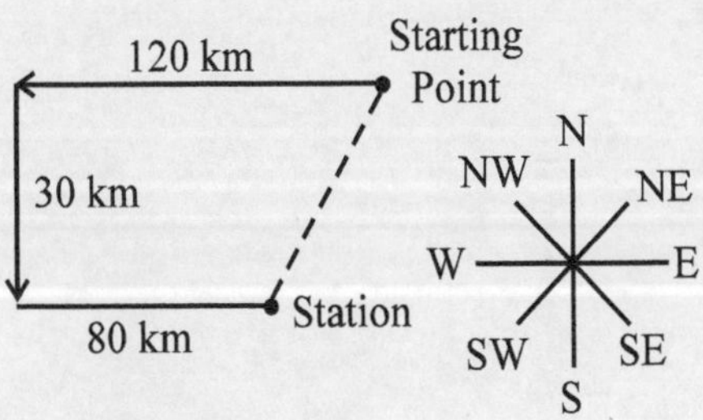

8. (c) : (40 + 20) = 60 metres South

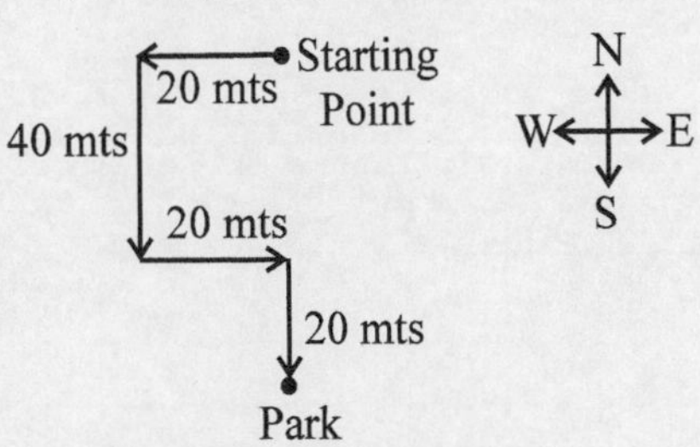

9. (a) : **Original Directions**

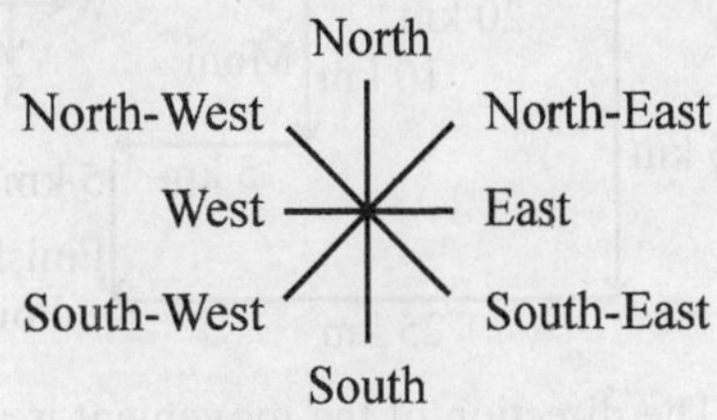

Changed Directions

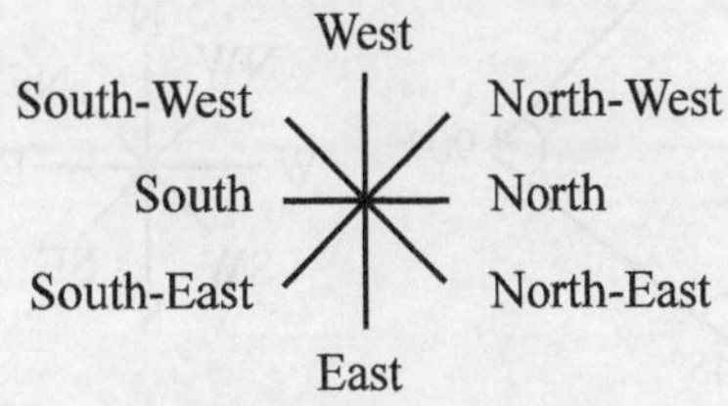

10. (d) :

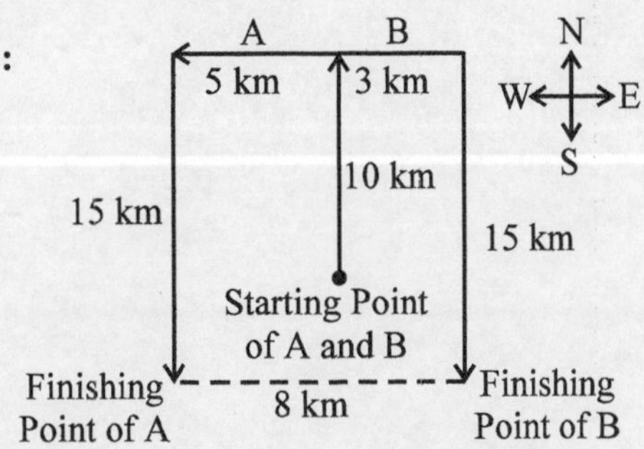

11. (d) :

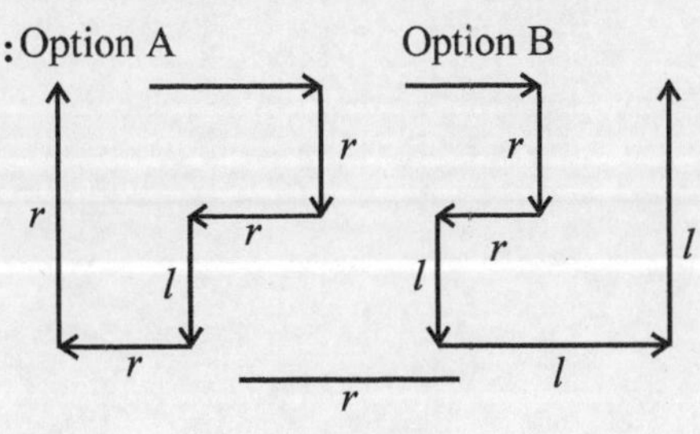

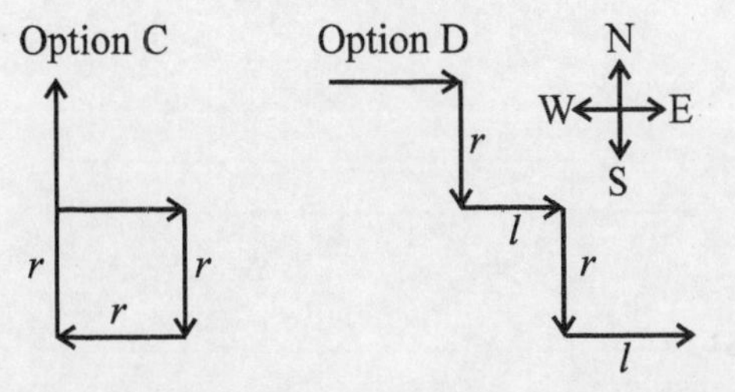

12. *(c)* **:**

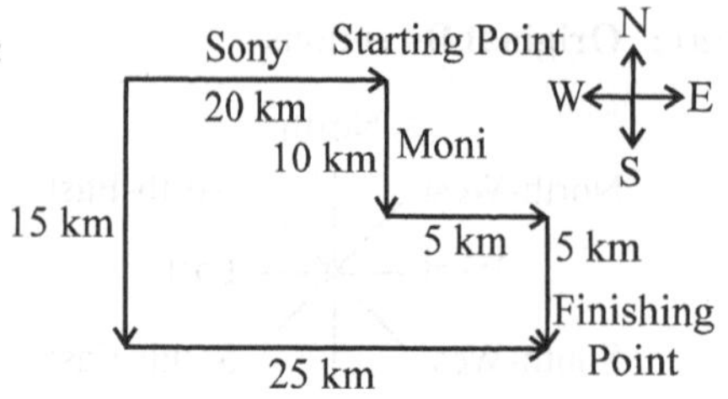

13. *(a)* **:** The direction of the movement is :

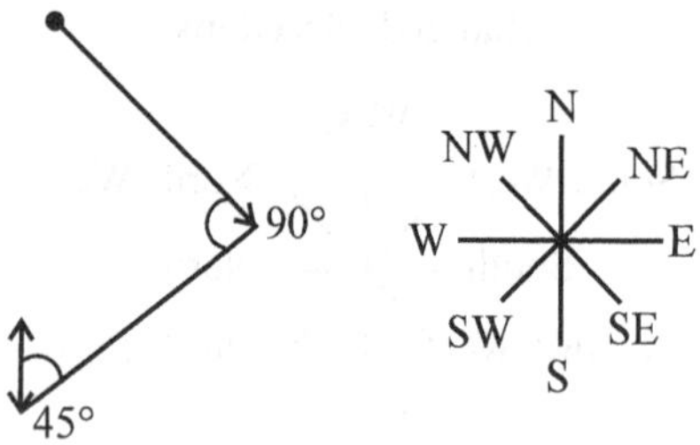

14. *(b)* **:** The track of both the friends is :

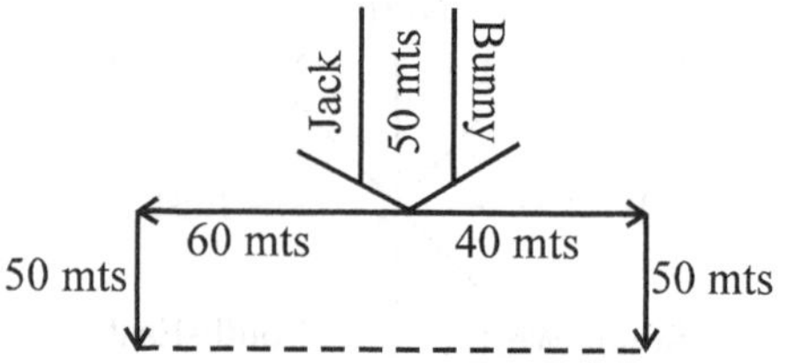

The two friends are 60 + 40 = 100 mts apart

15. *(d)* **:**

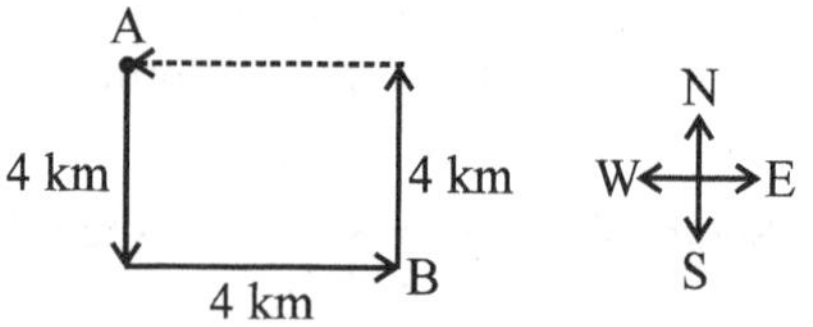

13 Blood Relationships

While attempting questions on blood relations, one should be clear of all the relation patterns that can exist between any two individuals. These type of questions are given mainly to test one's relationship ability.

Very well-known relations are :

Mother	Grandmother
Father	Grandfather
Son	Grandson
Daughter	Granddaughter
Brother	Brother-in-law
Sister	Sister-in-law
Niece	Father-in-law
Nephew	Mother-in-law
Uncle	Son-in-law
Aunt	Daughter-in-law
Husband	Cousin
Wife	

The patterns of some relationships which help in solving questions in these tests are :

Father's *or* Mother's Father	—	Grandfather (Paternal *or* Maternal)
Father's *or* Mother's Mother	—	Grandmother (Paternal *or* Maternal)
Father's *or* Mother's Son	—	Brother
Father's *or* Mother's Daughter	—	Sister
Father's Brother	—	Paternal Uncle
Father's Sister	—	Paternal Aunt
Mother's Brother	—	Maternal Uncle
Mother's Sister	—	Maternal Aunt
Uncle *or* Aunt's Son *or* Daughter	—	Cousin
Son's Wife	—	Daughter-in-law
Daughter's Husband	—	Son-in-law
Husband's *or* Wife's Brother	—	Brother-in-law
Husband's *or* Wife's Sister	—	Sister-in-law
Brother's Wife	—	Sister-in-law
Sister's Husband	—	Brother-in-law
Brother's Son	—	Nephew
Brother's Daughter	—	Niece

EXERCISE

Directions : *In each of the following questions keenly study the relationship mentioned between the persons, and then from the given options select the right relationship as the answer.*

1. A lady said, "The person standing there is my grandfather's only son's daughter". How is the lady related to the standing person?
(*a*) Sister
(*b*) Mother
(*c*) Aunt
(*d*) Cousin

2. Ajay is the brother of Vijay. Mili is the sister of Ajay. Sanjay is the brother of Rahul and Mehul is the daughter of Vijay. Who is Sanjay's Uncle?
(*a*) Rahul
(*b*) Ajay
(*c*) Mehul
(*d*) Data inadequate

3. A man introduced the boy coming with him as "He is son of the father of my wife's daughter". What relation did the boy bear to the man?
(*a*) Son-in-law
(*b*) Son
(*c*) Brother
(*d*) Father

4. If Amit's father is Billoo's father's only son and Billoo has neither a brother nor a daughter, what is the relationship between Amit and Billoo?
(*a*) Uncle — Nephew
(*b*) Father — Daughter
(*c*) Father — Son
(*d*) Cousins

5. Pointing to a woman in the photograph a man said, "She is the daughter of my grand-mother's only son. How is the woman related to the man?
(*a*) Mother (*b*) Daughter
(*c*) Sister-in-law (*d*) Sister

6. Pointing to a photograph, a woman said, "She is the only daughter of my mother's father." How is the woman related to the person in the photograph?
(*a*) Mother
(*b*) Grandmother
(*c*) Daughter
(*d*) Cannot be determined

7. Ram is the brother of Shyam and Mahesh is the father of Ram. Jagat is the brother of Priya and Priya is daughter of Shyam. Who is the uncle of Jagat ?
(*a*) Shyam
(*b*) Mahesh
(*c*) Ram
(*d*) Data insufficient

8. Introducing a man, a woman said, "His wife is the only daughter of my father". How is the man related to the woman?
(*a*) Husband
(*b*) Father
(*c*) Father-in-law
(*d*) Brother

9. If Maya is the only daughter of Richa's grandmother's brother, how is Maya's daughter related to Richa?
(*a*) Niece
(*b*) Cousin
(*c*) Aunt
(*d*) Mother

10. Pointing to a woman, a man said, "Her husband's mother is the wife of my father's only son". How is the man related to the woman?
(*a*) Son
(*b*) Brother-in-law
(*c*) Uncle
(*d*) Father-in-law

EXPLANATORY ANSWERS

1. (*a*) :

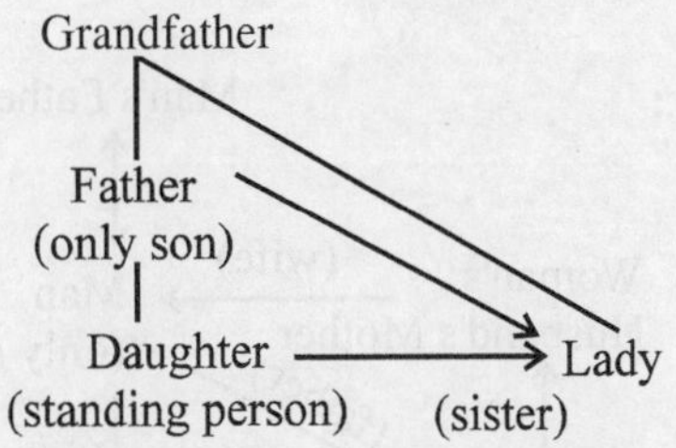

Lady's grandfather's son is lady's father and father's daughter will only be lady's sister.

2. (*d*) :

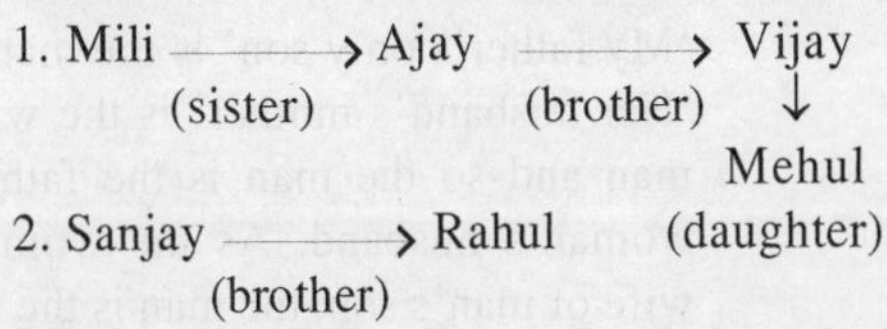

There are two sets of relationship. Information given is incomplete and no relation can be established between the two sets.

3. (*b*) : The relationship chart based on problem is :

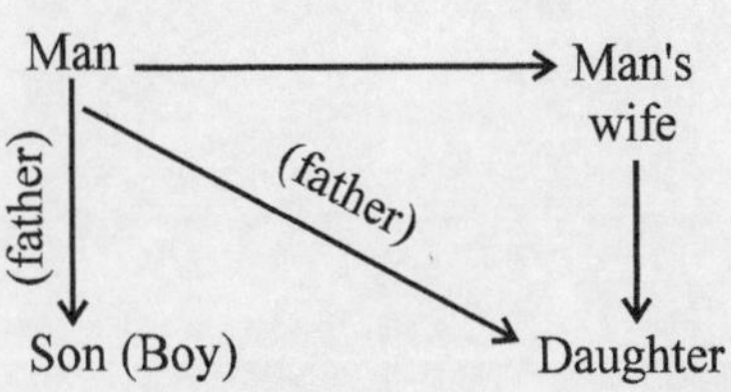

'Father of the man's wife's daughter' is the man himself and the boy in question is the man's son.

4. (*c*) : The relationship chart based on problem is :

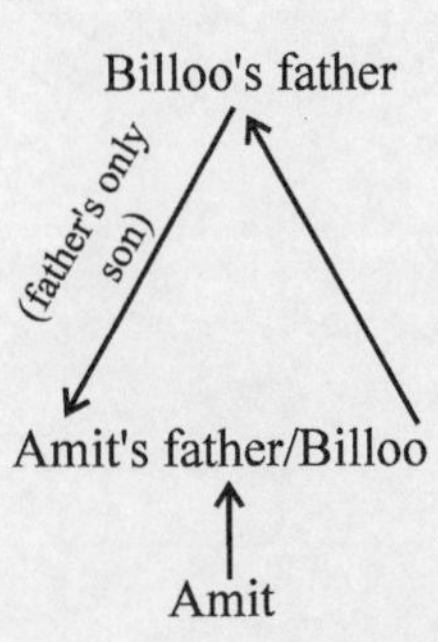

Amit's father is Billoo's father's only son means Billoo is the only son in question also, he is the father of Amit. It must be noted that Billoo has no brother which means he is single and also, when he has no daughter, Amit is his only son.

5. (*d*) :

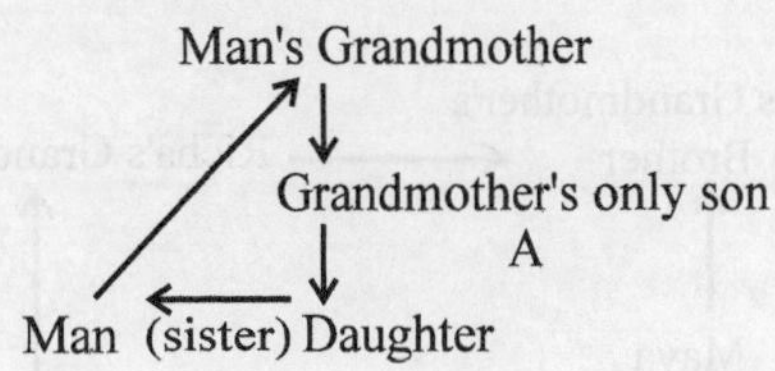

'My grandmother's only son' is the father of the man, and 'daughter of my grand-mother's only son' is the sister of the man.

6. (*c*) :

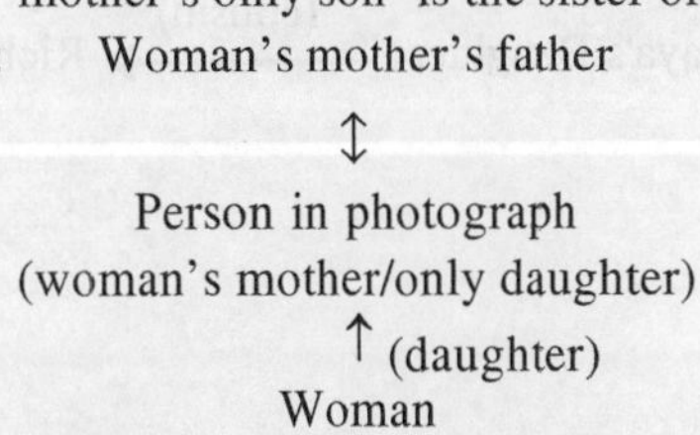

'Only daughter of my mother's father' is the person in the photograph and she is also the mother of the woman. So, the woman is the daughter of the person in the photo-graph.

7. (*c*) :

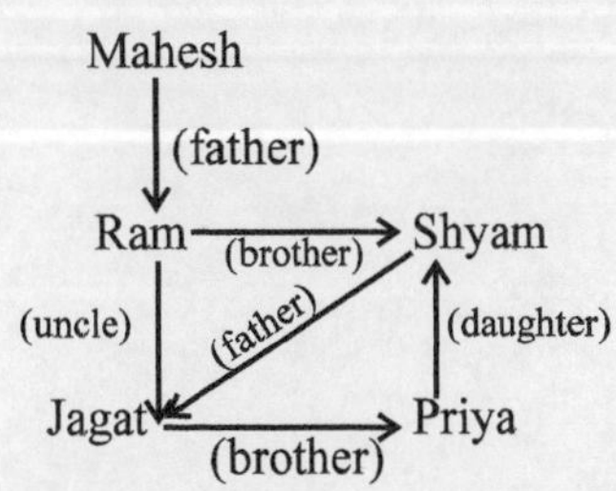

Jagat is brother of Priya and Priya is daughter of Shyam. So Shyam is also the father of Jagat. Ram is the brother of Shyam. So, Jagat's father's brother Ram is the uncle of Jagat.

8. (*a*) :

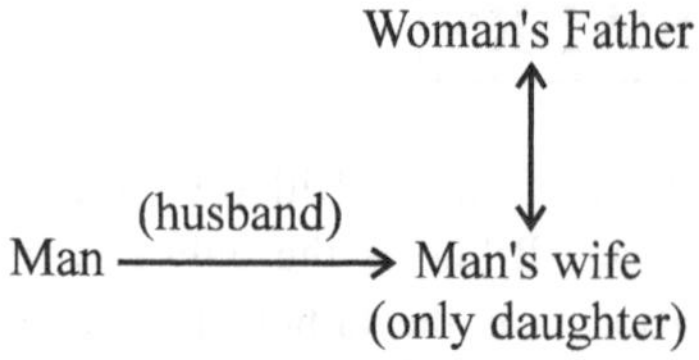

'Only daughter of my father' is the woman herself and the man is her husband.

9. (*b*) :

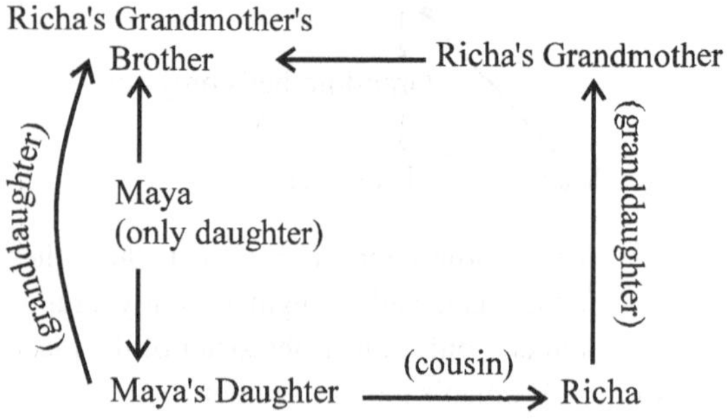

Both Maya's Daughter and Richa are granddaughters of a brother and a sister respectively. So Maya's daughter is the cousin of Richa.

10. (*d*) :

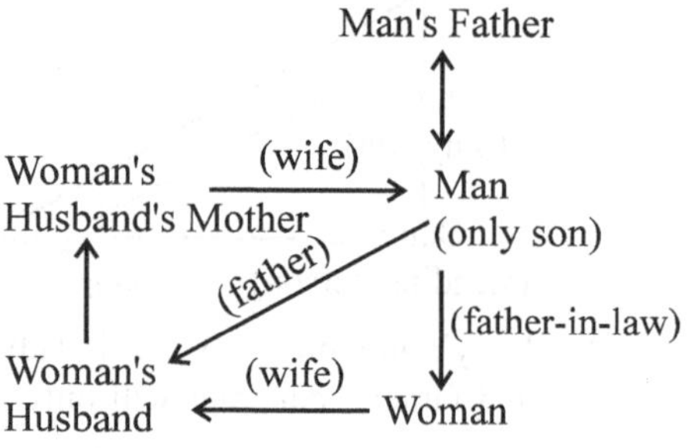

'My father's only son' is the man himself. 'Her husband's mother' is the wife of the man and so the man is the father of the woman's husband. As the woman is the wife of man's son, the man is the father-in-law of the woman.

14 Arranging in Order

In these type of questions arrangement of given options is done on the basis of dictionary, size, rank, weight, natural sequence etc in ascending or descending order.

EXERCISE

1. Which one would be a meaningful order of the following?

1. Key 2. Door
3. Lock 4. Room
5. Switch on

(*a*) 5 1 2 4 3 (*b*) 4 2 1 5 3
(*c*) 1 3 2 4 5 (*d*) 1 2 3 5 4

2. If the following words are rearranged in the alphabetical order as in a dictionary, which will be the third word?

(*a*) Amphibian
(*b*) Amorphous
(*c*) Ambiguous
(*d*) Amphidextrous

3. In a telephone directory, which of the following names will appear in the middle?

(*a*) Randhir (*b*) Randesh
(*c*) Rama (*d*) Ramesh

4. Which one would be a meaningful order of the following?

1. Mother 2. Child
3. Milk 4. Cry
5. Smile

(*a*) 3 2 1 5 4 (*b*) 2 4 1 3 5
(*c*) 1 5 2 4 3 (*d*) 2 4 3 1 5

5. Which would be the proper order of the following?

1. Rainbow 2. Rain
3. Sun 4. Happy
5. Child

(*a*) 4 2 3 5 1 (*b*) 4 5 1 2 3
(*c*) 2 1 4 3 5 (*d*) 2 3 1 5 4

6. Which would be the proper order of the following? (in ascending order)

1. Trillion 2. Thousand
3. Billion 4. Hundred
5. Million

(*a*) 4 2 5 3 1 (*b*) 1 5 3 2 4
(*c*) 4 2 3 5 1 (*d*) 1 2 3 4 5

7. Which would be the proper order of the following?

1. Country 2. Furniture
3. Forest 4. Wood
5. Trees

(*a*) 4 3 2 1 5 (*b*) 2 4 1 5 3
(*c*) 1 3 5 4 2 (*d*) 1 2 3 4 5

8. If the following words are arranged in natural order, what will come in the last place in ascending order?

1. Captain 2. Brigadier
3. Major 4. Lieutenant-General
5. Lieutenant

(*a*) Lientenant-General
(*b*) Brigadier
(*c*) Captain
(*d*) Major

9. If these words are arranged according to dictionary then what word will come in the third place?

1. Originality 2. Originally
3. Originator 4. Original
5. Originate

(*a*) Originality (*b*) Originator
(*c*) Originate (*d*) Originally

10. What will be the natural order of the following?
1. Independence Day
2. Christmas
3. Diwali
4. Holi
5. Republic Day

(*a*) 5 4 1 3 2 (*b*) 5 1 4 3 2
(*c*) 4 1 5 3 2 (*d*) 2 3 4 1 5

11. If the following words are arranged in ascending order what word will be in the fourth place?
1. Air commodore
2. Wing Commander
3. Pilot Officer
4. Squadron Leader
5. Air Marshal

(*a*) Air Marshal
(*b*) Air Commodore
(*c*) Wing Commander
(*d*) Pilot Officer

12. What will be the natural order of the following words according to size?
1. Dog 2. Horse
3. Ant 4. Giraffe
5. Mouse

(*a*) 3 5 1 2 4 (*b*) 3 1 5 2 4
(*c*) 3 5 1 4 2 (*d*) 3 5 2 1 4

EXPLANATORY ANSWERS

1. (*c*) : With the Key you open a Lock, then open the Door to enter the Room and Switch on the light.

2. (*b*) : The dictionary order of the words is—Ambiguous, Ambivalent, **Amorphous,** Amphibian, Amphidextrous.

3. (*b*) : In telephone directory the order of names is—Ramesh, Rana, **Randesh,** Randhir, Renmurthi.

4. (*b*) : When a Child Cries the Mother gives him Milk and then he Smiles.

5. (*d*) : When it rains in the Sun a Rainbow is formed and the Child is Happy to see it.

6. (*a*) : The words are arranged in order of increasing amount.

7. (*c*) : The proper order of the words is—Country, Forest, Trees, Wood, Furniture. In a Country there are Forests comprising Trees the Wood of which are used to make Furniture.

8. (*a*) : The arrangement of ranks in ascending order is—Lieutenant, Captain, Major, Brigadier, **Lieutenant-General.**

9. (*d*) : The dictionary order of words is—Original, Originality, **Originally,** Originate, Originator.

10. (*a*) : The natural order of National Holidays in Calendar is—Republic Day (January), Holi (March), Independence Day (August), Diwali (October/November), Christmas (December).

11. (*b*) : The arrangement of ranks in ascending order is—Pilot Officer, Squadron Leader, Wing Commander, **Air Commodore,** Air Marshal.

12. (*a*) : The natural order of living beings according to increasing size is—Ant, Mouse, Dog, Horse, Giraffe.

15 Calendar, Clock & Time

These are mathematical problem based on calculations of time by a clock or calendar and computations of speed or distances.

EXERCISE

1. If the day before yesterday was Thursday, when will Sunday be?
(*a*) Tomorrow (*b*) Day after tomorrow
(*c*) Today (*d*) Two days after today

2. Radha remembers that her father's birthday is after 16th but before 21st of March, while her brother Mangesh remembers that his father's birthday is before 22nd but after 19th of March. On which date is the birthday of their father?
(*a*) 19th (*b*) 20th
(*c*) 21st (*d*) Cannot be determined

3. A clock is so placed that at 12 noon its minute hand points towards north-east. In which direction does its hour hand point at 1.30 P.M.?
(*a*) East (*b*) West
(*c*) North (*d*) South

4. A couple married in 1980 had two children, one in 1982 and the other in 1984. Their combined ages will equal the years of the marriage in?
(*a*) 1986 (*b*) 1985
(*c*) 1987 (*d*) 1988

5. Manoj left home for the bus stop 15 minutes earlier than the usual time. It takes 10 minutes to reach the stop. He reached the stop at 8.40 a.m. What time does he usually leave home for the bus stop?
(*a*) 8.30 a.m. (*b*) 8.55 a.m.
(*c*) 8.45 p.m. (*d*) None of these

6. If the third day of a month is Monday, which of the following will be the fifth day from 21st of that month?
(*a*) Tuesday (*b*) Monday
(*c*) Wednesday (*d*) Thursday

7. Keshav runs a factory in three shifts of eight hours each with 210 employees. In each shift minimum of 80 employees are required to run the factory effectively. No employee can be allowed to work for more than 16 hours a day. At least how many employees will be required to work for 16 hours every day?
(*a*) 30 (*b*) 60
(*c*) Data inadequate (*d*) None of these

8. A clock shows the time as 3 : 30 p.m. If the minute hand gains 2 minutes every hour, how many minutes will the clock gain by 4 a.m.?
(*a*) 23 Minutes (*b*) 24 Minutes
(*c*) 25 Minutes (*d*) 26 Minutes

9. A train started from station 'A' and proceeded towards station 'B' at a speed of 48 km/hr. Forty-five minutes later another train started from station 'B' and proceeded towards station 'A' at 50 km/hr. If the distance between the two stations is 232 km, at what distance from station 'A' will the trains meet?
(*a*) 132 km (*b*) 144 km
(*c*) 108 km (*d*) 160 km

10. My uncle shall visit me after 64 days of my father's birthday. If my father's birthday falls on Tuesday, what shall be the day on my Uncle's visit?
(*a*) Wednesday (*b*) Sunday
(*c*) Tuesday (*d*) Monday

11. Arjun remembers that his mother's birthday is between fifteenth and twenty-first November. His sister remembers that their mother's birthday is between nineteenth and twenty-fifth November. If both of them remember correctly, on which day is their mother's birthday?
(*a*) Twentieth
(*b*) Twenty-first

(*c*) Twentieth or Twenty-first
(*d*) Twenty-second

12. If 3rd December 1999 is Sunday, what day is 3rd January 2000?
(*a*) Tuesday
(*b*) Wednesday
(*c*) Thursday
(*d*) Friday

13. Prabir starts for office every morning at 9.15 a.m. and reaches there at 9.55 a.m. On Wednesday he started five minutes later than the time he started on Friday. Three days out of five days in the week he started late, out of which Friday was one of the days. On how many days he started in time?
(*a*) Two (*b*) Three
(*c*) Four (*d*) One

EXPLANATORY ANSWERS

1. (*a*) : Thursday — Day-before-yesterday
Friday — Yesterday
Saturday — Today
Sunday — Tomorrow

2. (*b*) : Father's birthday

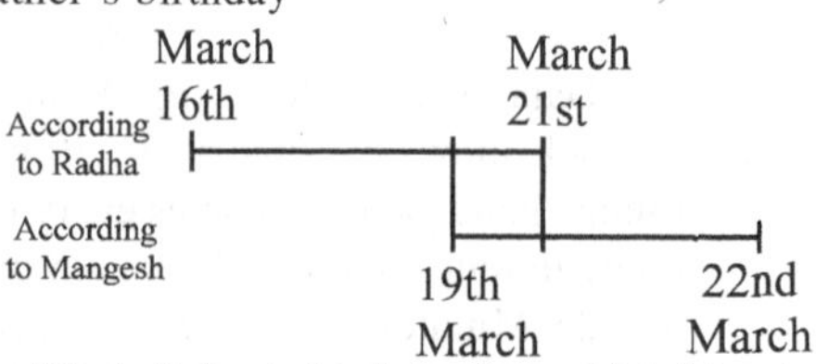

∴ Their father's birthday is on 20th March.

3. (*a*) :

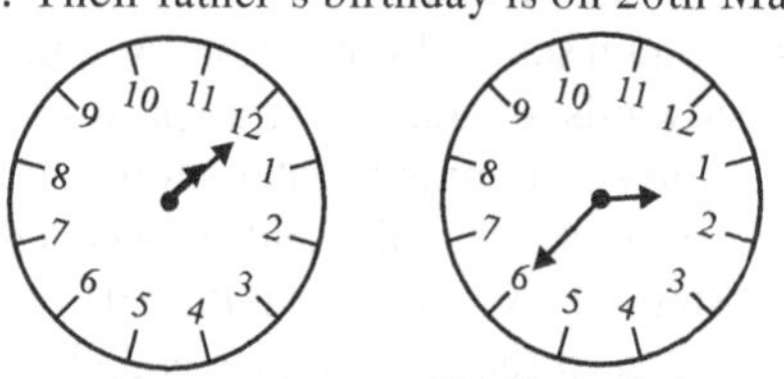

At 12 noon
At 1.30 p.m. the hour hand will point towards East.

4. (*a*) : 1982 — 2 years later — 1st child
1984 — 4 years later — 2nd child
Total age of children — 2 years.
1985 — 5 years later — Total age of children : 4 years.
1986 — 6 years later — Total age of children : 6 years.

5. (*d*) : Manoj reached the bus stop at 8.40 a.m. He left his home at 8:40 – 10 minutes = 8:30 a.m. He left 15 minutes earlier than usual, so his actual time of leaving home is 8:30 am + 15 minutes = 8:45 a.m.

6. (*c*) : 3rd day of the month is Monday
5th day from 21st is 26th
26 – 3 = 23 days
23 days later, 23/7 leaves 2 days.
So, two days ahead of Monday will be Wednesday.

7. (*d*) : 80 employees are required for double shift.

8. (*c*) : Hours between 3:30 p.m. and 4 a.m. are — 12½ hours. Number of minutes gained will be 12½ × 2 = 25 minutes.

9. (*a*) :

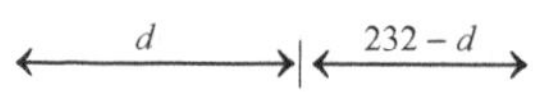

i.e., $\frac{d}{48} = \frac{232-d}{50} + \frac{3}{4}$

$\frac{d}{48} = \frac{464-2d+75}{100}$

$100\,d = (539 - 2d)\,48$

$100\,d = 25872 - 96\,d$

$196\,d = 25872$

$d = 25872 \div 196 = 132$ km.

10. (*a*) : My father's birthday is on Tuesday.
64 ÷ 7 gives 1 as remainder
So, 63rd day will be Tuesday and one day ahead is the day when uncle shall visit *i.e.,* on Wednesday.

11. (*a*) : Mother's birthday

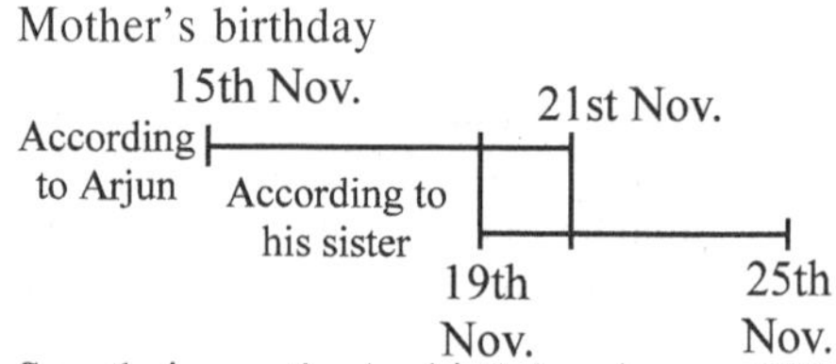

So, their mother's birthday is on 20th November.

12. (*b*) : 3rd December 1999 is Sunday. Number of days in-between 3rd December 1999 and 3rd January 2000 = 28 + 3 = 31 days 31 ÷ 7 gives 3 as remainder
So, 31st December 1999 will be Sunday and 3rd January 2000 will be 3 days ahad *i.e.* Wednesday.

13. (*a*) : Out of five days, he starts late on three days.

16 Rows and Ranks

These type of problems need easy calculations to find out the number of objects in a row, lane or queue or to find a person's rank in a class of certain number of students; or to find the total number of students.

EXERCISE

1. In a row of trees, one tree is fifth from either end of the row. How many trees are in the row?

(*a*) 11 (*b*) 8
(*c*) 10 (*d*) 9

2. Jaya ranks 5th in a class of 53. What is her rank from the bottom in the class?

(*a*) 49th (*b*) 48th
(*c*) 47th (*d*) 50th

3. Mohan ranks twenty-first in a class of sixty-five students. What will be his (Mohan's) rank if the lowest candidate is assigned rank 1?

(*a*) 44th (*b*) 45th
(*c*) 46th (*d*) Data inadequate

4. If Rahul finds that he is 12th from the right in a line of boys and 4th from the left, how many boys should be added to the line such that there are 28 boys in the line?

(*a*) 12 (*b*) 14
(*c*) 20 (*d*) 13

5. In a row of boys, Rajan is tenth from the right and Suraj is tenth from the left. When Rajan and Suraj interchange their positions, Suraj will be twenty-seventh from the left. Which of the following will be Rajan's position from the right?

(*a*) Tenth
(*b*) Twenty-sixth
(*c*) Twenty-ninth
(*d*) None of these

6. Mahesh and Suresh are ranked 11th and 12th respectively from the top in a class of 41 students. What will be their respective ranks from the bottom?

(*a*) 32nd and 33rd
(*b*) 29th and 30th
(*c*) 30th and 31st
(*d*) 31st and 30th

7. Uma ranked 8th from the top and 37th from bottom in a class. How many students are there in the class?

(*a*) 47 (*b*) 46
(*c*) 45 (*d*) None of these

8. In a queue, Sadiq is 14th from the front and Joseph is 17th from the end, while Jane is in between Sadiq and Joseph. If Sadiq be ahead of Joseph and there be 48 persons in the queue, how many persons are there between Sadiq and Jane?

(*a*) 5 (*b*) 6
(*c*) 7 (*d*) 8

9. Rohan ranked eleventh from the top and twenty-seventh from the bottom among the students who passed the annual examination in a class. If the number of students who failed in the examination was 12, how many students appeared for the examination?

(*a*) 48
(*b*) 49
(*c*) 50
(*d*) Cannot be determined

10. Some boys are sitting in a row. P is sitting fourteenth from the left and Q is seventh from the right. If there are four boys between P and Q, how many boys are there in the row?

(*a*) 19 (*b*) 21
(*c*) 25 (*d*) 23

EXPLANATORY ANSWERS

1. (*d*):

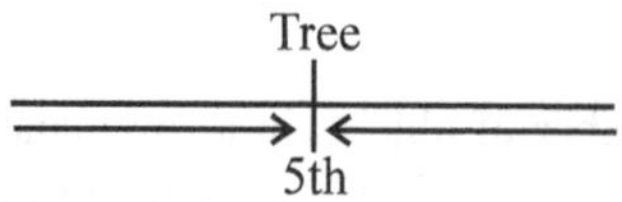

Total number of trees in the row are :
(5 + 5) –1 = 9.

2. (*a*) :

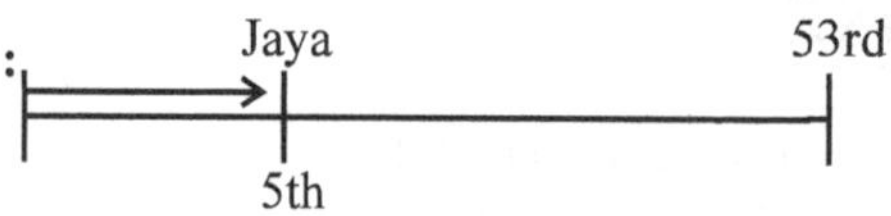

Jaya's rank from the bottom is :
(53 – 5) +1 = 49th.

3. (*b*) :

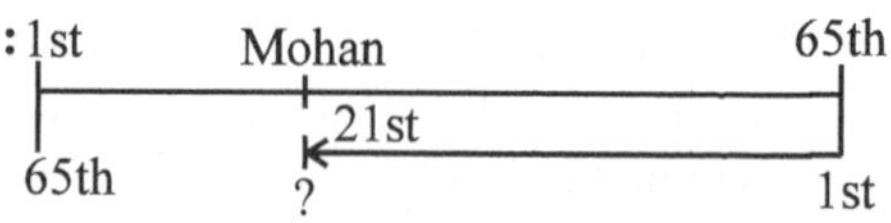

Note : Mohan's rank from the last or the question asked means the same.

Mohan's rank is (65 – 21) +1 = 45th.

4. (*d*) :

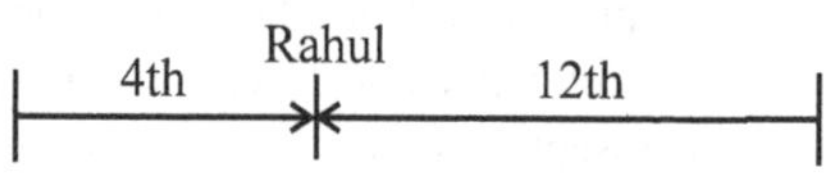

The number of boys in the line are :
(4 + 12) – 1 = 15

To make a line of 28 boys, (28 –15) *i.e.* 13 more boys are needed.

5. (*d*) :

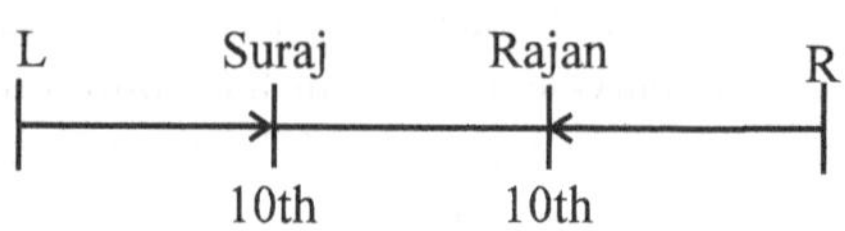

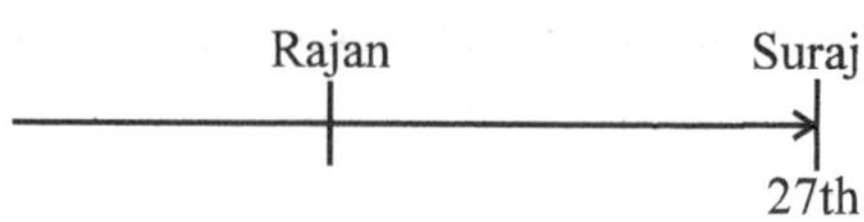

As the position of boys is equal from both ends, Rajan will also be 27th from the right after changing positions.

6. (*d*) :

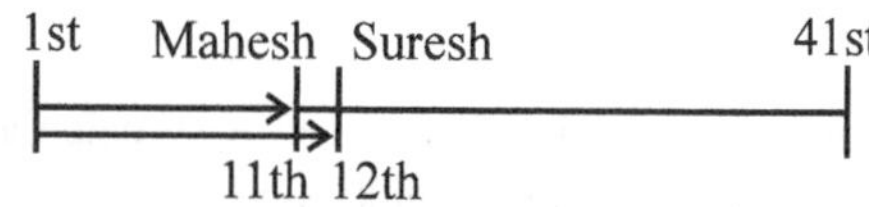

Mahesh's position from bottom is :
(41 – 11) + 1 = 31st

Suresh's position from bottom is :
(41 – 12) +1 = 30th.

7. (*d*) :

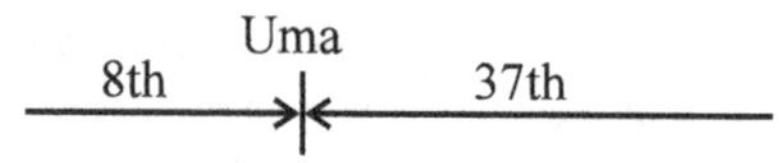

Total number of students in the class are :
(8 + 37) – 1 = 44.

8. (*c*) :

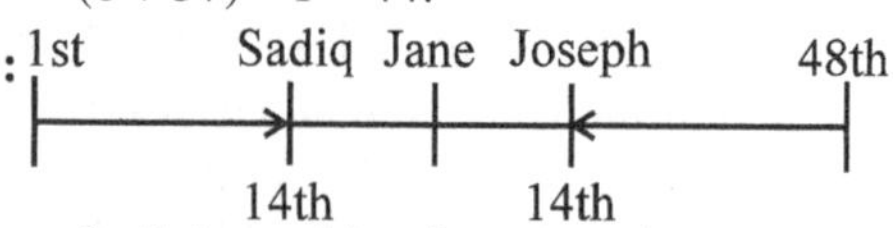

Sadiq's position from last is :
(48 – 14) + 1 = 35th

Number of persons between Sadiq and Joseph are (35 – 17) – 1 = 17

Jane is in-between Sadiq and Joseph *i.e.*, she's at 9th position from both the boys.

∴ there are 8 persons between Sadiq and Jane.

Note : (8 + 8) – 1 = 17.

9. (*b*) :

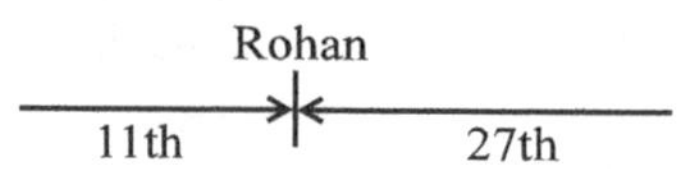

Number of students who passed the examination (11+ 27) – 1 = 37

Those who failed = 12

Total number of students who appeared in the examination = 37 + 12 = 49.

10. (*c*) :

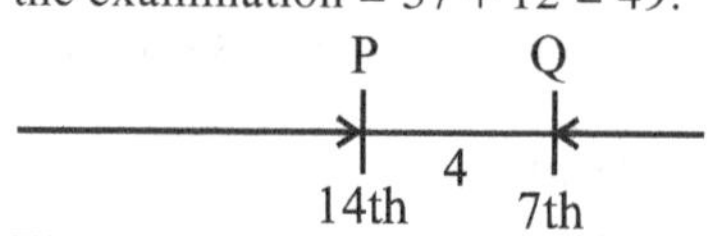

The number of boys in the row are :
(14 + 4 + 7) = 25.

17 Common Property

In this type of test, the questions contain either numbers or words or letters which have a common property. From the given set of options the candidate has to select the one which bears the same property.

EXERCISE

1. Out of the given alternatives, choose the one that belongs to the given number group.
Given number group : (49, 25, 9)
(*a*) (39, 26, 13) (*b*) (36, 16, 4)
(*c*) (64, 27, 8) (*d*) (36, 25, 16

2. Which one number is like the given number set : (363, 489, 579)?
(*a*) 281 (*b*) 382
(*c*) 471 (*d*) 562

3. Which set of numbers has the same property as the following numbers?
21, 38, 55
(*a*) 47, 64, 80 (*b*) 19, 36, 55
(*c*) 23, 40, 57 (*d*) 35, 62, 79

4. Which set of numbers is like the given number set : 1050, 210, 42?
(*a*) 75, 15, 3 (*b*) 60, 12, 2
(*c*) 125, 25, 6 (*d*) 95, 19, 3

5. Which set of numbers is like the given number set : 7, 77, 847?
(*a*) 9, 99, 989 (*b*) 1, 11, 131
(*c*) 6, 66, 726 (*d*) 8, 8, 948

6. Which of the following has the same property as RnTz, FnjK, BTbs, tfNL?
(*a*) FGhI (*b*) rRQd
(*c*) NOqB (*d*) GgTJ

7. Which set of numbers is like the given set : 53, 40, 27?
(*a*) 58, 27, 18 (*b*) 77, 63, 50
(*c*) 93, 80, 67 (*d*) 39, 26, 13

8. Which of the following words have same characteristics as Cap, Hat and Turban?
(*a*) Hair (*b*) Helmet
(*c*) Safety (*d*) Umbrella

9. Which set of letters is like the given set : WVU, EDC, LKJ?
(*a*) GHF (*b*) BAZ
(*c*) PON (*d*) WUT

10. Which number has the same property as the given numbers : 637, 399, 784?
(*a*) 161 (*b*) 535
(*c*) 493 (*d*) 257

EXPLANATORY ANSWERS

1. (*b*) : The numbers are squares of alternate numbers. $7^2 = 49, 5^2 = 25, 3^2 = 9$. Similarly, $6^2 = 36, 4^2 = 16, 2^2 = 4$.

2. (*c*) : The numbers are divisible by 3.

3. (*c*) : The difference between the numbers is 17, *i.e.*, $21 + 17 = 38; 38 + 17 = 55$. Similarly, $23 + 17 = 40; 40 + 17 = 57$.

4. (*a*) : The number divided by 5 is the next number, *i.e.*, $1050 \div 5 = 210; 210 \div 5 = 42$. Similarly $75 \div 5 = 15; 15 \div 5 = 3$.

5. (*c*) : The numbers are multiples of 11, *i.e.*, $7 \times 11 = 77; 77 \times 11 = 847$. Similarly $6 \times 11 = 66; 66 \times 11 = 726$.

6. (*b*) : Two letters are capital, two are small.

7. (*d*) : The difference between the numbers is 13 *i.e.* $53 - 13 = 40; 40 - 13 = 27$.
Similarly $39 - 13 = 26; 26 - 13 = 13$.

8. (*b*) : All three are worn on the head and so is helmet.

9. (*c*) : The letters are in reverse consecutive order.

10. (*a*) : The numbers are divisible by 7.

18 Symbol Substitution

Questions in these category are easy to attempt. Candidates must be quick in substituting symbols and calculations. The common pattern of questions asked are given below.

EXERCISE

1. If "+" means "–"; "–" means "×"; "×"means "÷" and "÷" means "+", then
$15 \times 5 \div 10 + 5 - 3 = ?$

(*a*) 9.5 (*b*) 0
(*c*) – 2 (*d*) 24

2. If "+" means "×"; "–" means "÷"; "÷"means "+" and "×" means "–", then what will be the value of $20 \div 40 - 4 \times 5 + 6 = ?$

(*a*) 60 (*b*) 1.67
(*c*) 150 (*d*) 0

3. If × stands for addition, $<$ for subtraction, + stands for division, $>$ for multiplication, – stands for equal to, ÷ for greater than, and = stands for less than, state which of the following is true?

(*a*) $5 \times 3 < 7 \div 8 + 4 \times 1$
(*b*) $3 \times 4 > 2 - 9 + 3 < 3$
(*c*) $5 > 2 + 2 = 10 < 4 \times 8$
(*d*) $3 \times 2 < 4 \div 16 > 2 + 4$

4. If $\rightarrow$ stands for subract, $\leftarrow$ stands for add, $\uparrow\uparrow\uparrow$ stands for multiply, $\downarrow\downarrow$ stands for divide, $\leftrightarrow$ for greater than, $\longleftrightarrow$ stands for equal to, then which of the following alternatives is true?

(*a*) $4 \leftarrow 6 \uparrow\uparrow 2 \longleftrightarrow 3 \rightarrow 12 \leftarrow 12$
(*b*) $10 \downarrow\downarrow 5 \uparrow\uparrow 5 \longleftrightarrow 9 \rightarrow 3 \leftarrow 4$
(*c*) $15 \uparrow\uparrow 2 \rightarrow 5 \longleftrightarrow 12 \downarrow\downarrow 4 \leftarrow 3$
(*d*) $13 \downarrow\downarrow 13 \leftarrow 1 \leftrightarrow 20 \rightarrow 5 \uparrow\uparrow 2$

5. If Δ denotes =; + denotes $>$, – denotes $<$, □ denotes ≠, × denotes $>$ and ÷ denotes $<$ then a + b – c denotes

(*a*) b Δ c □ a
(*b*) b □ a ÷ c
(*c*) a ÷ b × c
(*d*) b – a + c

6. If '✱' denotes '×', 'Δ' denotes '÷', '□' denotes '–', '●' denotes '+', 'α' denotes '=' and 'β' denotes ≠, then which of the following euations is correct?

(*a*) 2 □ 10 ✱ 4 Δ 5 α 5 ● 12 Δ 6
(*b*) 27 Δ 9 ● 6 β 3 ✱ 6 □ 9
(*c*) 4 Δ 2 ✱ 0 α 7 Δ 1 ✱ 0
(*d*) 5 ● 6 Δ 3 □ 2 α 8 Δ 4 ✱ 3

7. If $\downarrow$ stands for '÷', $\uparrow$ stands for '×', $\rightarrow$ stands for '+' and $\leftarrow$ stands for '–', then
$25 \downarrow 5 \rightarrow 3 \uparrow 6 \leftarrow 8 = ?$

(*a*) 9 (*b*) 12
(*c*) 16 (*d*) 15

8. If the + and × signs of the following equations are interchanged, which will be the correct equation?

(*a*) $7 \times 5 + 3 = 20$
(*b*) $4 + 9 \times 1 = 42$
(*c*) $6 \times 5 + 8 = 46$
(*d*) $2 + 11 \times 4 = 28$

9. If '+' stands for multiplication, '×' stands for addition, '÷' stands for subtraction and '–' stands for division, then what will be the result of the following equation?
$7 \times 4 \div 10 \times 2 + 5 = ?$

(*a*) 7 (*b*) 0
(*c*) 11 (*d*) 15

10. If 'A' means '÷', 'B' means '+', 'C' means '×' and 'D' means '–', then
12 C 4 A 24 D 10 B 1 = ?

(*a*) $11\frac{1}{3}$ (*b*) 23
(*c*) – 7 (*d*) $16\frac{4}{5}$

EXPLANATORY ANSWERS

1. (c) : $15 \div 5 + 10 - 5 \times 3$
$3 + 10 - 15 = -2$

2. (d) : $20 + 40 \div 4 - 5 \times 6$
$20 + 10 - 30 = 0$

3. (c) : *(a)* $5 + 3 - 7 > 8 \div 4 + 1$
$1 > 3$
(b) $3 + 4 \times 2 = 9 \div 3 - 3$
$11 = 0$
(c) $5 \times 2 \div 2 < 10 - 4 + 8$
$5 < 14$
(d) $3 + 2 - 4 > 16 \times 2 \div 4$
$1 > 8$

4. (b) : *(a)* $4 + 6 \times 2 = 3 - 12 + 12$
$16 = 3$
(b) $10 \div 5 \times 5 = 9 - 3 + 4$
$10 = 10$
(c) $15 \times 2 - 5 = 12 \div 4 + 3$
$25 = 6$
(d) $13 \div 13 + 1 > 20 - 5 \times 2$
$2 > 10$

5. (d) : What is given is a > b < c
The equations are :
(a) b = c ≠ a which is wrong
(b) b ≠ a < c which is wrong
(c) a < b > c which is wrong
(d) b < a > c which is correct
Therefore, *(d)* is the answer.

6. (c) : The solved equations will be :
(a) $2 - 10 \times 4 \div 5 = 5 + 12 \div 6$
$2 - 8 = 5 + 2$
$6 = 7$ which is wrong
(b) $27 \div 9 + 6 \neq 3 \times 6 - 9$
$3 + 6 \neq 18 - 9$
$9 \neq 9$ which is wrong
(c) $4 \div 2 \times 0 = 7 \div 1 \times 0$
$2 \times 0 = 7 \times 0$
$0 = 0$ which is correct
(d) $5 + 6 \div 3 - 2 = 8 \div 4 \times 3$
$5 = 6$ which is wrong

7. (d) : $25 \div 5 + 3 \times 6 - 8$
$5 + 18 - 8 = 15$

8. (c) : After interchanging the signs the equations are :
(a) $7 + 5 \times 3 = 22$ which is wrong
(b) $4 \times 9 + 1 = 37$ which is wrong
(c) $6 + 5 \times 8 = 46$ which is correct
(d) $2 \times 11 + 4 = 26$ which is wrong

9. (c) : $7 + 4 - 10 + 2 \times 5$
$7 + 4 - 10 + 10 = 11$

10. (c) : $12 \times 4 \div 24 - 10 + 1$
$2 - 10 + 1 = -7$

19 Missing Numbers

Playing with numbers and mathematical skills are needed to attempt these type of tests. The candidates have to work out the right combination of arithmetical symbols to arrive at the answer options which will take the place of the interrogation sign in the given questions.

EXERCISE

Directions : *In each question given below which one number can be placed at the sign of interrogation?*

1. 

(*a*) 693 (*b*) 939
(*c*) 981 (*d*) 993

2. 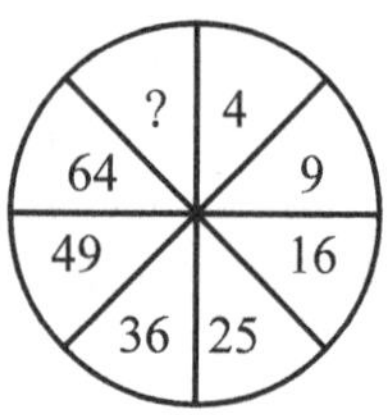

(*a*) 68 (*b*) 100
(*c*) 72 (*d*) 81

3. 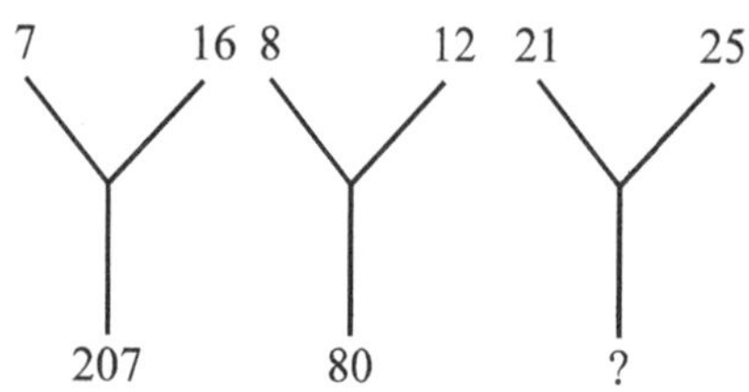

(*a*) 425 (*b*) 184
(*c*) 241 (*d*) 210

4. 

(*a*) 35 (*b*) 37
(*c*) 45 (*d*) 48

5. 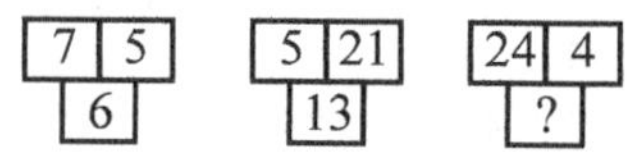

(*a*) 4 (*b*) 8
(*c*) 20 (*d*) 14

6.

14	9	4
12	7	2
10	5	0
16	11	?

(*a*) 9 (*b*) 6
(*c*) 3 (*d*) 7

7. 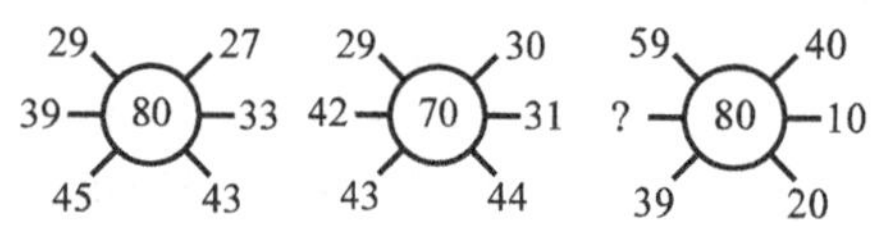

(*a*) 69 (*b*) 49
(*c*) 50 (*d*) 60

8. 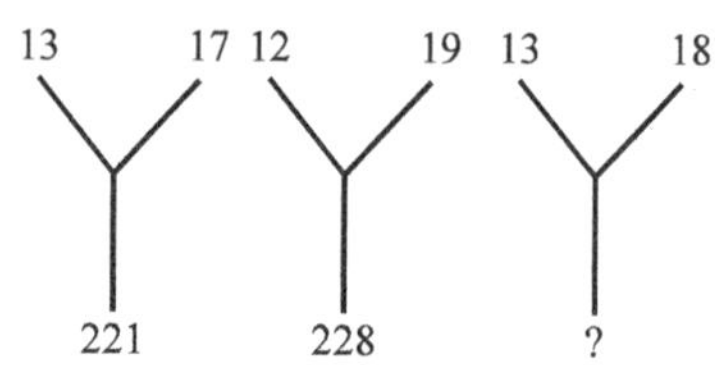

(*a*) 31 (*b*) 229
(*c*) 234 (*d*) 312

9. 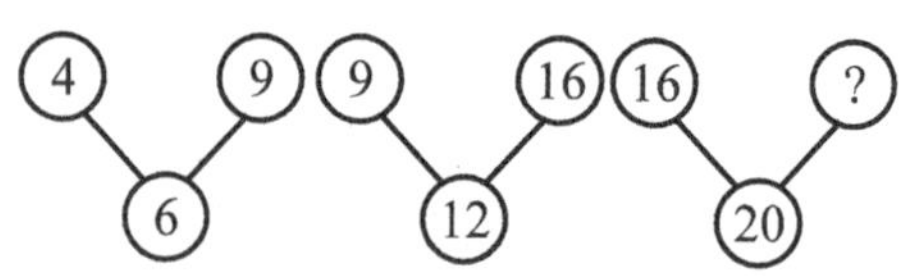

(*a*) 21 (*b*) 25
(*c*) 50 (*d*) 60

10.

51	(11)	61
64	(30)	32
35	(?)	43

(*a*) 25 (*b*) 27
(*c*) 32 (*d*) 37

11.

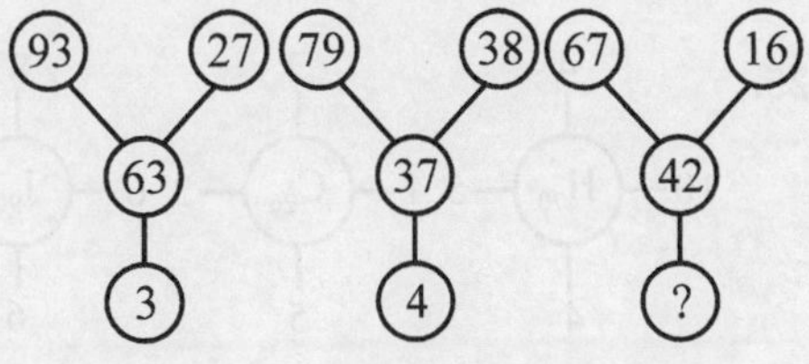

(*a*) 5 (*b*) 6
(*c*) 8 (*d*) 9

12.

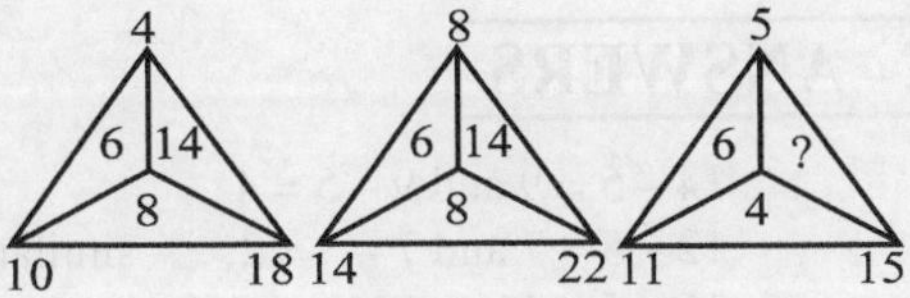

(*a*) 8 (*b*) 14
(*c*) 10 (*d*) 6

13.

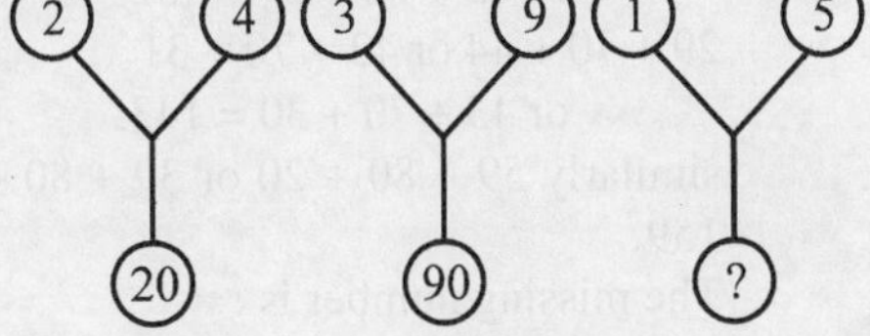

(*a*) 20 (*b*) 25
(*c*) 26 (*d*) 75

14.

27	22	50
13	12	26
9	2	?

(*a*) 12 (*b*) 39
(*c*) 18 (*d*) 24

15.

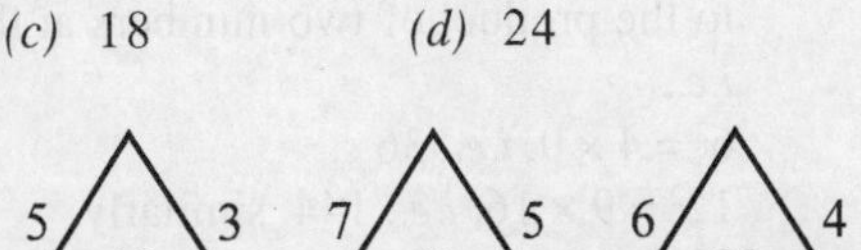

(*a*) 25 (*b*) 47
(*c*) 37 (*d*) 41

16.

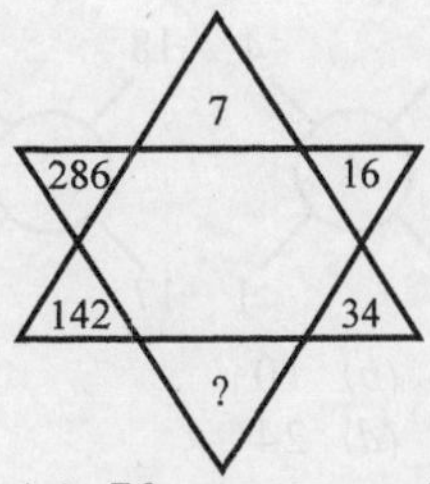

(*a*) 70 (*b*) 68
(*c*) 56 (*d*) 92

17.

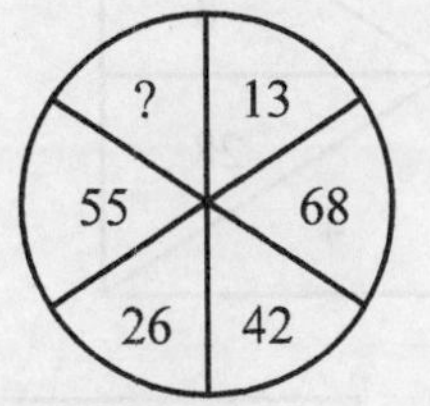

(*a*) 41 (*b*) 37
(*c*) 29 (*d*) 25

18.

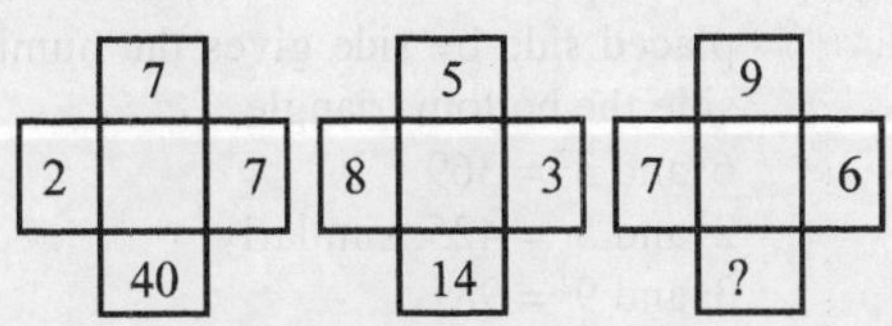

(*a*) 72 (*b*) 68
(*c*) 82 (*d*) 96

19.

42	(21)	22
78	(?)	84
162	(18)	99

(*a*) 12 (*b*) 13
(*c*) 60 (*d*) 72

20.

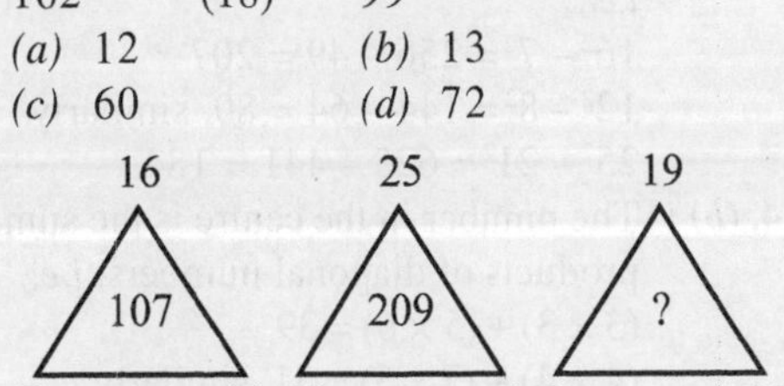

(*a*) 68 (*b*) 93
(*c*) 175 (*d*) 217

21.

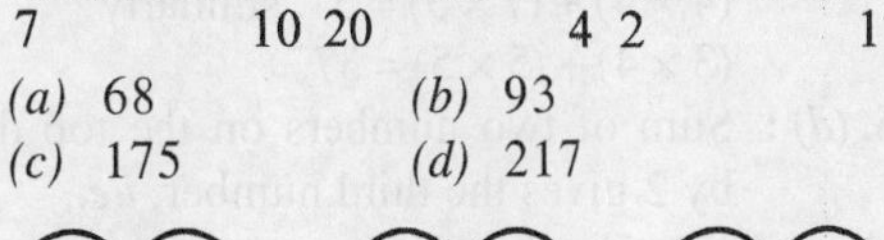

(*a*) 960 (*b*) 628
(*c*) 830 (*d*) 492

22. 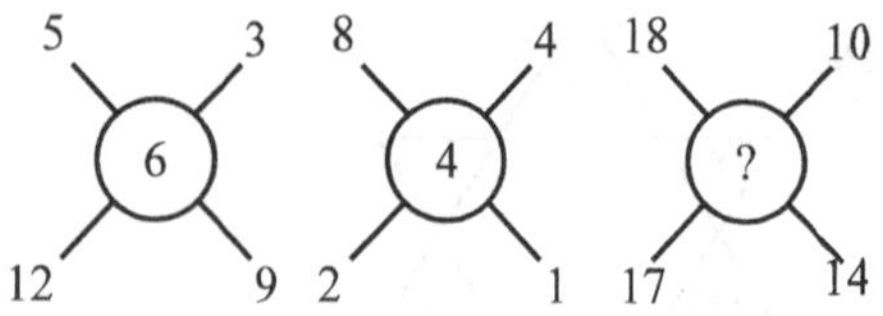

(*a*) 18 (*b*) 10
(*c*) 36 (*d*) 24

23. 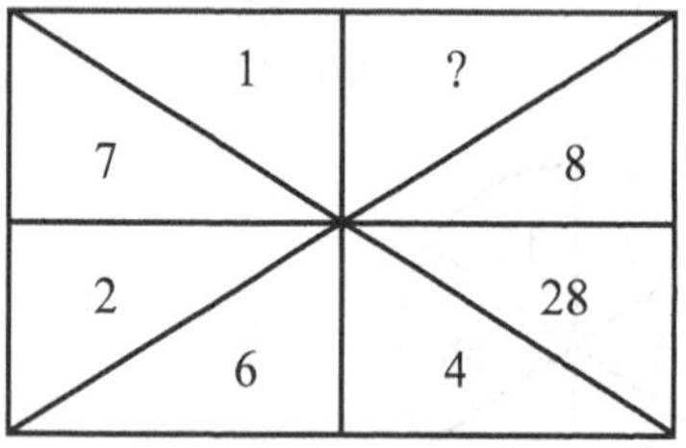

(*a*) 24 (*b*) 10
(*c*) 32 (*d*) 12

24. 6(40) 4
3(12) 3
7(?) 2

(*a*) 51 (*b*) 36
(*c*) 22 (*d*) 4

25. 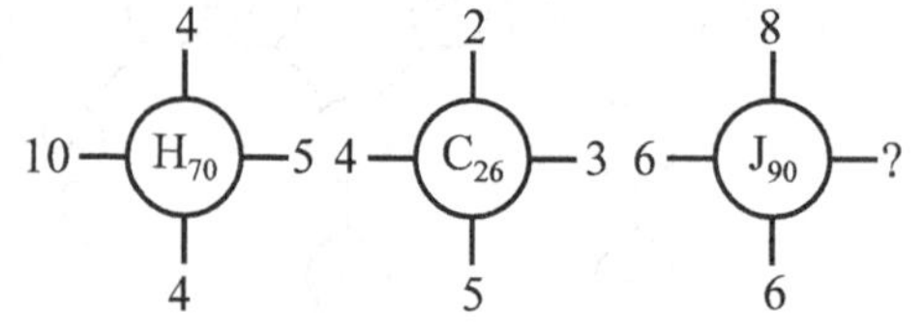

(*a*) 5 (*b*) 4
(*c*) 2 (*d*) 1

EXPLANATORY ANSWERS

1. ***(c)*** **:** The squares of two numbers on the top placed side by side gives the number inside the bottom triangle, *i.e.*,
6^2 and $3^2 = 369$
2^2 and $5^2 = 425$, similarly
3^2 and $9^2 = 981$.

2. ***(d)*** **:** Starting from number 4 the numbers are the squares of numbers in natural order *i.e.*, $2^2 = 4, 3^2 = 9, 4^2 = 16 \ldots\ldots 9^2 = 81$.

3. ***(b)*** **:** The number at the bottom is the difference of the squares of two numbers at the top, *i.e.*,
$16^2 - 7^2 = 256 - 49 = 207$
$12^2 - 8^2 = 144 - 64 = 80$, similarly
$25^2 - 21^2 = 625 - 441 = 184$.

4. ***(b)*** **:** The number in the centre is the sum of the products of diagonal numbers, *i.e.*,
$(3 \times 3) + (5 \times 6) = 39$
$(4 \times 4) + (7 \times 5) = 51$, similarly
$(3 \times 4) + (5 \times 5) = 37$.

5. ***(d)*** **:** Sum of two numbers on the top divided by 2 gives the third number, *i.e.*,
$(7 + 5) \div 2 = 6$
$(5 + 21) \div 2 = 13$, similarly
$(24 + 4) \div 2 = 14$.

6. ***(b)*** **:** The numbers in 2nd and 3rd columns are 5 less than the nunbers in 1st and 2nd columns respectively, *i.e.*,
$14 - 5 = 9$ and $9 - 5 = 4$
$12 - 5 = 7$ and $7 - 5 = 2, \ldots$ similarly
$16 - 5 = 11$ and $11 - 5 = 6$.

7. ***(a)*** **:** The sum of 3 numbers in each line in one figure is same, *i.e.*,
$29 + 80 + 43$ or $39 + 80 + 33$
or $45 + 80 + 27 = 152$
$29 + 70 + 44$ or $42 + 70 + 31$
or $43 + 70 + 30 = 143$,
similarly $59 + 80 + 20$ or $39 + 80 + 40 = 159$.
The missing number is :
$159 - (80 + 10) = 69$.

8. ***(c)*** **:** The number at the bottom is the product of two numbers at the top, *i.e.*,
$13 \times 17 = 221$
$12 \times 19 = 228$, similarly
$13 \times 18 = 234$.

9. ***(b)*** **:** Square of number at the bottom is equal to the product of two numbers at the top, *i.e.*,
$6^2 = 4 \times 9$, *i.e.*, 36
$12^2 = 9 \times 16$, *i.e.*, 144, similarly
$20^2 = 16 \times ?$, *i.e.*, 400. The missing number is $400 \div 16 = 25$.

10. ***(b)*** **:** The sum of the products of the digits of numbers in 1st and 3rd columns is the number in the 2nd column, *i.e.*,

$(5 \times 1) + (6 \times 1) = 11$
$(6 \times 4) + (3 \times 2) = 30$, similarly
$(3 \times 5) + (4 \times 3) = 27$.

11. ***(d)*** **:** The sum of numbers on right and centre subtracted from the number on the left gives the number at the bottom, *i.e.*,
$93 - (27 + 63) = 3$
$79 - (38 + 37) = 4$, similarly
$67 - (16 + 42) = 9$.

12. ***(c)*** **:** The number inside each triangle is the difference of the numbers at its base *i.e.*
$10 - 4 = 6$, $18 - 4 = 14$ and $18 - 10 = 8$
$14 - 8 = 6$, $22 - 8 = 14$ and $22 - 14 = 8$, similarly
$11 - 5 = 6$, $15 - 5 = 10$ and $15 - 11 = 4$.

13. ***(c)*** **:** The sum of squares of two numbers at the top gives the third number below, *i.e.*,
$2^2 + 4^2 = 20$
$3^2 + 9^2 = 90$, similarly
$1^2 + 5^2 = 26$.

14. ***(a)*** **:** The sum of numbers in 1st and 2nd column plus 1 is the number in the 3rd column, *i.e.*,
$27 + 22 + 1 = 50$
$13 + 12 + 1 = 26$, similarly
$9 + 2 + 1 = 12$.

15. ***(d)*** **:** The product of numbers on either side of the triangle plus the number at the base is the number inside the triangle, *i.e.*,
$(5 \times 3) + 4 = 19$
$(6 \times 4) + 5 = 29$, similarly
$(7 \times 5) + 6 = 41$.

16. ***(a)*** **:** Clockwise starting from number 7, the next number is obtained by doubling the number and adding 2, *i.e.*,
$(7 \times 2) + 2 = 16$
$(16 \times 2) + 2 = 34 \ldots$, similarly
$(34 \times 2) + 2 = 70$
$(70 \times 2) + 2 = 142$
$(142 \times 2) + 2 = 286$.

17. ***(c)*** **:** The difference between the numbers in opposite sectors is 13, *i.e.*,
$26 - 13 = 13$
$68 - 55 = 13$, similarly
The missing number is $42 - 13 = 29$
($42 + 13 = 55$ is not given as option).

18. ***(b)*** **:** The number at the bottom is obtained by subtracting the sum of two numbers in the centre grid line from the square of the number at the top, *i.e.*,
$7^2 - (2 + 7) = 40$
$5^2 - (8 + 3) = 14$, similarly
$9^2 - (7 + 6) = 68$.

19. ***(b)*** **:** The number inside the brackets is obtained by multiplying the number on the left by 2 and then dividing the product by the sum of digits of number on the right, *i.e.*,
$(42 \times 2) \div (2 + 2) = 21$
$(162 \times 2) \div (9 + 9) = 18$, similarly
$(78 \times 2) \div (8 + 4) = 13$.

20. ***(a)*** **:** Subtracting the sum of squares of two numbers at the base from the square of number at the apex gives the number inside the triangle, *i.e.*,
$16^2 - (7^2 + 10^2) = 107$
$25^2 - (20^2 + 4^2) = 209$, similarly
$19^2 - (2^2 + 17^2) = 68$.

21. ***(c)*** **:** The number in the centre is the product of all the 4 numbers minus 10, *i.e.*,
$(3 \times 5 \times 2 \times 6) - 10 = 170$
$(8 \times 1 \times 4 \times 9) - 10 = 278$, similarly
$(10 \times 6 \times 7 \times 2) - 10 = 830$.

22. ***(d)*** **:** The number inside the circle is the product of difference of two numbers above and difference of two numbers below, *i.e.*,
$(5 - 3)(12 - 9) = 6$
$(8 - 4)(2 - 1) = 4$, similarly
$(18 - 10)(17 - 14) = 24$.

23. ***(a)*** **:** Starting from number 1 anticlockwise the number in the diagonally opposite section is its multiplication by 4, *i.e.*,
$1 \times 4 = 4$, $7 \times 4 = 28$, $2 \times 4 = 8$, similarly
$6 \times 4 = 24$.

24. ***(a)*** **:** Square of the number on the left plus the number on the right is the number within brackets, *i.e.*,
$6^2 + 4 = 40$
$3^2 + 3 = 12$, similarly
$7^2 + 2 = 51$.

25. ***(b)*** **:** Letter H is 8th in order of alphabetical series. Taking the sum of numbers placed vertically outside the circle + 8; multiplying it by the number on the right; then subtracting from the product the number on the left, gives the number inside the circle, *i.e.*,

Step I $\rightarrow$ $4 + 8 + 4 = 16$

Step II $\rightarrow$ $16 \times 5 = 80$

Step III $\rightarrow$ $80 - 10 = 70$

Letter C is 3rd in order, so

Step I $\rightarrow$ $2 + 3 + 5 = 10$

Step II $\rightarrow$ $10 \times 3 = 30$

Step III $\rightarrow$ $30 - 4 = 26$

Similarly, J is 10th in order, so

Step I $\rightarrow$ $8 + 10 + 6 = 24$

Step II $\rightarrow$ $24 \times ?$

Step III $\rightarrow$ $(24 \times ?) - 6 = 90$

Simplifying the above equation :

$24 \times ? = 90 + 6$, *i.e.*, 96

$? = 96 \div 24 = 4$.

20 Matrices

In these type of questions, a set of numbers or letters are given in a figure which is divided into different cells. Some logic is applied to form a pattern in rows or columns. One of the cells is left empty. The candidates are required to analyse the logic and from the given options select one which will complete the given incomplete matrix.

EXERCISE

Directions (Qs. 1 to 5) : *In each question given below which one number when placed at the sign of interrogation shall complete the number matrix.*

1.

4	5	6
2	3	7
1	8	3
21	98	?

(*a*) 16 (*b*) 73
(*c*) 76 (*d*) 94

2.

3	6	8
5	8	4
4	7	?

(*a*) 9 (*b*) 8
(*c*) 7 (*d*) 6

3.

1	4	9	?
1	2	3	4
2	4	6	?

(*a*) 16 and 8 (*b*) 25 and 5
(*c*) 36 and 4 (*d*) 49 and 7

4.

7	16	9
5	21	16
9	?	4

(*a*) 29 (*b*) 21
(*c*) 13 (*d*) 42

5.

6	6	8
5	7	5
4	3	?
120	126	320

(*a*) 12 (*b*) 16
(*c*) 8 (*d*) 4

Directions (Qs. 6 to 10) : *In questions given below, a word is represented by only one set of numbers as given in any one of the alternatives. The sets of numbers given in the alternatives are represented by two classes of alphabets as in the 2 matrices given below. The columns and rows of matrix I are numbered from 0 to 4 and that of matrix II from 5 to 9. A letter from these matrices can be represented first by its row and next by column number. Identify the set for the word given in each question.*

6.

	0	1	2	3	4
0	E	A	T	S	H
1	A	H	T	A	S
2	E	H	A	S	T
3	H	E	A	T	S
4	S	H	T	A	E

	5	6	7	8	9
5	O	R	K	L	P
6	L	P	O	R	K
7	O	K	R	P	L
8	P	R	K	L	O
9	R	L	K	O	P

REAP

(*a*) 56, 00, 22, 59 (*b*) 68, 21, 22, 86
(*c*) 96, 00, 01, 99 (*d*) 86, 34, 24, 69

7.

	0	1	2	3	4
0	C	A	F	E	D
1	C	D	A	E	D
2	D	E	C	F	E
3	A	D	D	D	C
4	D	C	A	C	A

	5	6	7	8	9
5	T	R	R	S	M
6	S	T	M	R	S
7	R	S	P	T	P
8	P	S	T	R	T
9	P	M	P	M	S

FARM

(*a*) 02, 30, 85, 65 (*b*) 20, 31, 76, 68
(*c*) 23, 12, 68, 96 (*d*) 44, 43, 87, 57

8.

	0	1	2	3	4
0	C	H	H	N	N
1	I	N	C	B	B
2	N	E	C	H	I
3	I	C	N	E	I
4	B	B	E	C	I

	5	6	7	8	9
5	Y	P	S	P	K
6	K	T	S	R	R
7	K	Y	R	Y	Y
8	P	R	K	P	R
9	S	Y	S	T	S

PREY

(*a*) 82, 76, 34, 77 (*b*) 80, 70, 43, 12
(*c*) 94, 87, 43, 56 (*d*) 88, 77, 33, 79

9.

	0	1	2	3	4
0	D	K	A	E	C
1	C	D	K	A	E
2	K	C	E	A	D
3	K	C	D	E	A
4	E	D	A	K	C

	5	6	7	8	9
5	P	L	O	T	N
6	T	P	N	L	O
7	P	N	T	O	L
8	O	N	T	P	L
9	L	O	P	N	T

COLD

(*a*) 10, 85, 79, 24 (*b*) 31, 99, 77, 22
(*c*) 30, 66, 86, 43 (*d*) 44, 96, 95, 22

10.

	0	1	2	3	4
0	M	M	R	M	R
1	O	F	R	F	N
2	R	N	O	R	O
3	F	O	F	M	O
4	F	M	R	R	F

	5	6	7	8	9
5	T	G	J	T	G
6	P	J	G	G	U
7	U	T	P	T	J
8	U	T	T	J	P
9	G	U	G	T	P

TURF

(*a*) 57,86, 44, 11
(*b*) 86, 75, 20, 32
(*c*) 77, 68, 41, 44
(*d*) 89, 97, 12, 30

EXPLANATORY ANSWERS

1. (*d*) : $4^2 + 2^2 + 1^2 = 21$, *i.e.*, $16 + 4 + 1 = 21$
$5^2 + 3^2 + 8^2 = 98$, *i.e.*, $25 + 9 + 64 = 98$
$6^2 + 7^2 + 3^2 = 36 + 49 + 9 = 94$.

2. (*d*) : Sum of numbers in each row is 17, *i.e.*,
$3 + 6 + 8 = 17$
$5 + 8 + 4 = 17$
So, $17 - (4 + 7) = 6$.

3. (*a*) : The root of number in first row is the number in the second row and this number multiplied by 2 is the number in the third row, *i.e.*,
$\sqrt{1} = 1$ and $1 \times 2 = 2$
$\sqrt{4} = 2$ and $2 \times 2 = 4$
$\sqrt{9} = 3$ and $3 \times 2 = 6$
So, square of 4, *i.e.*, 16 in the first row and 4×2, *i.e.*, 8 in the third row completes the matrix.

4. (*c*) : $7 + 9 = 16$
$5 + 16 = 21$

5. *(c)* :

$$9 + 4 = 13.$$
$$6 \times 5 \times 4 = 120$$
$$6 \times 7 \times 3 = 126$$

So, 320 ÷ (8 × 5), *i.e.*, 8 in the third row completes the matrix.

6. *(a)* : R is represented by row 5, column 6
E by row 0, column 0
A by row 2, column 2
P by row 5, column 9.

7. *(c)* : F is represented by row 2, column 3
A by row 1, column 2
R by row 6, column 8
M by row 9, column 6.

8. *(d)* : P is represented by row 8, column 8
R by row 7, column 7
E by row 3, column 3
Y by row 7, column 9.

9. *(a)* : C is represented by row 1, column 0
O by row 8, column 5
L by row 7, column 9
D by row 2, column 4.

10. *(b)* : T is represented by row 8, column 6
U by row 7, column 5
R by row 2, column 0
F by row 3, column 2.

21 Alphabet Problems

Alphabet problems are fun to attempt. They are based on alphabetical series in natural as well as reverse order.

Natural Order

A B C D E F G H I J K L M N O P Q R S T U V W X Y Z

Reverse Order

Z Y X W V U T S R Q P O N M L K J I H G F E D C B A

Note : The series starts from A on reaching Z and from Z on reaching A. Of these A E I O U are vowels and the rest are consonants.

EXERCISE

1. Which letter should be ninth letter to the left of ninth letter from the right if the first half of the alphabet is reversed?

(a) I *(b)* D
(c) F *(d)* E

2. Starting from the fifth letter from the left, if twelve letters are written in reverse order, then which letter will be the seventh to the left of the fourteenth letter from the right?

(a) N *(b)* H
(c) L *(d)* O

3. What letter will come in the centre of sixth letter from the right and thirteenth letter from the left?

(a) Q *(b)* R
(c) P *(d)* S

4. If in the word "DISTURBANCE", the first letter is interchanged with the last letter, the second letter is interchanged with the tenth letter and so on, which letter would come after the letter "T" in the newly formed word?

(a) I *(b)* U
(c) N *(d)* S

5. If it is possible to make a meaningful word with the third, the fifth, the seventh and the tenth letters of the word PROJECTION, which of the following is the third letter of that word? If no such word can be made, give 'X' as the answer. If more than one such word can be made, give 'M' as the answer.

(a) T *(b)* N
(c) O *(d)* M

6. A meaningful word is made if we take the first, fourth, fifth, seventh, tenth, eleventh and the twelfth letters of the word "FELICITATIONS". Which of the following will be the fifth letter of that word from the right end of that word?

(a) T *(b)* C
(c) N *(d)* I

7. On rearranging the jumbled spelling of the word SKARTINS, a language is obtained. What is the fifth letter from the right of the rearranged word?

(a) N *(b)* K
(c) R *(d)* S

8. If the 1st, 3rd, 5th, 7th, 10th and 13th letters of the word "ENTERTAINMENT" are used to make a meaningful word, then what two letters will come in the centre?

(a) AM *(b)* TT
(c) RE *(d)* NA

9. On rearranging the jumbled spelling of the word GRUBY a sport is obtained. What is the letter in the centre?

(a) R *(b)* B
(c) G *(d)* U

10. If the letters 'ERVSECI' can be rearranged to form a meaningful word what will be the fifth letter from the right?

(a) R *(b)* V
(c) E *(d)* None of these

11. From the word HASTEN how many independent meaningful English words can be made without changing the order of the letters and using each letter only once?

(a) 1 *(b)* 2
(c) 3 *(d)* 4

EXPLANATORY ANSWERS

1. *(d)* : MLKJIGHFEDCBANOPQRSTUVWXYZ

9th 9th

2. *(d)* : ABCDPONMLKJIHGFEQRSTUVWXYZ

7th 14th

3. *(a)* :

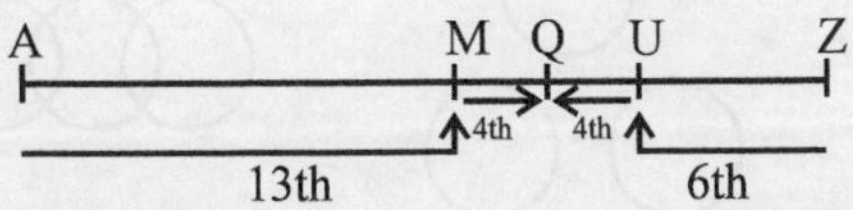

13th letter from left is 'M' and 6th letter from right is 'U'. The letter in the centre of 'M' and 'U' is 'Q'.

4. *(d)* : E C N A B R U T S I D

5. *(d)* : P R O J E C T I O N

The 3rd, 5th, 7th and 10th letters are OETN.

The words formed are TONE and NOTE.

6. *(b)* : F E L I C I T A T I O N S

The 1st, 4th, 5th, 7th, 10th, 11th and 12th lettes are FICTION.

The word is FICTION and 5th letter from right is 'C'.

7. *(d)* : The word is SANSKRIT and 5th letter from right is 'S'.

8. *(b)* : E N T E R T A I N M E N T

The 1st, 3rd, 5th 7th, 10th and 13th letters are ETRAMT.

The word formed is MATTER.

9. *(c)* : The sport is RUGBY. The letter in the centre is 'G'.

10. *(a)* : The word is SERVICE and fifth letter from right is 'R'.

11. *(b)* : The words formed are : HAS, TEN.

22 Logical Diagram

In these type of questions, a set of five different figures is given as options. Each figure represents a logical pattern of certain groups of related words wherein each word represents a class. One has to identify the most appropriate logical figure for the set of words given. Some of the relationships represented by these diagrams are given below. Understand the relationship patterns and then attempt the exercise following the explanation.

EXERCISE

Directions : *From the five logical Diagrams, select one which best illustrates the relationship among three given classes in the questions 1 to 10.*

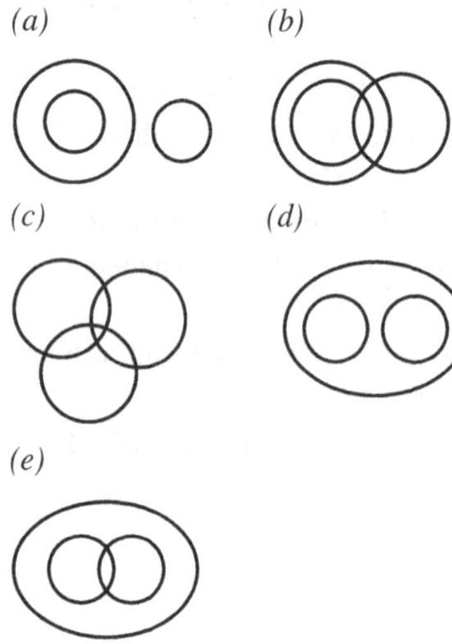

1. Birds, fruits, mangoes
2. Criminals, lawyers, bandits
3. Swimmers, bachelors, men
4. Smart, engineers, women
5. Vegetables, potatoes, brinjals
6. Grapes, sweet, fruit
7. Doctors, architects, humans
8. Scholars, people, Indians
9. Children, naughty, studious
10. Pens, pencils, stationery

Directions : *From the five logical diagrams select one which best illustrates the relationship among three given classes in questions 11 to 20.*

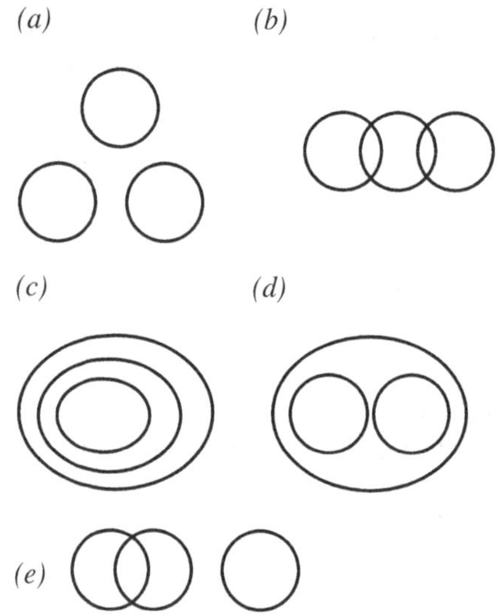

11. Ink, crayons, red
12. Canines, dogs, pups
13. Table, chair, stool
14. Ripe, mangoes, basket
15. Scholars, studious, illiterates
16. Cars, ships, means of conveyance
17. Age, number, thirteen
18. Country, state, continent
19. Father, parent, mother
20. Iron, metal, mercury

Directions : *From the five logical diagrams select one which best illustrates the relationship among three given classes in the questions 21 to 30.*

(a)

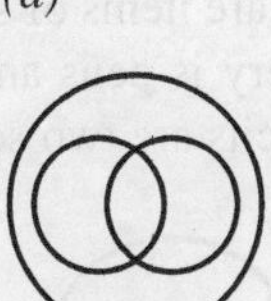

(b)

(c)

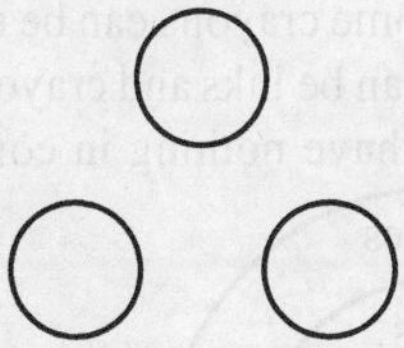

(d)

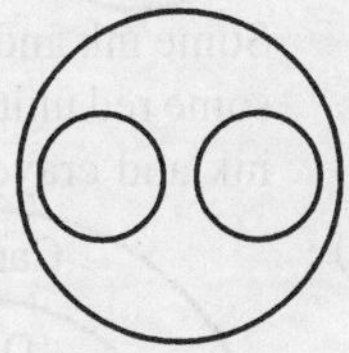

(e)

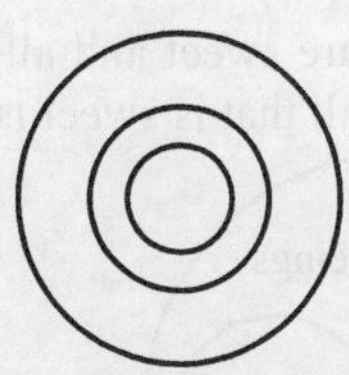

21. Lizards, Reptiles, Crocodiles
22. Whales, Tortoise, Fishes
23. Birds, Crows, Parrots
24. Sisters, Women, Mothers
25. Plants, Scientists, Men
26. Novels, Album, English
27. Sentences, Words, Paragraph
28. Beef, Mutton, Flesh
29. Principal, Student, Parent
30. Lily, Rose, Flower.

EXPLANATORY ANSWERS

1. *(a)* :

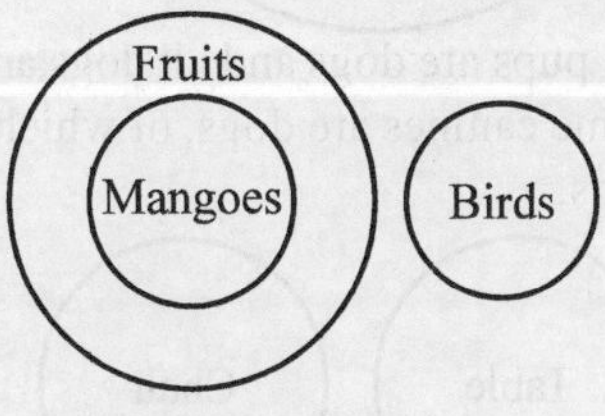

All mangoes are fruits, but neither fruits, nor mangoes can be birds.

2. *(a)* :

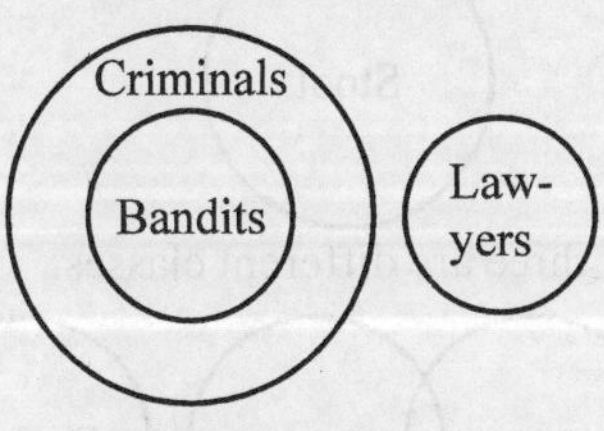

All bandits are criminal, but neither criminals nor bandits can be lawyers.

3. *(b)* :

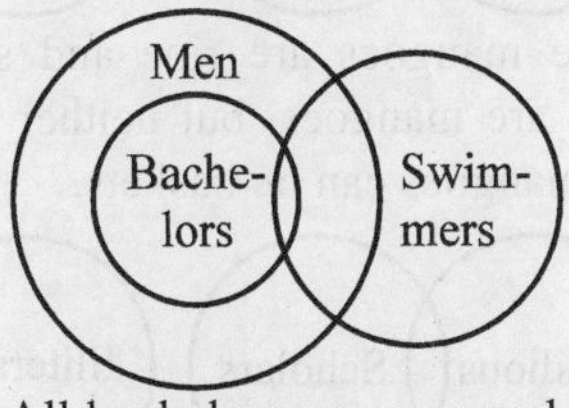

All bachelors are men and some men and bachelors can be swimmers.

4. *(c)* :

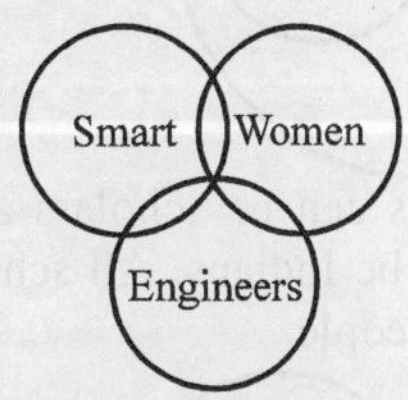

Some women can be smart and some women can be engineers and vice–versa. Some engineers can be women and some engineers can be smart and vice–versa.

5. *(d)* :

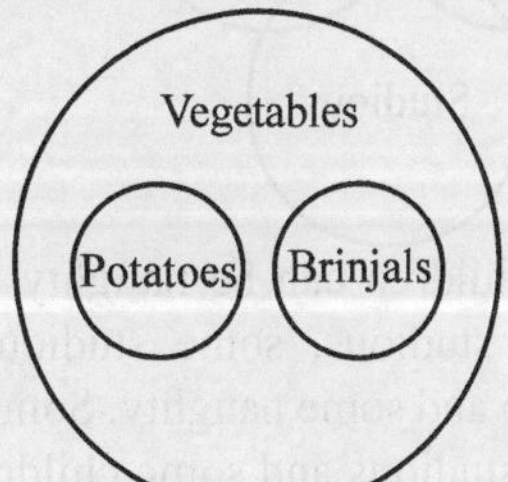

Potatoes and brinjals are vegetables but they have nothing in common. Some vegetables are potatoes and some are brinjals.

6. *(b)* :

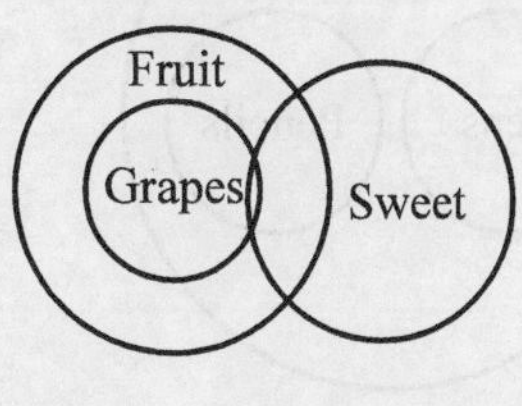

Some grapes are sweet and all grapes are fruit. But not all that is sweet is fruit.

7. *(d)* :

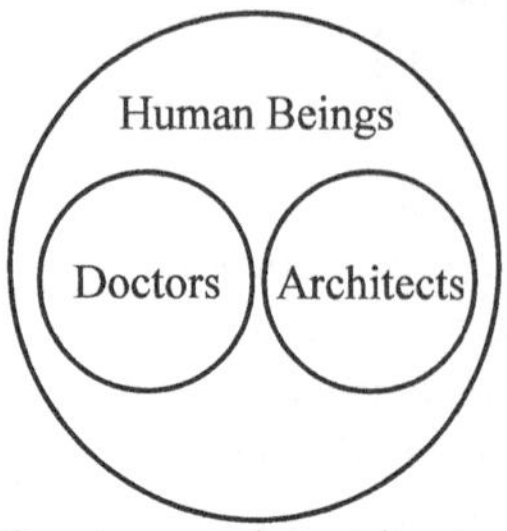

Doctors and architects are two separate classes, but all doctors and architects are humans and some humans are either doctors or architects.

8. *(e)* :

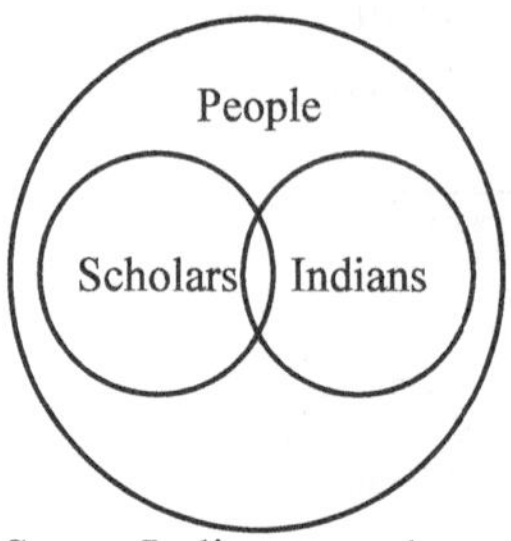

Some Indians can be scholars and some scholars can be Indians. All scholars and Indians are people.

9. *(c)* :

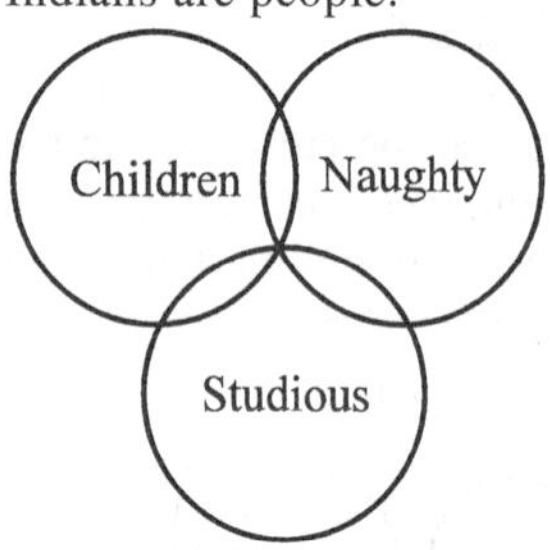

Some children can be naughty and some can be studious, some studious can be children and some naughty. Some naughty can be studious and some children.

10. *(d)* :

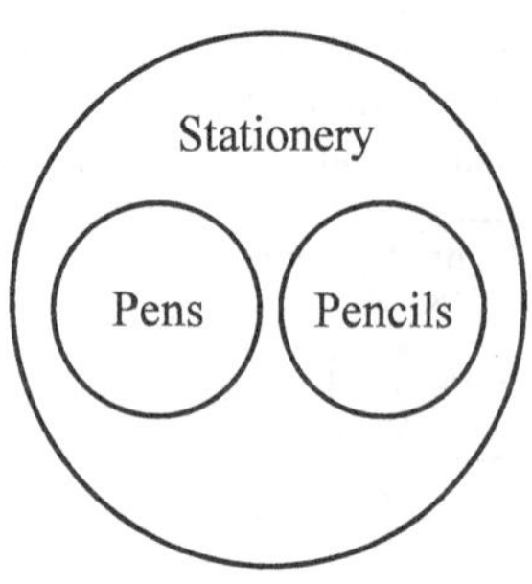

Pens and pencils both are items of stationery and some stationery is pens and pencils, but pens and pencils are two separate classes.

11. *(b)* :

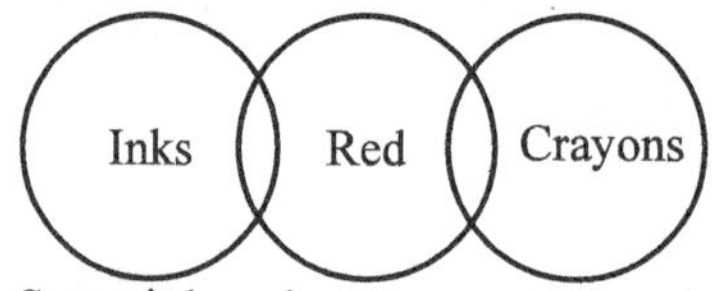

Some ink and some crayons can be red and some red units can be inks and crayons, but ink and crayon have nothing in common.

12. *(c)* :

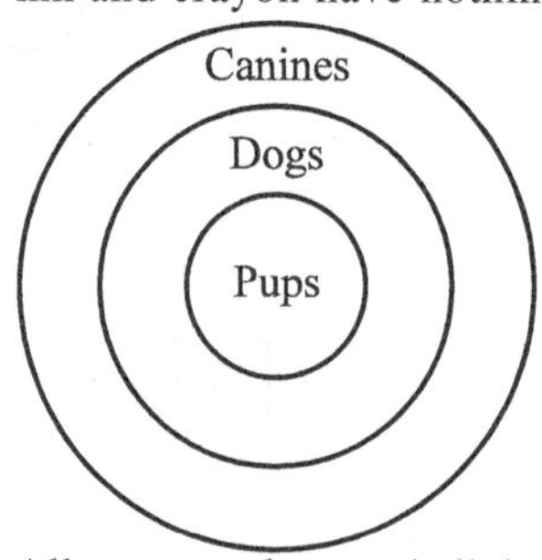

All pups are dogs and all dogs are canines. Some canines are dogs, of which some are pups.

13. *(a)* :

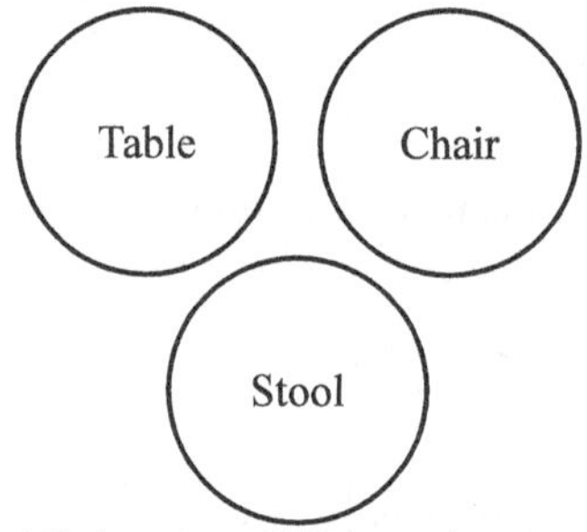

All three are different classes.

14. *(e)* :

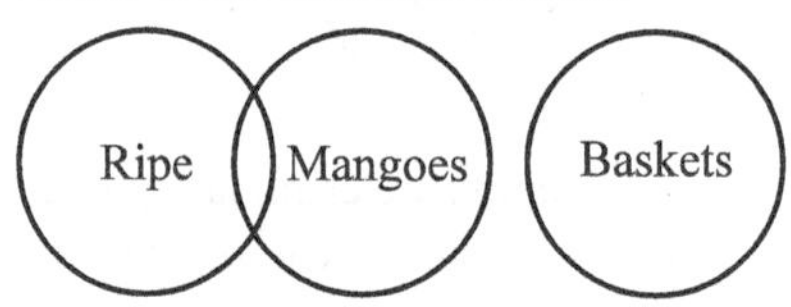

Some mangoes are ripe and some ripe units are mangoes, but neither ripe units nor mangoes can be baskets.

15. *(e)* :

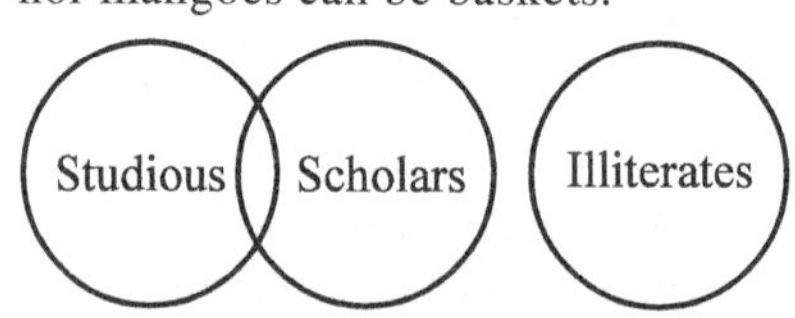

Some studious can be scholars and some scholars can be studious, but neither studious nor scholars can be illiterates.

16. *(d)* :

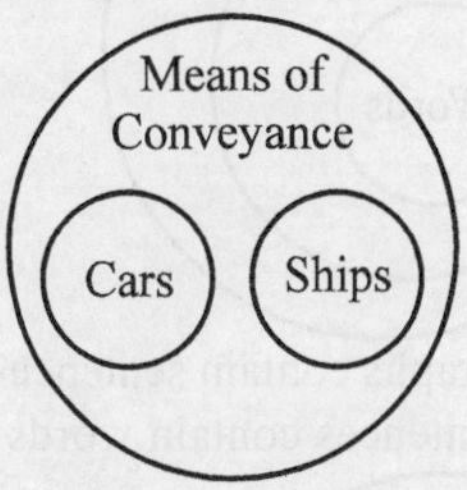

All cars and all ships are means of conveyance, but neither is contained in the other. Some means of conveyance are cars and some ships.

17. *(b)* :

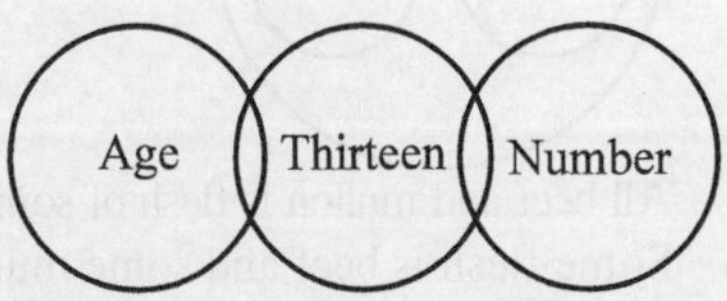

Some are aged thirteen and some numbers are thirteen. Some thirteen units are numbers and some ages. Age and number have nothing in common.

18. *(c)* :

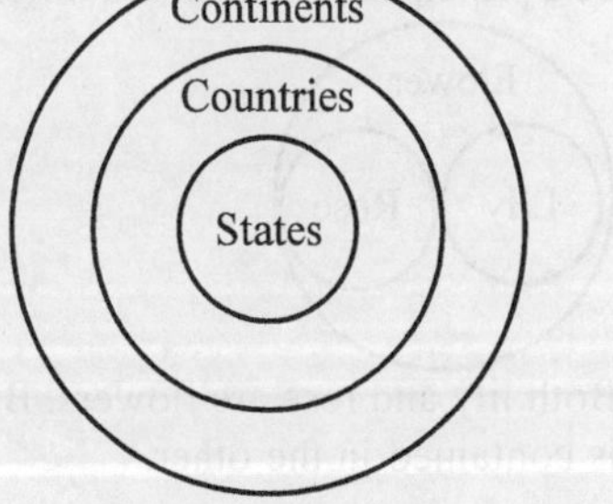

All continents contain countries within it and each country contains states within it.

19. *(d)* :

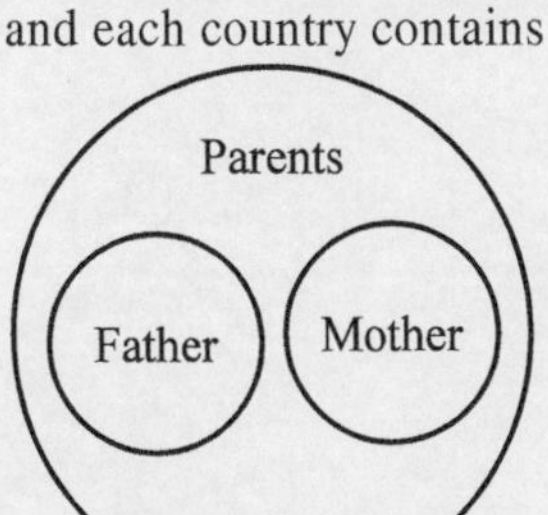

All fathers and mothers are parents, but they are two separate classes. Some of the parents are fathers and some are mothers.

20. *(d)* :

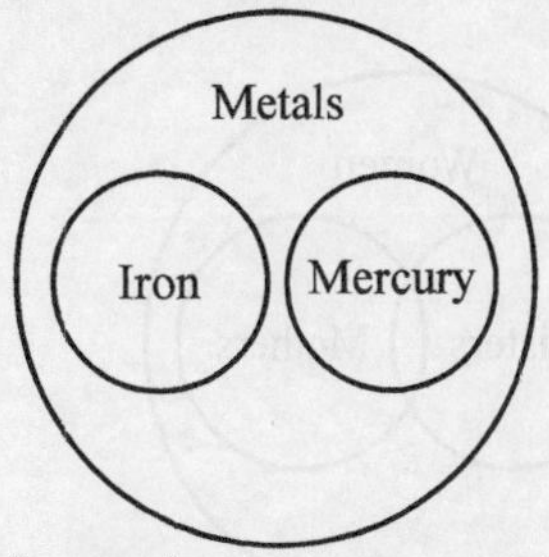

Iron and mercury are metals, but they have nothing in common. Some metals are iron and some mercury.

21. *(d)* :

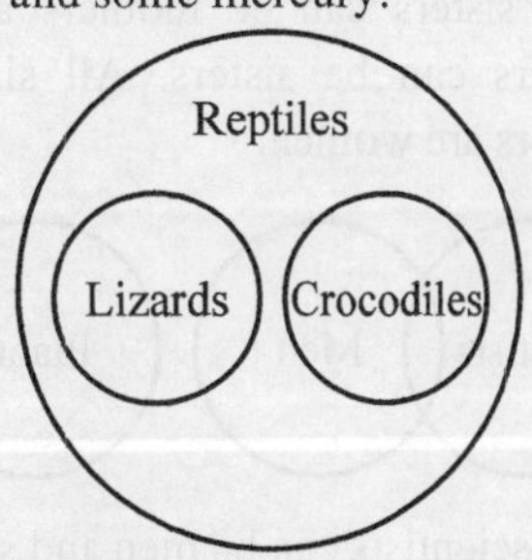

All lizards and crocodiles are reptiles, but neither is contained in the other. Some reptiles are lizards and some crocodiles.

22. *(c)* :

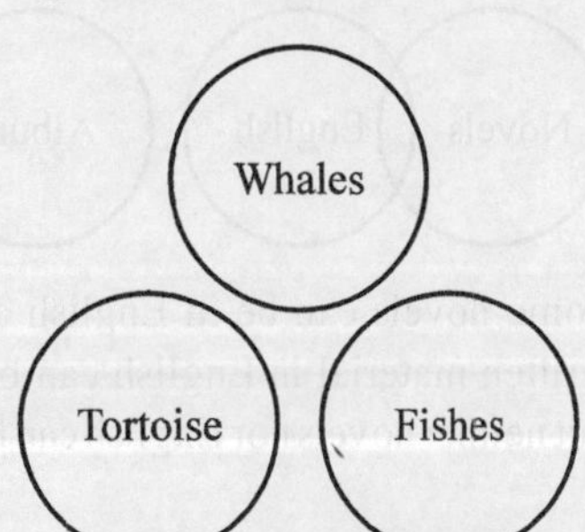

All three are different classes.

23. *(d)* :

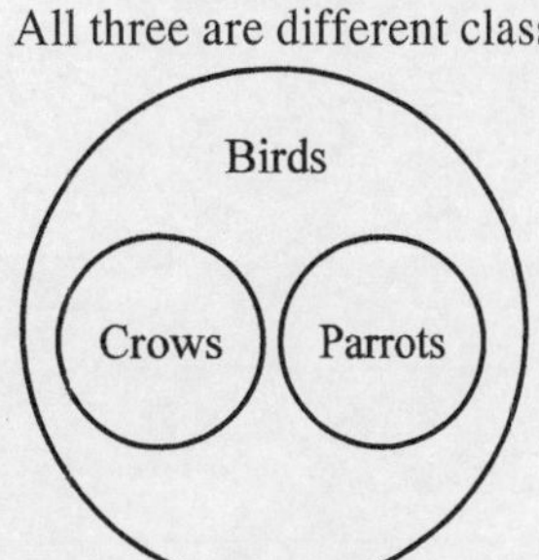

All crows and parrots are birds but neither is contained in the other. Some birds are crows and some parrots.

24. *(a)* :

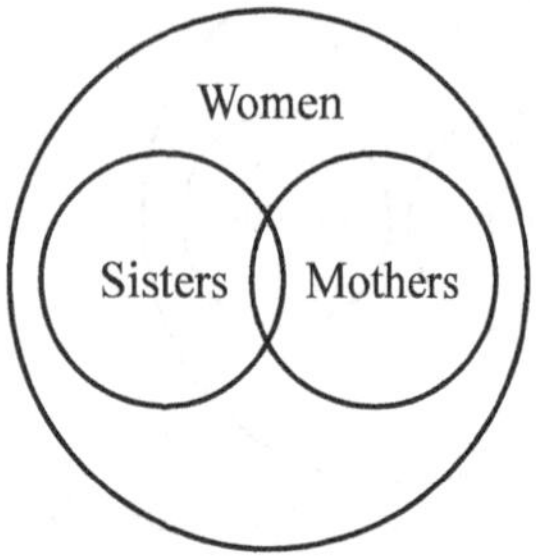

Some sisters can be mothers and some mothers can be sisters. All sisters and mothers are women.

25. *(b)* :

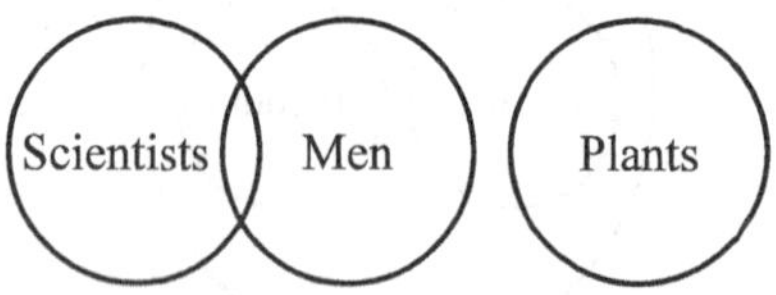

Some scientists can be men and some men can be scientists, but neither scientists nor men can be plants.

26. *(b)* :

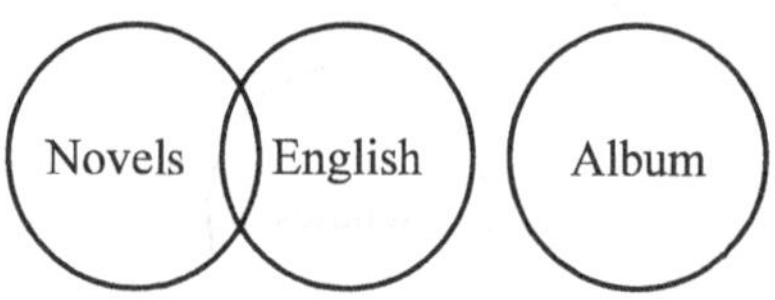

Some novels can be in English and some written material in English can be novels, but neither novels nor English can be album.

27. *(e)* :

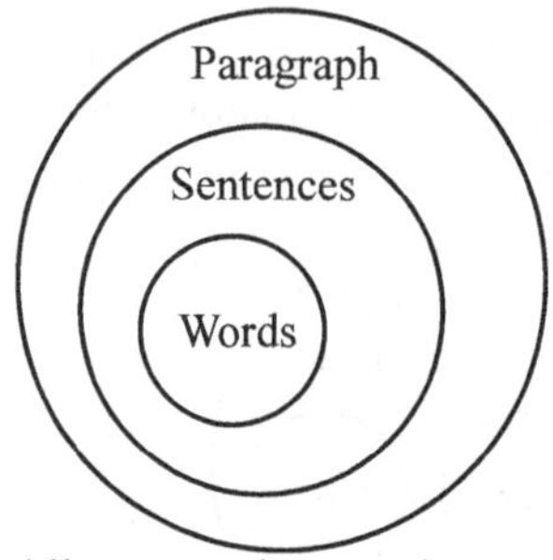

All paragraphs contain sentences within it and all sentences contain words within it.

28. *(d)* :

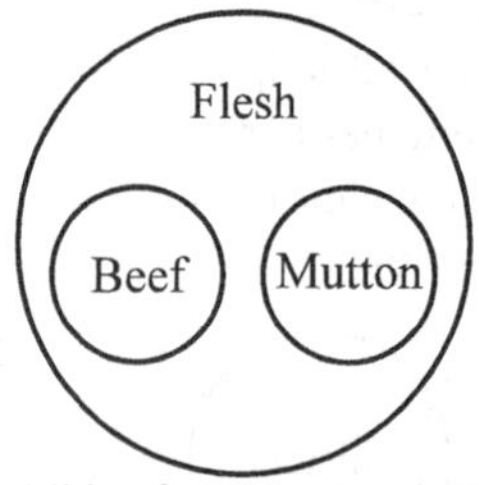

All beef and mutton is flesh of some animals. Some flesh is beef and some mutton.

29. *(b)* :

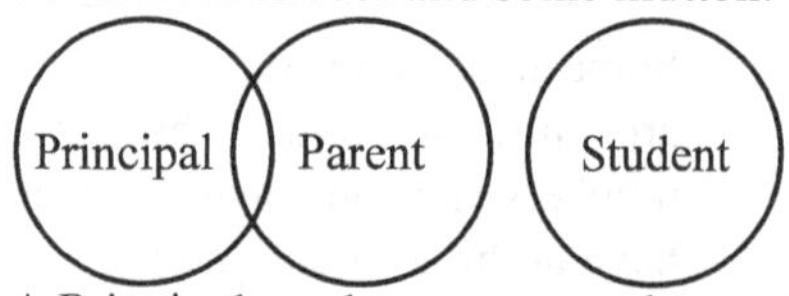

A Principal can be a parent and parent can be a principal. A student is a different class.

30. *(d)* :

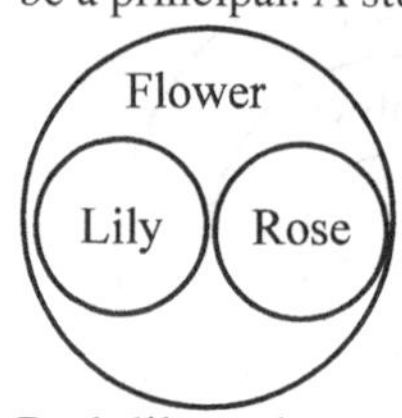

Both lily and rose are flowers. But neither is contained in the other.

23 Syllogism

In this reasoning pattern, the two premises are followed by two conclusions drawn from them. Five options *(a)*, *(b)*, *(c)*, *(d)* and *(e)* are given as answers. Based on the two statements the candidate has to select the right option as answer.

EXERCISE

Directions : *In each question below are given two statements followed by two conclusions numbered I and II. You have to take the two given statements to be true even if they seem to be at variance from commonly known facts and then decide which of the given conclusions logically follows from the two given statements, disregarding commonly known facts. Read both the statements and—*

Give answer (a) if only conclusion I follows; give answer (b) if only conclusion II follows; give answer (c) if either I or II follows; give answer (d) if neither I nor II follows and give answer (e) if both I and II follows.

1. *Statements* *I :* All tomatoes are red.
II : All grapes are tomatoes.
Conclusions I : All grapes are red.
II : Some tomatoes are grapes.

2. *Statements* *I :* All painters are smiling.
II : Some authors are painters.
Conclusions I : All smiling authors are painters.
II : Some authors are smiling.

3. *Statements* *I :* All peons in this office are efficient.
II : Ramu is not efficient.
Conclusions I : Ramu is not peon in this office.
II : Ramu should be more efficient.

4. *Statements* *I :* All weavers are hard working.
II : No hard working men are foolish.
Conclusions I : No weavers are foolish.
II : Some foolish are weavers.

5. *Statements* *I :* All fishes are cars.
II : All cars are vegetables.
Conclusions I : Some vegetables are cars.
II : Some vegetables are fishes.

6. *Statements* *I :* Some dogs are pups.
II : All horses are pups.
Conclusions I : Some dogs are horses.
II : Some horses are dogs.

7. *Statements* *I :* All beautiful women are mothers.
II : All mothers are understanding.
Conclusions I : All beautiful women are understanding.
II : All mothers are beautiful women.

8. *Statements* *I :* Some toys are tables.
II : No table is black.
Conclusions I : Some toys are black.
II : Some toys are not black.

9. *Statements* *I :* All rivers are mountains.
II : Some rivers are deserts.
Conclusions I : Some mountains are deserts.
II : Some deserts are not mountains.

10. *Statements* *I :* All men are horses.
II : All horses are elephants.
Conclusions I : All men are elephants.
II : All elephants are men.

Directions : *In the following questions, select the set of conclusion which logically follows from the given statements.*

11. *Statements* *I:* All foxes are plates.
II: All plates are trees.
Conclusions *I:* All foxes are trees.
II: All trees are foxes.
III: Some trees are foxes.
IV: Some trees are plates.

(*a*) All conclusions are correct.
(*b*) Only conclusions I, III, and IV follow.
(*c*) Only conclusions II, III, and IV follow.
(*d*) Only conclusions I and IV follow.
(*e*) None of the above.

12. *Statements* *I:* Some cubes are squares.
II: All squares are circles.
Conclusions *I:* All cubes are circles.
II: Some circles are cubes.
III: Some circles are squares.
IV: All squares are cubes.

(*a*) Only conclusion I follows.
(*b*) Only conclusion I, II and III follow.
(*c*) All conclusions are correct.
(*d*) Only conclusions II and III follow.
(*e*) None of the above.

13. *Statements* *I:* All cups are goats.
II: All goats are tins.
Conclusions *I:* All goats are cups.
II: All tins are goats.
III: No cups are tins.
IV: No tins are cups.

(*a*) Only conclusions III and IV follow.
(*b*) Only conclusios I and II follow.
(*c*) Only conclusions I, II and III follow.
(*d*) All conclusions are correct.
(*e*) None of the above.

14. *Statements* *I:* All bombs are bags.
II: Some bags are jets.
Conclusions *I:* All bombs are jets.
II: All jets are bombs.
III: Some jets are bombs.
IV: Some bombs are jets.

(*a*) Only conclusion III follows.
(*b*) Only conclusions I and II follow.
(*c*) All conclusions are correct.
(*d*) Only conclusions III and IV follow.
(*e*) None of these.

15. *Statements* *I:* Some thorns are jackets.
II: Some jackets are boats.
Conclusions *I:* No thorns are boats.
II: All jackets are boats.
III: Some boats are thorns.
IV: No jackets are thorns.

(*a*) Either conclusion I or IV follows.
(*b*) Either conclusion I or II follows.
(*c*) Either conclusion I or III follows.
(*d*) No conclusion is correct.
(*e*) All conclusions are correct.

EXPLANATORY ANSWERS

1. (*e*) **:** When all tomatoes are red and all grapes are tomatoes, then all grapes are also red. When all grapes are tomatoes, then some tomatoes must be grapes. Therefore, both conclusions I and II are correct.

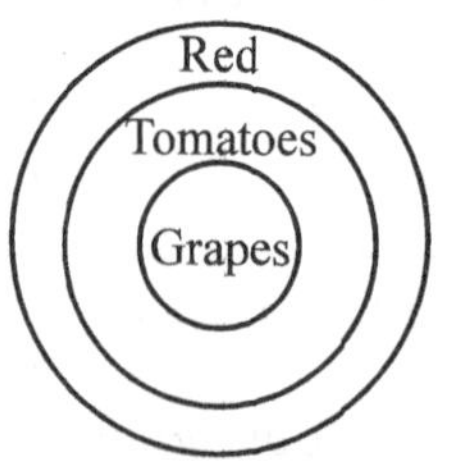

2. (*b*) **:** When all painters are smiling and some authors are painters, then some authors are smiling. Therefore, only conclusion II is correct.

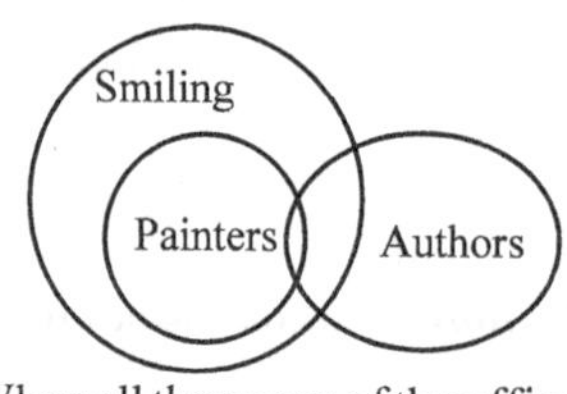

3. (*a*) **:** When all the peons of the office are efficient, then Ramu cannot be a peon in this office. Therefore, only conclusion I is correct.

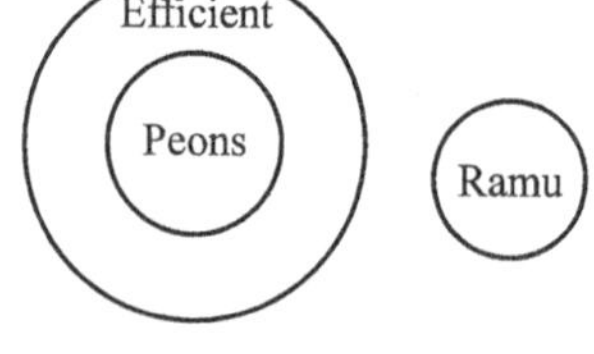

4. *(a)* **:** When all weavers are hardworking and no hardworking men are foolish, then no weavers are foolish. Therefore, only conclusion I is correct.

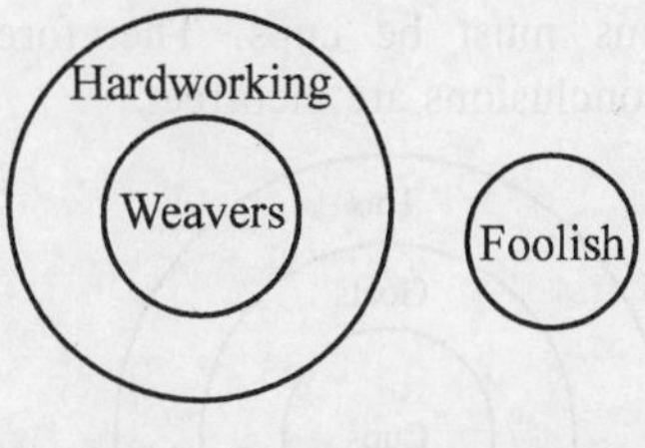

5. *(e)* **:** When all fishes are cars and all cars are vegetables, then all fishes will naturally be vegetables. This means that some vegetables are fishes. And when all cars are vegetables, then some vegetables will be cars naturally. Therefore, both the conclusions I and II are correct.

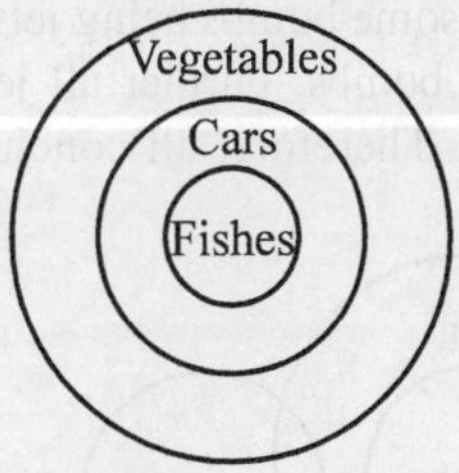

6. *(d)* **:** No relationship can be established between the two statements. Therefore, neither conclusion I nor conclusion II is correct.

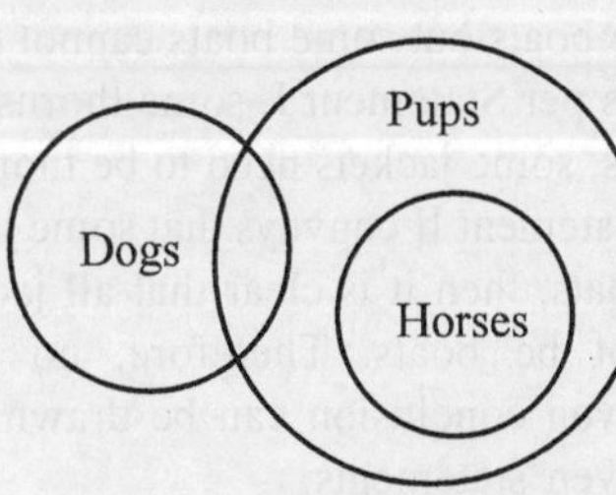

7. *(a)* **:** When all beautiful women are mothers and all mothers are understanding, then naturally all beautiful women are understanding. All mothers need not be beautiful women. Therefore, only conclusion I is correct.

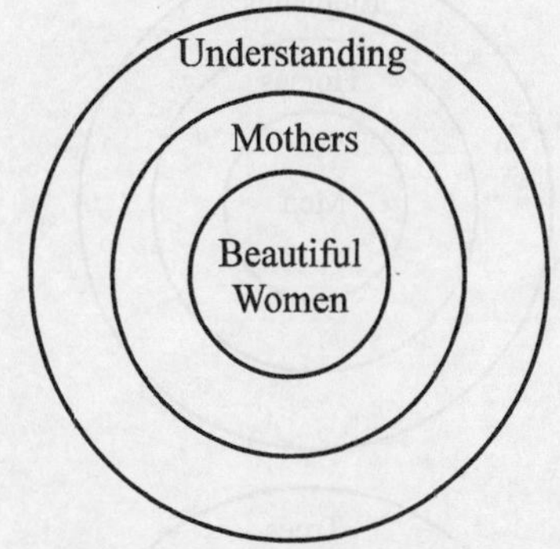

8. *(c)* **:** When some toys are tables and no table is black, then it is indicated that some toys can be black, as all toys are not tables. On the other hand, some toys may not be black. Therefore, there is a possibility that some toys may or may not be black. As such, either conclusion I or conclusion II can be correct.

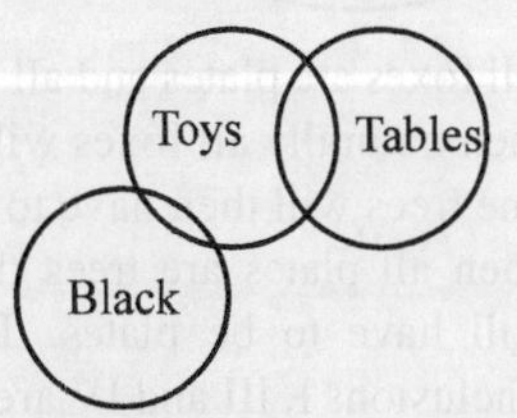

9. *(e)* **:** When all rivers are mountains and some rivers are deserts, then some deserts cannot be mountains and also, some mountains need not be deserts. Therefore, both conclusion I and conclusion II are correct.

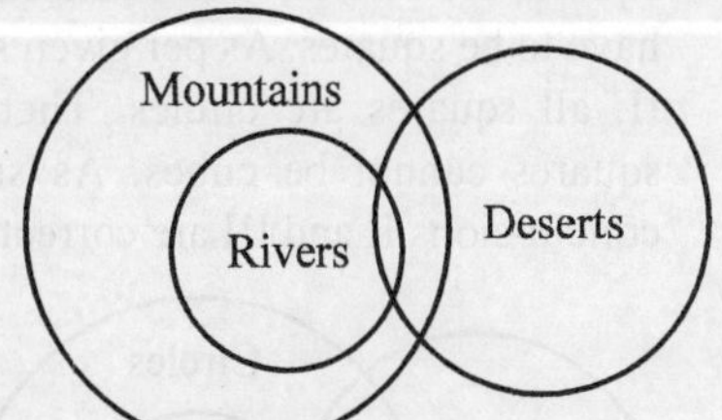

10. *(a)* **:** When all men are horses and all horses are elephants then, naturally all men are elephants, but all elephants need not be men. Therefore, only conclusion I is correct.

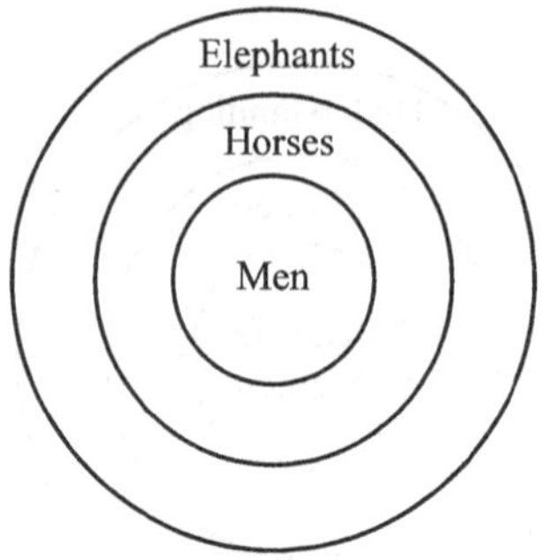

11. *(b)* :

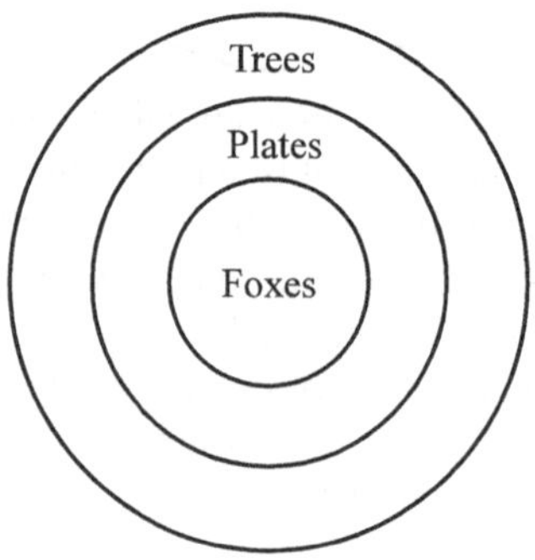

When all foxes are plates and all plates are trees, then naturally all foxes will be trees and some trees will then have to be foxes. And when all plates are trees then some trees will have to be plates. Therefore, only conclusions I, III and IV are correct.

12. *(d)* : When it is given that some cubes are squares and all squares are circles, then some cubes will naturally be circles, though all cubes cannot be circles. When some cubes are circles, then some circles will have to be cubes. And when all squares are circles, then some circles will have to be squares. As per given statement II, all squares are circles. Therefore all squares cannot be cubes. As such only conclu-sions II and III are correct.

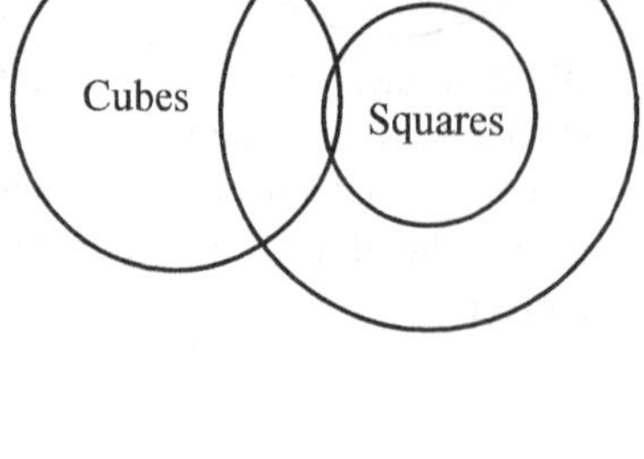

13. *(e)* : When all cups are goats, then only some goats can be cups. When all goats are tins, then only some tins can be goats. When all cups are goats and all goats are tins, then naturally all cups are tins and some tins must be cups. Therefore, all the conclusions are incorrect.

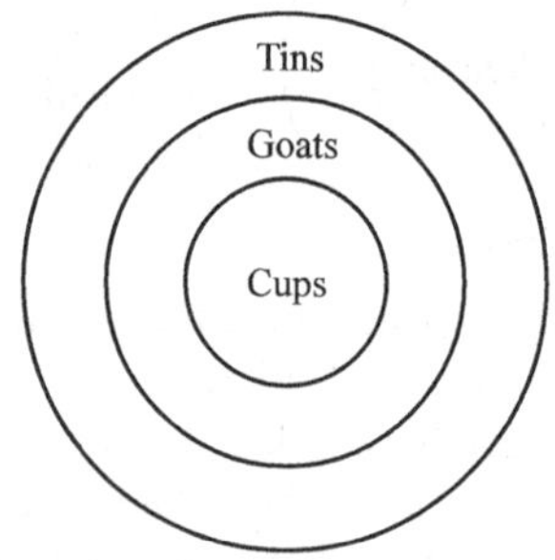

14. *(e)* : When all bombs are bags and some bags are jets then all bombs cannot be jets. 'Some bags' indicate that there is no chance of some bombs being jets, or some jets being bombs. Further all jets cannot be bombs. Therefore, all conclusions are incorrect.

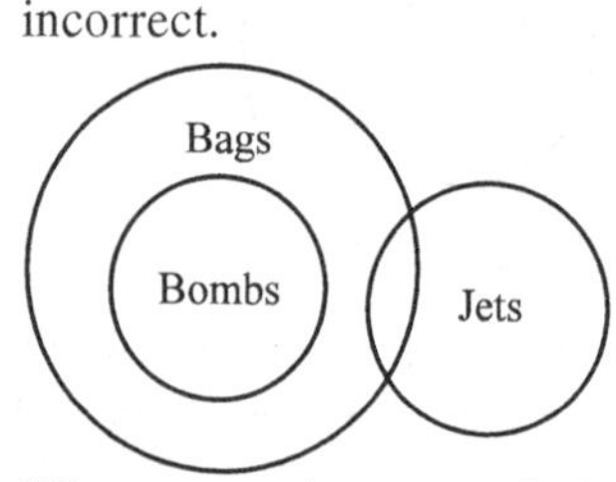

15. *(d)* : When some thorns are jackets and some jackets are boats, then some thorns may be boats but some boats cannot be thorns. As per Statement I, some thorns are jack-ets, some jackets need to be thorns. When Statement II conveys that some jackets are boats, then it is clear that all jackets can-not be boats. Therefore, no particular given conclusion can be drawn from the given statements.

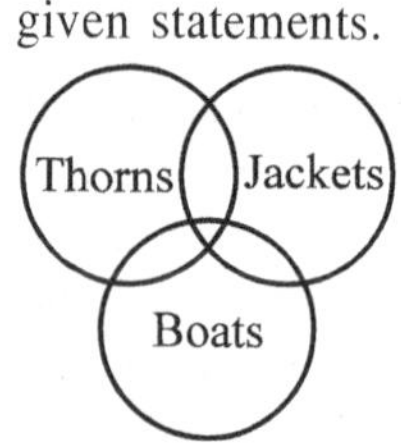

24 Venn Diagrams

In these type of questions, diagrammatic representation presents a logical illustration of particular class or statements based on which the questions are asked. A clear view of the diagram makes the concepts clear for attempting such questions.

EXERCISE

1. What is the number which is common to only two geometrical figures?

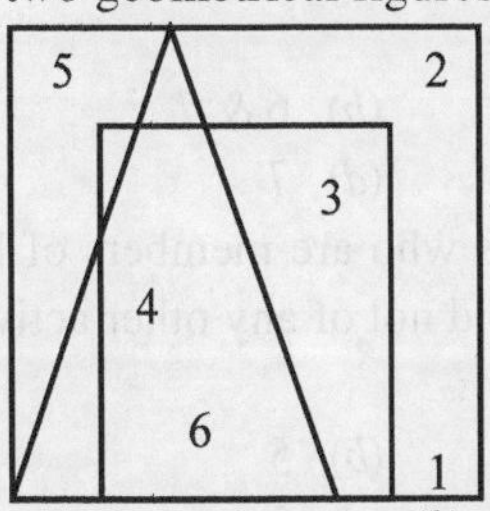

(*a*) 4 (*b*) 3

(*c*) 5 (*d*) 2

Directions (Qs. 2 and 3) : *In the following diagram, rectangle represents Hindi Announcers, circle represents English Announcers, square represents French Announcers, and triangle represents German Announcers.*

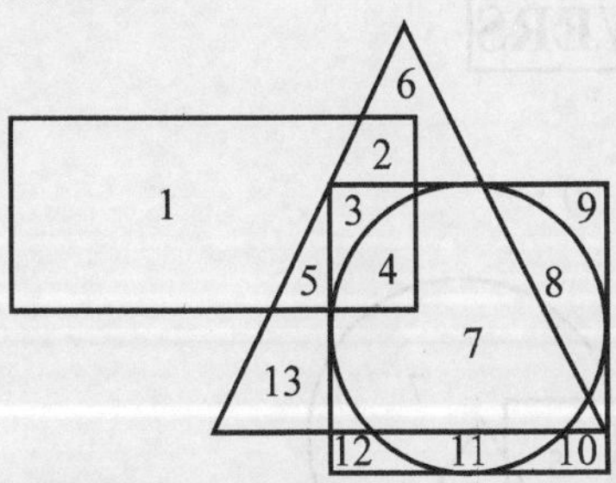

2. Which area represents those announcers who can present programmes in Hindi, French and German only?

(*a*) 1 (*b*) 2

(*c*) 3 (*d*) 4

3 Which area represents those announcers who can present programmes in French and English only?

(*a*) 7 (*b*) 9

(*c*) 11 (*d*) 13

Directions (Qs. 4 and 5) : *Study the diagram to answer these questions.*

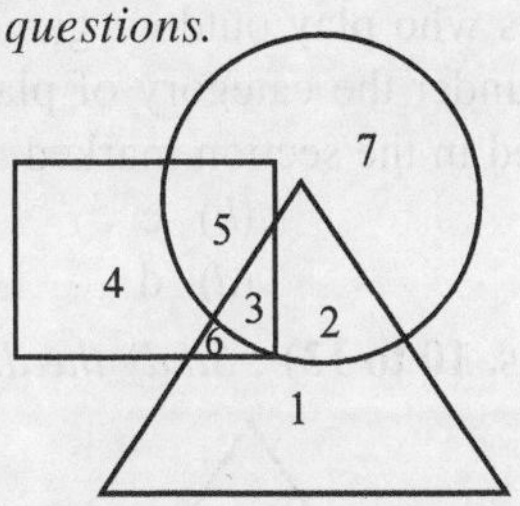

4. Which number is in all the geometrical figures?

(*a*) 5 (*b*) 6

(*c*) 2 (*d*) 3

5. Number 6 is in :

(*a*) Rectangle and triangle

(*b*) Circle and traingle

(*c*) Rectangle and circle

(*d*) Rectangle only

Directions (Qs. 6 to 9) : *In the following diagram*

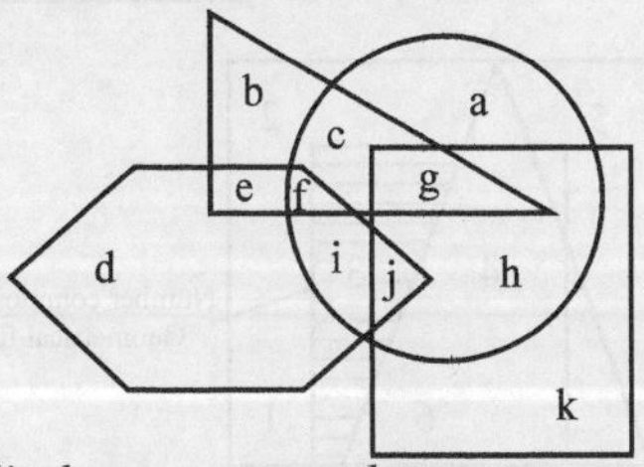

The Circle represents players
The Triangle represents outdoor games
The Hexagon represents indoor games and
The Square represents national level players
Study the diagram and answer the questions given below :

6. The letter in the section representing the players who play indoor games at national level is :

(*a*) f (*b*) i

(*c*) j (*d*) g

7. The letter representing the section of outdoor as well as indoor game players who do not play at the national level is :

(*a*) c (*b*) f
(*c*) e (*d*) i

8. The section representing national level players who do not play either outdoor or indoor games but still come under the category of players is :

(*a*) k (*b*) g
(*c*) c (*d*) h

9. Persons who play outdoor games but do not come under the category of players are represented in the section marked :

(*a*) b (*b*) c
(*c*) a (*d*) d

Directions (Qs. 10 to 13) : *Study the diagram given below.*

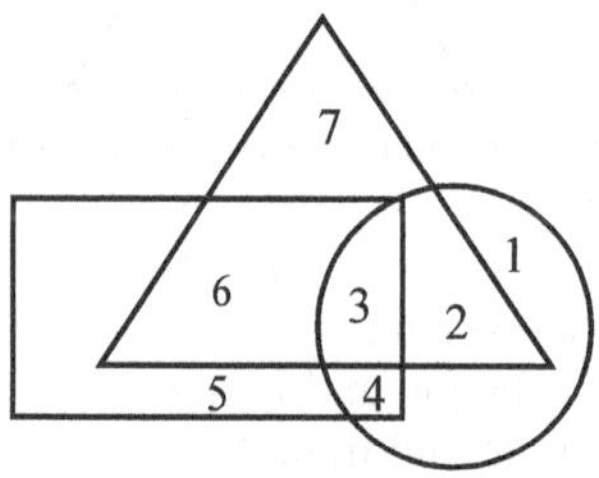

A college provides three different activities, students union represented by triangle, literary society represented by rectangle and social service league represented by circle.

10. Those who take part in both literary society and social service league but not in students union are represented by :

(*a*) 3 & 4 (*b*) 5 & 6
(*c*) 5 & 1 (*d*) 4

11. Those who take part in students union but not in social service league are represented by :

(*a*) 2 & 7 (*b*) 6 & 7
(*c*) 6 (*d*) 7

12. Those students who are members of literary society only and not of any other activity are represented by :

(*a*) 2 (*b*) 5
(*c*) 3 & 4 (*d*) 3

13. Those students who are members of all three groups are represented by :

(*a*) 2 (*b*) 3
(*c*) 4 (*d*) 6

EXPLANATORY ANSWERS

1. ***(b)*** **:**

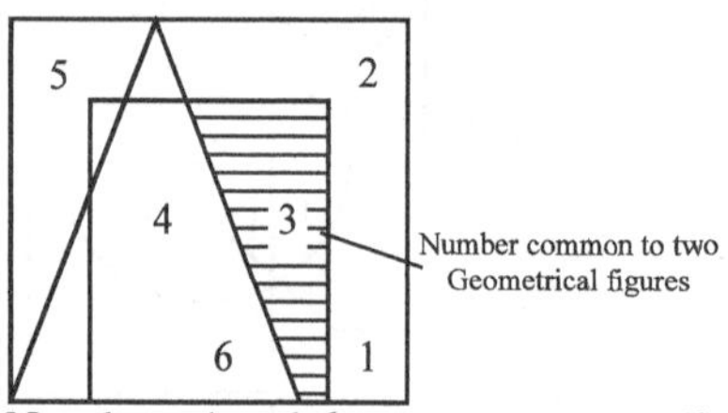

Note : Numbers 4 and 6 are common to all three geometrical figures.

2. ***(c)*****,** **3.** ***(c)*** **:**

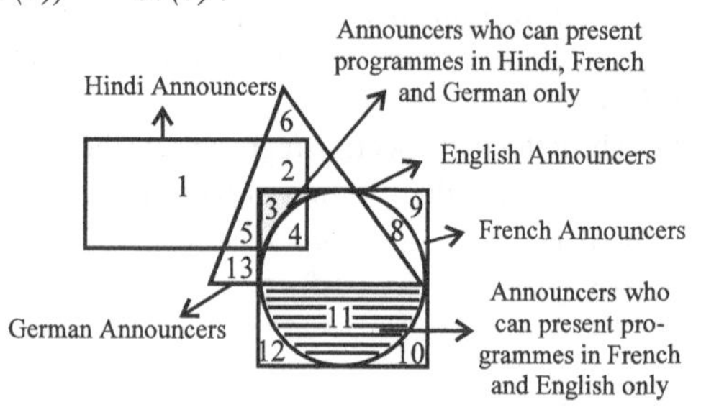

4. ***(d)*****,** **5.** ***(a)*** **:**

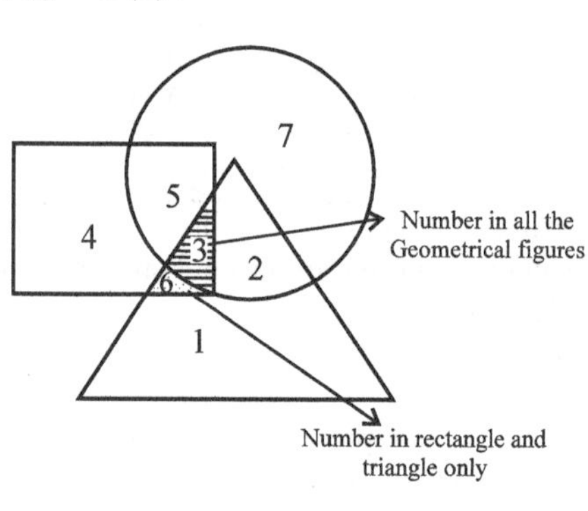

6. ***(c)*****,**
7. ***(b)*****,**
8. ***(d)*****,**
9. ***(a)*** **:**

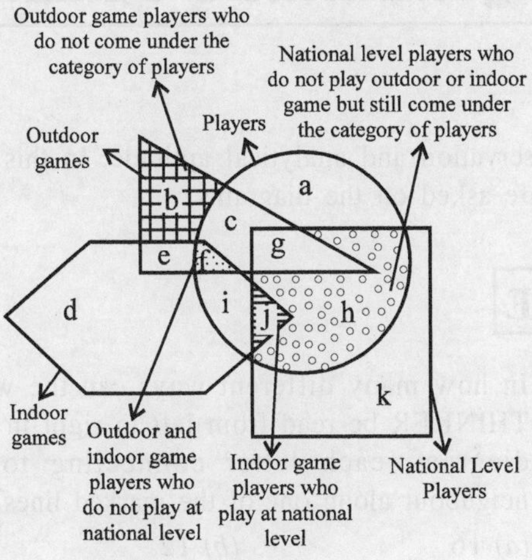

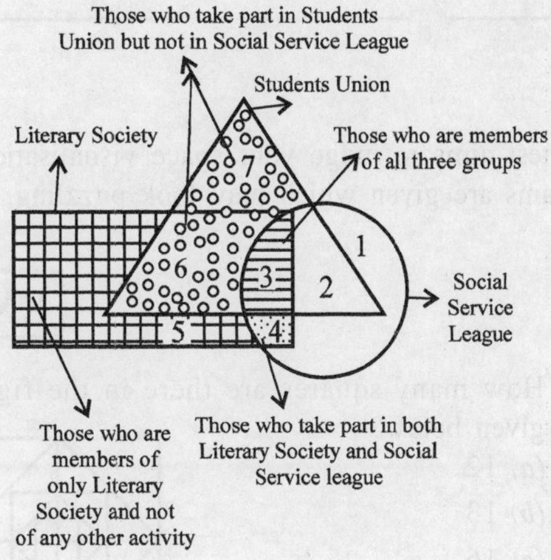

10. *(d)*, **11.** *(b)*, **12.** *(b)*, **13.** *(b)* :

25 Diagrammatic Puzzle

This test aims to judge your space visualisation, keen observation and analytical aptitude. In this test diagrams are given which may look puzzling. Questions are asked on the diagrams.

EXERCISE

1. How many squares are there in the figure given below?

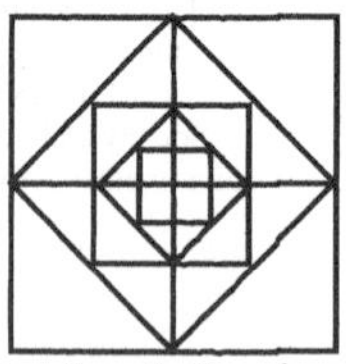

(*a*) 12

(*b*) 13

(*c*) 16

(*d*) 17

2. Find the number of squares in the following figure:

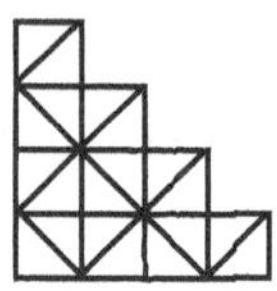

(*a*) 14

(*b*) 13

(*c*) 12

(*d*) 11

3. How many triangles are there in the figure given below?

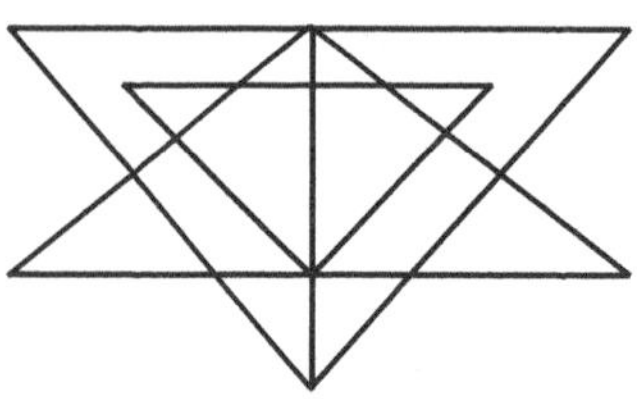

(*a*) 25 (*b*) 23

(*c*) 21 (*d*) 27

4.

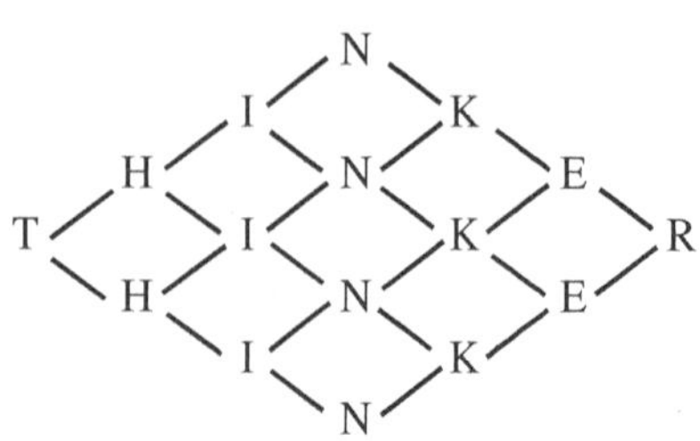

In how many different ways can the word THINKER be read from left to right in this diagram, each letter connecting to its neighbour along one of the marked lines.

(*a*) 16 (*b*) 12

(*c*) 8 (*d*) 20

5. Different designs can be made by placing a maximum of nine matchsticks. Which of the following designs cannot be made at all?

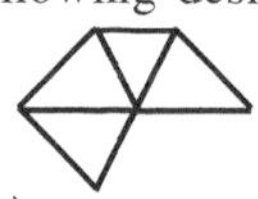

(A)

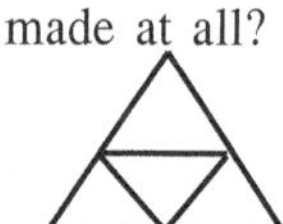

(B)

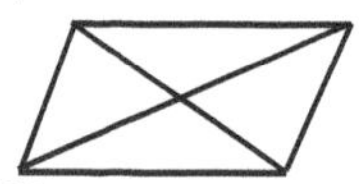

(C)

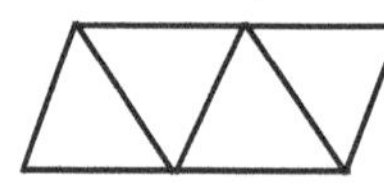

(D)

(*a*) A (*b*) B

(*c*) C (*d*) D

6. Two positions of a dice are shown below.

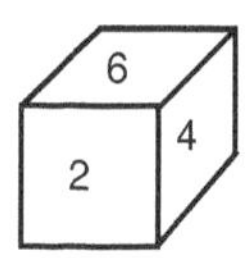

and

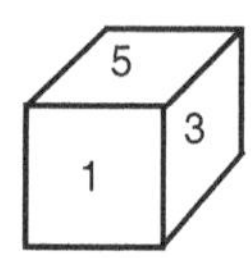

When 2 is at the bottom, what number will be at the top?

(*a*) 1 (*b*) 3

(*c*) 4 (*d*) 5

7. Six sides of a block are coloured Green, Blue, Red, Yellow, Orange and White in the following manner:

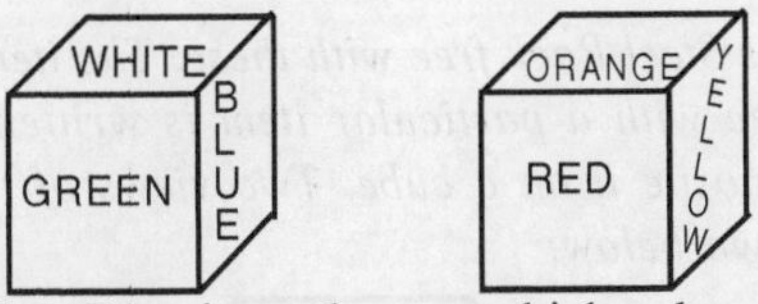

When Blue is on the top, which colour will be at the bottom?

(*a*) Orange (*b*) Red
(*c*) White (*d*) Yellow

8. Below are depicted the four different positions of a dice. Find the number of dots on the face opposite to the face with one dot.

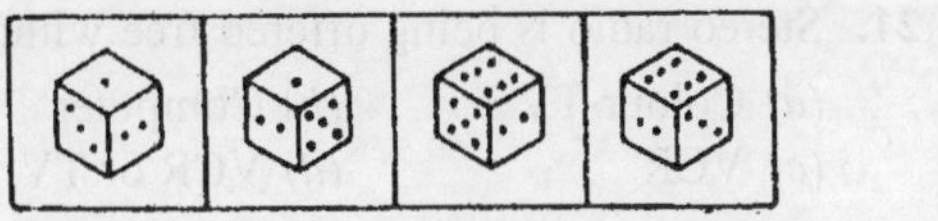

(*a*) 2 (*b*) 3
(*c*) 4 (*d*) 6

9. Two positions of a dice are shown below:

When 3 (three) dots are at the top, how many will be at the bottom?

(*a*) 1 (*b*) 2
(*c*) 4 (*d*) 5

Directions (Qs. 10 to 12): *Given below are three positions of the same cube having numbers 1 to 6 written on its six faces. Answer these questions after a careful study of the three positions of the cube.*

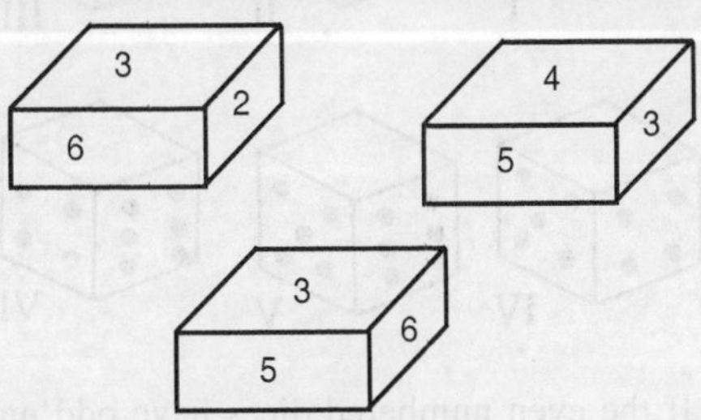

10. Which number occur's on the face opposite face 5?

(*a*) 5 (*b*) 3
(*c*) 2 (*d*) can't be determined

11. The face on the bottom in the first figure has the number:

(*a*) 5 (*b*) 1
(*c*) 4 (*d*) None of these

12. The number on the face opposite the face having number 6 is:

(*a*) 5 (*b*) 4
(*c*) 6 (*d*) 7

Directions (Qs. 13 to 15): *These questions are based on the following figures which depict three views of the same cube:*

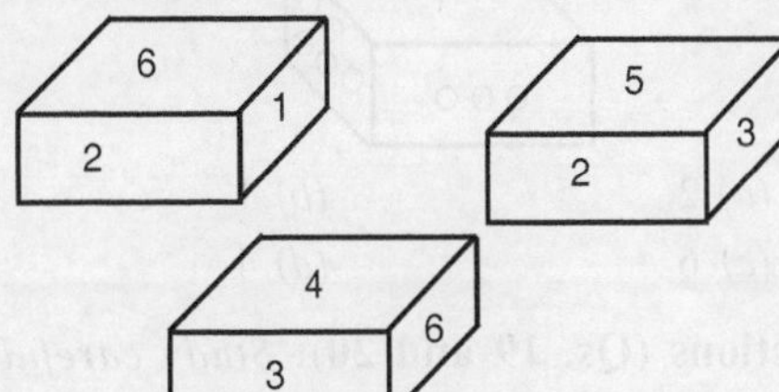

13. The number on the face opposite the face 1 is:

(*a*) 5 (*b*) 3
(*c*) 2 (*d*) 4

14. The numbers on the faces neighbouring the face marked 5 is:

(*a*) 1, 2, 3, 4 (*b*) 2, 3, 4, 6
(*c*) 1, 2, 4, 5 (*d*) 1, 3, 4, 6

15. Which of the following pairs does not correctly give the numbers on the opposite faces?

(*a*) 6-5 (*b*) 4-1
(*c*) 1-3 (*d*) 4-2

Directions (Qs. 16 to 18): *The figures given below show three positions of the same dice having 1, 2, 3, ...6 circles on its six faces. Answer these questions based on this dice.*

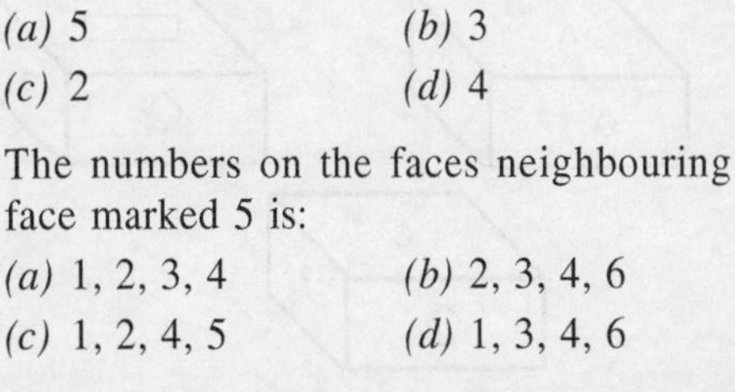

16. The number of circles on the face opposite to the one having three circles is:

(a) 6 (b) 5

(c) 7 (d) None of these

17. What is the number of circles on the face at the bottom of the first cube?

(a) 6 (b) 1

(c) 5 (d) None of these

18. How many circles will be there on the top face in the figure shown?

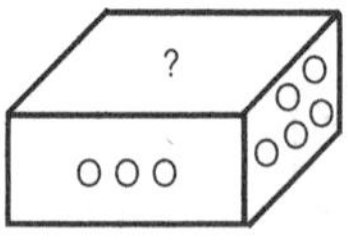

(a) 2 (b) 1

(c) 6 (d) 4

Directions (Qs. 19 and 20): *Study carefully the three views of the same cube shown below and then answer the questions.*

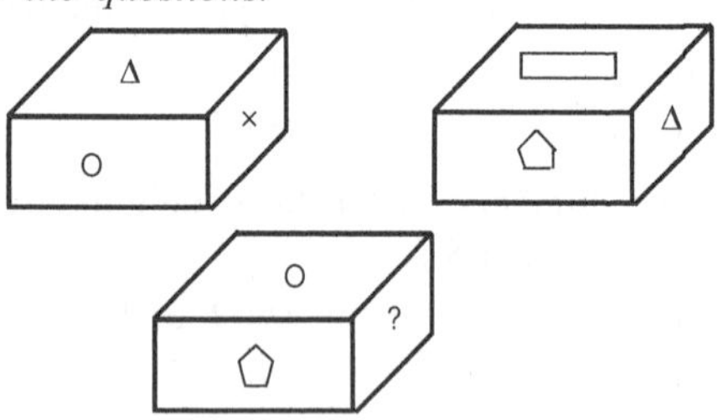

19. The figure on the face opposite the triangle is:

(a) pentagon

(b) circle

(c) question mark

(d) rectangle

20. Which of the following do not form correct pairs on opposite faces?

(a) circle-rectangle

(b) pentagon-cross

(c) rectangle-cross

(d) triangle-question mark

Directions (Qs. 21 and 22): *An electronics dealer selling colour TVs, VCRs and Computer (PCs) is offering Stereo Radio, Movable Trolley and Stainless Steel Rack free with these. The item which goes free with a particular item is written on the face opposite it on a cube. Two views of the cube are shown below:*

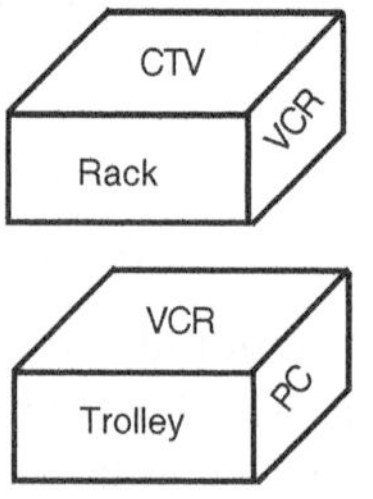

21. Stereo radio is being offered free with:

(a) Colour TV (b) Computer

(c) VCR (d) VCR or TV

22. The item offered free with the Computer is:

(a) Stainless Steel Rack

(b) Trolley

(c) Radio

(d) Radio or Trolley

Directions (Qs. 23 to 27): *In the following questions six dices with their top faces erased have been given. The opposite faces of the dices have dots which add up to thirteen. Work out the number of dots on the top faces, according to the question and spot your answer from amongst the given alternatives.*

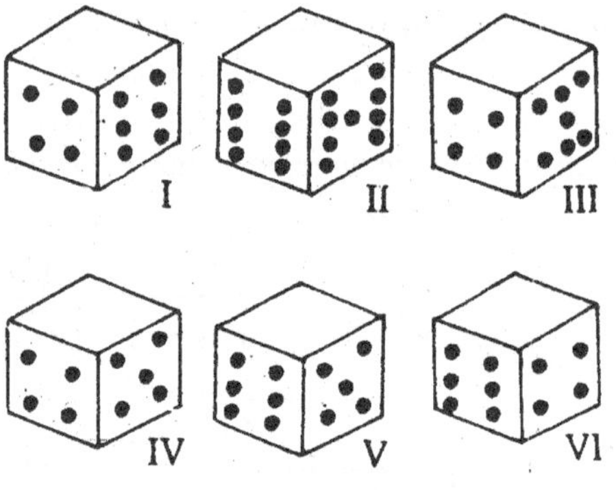

23. If the even numbered dices have odd number of dots at their top faces, what would be the total number of dots?

(a) 19 (b) 18

(c) 17 (d) 16

24. If dices, I, III and IV have odd number of dots at their top faces, what would be the total number of dots?

(*a*) 15 (*b*) 18
(*c*) 21 (*d*) 17

25. If dices, II, V and VI have even number of dots at their bottom faces, what would be the total number of dots?

(*a*) 18 (*b*) 20
(*c*) 16 (*d*) 24

26. If dices I, II and III have odd number of dots on their upper face and dices IV, V and VI have even number of dots on their bottom faces, then what would be the difference in the total number of top face dots between these two sets?

(*a*) 8 (*b*) 4
(*c*) 0 (*d*) 1

27. If the odd numbered dices have even number of dots at their bottom faces, what would be the total number of dots?

(*a*) 20 (*b*) 22
(*c*) 24 (*d*) 18

28. A cubical block with designs in its faces is presented as viewed from different directions. Find the design on the blank face?

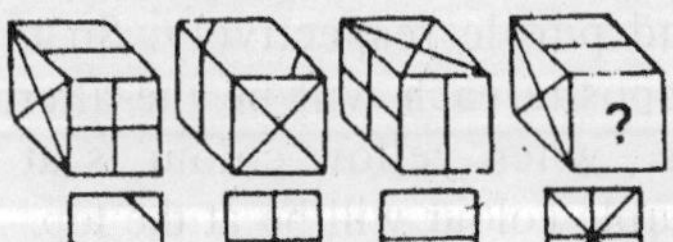

(*a*) (*b*) (*c*) (*d*)

Directions (Qs 29 to 30): *A cube is painted white on all sides. It is cut into 64 smaller cubes of equal size. Based on this information answer the question given below.*

29. How many smaller cubes are painted on one side only?

(*a*) 4 (*b*) 8
(*c*) 16 (*d*) 24

30. How many smaller cubes are not painted at all?

(*a*) 8 (*b*) 6
(*c*) 4 (*d*) 1

Directions: *A toy cube has pictures of different fruits on its six faces. The top face has the picture of orange. Banana is adjacent to melon and orange. Apple is not at the bottom of the cube and melon is opposite the peach.*

31. The neighbouring faces of the sixth fruit mango, do not have the picture of:

(*a*) apple (*b*) orange
(*c*) peach (*d*) banana

32. Which fruit is opposite the face having the picture of apple?

(*a*) Banana (*b*) Peach
(*c*) Orange (*d*) Mango

33. Which one of the following does not represent the correct pair of fruits on the opposite faces?

(*a*) Orange-Mango (*b*) Apple-Banana
(*c*) Apple-Mango (*d*) All of the above

34. A three centimetre cube has been painted blue on all its sides. It is cut into one centimetre cubes. How many cubes will be there with two sides painted blue?

(*a*) 8 (*b*) 4
(*c*) 6 (*d*) 12

35. A cube is coloured with different colours on each side. Red is at the base and white at the top. The colours green, yellow, blue and purple respectively are painted on the four sides of the cube, in the clockwise direction. When the yellow side is changed as the base of the cube, which colour will be on the top?

(*a*) BLUE (*b*) GREEN
(*c*) PURPLE (*d*) RED

36. A four centimetre cube has been painted blue on all its sides. It is then cut into one cm cubes. How many cubes will be there with only one side painted?

(*a*) 24 (*b*) 16
(*c*) 8 (*d*) 32

EXPLANATORY ANSWERS

1. *(d)*

2. *(a)*

3. *(d)*

4. *(d)*

5. *(c)*

6. *(b)*

7. *(b)*

8. *(d)*

9. *(c)*

10. *(c)* 6, 2, 4, 5 are neighbouring faces of 3. 1 is opposite to 3. Also, 5 has neighbours 4, 3, 6 and 1. Hence 2 is opposite to 5.

11. *(b)* 3 and 1 form opposite pairs as shown in the above explanations.

12. *(b)*

13. *(b)* Neighbours of face 3 are faces marked 2, 5, 4 and 6. Therefore face 1 must be opposite to 3.

14. *(a)* 1, 2, 3, 4 are neighbours of 6. Therefore 6 and 5 must be on opposite faces. Hence neighbours of 5 are also 1, 2, 3 and 4.

15. *(b)*

16. *(a)* 2, 4, 1 and 5 circles are neighbouring faces of 3.

17. *(c)* 5 circles' face has neighbouring faces with 1, 3, 2 and 6 circles. Hence 4 and 5 circles faces form opposite pairs.

18. *(a)*

19. *(c)* The neighbouring faces of the face having a triangle on it have circle, cross mark, rectangle and pentagon marked on these as can be seen from Fig. (1) and (3). Therefore, the question mark must be opposite the triangle.

20. *(c)* Pentagon is opposite cross mark.

21. *(c)* Since neighbouring faces of VCR have CTV, Rack, Trolley and PC, it follows that Stereo radio is written opposite the VCR and hence is offered free with it.

22. *(a)* Considering the neighbouring of rack (Fig. 1), these are VCR, CTV, radio (which is opposite to VCR) and Trolley (Personal Computer) cannot be its neighbour, because then it goes free with CTV, (which is not true). Hence Rack must be free with a Personal Computer.

23. *(b)*

24. *(a)*

25. *(d)*

26. *(c)*

27. *(d)*

28. *(b)*

29. *(d)*

30. *(a)*

[**Notes to Qs. 29 and 30.** Of the 64 smaller cubes, 8 are painted on 3 sides, 24 are painted on 2 sides, 24 are painted on one side and 8 are not painted at all.]

31. *(b)* Because mango is on the face opposite to orange.

32. *(a)* Banana is on the face opposite to apple.

33. *(c)* Apple is not at the bottom, so it cannot be opposite to orange, which is at the top. Melon and peach are opposite each other, so none of these will be opposite to orange. Also, banana is one of its neighbours. So, the sixth fruit mango must be opposite to orange, and at the bottom.

34. *(d)*

35. *(c)* The sides are painted green, yellow, blue and purple respectively. So the colour opposite each will be the alternate one, *i.e.*, when yellow colour is at the base purple colour will be at the top.

36. *(a)* One side of the cube has four such cubes, therefore six sides of the cube will have 24 such cubes with only one side painted.

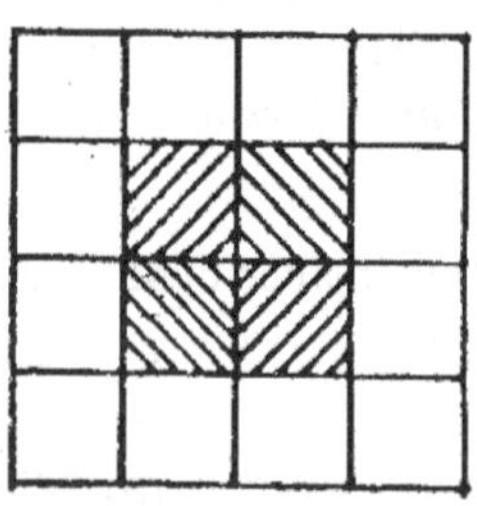

26 Non-Verbal Series

EXERCISE

Directions (Q. 1–10) : *In each of the following questions which one of the five answer figures given below should come after the problem figures if the sequence are continued?*

Problem Figures | **Answer Figures**

1. 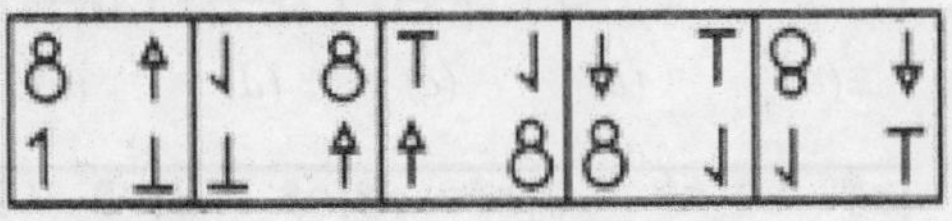 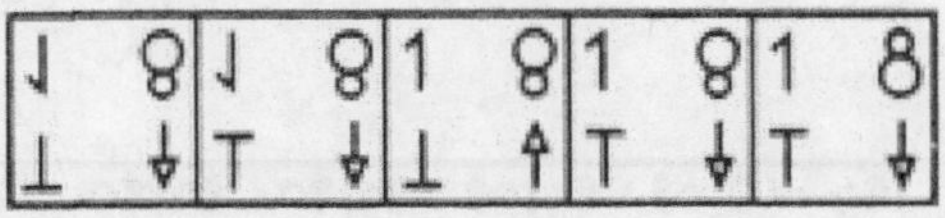

(a) (b) (c) (d) (e)

2. 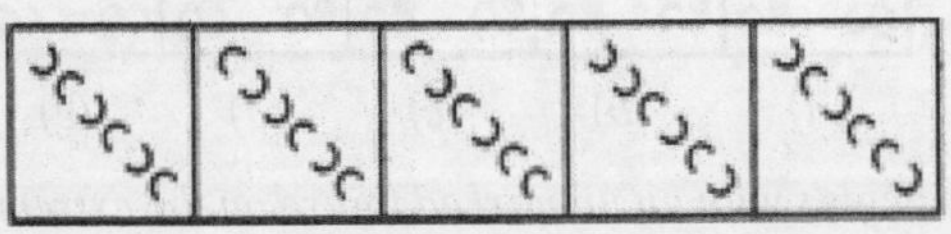 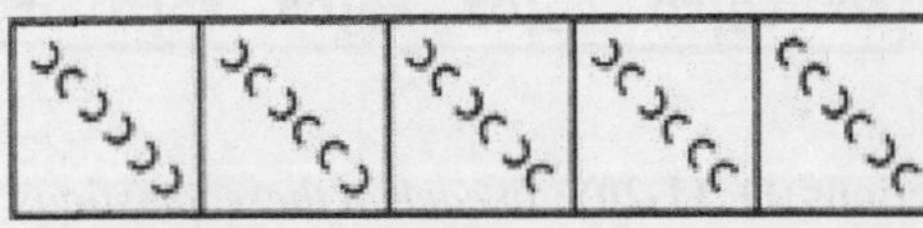

(a) (b) (c) (d) (e)

3. 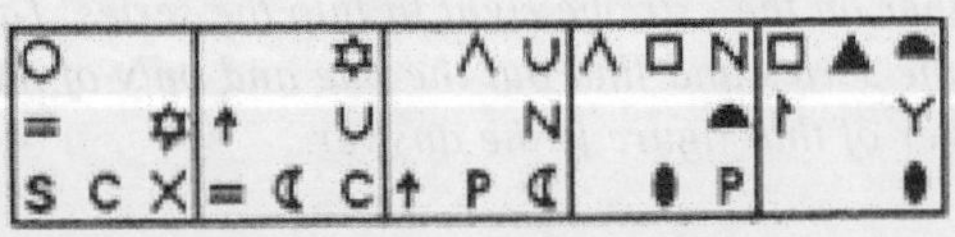 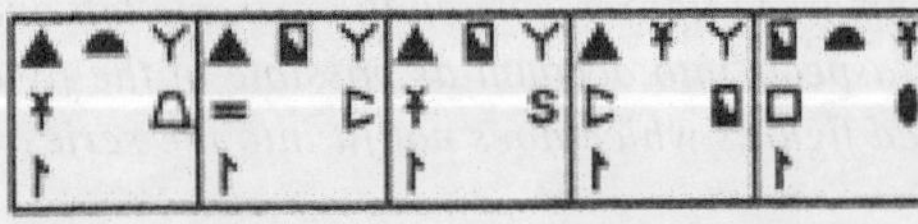

(a) (b) (c) (d) (e)

4.  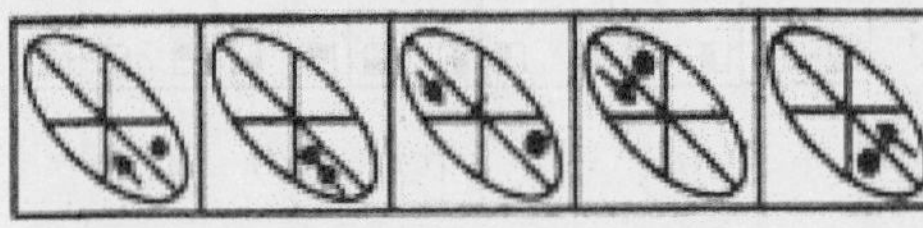

(a) (b) (c) (d) (e)

5.  

(a) (b) (c) (d) (e)

6.  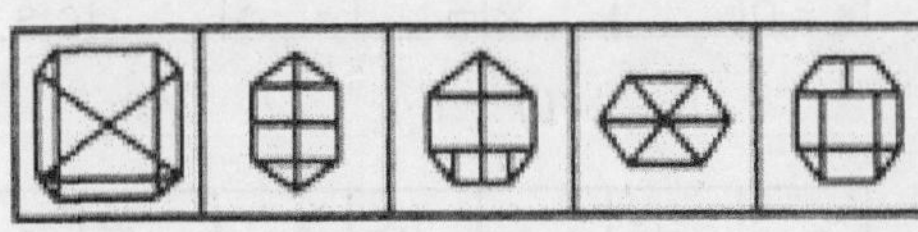

(a) (b) (c) (d) (e)

7.  

(a) (b) (c) (d) (e)

Problem Figures | **Answer Figures**

8.  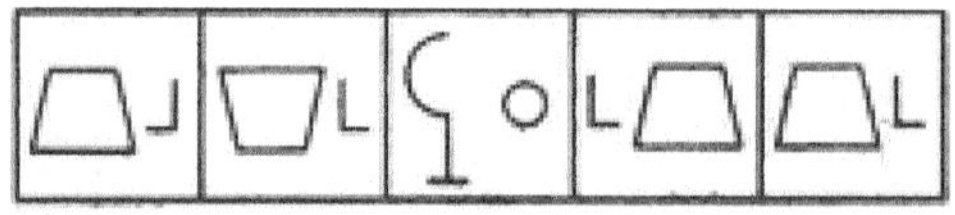

(a) (b) (c) (d) (e)

9. 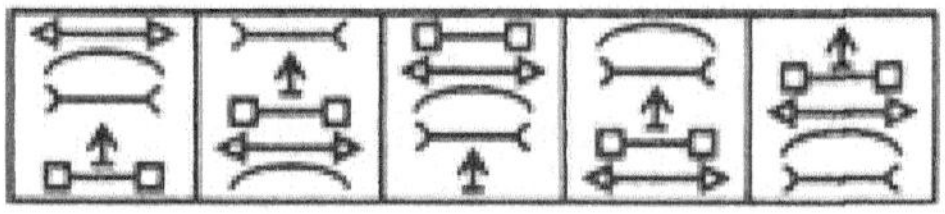 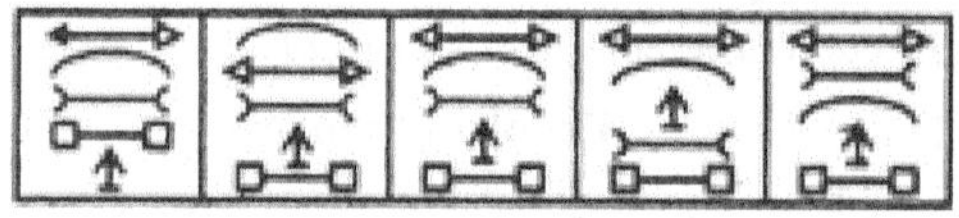

(a) (b) (c) (d) (e)

10. 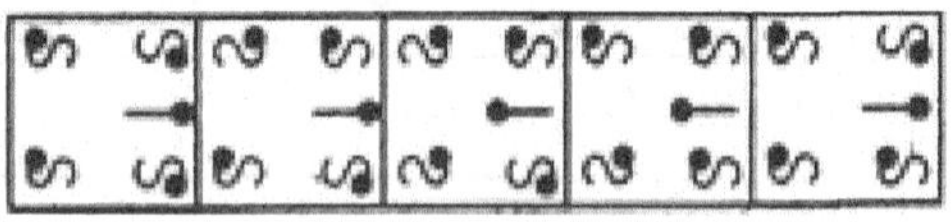 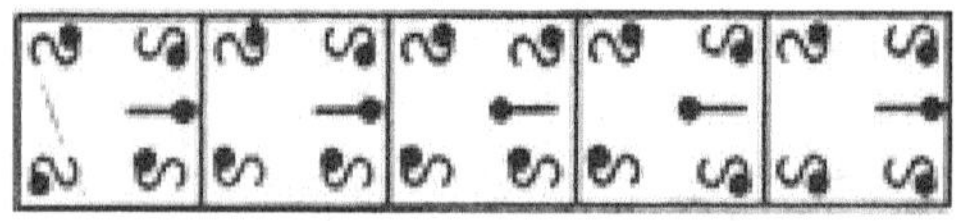

(a) (b) (c) (d) (e)

Directions (Q. 11-20) : *In each of these questions, a series begins with an unmarked figure on the extreme left in the row of figures. One and only one of the five lettered figures in the series does not fit into the series. The two unmarked figures, one on the extreme left and the other on the extreme right fit into the series. Take as many aspects into account as possible of the figures in the series and find out the one and only of the five marked figures which does not fit into the series. The letter of that figure is the answer.*

11. 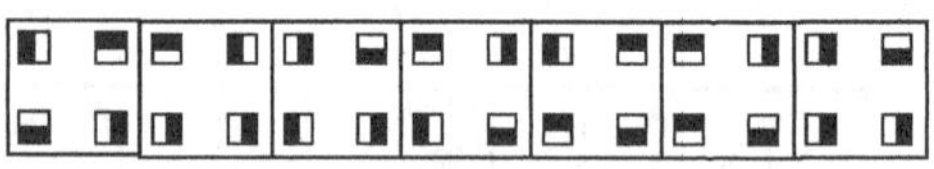

(a) (b) (c) (d) (e)

12. 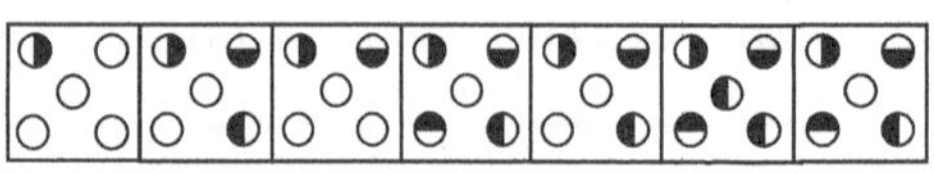

(a) (b) (c) (d) (e)

13. 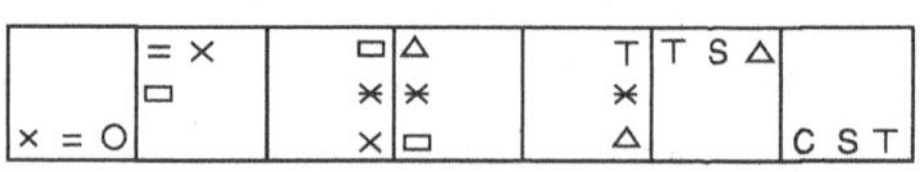

(a) (b) (c) (d) (e)

14. 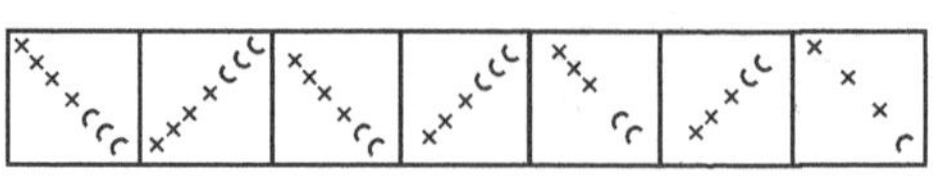

(a) (b) (c) (d) (e)

15. 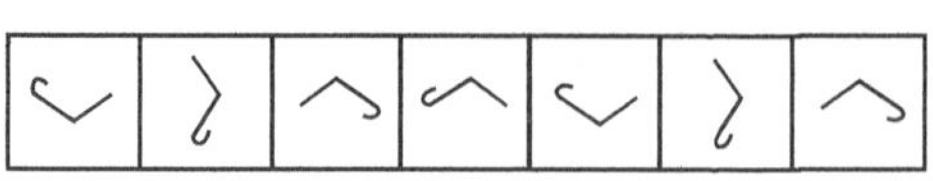

(a) (b) (c) (d) (e)

16. 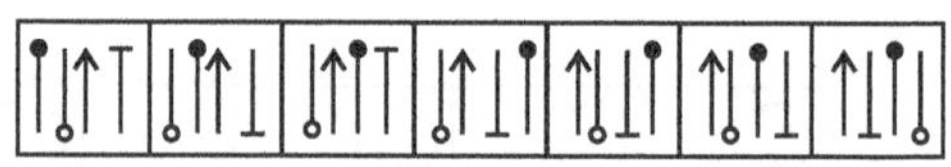

(a) (b) (c) (d) (e)

17. 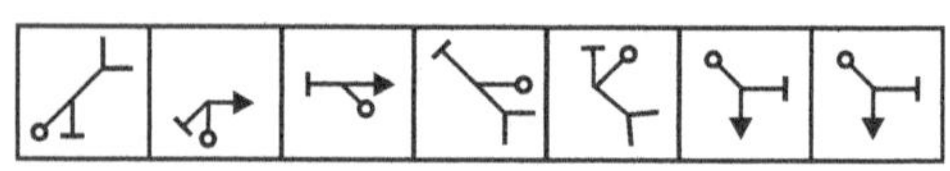

(a) (b) (c) (d) (e)

18. 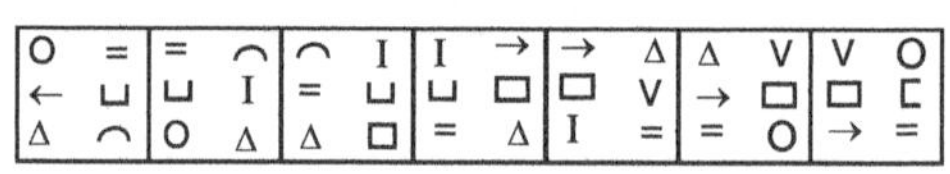

(a) (b) (c) (d) (e)

19. 

(a) (b) (c) (d) (e)

20. 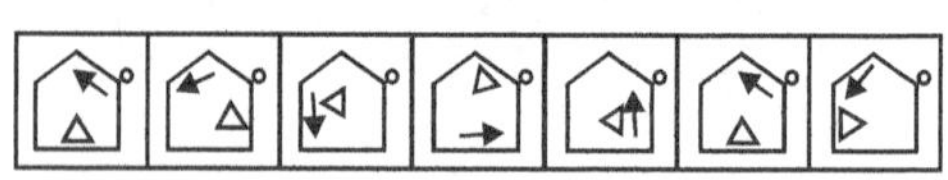

(a) (b) (c) (d) (e)

Directions (Q. 21–30) : *Each of the following questions consist of problem figures followed by answer figures. Select a figure from amongst the answer figures which will continue the same series or pattern as established by the problem figures.*

Problem Figures | **Answer Figures**

21. 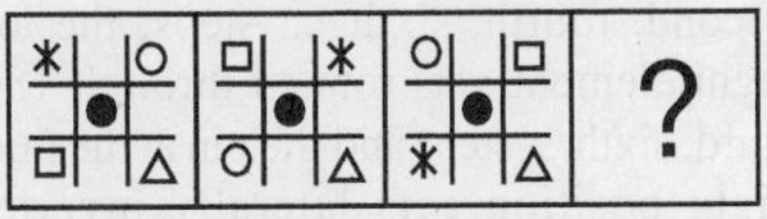 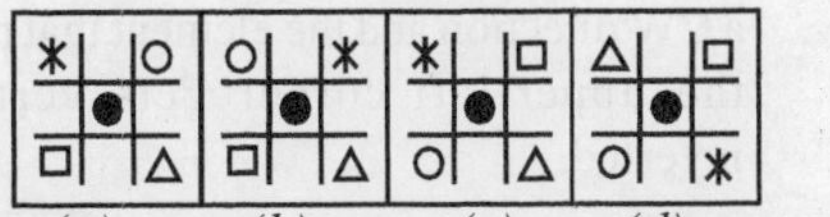

(a) (b) (c) (d)

22. 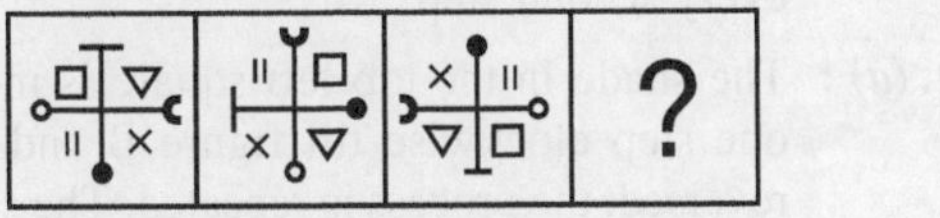 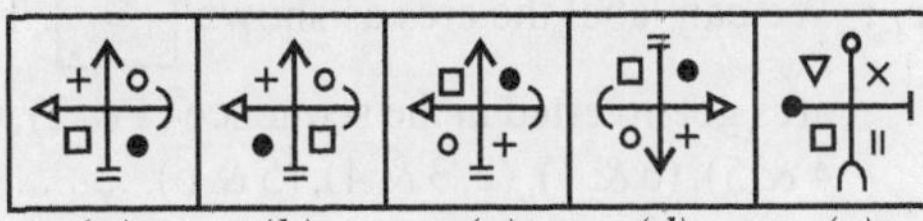

(a) (b) (c) (d) (e)

23.  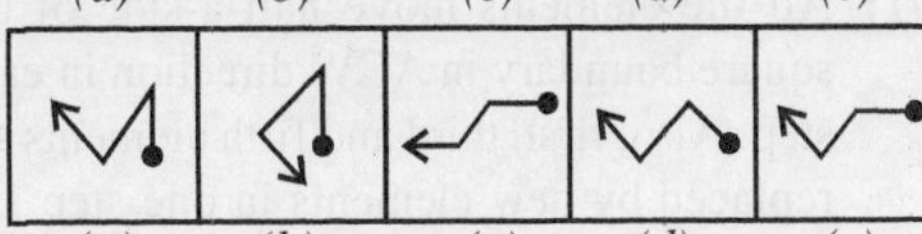

(a) (b) (c) (d) (e)

24. 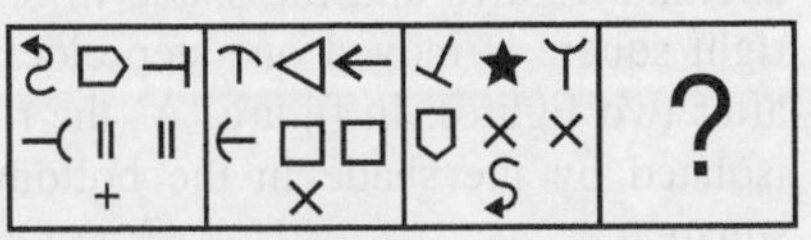 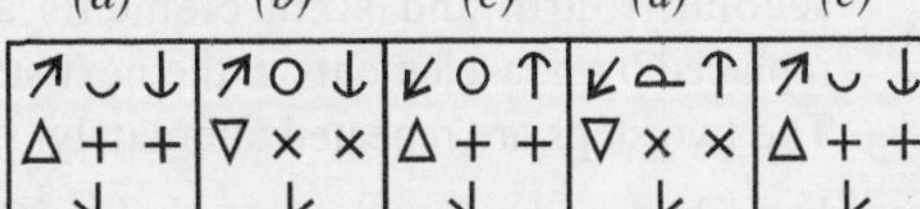

(a) (b) (c) (d) (e)

25. 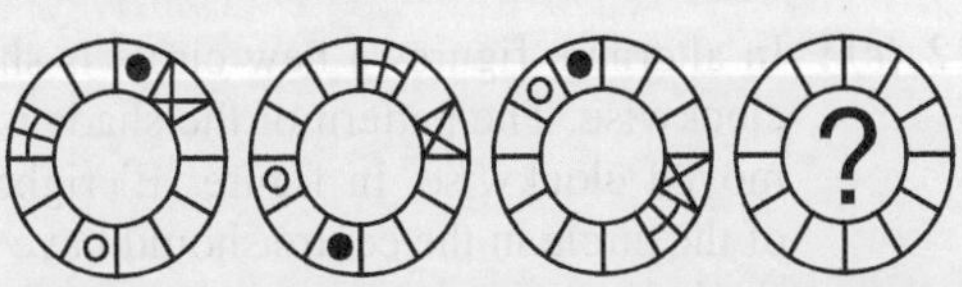 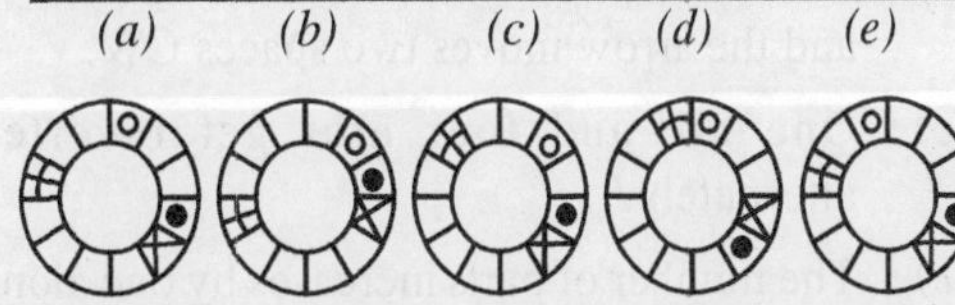

(a) (b) (c) (d) (e)

26.  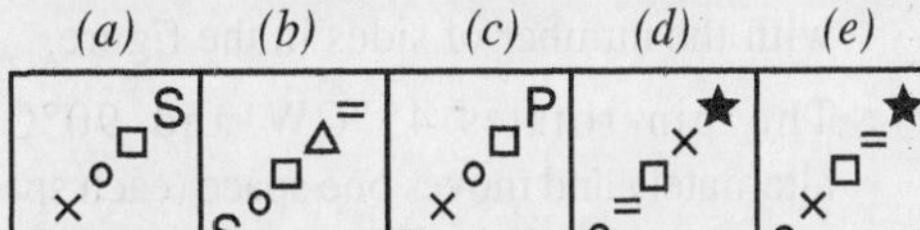

(a) (b) (c) (d) (e)

27. 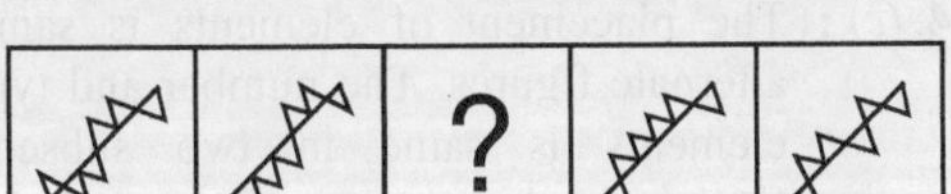 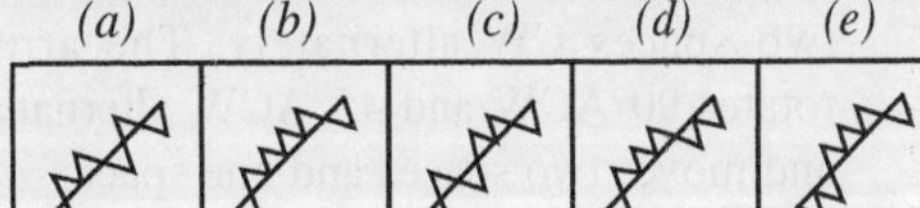

(a) (b) (c) (d) (e)

28.  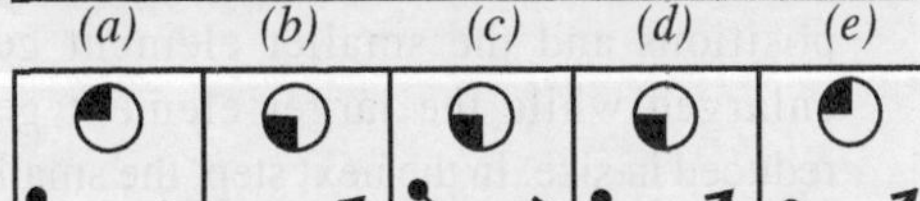

(a) (b) (c) (d) (e)

29. 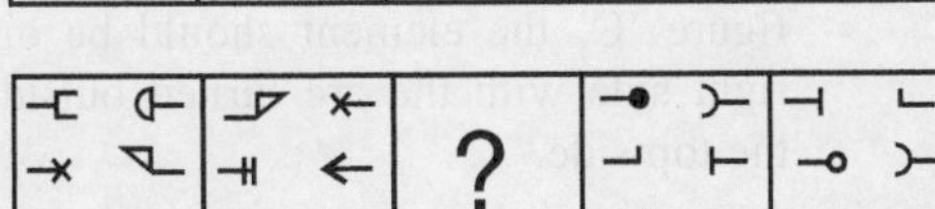 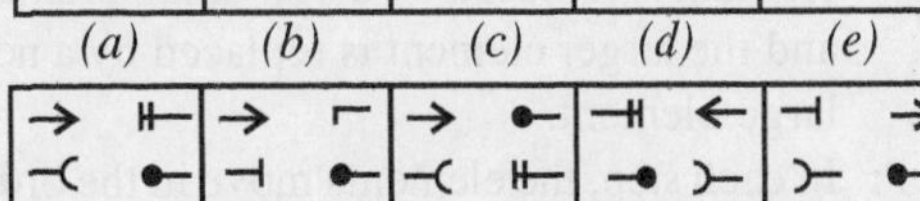

(a) (b) (c) (d) (e)

30. 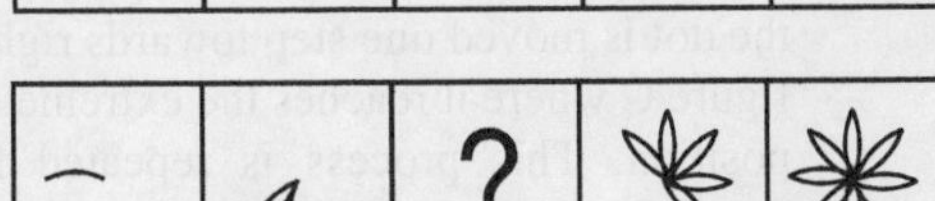 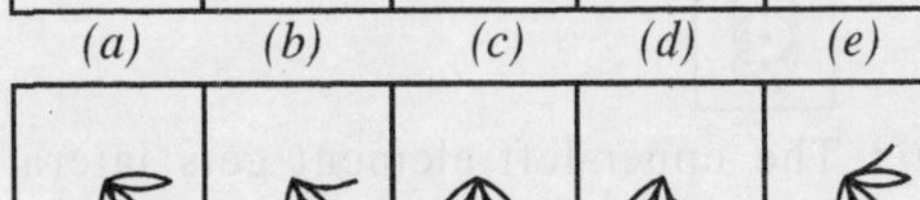

(a) (b) (c) (d) (e)

EXPLANATORY ANSWERS

1. *(d)* **:** In each step, all the elements move to the adjacent corner (of the square boundary) in a CW direction and the element that reaches the upper-left corner gets vertically inverted.

2. *(c)* **:** We can label the arcs as shown 

. The arcs get inverted in the sequence (1 & 2), (3, 4 & 5), (6 & 1), (2, 3 & 4), (5 & 6), ...

3. *(d)* **:** All the elements move half-a-side of the square boundary in ACW direction in each step. Also, first, third and fifth elements are replaced by new elements in one step and second, fourth and sixth elements are replaced by new elements in the next step. The two steps are repeated alternately.

4. *(a)* **:** In each step, the dot moves one space CW and the arrow moves two spaces CW.

5. *(c)* **:** One arc and four arcs get inverted alternately.

6. *(e)* **:** The number of parts increases by one along with the number of sides in the figure.

7. *(c)* **:** The pin rotates 45°CW and 90°CW alternately and moves one space (each space is equal to half-a-side of the square) and two spaces CW alternately. The arrow rotates 90°ACW and 45°ACW alternately and moves two spaces and one space.

8. *(e)* **:** In one step, the two elements interchange positions and the smaller element gets enlarged while the larger element gets reduced in size. In the next step, the smaller element is replaced by a new small element and the larger element is replaced by a new large element.

9. *(c)* **:** In each step, the elements move in the order 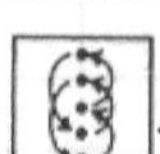.

10. *(b)* **:** The upper-left element gets laterally inverted in first, third, fifth. .... steps; the upper-right element gets rotated through 180° is first, fourth, seventh,.... steps; the lower-left element gets laterally inverted in second, fourth, sixth, ... steps; the lower-right element gets rotated through 180° in third, sixth,... steps and the pin at the middle-right position gets laterally inverted in every second step.

11. *(a)* **:** The shade in the top left square is moved one step clockwise till figure B and then reversed, the process is repeated. The shade in the top right square is moved one step anticlockwise till figure D and then reversed. The shade in the bottom left square is moved one step clockwise in alternate figures and the shade in bottom right square is moved one step clockwise after two figures. In figure 'A' the rule is isolated by the shade in the bottom left square.

12. *(e)* **:** In alternate figures a new circle is shaded clockwise. The pattern of the shade is also moved clockwise. In figure 'E' right half of the circle in the centre should have been shaded.

13. *(a)* **:** The three elements are placed either horizontally or vertically. In option 'A' neither of the placements can be applied.

14. *(c)* **:** The placement of elements is same in alternate figures. The number and type of elements is same in two subsequent figures. In this manner, figure 'C' should have four crosses and two C shapes.

15. *(c)* **:** The element is moved one step anticlockwise and the arc at one end is turned outside and inside alternately. In figure 'C' the element should be on the right side with the arc turned outside on the top side.

16. *(e)* **:** The left most element, line segment with the dot is moved one step towards right till figure C where it reaches the extreme right position. This process is repeated from figure D where the element on the extreme left, line segment with a circle, is moved.

In figure 'E' the placement of the elements does not follow the rule of the series.

17. *(e)* **:** The 'T' line is rotated 45° clockwise and the line with the circle 45° anticlockwise. The 'Y' shape and the arrow are repeated twice after two figures. In option E, the 'T' shape and the line with the circle are rotated by 90°.

18. *(e)* **:** First the elements in the four corners are moved one step anticlockwise, next the four elements from the top are moved one step anticlockwise and then the four elements from the bottom are moved one step anticlockwise. Of the remaining two elements, the one on the left is made new each time and then their places are interchanged. This process is repeated from figure D. In option 'E' open square should have been in place of circle to continue the series.

19. *(a)* **:** At each step the outermost figure is removed and a new figure is placed right in the centre of other two figures. In option 'A' the triangle is turned upside down, which violates the rule of the series.

20. *(a)* **:** The arrow is moved one step anticlockwise and the triangle one step clockwise. In figure 'A' the triangle should have been on the left side of the figure.

21. *(a)* **:** The places of star, circle and square are moved one step clockwise at each step.

22. *(e)* **:** The elements in the four quadrants are moved one step clockwise and the elements at the ends of the cross are moved one step anticlockwise in this series.

23. *(a)* **:** In alternate figures, the line with the dot is turned 90° clockwise and the arrow 180° clockwise.

24. *(e)* **:** In alternate figures, the element in the top left position is horizontally inverted and moved one and half steps anticlockwise, the top middle element is turned 90° clockwise and moved one step anticlockwise, the top right element is turned 135° clockwise and moved one step anticlockwise, the element at the bottom is replaced by a new element and moved to the top middle position, and the two identical elements are replaced by two new identical elements.

25. *(a)* **:** The cross and the circle move one and two steps clockwise respectively (at each step), the plus moves 3, 4 and 5 steps clockwise, and the dot 6, 5 and 4 steps clockwise.

26. *(a)* **:** At first step, the fifth or the bottom most element is moved to the second place from top, the second element moved to the fourth place, the fourth element is moved to the third place, the third element is moved to the first or the topmost place and the element on the top, which is made new, is moved to the last or the fifth place. At second step i.e., from second problem figure to third problem figure the above process is reversed. The bottom most element is the first and the top most element is the last or fifth. Hereafter, the process is repeated from the beginning. Option 'A' is the right answer.

27. *(c)* **:** Starting from the bottom, one triangle is moved to the opposite side at each step in upward order. Option 'C' fits into the question marked space.

28. *(c)* **:** The shade inside the circle is rotated clockwise in alternate figures; the line segment with a dot is rotated 135° clockwise in alternate figures and the arrow is rotated 135° anticlockwise in alternate figures. By this process answer figure 'C' completes the series.

29. *(a)* **:** At each step the elements are moved diagonally upward and then laterally inverted, and the top two elements are made new and placed at the bottom line. By this process, option figure 'A' completes the series.

30. *(a)* **:** The number of arcs making the petals of the flower are increased by one, one and half, two, two and half respectively at each step. Also, the flower is turned 45° anticlockwise. By this process, option 'A' is the right answer.

27 Non-Verbal Analogy

EXERCISE

TYPE-I

Directions (Q. 1-15): *The second figure in the first unit of the Problem Figures bears a certain relationship to the first figure. Similarly, one of the figures in the Answer Figures bears the same relationship to the first figures in the second unit of the Problem Figures. Locate the figure which would fit the questions marks.*

Problem Figures **Answer Figures**

1. 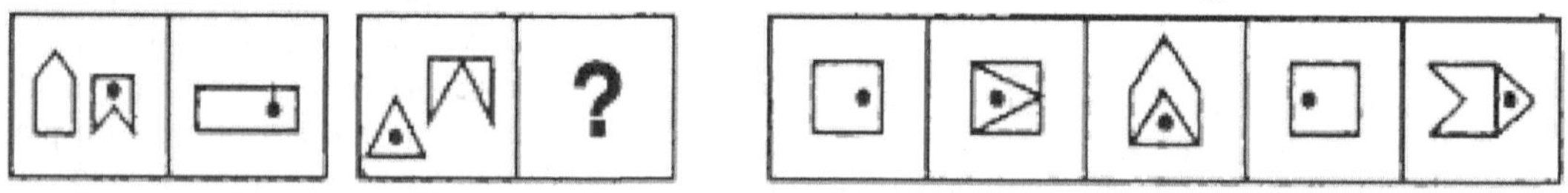

1 2 3 4 (a) (b) (c) (d) (e)

2. 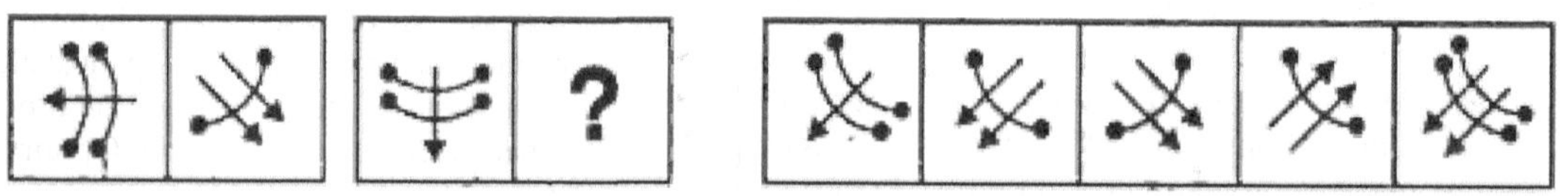

1 2 3 4 (a) (b) (c) (d) (e)

3. 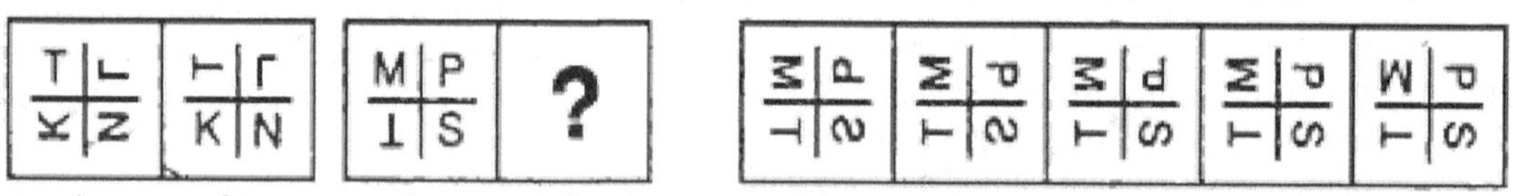

1 2 3 4 (a) (b) (c) (d) (e)

4. 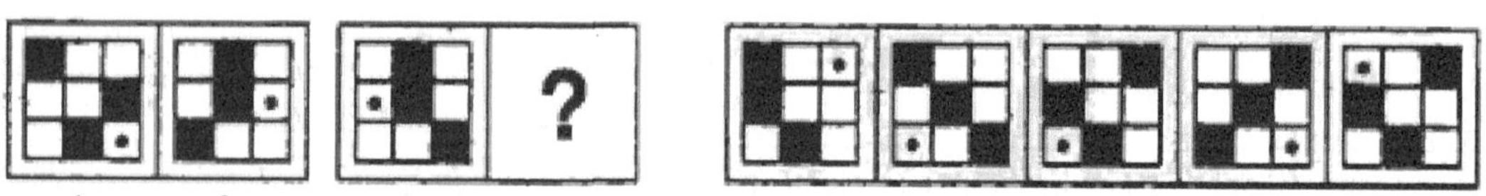

1 2 3 4 (a) (b) (c) (d) (e)

5. 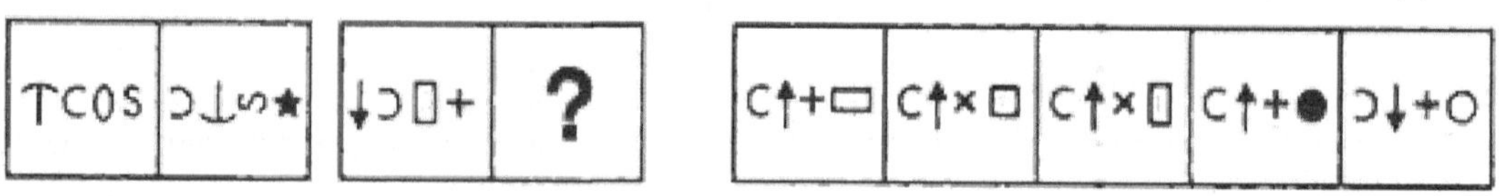

1 2 3 4 (a) (b) (c) (d) (e)

6. 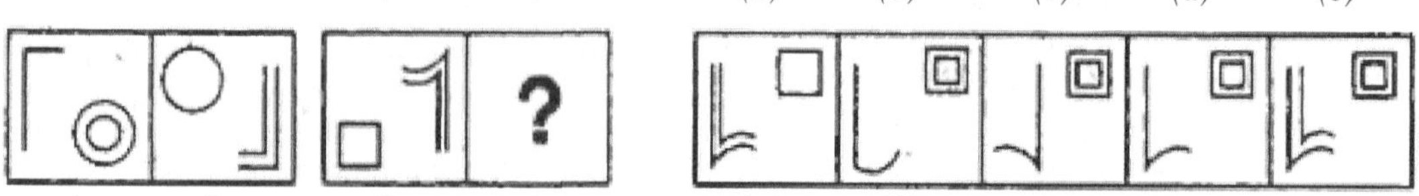

1 2 3 4 (a) (b) (c) (d) (e)

Problem Figures **Answer Figures**

7. 

1 2 3 4 (a) (b) (c) (d) (e)

8. 

1 2 3 4 (a) (b) (c) (d) (e)

9. 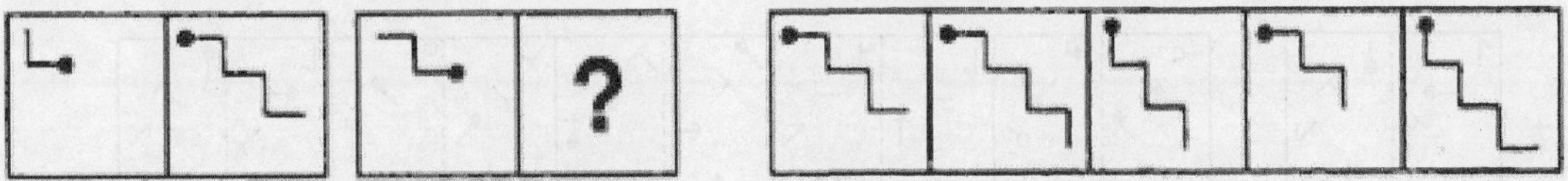

1 2 3 4 (a) (b) (c) (d) (e)

10. 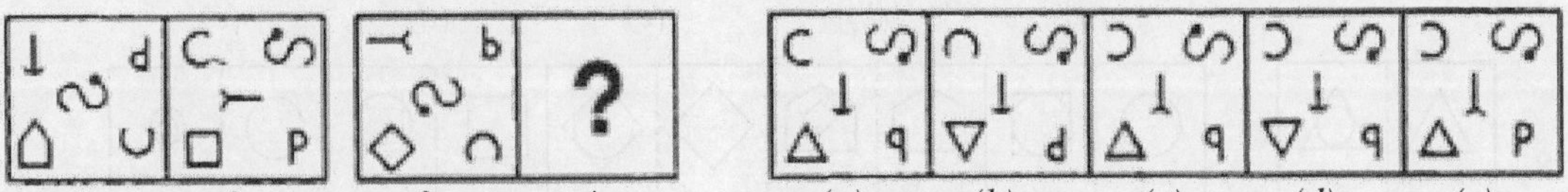

1 2 3 4 (a) (b) (c) (d) (e)

11. 

1 2 3 4 (a) (b) (c) (d) (e)

12. 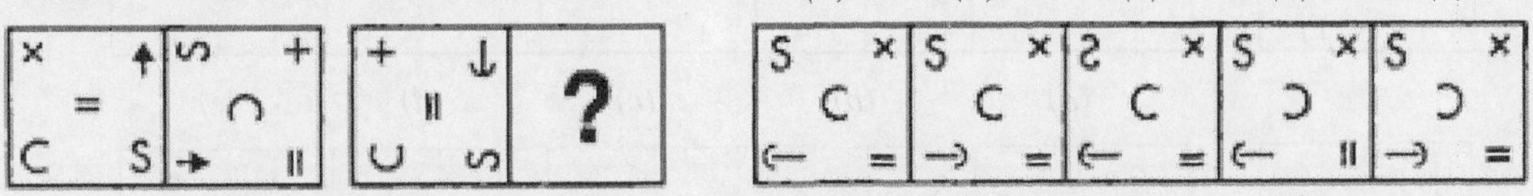

1 2 3 4 (a) (b) (c) (d) (e)

13. 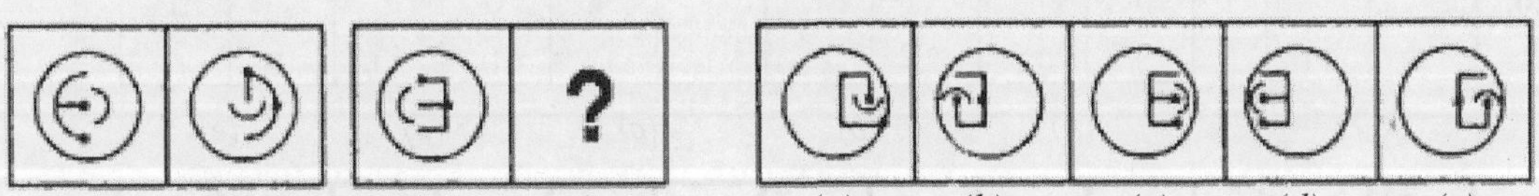

1 2 3 4 (a) (b) (c) (d) (e)

14. 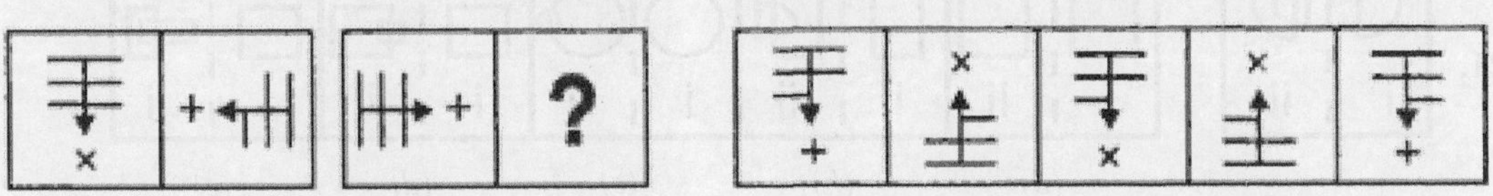

1 2 3 4 (a) (b) (c) (d) (e)

15. 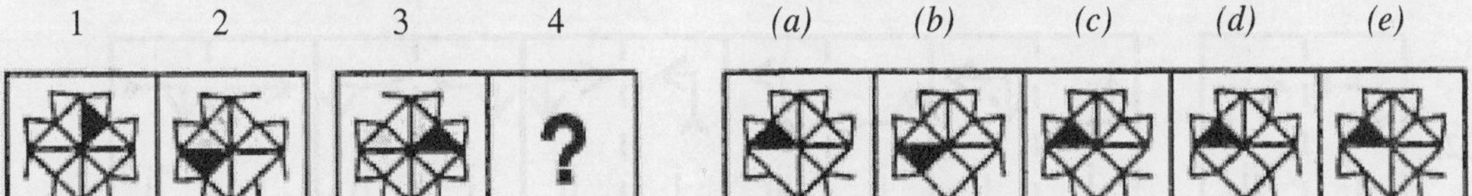

1 2 3 4 (a) (b) (c) (d) (e)

TYPE-II

Directions (Q. 16–30): *In each of the following questions, a related pair of figures is followed by five numbered pairs of figures. Select the pair that has a relationship* **similar** *to that in the unnumbered pair.*

Problem Figure | **Answer Figures**

16. 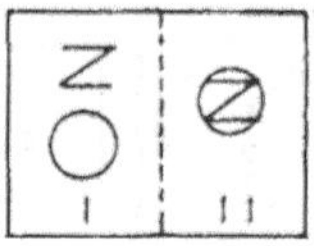 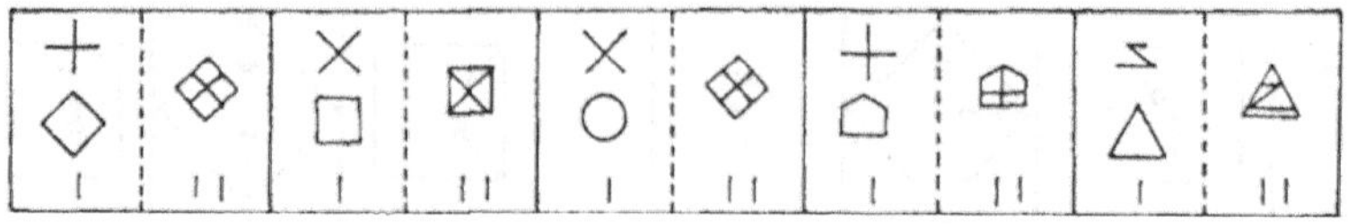

(a) *(b)* *(c)* *(d)* *(e)*

17. 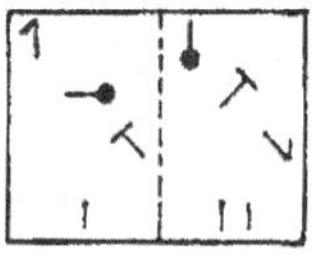 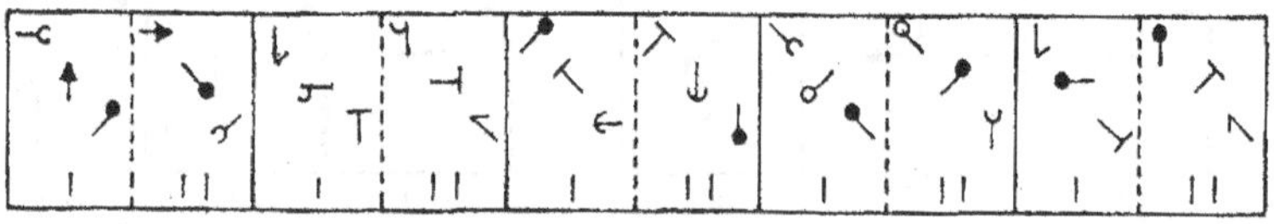

(a) *(b)* *(c)* *(d)* *(e)*

18. 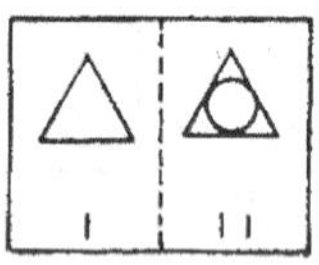 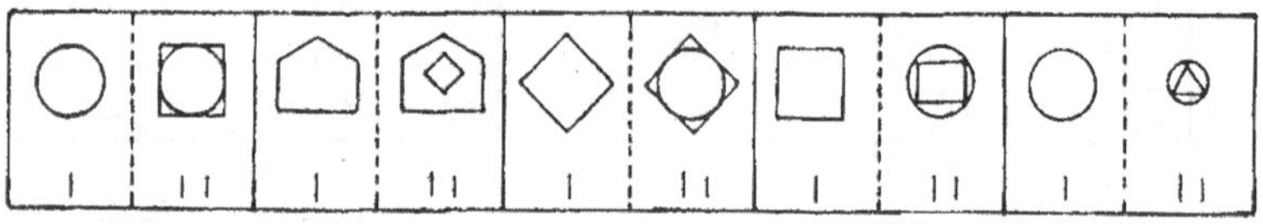

(a) *(b)* *(c)* *(d)* *(e)*

19. 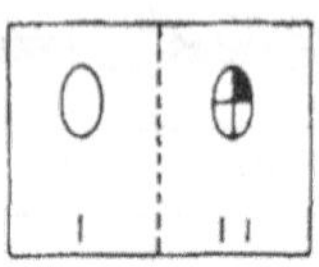 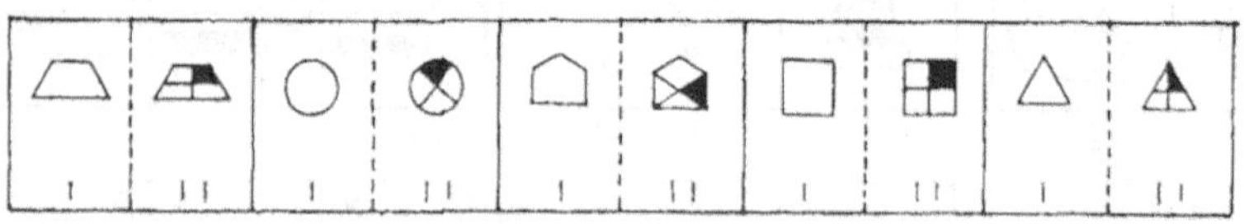

(a) *(b)* *(c)* *(d)* *(e)*

20. 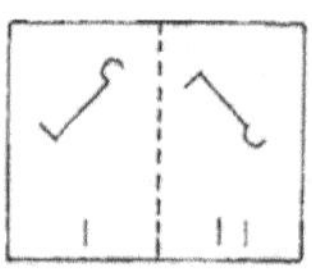 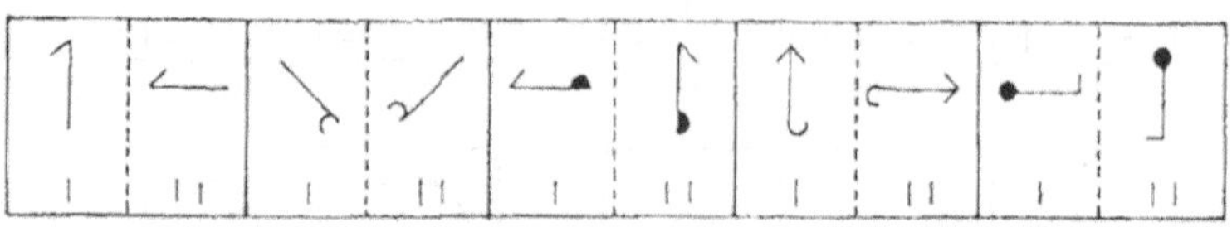

(a) *(b)* *(c)* *(d)* *(e)*

21. 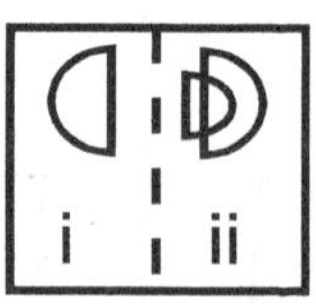 

(a) *(b)* *(c)* *(d)* *(e)*

22. 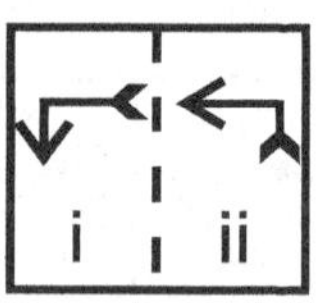 

(a) *(b)* *(c)* *(d)* *(e)*

Problem Figure **Answer Figures**

23.

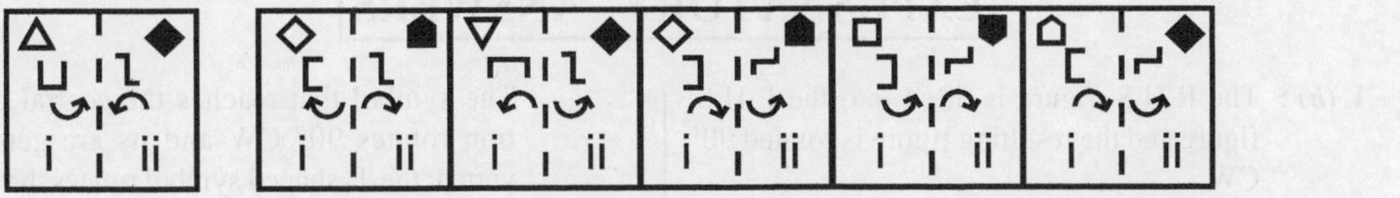

(a) (b) (c) (d) (e)

24.

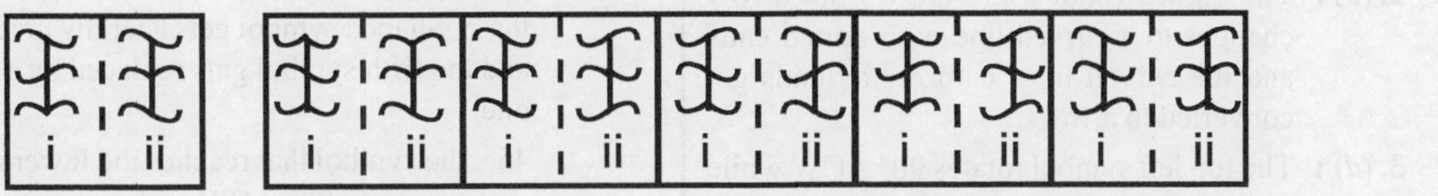

(a) (b) (c) (d) (e)

25.

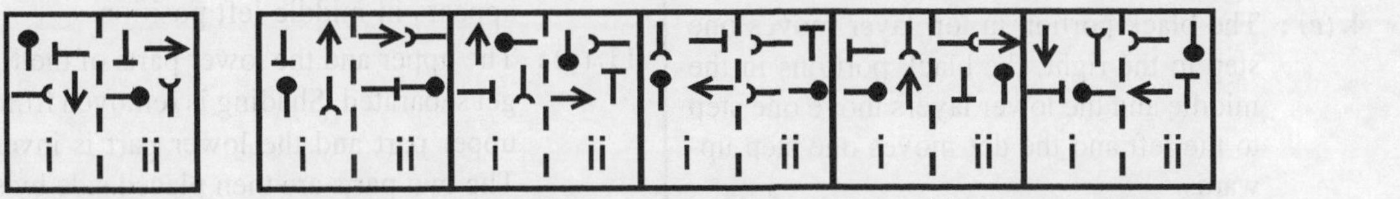

(a) (b) (c) (d) (e)

26.

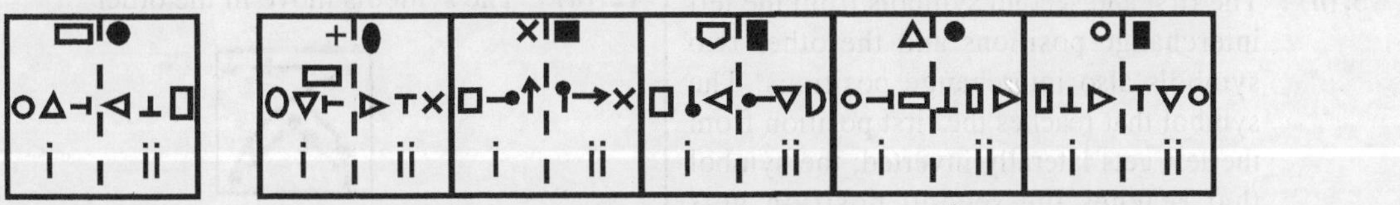

(a) (b) (c) (d) (e)

27.

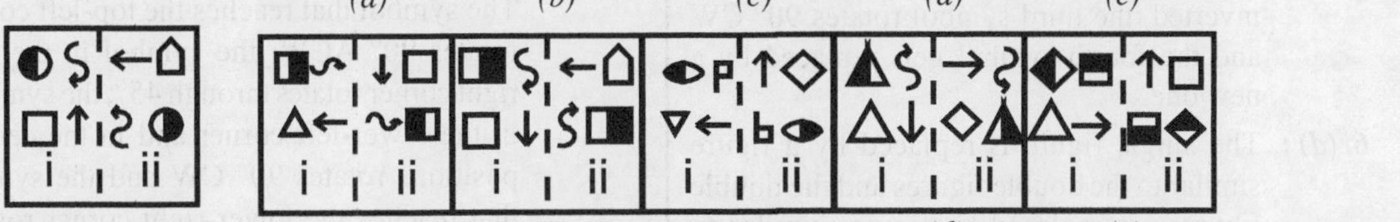

(a) (b) (c) (d) (e)

28.

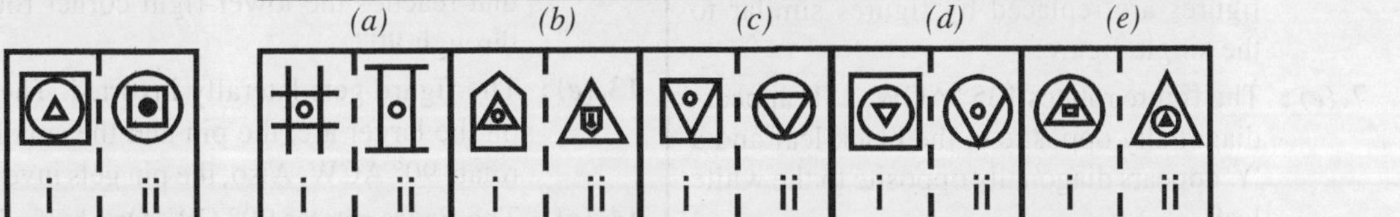

(a) (b) (c) (d) (e)

29.

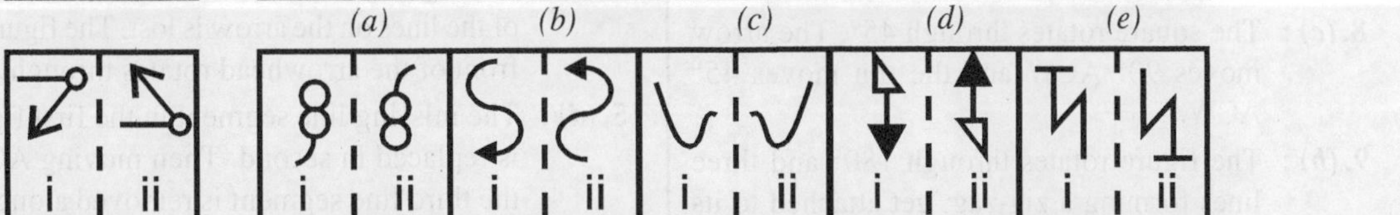

(a) (b) (c) (d) (e)

30.

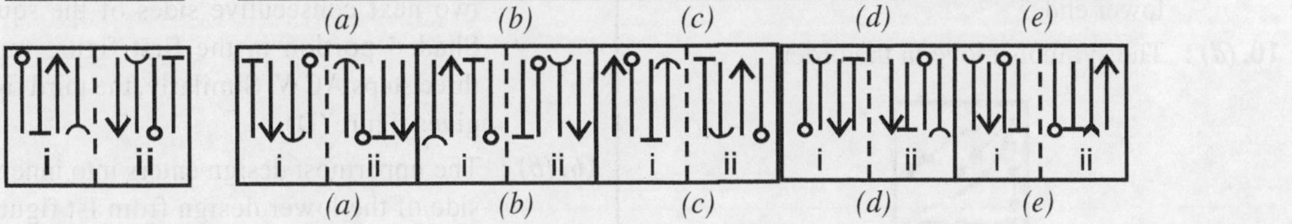

(a) (b) (c) (d) (e)

EXPLANATORY ANSWERS

1. *(b)* : The R.H.S. figure is fitted into the L.H.S. figure and the resulting figure is rotated 90° CW.

2. *(b)* : The figure rotates 45° ACW, the arrow changes to a curved line with dotted ends and the curved lines with dotted ends get converted to arrows.

3. *(d)* : The top left symbol rotates 90° ACW while all other symbols rotate 90° CW.

4. *(e)* : The black portion in top layer moves one step to the right; the black portions in the middle and the lower layers move one step to the left and the dot moves one step upwards.

5. *(d)* : The first and second symbols from the left interchange positions and the other two symbols also interchange positions. The symbol that reaches the first position from the left gets laterally inverted; the symbol that reaches the second position gets inverted, the third symbol rotates 90° CW and the fourth symbol gets replaced by a new one.

6. *(d)* : The single figure is replaced by a figure similar to the double figures and the double figures are replaced by figures similar to the single figure.

7. *(e)* : The figure rotates 135° ACW; a 'T' appears diagonally opposite to the black leaf and a 'Y' appears diagonally opposite to the white leaf.

8. *(c)* : The square rotates through 45°. The arrow moves 90° ACW and the pin moves 45° ACW.

9. *(b)* : The figure rotates through 180° and three lines forming a zig-zag, get attached to its lower end.

10. *(d)* : The symbols move in the order

The symbol that reaches the central position rotates 90° CW and its arc gets inverted; the 'P' shaped symbol rotates through 180°; the 'C' shaped symbol rotates 90° CW; the 'S' Shaped symbol gets laterally inverted and the fifth symbol gets replaced by a new one.

45°, the symbol that reaches the lower right corner rotates 90° ACW and a new symbol appears in middle-left position.

11. *(e)* : The upper and the lower parts of the figure get separated. Shading is removed from the upper part and the lower part is inverted. The two parts are then placed side by side.

12. *(a)* : The symbols move in the order

The symbol that reaches the top-left corner rotates 90° ACW; the symbol in the top-right corner rotates through 45°; the symbols in the lower-left corner and in the central positions rotates 90° CW and the symbol that reaches the lower-right corner rotates through 90°.

13. *(e)* : The figure gets laterally inverted. The dot on the larger arc, the pin and the small arc rotate 90° ACW. Also, the pin gets inverted.

14. *(c)* : The figure rotates 90° CW. One half of one of the lines on the arrow is lost. The figure in front of the arrowhead rotates through 45°.

15. *(d)* : The missing line segment in the first figure is replaced in second. Then moving ACW, the third line segment is removed along the two next consecutive sides of the square. Shaded portion in the first figure moves three steps ACW. Similarly, the third figure gives figure (D).

16. *(b)* : The uppermost design enters into innerside side of the lower design from Ist figure to the IInd figure.

17. (a) : In element I to II upper left design comes at lower right rotating 135° C.W. Middle design goes to upper left and rotates 90° CW. While lower right design goes to middle and it also rotates 90° C.W. The same changes occur in option A.

18. (e) : In element I to II and ellipse is put in the triangle. Similarly in option E a triangle is put in the ellipse.

19. (d) : From first figure to IInd figure, design is divided into four equal parts and right side of the upper portion becomes shaded.

20. (e) : From Ist figure to IInd figure, design is reversed after moving 90° anticlockwise direction.

21. (d) : The figure in the first part is laterally inverted and a similar but smaller design is placed on its left side in the second part.

22. (e) : The element in first part is moved by 90° and the places of short and long line segments are interchanged.

23. (c) : The number of sides making the top left figure is increased by one and a new figure is made, shaded and moved to the top right position. The element in the centre is turned 90° anticlockwise and the small line on the other side is turned by 180°. The element in the bottom right is turned upside down and moved to the bottom left position.

24. (a) : The direction of both arcs on the top, are on the middle right and arc on the bottom left in first part are turned to the other side in the second part.

25. (b) : From part one to part two, the element in the top left is turned 90° clockwise and the other three 90° anticlockwise, also the elements are moved one step anticlockwise.

26. (b) : From part one to part two, the top right element is turned by 90° and moved down, the lower right and middle elements are turned 90° clockwise and 90° anticlockwise respectively and moved to the left and the lower left element is shaded and moved up.

27. (a) : All the four elements exchange place diagonally and in doing so the top left element is laterally inverted, the top right element is horizontally inverted, the bottom right element is turned 90° anticlockwise and the number of lines making the element in bottom left is increased by one.

28. (e) : The innermost figure is removed and the new innermost figure also encloses the other two figures. The innermost and smallest figure is then shaded.

29. (b) : The design in the first part is horizontally inverted in the second.

30. (b) : All the elements in the first part are turned upside down and then 1st, 2nd, 3rd and 4th positioned elements become 3rd, 4th, 1st and 2nd elements in the second part.

28 Odd Man Out

In this type of reasoning a statement is followed by inferences drawn from it. From these inferences only one definitely follows which is the hidden proposition of the sentence and it is the right answer to the question.

EXERCISE

Directions (Q. 1–10) : *In each question below five figures are given. Four are similar in a certain way and so form a group. The question is— which one of the figures **does not** belong to that group?*

1. 

(a) (b) (c) (d) (e)

2. 

(a) (b) (c) (d) (e)

3. 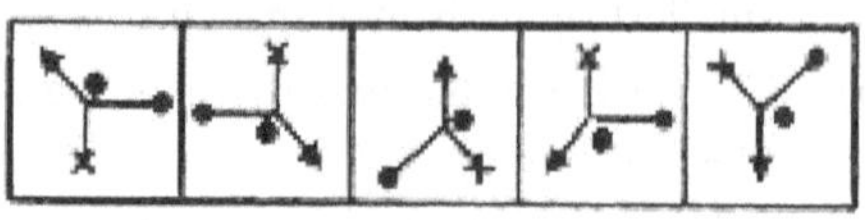

(a) (b) (c) (d) (e)

4. 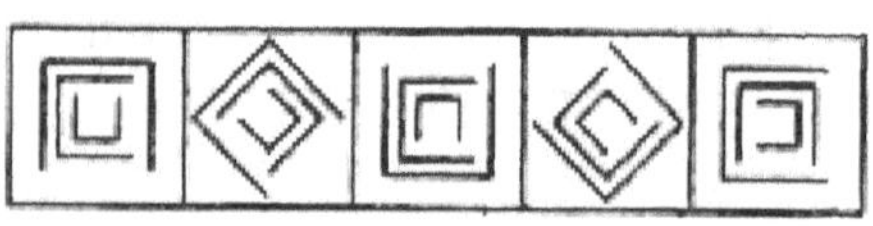

(a) (b) (c) (d) (e)

5. 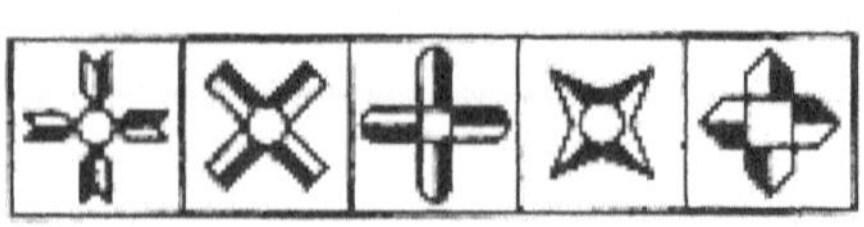

(a) (b) (c) (d) (e)

6. 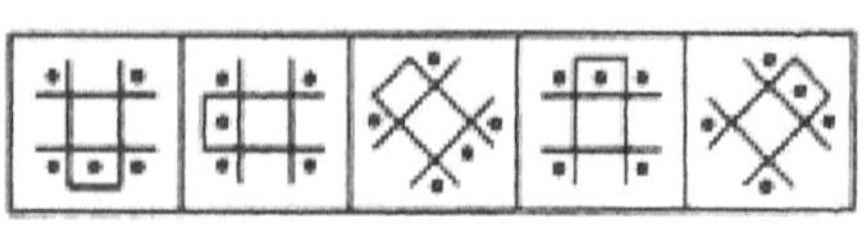

(a) (b) (c) (d) (e)

7. 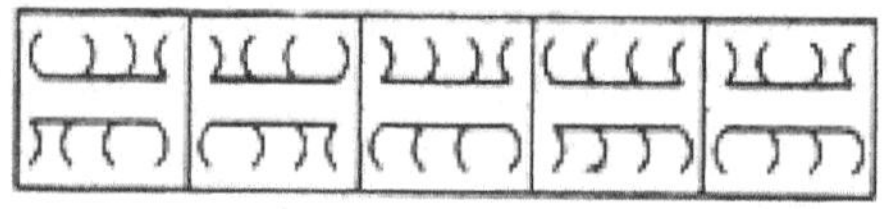

(a) (b) (c) (d) (e)

8. 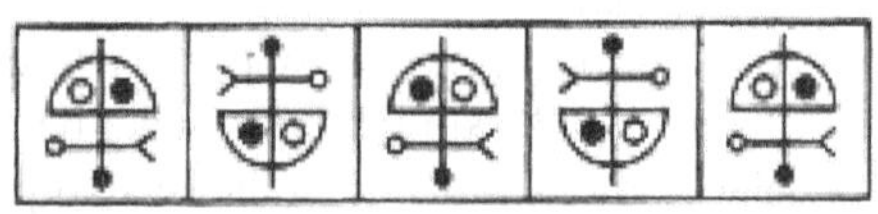

(a) (b) (c) (d) (e)

9. 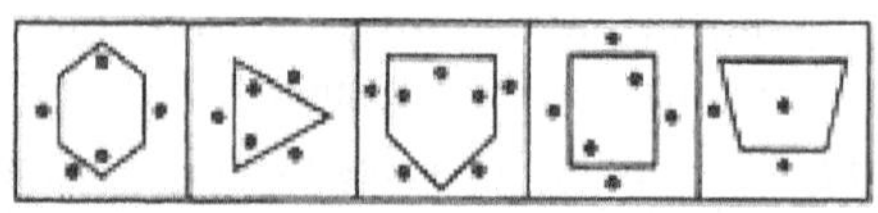

(a) (b) (c) (d) (e)

10. 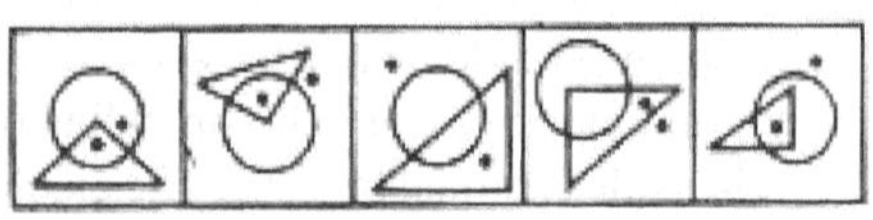

(a) (b) (c) (d) (e)

Directions (Q. 11–20) : *In each of the following questions, in four out of the five figures, element I is related to element II in the same particular way. Find out the figure in which the element I is **not** so related to element II.*

11. 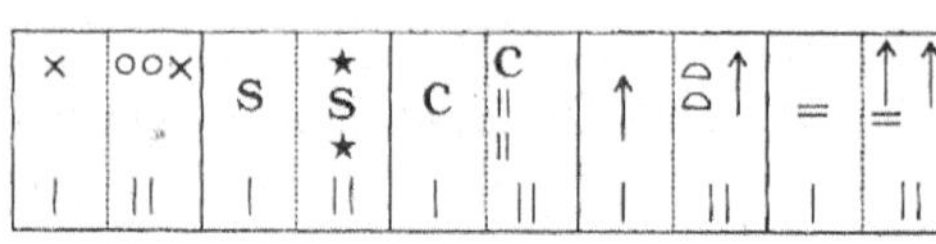

(a) (b) (c) (d) (e)

12. 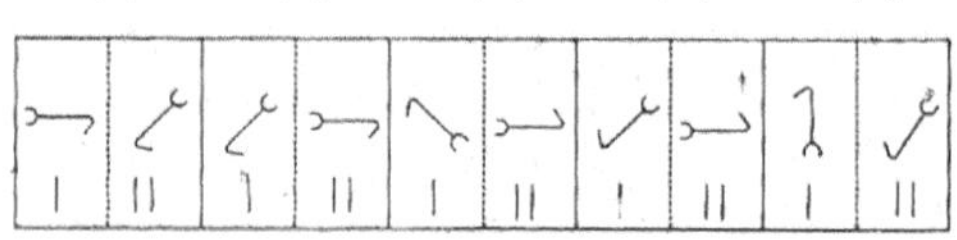

(a) (b) (c) (d) (e)

13. 

(a) (b) (c) (d) (e)

14. 

(a) (b) (c) (d) (e)

15. 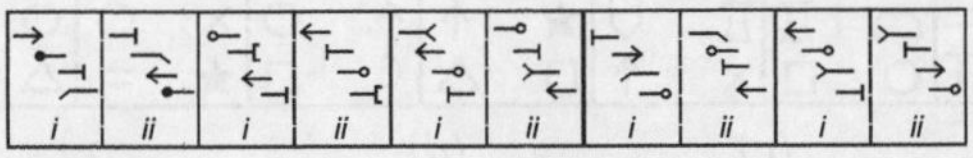

(a) (b) (c) (d) (e)

16. 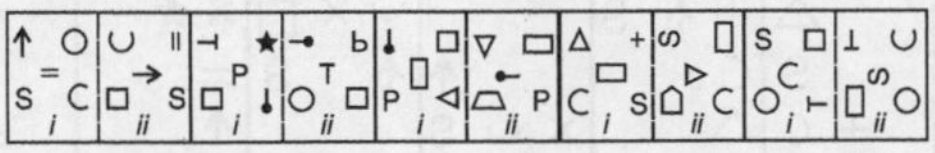

(a) (b) (c) (d) (e)

17. 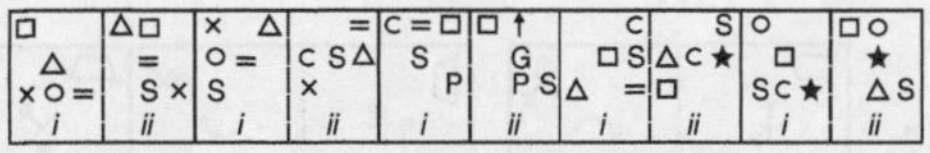

(a) (b) (c) (d) (e)

18. 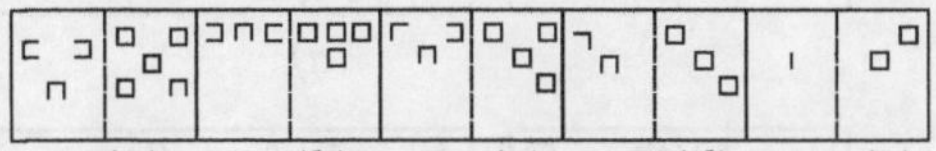

(a) (b) (c) (d) (e)

19. 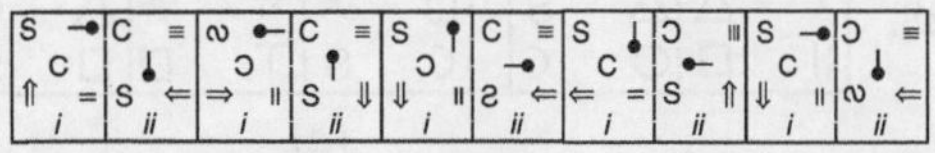

(a) (b) (c) (d) (e)

20. 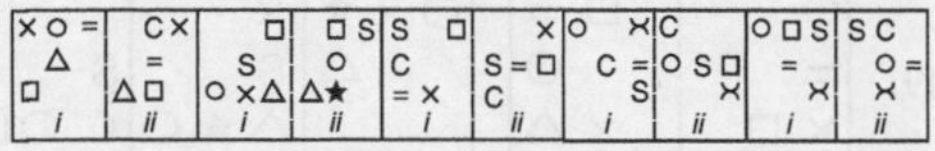

(a) (b) (c) (d) (e)

Directions (Q. 21–30) : *In each of the following questions, a related pair of figures (unnumbered) is followed by five numbered pairs of figures. Out of these five, four have relationship similar to that in the unnumbered pair. Only one pair of figures does not have similar relationship. Select that pair of figures which does not have a similar relationship to that in the unnumbered pair. Number of that pair is your answer.*

21. 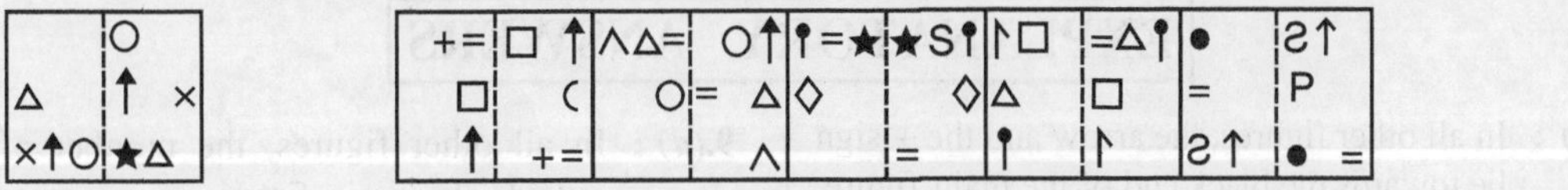

(a) (b) (c) (d) (e)

22. 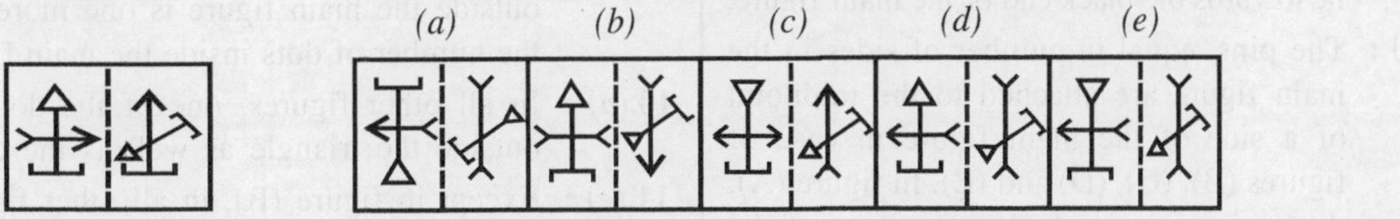

(a) (b) (c) (d) (e)

23. 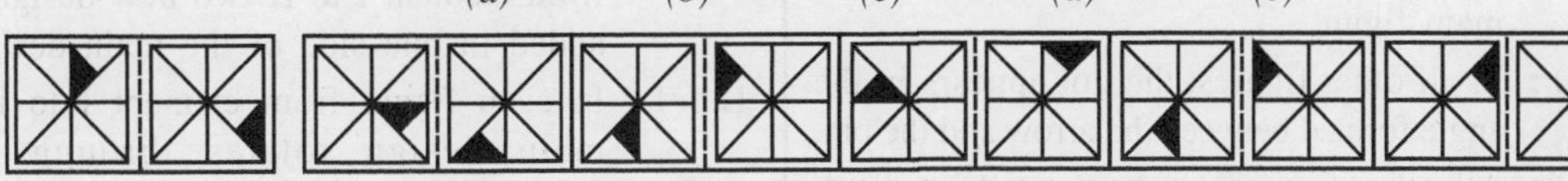

(a) (b) (c) (d) (e)

24. 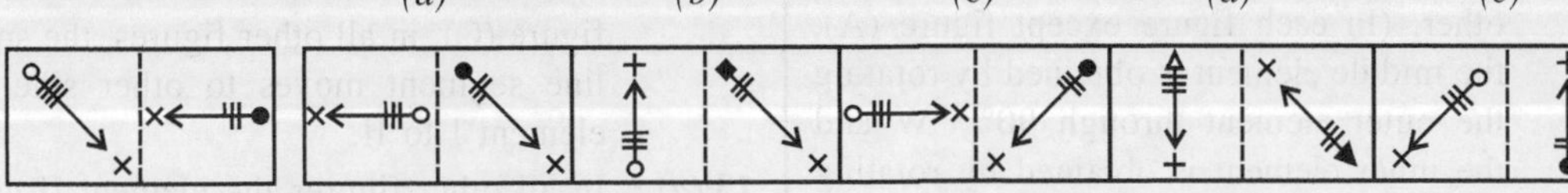

(a) (b) (c) (d) (e)

25. 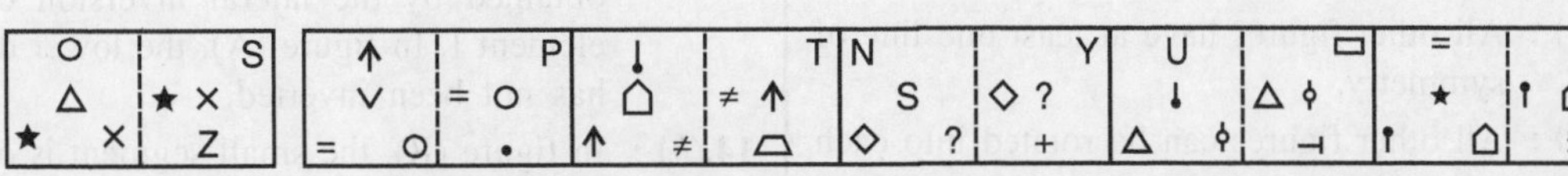

(a) (b) (c) (d) (e)

26. 

(a) (b) (c) (d) (e)

27. 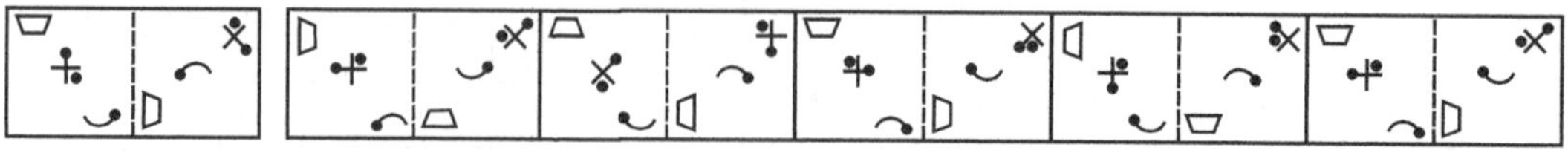

(a) (b) (c) (d) (e)

28. 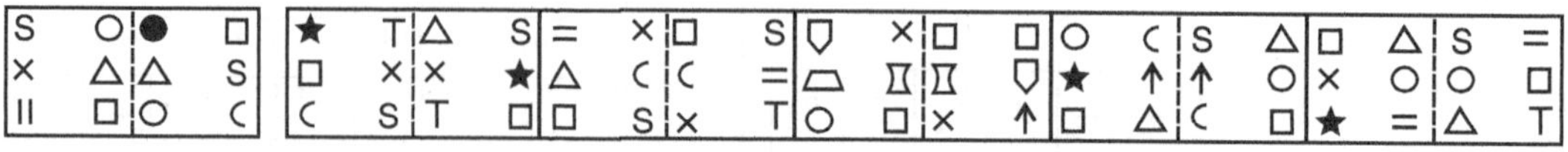

(a) (b) (c) (d) (e)

29. 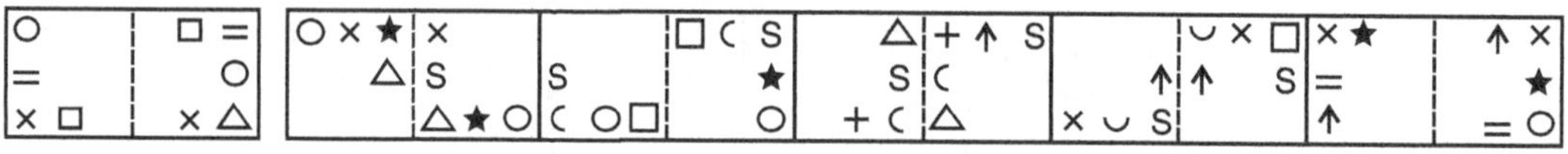

(a) (b) (c) (d) (e)

30. 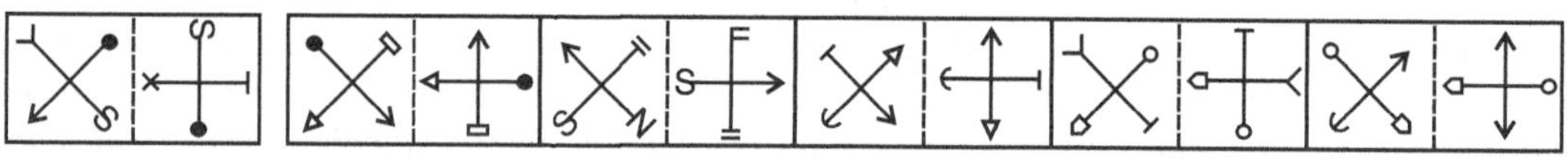

(a) (b) (c) (d) (e)

EXPLANATORY ANSWERS

1. (d) : In all other figures, the arrow and the + sign lie towards the black end of the main figure.

2.(a) : The pins, equal in number of sides in the main figure are attached to the midpoint of a side of the main figure in case of figures (B), (C), (D) and (E). In figure (A), these pins are attached to a vertex of the main figure.

3.(c) : In all other figures, the dot appears in the angle formed between the arrow and the pin.

4.(a) : All other figures can be rotated into each other. (In each figure except figure (A), the middle element is obtained by rotating the outer element through 90° CW and the inner element is obtained by rotating the middle element through 90° CW).

5.(c) : All other figures have at least one line of symmetry.

6.(c) : All other figures can be rotated into each other.

7.(e) : In each one of the other four figures, four arcs are curved towards the left and four other arcs are curved towards the right.

8.(c) : All other figures can be rotated into each other.

9.(d) : In all other figures, the number of dots outside the main figure is one more than the number of dots inside the main figure.

10.(a) : In all other figures, one of the dots lies outside the triangle as well as the circle.

11.(e) : Except in figure (B), in all other figures, from element I to II two new designs are added in one side of the main design.

12.(c) : In each figure from element I to II the main design rotates through 135° clockwise or anticlockwise. Except in figure (C), in all other figures, the smaller line segment moves to other side from element I to II.

13.(a) : In all other figures the element II can be obtained by the lateral inversion of the element I. In figure (A), the lower design has not been inverted.

14.(b) : In figure (B), the small segment is on the same side as that of the half shaded circle in both the elements.

15.(d) : The first design is inverted and moved to third place, the second design is moved to the fourth place, third design to the first place and fourth design is inverted and moved to the second place. Option (D) violates this.

16.*(b)* : In all other options the top-left element is moved to the centre with 90° clockwise rotation. Here, it is rotated anticlockwise.

17.*(d)* : All the designs are shifted in a set pattern one behind the other. The fourth design in all others is changed and placed in the last. Here, the fifth and last designs are changed.

18.*(a)* : In all other pair of figures, all incomplete squares in the first elements are completed and an extra square is added in the second element.

19.*(a)* : From element I to element II, the 'S' shape is turned 90° clockwise and moved down, the double arrow shape '⇒' is turned 90° clockwise and moved to the right, the two parallel lines one turned by 90°; one parallel line is added and all three lines are moved up, the line with a dot is turned 90° clockwise and moved to the centre and the 'C' shape in the centre is turned by 180° and moved to top left position. Here, the double arrow is turned anticlockwise.

20.*(c)* : Starting from one unit, all units are moved in a set pattern, the places of last two units moved are interchanged and the last unit is then made new. Here, no changes are made in the last two units.

21.*(d)* : From element I to element II clockwise the first unit is moved 2 steps forward, the second unit 1 step forward, the third unit 2½ steps forward and the fourth unit 3 steps forward. In option 'D' the third unit violates the rule.

22.*(e)* : From element I to element II, the horizontal bar is turned 135° anticlockwise and the unit at the lower end is turned by 180°. The vertical bar is turned 90° anticlockwise and the unit at the lower end is turned by 180°. In option 'E' one more unit at the top is turned by 180°.

23.*(e)* : In element II, the shade is moved two sections clockwise and shifted from the centre to the base. In option 'E' it is not so.

24.*(a)* : In element II, the arrow is turned 135° clock-wise. In option 'A' it is turned anticlockwise.

25.*(b)* : From element I to element II, the bottom right unit and bottom left unit are moved to the centre and middle left position respectively. The other two units are removed and two new elements are placed in the top right and bottom centre position respectively. In option 'B' the placement of bottom right and left elements is not right.

26.*(c)* : In element II, the shades are shifted one petal clockwise. In option 'C' one of the shades is not moved.

27.*(b)* : From element I to element II, the unit on the top left is turned 90° anticlockwise and moved to the bottom right corner position, the unit in the centre is turned 135° anticlockwise and moved to the top right position, and the unit in the bottom right is turned by 180° and moved to the centre. In option 'B', the middle unit is turned 135° clockwise.

28.*(a)* : From element I to element II, a new unit is placed in the top left position, the top left unit is moved to the middle right position, the middle right unit is moved to the left position, the middle left unit is replaced by a new unit and placed in bottom right position, the bottom right unit is moved to the top right position, and the top right unit is moved diagonally to replace the bottom left unit. In option 'A', the middle left unit is not changed when moved to the bottom right position.

29.*(e)* : From element I to element II starting anticlockwise, the first and second units are moved 1½ steps clockwise respectively, the third unit ½ step anticlockwise, the fourth unit 2 steps clockwise, and a new unit is placed ahead of the first unit. Option 'E' violates the rules.

30.*(e)* : In element II, the cross is turned 135° clockwise and then the positions of left and top units on the cross are interchanged. In option 'E' it is not so.

29 Completing An Incomplete Pattern

This test aims at judging the ability to comprehend correlations between geometric figures and diagrams and to perceive the structure of the design in its totality in order to select the appropriate part from amongst the answer figures for completion of each incomplete pattern.

In this test, a pattern/figure is given, a portion of which is left blank or incomplete. From the answer figures, you are required to select the figure which fits into the blank space in the incomplete figure.

EXERCISE

Directions (Qs. 1 to 18): *In each of the following questions a figure or a pattern or a design is given. A portion of that figure/pattern/design is blank or shown with a question mark. Below it are given four alternative figures. Choose a figure from the alternative figures which complete the given figure/pattern or design.*

1.

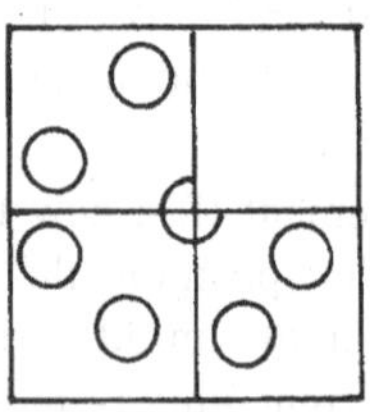

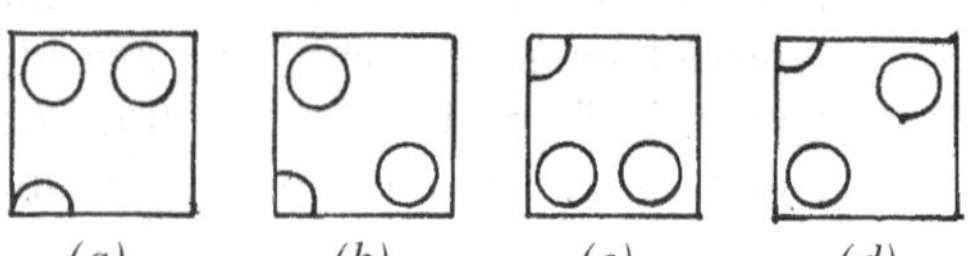

(a) (b) (c) (d)

2.

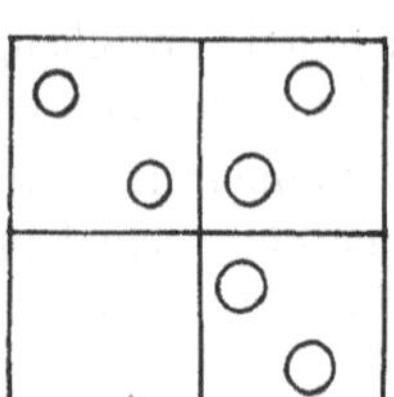

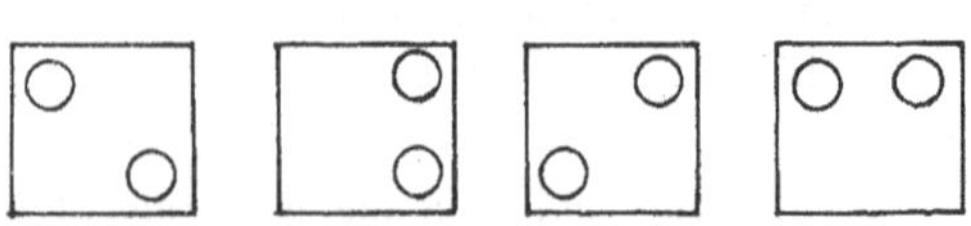

(a) (b) (c) (d)

3.

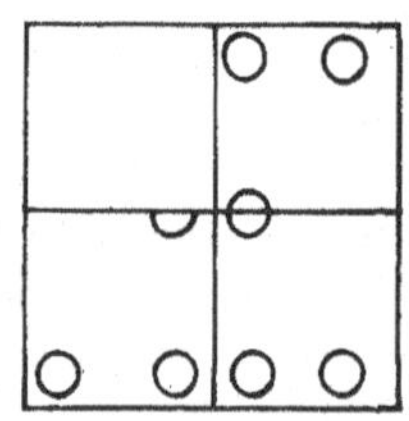

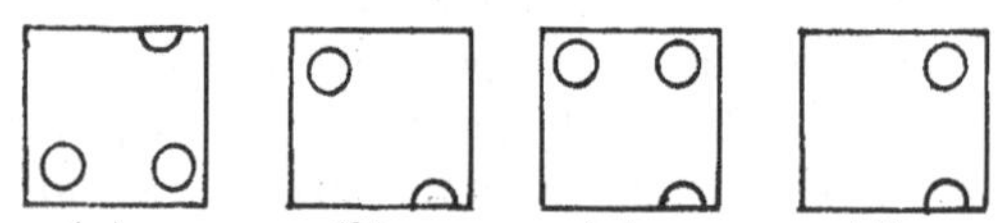

(a) (b) (c) (d)

4.

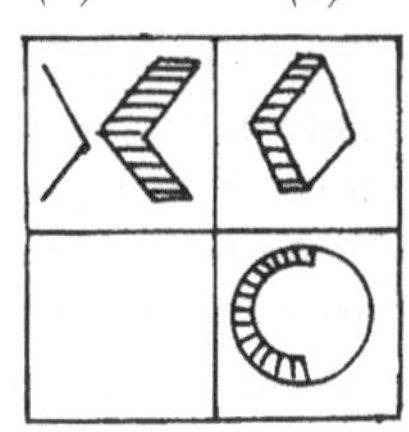

(a) (b) (c) (d)

5.

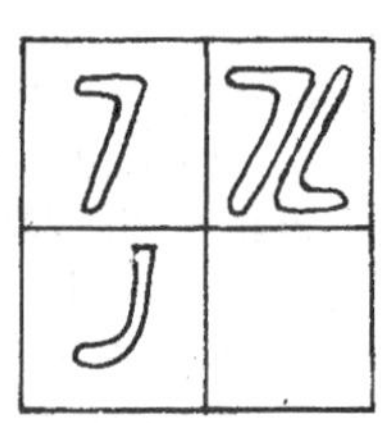

(a) (b) (c) (d)

6.

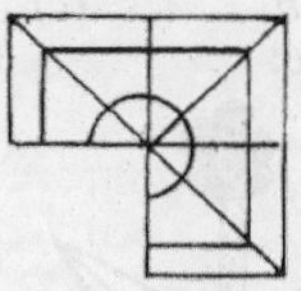

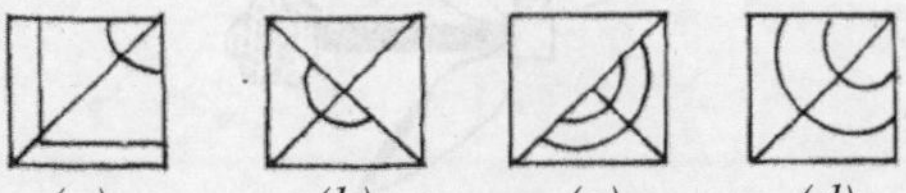

(a) (b) (c) (d)

7.

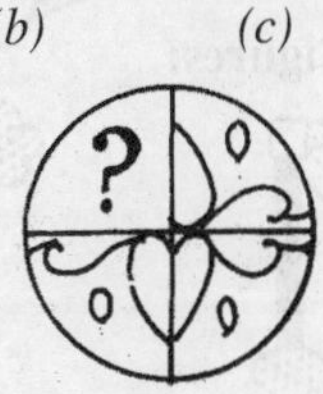

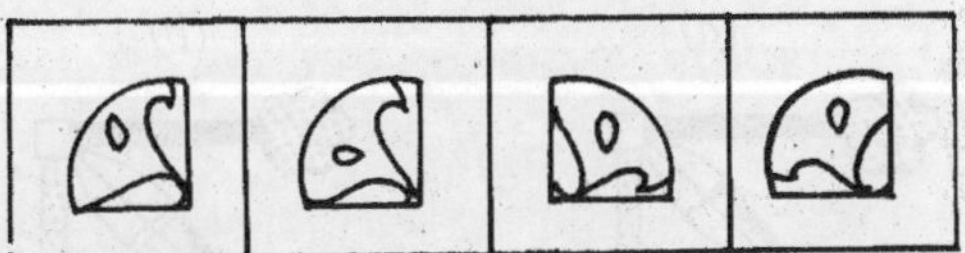

(a) (b) (c) (d)

8.

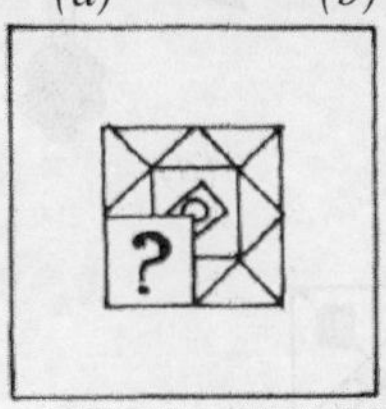

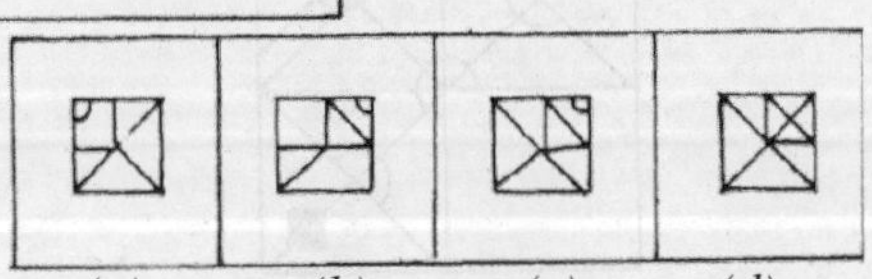

(a) (b) (c) (d)

9.

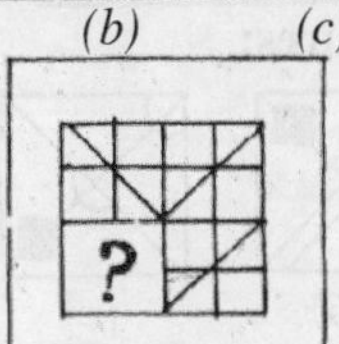

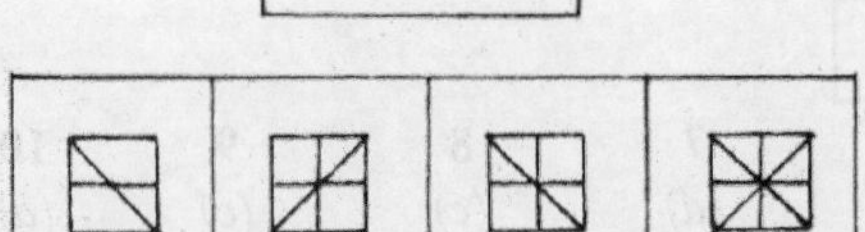

(a) (b) (c) (d)

10.

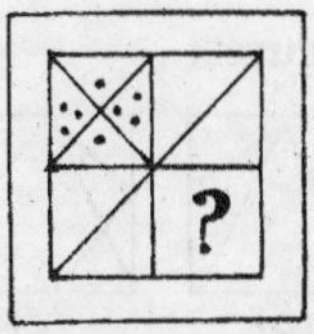

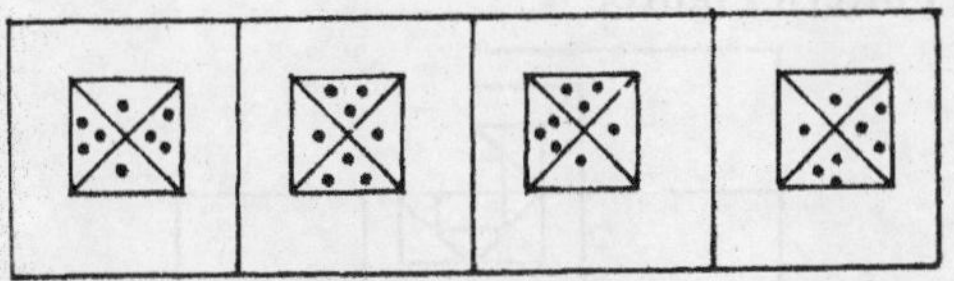

(a) (b) (c) (d)

11. Pattern Figure:

Alternative Figures:

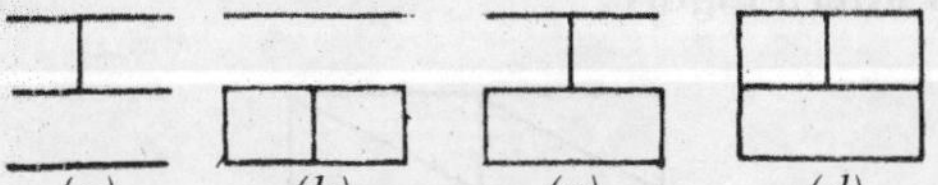

(a) (b) (c) (d)

12. Pattern Figure:

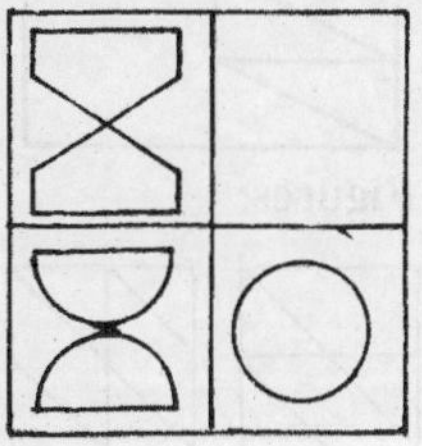

Alternative Figures:

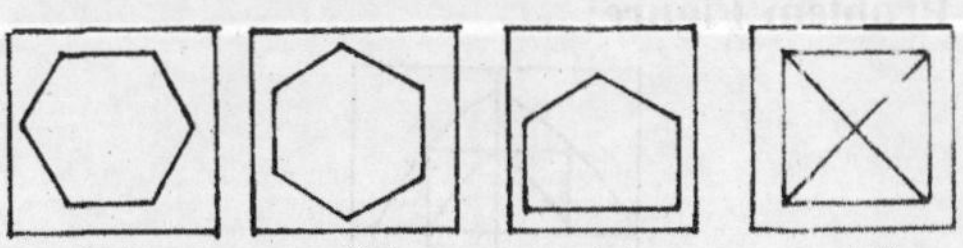

(a) (b) (c) (d)

13. Pattern Figure:

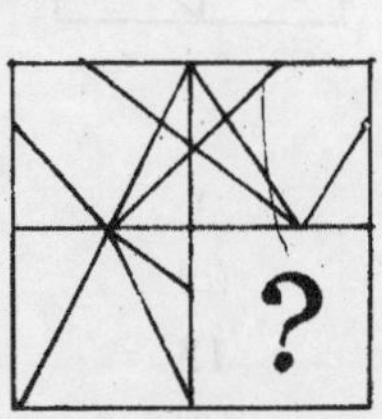

Alternative Figures:

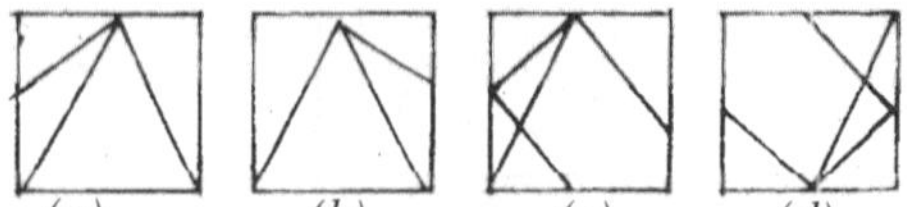

(a) (b) (c) (d)

14. Pattern Figure:

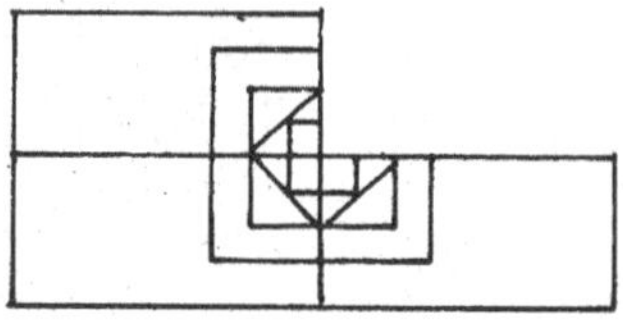

Alternative Figures:

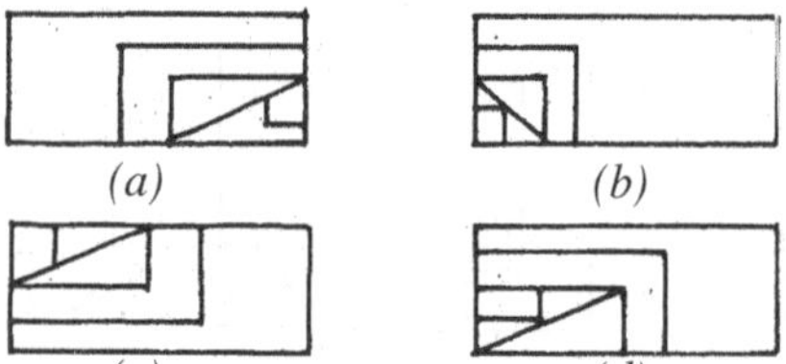

(a) (b) (c) (d)

15. Pattern Figure:

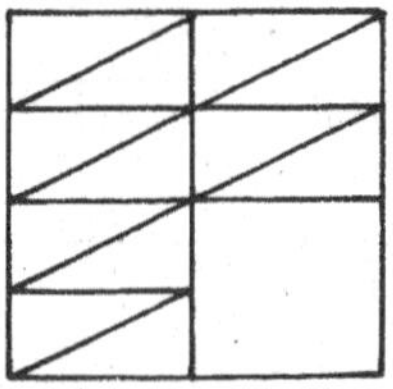

Alternative Figures:

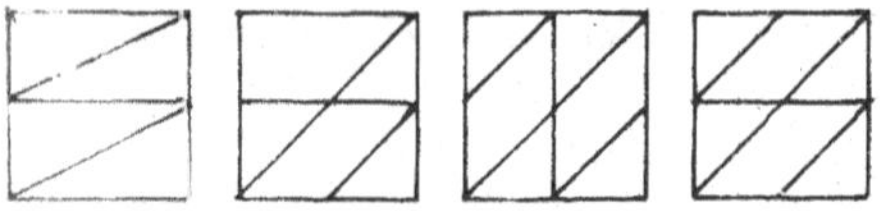

(a) (b) (c) (d)

16. Problem Figure:

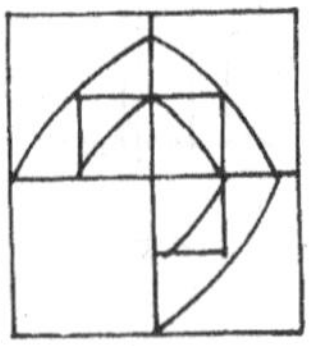

Alternative Figures:

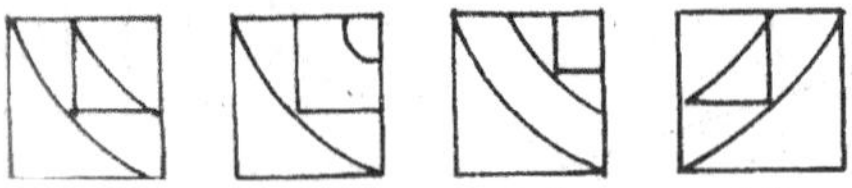

(a) (b) (c) (d)

17. Problem Figure:

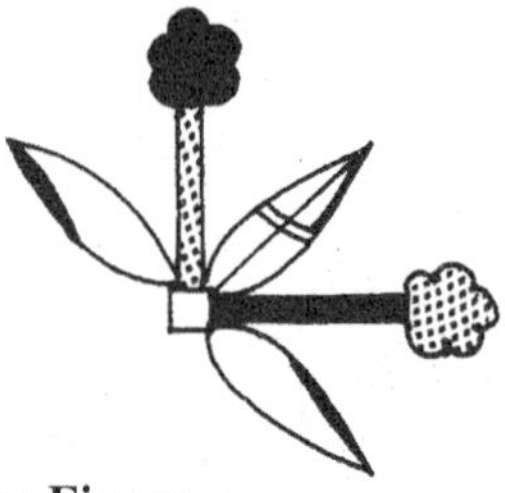

Alternative Figures:

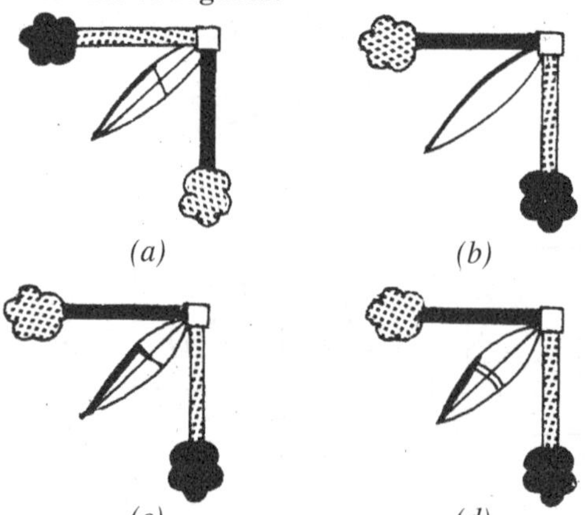

(a) (b) (c) (d)

18. Problem Figure:

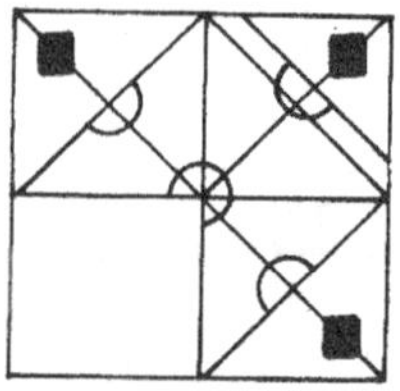

Alternative Figures:

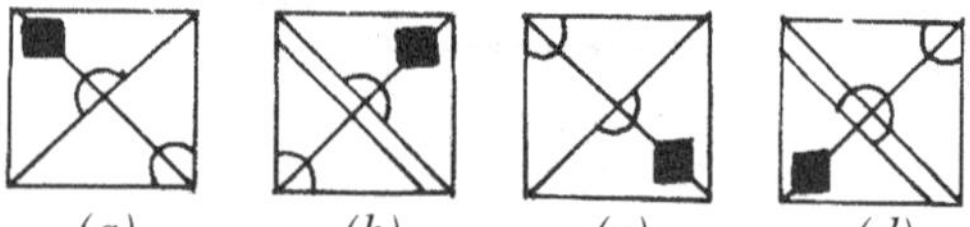

(a) (b) (c) (d)

ANSWERS

1	2	3	4	5	6	7	8	9	10
(b)	(c)	(c)	(b)	(c)	(a)	(d)	(c)	(c)	(a)

11	12	13	14	15	16	17	18
(c)	(b)	(a)	(b)	(a)	(a)	(d)	(d)

30 Spotting Hidden Pattern

In this test, the problem figure comprises just one figure.

Below it are given four alternative figures. Of these four alternative figures, one figure is such that the problem figure is hidden into it. Candidates must observe very keenly the problem figure. They must then try to make a search of that (problem figure) among the alternative figures. It requires undiluted shape perception and sharp analytical capability to pin point the hiddern figure/design out of a large and jumbled figure.

EXERCISE

Directions: *In each of the following questions a figure is given at the top. Below it are given four figure alternatives. In each question, the figure given at the top is hidden in one of the four alternatives. Choose that alternatives.*

1. Question Figure:

Alternative Figures:

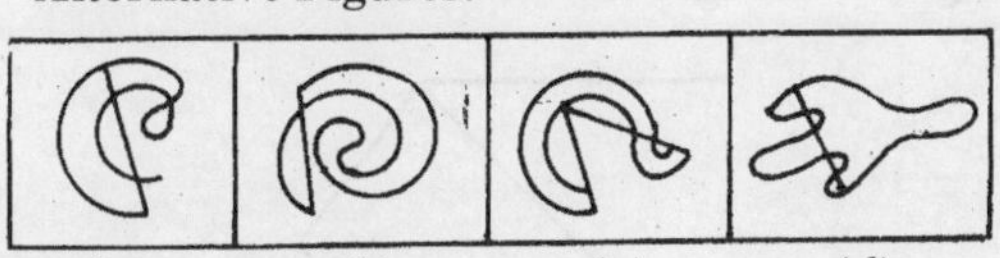

(a) (b) (c) (d)

2. Question Figure:

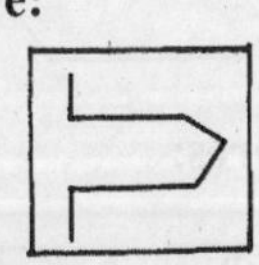

Alternative Figures:

(a) (b) (c) (d)

3. Question Figure:

Alternative Figures:

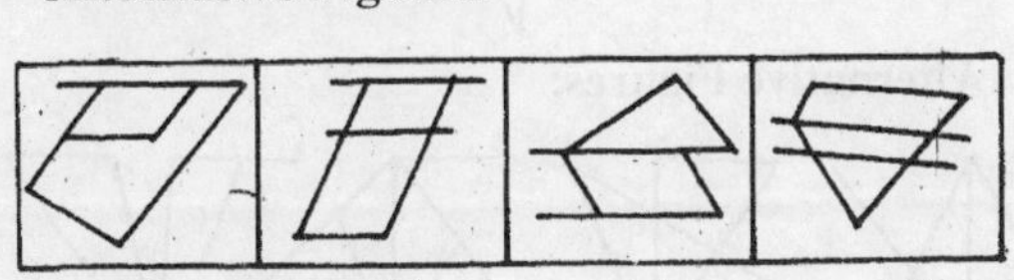

(a) (b) (c) (d)

4. Question Figure:

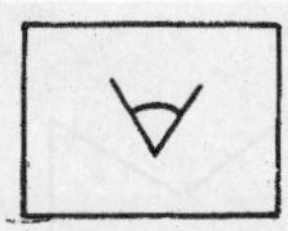

Alternative Figures:

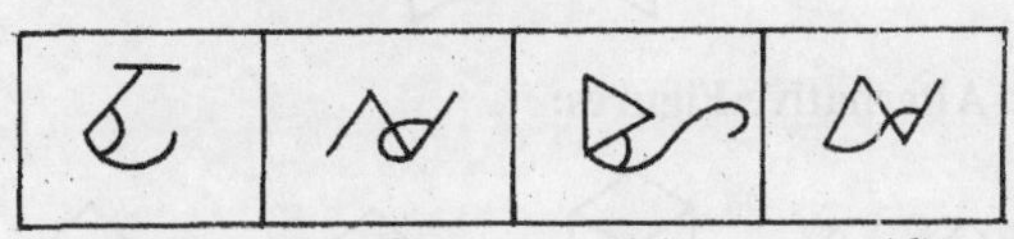

(a) (b) (c) (d)

5. Question Figure:

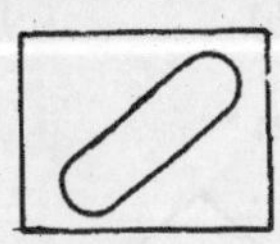

Alternative Figures:

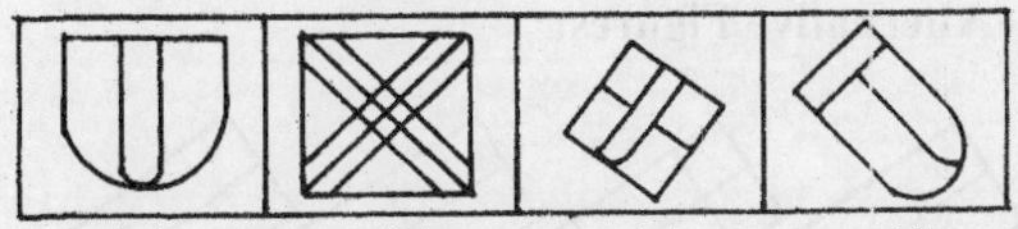

(a) (b) (c) (d)

6. Question Figure:

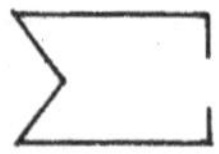

Alternative Figures:

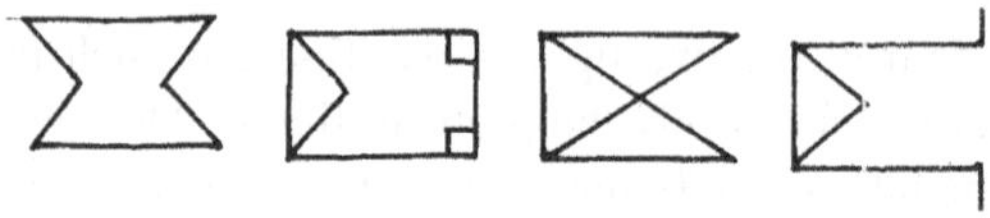

(a) (b) (c) (d)

7. Question Figure:

Alternative Figures:

(a) (b) (c) (d)

8. Question Figure:

Alternative Figures:

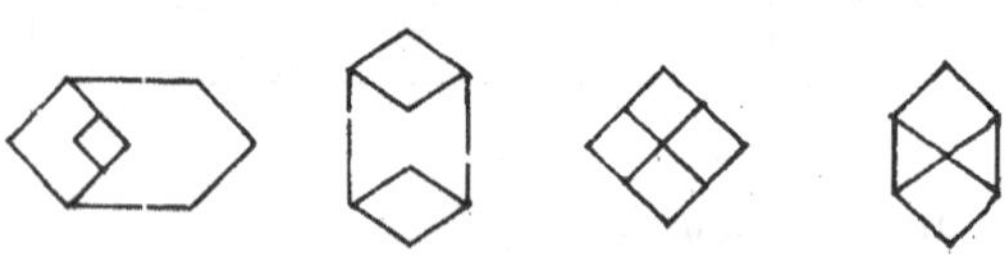

(a) (b) (c) (d)

9. Question Figure:

Alternative Figures:

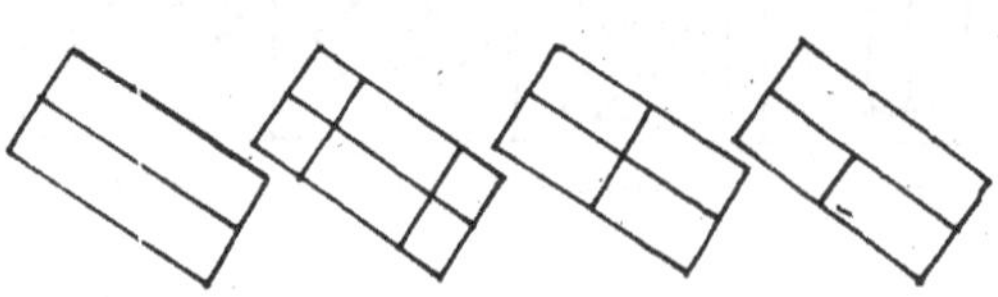

(a) (b) (c) (d)

10. Question Figure:

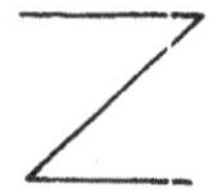

Alternative Figures:

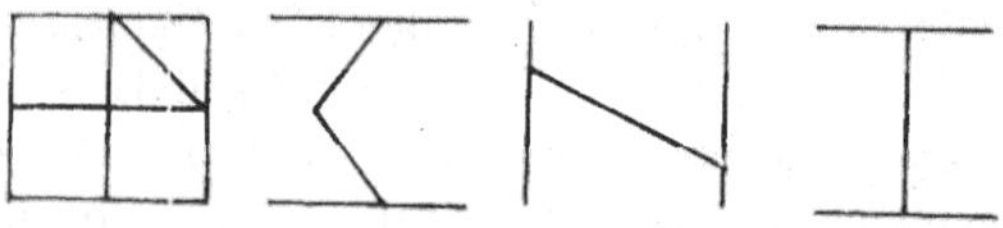

(a) (b) (c) (d)

11. Question Figure:

Alternative Figures:

(a) (b) (c) (d)

12. Question Figure:

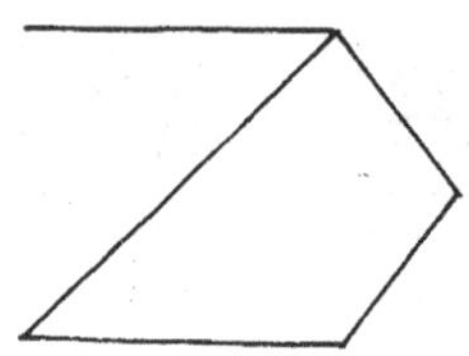

Alternative Figures:

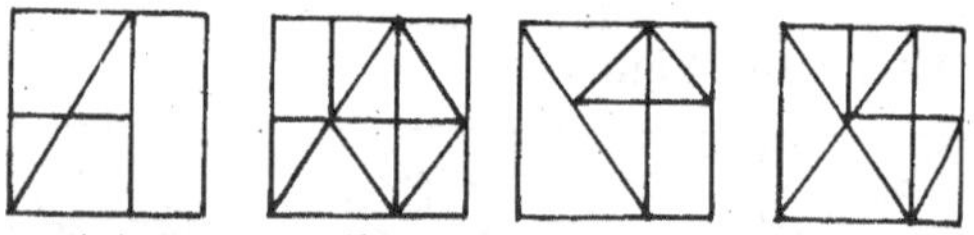

(a) (b) (c) (d)

13. Question Figure:

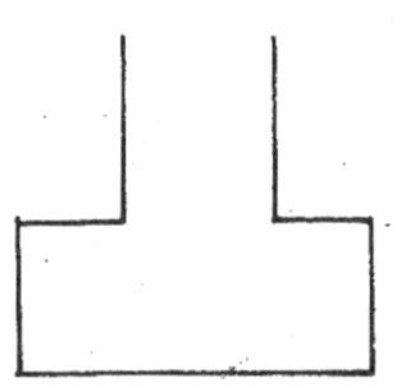

Alternative Figures:

(a) (b) (c) (d)

14. Question Figure:

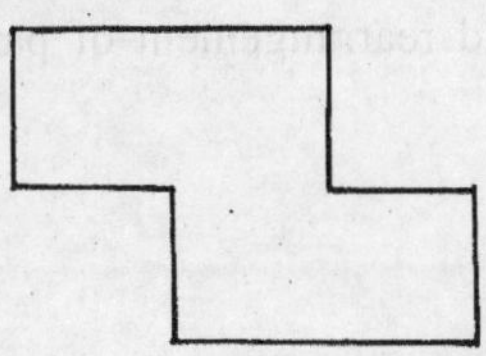

Alternative Figures:

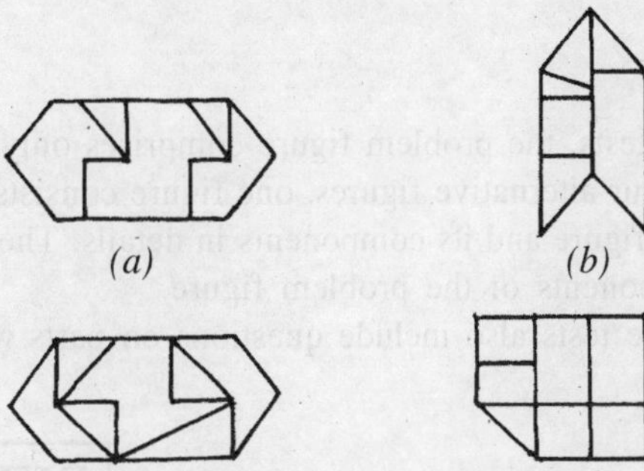

(a) (b) (c) (d)

ANSWERS

1	2	3	4	5	6	7	8	9	10
(b)	(a)	(c)	(d)	(b)	(b)	(b)	(b)	(d)	(c)
11	**12**	**13**	**14**						
(b)	(b)	(a)	(c)						

31 Components of Figures

In these tests, the problem figure comprises only one figure. Below it are given four alternative figures. Of the four alternative figures, one figure consists of all the components of the problem figure. Study the problem figure and its components in details. Then locate a figure from among the alternatives which has the components of the problem figure.

These tests also include questions on parts-whole perception and rearrangement of parts of a given figure.

EXERCISE

TYPE - I

Directions (Qs. 1 to 13): *In these questions a figure is given. Its components are given in one of the four alternative figures given below. Choose the alternative figure which has the components of the given figure.*

1. Given Figure:

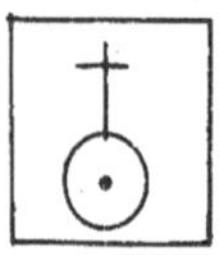

Alternative Figures:

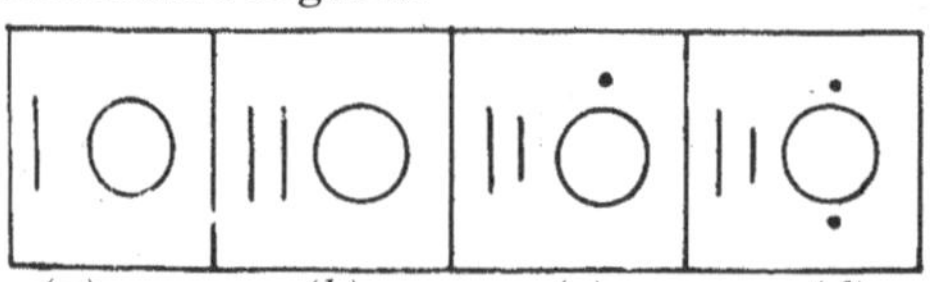

(a) (b) (c) (d)

2. Given Figure:

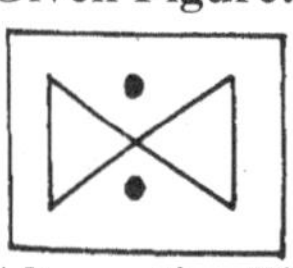

Alternative Figures:

(a)

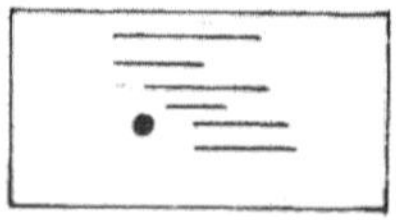

(b)

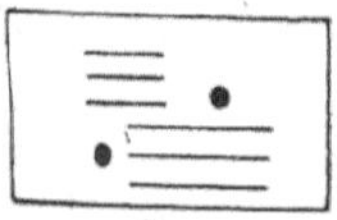

(c)

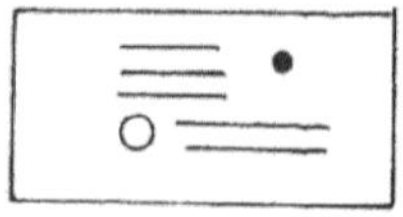

(d)

3. Given Figure:

Alternative Figures:

(a) (b) (c) (d)

4. Given Figure:

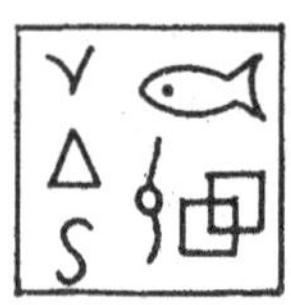

Alternative Figures:

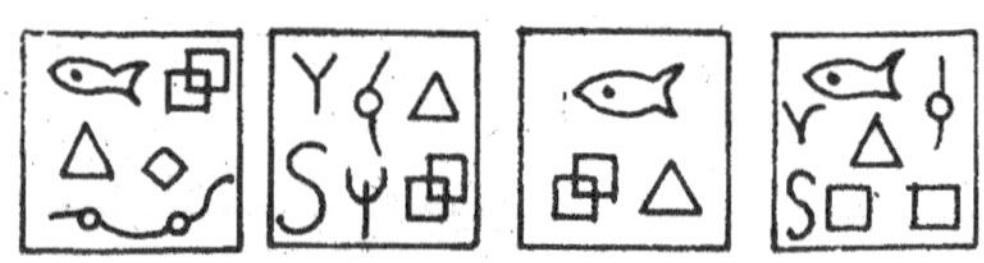

(a) (b) (c) (d)

5. Given Figure:

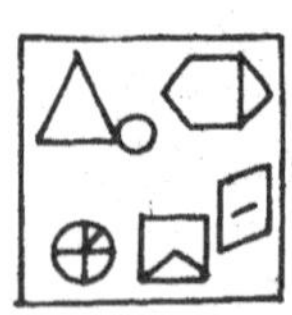

Alternative Figures:

(a)

(b)

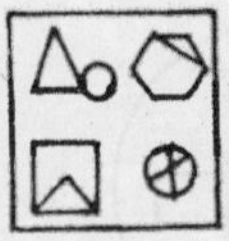
(c)

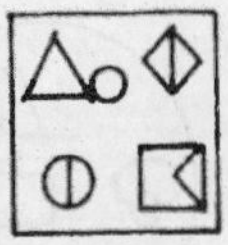
(d)

6. Given Figure:

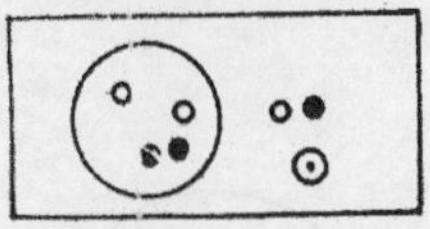

Alternative Figures:

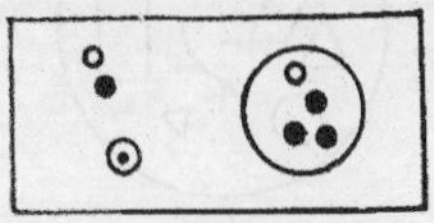
(a)

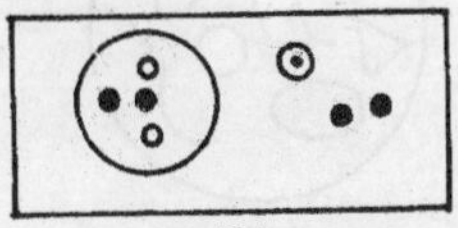
(b)

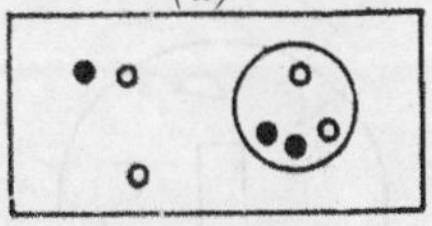
(c)

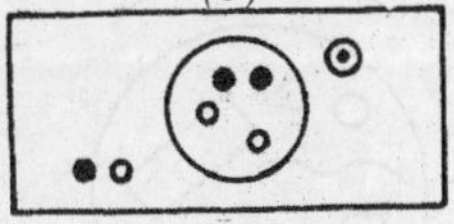
(d)

7. Given Figure:

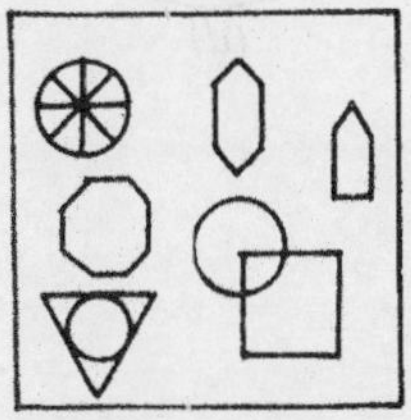

Alternative Figures:

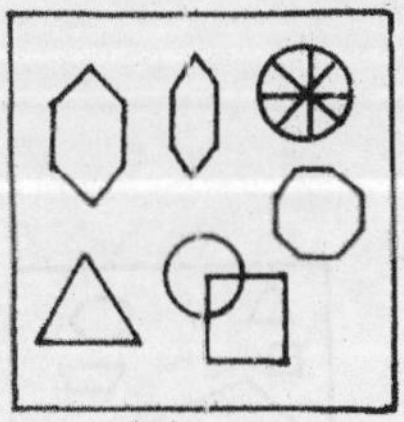
(a)

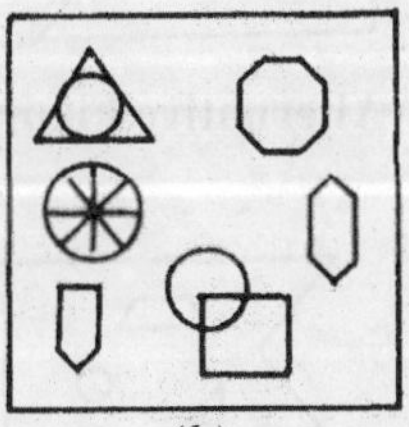
(b)

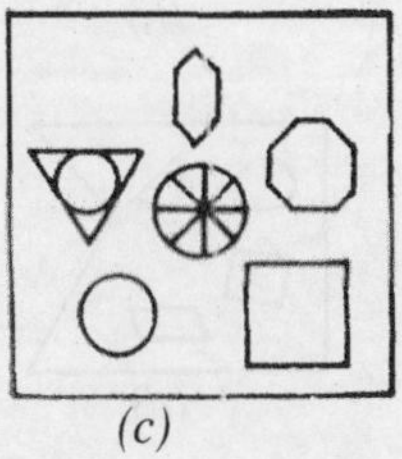
(c)

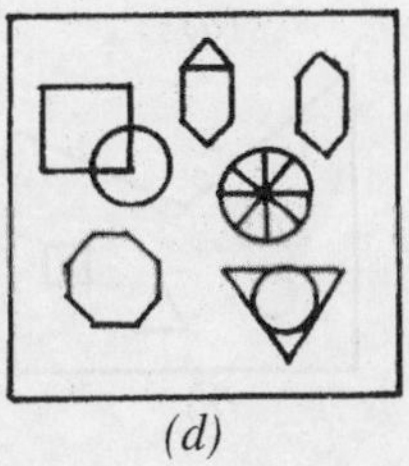
(d)

8. Given Figure:

Alternative Figures:

(a)

(b)

(c)

(d)

9. Given Figure:

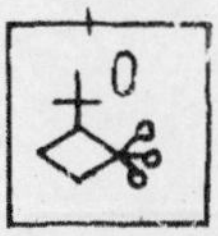

Alternative Figures:

(a)

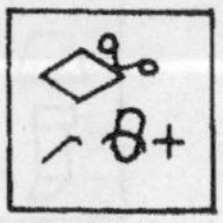
(b)

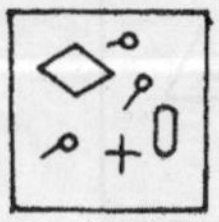
(c)

(d)

10. Given Figure:

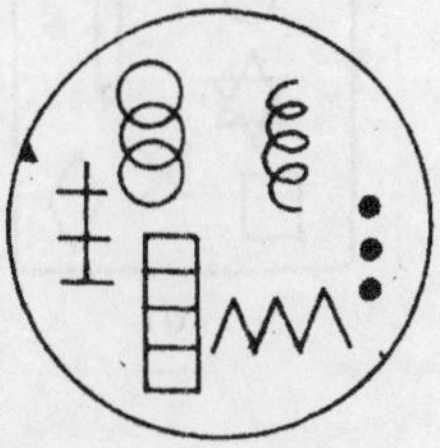

Alternative Figures:

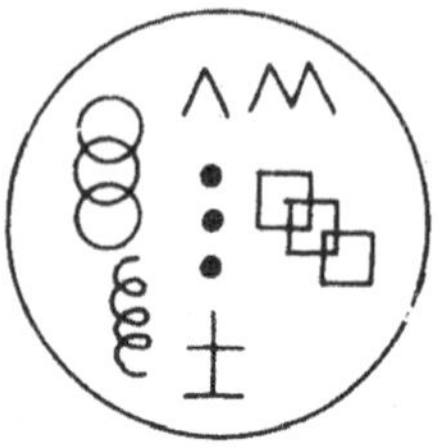
(a)

(b)

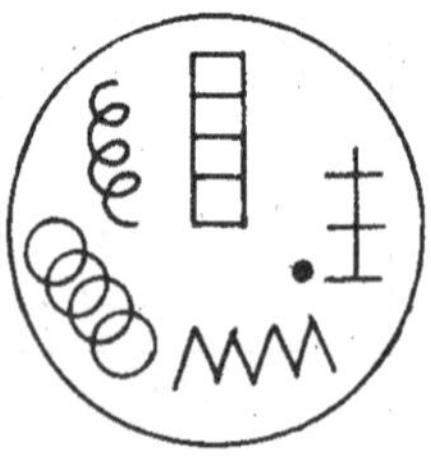
(c)

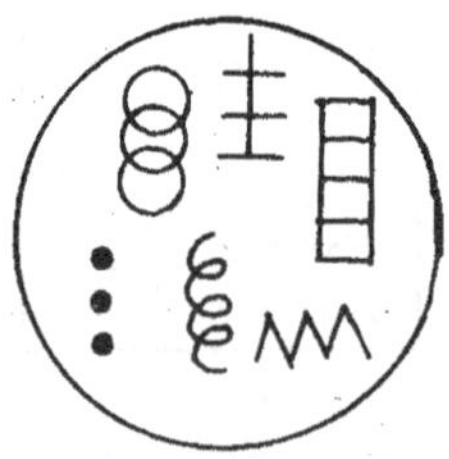
(d)

11. Given Figure:

Alternative Figures:

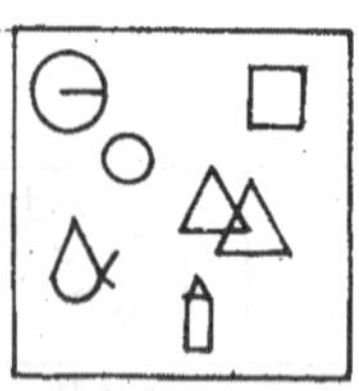
(a)

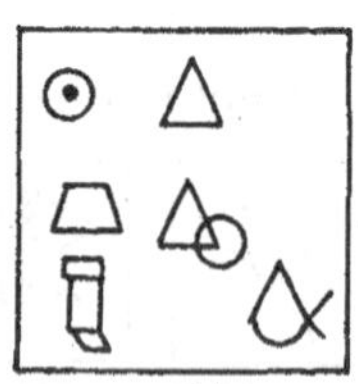
(b)

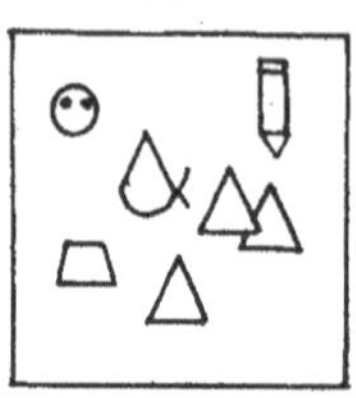
(c)

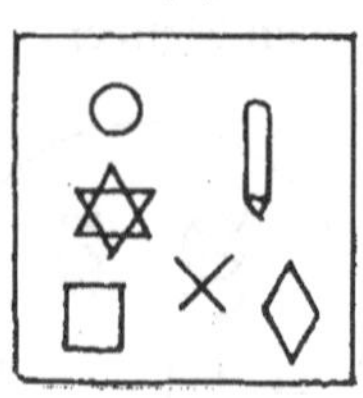
(d)

12. Given Figure:

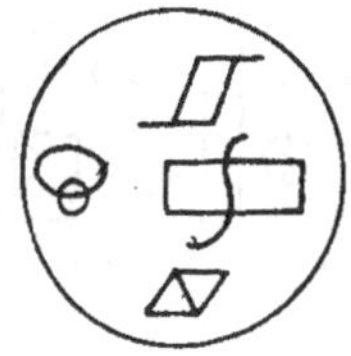

Alternative Figures:

(a)

(b)

(c)

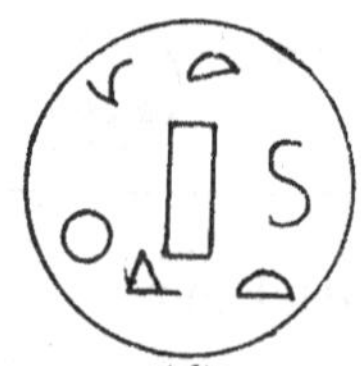
(d)

13. Given Figure:

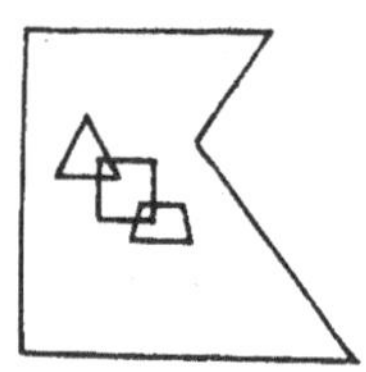

Alternative Figures:

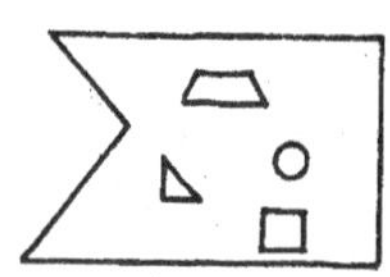
(a)

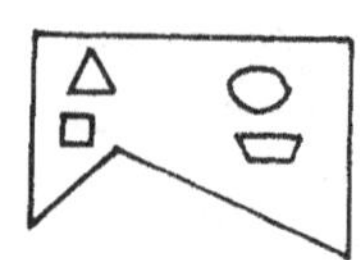
(b)

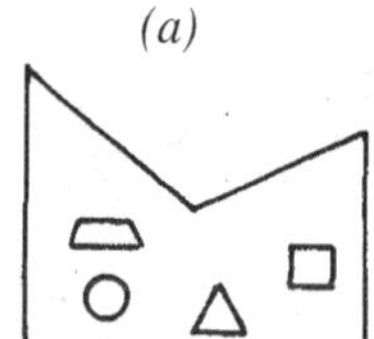
(c)

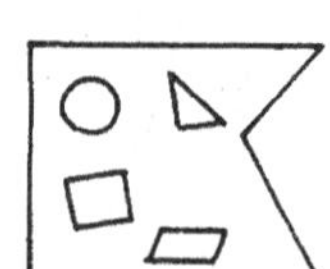
(d)

TYPE - II

Directions (Qs. 14 and 15): *In the following questions which of the alternatives will exactly make up the key figure?*

14. Key Figure:

Alternative Figures:

(a)

(b)

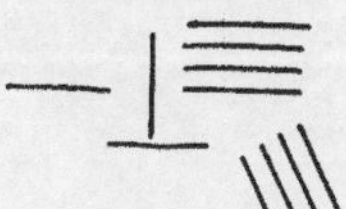

(c)

(d)

15. Key Figure:

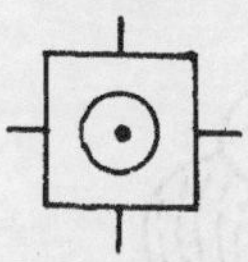

Alternative Figures:

(a)

(b)

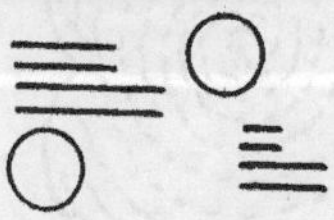

(c)

(d)

TYPE - III

Directions (Qs. 16 to 21): *In the Problem Figure you will find cut-out pieces of one of the response figures A, B, C or D given below. In each question identify the Response figure of which cut-out pieces are given in the problem figure.*

16. Problem Figure:

Answer Figures:

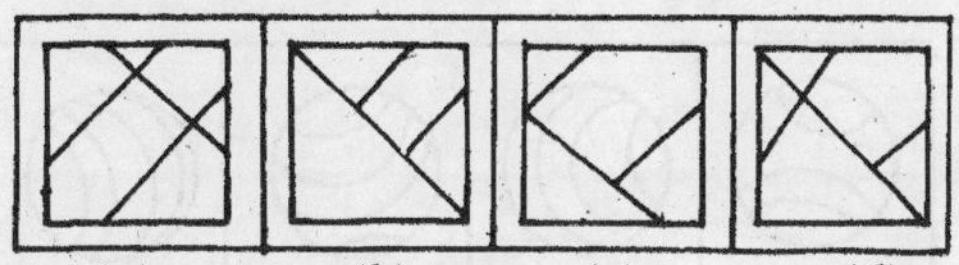

(a) (b) (c) (d)

17. Problem Figure:

Answer Figures:

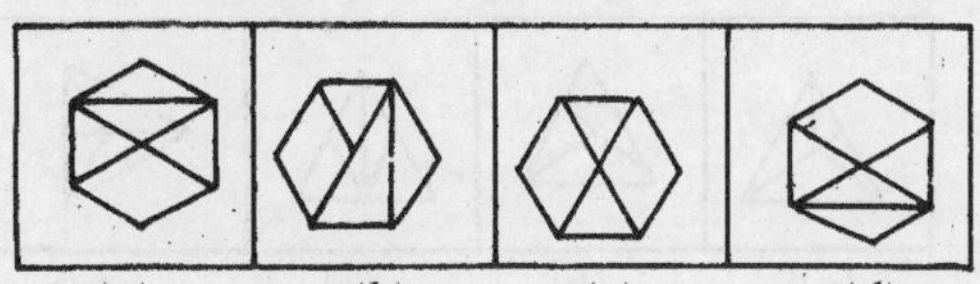

(a) (b) (c) (d)

18. Problem Figure:

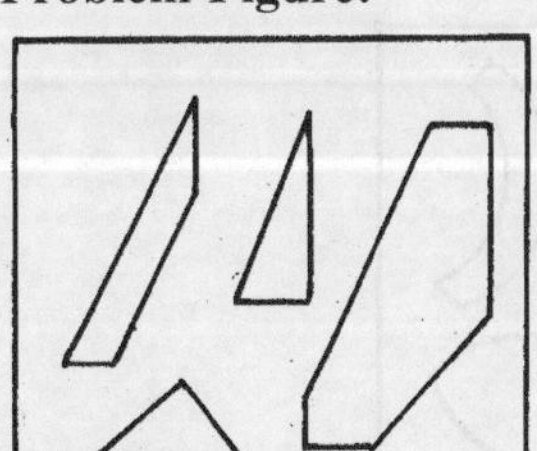

Answer Figures:

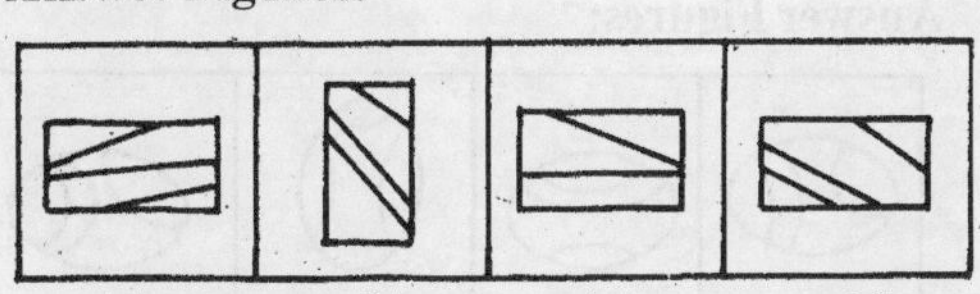

(a) (b) (c) (d)

19. Problem Figure:

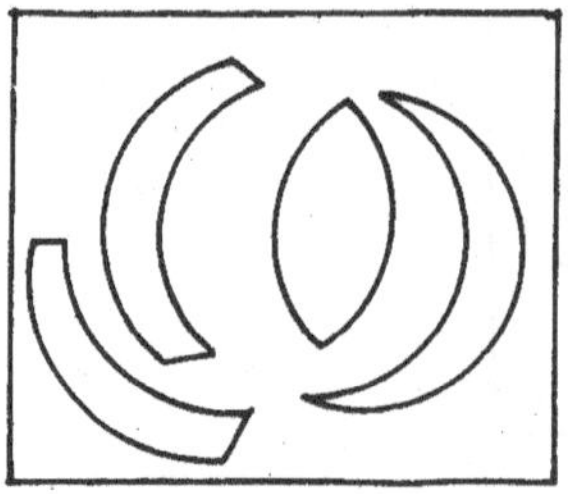

Answer Figures:

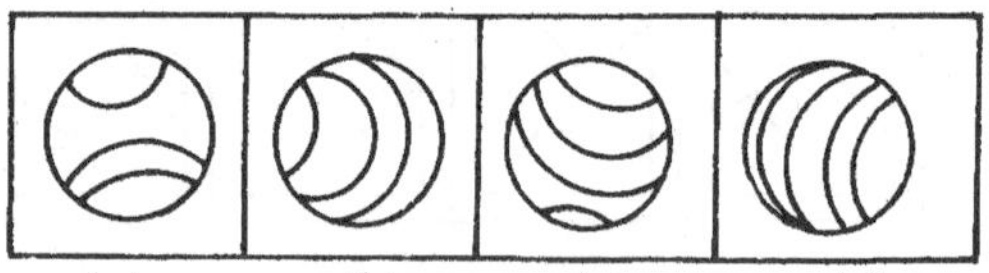

(a) (b) (c) (d)

20. Problem Figure:

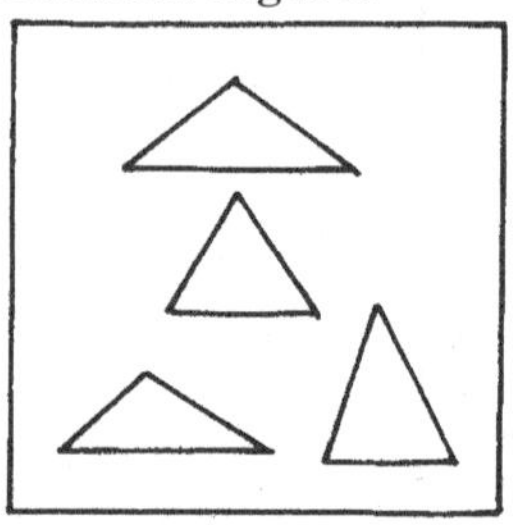

Answer Figures:

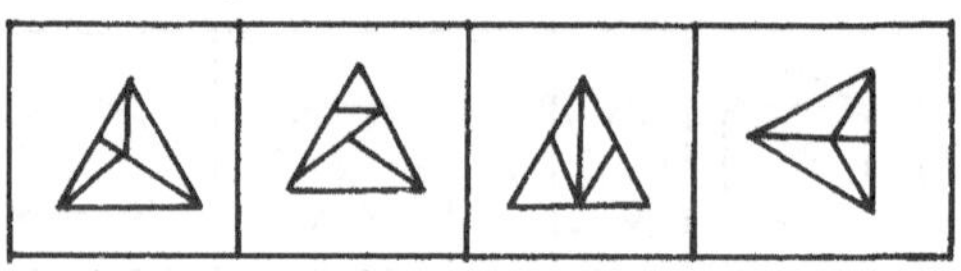

(a) (b) (c) (d)

21. Problem Figure:

Answer Figures:

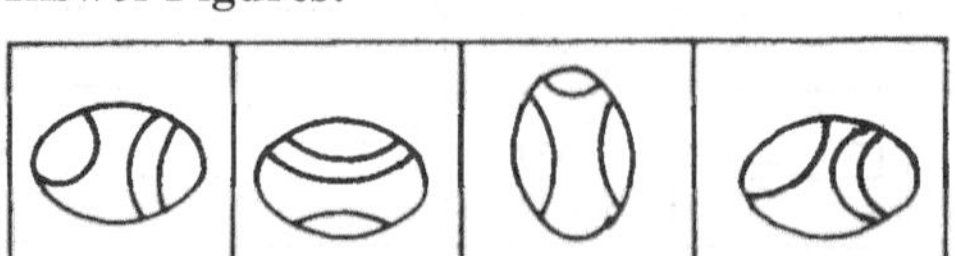

(a) (b) (c) (d)

TYPE - IV

Directions (Qs. 22 to 24): *In these questions, which figure is the rearrangement of the parts of the given figure.*

22. Given Figure:

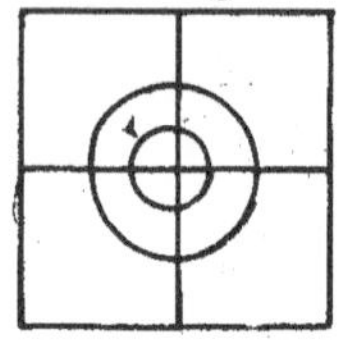

Answer Figures:

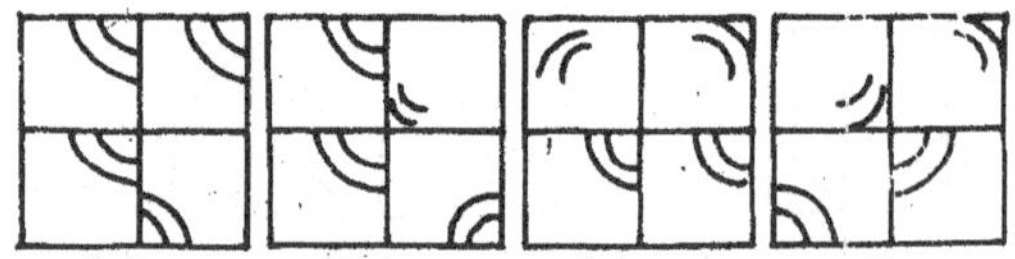

(a) (b) (c) (d)

23. Given Figure:

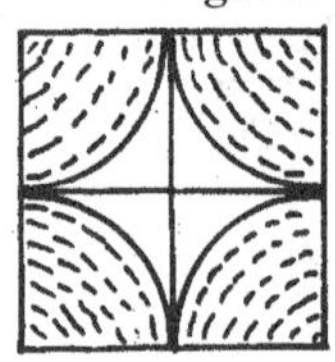

Answer Figures:

(a) (b)

(c) (d)

24. Given Figure:

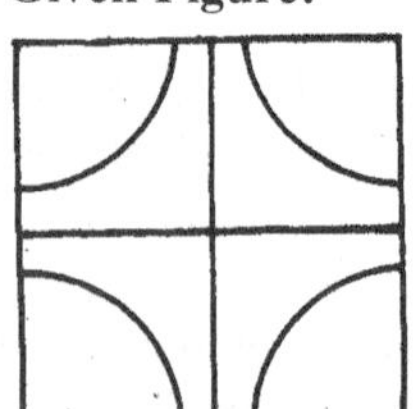

Answer Figures:

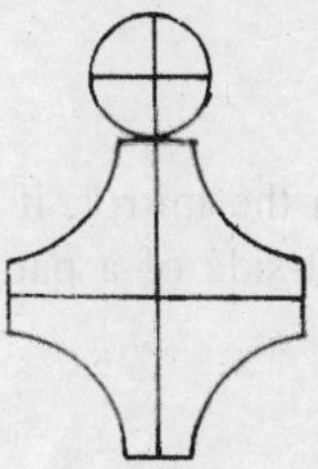

(a)

(b)

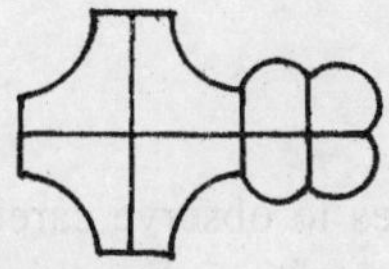

(c)

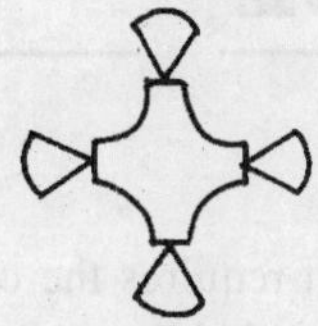

(d)

ANSWERS

1	2	3	4	5	6	7	8	9	10
(c)	*(a)*	*(c)*	*(d)*	*(b)*	*(d)*	*(b)*	*(a)*	*(c)*	*(d)*
11	**12**	**13**	**14**	**15**	**16**	**17**	**18**	**19**	**20**
(c)	*(a)*	*(c)*	*(b)*	*(a)*	*(c)*	*(b)*	*(d)*	*(d)*	*(c)*
21	**22**	**23**	**24**						
(d)	*(a)*	*(a)*	*(a)*						

32 Lateral Inversion

This test requires the candidates to observe carefully how a given figure will appear in the mirror, if the mairror is held at a particular position. For this test, you must remember that the left-side of a pattern appears to be on the right side in the mirror and vice-versa.

EXERCISE

Directions: *In the following questions, a figure is followed by four suggested mirror reflections of it. Assuming that the mirror is placed to the right of the figure, pick out the correct reflected figure.*

1. **Key Figure:**

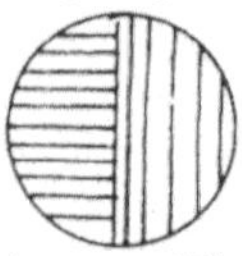

Answer Figures:

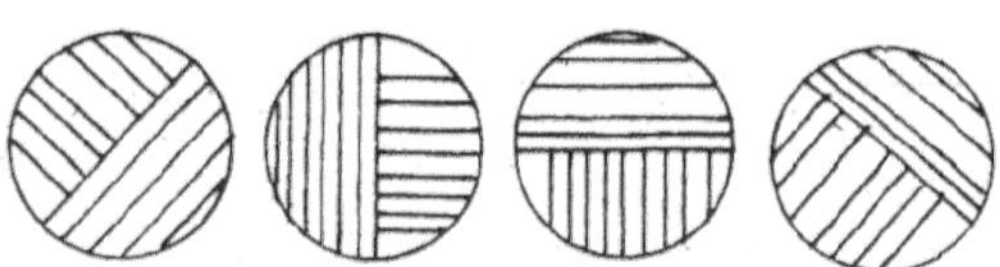

(a) (b) (c) (d)

2. **Key Figure:**

Answer Figures:

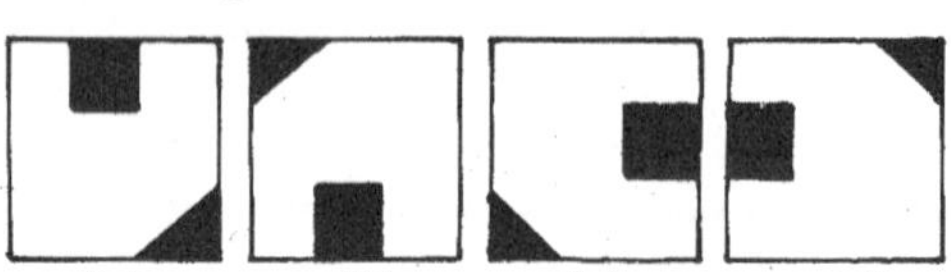

(a) (b) (c) (d)

3. **Key Figure:**

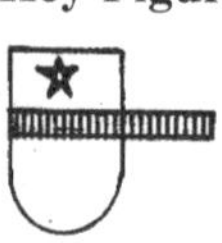

Answer Figures:

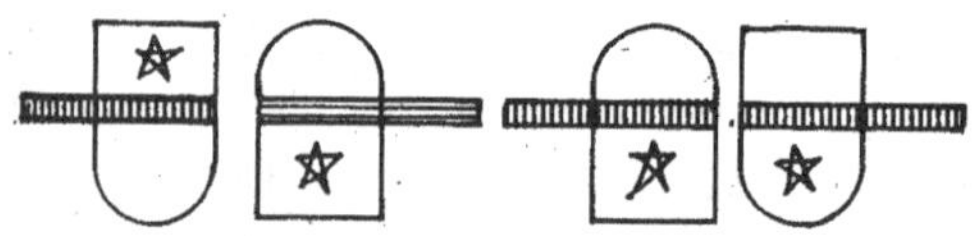

(a) (b) (c) (d)

4. **Key Figure:**

Answer Figures:

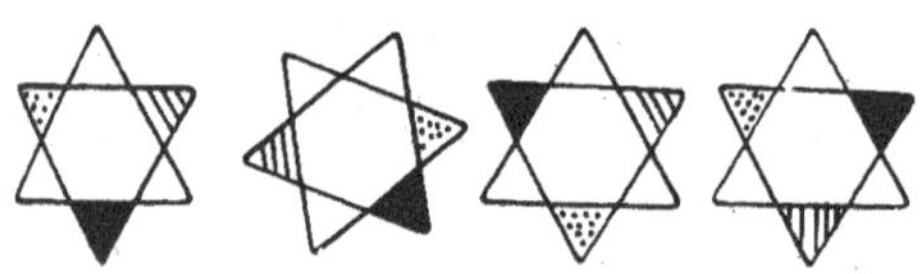

(a) (b) (c) (d)

5. **Key Figure:**

Answer Figures:

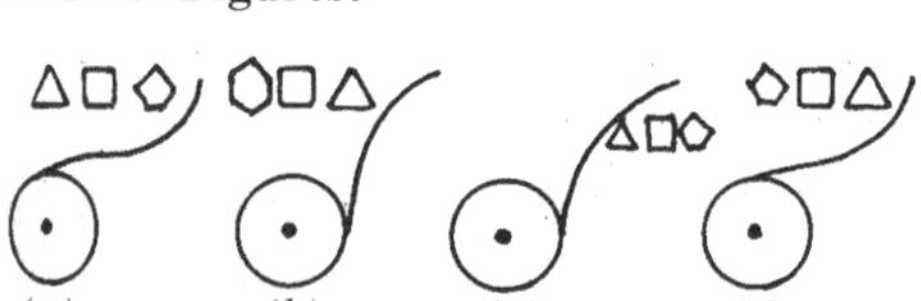

(a) (b) (c) (d)

6. Key Figure:

Answer Figures:

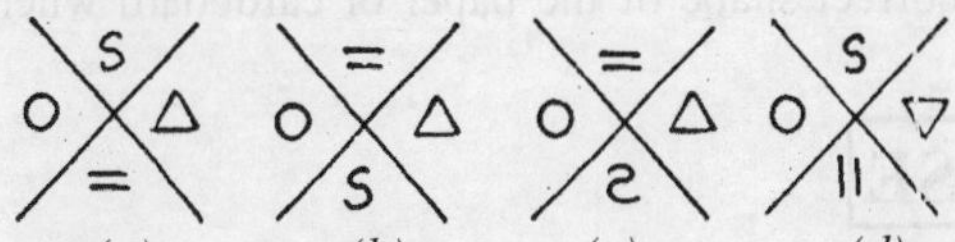

(a) (b) (c) (d)

7. Key Figure:

Answer Figures:

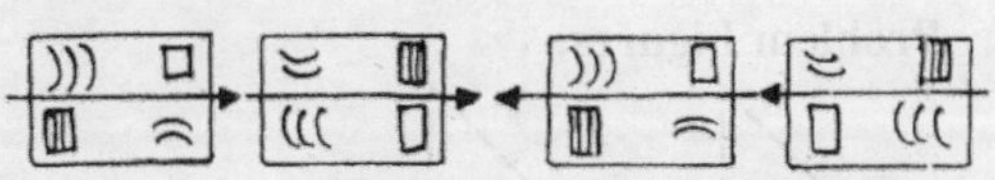

(a) (b) (c) (d)

Directions (Qs. 8 and 9): *In these questions, which of the Answer Figures is exactly the mirror image of the given figure when the mirror is held at AB?*

8. Given Figure:

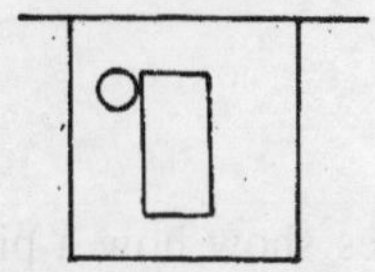

Answer Figures:

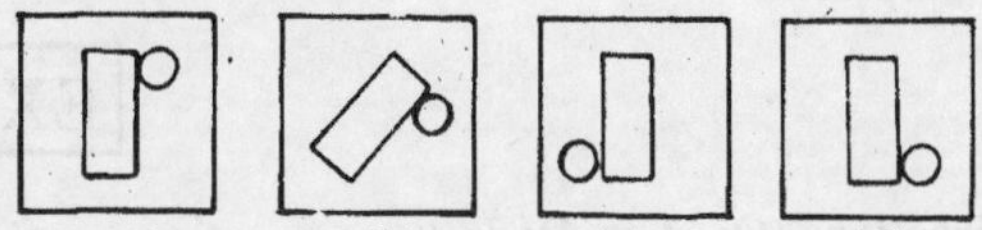

(a) (b) (c) (d)

9. Given Figure:

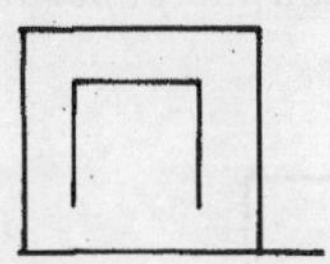

Answer Figures:

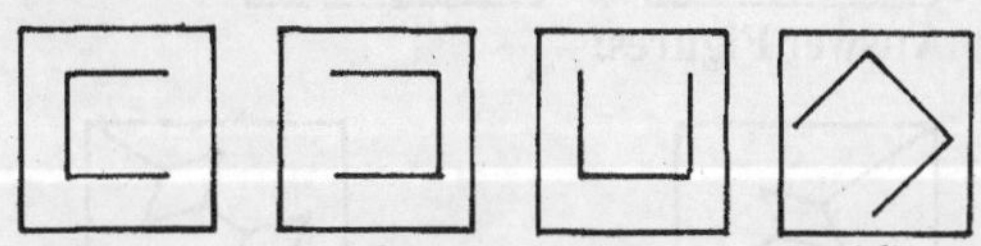

(a) (b) (c) (d)

ANSWERS

1	2	3	4	5	6	7	8	9
(b)	(c)	(a)	(c)	(d)	(c)	(d)	(c)	(c)

33 Folded or Unfolded Pattern

In this test, the problem figures show how a piece of paper or cardboard is folded and cut or punched. From the answer figures, you are required to choose the correct shape of the paper or cardboard when it is unfolded.

EXERCISE

Directions (Qs. 1 to 4): *In these questions, a piece of square paper is folded as shown below and a cut is made as marked. How would the paper look like when unfolded?*

1. Problem Figures:

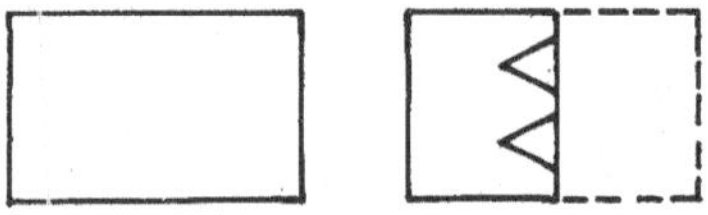

Answer Figures:

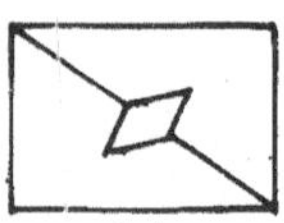

(a)

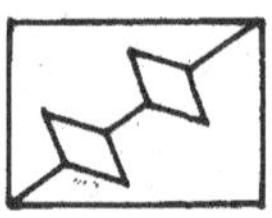

(b)

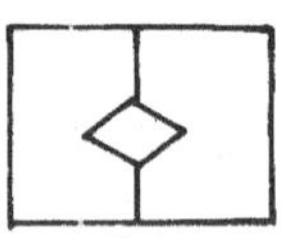

(c)

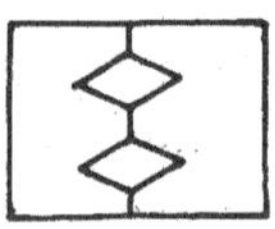

(d)

2. Problem Figures:

Answer Figures:

(a)

(b)

(c)

(d)

3. Problem Figure:

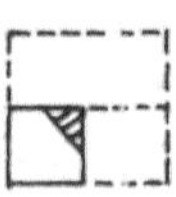

Answer Figures:

(a)

(b)

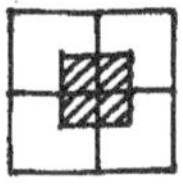

(c)

(d)

4. Problem Figures:

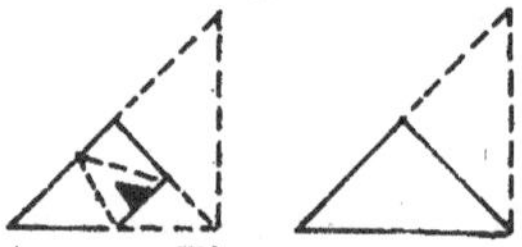

Answer Figures:

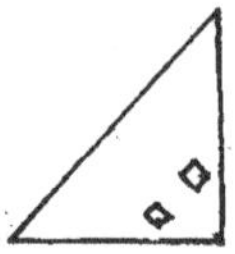

(a)

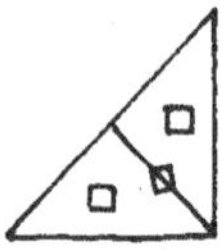

(b)

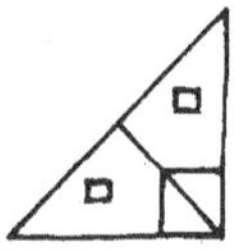

(c)

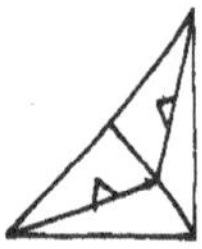

(d)

Directions (Qs. 5 to 9): *As shown below, a paper is folded and then cut. How will the paper look like, when unfolded?*

5. Problem Figures:

Answer Figures:

(a)

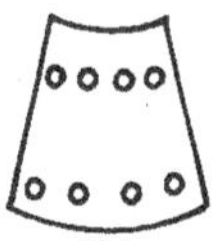

(b)

(c)

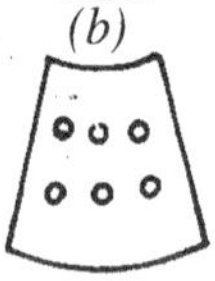

(d)

6. Problem Figures:

Answer Figures:

(a) (b)

(c) (d)

7. Problem Figures:

Answer Figures:

(a) (b)

(c) (d)

8. Problem Figures:

Answer Figures:

(a) (b)

(c) (d)

9. Problem Figures:

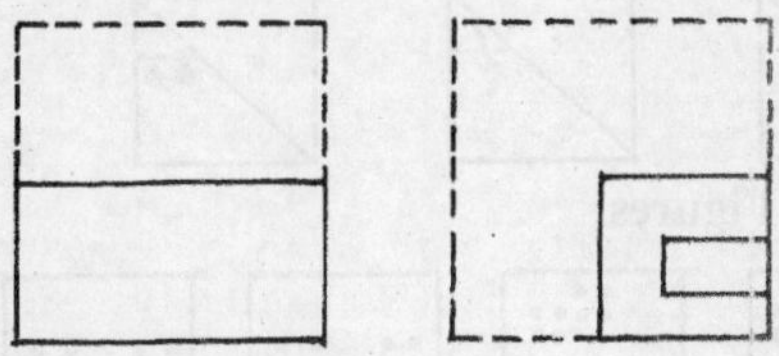

Answer Figures:

(a) (b)

(c) (d)

Directions (Qs. 10 to 14): *In these questions, a square/hexagonal sheet of paper has been folded and punched as shown by the top figures. You have to find out from amongst the four response figures how it will appear when opened?*

10. Problem Figures:

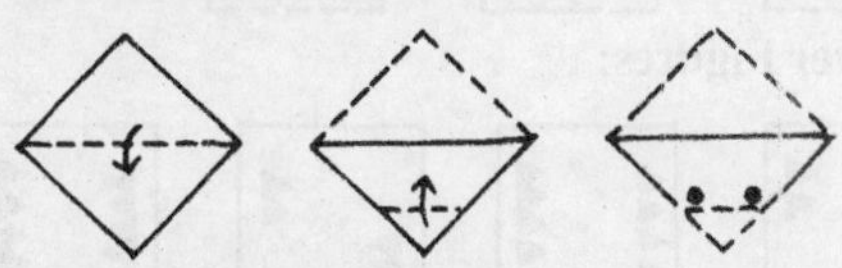

Answer Figures:

(a) (b) (c) (d)

11. Problem Figures:

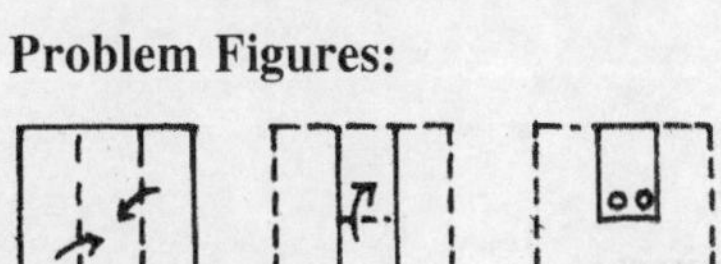

Answer Figures:

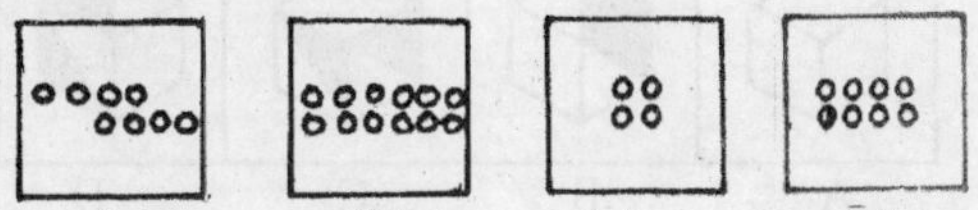

(a) (b) (c) (d)

12. Problem Figures:

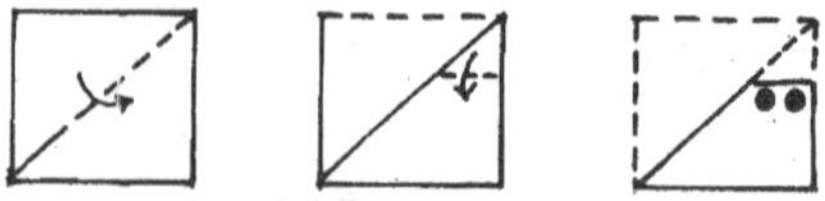

Answer Figures:

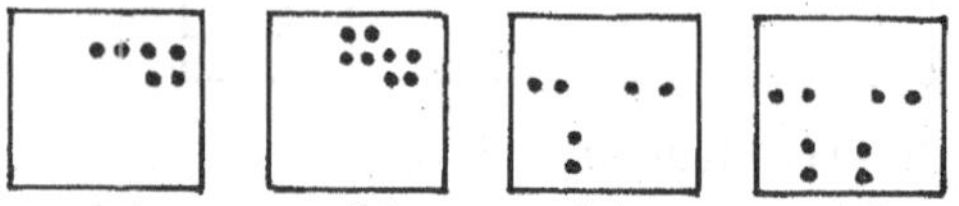

(a) (b) (c) (d)

13. Problem Figures:

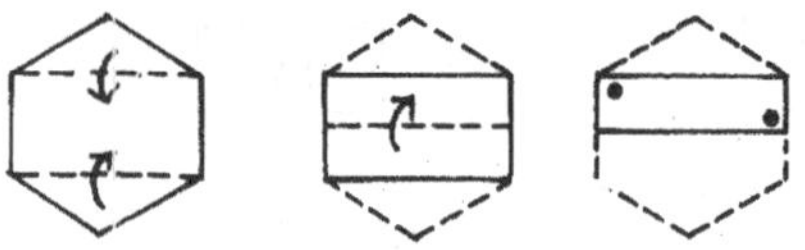

Answer Figures:

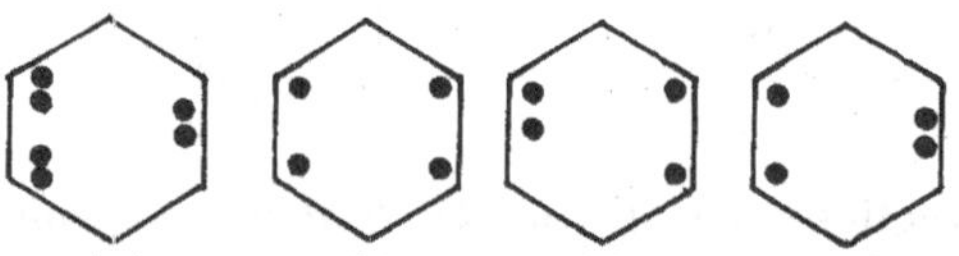

(a) (b) (c) (d)

14. Problem Figures:

Answer Figures:

(a) (b) (c) (d)

Directions (Qs. 15 to 19): *In each of the following questions, how does the figure look like when folded into a cube along the marked lines?*

15. Question Figure:

Answer Figures:

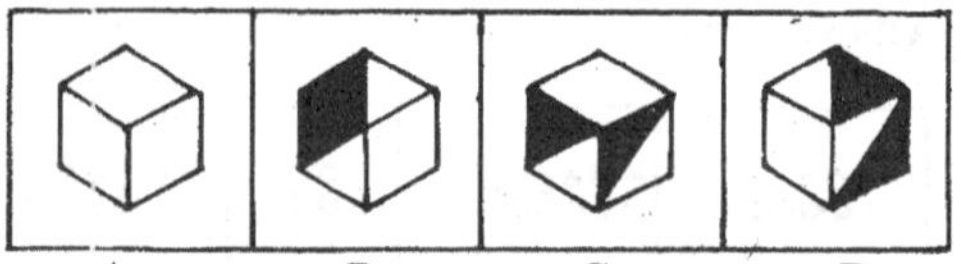

A B C D

(a) A and D (b) C and D
(c) A and B (d) B and C

16. Question Figure:

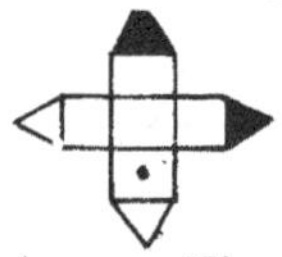

Answer Figures:

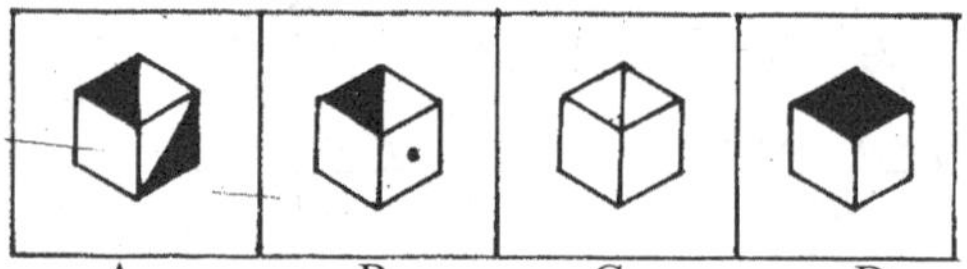

A B C D

(a) A and B (b) B and D
(c) B and C (d) A and D

17. Question Figure:

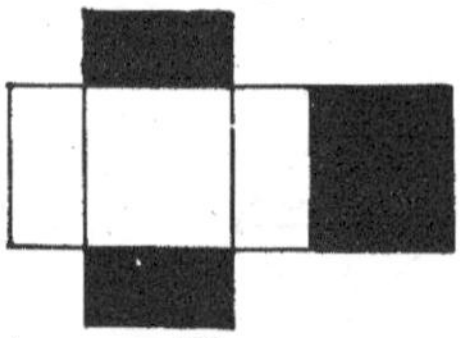

Answer Figures:

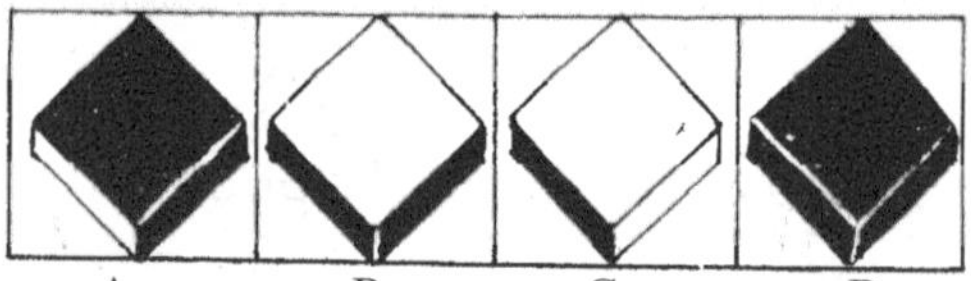

A B C D

(a) A and C (b) B and D
(c) B and C (d) A and D

18. Question Figure:

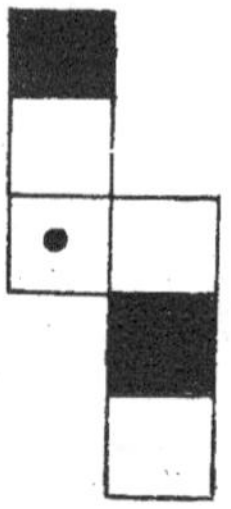

Answer Figures:

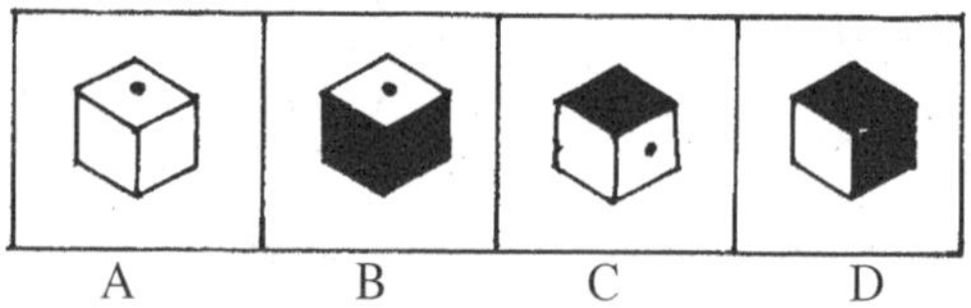

A B C D

(a) B and C (b) A, C and D
(c) B and D (d) A and D

19. Question Figure:

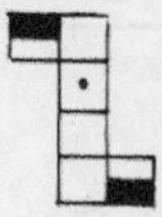

Answer Figures:

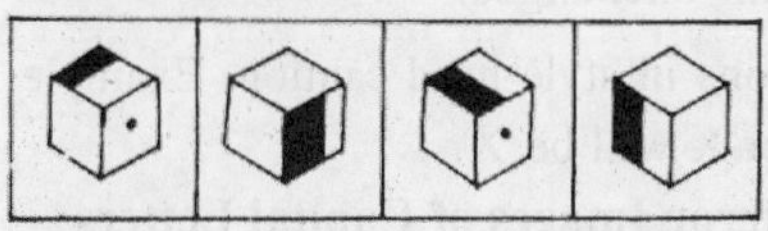

A B C D

(a) A and B *(b)* B and C

(c) B and D *(d)* A, B, C and D

Directions (Qs. 20 to 24): *In the following questions, a square/hexagon transparent sheet with a pattern is given. You have to find out from amongst the four alternatives as to how the pattern appear when the sheet is folded at the dotted line.*

20. Transparent sheet:

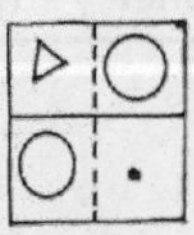

Response Figures:

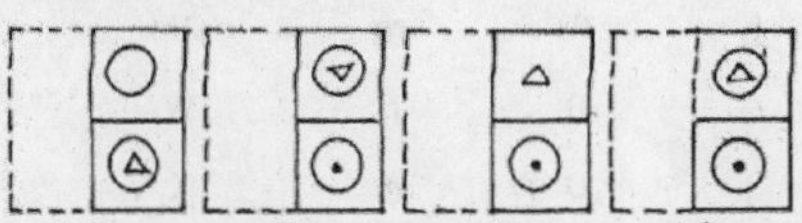

(a) *(b)* *(c)* *(d)*

21. Transparent sheet:

Response Figures:

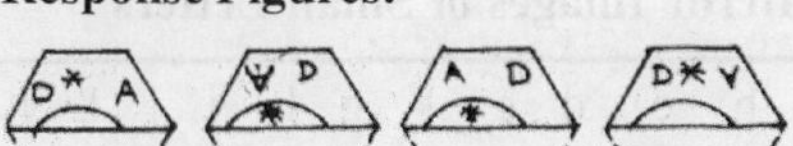

(a) *(b)* *(c)* *(d)*

22. Transparent sheet:

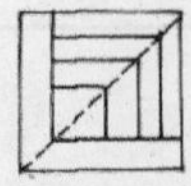

Response Figures:

(a) *(b)* *(c)* *(d)*

23. Transparent sheet:

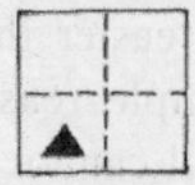

Response Figures:

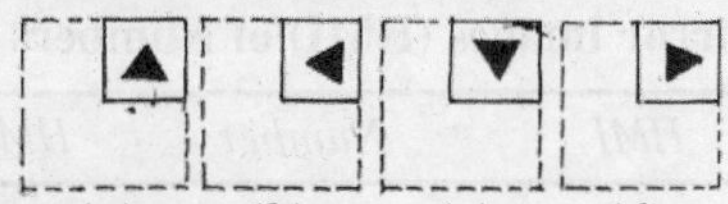

(a) *(b)* *(c)* *(d)*

24. Transparent sheet:

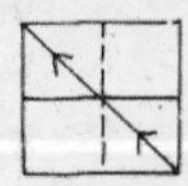

Response Figures:

(a) *(b)* *(c)* *(d)*

25. Find out the shape of the pattern which will be formed when the cardboard shown below is folded.

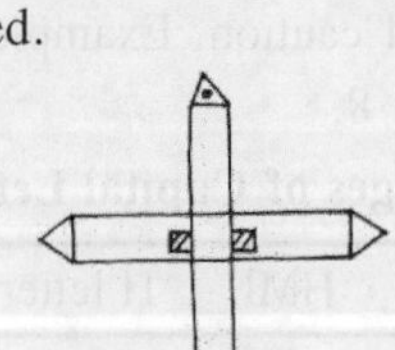

(a) *(b)* *(c)* *(d)*

ANSWERS

1	2	3	4	5	6	7	8	9	10
(d)	*(d)*	*(a)*	*(a)*	*(b)*	*(a)*	*(b)*	*(d)*	*(a)*	*(c)*
11	**12**	**13**	**14**	**15**	**16**	**17**	**18**	**19**	**20**
(b)	*(b)*	*(a)*	*(b)*	*(a)*	*(c)*	*(a)*	*(b)*	*(d)*	*(b)*
21	**22**	**23**	**24**	**25**					
(b)	*(a)*	*(c)*	*(a)*	*(d)*					

34 Mirror Images

These type of problems are based on the mirror images or reflections of number, letters and figures. While attempting such questions one must be able to visualise clearly the questioned reflections, be they on vertical plane or on horizontal plane. Study the chart and information given below. The visualisation of letters and numbers is easier than the visualisation of figures for the simple reason that the figures have many forms and all cannot be summed up.

Horizontal Mirror Images (HMI) of Numbers

Number	*HMI*	*Number*	*HMI*
0	0	5	ꙅ
1	I	6	ә
2	ꙅ	7	Ꞁ
3	Ɛ	8	8
4	ᔭ	9	ɘ

Note : HMI of 0 and 8 remain unchanged

Vertical Mirror Images (VMI) of Numbers

Numbers :	0	1	2	3	4	5	6	7	8	9
VMI :	0	I	ꙅ	3	ᔭ	ꙅ	ɘ	Ꞁ	8	ә

Note : VMI of 0, 3 and 8 remain unchanged.

Exceptions in style need caution. Example 3 will be 3, or 8 will be 8.

Horizontal Mirror Images of Capital Letters

Letter	HMI	Letter	HMI	H letter	HMI
A	A	J	Ⴑ	S	Ƨ
B	ꓭ	K	ꓘ	T	T
C	Ɔ	L	⅃	U	U
D	ꓷ	M	M	V	V
E	Ǝ	N	И	W	W
F	ꟻ	O	O	X	X
G	Ә	P	ꟼ	Y	Y
H	H	Q	Ϙ	Z	Ƹ
I	I	R	Я		

Note : HMI of A, H, I, M, O, T, U, V, W, X and Y remain unchanged.

Exceptions in style need caution. Example : A will be A, or X will be X.

Vertical Mirror Images of Capital Letters

Letters :	A	B	C	D	E	F	G	H	I	J	K	L	M
VMI :	∀	B	C	D	E	Ꮀ	Ͽ	H	I	ɿ	K	Γ	W

Letters :	N	O	P	Q	R	S	T	U	V	W	X	Y	Z
VMI :	И	O	b	Ó	ʁ	Ƨ	⊥	∩	Λ	M	X	⅄	Z

Note : VMI of C, D, E, H, I, K, O and X remain unchanged.

Horizontal Mirror Images of Small Letters

Letter	HMI	Letter	HMI	Letter	HMI
a	ɒ	j	į	s	ƨ
b	d	k	ʞ	t	ɟ
c	ɔ	l	l	u	u
d	b	m	m	v	v
e	ɘ	n	n	w	w
f	ʇ	o	o	x	x
g	ǫ	p	q	y	γ
h	ʜ	q	p	z	z
i	i	r	ɿ		

Note : HMI of o, v, w and x remain unchanged.

Vertical Mirror Images of Small Letters

Letter :	a	b	c	d	e	f	g	h	i	j	k	l	m
VMI :	ɑ	p	c	q	ɕ	ɟ	ɓ	ɥ	!	ɾ	ʞ	l	ɯ

Letter :	n	o	p	q	r	s	t	u	v	w	x	y	z
VMI :	u	o	b	d	ɹ	s	ʈ	n	ʌ	ʍ	x	λ	z

Note : VMI of c, o and x remain unchanged. Letter 1 has exceptions: if it is a straight vertical line – 1 then it remains unchanged.

Horizontal Mirror Images of Some Geometrical Shapes

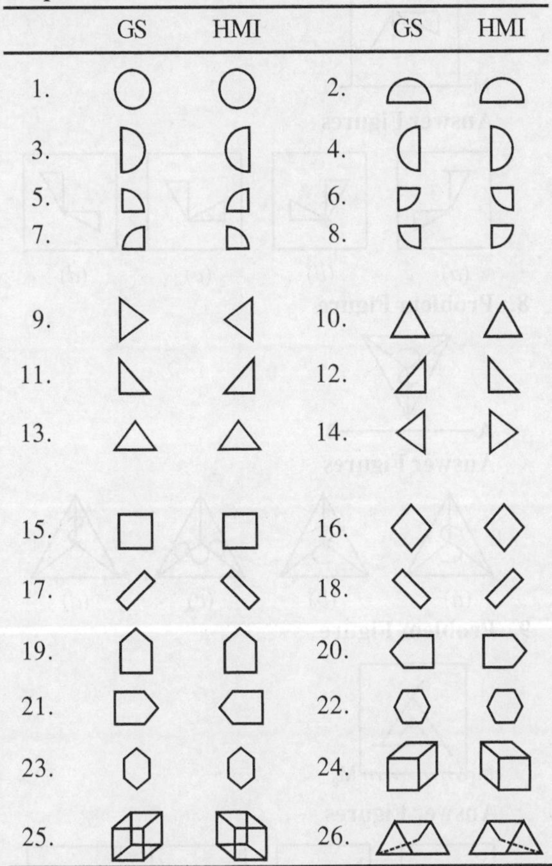

Vertical Mirror Images of Some Geometrical Shapes

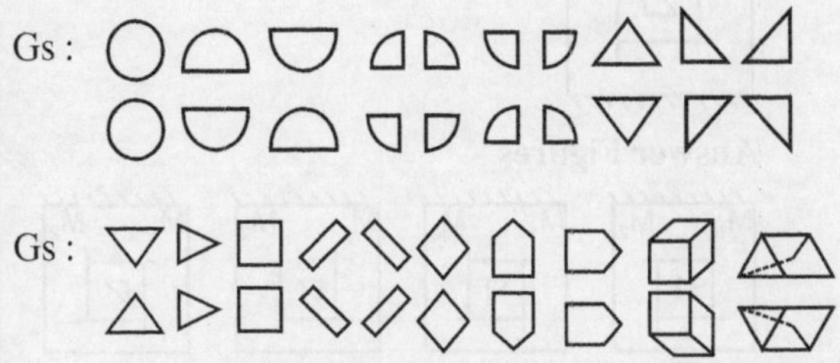

Horizontal and Vertical Mirror Images of some Signs and Symbols (SS)

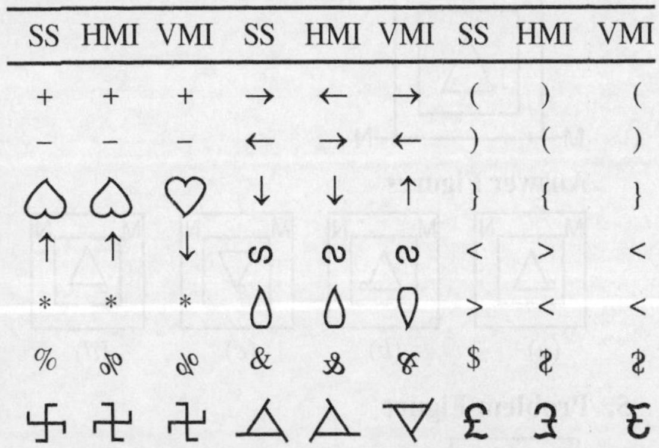

Note that the problems may be on numbers or letters or figures or signs or they may be a combination of all the above.

MULTIPLE CHOICE QUESTIONS

Directions (Qs. 1 to 20) : *In each question given below which one would be the mirror image of the given figure when the mirror is placed along the line shown in each figure.*

1. Problem Figure

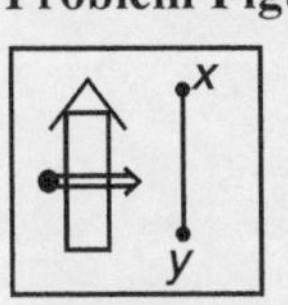

Answer Figures

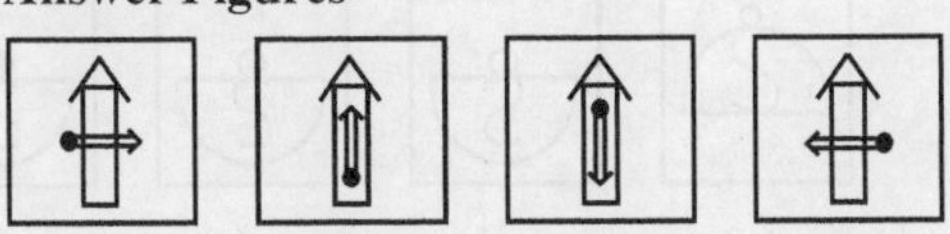

(*a*) (*b*) (*c*) (*d*)

2. Problem Figure

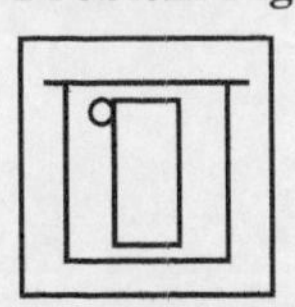

Answer Figures

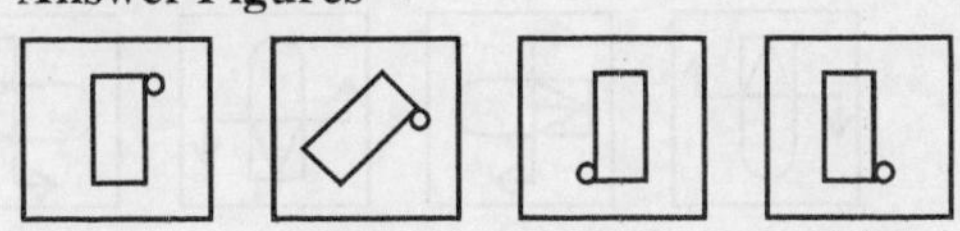

(*a*) (*b*) (*c*) (*d*)

3. Problem Figure

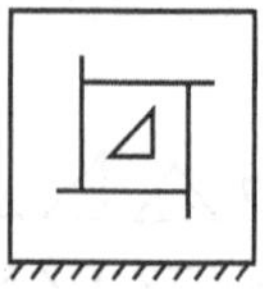

Answer Figures

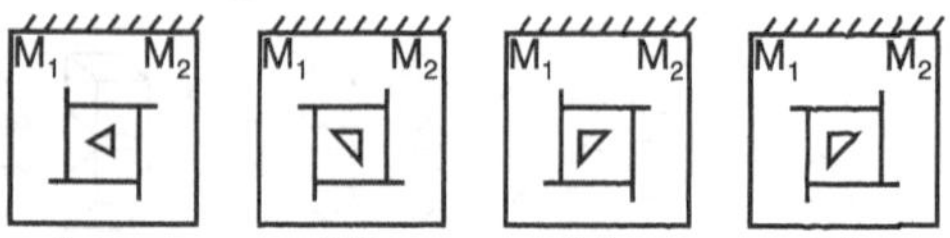

(*a*) (*b*) (*c*) (*d*)

4. Problem Figure

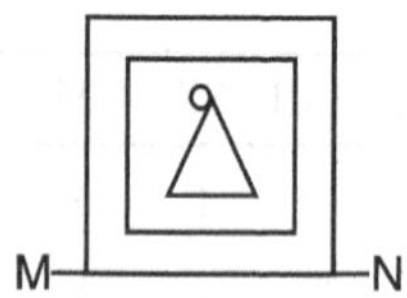

Answer Figures

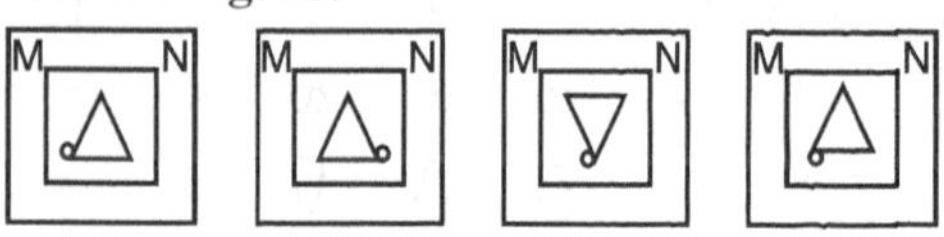

(*a*) (*b*) (*c*) (*d*)

5. Problem Figure

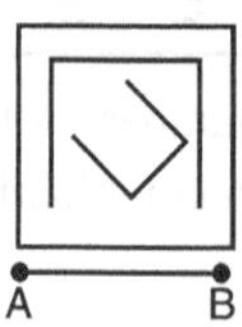

Answer Figures

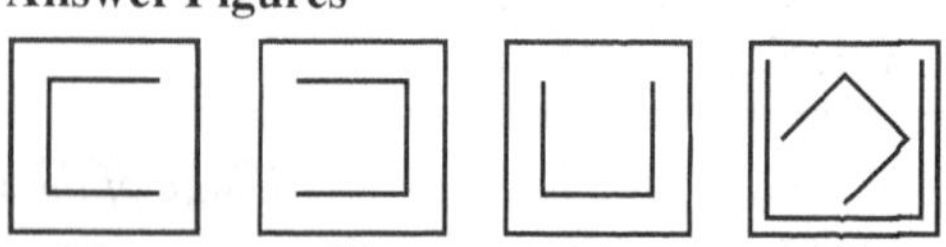

(*a*) (*b*) (*c*) (*d*)

6. Problem Figure

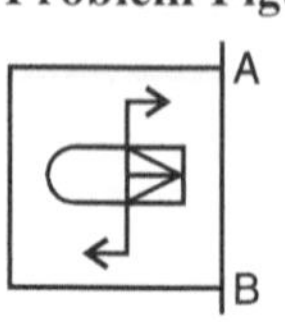

Answer Figures

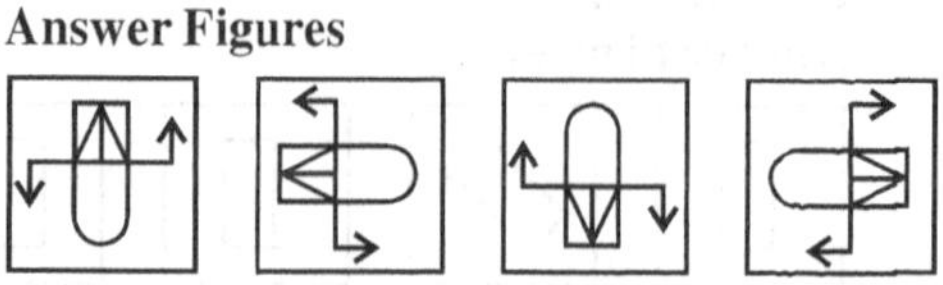

(*a*) (*b*) (*c*) (*d*)

7. Problem Figure

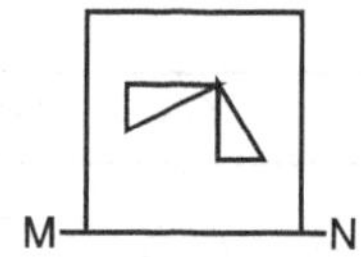

Answer Figures

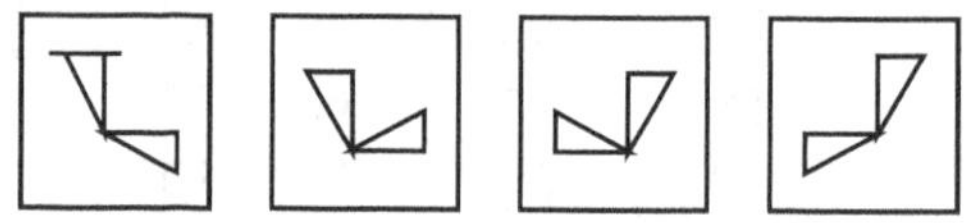

(*a*) (*b*) (*c*) (*d*)

8. Problem Figure

Answer Figures

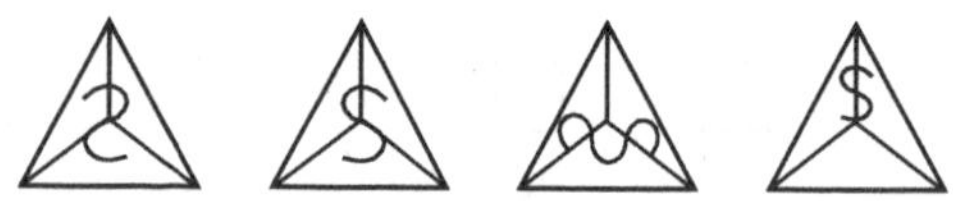

(*a*) (*b*) (*c*) (*d*)

9. Problem Figure

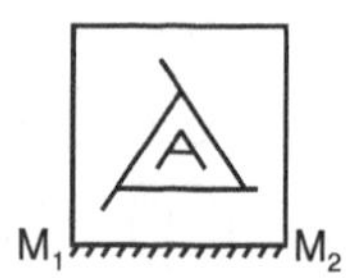

Answer Figures

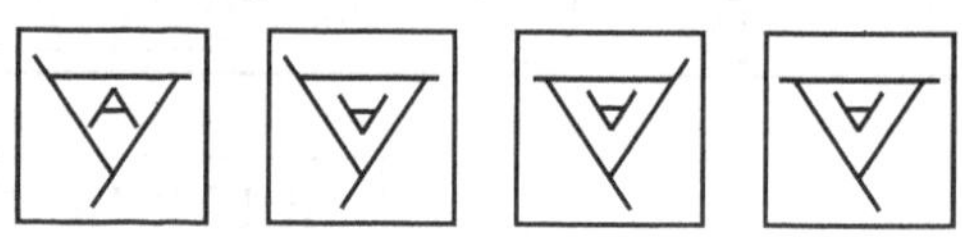

(*a*) (*b*) (*c*) (*d*)

10. Problem Figure

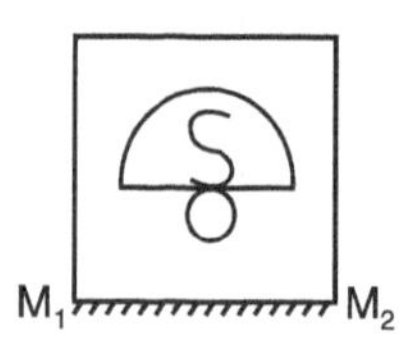

Answer Figures

(*a*) (*b*) (*c*) (*d*)

11. Problem Figure

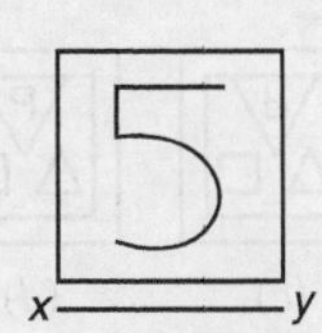

Answer Figures

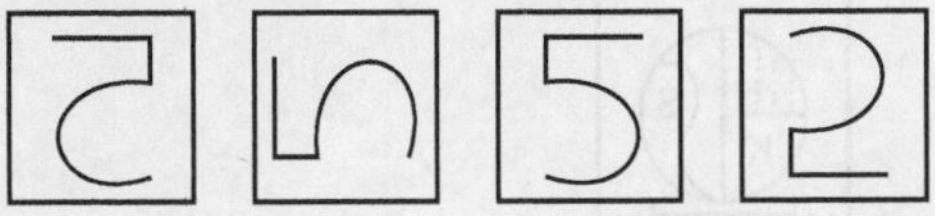

(a) (b) (c) (d)

12. Problem Figure

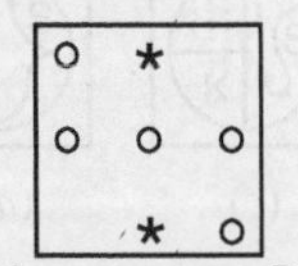

Answer Figures

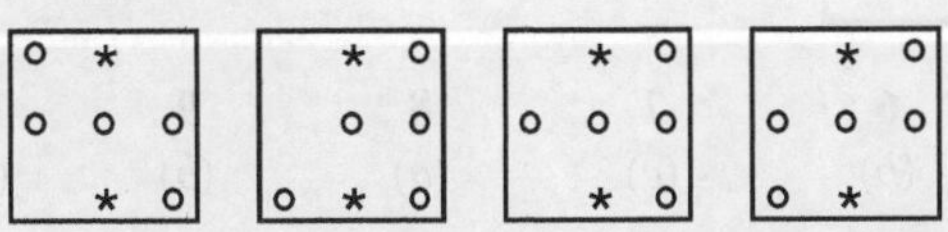

(a) (b) (c) (d)

13. Problem Figure

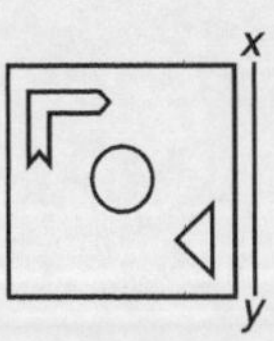

Answer Figures

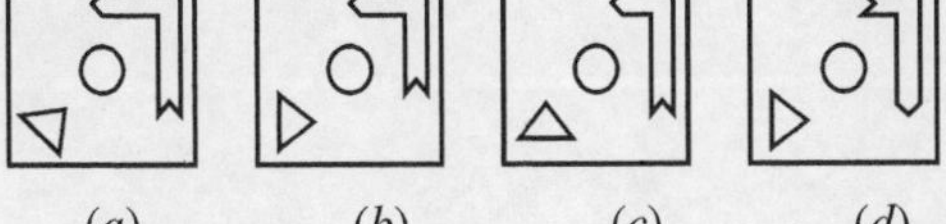

(a) (b) (c) (d)

14. Problem Figure

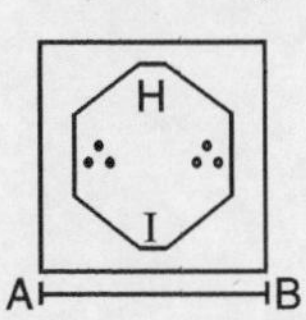

Answer Figures

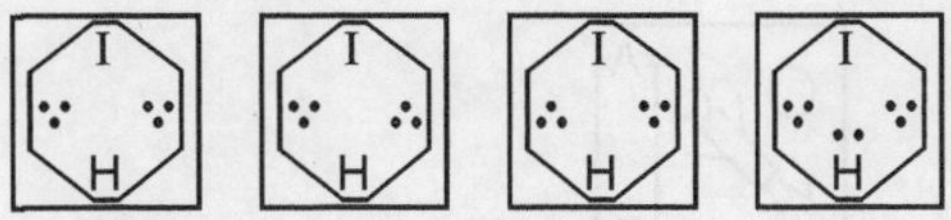

(a) (b) (c) (d)

15. Problem Figure

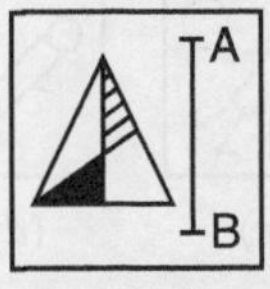

Answer Figures

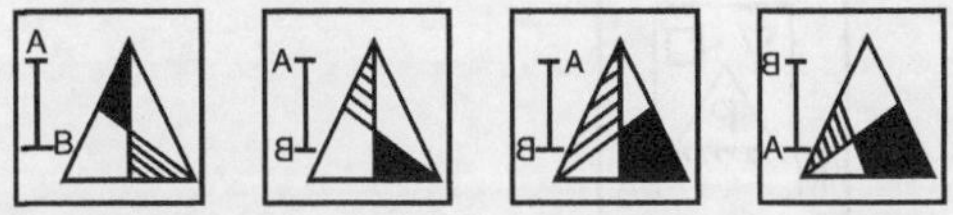

(a) (b) (c) (d)

16. Problem Figure

Answer Figures

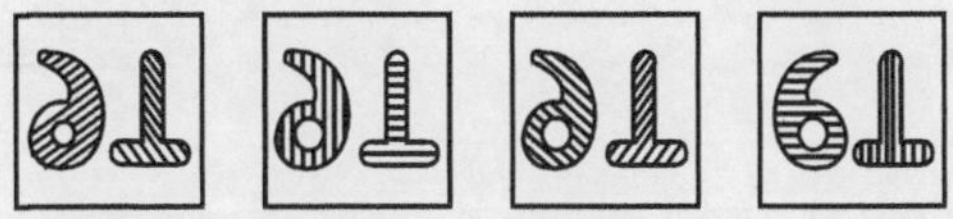

(a) (b) (c) (d)

17. Problem Figure

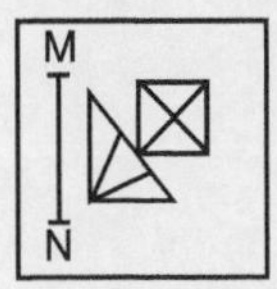

Answer Figures

(a) (b) (c) (d)

18. Problem Figure

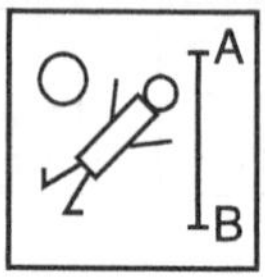

Answer Figures

(*a*) (*b*) (*c*) (*d*)

19. Problem Figure

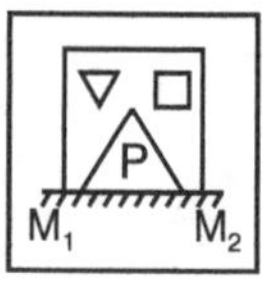

Answer Figures

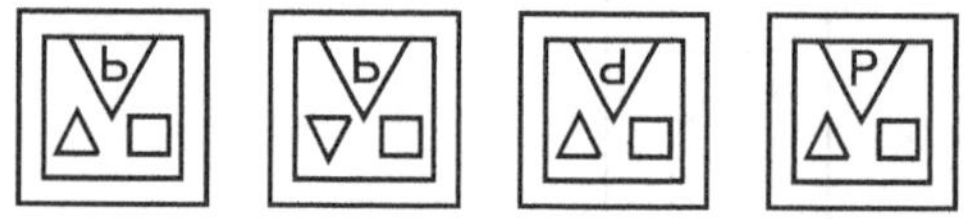

(*a*) (*b*) (*c*) (*d*)

20. Problem Figure

Answer Figures

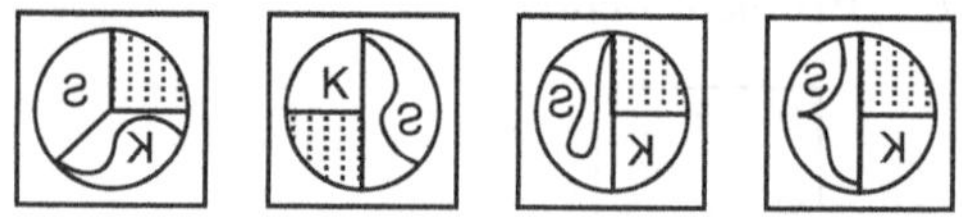

(*a*) (*b*) (*c*) (*d*)

ANSWERS

1	2	3	4	5	6	7	8	9	10
(*d*)	(*c*)	(*b*)	(*c*)	(*d*)	(*b*)	(*c*)	(*a*)	(*b*)	(*c*)
11	**12**	**13**	**14**	**15**	**16**	**17**	**18**	**19**	**20**
(*d*)	(*a*)	(*b*)	(*a*)	(*b*)	(*c*)	(*c*)	(*d*)	(*a*)	(*b*)

Elementary Mathematics

CHAPTER 1

Numbers

The development of the number system started with natural numbers. These are generally known as counting numbers.

Natural Numbers

Numbers which start from 1 are known as natural numbers. It is denoted by N. The smallest natural number is 1. It is written as,

$$N = \{1, 2, 3, ..., \infty\}$$

Whole Numbers

A number which starts from zero (0) is known as whole number. It is denoted by W. It is written as,

$$W = \{0, 1, 2, 3, ..., \infty\}$$

Integers

Natural numbers along with 0 and their negatives are known as integers. It is denoted by I. It is written as,

$$I = \{..., -4, -3, -2, -1, 0, 1, 2, 3, 4, ...\}$$

Even Numbers

A number which is divisible by 2 is known as even numbers.

Such as, 2, 4, 6, 10, 12, 128, 432 etc.

Odd Numbers

A number which is not divisible by 2 is known as odd numbers:

Such as, 1, 3, 5, 7, 9, 11, 13, 21, 29, 123 etc.

Prime Numbers

A number which is divided by itself is known as prime numbers. The smallest prime number is 2.

Such as, 2, 3, 5, 7, 11, 13, 17, 19, 23, ... etc.

Composite Numbers

A number which is divided by itself and others also is known as composite numbers. The smallest composite number is 4.

Such as, 4, 6, 8, 9, 10, 12, 14, 15, 16, 18, ... etc.

There are 25 prime numbers between 1 to 100.

Such as, 2, 3, 5, 7, 11, 13, 17, 19, 23, 29, 31, 37, 41, 43, 47, 53, 59, 61, 67, 71, 73, 79, 83, 89, 97.

Test, whether a given number is prime or composite: If we want to test any number more than 100, whether it is prime or not, take an integer larger than the approximate square root of that number. Let it be x. Test the divisibility of the given number by every prime number less than x. If it is not divisible by any of them, then it is prime; otherwise it is composite number.

EXAMPLE: Which of the following numbers are prime numbers?

(*i*) 421 (*ii*) 671

SOLUTION:

(*i*) The square root of 421 is nearly 21.
Prime numbers less than 21 are 2, 3, 5, 7, 11, 13, 17, 19. Clearly, 421 is not divisible by any of them. So, 421 is a prime number.

(*ii*) The square root of 671 is nearly 26.
Prime numbers less than 26 are 2, 3, 5, 7, 11, 13, 17, 19, 23. Out of these, 671 is divisible by 11. So, 671 is not a prime number. Hence it is composite number.

The formulae given below are quite useful for quick multiplication:

(*i*) $(a + b)^2 = a^2 + 2ab + b^2$

(*ii*) $(a - b)^2 = a^2 - 2ab + b^2$

(iii) $a^2 - b^2 = (a + b)(a - b)$

(iv) $a^2 + b^2 = (a + b)^2 - 2ab$

(v) $(a + b)^3 = a^3 + b^3 + 3ab(a + b)$

(vi) $(a - b)^3 = a^3 - b^3 - 3ab(a - b)$

(vii) $a^3 + b^3 = (a + b)(a^2 - ab + b^2)$

(viii) $a^3 - b^3 = (a - b)(a^2 + ab + b^2)$

EXAMPLE: Simplify the following.

(i) $\dfrac{348 \times 348 \times 348 + 252 \times 252 \times 252}{348 \times 348 - 348 \times 252 + 252 \times 252}$

(ii) $\dfrac{261 \times 261 \times 261 - 77 \times 77 \times 77}{261 \times 261 + 261 \times 77 + 77 \times 77}$

SOLUTION:

(i) $\dfrac{348 \times 348 \times 348 + 252 \times 252 \times 252}{348 \times 348 - 348 \times 252 + 252 \times 252}$

Let $348 = a$

and $252 = b$

$\therefore$ Given expression is written as

$$\frac{a \times a \times a + b \times b \times b}{a \times a - a \times b + b \times b} = \frac{a^3 + b^3}{a^2 - ab + b^2}$$

$$= \frac{(a+b)(a^2 - ab + b^2)}{(a^2 - ab + b^2)} = a + b$$

$= 348 + 252 = 600.$

(ii) $\dfrac{261 \times 261 \times 261 - 77 \times 77 \times 77}{261 \times 261 + 261 \times 77 + 77 \times 77}$

Let $261 = a$

and $77 = b$

$$\therefore \frac{a^3 - b^3}{a^2 + ab + b^2} = \frac{(a-b)(a^2 + ab + b^2)}{(a^2 + ab + b^2)} = a - b$$

$\therefore$ $261 - 77 = 184.$

If we divide a given number by another number, then

Dividend = (Divisor × Quotient) + Remainder

EXAMPLE: On dividing 18254 by a certain number, the quotient is 289 and the remainder is 47. Find the divisor.

SOLUTION: Here, Dividend = 18254

quotient = 289

remainder = 47

$$\therefore \quad \text{Divisor} = \frac{\text{Dividend} - \text{Remainder}}{\text{Quotient}}$$

$$= \frac{18254 - 47}{289} = \frac{18207}{289} = 63$$

Hence, divisor = 63.

EXAMPLE: What least number must be subtracted from 862 to get a number exactly divisible by 31?

SOLUTION: On dividing 862 by 31, the remainder obtained is 25.

Hence, the required number = 25.

MULTIPLE CHOICE QUESTIONS

1. The face value of 8 in the numeral 458926 is:

A. 8000 B. 8

C. 1000 D. 458000

2. $106 \times 106 + 94 \times 94 = x$, the value of x is:

A. 21032 B. 20032

C. 23032 D. 20072

3. If $m \times 48 = 173 \times 240$ then the value of m is:

A. 545 B. 685

C. 865 D. 495

4. $\left(1 - \frac{1}{3}\right)\left(1 - \frac{1}{4}\right)\left(1 - \frac{1}{5}\right)\ldots\left(1 - \frac{1}{n}\right) = x$

then the value of x is:

A. $\dfrac{1}{n}$ B. $\dfrac{2}{n}$

C. $\dfrac{2(n-1)}{n}$ D. $\dfrac{2}{n(n+1)}$

5. When simplified the product

$\left(2 - \frac{1}{3}\right)\left(2 - \frac{3}{5}\right)\left(2 - \frac{5}{7}\right)\ldots\left(2 - \frac{997}{999}\right)$ is

equal to:

A. $\dfrac{5}{999}$ B. $\dfrac{1001}{999}$

C. $\dfrac{1001}{3}$ D. None of these

6. Which number should replace both the asterisks in $\left(\frac{*}{21}\right)\times\left(\frac{*}{189}\right)=1$?

A. 21 B. 63
C. 3969 D. 147

7. In a division sum, the divisor is 12 times the quotient and 5 times the remainder. If the remainder be 48, then the dividend is:

A. 240 B. 576
C. 4800 D. 4848

8. What least number must be subtracted from 1294 so that the remainder when divided by 9, 11, 13 will leave in each case the same remainder 6?

A. 0 B. 1
C. 2 D. 3

9. If $\sqrt{\left(1+\frac{27}{169}\right)}=\left(1+\frac{x}{13}\right)$, then the value of x is:

A. 1 B. 3
C. 5 D. 7

10. If $\frac{x}{y}=\frac{3}{4}$, then the value of $\left(\frac{6}{7}+\frac{y-x}{y+x}\right)$ equals:

A. $\frac{5}{7}$ B. $1\frac{1}{7}$
C. 1 D. 2

11. The largest natural number by which the product of three consecutive even natural numbers is always divisible, is:

A. 16 B. 24
C. 48 D. 96

12. The least number of five digits which is exactly divisible by 12, 15 and 18 is:

A. 10080 B. 10800
C. 18000 D. 81000

13. The least number which when divided by 8, 9, 12, 16 and 20 leaves the same remainder 1 in each case is:

A. 712 B. 271
C. 721 D. 720

14. The value of 0.8693 + 0.092 + 0.87 + 0.4 equals:

A. 2.3213 B. 2.2331
C. 3.2313 D. 2.2313

15. The prime numbers between 1 to 50 are:

A. 8 B. 12
C. 15 D. 10

16. If $\frac{a}{b}=\frac{4}{3}$, then $\frac{3a+2b}{3a-2b}$ equals:

A. 6 B. 3
C. 5 D. –1

17. If $\sqrt{3^n}=81$, then n equals:

A. 2 B. 4
C. 6 D. 8

18. If $\sqrt{\frac{x}{196}}=\frac{72}{56}$, then x equals:

A. 18 B. 14
C. 324 D. 212

19. If $a \times 48 = 173 \times 240$, then the value of a is:

A. 545 B. 685
C. 865 D. 495

20. If $\frac{80}{x}=\frac{x}{20}$, then the value of x is:

A. 40 B. 400
C. 800 D. 1600

ANSWERS

1	2	3	4	5	6	7	8	9	10
B	D	C	B	C	B	D	B	A	C
11	**12**	**13**	**14**	**15**	**16**	**17**	**18**	**19**	**20**
C	A	C	D	C	B	D	C	C	A

EXPLANATORY ANSWERS

1. The face value of 8 in the numeral 458926 is 8.

2. $106 \times 106 + 94 \times 94 = x$

$$\Rightarrow (106)^2 + (94)^2 = x$$
$$\Rightarrow (100 + 6)^2 + (100 - 6)^2 = x$$
$$\Rightarrow 10000 + 1200 + 36 + 10000 - 1200 + 36 = x$$
$$\Rightarrow 20072 = x$$
$$\Rightarrow x = 20072.$$

3. $\because m = \dfrac{173 \times 240}{48} = 865.$

4. $\left(1-\dfrac{1}{3}\right)\left(1-\dfrac{1}{4}\right)\left(1-\dfrac{1}{5}\right)...\left(1-\dfrac{1}{n}\right) = x$

$$\because \quad 1-\frac{1}{3} = \frac{3-1}{3} = \frac{2}{3}$$
$$1-\frac{1}{4} = \frac{4-1}{4} = \frac{3}{4}$$
$$1-\frac{1}{5} = \frac{5-1}{5} = \frac{4}{5}$$
$$\vdots$$
$$1-\frac{1}{n} = \frac{n-1}{n}$$
$$\therefore \frac{2}{3}\times\frac{3}{4}\times\frac{4}{5}\times...\times\frac{n-2}{n-1}\times\frac{n-1}{n} = \frac{2}{n}$$

5. $\left(2-\dfrac{1}{3}\right)\left(2-\dfrac{3}{5}\right)\left(2-\dfrac{5}{7}\right)...\left(2-\dfrac{997}{999}\right)$

$$2-\frac{1}{3} = \frac{6-1}{3} = \frac{5}{3}$$
$$2-\frac{3}{5} = \frac{10-3}{5} = \frac{7}{5}$$
$$2-\frac{5}{7} = \frac{14-5}{7} = \frac{9}{7}$$
$$2-\frac{997}{999} = \frac{1998-997}{999} = \frac{1001}{999}$$
$$\therefore \frac{5}{3}\times\frac{7}{5}\times\frac{9}{7}\times...\times\frac{999}{997}\times\frac{1001}{999} = \frac{1001}{3}$$

6.
$$\frac{*}{21}\times\frac{*}{189} = 1$$
$$\frac{x^2}{21\times189} = 1$$
$$\Rightarrow x^2 = 21 \times 189 = 21 \times 21 \times 9$$
$$\Rightarrow x^2 = 21 \times 21 \times 3 \times 3$$
$$\Rightarrow x = 21 \times 3 = 63$$

7. Let quotient = Q and remainder = R

Then, divisor = 12Q = 5R

Now, R = 48

$\Rightarrow$ 12Q = 5 × 48 $\Rightarrow$ Q = 20

$\therefore$ Dividend = (20 × 240 + 48) = 4848

8. The number when divided by 9, 11, 13 leaving remainder 6 = (LCM of 9, 11, 13) + 6 = 1293

$\therefore$ Required number = (1294 – 1293) = 1

9.
$$\sqrt{\left(1+\frac{27}{169}\right)} = \left(1+\frac{x}{13}\right)$$
$$\Rightarrow \sqrt{\frac{169+27}{169}} = \frac{13+x}{13}$$
$$\Rightarrow \sqrt{\frac{196}{169}} = \frac{x+13}{13}$$
$$\Rightarrow \frac{14}{13} = \frac{x+13}{13}$$
$$\Rightarrow x + 13 = 14$$
$$\Rightarrow x = 1$$

10. $\because \dfrac{x}{y} = \dfrac{3}{4}$ then,

$$\frac{6}{7}+\frac{y-x}{y+x} = \frac{6}{7}+\frac{\frac{y}{y}-\frac{x}{y}}{\frac{y}{y}+\frac{x}{y}}$$

[Divide numerator and denominator by y.]

$$= \frac{6}{7}+\frac{1-\frac{3}{4}}{1+\frac{3}{4}} = \frac{6}{7}+\frac{\frac{1}{4}}{\frac{7}{4}}$$
$$= \frac{6}{7}+\frac{1}{7} = \frac{7}{7} = 1$$

11. It is 2 × 4 × 6 = 48

12. Least number of 5 digits is 10000.

LCM of 12, 15, 18 is 180.

On dividing 10000 by 180, the remainder is 100.

$\therefore$ The least number = 10000 + (180 – 100)
= 10080.

13. Least number = (LCM of 8, 9, 12, 16, 20) + 1

2	8,	9,	12,	16,	20
2	4,	9,	6,	8,	10
2	2,	9,	3,	4,	5
3	1,	9,	3,	2,	5
	1,	3,	1,	2,	5

$\therefore$ LCM = $2^4 \times 3^2 \times 5 = 720$

Hence, least number = (720 + 1) = 721.

14.

$$\begin{array}{r} 0.8693 \\ 0.092 \\ 0.87 \\ +\ 0.4 \\ \hline 2.2313 \end{array}$$

$\therefore$ The value of 0.8693 + 0.092 + 0.87 + 0.4
= 2.2313.

15. The prime numbers between 1 to 50 are 2, 3, 5, 7, 11, 13, 17, 19, 23, 29, 31, 37, 41, 43, 47.

Hence, there are 15 prime numbers between 1 to 50.

16. $\because \quad \dfrac{a}{b} = \dfrac{4}{3}$

$$\therefore \quad \frac{3a+2b}{3a-2b} = \frac{\frac{3a}{b} + \frac{2b}{b}}{\frac{3a}{b} - \frac{2b}{b}}$$

[Divide numerator and denominator by *b*.]

$$= \frac{3\left(\frac{4}{3}\right)+2}{3\left(\frac{4}{3}\right)-2} = \frac{4+2}{4-2}$$

$$= \frac{6}{2} = 3.$$

17. $\because \quad \sqrt{3^n} = 81 \quad \Rightarrow \quad 3^{\frac{n}{2}} = 3^4$

$\Rightarrow \quad \dfrac{n}{2} = 4 \quad \Rightarrow \quad n = 8.$

18. $\because \quad \sqrt{\dfrac{x}{196}} = \dfrac{72}{56} \Rightarrow \dfrac{x}{196} = \dfrac{72 \times 72}{56 \times 56}$

$\Rightarrow \quad x = \dfrac{72 \times 72 \times 196}{56 \times 56}$

$\Rightarrow \quad x = 18 \times 18 = 324.$

19. $\because \quad a \times 48 = 173 \times 240$

$\Rightarrow \quad a = \dfrac{173 \times 240}{48}$

$= 173 \times 5 = 865$

$\therefore$ The value of a = 865.

20. $\because \quad \dfrac{80}{x} = \dfrac{x}{20} \quad \Rightarrow \quad x^2 = 80 \times 20$

$\Rightarrow \quad x^2 = 1600 \quad \Rightarrow \quad x = 40$

Hence, the value of x = 40.

CHAPTER 2

HCF and LCM

FACTORS

The numbers are said to be factors of a given number when they exactly divide that number.

Example: Factors of 15 are 1, 3, 5 and 15 because each of these completely divides 15.

Highest Common Factor

The HCF of two or more than two numbers is the greatest number that divides each of them exactly. The highest common factor is also known as Greatest Common Divisor or Greatest Common Measure.

EXAMPLE: Let us consider two numbers 24 and 36. All possible factors of 24 are 1, 2, 3, 4, 6, 8, 12 and 24. All possible factors of 36 are 1, 2, 3, 4, 6, 9, 12, 18 and 36. The common factors of 24 and 36 are 1, 2, 3, 4, 6, 12. The greatest factor among these common factors is 12.

Hence, 12 is the HCF of 24 and 36.

EXAMPLE: Let us consider two numbers 18 and 30.

Now, $18 = 2 \times 3 \times 3$

and $30 = 2 \times 3 \times 5$

The factors common to the two numbers are 2 and 3. Hence the required HCF $= 2 \times 3 = 6$.

There are two methods of determining the HCF of two or more numbers.

(*i*) HCF by Factorization method

(*ii*) HCF by Division method.

HCF by Factorization Method

Express each one of the given number as the product of prime factors. Now choose common factors and take the product of these factors to obtain the required HCF.

EXAMPLE: Find the HCF of 126, 396 and 5400.

SOLUTION:

$$126 = 2 \times 3 \times 3 \times 7$$
$$396 = 2 \times 2 \times 3 \times 3 \times 11$$
$$5400 = 2 \times 2 \times 2 \times 3 \times 3 \times 3 \times 5 \times 5$$

Common factors are 2, 3 and 3.

Hence, the HCF $= 2 \times 3 \times 3 = 18$.

EXAMPLE: Find the HCF of 1056, 1584 and 2178.

SOLUTION: $1056 = 2^5 \times 3 \times 11$

$1584 = 2^4 \times 3^2 \times 11$

and $2178 = 2 \times 3^2 \times 11^2$

Hence, HCF $= (2 \times 3 \times 11) = 66$.

HCF by Division Method

Suppose we have to find the HCF of two given numbers. Divide the larger number by the smaller one. Now, divide the divisor by the remainder. Repeat the process of dividing the preceding divisor by the remainder last obtained till zero is obtained as remainder. The last divisor is the required HCF.

Suppose we have to find the HCF of three numbers. Then HCF of [(HCF of any two numbers) and (the third number)] gives the HCF of three given numbers. Similarly, the HCF of more than three numbers may be obtained.

EXAMPLE: Find the HCF of 48, 168 and 324.

SOLUTION: Firstly, we find the HCF of 48 and 168.

```
48) 1 6 8 (3
  – 1 4 4
    -------
      2 4) 4 8 (2
           4 8
           ---
            0
           ---
```

Thus, HCF of 48 and 168 = 24.

Now, we find the HCF of 24 and 324.

```
24) 3 2 4 (13
  − 2 4
    8 4
  − 7 2
    1 2) 2 4 (2
         2 4
           0
```

Thus, the HCF of 48, 168 and 324 is 12.

Lowest Common Multiple

The LCM of two or more numbers is the lowest or least number which is exactly divisible by each of them. In other words, it is the lowest number which contains each of them as a factor.

LCM by Factorization

Resolve each one of the given numbers into a product of prime factors. Then LCM is the product of highest powers of all the factors.

Example: Find the LCM of 72, 189 and 1026.

Solution: $72 = 2^3 \times 3^2$

$189 = 3^3 \times 7$

and $1026 = 2 \times 3^3 \times 19$

$\therefore$ $\text{LCM} = 2^3 \times 3^3 \times 7 \times 19$

$= 8 \times 27 \times 7 \times 19 = 28728$

Example: Find the LCM of 12, 15, 20 and 54 by short cut method.

Solution:

2	12,	15,	20,	54
2	6,	15,	10,	27
3	3,	15,	5,	27
5	1,	5,	5,	9
	1,	1,	1,	9

$\therefore$ $\text{LCM} = 2 \times 2 \times 3 \times 5 \times 9 = 540$

FORMULA

Product of two numbers = HCF × LCM.

$$\text{LCM} = \frac{\text{Product of numbers}}{\text{HCF}}$$

$$\text{HCF} = \frac{\text{Product of numbers}}{\text{LCM}}$$

$$\text{First number} = \frac{\text{LCM} \times \text{HCF}}{\text{2nd number}}$$

$$\text{2nd number} = \frac{\text{LCM} \times \text{HCF}}{\text{First number}}$$

HCF and LCM of Fractions

(*i*) $\text{HCF} = \dfrac{\text{HCF of numerators}}{\text{LCM of denominators}}$

(*ii*) $\text{LCM} = \dfrac{\text{LCM of numerators}}{\text{HCF of denominators}}$

Example: Find the HCF and LCM of $\frac{3}{4}, \frac{6}{8}, \frac{15}{64}$ and $\frac{12}{32}$.

Solution: $\text{HCF} = \dfrac{\text{HCF of 3, 6, 15, 12}}{\text{LCM of 4, 8, 64, 32}} = \dfrac{3}{64}$

$\text{LCM} = \dfrac{\text{LCM of 3, 6, 15, 12}}{\text{HCF of 4, 8, 64, 32}} = \dfrac{60}{4}$.

MULTIPLE CHOICE QUESTIONS

1. HCF of 1485 and 4356 is:

A. 189 B. 89
C. 99 D. 83

2. LCM of 18, 24, 42, 63 is:

A. 302 B. 604
C. 504 D. 404

3. Which of the following fractions is the greatest of all? $\frac{7}{8}, \frac{6}{7}, \frac{4}{5}, \frac{5}{6}$

A. $\frac{6}{7}$ B. $\frac{4}{5}$
C. $\frac{5}{6}$ D. $\frac{7}{8}$

4. Which of the following is in ascending order?

A. $\frac{5}{7}, \frac{7}{8}, \frac{9}{11}$ B. $\frac{5}{7}, \frac{9}{11}, \frac{7}{8}$
C. $\frac{7}{8}, \frac{5}{7}, \frac{9}{11}$ D. $\frac{9}{11}, \frac{7}{8}, \frac{5}{7}$

5. HCF of three numbers is 12. If they be in the ratio 1 : 2 : 3, the numbers are:
A. 12, 24, 36 B. 10, 20, 30
C. 5, 10, 15 D. 4, 8, 12

6. The largest natural number which exactly divides the product of any four consecutive natural numbers is:
A. 6 B. 12
C. 24 D. 120

7. The traffic lights at three different road crossings change after every 48 seconds, 72 seconds and 108 seconds respectively. If they all change simultaneously at 8 : 20 : 00 hrs; then they will again change simultaneously at:
A. 8 : 27 : 12 hrs B. 8 : 27 : 24 hrs
C. 8 : 27 : 36 hrs D. 8 : 27 : 48 hrs

8. The HCF of two numbers is 16 and their LCM is 160. If one of the number is 32, then the other number is:
A. 48 B. 80
C. 96 D. 112

9. The HCF of two numbers is 12 and their difference is also 12. The numbers are:
A. 66, 78 B. 70, 82
C. 94, 106 D. 84, 96

10. The largest number which exactly divides 210, 315, 147 and 161 is:
A. 3 B. 7
C. 21 D. 4410

11. The least perfect square number which is divisible by 3, 4, 5, 6 and 8 is:
A. 900 B. 1200
C. 2500 D. 3600

12. The smallest number which is divisible by 12, 15, 20 and is a perfect square, is:
A. 400 B. 900
C. 1600 D. 3600

13. The sum of two numbers is 216 and their HCF is 27. The numbers are:
A. 54, 162 B. 108, 108
C. 27, 189 D. None of these

14. The HCF and LCM of two numbers are 44 and 264 respectively. If the first number is divided by 2, the quotient is 44. The other number is:
A. 33 B. 66
C. 132 D. 264

15. The number of prime factors in $2^{222} \times 3^{333} \times 5^{555}$ is:
A. 3 B. 1107
C. 1110 D. 1272

16. The number of prime factors in the expression $(6)^{10} \times (7)^{17} \times (11)^{27}$ is:
A. 54 B. 64
C. 71 D. 81

17. Three measuring rods are 64 cm, 80 cm and 96 cm in length. The least length of cloth that can be measured exact number of times using any one of the above rod is:
A. 0.96 m B. 19.20 m
C. 9.60 m D. 96.00 m

18. The product of two numbers is 1600 and their HCF is 5. The LCM of the numbers is:
A. 320 B. 1605
C. 1595 D. 8000

19. About the number of pairs which have 16 as their HCF and 136 as their LCM, we can definitely say that:
A. Only one such pair exists
B. Only two such pairs exist
C. Many such pairs exist
D. No such pair exist

20. The total number of prime factors of the product $(8)^{20} \times (15)^{24} \times (7)^{15}$ is:
A. 59 B. 98
C. 123 D. 138

21. The LCM of two numbers is 85 and their product is 1020. Their HCF will be:
A. 16 B. 27
C. 12 D. 22

22. HCF of 420, 315 and 462 is:
A. 24 B. 28
C. 27 D. 21

23. Two numbers are in the ratio of 8 : 15. If their HCF is 4, the numbers are:
A. 32 and 60 B. 16 and 30
C. 80 and 150 D. 64 and 120

24. Three bells ring respectively at an interval of 15 seconds, 20 seconds and 24 seconds. If they ring continuously for 12 minutes then how many times during this period, will they ring together?
A. 2 times B. 6 times
C. 5 times D. 3 times

ANSWERS

1	2	3	4	5	6	7	8	9	10
C	C	D	B	A	C	A	B	D	B
11	**12**	**13**	**14**	**15**	**16**	**17**	**18**	**19**	**20**
D	B	C	C	C	B	C	A	D	C
21	**22**	**23**	**24**						
C	D	A	B						

EXPLANATORY ANSWERS

1.

```
1485) 4 3 5 6 (2
      2 9 7 0
      -------
      1 3 8 6) 1 4 8 5 (1
               1 3 8 6
               -------
                  9 9) 1 3 8 6 (14
                         9 9
                         -----
                         3 9 6
                         3 9 6
                         -----
                             0
```

$\therefore$ HCF of 1485 and 4356 is 99.

2.

2	18, 24, 42, 63
3	9, 12, 21, 63
3	3, 4, 7, 21
7	1, 4, 7, 7
	1, 4, 1, 1

LCM of 18, 24, 42, 63 = $2 \times 3^2 \times 7 \times 4 = 504$.

3. $\frac{7}{8} = 0.875$

$\frac{6}{7} = 0.857$

$\frac{4}{5} = 0.8$

$\frac{5}{6} = 0.833$

Clearly, 0.875 is the greatest of all.

Hence, $\frac{7}{8}$ is the greatest of all.

4. $\frac{5}{7} = 0.714$

$\frac{7}{8} = 0.875$

$\frac{9}{11} = 0.818$

Now, $0.714 < 0.818 < 0.875$

Hence, $\frac{5}{7} < \frac{9}{11} < \frac{7}{8}$.

5. Let the numbers be x, $2x$ and $3x$.
Then, their HCF = x
According to the question, $x = 12$
$\therefore$ The numbers are 12, 24, 36.

6. $1 \times 2 \times 3 \times 4 = 24$
$\therefore$ Required number = 24.

7. LCM of 48, 72, 108 = 432
432 seconds = 7 min 12 seconds.
So, the next simultaneous change will take place at 8 : 27 : 12 hrs.

8. Other number $= \frac{\text{LCM} \times \text{HCF}}{\text{One number}}$

$= \frac{160 \times 16}{32} = 80$

Hence, other number = 80.

9. 12 is not the HCF of given options A, B and C.
Hence, D is correct answer.
In 84, 96, 12 is HCF of 84 and 96
Difference of 96 – 84 = 12
So, required numbers are 84 and 96.

10. HCF of 210, 315, 147 and 161 = 7
Hence, the required number = 7.

11.

2	3, 4, 5, 6, 8
2	3, 2, 5, 3, 4
3	3, 1, 5, 3, 2
	1, 1, 5, 1, 2

LCM of 3, 4, 5, 6, 8
$= 2 \times 2 \times 3 \times 5 \times 2$

Required number
$= (2 \times 2 \times 3 \times 3 \times 5 \times 5 \times 2 \times 2)$
$= 3600$

12. LCM of 12, 15 and 20 = 60
Hence, required number = $60 \times 15 = 900$.

13. HCF of 54, 162 = 54
HCF of 108, 108 = 108
HCF of 27, 189 = 27
Hence, required numbers are 27 and 189.

14. According to the question,
First number = $2 \times 44 = 88$

$$\text{Other number} = \frac{\text{LCM} \times \text{HCF}}{\text{First number}}$$

$$= \frac{264 \times 44}{88} = 132$$

15. The number of prime factors in the given product = (222 + 333 + 555) = 1110

16. 2, 3, 7, 11 are prime numbers in the given expression. The number of prime factors in the given expression (10 + 10 + 17 + 27) = 64

17. Required length = (LCM of 64, 80, 96) cm
= 960 cm = 9.60 m.

18. $\text{LCM} = \frac{\text{Product of numbers}}{\text{HCF}} = \frac{1600}{5} = 320$

19. HCF is always a factor of LCM. So no two numbers exist with HCF = 16 and LCM = 136.

20. Since 2, 3, 5, 7 are prime numbers and the given expression is $(2^3)^{20} \times (3 \times 5)^{24} \times (7)^{15}$
i.e. $2^{60} \times 3^{24} \times 5^{24} \times 7^{15}$, so the number of prime factors in the given expression
= (60 + 24 + 24 + 15) = 123

21. LCM of two numbers × HCF of the numbers
= Product of the numbers
$\therefore \quad 85 \times \text{HCF} = 1020$

$$\text{HCF} = \frac{1020}{85} = 12$$

22.
```
315) 420 (1
     315
     ----------
     105) 315 (3
          315
          ---
           ×
          ---
```
Now HCF of 105 and 462.
```
105) 462 (4
     420
     ----------
      42) 105 (2
           84
          ----------
          21) 42 (2
              42
              ---
               ×
              ---
```
$\therefore$ Required HCF = 21

23. Let the numbers be $8x$ and $15x$
LCM of $8x$ and $15x = 120x$

$$\therefore \quad \text{HCF} = \frac{8x \times 15x}{120x}$$

$$4 = \frac{120x^2}{120x} = x$$

$\therefore$ Numbers are $8 \times 4 = 32$ and $15 \times 4 = 60$

24. LCM of 15, 20 and 24 = 120
$\because$ 12 minutes = $12 \times 60 = 720$ seconds
$\therefore$ Number of times the bells will ring together

$$12 \text{ minutes} = \frac{720}{120} = 6 \text{ times.}$$

3

CHAPTER

Simplification

Simplification means expressing in a simpler form. In order to simplify an expression we use the operations in the following order which is easily remembered as "BODMAS".

(*i*) Bracket (*ii*) Of (*iii*) Division (*iv*) Multiplication (*v*) Addition (*vi*) Subtraction.

'Of' means multiplication but it is operated even before division.

While removing brackets, first of all bar bracket '—' and after that small bracket '( )' is removed. Thereafter curley bracket '{ }' and at last square bracket '[ ]' is removed.

Example: Simplify: $100 \div 25 \times 6 + 16 - 32$

Solution: $100 \div 25 \times 6 + 16 - 32$

$= 4 \times 6 + 16 - 32$

$= 24 + 16 - 32$

$= 40 - 32 = 8$

Example: Simplify: $54 + 24 \div 4 - 8 \times 5 + 4 \times 3$

Solution: $54 + 24 \div 4 - 8 \times 5 + 4 \times 3$

$= 54 + 6 - 40 + 12$

$= 72 - 40 = 32$

Example: Simplify: $10 - \left[6 - \left\{7 - \left(6 - \overline{8 - 5}\right)\right\}\right]$

Solution: $10 - \left[6 - \left\{7 - \left(6 - 3\right)\right\}\right]$

$= 10 - [6 - \{7 - 3\}]$

$= 10 - [6 - 4] = 10 - 2 = 8.$

Example: Simplify: $\dfrac{12 \times 12 \times 12 - 1 \times 1 \times 1}{12 \times 12 + 12 \times 1 + 1 \times 1}$

Solution: Let $a = 12$ and $b = 1$

$$\therefore \quad \frac{a \times a \times a - b \times b \times b}{a \times a + a \times b + b \times b} = \frac{a^3 - b^3}{a^2 + ab + b^2}$$

$$= \frac{(a - b)(a^2 + ab + b^2)}{(a^2 + ab + b^2)}$$

$$= a - b = 12 - 1 = 11$$

Example: Simplify:

$$\frac{2.33 \times 2.33 \times 2.33 + 7.67 \times 7.67 \times 7.67}{2.33 \times 2.33 - 2.33 \times 7.67 + 7.67 \times 7.67}$$

Solution: Let $a = 2.33$ and $b = 7.67$

$$\frac{a^3 + b^3}{a^2 - ab + b^2} = \frac{(a + b)(a^2 - ab + b^2)}{(a^2 - ab + b^2)} = (a + b)$$

$$= 2.33 + 7.67 = 10$$

MULTIPLE CHOICE QUESTIONS

1. $\dfrac{48 - 12 \times 3 + 9}{12 - 9 \div 3}$ equals:

   A. 3   B. 21

   C. $\dfrac{7}{3}$ D. $\dfrac{1}{3}$

2. $\dfrac{69 - 14 \times 3 + 2}{9 \times 5 - (5)^2}$ equals:

   A. 1.45   B. 2.75

   C. 26.5   D. 265

3. If $\frac{17.28 \div x}{3.6 \times 0.2} = 2$ then, the value of x is:
A. 120 B. 1.20
C. 12 D. 0.12

4. $171 \div 19 \times 9$ equals:
A. 0 B. 1
C. 18 D. 81

5. $3120 \div 26 + 13 \times 30$ equals:
A. 2400 B. 3900
C. 536 D. None of these

6. $\frac{31}{10} \times \frac{3}{10} + \frac{7}{5} \div 20$ equals:
A. 0 B. 1
C. 100 D. $\frac{107}{200}$

7. The simplification of $1 + \cfrac{1}{2 + \cfrac{1}{1 - \cfrac{1}{3}}}$ yields the result:
A. $\frac{2}{7}$ B. $\frac{7}{9}$
C. $\frac{9}{7}$ D. $\frac{13}{7}$

8. The value of $1 + \frac{1}{4 \times 3} + \frac{1}{4 \times 3^2} + \frac{1}{4 \times 3^3}$ up to four places of decimals is:
A. 1.1202 B. 1.1203
C. 1.1204 D. None of these

9. $\frac{\frac{1}{2} \div 4 + 20}{\frac{1}{2} \times 4 + 20}$ equals:
A. $\frac{81}{88}$ B. $2\frac{3}{11}$
C. $\frac{161}{176}$ D. 1

10. $3 \div \left[(8-5) \div \left\{(4-2) \div \left(2 + \frac{8}{13}\right)\right\}\right]$ equals:
A. $\frac{13}{17}$ B. $\frac{68}{13}$
C. $\frac{17}{13}$ D. $\frac{13}{68}$

11. $10 - [9 - \{8 - (7 - 6)\}] - 5$ is equal to:
A. –5 B. 1
C. 3 D. 9

12. $\frac{\frac{1}{5} \div \frac{1}{5} \text{ of } \frac{1}{5}}{\frac{1}{5} \text{ of } \frac{1}{5} \div \frac{1}{5}}$ is equal to:
A. 1 B. 5
C. $\frac{1}{5}$ D. 25

13. The value of $1 + \cfrac{1}{1 + \cfrac{1}{1 + \cfrac{1}{9}}}$ is:
A. $\frac{29}{19}$ B. $\frac{10}{19}$
C. $\frac{29}{10}$ D. $\frac{10}{9}$

14. $\frac{3}{48}$ is what part of $\frac{1}{12}$?
A. $\frac{3}{7}$ B. $\frac{1}{12}$
C. $\frac{4}{3}$ D. None of these

15. How many $\frac{1}{8}$ s are there in $37\frac{1}{2}$?
A. 300
B. 400
C. 500
D. Cannot be determined

16. $\frac{885 \times 885 \times 885 + 115 \times 115 \times 115}{885 \times 885 + 115 \times 115 - 885 \times 115}$ is equal to:
A. 115 B. 770
C. 885 D. 1000

17. The value of $\frac{9^2 \times 18^4}{3^{16}}$ is:
A. $\frac{2}{3}$ B. $\frac{4}{9}$

C. $\frac{16}{81}$ D. $\frac{32}{243}$

18. $\left(1\frac{3}{5}-\frac{2}{3}\div\frac{12}{13}+\frac{7}{5}\times\frac{1}{3}\right)$ is equal to:

A. $1\frac{31}{90}$ B. $\frac{19}{30}$

C. $\frac{11}{30}$ D. 30

19. The value of $48\div 12\times\left(\frac{9}{8}\text{of}\frac{4}{3}\div\frac{3}{4}\text{of}\frac{2}{3}\right)$ is:

A. $1\frac{1}{3}$ B. $5\frac{1}{3}$

C. 3 D. 12

20. $(20\div 5)\div 2+(16\div 8)\times 2+(10\div 5)\times(3\div 2)$ is equal to

A. 9 B. 12

C. 15 D. 18

ANSWERS

1	2	3	4	5	6	7	8	9	10
C	A	C	D	D	B	C	B	C	A
11	**12**	**13**	**14**	**15**	**16**	**17**	**18**	**19**	**20**
C	D	A	D	A	D	C	A	D	A

EXPLANATORY ANSWERS

1. $\frac{48-12\times 3+9}{12-9\div 3}=\frac{48-36+9}{12-3}$

$=\frac{57-36}{9}=\frac{21}{9}=\frac{7}{3}.$

2. $\frac{69-14\times 3+2}{9\times 5-5^2}=\frac{69-42+2}{45-25}$

$=\frac{71-42}{20}=\frac{29}{20}=1.45.$

3. $17.28\div x=2\times 3.6\times 0.2$

$\Rightarrow\ \frac{17.28}{x}=1.44\Rightarrow 1.44\,x=17.28$

$\Rightarrow\ x=\frac{17.28}{1.44}=\frac{1728}{144}=12.$

4. $171\div 19\times 9=9\times 9=81.$

5. $3120\div 26+13\times 30=120+390=510.$

6. $\frac{31}{10}\times\frac{3}{10}+\frac{7}{5}\div 20=\frac{31}{10}\times\frac{3}{10}+\frac{7}{5}\times\frac{1}{20}$

$=\frac{93}{100}+\frac{7}{100}=\frac{93+7}{100}=\frac{100}{100}=1$

7. $1+\cfrac{1}{2+\cfrac{1}{1-\cfrac{1}{3}}}=1+\cfrac{1}{2+\cfrac{1}{\cfrac{3-1}{3}}}$

$=1+\cfrac{1}{2+\cfrac{1}{\cfrac{2}{3}}}=1+\cfrac{1}{2+\cfrac{3}{2}}$

$=1+\cfrac{1}{\cfrac{7}{2}}=1+\frac{2}{7}=\frac{9}{7}$

8. $1+\frac{1}{4\times 3}+\frac{1}{4\times 3^2}+\frac{1}{4\times 3^3}$

$=1+\frac{1}{12}+\frac{1}{36}+\frac{1}{108}=\frac{108+9+3+1}{108}$

$=\frac{121}{108}=1.1203$

9. $\cfrac{\frac{1}{2}\div 4+20}{\frac{1}{2}\times 4+20}=\cfrac{\frac{1}{8}+20}{2+20}=\cfrac{\frac{1+160}{8}}{22}$

$=\frac{161}{8\times 22}=\frac{161}{176}$

10. $3\div\left[(8-5)\div\left\{(4-2)\div\left(2+\frac{8}{13}\right)\right\}\right]$

$$= 3 \div \left[3 \div \left\{2 \div \frac{34}{13}\right\}\right]$$

$$= 3 \div \left[3 \div \left\{2 \times \frac{13}{34}\right\}\right] = 3 \div \left[3 \div \frac{13}{17}\right]$$

$$= 3 \div \left[3 \times \frac{17}{13}\right] = 3 \div \frac{51}{13}$$

$$= 3 \times \frac{13}{51} = \frac{13}{17}$$

11. $10 - [9 - \{8 - (7 - 6)\}] - 5$
$= 10 - [9 - \{8 - 1\}] - 5$
$= 10 - [9 - 7] - 5$
$= 10 - 2 - 5 = 10 - 7 = 3$

12. $$\frac{\frac{1}{5} \div \frac{1}{5} \text{ of } \frac{1}{5}}{\frac{1}{5} \text{ of } \frac{1}{5} \div \frac{1}{5}} = \frac{\frac{1}{5} \div \frac{1}{25}}{\frac{1}{25} \div \frac{1}{5}}$$

$$= \frac{\frac{1}{5} \times \frac{25}{1}}{\frac{1}{25} \times \frac{5}{1}} = \frac{\frac{5}{1}}{\frac{1}{5}} = \frac{5}{1} \times \frac{5}{1} = 25$$

13. $$1 + \cfrac{1}{1 + \cfrac{1}{1 + \cfrac{1}{9}}} = 1 + \cfrac{1}{1 + \cfrac{1}{\frac{10}{9}}}$$

$$= 1 + \cfrac{1}{1 + \frac{9}{10}} = 1 + \cfrac{1}{\frac{19}{10}} = 1 + \frac{10}{19} = \frac{29}{19}$$

14. Let x of $\frac{1}{12} = \frac{3}{48}$

$\Rightarrow \quad \frac{x}{12} = \frac{3}{48} \Rightarrow 48x = 36$

$\Rightarrow \quad x = \frac{36}{48} = \frac{3}{4}.$

15. Let n times $\frac{1}{8} = 37\frac{1}{2}$

$\Rightarrow \quad \frac{n}{8} = \frac{75}{2} \Rightarrow 2n = 8 \times 75$

$\Rightarrow \quad n = \frac{8 \times 75}{2} = 4 \times 75 = 300.$

16. $$\frac{885 \times 885 \times 885 + 115 \times 115 \times 115}{885 \times 885 + 115 \times 115 - 885 \times 115}$$
Let $a = 885$ and $b = 115$

$\therefore$ Given expression $= \frac{a^3 + b^3}{a^2 + b^2 - ab}$

$$= \frac{(a+b)(a^2 + b^2 - ab)}{(a^2 + b^2 - ab)} = a + b$$

$= 885 + 115 = 1000$

17. $$\frac{9^2 \times 18^4}{3^{16}} = \frac{3^4 \times (3 \times 6)^4}{3^{16}} = \frac{3^4 \times 3^4 \times 6^4}{3^{16}}$$

$$= \frac{3^4 \times 3^4 \times (3 \times 2)^4}{3^{16}}$$

$$= \frac{3^4 \times 3^4 \times 3^4 \times 2^4}{3^{16}} = \frac{3^{12} \times 2^4}{3^{16}}$$

$$= \frac{2^4}{3^4} = \frac{16}{81}$$

18. $$\left(1\frac{3}{5} - \frac{2}{3} \div \frac{12}{13} + \frac{7}{5} \times \frac{1}{3}\right)$$

$$= \frac{8}{5} - \frac{2}{3} \times \frac{13}{12} + \frac{7}{15}$$

$$= \frac{8}{5} - \frac{13}{18} + \frac{7}{15} = \frac{144 - 65 + 42}{90}$$

$$= \frac{186 - 65}{90} = \frac{121}{90} = 1\frac{31}{90}$$

19. $$48 \div 12 \times \left(\frac{9}{8} \text{ of } \frac{4}{3} \div \frac{3}{4} \text{ of } \frac{2}{3}\right)$$

$$= 48 \div 12 \times \left(\frac{3}{2} \div \frac{1}{2}\right)$$

$$= 48 \div 12 \times \left(\frac{3}{2} \times \frac{2}{1}\right)$$

$= 48 \div 12 \times 3 = 4 \times 3 = 12$

20. $(20 \div 5) \div 2 + (16 \div 8) \times 2 + (10 \div 5) \times (3 \div 2)$

$$= 4 \div 2 + 2 \times 2 + 2 \times \frac{3}{2}$$

$= 2 + 4 + 3 = 9$

4

CHAPTER

Surds and Indices

SURDS

If 'a' is a rational number and n is a positive integer such that nth root of 'a', *i.e.*, $a^{1/n}$ or $\sqrt[n]{a}$ is an irrational number, then $a^{1/n}$ is called a surd or radical.

In other words, an irrational root of a rational number is called a surd. The symbol '$\sqrt{}$' is known as surd sign or radical.

For example, $\sqrt{2} = 2^{1/2}$ = Square root of 2

$\sqrt[3]{5} = 5^{1/3}$ = Cube root of 5

Pure and Mixed Surds

Pure Surd: A surd which has unity only as rational factor, the other factor being irrational, is called a pure surd.

For example, $\sqrt{2}$, $\sqrt[3]{3}$, $\sqrt[5]{3}$ are pure surds.

Mixed Surd: A surd which has a rational factor other than unity, the other factor being irrational, is called a mixed surds.

For example, $2\sqrt{5}$ $3\sqrt[4]{7}$, $5\sqrt[3]{11}$ are mixed surds.

Rationalising Factor: When the product of two surds is a rational number, then each of them is called the rationalising factor (R.F.) of the other.

For example, $3\sqrt{5} \times \sqrt{5} = 3 \times 5 = 15$

$\therefore$ $\sqrt{5}$ is a rationalising factor of $3\sqrt{5}$.

Important Formulae Based on Surds

$\sqrt[n]{a} = a^{1/n}$ and it is called a surd of order n.

(*i*) $\sqrt[n]{a^n} = a$

(*ii*) $\sqrt[n]{ab} = \sqrt[n]{a}\,\sqrt[n]{b}$

(*iii*) $\sqrt{a} \times \sqrt{a} = a$

(*iv*) $\sqrt{a} \times \sqrt{b} = \sqrt{ab}$

(*v*) $\sqrt{a^2 b} = a\sqrt{b}$

(*vi*) $\left(\sqrt{a}+\sqrt{b}\right)^2 = a+b+2\sqrt{ab}$

(*vii*) $\left(\sqrt{a}-\sqrt{b}\right)^2 = a+b-2\sqrt{ab}$

(*viii*) $\left(\sqrt{a}+\sqrt{b}\right)\left(\sqrt{a}-\sqrt{b}\right) = a-b$ where a and b are positive rational numbers.

INDICES

Let n be a positive integer and 'a' be a real number. The continued product of n factors each equal to a *e.g.*, $a \times a \times a \times \ldots \times n$ times is written as a^n and is called "n^{th} power of a" or "a raised to the power n".

The expression a^n is termed as power function or simply power, a is called the base and n is called index or exponent of the power a^n.

For example, 2^2 = square of 2, 2^3 = cube of 2, etc.

Laws of Indices

(*i*) $a^m \times a^n = a^{m+n}$

(*ii*) $a^m \times a^n \times a^p \times \ldots = a^{m+n+p+\ldots}$

(*iii*) $\dfrac{a^m}{a^n} = a^{m-n}$, if $m > n$

(*iv*) $\dfrac{a^m}{a^n} = \dfrac{1}{a^{n-m}}$, if $m < n$

(*v*) $(a^m)^n = a^{mn}$

(*vi*) $(ab)^n = a^n b^n$

(*vii*) $a^0 = 1$

(*viii*) If $a^m = a^n$ then $m = n$

(*ix*) If $a^m = b^m$ then $a = b$

(*x*) $\dfrac{a^m}{a^m} = a^{m-m} = a^0 = 1$

MULTIPLE CHOICE QUESTIONS

1. If the infinite series is $x = \sqrt{6+\sqrt{6+\sqrt{6+...}}}$ then the value of x is:
A. 2.5 B. 3
C. 6 D. 8

2. If $\dfrac{9^n \cdot 3^2 \cdot 3^n - (27)^n}{3^{3m} \cdot 2^3} = \dfrac{1}{27}$, then the value of $(m-n)$ is:
A. 1 B. 2
C. $\sqrt{3}$ D. $\sqrt{\dfrac{2}{3}}$

3. If $x = \dfrac{\sqrt{5}+\sqrt{3}}{\sqrt{5}-\sqrt{3}}$ and $y = \dfrac{\sqrt{5}-\sqrt{3}}{\sqrt{5}+\sqrt{3}}$, then $(x+y)$ is equal to:
A. 8 B. 6
C. $2\sqrt{15}$ D. $2\left(\sqrt{5}+\sqrt{3}\right)$

4. $2^{x+1} + 2^{x+3} = 2560$, then x is equal to:
A. 12 B. 11
C. 8 D. 6

5. If $\dfrac{5+2\sqrt{3}}{7+4\sqrt{3}} = a + b\sqrt{3}$, then b is equal to:
A. –6 B. 6
C. –11 D. 11

6. If $\dfrac{(21)^{5.36}}{(21)^{3.47}} = (21)^x$, then the value of x is:
A. 8.88 B. 1.54
C. 9.32 D. 1.89

7. $\sqrt{24}+\sqrt{12}$ equal to:
A. $\sqrt{36}$ B. $2\sqrt{6}+2\sqrt{3}$
C. $6\sqrt{2}$ D. $\sqrt{288}$

8. If $a^b = 64$, where a and b are positive integers then $(a-b)^{a+b-4}$ is:
A. 0 B. 1
C. 2 D. $\dfrac{1}{2}$

9. The value of $\dfrac{5^{10+n} \cdot 25^{3n-4}}{5^{7n}}$ is:
A. 5 B. 8
C. 25 D. 16

10. $3^x - 3^{x-1} = 18$, then the value of x^x is:
A. 3 B. 8
C. 27 D. 216

11. If $x = \sqrt{10+\sqrt{25+\sqrt{121}}}$, then x is equal to:
A. –2 only B. 2 only
C. ± 4 D. 4 only

12. If $a^x = b^y = c^z$ and $b^2 = ac$, then y is equal to:
A. $\dfrac{xz}{x+z}$ B. $\dfrac{xz}{2(x-z)}$
C. $\dfrac{xz}{2(z-x)}$ D. $\dfrac{2xz}{x+z}$

13. $\dfrac{5^{n+3} - 6 \times 5^{n+1}}{9 \times 5^n - 5^n \times 2^2}$ is equal to:
A. 5 B. 19
C. 25 D. 95

14. The value of $\left(\dfrac{x^a}{x^b}\right)^{(a+b)} \times \left(\dfrac{x^b}{x^c}\right)^{(b+c)} \times \left(\dfrac{x^c}{x^a}\right)^{(c+a)}$ is equal to:
A. 0 B. 2
C. 1 D. 3

15. If $\sqrt{3^n} = 729$, then the value of n is:
A. 12 B. 8
C. 10 D. 6

16. The value of $4\sqrt{3} - 3\sqrt{12} + 2\sqrt{75}$ is:
A. $2\sqrt{3}$ B. $4\sqrt{3}$
C. $6\sqrt{3}$ D. $8\sqrt{3}$

17. The value of $\sqrt{50} - \sqrt{98} + \sqrt{162}$ is:
A. $5\sqrt{2}$ B. $7\sqrt{2}$
C. $3\sqrt{2}$ D. $4\sqrt{2}$

18. If $x = 1-\sqrt{2}$, the value of $\left(x-\frac{1}{x}\right)^3$ is:

A. 1 B. 4
C. 8 D. 2

19. If $a = 7-4\sqrt{3}$, then the value of $\sqrt{a}+\frac{1}{\sqrt{a}}$ is equal to:

A. 1 B. 4
C. 2 D. 3

20. The value of $\frac{4\sqrt{18}}{\sqrt{12}}-\frac{8\sqrt{75}}{\sqrt{32}}+\frac{9\sqrt{2}}{\sqrt{3}}$ is:

A. 0 B. 2
C. 1 D. 3

21. $\sqrt[3]{8^4}$ is equivalent to:

A. 15 B. 9
C. 16 D. 25

22. What will be the value of $\left(\sqrt{80}+3\sqrt{245}=\sqrt{125}\right)$?

A. $18\sqrt{5}$ B. $20\sqrt{5}$
C. $22\sqrt{5}$ D. $28\sqrt{2}$

23. Value of $\left(\frac{\sqrt{5}+\sqrt{3}}{\sqrt{5}-\sqrt{3}}\right)$ will be equivalent to:

A. $4+\sqrt{15}$ B. $3-\sqrt{15}$
C. $2+\sqrt{15}$ D. $4-\sqrt{15}$

ANSWERS

1	2	3	4	5	6	7	8	9	10
B	A	A	C	A	D	B	B	C	C
11	**12**	**13**	**14**	**15**	**16**	**17**	**18**	**19**	**20**
D	D	B	C	A	D	B	C	B	A
21	**22**	**23**							
C	B	A							

EXPLANATORY ANSWERS

1. $x = \sqrt{6+x}$

Squaring both sides

$$x^2 = 6+x$$
$$\Rightarrow x^2-x-6 = 0$$
$$\Rightarrow x^2-3x+2x-6 = 0$$
$$\Rightarrow x(x-3)+2(x-3) = 0$$
$$\Rightarrow (x-3)(x+2) = 0$$
$$\Rightarrow x = 3 \text{ or } x = -2$$

But x cannot be -2.

Hence, the required value of x is 3.

2. $$\frac{9^n \cdot 3^2 \cdot 3^n-(27)^n}{3^{3m}\cdot 2^3} = \frac{1}{27}$$

$$\Rightarrow \frac{3^{2n}\times 9\times 3^n-3^{3n}}{8\times 3^{3m}} = \frac{1}{3^3}$$

$$\Rightarrow \frac{3^{3n}(9-1)}{8\,3^{3m}} = 3^{-3}$$

$$\Rightarrow 3^{3n-3m} = (3)^{-3}$$
$$\Rightarrow 3m-3n = 3$$
$$\Rightarrow 3(m-n) = 3$$
$$\Rightarrow m-n = \frac{3}{3} = 1$$

3. $$x = \frac{\sqrt{5}+\sqrt{3}}{\sqrt{5}-\sqrt{3}}\times\frac{\sqrt{5}+\sqrt{3}}{\sqrt{5}+\sqrt{3}} = \frac{\left(\sqrt{5}+\sqrt{3}\right)^2}{5-3}$$

$$\Rightarrow x = \frac{5+3+2\sqrt{15}}{2} = \frac{8+2\sqrt{15}}{2} = \frac{2\left(4+\sqrt{15}\right)}{2}$$

$$\therefore x = 4+\sqrt{15}$$

Again, $$y = \frac{\sqrt{5}-\sqrt{3}}{\sqrt{5}+\sqrt{3}}\times\frac{\sqrt{5}-\sqrt{3}}{\sqrt{5}-\sqrt{3}}$$

$$= \frac{\left(\sqrt{5}-\sqrt{3}\right)^2}{5-3}$$

$$\Rightarrow \quad y = \frac{5+3-2\sqrt{15}}{2}$$

$$= \frac{8-2\sqrt{15}}{2} = \frac{2\left(4-\sqrt{15}\right)}{2}$$

$$\Rightarrow \quad y = 4-\sqrt{15}$$

$$\therefore \quad x+y = 4+\sqrt{15}+4-\sqrt{15} = 8$$

4. $2^{x+1} + 2^{x+3} = 2560$

$\Rightarrow \quad 2^x \times 2 + 2^x \times 2^3 = 2560$

$\Rightarrow \quad 2 \times 2^x + 8 \times 2^x = 2560$

$\Rightarrow \quad 2^x (2+8) = 2560$

$\Rightarrow \quad 2^x = 256 = 2^8$

$\Rightarrow \quad x = 8$

5. $\because \quad \dfrac{5+2\sqrt{3}}{7+4\sqrt{3}} = a+b\sqrt{3}$

$$\frac{5+2\sqrt{3}}{7+4\sqrt{3}} \times \frac{7-4\sqrt{3}}{7-4\sqrt{3}} = \frac{35-20\sqrt{3}+14\sqrt{3}-24}{49-48}$$

$$= \frac{11-6\sqrt{3}}{1}$$

Comparing then we get,

$a = 11, b = -6$

Hence, $b = -6$.

6. $\dfrac{(21)^{5.36}}{(21)^{3.47}} = (21)^x$

$\Rightarrow \quad (21)^{5.36-3.47} = (21)^x$

$\Rightarrow \quad x = 1.89$

7. $\sqrt{24}+\sqrt{12} = 2\sqrt{6}+2\sqrt{3}$

8. $a^b = 64 = (4)^3 \Rightarrow a = 4, b = 3$

$\therefore (a-b)^{a+b-4} = (4-3)^{4+3-4} = (1)^3 = 1$

9. $\dfrac{5^{10+n} \cdot 25^{3n-4}}{5^{7n}} = \dfrac{5^{10} \times 5^n \times (5^2)^{3n-4}}{5^{7n}}$

$$= \frac{5^{10} \times 5^n \times 5^{6n} \times 5^{-8}}{5^{7n}}$$

$$= \frac{5^{10-8} \times 5^{7n}}{5^{7n}} = 5^2 \times 5^{7n-7n}$$

$= 25 \times 5^0 = 25 \times 1 = 25$

10. $3^x - 3^{x-1} = 18$

$\Rightarrow \quad 3^x - 3^x \times 3^{-1} = 18$

$\Rightarrow \quad 3^x\left(1-\dfrac{1}{3}\right) = 18$

$\Rightarrow \quad 3^x\left(\dfrac{2}{3}\right) = 18$

$\Rightarrow \quad 3^x = \dfrac{18\times 3}{2} = 27$

$\Rightarrow \quad 3^x = (3)^3 \Rightarrow x = 3$

$\therefore \quad x^x = (3)^3 = 27$

11. $x = \sqrt{10+\sqrt{25+\sqrt{121}}}$

$\Rightarrow \quad x = \sqrt{10+\sqrt{25+11}}$

$\Rightarrow \quad x = \sqrt{10+\sqrt{36}}$

$\Rightarrow \quad x = \sqrt{10+6} = \sqrt{16}$

$\Rightarrow \quad x = 4$

12. Let $a^x = b^y = c^z = k$

then $a = k^{\frac{1}{x}}$, $b = k^{\frac{1}{y}}$, $c = k^{\frac{1}{z}}$

Now, $\quad b^2 = ac$

$\Rightarrow \quad \left(k^{\frac{1}{y}}\right)^2 = k^{\frac{1}{x}} \cdot k^{\frac{1}{z}}$

$\Rightarrow \quad k^{\frac{2}{y}} = k^{\frac{1}{x}+\frac{1}{z}}$

$\Rightarrow \quad \dfrac{2}{y} = \dfrac{z+x}{xz}$

$\Rightarrow \quad 2xz = y(x+z)$

$\Rightarrow \quad y = \dfrac{2xz}{x+z}$

13. $\dfrac{5^{n+3}-6\times 5^{n+1}}{9\times 5^n - 5^n \times 2^2} = \dfrac{5^n \times 5^3 - 6 \times 5^n \times 5}{9\times 5^n - 4\times 5^n}$

$$= \frac{5^n(125-30)}{5^n(9-4)} = 5^0 \times \frac{95}{5}$$

$= 1 \times 19 = 19.$

14. $\left(\dfrac{x^a}{x^b}\right)^{(a+b)} \times \left(\dfrac{x^b}{x^c}\right)^{(b+c)} \times \left(\dfrac{x^c}{x^a}\right)^{(c+a)}$

$= \left(x^{a-b}\right)^{(a+b)} \times \left(x^{b-c}\right)^{(b+c)} \times \left(x^{c-a}\right)^{c+a}$

$= x^{a^2-b^2} \times x^{b^2-c^2} \times x^{c^2-a^2}$

$= x^{a^2-b^2+b^2-c^2+c^2-a^2}$

$= x^0 = 1$

15. $\sqrt{3^n} = 729 \Rightarrow 3^{n/2} = 3^6$

$\Rightarrow \quad \frac{n}{2} = 6$

$\Rightarrow \quad n = 12.$

16. $4\sqrt{3} - 3\sqrt{12} + 2\sqrt{75}$

$= 4\sqrt{3} - 3\sqrt{2\times 2\times 3} + 2\sqrt{5\times 5\times 3}$

$= 4\sqrt{3} - 6\sqrt{3} + 10\sqrt{3}$

$= \sqrt{3}(4 - 6 + 10) = 8\sqrt{3}$

17. $\sqrt{50} - \sqrt{98} + \sqrt{162}$

$= \sqrt{5\times 5\times 2} - \sqrt{7\times 7\times 2} + \sqrt{3\times 3\times 3\times 3\times 2}$

$= 5\sqrt{2} - 7\sqrt{2} + 9\sqrt{2}$

$= 14\sqrt{2} - 7\sqrt{2} = 7\sqrt{2}$

18. $\because \quad x = 1 - \sqrt{2}$

$$\frac{1}{x} = \frac{1}{1-\sqrt{2}} \times \frac{1+\sqrt{2}}{1+\sqrt{2}} = \frac{1+\sqrt{2}}{1-2}$$

$$\therefore \quad \frac{1}{x} = \frac{1+\sqrt{2}}{-1} = -1-\sqrt{2}$$

$$x - \frac{1}{x} = 1-\sqrt{2}-\left(-1-\sqrt{2}\right)$$

$$= 1-\sqrt{2}+1+\sqrt{2} = 2$$

$$\therefore \quad \left(x-\frac{1}{x}\right)^3 = (2)^3 = 8$$

19. $\because \quad a = 7 - 4\sqrt{3}$

$$\frac{1}{a} = \frac{1}{7-4\sqrt{3}} \times \frac{7+4\sqrt{3}}{7+4\sqrt{3}}$$

$$= \frac{7+4\sqrt{3}}{49-48} = \frac{7+4\sqrt{3}}{1}$$

$$a + \frac{1}{a} = 7-4\sqrt{3}+7+4\sqrt{3} = 14$$

$$a + \frac{1}{a} + 2 = 14 + 2$$

$$a + \frac{1}{a} + 2 = 16$$

$$\left(\sqrt{a} + \frac{1}{\sqrt{a}}\right)^2 = 4^2$$

$$\therefore \quad \sqrt{a} + \frac{1}{\sqrt{a}} = 4$$

20. $\frac{4\sqrt{18}}{\sqrt{12}} - \frac{8\sqrt{75}}{\sqrt{32}} + \frac{9\sqrt{2}}{\sqrt{3}}$

$$= \frac{4\times 3\sqrt{2}}{2\sqrt{3}} - \frac{8\times 5\sqrt{3}}{4\sqrt{2}} + \frac{9\sqrt{2}}{\sqrt{3}}$$

$$= \frac{6\sqrt{2}}{\sqrt{3}} \times \frac{\sqrt{3}}{\sqrt{3}} - \frac{10\sqrt{3}}{\sqrt{2}} \times \frac{\sqrt{2}}{\sqrt{2}} + \frac{9\sqrt{2}}{\sqrt{3}} \times \frac{\sqrt{3}}{\sqrt{3}}$$

$$= \frac{6\sqrt{6}}{3} - \frac{10\sqrt{6}}{2} + \frac{9\sqrt{6}}{3}$$

$$= 2\sqrt{6} - 5\sqrt{6} + 3\sqrt{6}$$

$$= 5\sqrt{6} - 5\sqrt{6} = 0$$

21. $\sqrt[3]{8^4} = (8)^{4/3} = (2^3)^{4/3} = 2^4 = 16$

22. $\sqrt{80} + 3\sqrt{245} - \sqrt{125}$

$$= \sqrt{16\times 5} + 3\sqrt{49\times 5} - \sqrt{25\times 5}$$

$$= 4\sqrt{5} + 21\sqrt{5} - 5\sqrt{5}$$

$$= 25\sqrt{5} - 5\sqrt{5} = 20\sqrt{5}$$

23. $\frac{\sqrt{5}+\sqrt{3}}{\sqrt{5}-\sqrt{3}} = \frac{\sqrt{5}+\sqrt{3}}{\sqrt{5}-\sqrt{3}} \times \frac{\sqrt{5}+\sqrt{3}}{\sqrt{5}+\sqrt{3}}$

$$= \frac{(\sqrt{5}+\sqrt{3})^2}{(\sqrt{5})^2 - (\sqrt{3})^2}$$

$$= \frac{5+3+2\sqrt{15}}{5-3}$$

$$= \frac{8+2\sqrt{15}}{2} = \frac{2(4+\sqrt{15})}{2}$$

$$= 4 + \sqrt{15}$$

5

CHAPTER

Ratio and Proportion

RATIO

When comparison is made by dividing one quantity by another of the same kind, the result is called ratio. If a and b are two numbers, ratio of a to b is denoted by $a : b$ or $\frac{a}{b}$. Here a is called first term and b is called the second term. The first term is also called antecedent and the second term is also called consequent.

Example: The ratio 3 : 10 represents $\frac{3}{10}$ with antecedent 3 and consequent 10.

The multiplication or division of each term of a ratio by a same non-zero number does not effect the ratio.

PROPORTION

Equality of two ratios is called proportion. If $a : b = c : d$, then a, b, c, d are called in proportion. In a proportion $a : b :: c : d$, then a and d are called extremes and b and c are called means.

Product of extremes = Product of means

Comparison of Ratio: Suppose $\frac{a}{b} > \frac{c}{d}$ then we say that $a : b > c : d$.

Compounded Ratio: The compound ratio of the ratios $a : b$, $c : d$ and $e : f$ is $ace : bdf$.

Duplicate Ratio: The duplicate ratio of $a : b$ is $a^2 : b^2$.

Triplicate Ratio: The triplicate ratio of $a : b$ is $a^3 : b^3$.

Sub-duplicate and Sub-triplicate ratios

The sub-duplicate and Sub-triplicate ratios of ratio $a : b$ are $a^{1/2} : b^{1/2}$ and $a^{1/3} : b^{1/3}$ respectively.

Mean Proportional: Mean proportional between a and b is $\sqrt{ab}$.

Third Proportional: The third proportional to a, b is the fourth proportional to a, b, b.

Fourth Proportional: If $a : b :: c : d$ is a proportion, then d is called the fourth proportional to a, b, c.

Example: If A : B = 3 : 4 and B : C = 8 : 9 then find A : C.

Solution: $A : B = 3 : 4 \Rightarrow \frac{A}{B} = \frac{3}{4}$

$B : C = 8 : 9 \Rightarrow \frac{B}{C} = \frac{8}{9}$

$$\frac{A}{C} = \frac{A}{B} \times \frac{B}{C} = \frac{3}{4} \times \frac{8}{9} = \frac{2}{3}$$

$\Rightarrow \quad A : C = 2 : 3$

Example: If 15% of A is the same as 20% of B, then find A : B.

Solution: Given : 15% of A = 20% of B

$\Rightarrow \quad \frac{15}{100} \times A = \frac{20}{100} \times B$

$\Rightarrow \quad 3A = 4B$

$\Rightarrow \quad \frac{A}{B} = \frac{4}{3}$

$\Rightarrow \quad A : B = 4 : 3$

Example: A stick 1.4 m long casts a shadow 1.3 m long at the same time when a pole casts a shadow 5.2 m long. Find the length of the pole.

Solution: Clearly, more is the length of shadow, more is the length of the object.

Let the length of the pole be x metres.

Then, $1.3 : 5.2 :: 1.4 : x$

$$\Rightarrow \quad \frac{1.3}{5.2} = \frac{1.4}{x}$$

$$\Rightarrow \quad \frac{1}{4} = \frac{1.4}{x}$$

$$\Rightarrow \quad x = 1.4 \times 4 = 5.6$$

Hence, the length of the pole is 5.6 m.

MULTIPLE CHOICE QUESTIONS

1. If A : B = 2 : 3 and B : C = 4 : 5, then C : A is equal to:

A. 15 : 8 B. 12 : 10
C. 8 : 5 D. 8 : 15

2. If 10% of x is the same as 20% of y, then $x : y$ is equal to:

A. 1 : 2 B. 2 : 1
C. 5 : 1 D. 10 : 1

3. The mean proportional to $6+\sqrt{27}$ and $6-\sqrt{27}$ is:

A. 3 B. 9
C. 10 D. $\sqrt{10}$

4. If $x : y = 9 : 11$, the value of $\frac{5x+3y}{3x+5y}$ is:

A. 45 : 55 B. 18 : 22
C. 37 : 41 D. 39 : 41

5. If $a + b : b + c : c + a = 6 : 7 : 8$ and $a + b + c = 14$, then the value of c is:

A. 14 B. 7
C. 8 D. 6

6. Two numbers are in the ratio 2 : 3. If 5 is added to each number, the ratio becomes 5 : 7. The bigger number is:

A. 30 B. 40
C. 60 D. 20

7. What should be added to each of the numbers 12, 30, 40 and 86, so that they are in proportion?

A. 6 B. 4
C. –6 D. –4

8. The ratio of males and females of a village is 5 : 3. If there are 800 males in the village, females are:

A. 240 B. 480
C. 840 D. 488

9. In a mixture of 60 litres, the ratio of ethanol to ether is 4 : 1. How much ether must be added to the mixture to make this ratio 2 : 1?

A. 10 litres B. 12 litres
C. 18 litres D. 24 litres

10. The proportion of zinc and copper in a brass piece is 4 : 5. How much zinc will be there in 180 kg of such a piece?

A. 40 kg B. 80 kg
C. 100 kg D. 120 kg

11. The prices of a scooter and a television set are in the ratio 3 : 2. If a scooter costs ₹ 6000 more than the television set, the price of the television set is:

A. ₹ 18000 B. ₹ 12000
C. ₹ 10000 D. ₹ 6000

12. The weight of a 13 metres long iron rod be 23.4 kg. The weight of 6 metres long of such rod will be:

A. 7.2 kg B. 12.4 kg
C. 10.8 kg D. 18 kg

13. The ratio between the ages of Gayatri and Savitri is 6 : 5 and the sum of their ages is 44 years. The ratio of their ages after 8 years will be:

A. 5 : 6 B. 7 : 8
C. 8 : 7 D. 14 : 13

14. Two numbers are such that the ratio between them is 3 : 5 but if each is increased by 10, the ratio between them becomes 5 : 7. The numbers are:

A. 3, 5 B. 7, 9
C. 13, 22 D. 15, 25

15. In a factory the ratio of male workers to female workers was 5 : 3. If the number of female workers was less by 40, the total number of workers in the factory was:

A. 100 B. 500
C. 160 D. 200

16. If $a : b = 2 : 3$, $b : c = 4 : 5$ and $c : d = 6 : 7$, then $a : d$ is equal to:

A. 2 : 7 B. 7 : 8
C. 16 : 35 D. 4 : 13

17. A bag contains one rupee, fifty paise and 25 paise coins in the ratio of 2 : 3 : 4. If the total amount is ₹ 180, the number of fifty paise coins is:

A. 120 B. 60
C. 40 D. 240

18. $\frac{3}{7}$ of $\frac{7}{8}$ of a number is equal to the 25% of 45% of another number. The ratio of first number and second number is:

A. 3 : 7 B. 9 : 10
C. 3 : 10 D. None of the above

19. The ratios of milk and water in four solutions are 1 : 2, 2 : 3, 3 : 2 and 7 : 8 respectively. If their equal quantities are mixed together, then the ratio of milk and water in the new solution will be:

A. 13 : 15 B. 7 : 9
C. 9 : 11 D. 11 : 9

20. A number is divided into parts such that the sum of 5 times of the first part and 18 times of the second part is equal to 7 times of the number. The ratio of two parts is:

A. 5 : 7 B. 9 : 8
C. 1 : 7 D. 11 : 2

21. If $x : y :: 5 : 2$, then $8x + 9y : 8x + 2y$ is equal to:

A. 22 : 29 B. 29 : 22
C. 31 : 29 D. 21 : 29

22. If 76 is divided in to the ratios of 7, 5, 3 and 4, then the smallest part will be:

A. 14 B. 18
C. 32 D. 12

23. The sum of two numbers is 70 and their difference is 16. Ratio of these two numbers is:

A. 43 : 27 B. 27 : 64
C. 43 : 16 D. 25 : 64

24. Two numbers are in the ratio of 12 and 19. If the sum of these two numbers is 217, the value of smallest number is:

A. 81 B. 64
C. 70 D. 84

ANSWERS

1	2	3	4	5	6	7	8	9	10
A	B	A	D	D	A	A	B	B	B
11	**12**	**13**	**14**	**15**	**16**	**17**	**18**	**19**	**20**
B	C	C	D	C	C	A	C	C	D
21	**22**	**23**	**24**						
B	D	A	D						

EXPLANATORY ANSWERS

1. $\frac{A}{B} = \frac{2}{3}$ and $\frac{B}{C} = \frac{4}{5}$

$$\Rightarrow \frac{A}{B}\times\frac{B}{C} = \frac{2}{3}\times\frac{4}{5} \Rightarrow \frac{A}{C} = \frac{8}{15}$$

$$\Rightarrow \frac{C}{A} = \frac{15}{8}$$

Hence, C : A = 15 : 8.

2. 10% of x = 20% of y

$$\Rightarrow \frac{10}{100}x = \frac{20}{100}y \Rightarrow \frac{x}{10} = \frac{y}{5}$$

$$\Rightarrow \frac{x}{y} = \frac{10}{5} \Rightarrow x : y = 2 : 1$$

3. Mean proportional $= \sqrt{(6+\sqrt{27})(6-\sqrt{27})}$

$$= \sqrt{36-27} = \sqrt{9} = 3$$

4. $\because \frac{x}{y} = \frac{9}{11}$

$$\frac{5x+3y}{3x+5y} = \frac{\frac{5x}{y}+\frac{3y}{y}}{\frac{3x}{y}+\frac{5y}{y}} = \frac{5\left(\frac{x}{y}\right)+3}{3\left(\frac{x}{y}\right)+5}$$

$$= \frac{5\times\frac{9}{11}+3}{3\times\frac{9}{11}+5} = \frac{\frac{45+33}{11}}{\frac{27+55}{11}} = \frac{78}{82} = \frac{39}{41}$$

Hence, the value of $\frac{5x+3y}{3x+5y} = \frac{39}{41}$.

5. Given : $a + b = 6x,\ b + c = 7x$
and $c + a = 8x$ ...(*i*)
and $a + b + c = 14$ ...(*ii*)
Adding Eq. (*i*)
$$a + b + b + c + c + a = 6x + 7x + 8x$$
$$\Rightarrow \quad 2(a + b + c) = 21x$$
$$\Rightarrow \quad 2 \times 14 = 21x \quad \text{[from Eq. (ii)]}$$
$$\Rightarrow \quad x = \frac{28}{21} = \frac{4}{3}$$
$$\therefore \quad a + b = 6x = 6 \times \frac{4}{3} = 8$$
$$\because \quad a + b + c = 14 \Rightarrow c = 14 - 8 = 6$$

6. Let the two numbers are a and b
According to the question,
$$\frac{a}{b} = \frac{2}{3} \Rightarrow 3a = 2b \Rightarrow b = \frac{3a}{2}$$
Now, $$\frac{a+5}{b+5} = \frac{5}{7} \Rightarrow 7a + 35 = 5b + 25$$
$$\Rightarrow \quad 7a - 5b = -10$$
$$\Rightarrow \quad 7a - 5\left(\frac{3a}{2}\right) = -10$$
$$\Rightarrow \quad 14a - 15a = -20 \Rightarrow -a = -20$$
$$\Rightarrow \quad a = 20,\ b = 3 \times \frac{20}{2} = 30$$
Hence, the bigger number is 30.

7. Let x be added to each of the numbers.
Then, $(12 + x) : (30 + x) : : (40 + x) : (86 + x)$
$$\Rightarrow \quad \frac{12+x}{30+x} = \frac{40+x}{86+x}$$
$$\Rightarrow (12 + x)(86 + x) = (30 + x)(40 + x)$$
$$\Rightarrow 12 \times 86 + 12x + 86x + x^2 = 30 \times 40 + 30x + 40x + x^2$$
$$\Rightarrow \quad 1032 + 98x = 1200 + 70x$$
$$\Rightarrow \quad 28x = 168 \Rightarrow x = 6$$

8. Ratio of Males : Females = 5 : 3
$$\Rightarrow \quad \frac{800}{x} = \frac{5}{3} \Rightarrow 5x = 3 \times 800$$
$$\Rightarrow \quad x = \frac{3 \times 800}{5} = 3 \times 160 = 480$$
Hence, number of females = 480.

9. Let ethanol = $4x$ and ether = $1x$
$4x + 1x = 60 \Rightarrow 5x = 60 \Rightarrow x = 12$
Quantity of ethanol = 12 × 4 = 48 litres
Quantity of ether = 1 × 12 = 12 litres
Let m litres of ether be added to mixture to get the desired ratio. Then,
$$\frac{48}{12+m} = \frac{2}{1} \Rightarrow 24 + 2m = 48$$
$$\Rightarrow \quad 2m = 24 \Rightarrow m = 12$$
Hence, 12 litres of ether is to be added.

10. In 9 kg of brass, zinc = 4 kg
$\therefore$ In 180 kg of brass, zinc = $\frac{4}{9} \times 180 = 80$ kg.

11. Let the prices of a scooter and a television be ₹ $3x$ and $2x$ respectively.
According to the question,
$3x - 2x = 6000 \Rightarrow x = 6000$
$\therefore$ Price of a television = 2 × 6000 = ₹ 12000.

12. Weight of 13 m long iron rod = 23.4 kg
Weight of 6 m long iron rod
$$= \frac{23.4}{13} \times 6 \text{ kg} = 1.8 \times 6 = 10.8 \text{ kg.}$$

13. Let present age of Gayatri = $6x$ years and present age of Savitri = $5x$ years.
According to the question,
$$6x + 5x = 44 \Rightarrow 11x = 44 \Rightarrow x = 4$$
Gayatri's age = 6 × 4 = 24 years
Savitri's age = 5 × 4 = 20 years
After 8 years their ages will be 32 years and 28 years.
Ratio of their ages after 8 years = $\frac{32}{28} = 8 : 7$.

14. Let numbers are x and y
$$\frac{x}{y} = \frac{3}{5}$$
$$\Rightarrow \quad 5x = 3y \Rightarrow x = \frac{3y}{5}$$
According to the question,
$$\frac{x+10}{y+10} = \frac{5}{7} \Rightarrow 7x + 70 = 5y + 50$$
$$\Rightarrow \quad 7x - 5y = -20$$
$$\Rightarrow \quad 7\left(\frac{3y}{5}\right) - 5y = -20$$
$$\Rightarrow \quad 21y - 25y = -100$$
$$\Rightarrow \quad 4y = 100 \Rightarrow y = 25$$
$$\therefore \quad x = \frac{3 \times 25}{5} = 15$$
Hence, numbers are 15 and 25.

15. Let the number of male and female workers be $5x$ and $3x$ respectively.
According to the question,
$5x - 3x = 40 \Rightarrow 2x = 40 \Rightarrow x = 20$
$\therefore$ Number of male $= 5 \times 20 = 100$
and number of female $= 3 \times 20 = 60$
Hence, total number of workers $= 100 + 60 = 160$.

16. $\frac{a}{b} = \frac{2}{3}, \frac{b}{c} = \frac{4}{5}$ and $\frac{c}{d} = \frac{6}{7}$

$$\therefore \frac{a}{d} = \frac{a}{b}\times\frac{b}{c}\times\frac{c}{d} = \frac{2}{3}\times\frac{4}{5}\times\frac{6}{7} = \frac{16}{35}$$

Hence, $a : d = 16 : 35$.

17. One rupee : Fifty paise : Twenty-five paise

$$2 \times 1 : 3\times\frac{50}{100} : 4\times\frac{25}{100}$$
$$2 : \frac{3}{2} : 1$$
$$4 : 3 : 2$$

Amount of fifty paise coins

$$= \frac{3}{4+3+2}\times 180$$
$$= \frac{3}{9}\times 180 = ₹\ 60$$

$\therefore$ Number of fifty paise coins $= 60 \times 2 = 120$.

18. Let first number be x and second number be y.

$$\frac{3}{7}\times\frac{7}{8}x = \frac{25}{100}\times\frac{45}{100}\times y$$
$$\Rightarrow \frac{3}{8}x = \frac{1}{4}\times\frac{9}{20}y \Rightarrow \frac{3x}{8} = \frac{9y}{80}$$
$$\Rightarrow 240x = 72y \Rightarrow \frac{x}{y} = \frac{72}{240} = \frac{3}{10}$$

Hence, ratio of first number and second number $= 3 : 10$.

19. Required ratio

$$= \left(\frac{1}{1+2}+\frac{2}{2+3}+\frac{3}{3+2}+\frac{7}{7+8}\right) : \left(\frac{2}{1+2}+\frac{3}{2+3}+\frac{2}{3+2}+\frac{8}{7+8}\right)$$
$$= \left(\frac{1}{3}+\frac{2}{5}+\frac{3}{5}+\frac{7}{15}\right) : \left(\frac{2}{3}+\frac{3}{5}+\frac{2}{5}+\frac{8}{15}\right)$$
$$= \left(\frac{1}{3}+\frac{5}{5}+\frac{7}{15}\right) : \left(\frac{2}{3}+\frac{5}{5}+\frac{8}{15}\right)$$
$$= \left(\frac{5+15+7}{15}\right) : \left(\frac{10+15+8}{15}\right)$$

$= 27 : 33 = 9 : 11$.

20. Let first part $= x$, second part $= y$

Then, $5x + 18y = 7(x + y)$
$\Rightarrow 5x + 18y = 7x + 7y$
$\Rightarrow 18y - 7y = 7x - 5x$
$\Rightarrow 11y = 2x$
$\Rightarrow \frac{x}{y} = \frac{11}{2}$

$\therefore$ The ratio of two parts is $11 : 2$.

21. $\because x : y :: 5 : 2$

$\Rightarrow \frac{x}{y} = \frac{5}{2}$
$\Rightarrow 2x = 5y \Rightarrow 8x = 20y$
$\Rightarrow 8x + 9y = 20y + 9y = 29y$
and $8x + 2y = 20y + 2y = 22y$

$$\therefore \frac{8x+9y}{8x+2y} = \frac{29y}{22y} = \frac{29}{22}$$

22. We have to divide 76 in the ratio of
$7 : 5 : 3 : 4$
Sum of proportionals $= 7 + 5 + 3 + 4 = 19$

$$\therefore \text{Smallest share} = \frac{3}{19}\times 76 = 12$$

23. Let numbers are x and y
According to the question,
$x + y = 70$ ...(*i*)
and $x - y = 16$ ...(*ii*)
Solving (*i*) and (*ii*) we get $x = 43$
and $y = 27$
$\therefore$ Ratio of the numbers $= 43 : 27$

24. Ratio of two numbers $= 12 : 19$

$$\therefore \text{Value of the smaller number} = \frac{12}{31}\times 217 = 84$$

6

CHAPTER

Partnership

Partnership is a form of association of two or more persons who contribute resources like money together in order to carry on a business. It may be of simple or compound type.

Simple partnership is one in which the capitals of the partners are invested for the same time. The profits or losses are divided among the partners in the ratio of their investments.

Compound partnership is one in which the capitals of the partners are invested for different periods. In such cases, equivalent capitals are calculated for each partner by multiplying their capital contributions with time. The profits or losses are then divided in the ratio of these equivalent capitals. Thus, the ratio of profits is directly proportional to both capital invested as well as time.

The partner who invests the money in the business as well as takes part in its management, is known as **Working partner**.

The partner who only invests the money in the business and does not work, is known as **Sleeping partner**.

A working partner gets either monthly payment or a share in the profit for his contribution in the management of the business. This payment is deducted from the total profit before its distribution.

EXAMPLE: A, B and C invest ₹ 15000, ₹ 20000 and ₹ 25000 respectively in a business. The profit earned is ₹ 1200. Find the share of each in the profit.

SOLUTION: This is a case of simple partnership

Ratio of investments,	A	: B	: C
	= 15000	: 20000	: 25000
	= 3	: 4	: 5

Sum of the ratios = 3 + 4 + 5 = 12

Share in the profit

$$\text{For A} = \frac{3}{12} \times 1200 = ₹\,300$$

$$\text{For B} = \frac{4}{12} \times 1200 = ₹\,400$$

$$\text{For C} = \frac{5}{12} \times 1200 = ₹\,500$$

EXAMPLE: A and B are partners in a firm. A invests ₹ 15000 and B ₹ 25000. A is the working partner and gets 20% of the profit for his contribution in the management of the firm. B is the sleeping partner. If the profit is ₹ 475, find the share of each.

SOLUTION: First we have to deduct the payment to be made to A from the total profit for his contribution in the management of the firm.

20% of ₹ 475 = ₹ 95

Balance profit = 475 – 95 = ₹ 380

This has to be divided between A and B in the ratio of their investments *i.e.,* ₹ 15000 : ₹ 25000 = 3 : 5

$$\text{A's share} = ₹\,380 \times \frac{3}{8} = ₹\,142.5$$

$$\text{B's share} = ₹\,380 \times \frac{5}{8} = ₹\,237.5$$

Finally, A gets a total of (95 + 142.5) = ₹ 237.5 and B gets = ₹ 237.5

EXAMPLE: In a business A and B gained some amount in a certain ratio. B and C received the profit in the ratio as that of A and B. If B received ₹ 6400 and C received ₹ 10,000 then find the amount invested by B.

SOLUTION: Let the ratio of A's and B's profit be $\frac{a}{b}$.

Hence, the ratio of B's and C's profit = $\frac{a}{b}$

Thus, $A : B : C = a : b : \frac{b^2}{a}$

when A's profit, $a =$ ₹ 6400

and C's profit, $\frac{b^2}{a} =$ ₹ 10,000

$\Rightarrow \quad b^2 = 10{,}000 \times 6400 = 100 \times 100 \times 80 \times 80$

$\Rightarrow \quad b = 100 \times 80 = 8000$

Hence, the amount invested by B = ₹ 8000.

MULTIPLE CHOICE QUESTIONS

1. A, B and C share the profit in the ratio of 3 : 5 : 7. If the gain is ₹ 2040, then C's share is:
A. ₹ 360 B. ₹ 600
C. ₹ 952 D. ₹ 120

2. A, B and C started a business with ₹ 47000. A puts in ₹ 5000 more than B and B ₹ 3000 more than C. The share of A out of the profit of ₹ 14100 will be:
A. ₹ 3600 B. ₹ 4500
C. ₹ 6000 D. ₹ 6300

3. A starts a business with ₹ 5000. After 4 months B joins him with a sum of ₹ 4000. In the end of the year there is a profit of ₹ 8970. The share of A in the profit will be:
A. ₹ 3120 B. ₹ 4020
C. ₹ 5850 D. ₹ 6360

4. A, B, C are three partners in a business. The profit share of A is $\frac{3}{16}$ of the profit and B's share is $\frac{1}{4}$ of the profit. If C receives ₹ 243, then the amount received by B will be:
A. ₹ 90 B. ₹ 96
C. ₹ 108 D. ₹ 120

5. A, B and C share the profit in the ratio 2 : 3 : 7. If the average gain is ₹ 8000, then B's share is:
A. ₹ 2000 B. ₹ 1000
C. ₹ 1500 D. ₹ 3000

6. Ashok started a business investing ₹ 90,000. After 3 months Shabir joined him with a capital of ₹ 1,20,000. If at the end of one year the total profit made by them was ₹ 96,000, what will be the difference between their shares?
A. ₹ 24000 B. ₹ 8000
C. ₹ 20000 D. None of these

7. Mahesh received ₹ 6000 as his share out of the total profit of ₹ 9000 which he and Ram entered at the end of one year. If Mahesh invested ₹ 20,000 for 6 months, whereas Ram invested his amount for the whole year, what was the amount invested by Ram?
A. ₹ 4000 B. ₹ 5000
C. ₹ 3000 D. ₹ 6000

8. A and B started a business jointly. A's investment was thrice the investment of B and the period of his investment was two times the period of investment of B. If B received ₹ 40,000 as profit, then their total profit is:
A. ₹ 2,40,000 B. ₹ 28000
C. ₹ 24000 D. ₹ 2,80,000

9. Anil started a business investing ₹ 70,000. After 8 months Vimal joined him with a capital of ₹ 1,80,000. In what ratio should Anil and Vimal share the profit after two years?
A. 8 : 7 B. 7 : 5
C. 7 : 6 D. None of these

10. A, B and C starts a business. A invests ₹ 3,20,000 for four months. B invests ₹ 5,10,000 for three months and C invests ₹ 2,70,000 for five months. If at the end of year there is a profit of ₹ 1,24,800, then share of B is:
A. ₹ 79000 B. ₹ 49200
C. ₹ 50000 D. ₹ 45900

11. A, B and C contract a work for ₹ 550. Together A and B are to do $\frac{7}{11}$ of the work. The share of C should be:
A. ₹ 400 B. ₹ 300
C. ₹ 200 D. ₹ $183\frac{1}{3}$

12. Jagmohan, Rooplal and Pankaj rented a video cassette for one week at a rent of ₹ 350. If they use it for 6 hrs, 10 hrs and 12 hrs respectively, the rent to be paid by Pankaj is:
A. ₹ 75 B. ₹ 125
C. ₹ 35 D. ₹ 150

13. Manoj got ₹ 6000 as his share out of the total profit of ₹ 9000 which he and Ramesh earned at the end of one year. If Manoj invested ₹ 20,000 for 6 months, whereas Ramesh invested his amount for the whole year, the amount invested by Ramesh was:

A. ₹ 60,000 B. ₹ 10,000
C. ₹ 4000 D. ₹ 5000

14. A, B and C invest ₹ 2000, ₹ 3000 and ₹ 4000 in a business. After one year A removed his money, B and C continued the business for one more year. If the net profit after 2 years be ₹ 3200, then A's share in the profit is:

A. ₹ 1000 B. ₹ 600
C. ₹ 800 D. ₹ 400

15. A and B enter into partnership investing ₹ 12000 and ₹ 16000 respectively. After 8 months, C also joins the business with a capital of ₹ 15000. The share of C in a profit of ₹ 46500 after 2 years will be:

A. ₹ 12000 B. ₹ 14400
C. ₹ 19200 D. ₹ 21200

16. A, B and C rent a pasture. A puts in 10 oxen for 7 months, B 12 oxen for 5 months and C 15 oxen for 3 months for grazing. If the rent of the pasture is ₹ 175, how much must C pay as his share of rent?

A. ₹ 45 B. ₹ 50
C. ₹ 55 D. ₹ 60

17. Sumit started software business with ₹ 50,000. After 6 months Nitin joined him with ₹ 80,000. After three years they earned ₹ 24500 as profit. What is the share of Sumit in the profit?

A. ₹ 11500 B. ₹ 9050
C. ₹ 10500 D. ₹ 9500

18. A starts a business with ₹ 3500 and after 5 months B joins A as his partner. After a year, the profit is divided in the ratio 2 : 3. What is B's contribution in the capital?

A. ₹ 8000 B. ₹ 8500
C. ₹ 9000 D. ₹ 750

19. M, P and Q together started a business. M invested ₹ 6500 for 6 months, P invested ₹ 8400 for 5 months and Q invested ₹ 10000 for 3 months. M is working member for which he gets 5% extra profit. If the total gain is ₹ 7400, then Q's share is:

A. ₹ 1500
B. ₹ 2100
C. ₹ 3200
D. None of the above

20. Sarita started a business by investing ₹ 50,000. After 6 months Abhishek joined her by investing ₹ 75000. After his 6 months Nisha joined with ₹ 125000. What is the ratio of profit share after 2 years among Sarita, Abhishek and Nisha?

A. 4 : 5 : 6 B. 8 : 9 : 10
C. 8 : 9 : 12 D. 4 : 5 : 8

21. A and B started a business with the investment of ₹ 80000 and ₹ 60000 respectively. At the end of the year total profit in the business will be divided between them in the ratio of:

A. 2 : 3 B. 3 : 4
C. 2 : 1 D. 4 : 3

22. A and B started a business in partnership with the investment of ₹ 4000 and ₹ 6000 respectively. If at the end of the year total profit is ₹ 2250, what will each of them get?

A. ₹ 900, ₹ 1350 B. ₹ 800, ₹ 1450
C. ₹ 1000, ₹ 1250 D. ₹ 1200, ₹ 1050

23. Sonu, Monu and Mohit together start a business with the investment of ₹ 1800, ₹ 1500 and ₹ 1600 respectively. If at the end of the year, Monu gains a profit of ₹ 900 the total profit in the business is:

A. ₹ 2880 B. ₹ 2940
C. ₹ 3200 D. ₹ 3240

ANSWERS

1	2	3	4	5	6	7	8	9	10
C	C	C	C	A	D	B	D	D	D
11	**12**	**13**	**14**	**15**	**16**	**17**	**18**	**19**	**20**
C	D	D	D	A	A	C	C	D	B
21	**22**	**23**							
D	A	B							

EXPLANATORY ANSWERS

1. C's share = $\frac{7}{15} \times 2040$ = ₹ 952.

2. Let C's capital be ₹ x

Then B's capital = ₹ $(x + 3000)$

and A's capital = ₹ $(x + 3000 + 5000) = x + 8000$

$\Rightarrow \quad x + (x + 3000) + (x + 8000) = 47000$

$\Rightarrow \quad 3x + 11000 = 47000$

$\Rightarrow \quad 3x = 47000 - 11000$

$= 36000$

$\Rightarrow \quad x = 12000$

Thus, capital of A, B and C are ₹ 20000, ₹ 15000 and ₹ 12000 respectively.

∴ Profit sharing ratio = 20 : 15 : 12

∴ Profit of A = $\frac{20}{47} \times 14100$ = ₹ 6000

3. ₹ 5000 × 12 = ₹ 60,000 for A

₹ 4000 × (12 – 4) = 4000 × 8 = ₹ 32000 for B

Ratio of profit sharing = 60000 : 32000

= 60 : 32 = 15 : 8

∴ Share of A in the profit = $\frac{15}{23} \times 8970$

= 15 × 390 = ₹ 5850

4. Let the profit be ₹ 1. Then,

$$A : B : C = \frac{3}{16} : \frac{1}{4} : \left[1 - \left(\frac{3}{16} + \frac{1}{4}\right)\right]$$

$$= \frac{3}{16} : \frac{1}{4} : \frac{9}{16}$$

$$= \frac{3}{16} : \frac{4}{16} : \frac{9}{16} \text{ i.e., } 3 : 4 : 9$$

when C's share is ₹ 9, then B's share = ₹ 4

when C's share is ₹ 243, then B's share

$= \frac{4 \times 243}{9}$ = ₹ 108

5. B's share $= \frac{3}{2+3+7} \times 8000$

$= \frac{3 \times 8000}{12}$ = ₹ 2000

6. The ratio of their investment

$= 12 \times 90000 : (12 - 3) \times 120000$

$= 12 \times 9 : 9 \times 12 = 1 : 1$

Ashok's share = $\frac{1}{1+1} \times 96000$ = ₹ 48000

Shabir's share = $\frac{1}{1+1} \times 96000$ = ₹ 48000

Difference between their shares

= ₹ 48000 – ₹ 48000 = 0.

7. The ratio of their profit

= ₹ 6000 : ₹ (9000 – 6000)

= ₹ 6000 : ₹ 3000 = 2 : 1

Let ₹ x be the amount invested by Ram.

The ratio of their profit = The ratio of their investment

$\Rightarrow \quad 2 : 1 = 6 \times 20000 : 12 \times x$

$\Rightarrow \quad \frac{2}{1} = \frac{6 \times 20000}{12 \times x} \Rightarrow 2x = 10000$

$\Rightarrow \quad x = 5000$

∴ The investment of Ram is ₹ 5000.

8. Let ₹ x be the investment of B and n years be the period of investment of B.

Given : A's investment = 3 × ₹ x = ₹ $3x$

and period of investment of A = $2n$ years

∴ The ratio of investment of A and B

$= 2n \times 3x : n \times x$

$= 6nx : nx = 6 : 1$

Let the total profit be ₹ y

Given B's share in profit = ₹ 40,000

$\Rightarrow \frac{1}{6+1} \times y$ = ₹ 40,000 $\Rightarrow y$ = ₹ 2,80,000

∴ Total profit is ₹ 2,80,000.

9. The ratio of Anil's and Vimal's share in the profit

= Ratio of their investments

= 24 × 70000 : 16 × 180000

= 24 × 7 : 16 × 18 = 7 : 12

10. The ratio of investments of A, B and C

= 4 × 320000 : 3 × 510000 : 5 × 270000

= 4 × 32 : 3 × 51 : 5 × 27

= 128 : 153 : 135

Total profit after 1 year = ₹ 124800

Share of B = ₹ $\frac{153}{128+153+135} \times 124800$

= ₹ $\frac{153}{416} \times 124800$ = ₹ 45900

11. C's share = ₹ $\left(550 \times \frac{4}{11}\right)$ = ₹ 200

12. Ratio of rents = 6 : 10 : 12 = 3 : 5 : 6

$\therefore$ Pankaj's share of rent = ₹$\left(350\times\frac{6}{14}\right)$ = ₹ 150

13. Let amount invested by Ramesh be ₹ x

$\therefore$ 20000 × 6 : 12x = 6000 : 3000

i.e., $\frac{12x}{120000}=\frac{3000}{6000}$ or x = ₹ 5000

14. Ratio of investments

= (2000 × 1) : (3000 × 2) : (4000 × 2)

= 1 : 3 : 4

$\therefore$ A's share = ₹$\left(3200\times\frac{1}{8}\right)$ = ₹ 400.

15. Ratio of investments

= (12000 × 24) : (16000 × 24) : (15000 × 16)

= 6 : 8 : 5

C's share of profit = ₹$\left(45600\times\frac{5}{19}\right)$ = ₹ 12000

16. Ratio of A, B and C shares in the rent

= 7 × 10 : 5 × 12 : 3 × 15 = 14 : 12 : 9

$\therefore$ Rent paid by C = $\frac{9}{14+12+9}\times 175$

= $\frac{9}{35}\times 175$ = ₹ 45

17. Ratio of investments

= $50000\times 3 : 80000\times\frac{5}{2}$

$\left[2\frac{1}{2}\text{ years} = \frac{5}{2}\text{ years}\right]$

= 15 : 20 = 3 : 4

Sumit's share = $\frac{3}{3+4}\times 24500$

= $\frac{3}{7}\times 24500$

= 3 × 3500 = ₹ 10500

18. Let B's contribution be x_2 for (12 – 5) = 7 months

Then, $t_1x_1 : t_2x_2 = 2 : 3$

$\Rightarrow$ 12 × 3500 : 7 × x_2 = 2 : 3

$\Rightarrow$ 2 × 7 × x_2 = 3 × 12 × 3500

$\therefore$ $x_2=\frac{3\times 12\times 3500}{2\times 7}$

= ₹ 9000

19. Total profit = ₹ 7400

M's extra share = $7400\times\frac{5}{100}$ = ₹ 370

Remaining profit = 7400 – 370 = ₹ 7030

Profit share ratio = M : P : Q

= 6 × 6500 : 5 × 8400 : 3 × 10000

= 13 : 14 : 10

$\therefore$ Q's share = $\frac{10}{13+14+10}\times 7030$

= $\frac{10}{37}\times 7030$ = ₹ 1900

20. Required ratio = $t_1x_1 : t_2x_2 : t_3x_3$

= 24 × 50000 : (24 – 6) × 75000 : (24 – 12) × 125000

= 24 × 50 : 18 × 75 : 12 × 125

= 24 × 2 : 18 × 3 : 12 × 5 [dividing by 25]

= 4 × 2 : 3 × 3 : 2 × 5 [dividing by 6]

= 8 : 9 : 10

21. The two partners invest their capitals for the same period

$\therefore$ Profit will be divided between them in the ratio of their capitals

$\therefore$ Ratio between their profits = 80000 : 60000

= 4 : 3

22. A and B ivest their capitals for the same period.

Ratio between the profits of A and B

= 4000 : 6000 = 2 : 3

Sum of proportionals = 2 + 3 = 5

Total profit = ₹ 2250

$\therefore$ A's share = $\frac{2}{5}\times 2250$ = ₹ 900

B's share = $\frac{3}{5}\times 2250$ = ₹ 1350

23. Sonu, Monu and Mohit invest their capitals for the same period

Ratio of their profits = 1800 : 1500 : 1600

= 18 : 15 : 16

Sum of proportionals = 18 + 15 + 16 = 49

Mohit's profit = ₹ 900

$\therefore$ Total profit in the business = $\frac{900}{15}\times 49$

= ₹ 2940

7 CHAPTER

Average

The sum of all the quantities of same kind divided by their number is called average (or mean) of those quantities.

FORMULAE

1. $\text{Average} = \left(\dfrac{\text{Sum of observations}}{\text{Number of observations}}\right)$
2. Sum of the first n natural numbers
$= 1 + 2 + 3 + ... + n = \dfrac{n(n+1)}{2}$
3. Sum of the squares of the first n natural numbers
$= 1^2 + 2^2 + ... + n^2 = \dfrac{n(n+1)(2n+1)}{6}$
4. Sum of the cubes of the first n natural numbers
$= 1^3 + 2^3 + ... + n^3 = \left\{\dfrac{n(n+1)}{2}\right\}^2$
5. Sum of the first n odd numbers
$= 1 + 3 + 5 + ... + (2n - 1) = n^2$
6. Distance between two stations P and Q is x km. A person covers the journey from P to Q at 'a' km/hr and returns back to P with a uniform speed of 'b' km/hr. Then the average speed of the person during the whole journey
$= \dfrac{2ab}{a+b}$ km/hr.

Different kinds of mean or average:

(*a*) Arithmetic mean
(*b*) Geometric mean
(*c*) Harmonic mean

(*a*) **Arithmetic Mean:** It is most popularly used of all the averages. For example, average income, average profit, average mileage etc. As defined earlier, it is the sum total of all values of items divided by the total number of items. For detailed discussion we will confine ourselves to Arithmetic Mean only because this is the most relevant of all the average for us.
Let $x_1, x_2, x_3, ..., x_n$ be the n values of x.
Their average is denoted by $\bar{x}$ and given by

$$\bar{x} = \frac{\text{Sum of observations}}{\text{Total number of observations}}$$

or $$\bar{x} = \frac{x_1 + x_2 + x_3 + ... + x_n}{n}$$

(*b*) **Geometric Mean :** For observations $x_1, x_2, x_3, ..., x_n$ the geometric mean denoted by G.M. is defined as:

$$\text{G.M.} = (x_1 . x_2 . x_3 ... x_n)^{1/n}$$

It is useful in calculating averages of ratios such as average population, growth rate, average percentage increase etc.

(*c*) **Harmonic Mean:** It is defined as

$$\text{H.M.} = \frac{n}{\frac{1}{x_1} + \frac{1}{x_2} + ... + \frac{1}{x_n}}.$$

Example: Find the average of first ten prime numbers.

Solution: First ten prime numbers are 2, 3, 5, 7, 11, 13, 17, 19, 23 and 29.

$$\therefore \text{Average} = \frac{2+3+5+7+11+13+17+19+23+29}{10}$$

$$= \frac{129}{10} = 12.9$$

EXAMPLE: If x_1, x_2, x_3, x_4, x_5 are five consecutive odd numbers then find the average of these numbers.

SOLUTION: Since x_1 is the first odd number.

$$\therefore \quad x_2 = x_1 + 2$$
$$x_3 = x_2 + 2 = x_1 + 4$$
$$x_4 = x_3 + 2 = x_1 + 6$$
$$x_5 = x_4 + 2 = x_1 + 8$$

$$\therefore \text{ Average} = \frac{x_1 + x_1 + 2 + x_1 + 4 + x_1 + 6 + x_1 + 8}{5}$$

$$= \frac{5x_1 + 20}{5} = \frac{5(x_1 + 4)}{5} = x_1 + 4$$

EXAMPLE: If the average of four consecutive even numbers is 27, then find the largest of these numbers.

SOLUTION: Let x be the first even number in the series of four consecutive even numbers.

$\therefore$ 2nd even number = $x + 2$

3rd even number = $x + 4$

4th even number = $x + 6$

$$\text{Average} = \frac{x + x + 2 + x + 4 + x + 6}{4}$$

$$\Rightarrow \quad 27 = \frac{4x + 12}{4}$$
$$\Rightarrow \quad 4x + 12 = 27 \times 4 = 108$$
$$\Rightarrow \quad 4x = 96$$
$$\Rightarrow \quad x = 24$$

Largest number in this series is $x + 6$

i.e., $24 + 6 = 30$

EXAMPLE: The average of eight numbers is 14. The average of six of these numbers is 16. What is the average of the remaining two numbers?

SOLUTION: Sum of the eight numbers = $14 \times 8 = 112$

Sum of six of these eight numbers = $16 \times 6 = 96$

$\therefore$ Sum of the remaining two numbers = $112 - 96 = 16$

$\therefore$ Average of the remaining two numbers = $\frac{16}{2} = 8$

EXAMPLE: What is the average of first 30 multiples of 7?

SOLUTION: Required Average

$$= \frac{7 + 14 + 21 + ... + 210}{30}$$
$$= \frac{7(1 + 2 + 3 + ... + 30)}{30}$$
$$= \frac{7 \times 30(30 + 1)}{2 \times 30}$$
$$= \frac{7 \times 31}{2} = \frac{217}{2} = 108.5$$

EXAMPLE: The average of 11 results is 50. If the average of first six results is 49 and that of last six is 52, find the sixth result.

SOLUTION: Sum of 11 results = $11 \times 50 = 550$

Sum of first 6 results $6 \times 49 = 294$

Sum of last 6 results = $6 \times 52 = 312$

$\therefore$ 6th result = $294 + 312 - 550$

$= 56$

EXAMPLE: The average age of three boys is 15 years. If their ages are in the ratio 3 : 5 : 7. What is the age of the youngest boy?

SOLUTION: Let the ages of the three boys be $3x$, $5x$ and $7x$.

$$\text{Average age} = \frac{3x + 5x + 7x}{3} = 5x$$

and $5x = 15 \Rightarrow x = 3$

The age of the youngest boy = $3x = 3 \times 3 = 9$ years.

EXAMPLE: The average of 100 observations is 45. It was later found that two observations 19 and 31 were incorrectly recorded as 91 and 13. Find the correct average.

SOLUTION: Sum of 100 observations

$= 100 \times 45 = 4500$

New sum of 100 observations

$= 4500 + (19 + 31) - (91 + 13)$

$= 4500 + 50 - 104 = 4446$

$$\text{Correct average} = \frac{4446}{100} = 44.46$$

MULTIPLE CHOICE QUESTIONS

1. The average of first five multiples of 3 is:
A. 3 B. 9
C. 12 D. 15

2. The average of 25 results is 18, that of first 12 is 14 and of the last 12 is 17. Thirteenth result is:
A. 78 B. 85
C. 28 D. 72

3. Out of three numbers, the first is twice the second and is half of the third. If the average of the three numbers is 56, the three numbers in order are:
A. 48, 96, 24 B. 48, 24, 96
C. 96, 24, 48 D. 96, 48, 24

4. The sum of three numbers is 98. If the ratio between first and second be 2 : 3 and that between second and third be 5 : 8, then the second number is:
A. 30 B. 20
C. 58 D. 48

5. The average age of a committee of seven trustees is the same as it was 5 years ago; a young man having been substituted for one of them. The new man compared to the replaced old man, is younger in age by:
A. 5 years B. 7 years
C. 12 years D. 35 years

6. The average expenditure of a man for the first five months is ₹ 120 and for the next seven months is ₹ 130. His monthly average income if he saves ₹ 290 in that year, is:
A. ₹ 160 B. ₹ 170
C. ₹ 150 D. ₹ 140

7. The average salary of 20 workers in an office is ₹ 1900 per month. If the manager's salary is added, the average becomes ₹ 2000 per month. The manager's salary is:
A. ₹ 24000 B. ₹ 25200
C. ₹ 45600 D. None of these

8. The average temperature of first 3 days is 27°C and of the next 3 days is 29°C. If the average of the whole week is 28.5°C, the temperature of the last day is:
A. 31.5°C B. 10.5°C
C. 21°C D. 42°C

9. A cricketer scored 180 runs in the first test and 258 runs in the second. How many runs should he score in the third test so that his average score in the three tests would be 230 runs?
A. 219 B. 242
C. 334 D. None of these

10. The average of first five prime numbers is:
A. 5.0 B. 5.2
C. 5.6 D. 6.0

11. The average weight of 3 men A, B and C is 84 kg. Another man D joins the group and the average now becomes 80 kg. If another man E, whose weight is 3 kg more than that of D, replaces A, then average weight of B, C, D and E becomes 79 kg. The weight of A is:
A. 70 kg B. 72 kg
C. 75 kg D. 80 kg

12. The average age of A, B, C, D 5 years ago was 45 years. By including x, the present average of all the five is 49 years. The present age of x is:
A. 64 years B. 48 years
C. 45 years D. 40 years

13. The average height of 30 boys, out of a class of 50, is 160 cm. If the average height of the remaining boys is 165 cm, the average height of the whole class (in cm) is:
A. 161 B. 162
C. 163 D. 164

14. The average age of an adult class is 40 years. 12 new students with an average age of 32 years join the class, thereby decreasing the average of the class by 4 years. The original strength of the class was:
A. 10 B. 11
C. 12 D. 15

15. If a, b, c, d, e are five consecutive odd numbers, their average is:
A. $5(a+4)$ B. $\frac{abcde}{5}$
C. $5(a+b+c+d+e)$ D. None of these

16. Of the three numbers, second is twice the first and is also thrice the third. If the average of the three numbers is 44, the largest number is:
A. 24 B. 36
C. 72 D. 108

17. The average of 50 numbers is 38. If two numbers namely, 45 and 55 are discarded, the average of remaining number is:

A. 36.50 B. 37.00
C. 37.50 D. 37.52

18. The average height of 30 girls out of a class of 40 is 160 cm and that of the remaining girls is 156 cm. The average height of the whole class is:

A. 158 cm B. 158.5 cm
C. 159 cm D. 159.5 cm

19. The average of n numbers is x. If 36 is subtracted from any two numbers each, then new average is $(x - 8)$. The value of n is:

A. 6 B. 8
C. 9 D. 72

20. The average salary of male employees in a firm is ₹ 520 and that of female employees is ₹ 420. The mean salary of all the employees is ₹ 500. The percentage of female employees is:

A. 40% B. 30%
C. 25% D. 20%

ANSWERS

1	**2**	**3**	**4**	**5**	**6**	**7**	**8**	**9**	**10**
B	A	B	A	D	C	D	A	D	C
11	**12**	**13**	**14**	**15**	**16**	**17**	**18**	**19**	**20**
C	C	B	C	D	C	C	C	C	D

EXPLANATORY ANSWERS

1. Average $= \dfrac{3(1+2+3+4+5)}{5} = \dfrac{(3\times15)}{5} = 9$

2. Thirteenth result
$= [(25 \times 18) - (12 \times 14 + 12 \times 17)]$
$= [450 - (168 + 204)]$
$= 450 - 372 = 78.$

3. Let the numbers be $2x$, x and $4x$.

$$\text{Average} = \frac{2x+x+4x}{3} = \frac{7x}{3}$$

According to the question,

$$\frac{7x}{3} = 56$$

$\Rightarrow \quad 7x = 3 \times 56$

$\Rightarrow \quad x = \dfrac{3\times56}{7} = 24$

Hence, the numbers in order are 48, 24 and 96.

4. Let the numbers be x, y, z, then

$x + y + z = 98$

$\dfrac{x}{y} = \dfrac{2}{3}$ and $\dfrac{y}{z} = \dfrac{5}{8}$

$\therefore \quad x = \dfrac{2y}{3}$ and $z = \dfrac{8y}{5}$

So, $\dfrac{2y}{3} + y + \dfrac{8y}{5} = 98$

$\Rightarrow \quad \dfrac{10y+15y+24y}{15} = 98$

$\Rightarrow \quad 49y = 15 \times 98$

$\Rightarrow \quad y = \dfrac{15\times98}{49} = 30$

5. During these five years, the total age would have increased by $(7 \times 5) = 35$ years. But, it remains the same as it was 5 years ago.
$\therefore$ The new man is younger than the replaced old man by 35 years.

6. Total income for 12 months
$= ₹\ (120 \times 5 + 130 \times 7 + 290)$
$= ₹\ 1800$

Average monthly income $= ₹\dfrac{1800}{12} = ₹150$

7. Total salary of 20 workers
$= 20 \times 1900 = ₹\ 38000$

Total salary of 20 workers and manager
$= 21 \times 2000 = ₹\ 42000$

Monthly salary of the manager
$= 42000 - 38000 = ₹\ 4000.$

8. Total temperature of first 3 days
$= 27 \times 3 = 81°C$

Total temperature of next 3 days
$= 29 \times 3 = 87°C$

Total temperature of 7 days

$= 28.5 \times 7 = 199.5°C$

Temperature of the last day

$= 199.5 - (81 + 87)$

$= 199.5 - 168 = 31.5°C$

9. Let runs he should score in third test be x :

Then, $\frac{180+258+x}{3} = 230$

$\Rightarrow \quad x = 690 - 438 = 252.$

10. Average $= \frac{2+3+5+7+11}{5} = \frac{28}{5} = 5.6.$

11. Weight of D = $(80 \times 4 - 84 \times 3)$ kg = 68 kg

Weight of E = $(68 + 3)$ kg = 71 kg

(B + C + D + E)'s weight = (79×4) kg = 316 kg

$\therefore$ (B + C)'s weight

$= [316 - (68 + 71)]$ kg = 177 kg

Hence, A's weight

$= [(84 \times 3) - 177]$kg = 75 kg

12. Total age of A, B, C and D 5 years ago

$= (45 \times 4)$ years = 180 years.

Total present age of A, B, C, D and x

$= (49 \times 5)$ years = 245 years.

Present age of A, B, C and D

$= (180 + 5 \times 4)$ years = 200 years.

$\therefore$ Present age of x = 45 years.

13. Total height of 30 boys = $30 \times 160 = 4800$

Total height of 20 boys = $20 \times 165 = 3300$

Total height of 50 boys = 8100

Average height of 50 boys = $\frac{8100}{50} = 162.$

14. $40x + 12 \times 32 = (12 + x) \times 36$

$\Rightarrow \quad 40x + 384 = 432 + 36x$

$\Rightarrow \quad 4x = 432 - 384 = 48$

$\Rightarrow \quad x = \frac{48}{4} = 12$

Hence, the original strength of the class was 12.

15. Average $= \frac{a+a+2+a+4+a+6+a+8}{5}$

$= \frac{5a+20}{5} = \frac{5(a+4)}{5} = a+4$

16. Let the numbers be x, $2x$ and $\frac{2x}{3}$.

$$\text{Average} = \frac{x+2x+\frac{2x}{3}}{3}$$

$\Rightarrow \quad \frac{11x}{9} = 44$

$\Rightarrow \quad x = \frac{44 \times 9}{11} = 36$

So, the numbers are 36, 72 and 24.

Hence, the largest one is 72.

17. Total of 50 numbers = $50 \times 38 = 1900$

Average of 48 numbers $= \frac{1900-(45+55)}{48}$

$= \frac{1800}{48} = 37.50$

18. The average of the whole class

$= \frac{(30 \times 160 + 10 \times 156)}{40} = \frac{4800+1560}{40}$

$= \frac{6360}{40} = 159$ cm

19. $\frac{nx-36-36}{n} = x - 8$

$\Rightarrow \quad nx - 72 = nx - 8n$

$\Rightarrow \quad 8n = 72$

$\Rightarrow \quad n = 9$

20. Let the total employees be 100.

n_1 = number of females = x

n_2 = number of males = $100 - x$

$$\bar{x} = \frac{n_1\bar{x}_1 + n_2\bar{x}_2}{n_1 + n_2}$$

$\Rightarrow \quad 500 = \frac{x \times 420 + (100-x) \times 520}{100}$

$\Rightarrow \quad 500 = \frac{42x + 5200 - 52x}{10}$

$\Rightarrow \quad 5000 = 5200 - 10x$

$\Rightarrow \quad 10x = 200$

$\Rightarrow \quad x = 20$ *i.e.*, 20%.

8

CHAPTER

Profit and Loss

Cost Price (CP)

The price at which an article is purchased is called the cost price of the article.

Selling Price (SP)

The price at which an article is sold is called the selling price of the article.

Profit or Gain

If SP is greater than the CP, the seller is said to have a profit or gain.

Clearly, Gain = SP – CP

Loss

If SP is less than CP, the seller is said to have a loss.

Clearly, Loss = CP – SP

Profit or loss per cent is calculated on cost price.

$$\text{Profit \%} = \frac{\text{Profit}}{\text{CP}} \times 100$$

$$\text{Loss \%} = \frac{\text{Loss}}{\text{CP}} \times 100$$

$$\text{SP} = \frac{\text{CP} \times (100 + \text{Profit\%})}{100}, \text{ if there is gain}$$

$$\text{SP} = \frac{\text{CP} \times (100 - \text{Loss\%})}{100}, \text{ if there is loss}$$

$$\text{CP} = \text{SP} \times \left(\frac{100}{100 + \text{Profit\%}}\right), \text{ if there is gain}$$

$$\text{CP} = \text{SP} \times \left(\frac{100}{100 - \text{Loss\%}}\right), \text{ if there is loss}$$

If an article is sold at a gain of 20%,

then, SP = (120% of CP)

If an article is sold at a loss of 20%,

then, SP = (80% of CP)

Overheads

The expenses incurred on transportation, rent, personnel salary, maintenance, packaging, advertisements and the like are included under the general heading of overheads. These overhead and the profit when added to the cost price determine the selling price. If the overheads are not separately mentioned in the problem, we assume it to be zero or else these have been included in the cost price itself.

Discount

It is an offer made by the seller to the buyer for reduction in price to be paid. There are several cases where discounts are allowed. For instance, to dispose off old goods, to increase its market share when the customer is ready to pay the whole amount in cash instead of instalment and so on. It is subtracted from the original price and is usually expressed as per cent or a fraction of the marked price. The price obtained after deducting the discount from the original price is the selling price which the customer has to pay.

Example: If an article is purchased for ₹ 570 and sold for ₹ 518.70, find the lost per cent.

Solution: CP = ₹ 570

SP = ₹ 518.70

∴ Loss = CP – SP

= 570 – 518.70 = ₹ 51.30

$$\text{Loss \%} = \frac{\text{Loss}}{\text{CP}} \times 100 = \frac{51.30}{570} \times 100$$

$$= \frac{5130}{570} = \frac{513}{57} = 9\%$$

EXAMPLE: A man buys a TV for ₹ 16,000. After two years he sells it for ₹ 12800. Find his loss per cent.

SOLUTION: $\text{Loss \%} = \frac{\text{Loss}}{\text{CP}} \times 100$

$$= \frac{16000-12800}{16000} \times 100$$

$$= \frac{3200}{16000} \times 100 = 20\%$$

EXAMPLE: Mohan sells his watch at a loss of ₹ 500 for ₹ 1000. Find the cost price and loss per cent.

SOLUTION: $\text{CP} = \text{SP} + \text{Loss}$

$$= 1000 + 500 = ₹\ 1500$$

$$\text{Loss \%} = \frac{\text{Loss}}{\text{CP}} \times 100 = \frac{500}{1500} \times 100$$

$$= \frac{100}{3} = 33\frac{1}{3}\%$$

EXAMPLE: Ravi buys an article for ₹ 5000 and sells it at 20% gain. Find it selling price.

SOLUTION: $\text{Profit} = 20\% \text{ of CP} = \frac{20}{100} \times 5000$

$\Rightarrow$ $\text{Profit} = ₹\ 1000$

$$\text{SP} = \text{CP} + \text{Profit}$$

$$= 5000 + 1000$$

$$= ₹\ 6000$$

EXAMPLE: A man sells an article at 20% gain for ₹ 3600. Find its cost price.

SOLUTION: Let CP = ₹ 100

then SP = 100 + 20 = ₹ 120

When SP ₹ 120 then CP = ₹ 100

When SP ₹ 3600 then CP = $\frac{100}{120} \times 3600$

Hence CP = ₹ 3000

EXAMPLE: The cost price of 6 pens is equal to the selling price of 4 pens. Find the profit per cent.

SOLUTION: SP of 4 pens = CP of 6 pens

SP of 2 pens = CP of $\frac{6}{4} \times 2 = 3$ pens

Profit = CP of 3 pens

investment = CP of 6 pens

$$\text{Profit \%} = \frac{3}{6} \times 100 = 50\%$$

Alternatively:

Let the CP of 1 pen be ₹ x.

$\therefore$ CP of 6 pens = ₹ $6x$

Also, SP of 4 pens = ₹ $6x$

$\therefore$ SP of 6 pens = $\frac{6x}{4} \times 6 = ₹\ 9x$

$$\text{Profit} = \text{SP} - \text{CP} = 9x - 6x = 3x$$

$$\text{Profit \%} = \frac{3x}{6x} \times 100 = 50\%$$

EXAMPLE: If CP of 20 tables is equal to the SP of 25 tables. Find the loss percent.

SOLUTION: Let the CP of 1 table be ₹ x.

$\therefore$ CP of 20 tables = ₹ $20x$

Also, SP of 25 tables = ₹ $20x$

$\therefore$ SP of 20 tables = ₹ $\frac{20x}{25} \times 20 = ₹\ 16x$

$$\text{Loss} = 20x - 16x = 4x$$

$$\text{Loss \%} = \frac{\text{Loss}}{\text{CP}} \times 100$$

$$= \frac{4x}{20x} \times 100 = 20\%$$

EXAMPLE: Ram sold a book at a profit of 6%. Had he sold it for ₹ 2 more he would have gained 10%. Find the cost price of the book.

SOLUTION: (10% – 6%) of CP = 4% of CP = ₹ 2

$\Rightarrow$ $\frac{4}{100} \times \text{CP} = 2$

$\Rightarrow$ $\text{CP} = \frac{200}{4} = ₹\ 50$

EXAMPLE: An article is sold for ₹ 4600 at a gain of 15%. What would be the profit or loss per cent if it is sold for ₹ 3600?

SOLUTION: $\text{CP} = 4600 \times \frac{100}{115} = ₹\ 4000$

$$\text{Loss \%} = \frac{4000-3600}{4000} \times 100 = 10\%$$

MULTIPLE CHOICE QUESTIONS

1. A loss of 5% was suffered by selling a plot for ₹ 4085. The cost price of the plot was:
A. ₹ 4350　B. ₹ 4259.25
C. ₹ 4200　D. ₹ 4300

2. On selling an article for ₹ 240, a trader loses 4%. In order to gain 10%, he must sell that article for:
A. ₹ 264.00　B. ₹ 273.20
C. ₹ 275.00　D. ₹ 280.00

3. A man purchased a watch for ₹ 400 and sold it at a gain of 20% of the selling price. The selling price of the watch is:
A. ₹ 300　B. ₹ 320
C. ₹ 440　D. ₹ 500

4. If 5% more is gained by selling an article for ₹ 350 than by selling it for ₹ 340, the cost of the article is:
A. ₹ 50　B. ₹ 160
C. ₹ 200　D. ₹ 225

5. Profit after selling a commodity for ₹ 425 is same as loss after selling it for ₹ 355. The cost of the commodity is:
A. ₹ 385　B. ₹ 390
C. ₹ 395　D. ₹ 400

6. The cost price of an article, which on being sold at a gain of 12% yields ₹ 6 more than when it is sold at a loss of 12%, is:
A. ₹ 30　B. ₹ 25
C. ₹ 20　D. ₹ 24

7. The CP of an article which is sold at a loss of 25% for ₹150, is:
A. ₹ 125　B. ₹ 175
C. ₹ 200　D. ₹ 225

8. When the price of pressure cooker was increased by 15%, its sale fell down by 15%. The effect on the money receipt was:
A. no effect　B. 15% decrease
C. 7.5% increase　D. 2.25% decrease

9. A man sells 320 mangoes at the cost price of 400 mangoes. His gain per cent is:
A. 10%　B. 25%
C. 15%　D. 20%

10. By selling 12 oranges for one rupee a man loses 20%. How many for a rupee should he sell to get a gain of 20%?
A. 5　B. 8
C. 10　D. 15

11. A man sells a car to his friend at 10% loss. If the friend sells it for ₹ 54000 and gains 20%, the original CP of the car was:
A. ₹ 25000　B. ₹ 37500
C. ₹ 50000　D. ₹ 60000

12. The loss incurred on selling an article for ₹ 270 is as much as the profit made after selling it at 10% profit. The CP of the article is:
A. ₹ 90　B. ₹ 110
C. ₹ 363　D. ₹ 300

13. An item costing ₹ 200 is being sold at 10% loss. If the price is further reduced by 5%, the selling price will be:
A. ₹ 179　B. ₹ 175
C. ₹ 171　D. ₹ 170

14. A trader lists his articles 20% above CP and allows a discount of 10% on cash payment. His gain per cent is:
A. 10%　B. 6%
C. 8%　D. 5%

15. A discount series of 10%, 20% and 40% is equal to a single discount of:
A. 50%　B. 56.80%
C. 70%　D. 70.28%

16. An umbrella marked at ₹ 80 is sold for ₹ 68, the rate of discount is:
A. 12%　B. 15%
C. $17\frac{11}{17}\%$　D. 20%

17. A reduction of 20% in the price of mangoes enables a person to purchase 12 more for ₹ 15. The price of 16 mangoes before reduction was:
A. ₹ 5　B. ₹ 6
C. ₹ 7　D. ₹ 9

18. Tarun bought a TV with 20% discount on the labelled price. Had he bought it with 25% discount, he would have saved ₹ 500. At what price did he buy the TV?
A. ₹ 5,000　B. ₹ 10,000
C. ₹ 12,000　D. None of these

19. If a commission of 10% is given on the marked price of a book, the publisher gains 20%. If the commission is increased to 15%, the gain is:

A. $16\frac{2}{3}\%$ B. $13\frac{1}{3}\%$

C. $15\frac{1}{6}\%$ D. None of these

20. There would be 10% loss if rice is sold at ₹ 5.40 per kg. At what price per kg should it be sold to earn a profit of 20%?

A. ₹ 7.20 B. ₹ 7.02
C. ₹ 6.48 D. ₹ 6

21. A merchant sold two cows for ₹ 8400 and ₹ 8800 respectively. If he earns profit of 20% on the first and 10% on the second, his total profit is:

A. ₹ 4200 B. ₹ 2100
C. ₹ 2400 D. ₹ 2200

22. By selling an article for ₹ 4080 a man loes 15%. Cost price of article is:

A. ₹ 4800 B. ₹ 4500
C. ₹ 5000 D. ₹ 5180

ANSWERS

1	2	3	4	5	6	7	8	9	10
D	C	D	C	B	B	C	D	B	B
11	**12**	**13**	**14**	**15**	**16**	**17**	**18**	**19**	**20**
C	D	C	C	B	B	A	D	B	A
21	**22**								
D	A								

EXPLANATORY ANSWERS

1. Loss = 5%, SP = ₹ 4085

Let CP = ₹ 100

∴ SP = ₹ 100 − 5 = ₹ 95

When SP ₹ 95 then CP = ₹ 100

When SP ₹ 4085 then CP = $\frac{100}{95} \times 4085$

= 4300

Hence, the cost price of the plot was ₹ 4300.

2. Loss = 4%, SP = ₹ 240

Let CP = ₹ 100

∴ SP = 100 − 4 = 96

When SP ₹ 96 then CP = ₹ 100

When SP ₹ 240 then CP = $\frac{100}{96} \times 240$ = ₹ 250

Again 100 + 10 = 110

When CP 100 then SP = ₹ 110

When CP 250 then SP = $\frac{110}{100} \times 250$ = ₹ 275

3. Let SP = ₹ x

then, profit = $\frac{20}{100} \times x$ = ₹ $\frac{x}{5}$

CP = SP − profit = $x - \frac{x}{5}$ = ₹ $\frac{4x}{5}$

According to the question,

$$\frac{4x}{5} = 400 \quad \Rightarrow \quad 4x = 2000$$

$\Rightarrow$ $x = 500$

Hence, selling price of the watch = ₹ 500.

4. Let CP = ₹ x

Then, if SP = ₹350

Profit = SP − CP = ₹ $(350 - x)$

if SP = ₹ 340 then, profit = ₹ $(340 - x)$

$\therefore (350 - x) - (340 - x) = \frac{5}{100}x$

$\Rightarrow 10 = \frac{5}{100}x \quad \Rightarrow x = 200$

Hence, the cost of the article = ₹ 200.

5. Let CP = ₹ x,

then, $425 - x = x - 355 \Rightarrow 2x = 780$

$\Rightarrow x = 390$

Hence, the cost of commodity is ₹ 390.

6. Let CP of the article = ₹ x

Then, SP when profit is 12%

$$= \left(\frac{12x}{100}+x\right) = \frac{112x}{100}$$

$$\therefore \quad \frac{112x}{100}-\frac{88x}{100} = 6$$

$$\Rightarrow \quad 24x = 600$$

$$\Rightarrow \quad x = \frac{600}{24} = 25$$

∴ CP of the article is ₹ 25.

7. 100 – 25 = 75

When SP 75 then CP = ₹ 100

When SP 150 then CP = ₹ $\frac{100}{75}\times 150 =$ ₹ 200

8. Let the original cost of each cooker be ₹ 1 and let the number sold originally be 100.

Total sale proceed = ₹ (100 × 1) = ₹ 100

New rate = (115% of ₹ 1) = ₹ 1.15

Number sold now = 85

∴ Sale proceed now = ₹(1.15 × 85) = ₹ 97.75

So, there is a decrease of 2.25% in the money receipt.

9. Let CP of each mango be ₹ 1.

Then, CP of 400 mangoes = ₹ 400

∴ CP of 320 mangoes = ₹ 320

SP of 320 mangoes = ₹ 400

Profit = 400 – 320 = ₹ 80

$$\text{Profit\%} = \frac{80}{320}\times 100 = 25\%$$

10. SP = ₹ 1, Loss = 20%

$$\Rightarrow \text{CP} = \left(\frac{100}{80}\times 1\right) \Rightarrow \text{CP} = ₹\frac{5}{4}$$

Now, CP = ₹ $\frac{5}{4}$, gain, 20%

$$\Rightarrow \text{SP} = \frac{120}{100}\times\frac{5}{4} = ₹\frac{3}{2}$$

For ₹ $\frac{3}{2}$, he must sell 12 oranges

For ₹ 1, he must sell $\left(12\times\frac{2}{3}\right) = 8$ oranges.

11. SP = ₹ 54000 and gain earned = 20%

$$\text{CP} = ₹\left(\frac{100}{120}\times 54000\right) = ₹\ 45000$$

Now, SP = ₹ 45000 and Loss = 10%

$$\therefore \text{CP} = ₹\left(\frac{100}{90}\times 45000\right) = ₹\ 50000$$

12. Let CP be ₹ x. Then,

$$x - 270 = 10\% \text{ of } x = \frac{x}{10}$$

$$\Rightarrow \quad x - \frac{x}{10} = 270$$

$$\Rightarrow \quad 9x = 10 \times 270$$

$$\Rightarrow \quad x = \frac{10\times 270}{9}$$

$$\Rightarrow \quad x = 300$$

∴ CP of the article is ₹ 300.

13. SP = 90% of ₹ 200 = ₹ 180

Further, SP = (95% of ₹180) = ₹ 171

14. Let CP = ₹ 100. Then, MP = ₹ 120.

$$\text{SP} = 90\% \text{ of } ₹\ 120 = \frac{90}{100}\times 120 = ₹\ 108$$

Profit = SP – CP = 108 – 100 = ₹ 8

$$\text{Profit \%} = \frac{\text{Profit}}{\text{CP}}\times 100 = \frac{8}{100}\times 100 = 8\%$$

15. Let original price = ₹ 100

Price after 1st discount = ₹ 90

Price after 2nd discount

$$= ₹\left(\frac{80}{100}\times 90\right) = ₹\ 72$$

Price after 3rd discount

$$= ₹\left(\frac{60}{100}\times 72\right) = ₹\ 43.20$$

∴ Single discount = 100 – 43.20 = 56.8%.

16. Marked price = ₹ 80

SP = ₹ 68

Discount = MP – SP = 80 – 68 = ₹ 12

$$\text{Discount \%} = \frac{\text{discount}}{\text{MP}}\times 100$$

$$= \frac{12}{80}\times 100 = 15\%$$

17. Suppose the price of 1 mango be x paise.

Number of mangoes for ₹ 15 = $\frac{1500}{x}$

New price of one mango

$$= (80\% \text{ of } x) = \frac{4x}{5} \text{ paise}$$

Number of mangoes for ₹ 15 = $\left(\frac{1500 \times 5}{4x}\right)$

$$\therefore \quad \frac{7500}{4x} - \frac{1500}{x} = 12 \Rightarrow x = 31.25$$

∴ Cost of 16 mangoes before reduction

$$= ₹\left(\frac{31.25 \times 16}{100}\right) = ₹\ 5$$

18. Let SP of TV (by trader) = ₹ 100

If SP is ₹ 80, MP = ₹ 100

If SP is ₹ 100, MP = $₹\left(\frac{100}{80} \times 100\right) = ₹\ 125$

Now, if discount is 25%

then SP = (75% of ₹ 125)

$$= \frac{75}{100} \times 125 = ₹\frac{375}{4}$$

Difference between two SP

$$= \left(100 - \frac{375}{4}\right) = ₹\frac{25}{4}$$

When difference is $₹\frac{25}{4}$ then SP = ₹ 100

When difference is ₹ 500 then SP = $\frac{100}{\frac{25}{4}} \times 500$

$$= \frac{100 \times 4 \times 500}{25} = ₹\ 8000$$

19. Let marked price be ₹ 100.

SP with 10% discount = ₹ 90

∴ 120% of CP = ₹ 90

$$\Rightarrow \quad \frac{120}{100} \times CP = 90$$

$$\Rightarrow \quad CP = \frac{90 \times 100}{120} = ₹\ 75$$

SP with 15% commission = ₹ 85

Profit = ₹ 85 – ₹ 75 = ₹ 10

$$\text{Profit\%} = \frac{10}{75} \times 100 = \frac{40}{3} = 13\frac{1}{3}\%$$

20. Let CP per kg be ₹ x. Then,

x – 10% of x = 5.40

$$\Rightarrow \quad x - \frac{10}{100} \times x = 5.40$$

$$\Rightarrow \quad 9x = 54$$

$$\Rightarrow \quad x = 6$$

∴ SP = ₹ [6 + 20% of 6]

$$= ₹\left[6 + \frac{20}{100} \times 6\right]$$

$$= ₹\left[6 + \frac{120}{100}\right]$$

= ₹ (6 + 1.20) = ₹ (7.20)

Hence, SP is ₹ 7.20.

21. For the First Cow:

SP = ₹ 8400

$$CP = 8400 \times \frac{100}{120} = ₹\ 7000$$

∴ Profit = 8400 – 7000 = ₹ 1400

For the second cow:

SP = ₹ 8800

Profit = 10%

$$\therefore \quad CP = 8800 \times \frac{100}{110} = ₹\ 8000$$

Profit = 8800 – 8000 = ₹ 800

Hence, total profit = 1400 + 800 = ₹ 2200

22. S.P. of the article = ₹ 4080

Loss = 15%

$$\therefore \quad CP = \frac{SP}{\left(1 - \frac{\text{Loss\%}}{100}\right)} = \frac{SP \times 100}{100 - \text{loss\%}}$$

$$\text{Hence,} \quad CP = \frac{4080 \times 100}{(100 - 15)}$$

$$= \frac{4080 \times 100}{85} = ₹\ 4800$$

9

CHAPTER

Simple and Compound Interest

In any money transaction there is a **lender** who gives money, and a **borrower** who receives money. The amount of loan borrowed, is called the principal (P). The borrower pays a certain amount for the use of this money. This is called **Interest (I)**. Interest is always calculated on the principal borrowed. The borrowing is for a specified **Time (t)** and on specified terms. The specified term is expressed as per cent of the principal and is called rate of interest.

The sum of the principal and the interest is called the **Amount (A)**. In general, the rate of interest may be yearly, half yearly, quarterly or monthly as mutually agreed upon by both parties at the time of transaction. Depending upon the period of rate of interest, time is expressed in multiples of this period.

Interest is of two kinds—**Simple Interest and compound Interest**. If the interest is calculated only, on a certain sum borrowed it is called Simple Interest.

The simple interest (SI) on a principal P at R% per annum for T years is given by:

$$SI = \frac{P \times R \times T}{100}$$

$$\therefore \quad P = \frac{SI \times 100}{R \times T}$$

$$\therefore \quad R = \frac{SI \times 100}{P \times T}$$

$$\therefore \quad T = \frac{SI \times 100}{P \times R}$$

Compound Interest differs from Simple Interest that in CI the interest for the future period is calculated not only on the principal but also on the interest earned until the previous period. Thus, the total interest earned in case of CI is not uniformly distributed over time units whereas in Simple Interest it is uniformly distributed. The interest due at the end of the first unit of time is added to the principal and the amount so obtained becomes the principal for the second unit. Similarly, the amount after the 2nd unit of time becomes the principal for the third unit of time and continues till the last unit of time.

The difference between the final amount (A) obtained at the last unit of time and the original principal is called the **Compound Interest**.

Important Relations

Principal = ₹ P (in rupees)

Rate = R % (in per cent per annum)

Time period = T years (in years)

Amount = ₹ A (in rupees)

I. When interest is compounded annually,

$$A = P\left[1 + \frac{R}{100}\right]^T$$

II. When interest is compounded half-yearly,

$$A = P\left[1 + \frac{R/2}{100}\right]^{2T} = P\left[1 + \frac{R}{200}\right]^{2T}$$

[R is divided by 2 and T is multiplied by 2.]

III. When interest is compounded quarterly,

$$A = P\left[1+\frac{R/4}{100}\right]^{4T} = P\left[1+\frac{R}{400}\right]^{4T}$$

[R is divided by 4 and T is multiplied by 4.]

IV. When interest is $R_1\%$ for first year, $R_2\%$ for 2nd year and $R_3\%$ for third year;

$$A = P\left[1+\frac{R_1}{100}\right]\left[1+\frac{R_2}{100}\right]\left[1+\frac{R_3}{100}\right]$$

V. CI = A – P

Example: Find the simple interest on ₹ 1000 for 3 years at 10% p.a.

Solution: $SI = \frac{P\times R\times T}{100} = \frac{1000\times 10\times 3}{100} =$ ₹ 300

Example: Find the amount of ₹ 600 in 4 years at 3% p.a.

Solution: $SI = \frac{P\times R\times T}{100} = \frac{600\times 3\times 4}{100} =$ ₹ 72

∴ Amount = P + SI = 600 + 72 = ₹ 672

Example: In what time will ₹ 7000 give ₹ 3675 as interest at the rate of 7% p.a. simple interest?

Solution: $T = \frac{SI\times 100}{P\times R} = \frac{3675\times 100}{7000\times 7}$

$= \frac{15}{2} = 7\frac{1}{2}$ years.

Example: At what rate per annum will a sum of ₹ 5000 amount to ₹ 6000 in 4 years?

Solution: SI = A – P = 6000 – 5000 = ₹ 1000

$R = \frac{SI\times 100}{P\times T} = \frac{1000\times 100}{5000\times 4} = 5\%$

Example: In how many years will a sum of money double itself at 5% rate of interest?

Solution: A sum doubles itself when amount of interest becomes equal to the principal

SI = P, R = 5%

∴ $T = \frac{100\times P}{P\times 5} = 20$ years

Example: A certain sum amounts to ₹ 115200 in 2 years and to ₹ 165888 in 4 years. Find the sum and rate per cent.

Solution: Here, amount on ₹ 115200 for 2 years at CI is ₹ 165888

$$\therefore\quad 115200\left(1+\frac{R}{100}\right)^2 = 165888$$

$$\left(1+\frac{R}{100}\right)^2 = \frac{165888}{115200} = 1.44$$

$$\therefore\quad 1+\frac{R}{100} = 1.2$$

$$\frac{R}{100} = 1.2 - 1 = 0.2$$

$$\Rightarrow\quad R = 0.2\times 100 = 20\%$$

Amount after 2 years is ₹ 115200

$$\therefore\quad P\left(1+\frac{20}{100}\right)^2 = 115200$$

$$\Rightarrow\quad P = \frac{115200}{\left(1+\frac{20}{100}\right)^2} = \frac{115200}{1.44} = 80000$$

∴ Principal = ₹ 80000

Example: A sum of money doubles itself at CI in 15 years. In how many years will it become eight times?

Solution: $P\left(1+\frac{R}{100}\right)^{15} = 2P$

$$\Rightarrow\quad \left(1+\frac{R}{100}\right)^{15} = 2$$

Let T be the required number of years that makes the principal 8 times of it.

$$\therefore\quad P\left(1+\frac{R}{100}\right)^{T} = 8P$$

$$\Rightarrow\quad \left(1+\frac{R}{100}\right)^{T} = 8 = (2)^3$$

$$\Rightarrow\quad \left(1+\frac{R}{100}\right)^{T} = \left[\left(1+\frac{R}{100}\right)^{15}\right]^3$$

$$\Rightarrow\quad \left(1+\frac{R}{100}\right)^{T} = \left(1+\frac{R}{100}\right)^{45}$$

$$\Rightarrow\quad T = 45 \text{ years}$$

Hence, required number of years is 45 years.

Example: The difference between simple and compound interest on a sum of money at 5% p.a. for 2 years is ₹ 25. Find the sum.

Solution: Let P = ₹ 100

$$SI = \frac{P \times R \times T}{100} = \frac{100 \times 5 \times 2}{100} = ₹\,10$$

$$A = P\left(1 + \frac{R}{100}\right)^T = 100\left(1 + \frac{5}{100}\right)^2$$

$$= \frac{100 \times 21 \times 21}{400} = ₹\,\frac{441}{4}$$

$$CI = A - P = \frac{441}{4} - 100 = ₹\,\frac{41}{4}$$

$$CI - SI = \frac{41}{4} - 10 = \frac{41 - 40}{4} = ₹\,\frac{1}{4}$$

When difference ₹ $\frac{1}{4}$ then P = ₹ 100

When difference ₹ 25 then P = 100 × 4 × 25 = ₹ 10000

Hence, sum = ₹ 10000.

MULTIPLE CHOICE QUESTIONS

1. The simple interest on ₹ 500 for 6 years at 5% p.a. is:
A. ₹ 250 B. ₹ 150
C. ₹ 140 D. ₹ 120

2. A certain sum of money at SI amounts to ₹ 1012 in $2\frac{1}{2}$ years and to ₹ 1067.20 in 4 years. The rate of interest per annum is:
A. 2.5% B. 3%
C. 4% D. 5%

3. ₹ 1200 amounts to ₹ 1632 in 4 years at a certain rate of simple interest. If the rate of interest is increased by 1%, it would amount to how much?
A. ₹ 1635 B. ₹ 1644
C. ₹ 1670 D. ₹ 1680

4. A man will get ₹ 87 as simple interest on ₹ 725 at 4% per annum in:
A. 3 years B. 3½ years
C. 4 years D. 5 years

5. At simple interest, a sum doubles after 20 years. The rate of interest per annum is:
A. 5% B. 10%
C. 20% D. Data inadequate

6. A lent ₹ 600 to B for 2 years and ₹ 150 to C for 4 years and received altogether from both ₹ 90 as simple interest. The rate of interest is:
A. 12% B. 10%
C. 5% D. 4%

7. Interest on a certain sum of money for $2\frac{1}{3}$ years at $3\frac{3}{4}\%$ per annum is ₹ 210. The sum is:
A. ₹ 2800 B. ₹ 1580
C. ₹ 2400 D. None of these

8. A certain sum of money at simple interest amounts to ₹ 1260 in 2 years and to ₹ 1350 in 5 years. The rate per cent per annum is:
A. 2.5% B. 3.75%
C. 5% D. 7.5%

9. A sum of money doubles itself in 5 years. It will become 4 times itself in:
A. 10 years B. 12 years
C. 15 years D. 20 years

10. The simple interest on a sum of money will be ₹ 600 after 10 years. If the principal is trebled after 5 years, the total interest at the end of 10 years will be:
A. ₹ 600 B. ₹ 900
C. ₹ 1200 D. Data inadequate

11. ₹ 800 amounts to ₹ 920 in 3 years at simple interest. If the interest rate is increased by 3%, it would amount to how much?
A. ₹ 1056 B. ₹ 1112
C. ₹ 1182 D. ₹ 992

12. A sum of money at simple interest amounts to ₹ 2240 in 2 years and ₹ 2600 in 5 years. The sum is:
A. ₹ 1880 B. ₹ 2000
C. ₹ 2120 D. Data inadequate

13. If ₹ 7500 are borrowed at CI at the rate of 4% per annum, then after 2 years the amount to be paid is:

A. ₹ 8082 B. ₹ 7800
C. ₹ 8100 D. ₹ 8112

14. Simple interest on a sum at 4% per annum is ₹ 80 in 2 years. The compound interest on the same sum for the same period is:

A. ₹ 81.60 B. ₹ 160
C. ₹ 1081.60 D. None of these

15. ₹ 800 at 5% per annum compound interest will amount to ₹ 882 in:

A. 1 year B. 2 years
C. 3 years D. 4 years

16. What is the principal amount which earns ₹ 132 as compound interest for the second year at 10% per annum?

A. ₹ 1000 B. ₹ 1200
C. ₹ 1320 D. None of these

17. The difference between the compound interest and the simple interest on a certain sum at 5% per annum for 2 years is ₹ 1.50. The sum is:

A. ₹ 600 B. ₹ 500
C. ₹ 400 D. ₹ 300

18. The compound interest on a certain sum of money for 2 years at 10% per annum is ₹ 420. The simple interest on the same sum at the same rate and for the same time will be:

A. ₹ 350 B. ₹ 375
C. ₹ 380 D. ₹ 400

19. A sum amounts to ₹ 2916 in 2 years and to ₹ 3149.28 in 3 years at compound interest. The sum is :

A. ₹ 1500 B. ₹ 2000
C. ₹ 2500 D. ₹ 3000

20. A sum of money amounts to ₹ 10648 in 3 years and ₹ 9680 in 2 years. The rate of interest is:

A. 5% B. 10%
C. 15% D. 20%

ANSWERS

1	2	3	4	5	6	7	8	9	10
B	C	D	A	A	C	C	A	C	C
11	**12**	**13**	**14**	**15**	**16**	**17**	**18**	**19**	**20**
D	B	D	A	B	B	A	D	C	B

EXPLANATORY ANSWERS

1. $SI = \frac{P \times R \times T}{100} = \frac{500 \times 5 \times 6}{100} = ₹\ 150$

2. SI for $1\frac{1}{2}$ years = 1067.20 – 1012 = ₹ 55.20

SI for $2\frac{1}{2}$ years = $55.20 \times \frac{2}{3} \times \frac{5}{2}$ = ₹ 92

∴ Principal = ₹ (1012 – 92) = ₹ 920

$R = \frac{SI \times 100}{P \times T} = \frac{92 \times 100 \times 2}{920 \times 5} = 4\%$

3. $R = \frac{SI \times 100}{P \times T} = \frac{432 \times 100}{1200 \times 4} = 9\%$

New rate = (9 + 1)% = 10%

$SI = \frac{P \times R \times T}{100} = \frac{1200 \times 10 \times 4}{100} = ₹\ 480$

Amount = P + SI = 1200 + 480 = ₹ 1680

4. $T = \frac{SI \times 100}{P \times R} = \frac{87 \times 100}{725 \times 4} = 3$ years

5. Let P be ₹ x then A = ₹ $2x$

SI = A – P = $2x - x$ = ₹ x

$R = \frac{SI \times 100}{P \times T} = \frac{x \times 100}{x \times 20} = 5\%$

6. $SI = \frac{P \times R \times T}{100} = \frac{600 \times R \times 2}{100} = 12R$

Again $SI = \frac{P \times R \times T}{100} = \frac{150 \times R \times 4}{100} = 6R$

Total SI = 12R + 6R = 18R

According to the question,

$$18R = 90 \Rightarrow R = \frac{90}{18} = 5\%$$

7. $T = 2\frac{1}{3} = \frac{7}{3}$ years,

$$R = 3\frac{3}{4}\% = \frac{15}{4}\%$$

$$P = \frac{SI \times 100}{P \times T} = \frac{210 \times 100}{\frac{15}{4} \times \frac{7}{3}}$$

$$= \frac{210 \times 100 \times 4 \times 3}{15 \times 7} = ₹\ 2400$$

8. SI for 3 years = ₹ 1350 – ₹ 1260 = ₹ 90

SI for 1 year = $\frac{90}{3}$ = ₹ 30

SI for 2 years = ₹ 30 × 2 = ₹ 60

P = A – SI = 1260 – 60 = ₹ 1200

$$R = \frac{SI \times 100}{P \times T} = \frac{60 \times 100}{1200 \times 2} = \frac{5}{2} = 2.5\%$$

9. Let P be ₹ x, A = ₹ $2x$,

SI = $2x - x$ = ₹ x

$$R = \frac{SI \times 100}{P \times T} = \frac{x \times 100}{x \times 5} = 20\%$$

Again, P = ₹ x, A = $4x$,

SI = $4x - x = 3x$

$$T = \frac{SI \times 100}{P \times R} = \frac{3x \times 100}{x \times 20} = 15 \text{ years}$$

10. Let P be ₹ x

SI = ₹ 600, T = 10 years.

$$R = \frac{SI \times 100}{P \times T} = \frac{600 \times 100}{x \times 10} = \frac{6000}{x}\%$$

SI for first 5 years = $\frac{x \times 5 \times 6000}{100 \times x}$ = ₹ 300

SI for last 5 years = $\frac{3x \times 5 \times 6000}{100 \times x}$ = ₹ 900

Total interest at the end of 10 years

= 900 + 300 = ₹ 1200.

11. P = ₹ 800, SI = 920 – 800 = ₹ 120

T = 3 years

$$R = \frac{SI \times 100}{P \times T} = \frac{120 \times 100}{800 \times 3} = 5\%$$

New rate = 8% (increase 3%)

$$SI = \frac{P \times R \times T}{100} = \frac{800 \times 8 \times 3}{100} = ₹\ 192$$

∴ A = P + SI = 800 + 192 = ₹ 992.

12. SI for 3 years = 2600 – 2240 = ₹ 360

SI for 2 years = $\frac{360}{3} \times 2$ = ₹ 240

∴ Sum = 2240 – 240 = ₹ 2000

13. $A = P\left(1 + \frac{R}{100}\right)^T = 7500\left(1 + \frac{4}{100}\right)^2$

$$= 7500 \times \frac{26}{25} \times \frac{26}{25} = ₹\ 8112$$

14. $P = \frac{SI \times 100}{T \times R} = \frac{80 \times 100}{4 \times 2} = ₹\ 1000$

$$A = P\left(1 + \frac{R}{100}\right)^T = 1000\left(1 + \frac{4}{100}\right)^2$$

$$= 1000 \times \frac{26}{25} \times \frac{26}{25} = 1081.60$$

CI = A – P = 1081.60 – 1000 = ₹ 81.60

15. Let time = x years

$$A = P\left(1 + \frac{R}{100}\right)^T$$

$$882 = 800\left(1 + \frac{5}{100}\right)^x$$

$$\Rightarrow \frac{882}{800} = \left(\frac{21}{20}\right)^x$$

$$\Rightarrow \left(\frac{21}{20}\right)^2 = \left(\frac{21}{20}\right)^x \Rightarrow x = 2$$

∴ Time = 2 years

16. Let x be the principal at the end of first year

Then, $\frac{x \times 10 \times 1}{100} = 132 \Rightarrow x = 1320$

Let y be the original principal

Then, $y + \frac{y \times 10 \times 1}{100} = 1320$

$\Rightarrow$ $y = 1200$

17. Let $P = ₹\ 100$

$$SI = \frac{P \times R \times T}{100} = \frac{100 \times 5 \times 2}{100} = ₹\ 10$$

$$A = P\left(1+\frac{R}{100}\right)^T = 100\left(1+\frac{5}{100}\right)^2$$

$$= 100 \times \frac{21}{20} \times \frac{21}{20} = \frac{441}{4}$$

$$CI = A - P = \frac{441}{4} - 100 = \frac{41}{4}$$

$$CI - SI = \frac{41}{4} - 10 = ₹\frac{1}{4}$$

When difference $₹\frac{1}{4}$ then $P = ₹\ 100$

When difference ₹ 1.5 then $P = \frac{100}{1/4} \times 1.5$

$$\Rightarrow P = \frac{100 \times 4 \times 15}{10} = ₹\ 600$$

18. Let $P = ₹\ 100$

$$A = P\left(1+\frac{R}{100}\right)^T = 100\left(1+\frac{10}{100}\right)^2$$

$$= 100 \times \frac{11}{10} \times \frac{11}{10} = ₹\ 121$$

$CI = A - P = 121 - 100 = ₹\ 21$

When CI ₹ 21 then $P = ₹\ 100$

When CI ₹ 420 then $P = \frac{100}{21} \times 420 = ₹\ 2000$

$$SI = \frac{P \times R \times T}{100} = \frac{2000 \times 10 \times 2}{100} = ₹\ 400$$

19. $A = P\left(1+\frac{R}{100}\right)^T$

$$P\left(1+\frac{R}{100}\right)^3 = 3149.28 \quad ...(i)$$

and $$P\left(1+\frac{R}{100}\right)^2 = 2916 \quad ...(ii)$$

Dividing (*i*) by (*ii*) we get

$$1+\frac{R}{100} = \frac{3149.28}{2916}$$

$$\Rightarrow \frac{R}{100} = \frac{3149.28}{2916} - 1$$

$$= \frac{3149.28 - 2916}{2916} = \frac{233.28}{2916}$$

$$R = \frac{233.28 \times 100}{2916} = 8\%$$

Now, $$P\left(1+\frac{R}{100}\right)^2 = 2916$$

$$\Rightarrow P\left(1+\frac{8}{100}\right)^2 = 2916$$

$$\Rightarrow P\left(\frac{27}{25} \times \frac{27}{25}\right) = 2916$$

$$P = \frac{25 \times 25 \times 2916}{27 \times 27} = ₹\ 2500$$

20. $$10648 = P\left(1+\frac{R}{100}\right)^3 \quad ...(i)$$

and $$9680 = P\left(1+\frac{R}{100}\right)^2 \quad ...(ii)$$

Dividing (*i*) by (*ii*), we get

$$\frac{10648}{9680} = 1+\frac{R}{100}$$

$$\Rightarrow \frac{R}{100} = \frac{1}{10} \Rightarrow R = 10\%$$

10

CHAPTER

Time and Work

Performing or doing work of any amount involves efforts of person (S) over a period of time. Therefore, the number of persons (P), the quantity of work (W) and the period of time (T) are important variables in problems related to "Time and Work". Moreover time (T) taken to do a work depends not only on how many persons are employed to do it but also on how efficient they are. Efficiency here means rate of doing same work. This aspect comes into picture when the problem involves comparison of work done by different categories of persons. For instance, efficiencies of man, woman, boy, girl in general are different. Even efficiency of one man may not be same as that of other; but unless otherwise specifically stated in the problem, all men or women working in a group are assumed to do work with equal efficiency.

The problems on Time and Work can be solved by following two methods:

(*i*) Ratio and proportion method

(*ii*) Unitary method

(*i*) **Ratio and Proportion Method:** Since problems concerning to Time and Work have proportional relation, these can be solved by this method. We have tried to solve questions based on Time and Work in the chapter mentioned.

(*ii*) **Unitary Method:** This is a very simple and useful method. The term 'Unitary' is self-evident. In this method, we first proceed to reduce the problem to either work done by one person or work done in 1 day and so on as per the requirement of the problem. Let us try to understand it.

(*a*) If a man can do a piece of work in 10 days he will do $\frac{1}{10}$ of the work in 1 day. Conversely, if a man can do $\frac{1}{10}$ of the work in 1 day, he will do the work in 10 days.

(*b*) If the number of men engaged to do a piece of work be changed in the ratio 5 : 4, the time required for the work will be changed in the ratio 4 : 5.

(*c*) If A is x times as good a workman as B, then A will take $\frac{1}{x}$ of the time that B takes to do a certain work.

All the above points can be summarised into one and can be written in the following form:

If M_1 persons can do W_1 works in D_1 days and M_2 persons can do W_2 works in D_2 days then we have a very general formula in the relationship of

$$M_1 D_1 W_2 = M_2 D_2 W_1$$

The above relationship can be taken as a very basic and all-in-one formula we also derive:

(*i*) More men less days and conversely more days less men.

(*ii*) More men more work and conversely more work more men.

(*iii*) More days more work and conversely more work more days.

$$M_1 D_1 T_1 W_2 = M_2 D_2 T_2 W_1$$

EXAMPLE: 5 men can prepare 10 toys in 6 days working 6 hrs a day. How many days can 12 men prepare 16 toys working 8 hrs a day?

SOLUTION: $M_1 D_1 T_1 W_2 = M_2 D_2 T_2 W_1$

$$5 \times 6 \times 6 \times 16 = 12 \times D_2 \times 8 \times 10$$

$$D_2 = \frac{5 \times 6 \times 6 \times 16}{12 \times 8 \times 10} = 3 \text{ days.}$$

EXAMPLE: A can reap a field in 8 days, which B alone can reap in 12 days. In how many days, both together, can reap this field?

SOLUTION: A's 1 day's work $= \frac{1}{8}$

B's 1 day's work $= \frac{1}{12}$

(A + B)'s 1 day's work $= \left(\frac{1}{8}+\frac{1}{12}\right)$

$= \frac{3+2}{24} = \frac{5}{24}$

$\therefore$ Both together can reap the field in $\frac{24}{5}$ days

$= 4\frac{4}{5}$ days.

EXAMPLE: A and B together can do a piece of work in 12 days, B alone can finish it in 30 days. In how many days can A alone finish the work?

SOLUTION: (A + B)'s 1 day's work $= \frac{1}{12}$

B's 1 day's work $= \frac{1}{30}$

$\therefore$ A's 1 day's work $= \frac{1}{12}-\frac{1}{30}$

$= \frac{5-2}{60} = \frac{3}{60} = \frac{1}{20}$

Hence, A alone can finish the work in 20 days.

EXAMPLE: A and B can do a piece of work in 12 days, C and A in 20 days and B and C in 15 days. In how many days will they finish it together and separately?

SOLUTION: (A + B)'s 1 day's work $= \frac{1}{12}$

(B + C)'s 1 day's work $= \frac{1}{15}$

(C + A)'s 1 day's work $= \frac{1}{20}$

Adding, 2(A + B + C)'s 1 day's work

$= \left(\frac{1}{12}+\frac{1}{15}+\frac{1}{20}\right) = \frac{5+4+3}{60}$

$= \frac{12}{60} = \frac{1}{5}$

or (A + B + C)'s 1 day's work $= \frac{1}{10}$

$\therefore$ A, B, C together can finish the work in 10 days.

Now, C's 1 day's work $= \frac{1}{10}-\frac{1}{12} = \frac{1}{60}$

$\therefore$ C alone can finish the work in 60 days.

Similarly B's 1 day's work $= \frac{1}{10}-\frac{1}{20} = \frac{1}{20}$

$\therefore$ B alone can finish the work in 20 days.

A's 1 day's work $= \frac{1}{10}-\frac{1}{15} = \frac{1}{30}$

$\therefore$ A alone can finish the work in 30 days.

EXAMPLE: A can do a piece of work in 25 days and B can finish it in 20 days. They work together for 5 days and then A goes away. In how many days will B finish the work?

SOLUTION: (A + B)'s 5 days work $= 5\left(\frac{1}{25}+\frac{1}{20}\right) = \frac{9}{20}$

Remaining work $= 1-\frac{9}{20} = \frac{11}{20}$

Now, $\frac{1}{20}$ work is finished by B in 1 day

$\therefore$ $\frac{11}{20}$ work will be finished by B in $\left(\frac{20\times 11}{20}\right)$ = 11 days.

EXAMPLE: A is thrice as good a workman as B and is therefore able to finish a piece of work in 60 days less than B. Find the time in which they can do it, working together.

SOLUTION: Ratio of work done by A and B in the same time = 3 : 1

Ratio of time taken by A and B = 1 : 3

Suppose B takes x days to finish a work

then, A takes $(x – 60)$ days

$\therefore$ $\frac{x-60}{x} = \frac{1}{3}$ or $3(x-60) = x \Rightarrow x = 90$

$\therefore$ B can finish the work in 90 days.

A can finish the work in (90 – 60) = 30 days

Both finish the work $= \left[\frac{1}{30}+\frac{1}{90} = \frac{2}{45}\right]$

$= \frac{45}{2} = 22\frac{1}{2}$ days.

EXAMPLE: A certain number of men complete a piece of work in 60 days. If there were 8 men more, the work could be finished in 10 days less. How many men were originally there?

SOLUTION: Let the original number of men be x.

Now, x men can finish the work in 60 days

and $(x + 8)$ men can finish it in $(60 - 10)$ *i.e.*, 50 days.

$$\therefore \quad x + 8 : x :: 60 : 50$$

$$\Rightarrow \quad \frac{x+8}{x} = \frac{60}{50} = \frac{6}{5}$$

$$\Rightarrow \quad 6x = 5x + 40 \Rightarrow x = 40$$

Hence, the original number of men = 40.

EXAMPLE: If 4 men or 6 boys can finish a piece of work in 20 days, in how many days can 6 men and 11 boys finish it?

SOLUTION: 4 men = 6 boys

$$\therefore \quad 6 \text{ men} = \frac{6}{4} \times 6 = \frac{36}{4} = 9 \text{ boys}$$

6 men + 11 boys = 9 + 11 = 20 boys

Now, 6 boys can finish a work in 20 days.

1 boy can finish the same work in 6×20 days.

20 boys can finish the same work in $\frac{6 \times 20}{20}$

$= 6$ days.

EXAMPLE: If 12 men can build a wall 360 m long in 54 days, how many days will it take to build a similar wall 160 m long, if 16 men working on it?

SOLUTION: 12 men can build 360 m long wall in 54 days.

1 man can build 360 m long wall in 54×12 days.

1 man can build 1 m long wall in $\frac{54 \times 12}{360}$ days

16 men can build 1 m long wall in $\frac{54 \times 12}{360 \times 16}$ days

16 men can build 160 m long wall in $\frac{54 \times 12 \times 160}{360 \times 16}$ days

$= 18$ days.

EXAMPLE: If 3 persons weave 168 carpets in 7 days, how many carpets will 8 persons weave in 5 days?

SOLUTION: 3 persons can weave in 7 days 168 carpets

1 person can weave in 7 days = $\frac{168}{3}$ carpets

1 person can weave in 1 day = $\frac{168}{3 \times 7}$ carpets

8 persons can weave in 1 day = $\frac{168 \times 8}{3 \times 7}$ carpets

8 persons can weave in 5 days = $\frac{168 \times 8 \times 5}{3 \times 7}$ carpets

$= 320$ carpets

EXAMPLE: Mukesh can do a job in 12 days while Manoj can do the same job in 15 days. They undertake to complete the job for ₹ 5400. What will be the share of each in the income?

SOLUTION: Mukesh's 1 day's work = $\frac{1}{12}$

Manoj's 1 day's work = $\frac{1}{15}$

Ratio of their 1 day's work = $\frac{1}{12} : \frac{1}{15} = 5 : 4$

$\therefore$ Mukesh's share = ₹ $\frac{5}{9} \times 5400$ = ₹ 3000

Manoj's share = ₹ $\frac{4}{9} \times 5400$ = ₹ 2400

MULTIPLE CHOICE QUESTIONS

1. A and B can together do a piece of work in 15 days. B alone can do it in 20 days. In how many days can A alone do it?

A. 30 days B. 40 days
C. 45 days D. 60 days

2. A can do a piece of work in 30 days while B can do it in 40 days. A and B working together can do it in:

A. 70 days B. $42\frac{3}{4}$ days
C. $27\frac{1}{7}$ days D. $17\frac{1}{7}$ days

3. A can do $\frac{1}{3}$ of the work in 5 days and B can do $\frac{2}{5}$ of the work in 10 days. In how many days both A and B together can do the work?

A. $7\frac{3}{4}$ days B. $8\frac{4}{5}$ days

C. $9\frac{3}{8}$ days D. 10 days

4. A, B and C can do a piece of work in 6, 12 and 24 days respectively. They altogether will complete the work in:

A. $3\frac{3}{7}$ days B. $\frac{7}{24}$ days

C. $4\frac{4}{5}$ days D. $\frac{5}{24}$ days

5. A, B and C contract a work for ₹ 550. Together A and B are to do $\frac{7}{11}$ of the work. The share of C should be:

A. ₹ $183\frac{1}{3}$ B. ₹ 200

C. ₹ 300 D. ₹ 400

6. A and B finish a job in 12 days while A, B and C can finish it in 8 days. C alone will finish the job in:

A. 20 days B. 14 days

C. 24 days D. 16 days

7. 12 men can complete a work in 8 days. Three days after they started the work, 3 more men joined them. In how many days will all of them together complete the remaining work?

A. 2 B. 4

C. 5 D. 6

8. Mahesh and Umesh can complete a work in 10 and 15 days respectively. Umesh starts the work and after 5 days Mahesh joins him. In all, the work would be completed in:

A. 9 days B. 7 days

C. 11 days D. None of these

9. Sunil completes a work in 4 days whereas Dinesh completes the work in 6 days. Ramesh works $1\frac{1}{2}$ times as fast as Sunil. How many days it will take for the three together to complete the work?

A. $\frac{7}{12}$ B. $1\frac{5}{12}$

C. $1\frac{5}{7}$ D. None of these

10. A can complete a work in 6 days and B in 5 days. They work together, finish the job and receive ₹ 220 as wages. B's share should be:

A. ₹ 120 B. ₹ 110

C. ₹ 100 D. ₹ 90

11. 12 men and 8 children can finish a piece of work in 9 days. If each child takes twice the time taken by a man to finish the work, in how many days will 12 men finish the same work?

A. 8 days B. 15 days

C. 9 days D. 12 days

12. A, B and C together earn ₹ 150 per day while A and C together earn ₹ 94 and B and C together earn ₹ 76. The daily earning of C is:

A. ₹ 75 B. ₹ 56

C. ₹ 34 D. ₹ 20

13. If 5 men or 9 women can finish a piece of work in 19 days, 3 men and 6 women will do the same work in:

A. 10 days B. 12 days

C. 13 days D. 15 days

14. A can do a piece of work in 12 days. B is 60% more efficient than A. The number of days, it takes B to do the same piece of work, is:

A. $7\frac{1}{2}$ days B. $6\frac{1}{4}$ days

C. 8 days D. 6 days

15. A and B can do a piece of work in 45 and 40 days respectively. They began the work together, but A leaves after some days and B finished the remaining work in 23 days. After how many days did A leave?

A. 6 days B. 8 days

C. 9 days D. 12 days

16. 12 men can complete a work within 9 days. After 3 days they started the work, 6 men joined them to replace 2 men. How many days will they take to complete the remaining work?

A. 2 days B. 3 days
C. 4 days D. $4\frac{1}{2}$ days

17. 10 men can finish a piece of work in 10 days whereas it takes 12 women to finish it in 10 days. If 15 men and 6 women undertake to complete the work, how many days will they take to complete it?
A. 2 days B. 4 days
C. 5 days D. 11 days

18. A can do a piece of work in 80 days. He works at it for 10 days and then B alone finishes the work in 42 days. The two together could complete the work in:
A. 24 days B. 25 days
C. 30 days D. 35 days

19. A and B can together finish a work in 30 days. They worked for it for 20 days and then B left. The remaining work was done by A alone in 20 more days. A alone can finish the work in:
A. 48 days B. 50 days
C. 54 days D. 60 days

20. A can complete a job in 9 days, B in 10 days and C in 15 days. B and C start the work and are forced to leave after 2 days. The time taken by A alone to complete the remaining work is:
A. 13 days B. 10 days
C. 9 days D. 6 days

ANSWERS

1	2	3	4	5	6	7	8	9	10
D	D	C	A	B	C	B	A	D	A
11	**12**	**13**	**14**	**15**	**16**	**17**	**18**	**19**	**20**
D	D	D	A	C	D	C	C	D	D

EXPLANATORY ANSWERS

1. $(A+B)$'s 1 day's work $= \frac{1}{15}$

B's 1 day's work $= \frac{1}{20}$

A's 1 day's work $= \frac{1}{15} - \frac{1}{20} = \frac{4-3}{60} = \frac{1}{60}$

$\therefore$ A can do this work alone in 60 days.

2. A's 1 day's work $= \frac{1}{30}$

B's 1 day's work $= \frac{1}{40}$

$(A+B)$'s 1 day's work $= \frac{1}{30} + \frac{1}{40}$

$= \frac{4+3}{120} = \frac{7}{120}$

$\therefore$ Both together will finish the work in $\frac{120}{7}$

$= 17\frac{1}{7}$ days.

3. $\frac{1}{3}$ of the work is done by A in 5 days.

$\therefore$ Whole work will be done by A in 3×5
$= 15$ days

$\frac{2}{5}$ of the work is done by B in 10 days.

Whole work will be done by B in $\left(10 \times \frac{5}{2}\right)$
$= 25$ days

$(A+B)$'s 1 day's work $= \frac{1}{15} + \frac{1}{25} = \frac{5+3}{75} = \frac{8}{75}$

$\therefore$ Both together can finish it in $\frac{75}{8} = 9\frac{3}{8}$ days.

4. A's 1 day's work $= \frac{1}{6}$

B's 1 day's work $= \frac{1}{12}$

C's 1 day's work $= \frac{1}{24}$

$(A + B + C)$'s 1 day's work $= \frac{1}{6} + \frac{1}{12} + \frac{1}{24}$

$= \frac{4+2+1}{24} = \frac{7}{24}$

∴ They all together will complete the work in

$\frac{24}{7}$ days $= 3\frac{3}{7}$ days

5. Work to be done by C $= \left(1 - \frac{7}{11}\right) = \frac{4}{11}$

$\therefore (A + B) : C = \frac{7}{11} : \frac{4}{11} = 7 : 4$

∴ C's share = ₹ $\frac{4}{11} \times 550$ = ₹ 200

6. $(A + B)$'s 1 day's work $= \frac{1}{12}$

$(A + B + C)$'s 1 day's work $= \frac{1}{8}$

C's 1 day's work $= \frac{1}{8} - \frac{1}{12} = \frac{3-2}{24} = \frac{1}{24}$

Hence, C will complete the work in 24 days.

7. 1 man's 1 day's work $= \frac{1}{96}$

12 men's 3 day's work $= \frac{12}{96} \times 3 = \frac{3}{8}$

Remaining work $= \left(1 - \frac{3}{8}\right) = \frac{5}{8}$

15 men's 1 day's work $= \frac{15}{96}$

Now, $\frac{15}{96}$ work is done by them in 1 day

∴ $\frac{5}{8}$ work will be done by them in $\frac{96}{15} \times \frac{5}{8}$

= 4 days

8. Umesh's 5 day's work $= \frac{5}{15} = \frac{1}{3}$

Remaining work $= \left(1 - \frac{1}{3}\right) = \frac{2}{3}$

Now, $\left(\frac{1}{10} + \frac{1}{15}\right)$ work is done by A and B in 1 day.

∴ $\frac{2}{3}$ work will be done by A and B in $6 \times \frac{2}{3}$

= 4 days.

So, the work would be completed in (5 + 4)

= 9 days.

9. Time taken by Ramesh alone $= \frac{2}{3} \times 4 = \frac{8}{3}$ days

∴ Their 1 day's work $= \left(\frac{1}{4} + \frac{1}{6} + \frac{3}{8}\right)$

$= \frac{6+4+9}{24} = \frac{19}{24}$

So, together they can finish the work in $\frac{24}{19}$ days

$= 1\frac{5}{19}$ days.

10. Ratio of time taken by A and B = 6 : 5

Ratio of work done in same time = 5 : 6

So, the money is to be divided among A and B in the ratio 5 : 6.

∴ B's share = ₹ $\frac{6}{11} \times 220$ = ₹ 120

11. 2 children = 1 man

∴ 8 children + 12 men = 4 + 12 = 16 men

Now, less men, more days

$12 : 16 :: 9 : x \Rightarrow \frac{12}{16} = \frac{9}{x} \Rightarrow x = 12$ days

12. B's daily earning = ₹ (150 – 94) = ₹ 56

A's daily earning = ₹ (150 – 76) = ₹ 74

C's daily earning = ₹ [150 – (56 + 74)] = ₹ 20

13. 5 men = 9 women ⇒ 1 man $= \frac{9}{5}$ women

∴ 3 men + 6 women $= \left(3 \times \frac{9}{5} + 6\right) = \frac{57}{5}$ women

Now, 9 women can do the work in 19 days

∴ $\frac{57}{5}$ women can do it in $\frac{9 \times 19 \times 5}{57}$ = 15 days

14. A's 1 day's work $= \frac{1}{12}$

B's 1 day's work $= \frac{1}{12} + 60\%$ of $\frac{1}{12} = \frac{2}{15}$

Hence, B can do the whole work in $\frac{15}{2}$

$= 7\frac{1}{2}$ days.

15. B's 23 day's work = $\frac{23}{40}$

Remaining work = $\left(1-\frac{23}{40}\right) = \frac{17}{40}$

Now, (A + B)'s 1 day's work = $\left(\frac{1}{45}+\frac{1}{40}\right) = \frac{17}{360}$

$\frac{17}{360}$ work is done by A and B in 1 day

$\frac{17}{40}$ work is done by A and B in $\frac{360}{17} \times \frac{17}{40}$

= 9 days.

Hence, A left after 9 days.

16. 12 men can complete $\frac{1}{3}$ of the work in 3 days

and the remaining $\frac{2}{3}$ of the work in 6 days

1 man can complete $\frac{2}{3}$ of the work in 12×6

= 72 days

$\therefore$ 12 – 2 + 6 = 16 men can complete

$\frac{2}{3}$ of the work in $\frac{72}{16} = \frac{9}{2} = 4\frac{1}{2}$ days.

17. 10 men = 12 women $\Rightarrow$ 1 man = $\frac{6}{5}$ women

$\therefore$ 15 men + 6 women = $15 \times \frac{6}{5} + 6$

= 18 + 6 = 24 women

12 women can do the work in 10 days

24 women can do the same work in $\frac{10 \times 12}{24}$

= 5 days

18. A's 10 day's work = $\frac{10}{80} = \frac{1}{8}$

$\left(1-\frac{1}{8}\right)$ work is done by B in 42 days

Therefore, B alone can finish the work in $\frac{42 \times 8}{7}$

= 48 days

B's 1 day's work = $\frac{1}{48}$

(A + B)'s 1 day's work = $\frac{1}{80} + \frac{1}{48}$

$= \frac{3+5}{240} = \frac{8}{240} = \frac{1}{30}$

$\therefore$ A and B together can do the work in 30 days.

19. (A + B)'s 20 day's work = $20 \times \frac{1}{30} = \frac{2}{3}$

Remaining work = $\left(1-\frac{2}{3}\right) = \frac{1}{3}$

$\frac{1}{3}$ work is done by A in 20 days

whole work can be done by A in (3 × 20)

= 60 days.

20. (B + C)'s 2 day's work = $2\left(\frac{1}{10}+\frac{1}{15}\right) = \frac{1}{3}$

Remaining work = $1 - \frac{1}{3} = \frac{2}{3}$

Now, $\frac{1}{9}$ work is done by A in 1 day

$\therefore$ $\frac{2}{3}$ work will be done by A in $9 \times \frac{2}{3}$ = 6 days

11

CHAPTER

Area and Perimeter

The area of any figure is the amount of surface enclosed within its boundary lines. It is measured by the number of square metres or square centimetres or square inches (or some other units of square measure) it contains.

Perimeter

Perimeter of a geometrical figure is the total length of the sides enclosing the figure.

Triangle

A triangle is a plane figure bounded by three sides. It includes three angles. It is denoted by the symbol Δ. The sum of angles of a triangle is 180°.

(*i*) **Equilateral Triangle:** A triangle in which all sides are equal is called an equilateral triangle.

(*ii*) **Isosceles Triangle:** A triangle in which two sides are equal is called an isosceles triangle.

(*iii*) **Scalene Triangle:** A triangle in which all sides are different or unequal is called scalene triangle.

(*iv*) **Right Angled Triangle:** A triangle having one of the angles equal to 90° is called a right angled triangle. The side opposite to the right angle of a triangle is called its hypotenuse.

Quadrilateral

A plane figure bounded by four straight lines is called a quadrilateral.

Various Types of Quadrilaterals:

(*i*) **Rectangle:** A quadrilateral whose opposite sides are equal and all angles are at right angles. The diagonals of a rectangle are equal.

(*ii*) **Square:** A rectangle having all sides are equal is called a square.

(*iii*) Parallelogram : A quadrilateral whose opposite sides are equal and parallel is called parallelogram.

(*iv*) **Rhombus:** A parallelogram having all the sides equal is called a rhombus. Diagonals of a rhombus are not equal and they bisect each other at right angles.

(*v*) **Trapezium:** A quadrilateral having one pair of opposite sides parallel, is called a trapezium.

Circle

The path traced by a point which moves in such a way that its distance from a fixed point is always same, is called a circle. The fixed point is called its centre and fixed distance is called its radius. The length of the whole path of a circle is called its circumference.

(*i*) **Arc:** Any part of the circumference of a circle is called an arc.

(*ii*) **Chord:** The straight line joining the ends of an arc of a circle is called a chord.

(*iii*) **Diameter:** The chord passing through the centre of a circle is called its diameter.

The diameter of a circle divides the circle into two equal parts, each one of which is called a semi-circle.

(*iv*) **Segment:** The area enclosed by an arc and a chord is called a segment.

(*v*) **Sector:** The area bounded by an arc and two radii is called a sector.

Formulae for Area of Various Figures:

(*i*) **Rectangle:**

Area of rectangle = $l \times b$

Perimeter of rectangle = $2\,(l + b)$.

(ii) **Square:**

Area of square = $(\text{side})^2$

Perimeter of square = 4 × side

Area of room = $l \times b$

Area of 4 walls of a room = $2(l + b) \times h$

(iii) **Parallelogram:**

Area of $||^{gm} = b \times h$

Area of rhombus = $\frac{1}{2} \times d_1 \times d_2$.

(iv) **Trapezium:**

Area of trapezium = $\frac{1}{2}$ (sum of parallel sides) × (distance between them)

(v) **Triangle:**

(*a*) Area of right triangle = $\frac{1}{2} \times b \times h$

(*b*) Area of equilateral triangle = $\frac{\sqrt{3}}{4} \times (\text{side})^2$

(*c*) Area of scalene triangle

$$= \sqrt{s(s-a)(s-b)(s-c)}$$

where, $s = \frac{a+b+c}{2}$

(vi) **Circle:**

(*a*) Area of circle = πr^2

(*b*) Circumference of a circle = $2\pi r$

(*c*) Length of arc = $\frac{\theta}{360} \times 2\pi r$

(*d*) Area of sector = $\frac{\theta}{360} \times \pi r^2$

Polygon

A polygon is plane figure bounded by multiple number of sides. Normally, it is used for figures enclosed by more than four sides: *e.g.*, pentagon, hexagon, octagon etc.

Regular Polygon

It is a polygon whose all sides are equal.

For a regular polygon of n equal sides, its vertex angle θ is given by

$$\theta = \left(\frac{n-2}{n}\right) \times 180°$$

Example: Find the area and perimeter of a rectangle whose length is 25 m and breadth is 15 m.

Solution: Area of rectangle $= l \times b$

$= 25 \times 15 = 375 \text{ m}^2$

Perimeter of rectangle $= 2(l + b)$

$= 2(25 + 15) = 80$ m

Example: Find the area of a rectangle whose one side is 6 m and the diagonal is 10 m.

Solution: Another side of rectangle = $\sqrt{(10)^2 - (6)^2}$

$= \sqrt{100-36} = \sqrt{64} = 8$ m

Area of rectangle $= l \times b = 8 \times 6 = 48 \text{ m}^2$

Example: Find area and perimeter of a square whose each side is 12 cm.

Solution: Area of square = $(\text{side})^2 = (12)^2 = 144 \text{ cm}^2$

Perimeter of square = 4 × side = 4 × 12 = 48 cm

Example: Find the area of a parallelogram whose base is 35 m and altitude 18 m.

Solution: Area of parallelogram = $b \times h$

$= 35 \times 18 = 630 \text{ m}^2$

Example: Find the area of a rhombus one side of which measures 20 cm and one diagonal 24 cm.

Solution: Since the diagonals of a rhombus bisect at right angles, so one side and half of each of the diagonals form a right angled triangle. In this right angled triangle,

One side = 20 cm, another side = $\frac{24}{2} = 12$ cm

Third side = $\sqrt{(20)^2 - (12)^2} = \sqrt{400-144}$

$= \sqrt{256} = 16$ cm

Hence other diagonal = 16 × 2 = 32 cm

Area of rhombus = $\frac{1}{2} \times d_1 \times d_2$

$= \frac{1}{2} \times 24 \times 32 = 12 \times 32$

$= 384 \text{ cm}^2$

Example: Find the area of an equilateral triangle each of whose sides measures 12 cm.

Solution: Area of equilateral triangle

$= \frac{\sqrt{3}}{4} (\text{side})^2 = \frac{\sqrt{3}}{4} \times (12)^2$

$$= \frac{\sqrt{3}}{4} \times 144 = 36\sqrt{3}\ \text{cm}^2$$

$$= 36 \times 1.73 = 62.28\ \text{cm}^2$$

EXAMPLE: Find the area of a triangle whose sides are 40 cm, 41 cm and 9 cm respectively.

SOLUTION: $s = \dfrac{a+b+c}{2} = \dfrac{9+40+41}{2}$

$$= \frac{90}{2} = 45\ \text{cm}$$

$$\text{Area of triangle} = \sqrt{s(s-a)(s-b)(s-c)}$$

$$= \sqrt{45(45-9)(45-40)(45-41)}$$

$$= \sqrt{45 \times 36 \times 5 \times 4}$$

$$= \sqrt{225 \times 144}$$

$$= 15 \times 12 = 180\ \text{cm}^2$$

EXAMPLE: Find the circumference and the area of a circle of radius 3.5 cm.

SOLUTION: Circumference $= 2\pi r$

$$= 2 \times \frac{22}{7} \times 3.5 = 22\ \text{cm}$$

$$\text{Area of circle} = \pi r^2 = \frac{22}{7} \times 3.5 \times 3.5$$

$$= 38.5\ \text{cm}^2$$

EXAMPLE: In a circle of radius 35 cm, an arc subtends an angle of 72° at the centre. Find the length of the arc and the area of the sector.

SOLUTION: Length of arc $= \dfrac{\theta}{360} \times 2\pi r$

$$= \frac{72}{360} \times 2 \times \frac{22}{7} \times 35$$

$$= 44\ \text{cm}$$

$$\text{Area of the sector} = \frac{\theta}{360} \times \pi r^2$$

$$= \frac{72}{360} \times \frac{22}{7} \times 35 \times 35$$

$$= 770\ \text{cm}^2$$

EXAMPLE: Find the area of a trapezium whose parallel sides are 77 cm, 60 cm and the other sides are 25 cm and 26 cm.

SOLUTION:

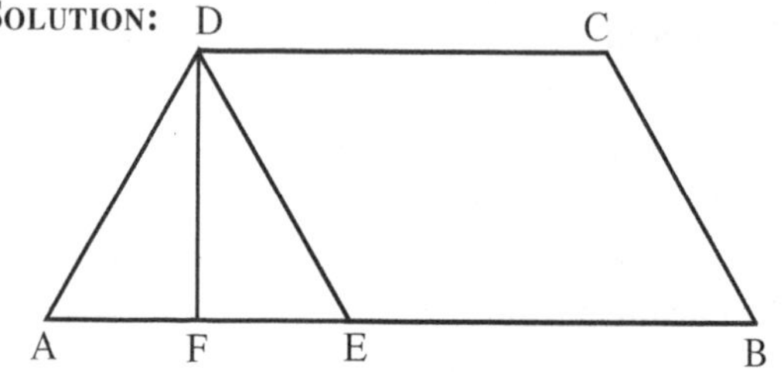

Let ABCD be the given trapezium in which AB = 77 cm, CD = 60 cm, BC = 25 cm, AD = 26 cm.

Draw DE || BC and DF ⊥ AB

Now, $\quad DE = BC = 25\ \text{cm}$

$$AE = AB - EB = AB - CD$$

$$= 77 - 60 = 17\ \text{cm}$$

In ΔDAE, $\quad s = \dfrac{17+25+26}{2} = \dfrac{68}{2} = 34\ \text{cm}$

$$\text{Area of } \Delta DAE = \sqrt{34(34-17)(34-25)(34-26)}$$

$$= \sqrt{34 \times 17 \times 9 \times 8} = 204\ \text{cm}^2$$

$$\text{Again area of } \Delta DAE = \frac{1}{2} \times AE \times DF$$

$$204 = \frac{1}{2} \times 17 \times DF$$

$$\Rightarrow \quad DF = \frac{2 \times 204}{17} = 24\ \text{cm}$$

$$\therefore \text{ Area of trapezium ABCD} = \frac{1}{2}(AB + CD) \times DF$$

$$= \frac{1}{2}(77 + 60) \times 24$$

$$= \frac{1}{2} \times 137 \times 24$$

$$= 1644\ \text{cm}^2$$

EXAMPLE: A copper wire when bent in the form of a square, encloses an area of 484 cm^2. If the same wire is bent in the form of circle, find the area enclosed by it.

SOLUTION: Area of the square = 484 cm^2

$$\text{Side} = \sqrt{484} = 22\ \text{cm}$$

$$\text{Length of wire} = \text{Perimeter of square}$$

$$= 4 \times \text{side} = 4 \times 22$$

$$= 88\ \text{cm}$$

Let r be the radius of the circle.

$\therefore$ Circumference of circle = Perimeter of square

$$\therefore \quad 2\pi r = 88 \Rightarrow r = \frac{88}{2\pi}$$

$$= \frac{88 \times 7}{2 \times 22} = 14 \text{ cm}$$

$$\text{Area of circle} = \pi r^2 = \frac{22}{7} \times 14 \times 14$$

$$= 616 \text{ cm}^2$$

Example: A bicycle wheel makes 5000 revolutions in moving 11 km. Find the diameter of the wheel.

Solution: Distance covered by the wheel in 1 revolution

$$= \frac{\text{Distance covered}}{\text{Number of revolutions}} = \frac{11}{5000} \text{ km}$$

$$= \frac{11 \times 1000 \times 100}{5000} \text{ cm} = 220 \text{ cm}$$

$\therefore$ Circumference of the wheel = 220 cm

$$2\pi r = 220 \Rightarrow 2 \times \frac{22}{7} \times r = 220$$

$$\Rightarrow \quad r = \frac{220 \times 7}{44} = 35 \text{ cm}$$

Hence, diameter of the wheel = 35 × 2 = 70 cm

Example: The perimeter of a square is 44 cm and circumference of a circle is 44 cm. Which area is greater and by how much?

Solution: Side of square = $\frac{44}{4}$ = 11 cm

Area of square = $(11)^2 = 121$ cm^2

Circumference of a circle = $2\pi r$

$$\Rightarrow \quad 44 = 2 \times \frac{22}{7} \times r$$

$$\Rightarrow \quad r = \frac{44 \times 7}{44} = 7 \text{ cm}$$

$$\text{Area of circle} = \pi r^2$$

$$= \frac{22}{7} \times 7 \times 7 = 154 \text{ cm}^2$$

Clearly, area of circle > area of square

Difference = 154 – 121 = 33 cm^2.

Example: A sheet of paper is in the form of a rectangle ABCD in which AB = 40 cm and AD = 28 cm. A semi-circular portion with BC as diameter is cut off. Find the area of the remaining paper.

Solution:

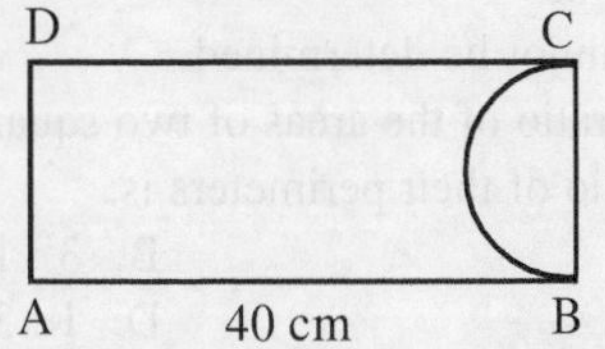

$$\text{Area of ABCD} = 40 \times 28 = 1120 \text{ cm}^2$$

$$\text{Area of semicircle} = \frac{1}{2}\pi r^2$$

$$= \frac{1}{2} \times \frac{22}{7} \times 14 \times 14$$

$$= 22 \times 14 = 308 \text{ cm}^2$$

Area of the remaining paper = 1120 – 308 = 812 cm^2

MULTIPLE CHOICE QUESTIONS

1. The length of a plot is four times its breadth. A playground measuring 1200 square metres occupies a third of the total area of the plot. What is the length of the plot, in metres?

A. 20 B. 30
C. 60 D. None of these

2. The width of a rectangular hall is $\frac{3}{4}$ of its length. If the area of the hall is 300 m^2, then the difference between its length and width is:

A. 3 m B. 4 m
C. 5 m D. 15 m

3. The length and breadth of a rectangular piece of land are in ratio of 5 : 3. The owner spent ₹ 3000 for surrounding it from all the sides at ₹ 7.50 per metre. The difference between its length and breadth is:

A. 50 m
B. 100 m
C. 150 m
D. 200 m

4. A room 8 m × 6 m is to be carpeted by a carpet 2 m wide. The length of carpet required is:

A. 12 m B. 36 m
C. 24 m D. 48 m

5. The length of a rectangle is increased by 60%. By what per cent would the width have to be decreased to maintain the same area?

A. $37\frac{1}{2}\%$ B. 60%
C. 75% D. 120%

6. A man walked 20 m to cross a rectangular field diagonally. If the length of the field is 16 m, the breadth of the rectangle is:

A. 4 m
B. 16 m
C. 12 m
D. Cannot be determined

7. If the ratio of the areas of two squares is 9 : 1, the ratio of their perimeters is:

A. 9 : 1 B. 3 : 1
C. 3 : 4 D. 1 : 3

8. The perimeter of both, a square and a rectangle are each equal to 48 m and the difference between their areas is 4 m^2. The breadth of the rectangle is:

A. 10 m B. 12 m
C. 14 m D. None of these

9. Area of a square with side x is equal to the area of a triangle with base x. The altitude of the triangle is:

A. $\frac{x}{2}$ B. x
C. $2x$ D. $4x$

10. If only the length of the rectangular plot is reduced to $\frac{2}{3}$rd of its original length, the ratio of original area to reduced area is:

A. 2 : 3 B. 3 : 2
C. 1 : 2 D. None of these

11. If the radius of a circle be reduced by 50%, its area is reduced by:

A. 25% B. 50%
C. 75% D. 100%

12. The perimeter of a rhombus is 52 m while its longer diagonal is 24 m. Its other diagonal is:

A. 5 m B. 10 m
C. 20 m D. 28 m

13. The circumference of a circle is 352 m, then its area in m^2 is:

A. 9856 B. 8956
C. 6589 D. 5986

14. A wheel makes 100 revolutions in covering a distance of 88 km. The diameter of the wheel is:

A. 240 m B. 400 m
C. 280 m D. 140 m

15. If the diameter of a circle is increased by 100%, its area is increased by:

A. 100% B. 200%
C. 300% D. 400%

16. The area of a sector of a circle of radius 5 cm formed by an arc of length 3.5 cm, is:

A. 35 cm^2 B. 17.5 cm^2
C. 8.75 cm^2 D. 55 cm^2

17. A circular wire of radius 42 cm is cut and bent in the form of a rectangle whose sides are in the ratio 6 : 5. The smaller side of the rectangle is:

A. 30 cm B. 60 cm
C. 72 cm D. 132 cm

18. The length of a minute hand on a wall clock is 7 cm. The area swept by the minute hand in 30 minutes is:

A. 147 cm^2 B. 210 cm^2
C. 154 cm^2 D. 77 cm^2

19. A circle and a square have same area. The ratio of the side of the square and the radius of the circle is:

A. $\sqrt{\pi} : 1$ B. $1 : \sqrt{\pi}$
C. $1 : \pi$ D. $\pi : 1$

20. The dimensions of the floor of a rectangular hall are 4 m × 3 m. The floor of the hall is to be tiled fully with 8 cm × 6 cm rectangular tiles without breaking tiles to smaller sizes. The number of tiles required is:

A. 4800 B. 2600
C. 2500 D. 2400

ANSWERS

1	2	3	4	5	6	7	8	9	10
D	C	A	C	A	C	B	A	C	B
11	**12**	**13**	**14**	**15**	**16**	**17**	**18**	**19**	**20**
C	B	A	C	C	C	B	D	A	C

EXPLANATORY ANSWERS

1. Area of the plot = 3 × 1200 = 3600 m^2
Let breadth be x m. Then length = $4x$ m
According to the question,
$4x \times x = 3600 \Rightarrow x^2 = 900 \Rightarrow x = 30$
Hence, length of the plot = 4 × 30 = 120 m.

2. Let length be x m, then breadth = $\frac{3x}{4}$ m

Area of the hall = $x \times \frac{3x}{4} = \frac{3x^2}{4}$

According to the question,

$\frac{3x^2}{4} = 300 \Rightarrow x^2 = 400 \Rightarrow x = 20$

Length = 20 m and breadth = $\frac{3}{4} \times 20 = 15$ m

Difference = 20 – 15 = 5 m

3. Let length = $5x$ m and breadth = $3x$ m
Perimeter of rectangle = $2(5x + 3x) = 16x$ m

But perimeter = $\frac{\text{Total cost}}{\text{Rate}} = \frac{3000}{7.50} = 400$ m

Now, $16x = 400 \Rightarrow x = 25$
length = $5x = 5 \times 25 = 125$ m
breadth = $3x = 25 \times 3 = 75$ m
Difference = 125 – 75 = 50 m

4. Length of the carpet = $\frac{8 \times 6}{2} = 24$ m.

5. Initially, let length = x and breadth = y
Let new breadth = z.

Then new length = $\frac{160x}{100} = \frac{8x}{5}$

$\therefore \quad \frac{8x}{5} \times z = xy \Rightarrow z = \frac{5y}{8}$

Decrease in breadth = $\left(y - \frac{5y}{8}\right) = \frac{3y}{8}$

$\therefore$ Decrease per cent = $\frac{3y}{8} \times \frac{1}{y} \times 100$

$= \frac{75}{2} = 37.5\% =$

6. Breadth = $\sqrt{(20)^2 - (16)^2}$

$= \sqrt{400 - 256} = \sqrt{144} = 12$ m.

7. Let the areas of the squares be $(9x^2)$ m^2 and (x^2) m^2
Then, their sides are $3x$ m and x m respectively

Ratio of their perimeters = $\frac{12x}{4x} = 3:1$

8. Let length of rectangle = x m
and breadth of rectangle = y m
Also, let the side of the square be z m
According to the question,
$2(x + y) = 4z = 48$
$x + y = 24$ and $z = 12$
Also, $z^2 - xy = 4$
$\Rightarrow \quad (12)^2 - 4 = xy$
$\Rightarrow \quad xy = 140$
$\because \quad x + y = 24$ and $xy = 140$
$(x - y)^2 = (x + y)^2 - 4xy$
$\Rightarrow \quad (x - y)^2 = (24)^2 - 4(140)$
$\Rightarrow \quad (x - y)^2 = 576 - 560 = 16$
$\Rightarrow \quad x - y = 4$
Now, $x + y = 24$
$x - y = 4$
Solving and get $x = 14$, $y = 10$
Hence, breadth of rectangle = 10 m.

9. According to the question,

$x^2 = \frac{1}{2} \times x \times h$

$\Rightarrow \quad h = \frac{2x^2}{x} = 2x$

10. Let length = x and breadth = y

New length = $\frac{2}{3}x$

$\therefore \frac{\text{Original area}}{\text{Reduced area}} = \frac{xy}{\frac{2}{3}xy} = \frac{3}{2} = 3:2$

11. Original area = πr^2, New area = $\pi\left(\frac{r}{2}\right)^2 = \frac{\pi r^2}{4}$

Reduction in area = $\pi r^2 - \frac{\pi r^2}{4} = \frac{3\pi r^2}{4}$

Reduction per cent = $\frac{3\pi r^2}{4} \times \frac{1}{\pi r^2} \times 100 = 75\%$

12. Side of rhombus = $\frac{52}{4}$ = 13 m

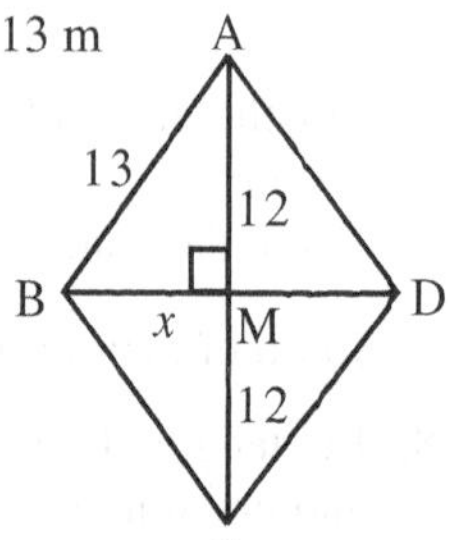

In ΔABM,

$x^2 = (13)^2 - (12)^2$

$x^2 = 169 - 144$

$x^2 = 25$

$\Rightarrow x = 5$ m

$\therefore$ Another diagonal

= 2 × 5 = 10 m

13. Circumference of a circle = $2\pi r$

$\Rightarrow 352 = 2 \times \frac{22}{7} \times r$

$\Rightarrow r = \frac{352 \times 7}{44} = 56$ m

Area of circle = $\pi r^2 = \frac{22}{7} \times 56 \times 56$

= 9856 m^2

14. Distance travelled in 1 revolution = $\frac{88 \times 1000}{100}$

= 880 m

Circumference of a wheel = $2\pi r$

$\therefore 880 = 2 \times \frac{22}{7} \times r$

$\Rightarrow r = \frac{880 \times 7}{44} = 140$ m

$\therefore$ Diameter of the wheel = 140 × 2 = 280 m

15. Original area = $\pi\left(\frac{d}{2}\right)^2 = \frac{\pi d^2}{4}$

New area = $\pi \times \left(\frac{2d}{2}\right)^2 = \pi d^2$

Increase in area = $\pi d^2 - \frac{\pi d^2}{4} = \frac{3\pi d^2}{4}$

$\therefore$ Increase per cent = $\frac{3\pi d^2}{4} \times \frac{4}{\pi d^2} \times 100$

= 300%

16. Area of sector = $\left(\frac{1}{2} \times r^2 \times \frac{\text{arc}}{r}\right)$

$= \frac{1}{2} \times 5 \times 3.5 = 8.75 \text{ cm}^2$

17. Circumference of a circle = $2\pi r$

$= 2 \times \frac{22}{7} \times 42 = 264$ cm

Let length of rectangle = $6x$

and breadth of rectangle = $5x$.

$\therefore 2(6x + 5x) = 264$

$\Rightarrow 22x = 264 \Rightarrow x = 12$

Hence, smaller side of rectangle

$= 5x = 5 \times 12 = 60$ cm

18. Angle formed in 30 minutes = $\frac{360}{60} \times 30 = 180°$

Area swept = $\frac{\theta}{360}\pi r^2$

$= \frac{180}{360} \times \frac{22}{7} \times 7 \times 7 = 77 \text{ cm}^2$.

19. $\because$ Area of square = Area of circle

$\Rightarrow x^2 = \pi r^2 \Rightarrow \frac{x}{r} = \sqrt{\pi}$

$\Rightarrow \frac{x}{r} = \frac{\sqrt{\pi}}{1} \Rightarrow x : r = \sqrt{\pi} : 1$

20. Area of the floor = 400 × 300 cm^2

Area of each tile = 8 × 6 cm^2

$\therefore$ Number of tiles = $\frac{400 \times 300}{8 \times 6} = 2500$

12

CHAPTER

Volume and Surface Area

We know that every real object occupies some space. It is usually specified by its three dimensions—length, breadth and depth (or height or thickness). It may be a solid or a hollow object. In case of circular, cylindrical and spherical object the specifying dimensions may change to radius, angle etc. The amount of space occupied by the object is called its volume. Its unit of measurement is m^3, cm^3, $(\text{inches})^3$ etc. The area of the surfaces (plane/curved) of the object is called its surface area.

A Cuboid and A Cube

The solid like wooden boxes, tea containers, match box etc. which have six faces, each of which is a rectangle, are called cuboids. It has 12 edges.

A cuboid in which every face is a square is called a cube. Length of each face of a cube is called its edge.

Prism

A right prism is a solid in which the two ends are congruent parallel figures and the side faces are rectangles. The total area of side faces of a prism is called the lateral surface of the prism.

Cylinder

The solid generated by the revolution of a rectangle about one of its sides as axis is called a cylinder.

Pyramid

A solid whose base is a plane rectilinear figure having the side faces as triangles meeting at a common vertex is called a pyramid. When the base of a pyramid is a triangle, the pyramid is called a tetrahedron.

Cone

The solid generated by the revolution of a right angled triangle about one of the sides containing the right angle as the axis is called a right circular cone.

The perpendicular distance from the vertex to the base is called the height of the cone and the length of slant face from vertex to the base is called the slant height of the cone.

Frustum

If a cone is cut by a plane parallel to the base so as to divide the cone into two parts, then the lower part is called the frustum of the cone.

Sphere

When a semicircle moves about its diameter, the solid generated is called a sphere.

Formulae

Cuboid:

Volume of cuboid = $l \times b \times h$ cubic units

Whole surface area = $2(lb + bh + hl)$ square units

Diagonal of cuboid = $\sqrt{l^2 + b^2 + h^2}$ units

Area of 4 walls of a room = $2(l + b) \times h$ square units

Cube:

Volume of cube = a^3 cubic units

Side of cube = $\sqrt[3]{\text{Volume}}$

Lateral surface area = $4a^2$ square units

Total surface area = $6a^2$ square units

Diagonal of the cube = $\left(\sqrt{3}\,a\right)$ units

Cylinder:

Volume of cylinder = $\pi r^2 h$ cubic units

Lateral surface area = $2\pi rh$ square units

Total surface area = $2\pi r(h + r)$ square units

Cone:

Volume of cone = $\frac{1}{3}\pi r^2 h$ cubic units

Lateral surface area = πrl square units

Total surface area = $\pi r(l + r)$ square units

Slant height (l) = $\sqrt{r^2 + h^2}$

Sphere:

Volume of sphere = $\frac{4}{3}\pi r^3$ cubic units

Surface area = $4\pi r^2$ square units

Hemisphere:

Volume = $\frac{2}{3}\pi r^3$ cubic units

Lateral surface area = $2\pi r^2$ square units

Total surface area = $3\pi r^2$ square units

Frustum:

Volume = $\frac{1}{3}\pi h(r_1^2 + r_1 r_2 + r_2^2)$ cubic units

Curved surface area = $\pi(r_1 + r_2) \times l$ square units

Total surface area = $\pi\left[r_1^2 + r_2^2 + (r_1 + r_2)l\right]$ square units

Pyramid:

Volume = $\frac{1}{2} \times$ (area of base) $\times$ height cubic units

EXAMPLE: The dimensions of a metallic cuboid are 100 cm × 80 cm × 64 cm. It is melted and recast into cube. Find the total surface area of the cube.

SOLUTION: Volume of cuboid = $l \times b \times h$

$= 100 \times 80 \times 64$

$= 512000 \text{ cm}^3$

Volume of cube = a^3

According to the question,

$a^3 = 512000$

$\Rightarrow \quad a^3 = 8 \times 8 \times 8 \times 10 \times 10 \times 10$

$\Rightarrow \quad a = 8 \times 10 = 80$ cm

Total surface area of cube = $6a^2 = 6 \times 80 \times 80 = 38400$

Hence, total surface area of cube is 38400 cm^2.

EXAMPLE: Three cubes whose edges measure 3 cm, 4 cm and 5 cm respectively form a single cube. Find the total surface area of the new cube.

SOLUTION: Let the edge of new cube = x cm

$x^3 = 3^3 + 4^3 + 5^3$

$= 27 + 64 + 125 = 216 \text{ cm}^3$

$\Rightarrow \quad x^3 = 6 \times 6 \times 6 \Rightarrow x = 6$ cm

Total surface area of cube = $6(x)^2 = 6 \times 6 \times 6 = 216 \text{ cm}^2$

Hence, total surface area of new cube = 216 cm^2.

EXAMPLE: The capacity of a cylindrical tank is 6160 m^3. If the radius of its base is 14 m, find the depth of the tank.

SOLUTION: Volume of cylinder = $\pi r^2 h$

$\pi r^2 h = 6160$

$\Rightarrow \quad \frac{22}{7} \times 14 \times 14 \times h = 6160$

$\Rightarrow \quad h = \frac{6160}{44 \times 14} = 10$ m

Hence, depth of the tank is 10 m.

EXAMPLE: How many bullets can be made out of a lead cylinder 28 cm high and 6 cm radius, each bullet being 1.5 cm in diameter?

SOLUTION: Number of bullets

$$= \frac{\text{Volume of cylinder}}{\text{Volume of 1 bullet}}$$

$$= \frac{\pi \times 6 \times 6 \times 28}{\frac{4}{3} \times \pi \times 0.75 \times 0.75 \times 0.75}$$

$$= \frac{6 \times 6 \times 28 \times 3}{4 \times \frac{3}{4} \times \frac{3}{4} \times \frac{3}{4}} = \frac{6 \times 6 \times 28 \times 4 \times 4 \times 3}{3 \times 3 \times 3}$$

$= 1792$

EXAMPLE: A metal sphere of diameter 42 cm is dropped into a cylindrical vessel, which is partly filled with water. The diameter of the vessel is 1.68 metres. If the sphere is completely submerged, find by how much the surface of water will rise.

SOLUTION: Radius of the sphere = 21 cm

Volume of sphere = $\frac{4}{3}\pi r^3$

$= \frac{4}{3} \times \frac{22}{7} \times 21 \times 21 \times 21$

$= 38808 \text{ cm}^3$

Volume of water displaced by sphere = 38808 cm^3

Let water rise by h cm.

$$\text{Volume of cylinder} = \pi r^2 h$$

$$\frac{22}{7} \times 84 \times 84 \times h = 38808$$

$$\Rightarrow \quad h = \frac{38808 \times 7}{22 \times 84 \times 84} = \frac{7}{4} = 1.75 \text{ cm}$$

EXAMPLE: A tent is in the form of a right circular cylinder surmounted by a cone. The diameter of cylinder is 24 m. The height of the cylindrical portion is 11 m while the vertex of the cone is 16 m above the ground. Find the area of the canvas required for the tent.

SOLUTION: Lateral surface area of cylinder = $2\pi rh$

$$= 2 \times \frac{22}{7} \times 12 \times 11 = \frac{5808}{7} \text{ m}^2$$

Height of cone = 16 – 11 = 5 m

Radius of cone = 12 m

$$\text{Slant height } l = \sqrt{r^2 + h^2} = \sqrt{12^2 + 5^2}$$

$$= \sqrt{169} = 13 \text{ m}$$

Lateral surface area of cone = πrl

$$= \frac{22}{7} \times 12 \times 13 = \frac{3432}{7} \text{ m}^2$$

$$\text{Area of canvas} = \frac{5808}{7} + \frac{3432}{7}$$

$$= \frac{9240}{7} = 1320 \text{ m}^2$$

EXAMPLE: The slant height of the frustum of a cone is 20 cm and the height of the frustum is 16 cm. The radius of the smaller circle is 8 cm. Find the volume and total surface area of the frustum.

SOLUTION: $l = \sqrt{h^2 + (R - r)^2} = \sqrt{16^2 + (R - 8)^2}$

$$\Rightarrow \quad 20 = \sqrt{256 + R^2 - 16R + 64}$$

$$= \sqrt{R^2 - 16R + 320}$$

$$\Rightarrow R^2 - 16R + 320 = 400$$

$$\Rightarrow R^2 - 16R - 80 = 0 \Rightarrow R = 20 \text{ cm}$$

$$\text{Volume of frustum} = \frac{1}{3}\pi h(R^2 + r^2 + Rr)$$

$$= \frac{1}{3} \times \frac{22}{7} \times 16(400 + 64 + 160)$$

$$= \frac{73216}{7} \text{ cm}^3$$

$$\text{Total surface area} = \pi(R^2 + r^2 + Rl + rl)$$

$$= \frac{22}{7}(400 + 64 + 400 + 160)$$

$$= \frac{22}{7} \times 1024 = \frac{22528}{7}$$

$$= 3218.28 \text{ cm}^2$$

EXAMPLE: The length of a garden roller is 2 m and diameter is 1.4 m. How much area will it cover in 10 revolutions?

SOLUTION: Area covered

= Curved surface × no. of revolutions

= $2\pi rh \times 10$

$$= 2 \times \frac{22}{7} \times 0.7 \times 2 \times 10 = 88 \text{ m}^2$$

EXAMPLE: A cylinder is made by lead whose radius is 4 cm and height is 10 cm. By melting it how many spheres of radius 2 cm can be made?

SOLUTION: Given, radius of the cylinder = 4 cm

and height of the cylinder = 10 cm

$$\therefore \quad \text{Volume of the cylinder} = \pi r^2 h = \pi(4)^2 \times 10$$

$$= 160\pi \text{ cm}^3$$

$$\text{Volume of sphere} = \frac{4}{3}\pi r^3 = \frac{4}{3}\pi(2)^3$$

$$= \frac{32}{3}\pi \text{ cm}^3$$

$$\therefore \quad \text{Number of spheres} = \frac{\text{Volume of cylinder}}{\text{Volume of one sphere}}$$

$$= \frac{160\pi}{\frac{32}{3}\pi} = \frac{160 \times 3}{32} = 15$$

Hence, number of spheres that can be made are 15.

MULTIPLE CHOICE QUESTIONS

1. The surface area of a cube is 726 m^2. The volume of cube is:

A. 1300 m^3 B. 1331 m^3
C. 1452 m^3 D. 1542 m^3

2. Sum of the length, width and depth of a cuboid is s and its diagonal is d. Its surface area is:

A. s^2 B. d^2
C. $s^2 - d^2$ D. $s^2 + d^2$

3. A wooden box of dimensions 8 m × 7 m × 6 m is to carry rectangular boxes of dimensions 8 cm × 7 cm × 6 cm. The maximum number of boxes that can be carried in 1 wooden box is:

A. 1200000 B. 1000000
C. 9800000 D. 7500000

4. The length of the longest rod that can be placed in a room 30 m long, 24 m broad and 18 m high is:

A. 30 m B. $15\sqrt{2}$ m
C. 60 m D. $30\sqrt{2}$ m

5. If the volume of two cubes are in the ratio 8 : 1, the ratio of their edges is:

A. 8 : 1 B. $2\sqrt{2} : 1$
C. 2 : 1 D. None of these

6. A metal sheet 27 cm long 8 cm broad and 1 cm thick is melted into a cube. The difference between the surface areas of two solids will be:

A. 284 cm^2 B. 296 cm^2
C. 286 cm^2 D. 300 cm^2

7. If each edge of a cube is increased by 50%, the percentage increase in surface area is:

A. 50% B. 75%
C. 100% D. 125%

8. If a right circular cone of vertical height 24 cm has a volume of 1232 cm^3, then the area of its curved surface in cm^2 is:

A. 1254 B. 704
C. 550 D. 154

9. Two cubes have volumes in the ratio 1 : 27. The ratio of their surface areas is:

A. 1 : 3 B. 1 : 8
C. 1 : 9 D. 1 : 18

10. If the volumes of two cones are in the ratio 1 : 4 and their diameters are in the ratio 4 : 5, then the ratio of their heights is:

A. 1 : 5 B. 5 : 4
C. 5 : 16 D. 25 : 64

11. The radius of a wire is decreased to one-third. If volumes remains the same, length will increase:

A. 1 time B. 3 times
C. 6 times D. 9 times

12. A cylindrical piece of metal of radius 2 cm and height 6 cm is shaped into a cone of same radius. The height of cone is:

A. 18 cm B. 14 cm
C. 12 cm D. 8 cm

13. If 1 cubic cm of cast iron weight 21 g then the weight of a cast iron pipe of length 1 m with a bore of 3 cm and in which the thickness of the metal is 1 cm, is:

A. 21 kg B. 24.2 kg
C. 26.4 kg D. 18.6 kg

14. The number of solid spheres, each of diameter 6 cm, that could be moulded to form a solid metal cylinder of height 45 cm and diameter 4 cms, is:

A. 3 B. 4
C. 5 D. 6

15. A right cylinder and a right circular cone have the same radius and the same volume. The ratio of the height of the cylinder to that of the cone is:

A. 3 : 5 B. 2 : 5
C. 3 : 1 D. 1 : 3

16. If a solid sphere of radius 10 cm is moulded into 8 spherical solid balls of equal radius, then surface area of each ball (in cm^2) is:

A. 100π B. 75π
C. 60π D. 50π

17. The radii of two spheres are in the ratio 1 : 2. The ratio of their surface areas, is:

A. 1 : 2 B. 1 : 4
C. $1 : \sqrt{2}$ D. 3 : 8

18. The radii of two cylinders are in the ratio 2 : 3 and their heights are in the ratio 5 : 3, then their volumes will be in ratio:

A. 4 : 9 B. 27 : 20
C. 20 : 27 D. 9 : 4

19. The volume of a hemisphere is 19404 cm^3. The total surface area is:

A. 2772 cm^2 B. 4158 cm^2
C. 5544 cm^2 D. 1386 cm^2

20. If the volume and surface area of a sphere are numerically the same, then its radius is:

A. 1 unit B. 2 units
C. 3 units D. 4 units

ANSWERS

1	2	3	4	5	6	7	8	9	10
B	C	B	D	C	C	D	C	C	D
11	**12**	**13**	**14**	**15**	**16**	**17**	**18**	**19**	**20**
D	A	C	C	D	A	B	C	B	C

EXPLANATORY ANSWERS

1. Surface area of cube = $6a^2$

$6a^2 = 726 \Rightarrow a^2 = \frac{726}{6} = 121 \Rightarrow a = 11$ m

Volume of cube = $a^3 = 11 \times 11 \times 11 = 1331$ m^3

2. $l + b + h = s$

and $\sqrt{l^2 + b^2 + h^2} = d \Rightarrow l^2 + b^2 + h^2 = d^2$

$(l + b + h)^2 = s^2$

$\Rightarrow l^2 + b^2 + h^2 + 2(lb + bh + hl) = s^2$

$\Rightarrow d^2 + 2(lb + bh + hl) = s^2$

$\Rightarrow 2(lb + bh + hl) = s^2 - d^2$

$\therefore$ Surface area = $(s^2 - d^2)$.

3. Number of boxes = $\frac{800 \times 700 \times 600}{8 \times 7 \times 6} = 1000000$

4. Diagonal of cuboid = $\sqrt{l^2 + b^2 + h^2}$

$\therefore$ Length of longest rod = $\sqrt{30^2 + 24^2 + 18^2}$

$= \sqrt{900 + 576 + 324} = \sqrt{1800}$

$= \sqrt{30 \times 30 \times 2} = 30\sqrt{2}$ m

5. Let their volumes be $8x^3$ and x^3.

Then, their sides are $2x$ and x

$\therefore$ Ratio of their edges = 2 : 1

6. Volume of sheet = $27 \times 8 \times 1 = 216$ cm^3

Volume of cube formed = 216 cm^3

Side of cube = $\sqrt[3]{216} = 6$ cm

Surface area of cuboid = $2(lb + bh + hl)$

$= 2(27 \times 8 + 8 \times 1 + 1 \times 27) = 502$ cm^2

Surface area of cube = $6(\text{side})^2 = 6 \times 36 = 216$ cm^2

Difference in areas = $502 - 216 = 286$ cm^2

7. Let original length of cube = x

then, its surface area = $6x^2$

New edge = $\left(\frac{150}{100}x\right) = \frac{3}{2}x$

New surface area = $6 \times \left(\frac{3}{2}x\right)^2$

$= 6 \times \frac{9}{4}x^2 = \frac{27}{2}x^2$

Increase in surface area = $\left(\frac{27}{2} - 6\right)x^2 = \frac{15}{2}x^2$

$\therefore$ Increase % = $\frac{15x^2/2}{6x^2} \times 100$

$= \frac{15x^2}{12x^2} \times 100 = 125\%$

8. Volume of cone = 1232

$\Rightarrow \frac{1}{3}\pi r^2 h = 1232$

$\Rightarrow \frac{1}{3} \times \frac{22}{7} \times r^2 \times 24 = 1232$

$\Rightarrow r^2 = \frac{3 \times 7 \times 1232}{22 \times 24} = 49 \Rightarrow r = 7$ cm

$\Rightarrow l = \sqrt{r^2 + h^2} = \sqrt{7^2 + 24^2} = \sqrt{625} = 25$ cm

Lateral surface area of cone = $\pi r l$

$= \frac{22}{7} \times 7 \times 25 = 22 \times 25 = 550$ cm^2

9. Let their volumes are x^3 and $27x^3$.

Then, their sides are x and $3x$.

Ratio of their surface areas = $\frac{6x^2}{6(3x)^2} = \frac{x^2}{9x^2}$

$= 1 : 9$

10. Let the diameters of the bases of the cones be $4r$ and $5r$. Let their heights be h and H.

then, $$\frac{\frac{1}{3}\pi \times \left(\frac{4r}{2}\right)^2 \times h}{\frac{1}{3}\pi\left(\frac{5r}{2}\right)^2 \times H} = \frac{1}{4}$$

$$\Rightarrow \quad \frac{16}{25} \times \frac{h}{H} = \frac{1}{4}$$

$$\Rightarrow \quad \frac{h}{H} = \frac{25}{64}$$

11. Let original radius $= r$
and original length $= h$

New radius $= \frac{1}{3}r$

Let new length = H

then, $$\pi r^2 h = \pi\left(\frac{1}{3}r\right)^2 \times H = \frac{\pi r^2 H}{9}$$

$\therefore \quad H = 9h$

Thus length becomes 9 times.

12. Volume of cone = Volume of cylinder

$$\frac{1}{3}\pi r^2 h = \pi r^2 h$$

$$\Rightarrow \quad \frac{1}{3} \times \frac{22}{7} \times 2 \times 2 \times h = \frac{22}{7} \times 2 \times 2 \times 6$$

$$\Rightarrow \quad \frac{h}{3} = 6 \Rightarrow h = 18 \text{ cm}$$

$\therefore$ Height of cone = 18 cm

13. Diameter = 3 cm, h = 1 m = 100 cm

$\therefore$ Radius $= \frac{3}{2}$ cm = 1.5 cm

thickness = 1 cm

$\therefore \quad R = 1.5 + 1 = 2.5$ cm

$r = 1.5$ cm

Volume of metal $= \pi(R^2 - r^2) \times h$
$= \pi[(2.5)^2 - (1.5)^2] \times 100$
$= \pi[4] \times 100 = \pi \times 400 \text{ cm}^3$

$\because \quad 1 \text{ cm}^3 = 21$ g

$\therefore \quad \pi \times 400 \text{ cm}^3 = 21 \times \pi \times 400$ g

$$= 21 \times \frac{22}{7} \times \frac{400}{1000} \text{ kg}$$

= 26.4 kg

14. Number of spheres $= \frac{\text{Volume of cylinder}}{\text{Volume of sphere}}$

$$= \frac{\pi \times 2 \times 2 \times 45}{\frac{4}{3}\pi \times (3)^3} = \frac{4 \times 45 \times 3}{4 \times 27} = 5$$

15. Volume of cylinder = Volume of cone

$$\pi r^2 h = \frac{1}{3}\pi r^2 H$$

$$\Rightarrow \quad 3h = H \Rightarrow \frac{h}{H} = \frac{1}{3}$$

16. $$\frac{4}{3}\pi R^3 = 8 \times \frac{4}{3}\pi r^3$$

$$\Rightarrow \quad \frac{4}{3}\pi \times 10 \times 10 \times 10 = 8 \times \frac{4}{3}\pi r^3$$

$$\Rightarrow \quad 8r^3 = 1000 \Rightarrow r^3 = \frac{1000}{8}$$

$$\Rightarrow \quad r^3 = 125 \Rightarrow r = 5 \text{ cm}$$

Surface area of each ball $= 4\pi r^2$
$= 4 \times \pi \times 5^2$
$= 100\ \pi \text{ cm}^2$

17. Let the radii of spheres are r and $2r$.

Ratio of surface areas $= \frac{4\pi r^2}{4\pi(2r)^2} = \frac{r^2}{4r^2} = 1 : 4$

18. Let the radii of cylinders are $2r$ and $3r$
and heights are $5x$ and $3x$
Ratio of their volumes

$$= \frac{\pi(2r)^2 \times 5x}{\pi(3r)^2 \times 3x} = \frac{4r^2 \times 5}{9r^2 \times 3} = \frac{20}{27}$$

19. Volume of hemisphere = 19404

$$\Rightarrow \quad \frac{2}{3}\pi r^3 = 19404 \Rightarrow \frac{2}{3} \times \frac{22}{7} r^3 = 19404$$

$$\Rightarrow \quad r^3 = \frac{3 \times 19404 \times 7}{2 \times 22} = 9261$$

$$\Rightarrow \quad r = 21 \text{ cm}$$

Surface area $= 3\pi r^2 = 3 \times \frac{22}{7} \times 21 \times 21$
$= 4158 \text{ cm}^2$

20. $$\frac{4}{3}\pi r^3 = 4\pi r^2$$

$$\Rightarrow \quad \frac{r}{3} = 1 \Rightarrow r = 3 \text{ units}$$

13

CHAPTER

Data Interpretation

The collection of figures and facts in every field is called the statistical data. There are three types of statistical data.

(*a*) **Primary data:** The data collected by the investigator or the statistician to be used or integrated himself are called primary data. It is more reliable and relevant because it is collected by the investigator himself for the first time for his study.

(*b*) **Secondary data:** The data which are collected originally by someone else and used and interpreted by others for statistical analysis are called secondary data.

(*c*) **Grouped data:** When primary data is arranged in classes or groups to bring out certain sailent feature of the data is called grouped data.

Graphical Representation of Data

A graph is a visual form for presentation of data, highlighting their basic facts and relationship.

The word graph, chart and diagram are used interchangeably for the pictorial representation of data. However, the visual form made by using rectangular coordinate system is called a graph. In general, the other pictorial representation in which the coordinate system is not used are called diagrams or charts.

Variate: The quantity that we measure from observation-to-observation is called a variate.

Class-Interval: Every data is generally divided into small group using some interval is said to be in class-interval, *e.g.*, 0–5, 5–10, 10–15 etc.

Class-Size: The difference between the true upper limit and true lower limit of a class gives the size of a class-interval, *e.g.*, class-size of the class-interval 0–5 is 5.

Mid Value: The variable value which is mid-way between the lower and upper limit of a class is called its mid-value, *e.g.*, mid-value of class-interval 0–5 is $\frac{0+5}{2} = 2.5$.

Frequency: The number of observations corresponding to particular class is said to be the frequency of that class, *e.g.*, frequency of the interval 5–10 is 6. It means 6 persons have got 5 or more articles but less than 10.

Cumulative Frequency: The sum of the preceding frequencies is called cumulative frequency. Last frequency of cumulative frequency column is equal to the sum of the frequencies.

Class Limit: Every interval has two limits. Lower number of the interval is called lower limit while upper number of the interval is called upper limit, *e.g.*, in class-interval 0–5, 0 is lower limit while 5 is the upper limit.

Histogram

A statistical graph that represents by the height of a rectangular column the number of times that each class of result occurs in a sample or experiment, *e.g.*, the following table represents the number of matured persons in age group (15–20) in a city.

Age Group	Number of persons
15–20	200
20–25	350
25–30	475
30–35	600
35–40	750
40–45	900
45–50	100

Then the histogram of the data is given below:

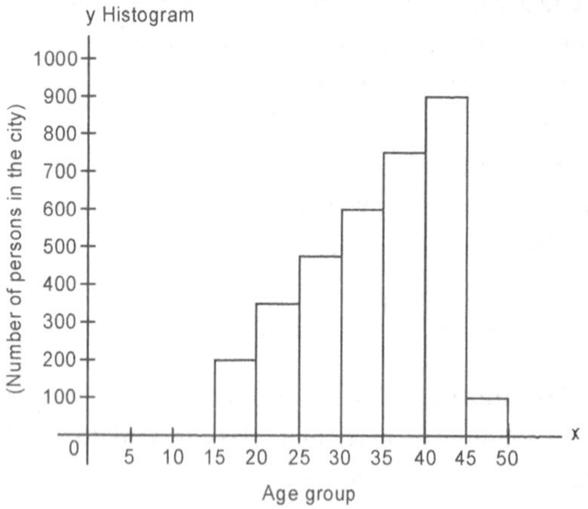

Bar Chart

A graph consisting of bars whose lengths are proportional to quantities in a set of data. It can be used when one axis cannot have a numerical scale, *e.g.*, to show how many different columns of flowers grow from a packet of mixed seeds, *e.g.*,

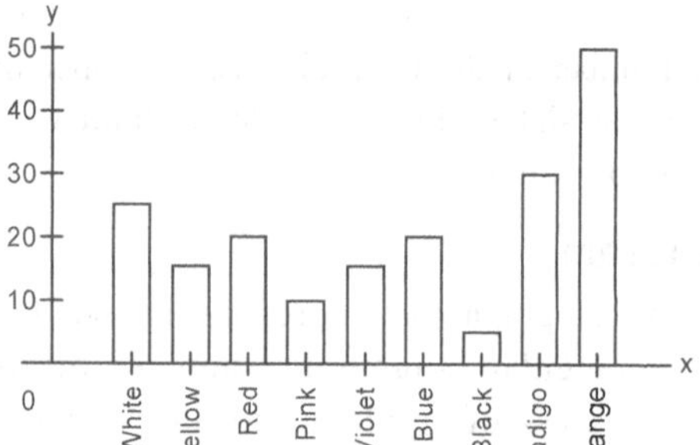

Pie Chart

A diagram in which proportions are illustrated as sectors of a circle. The relative area of the sectors representing the different proportions, *e.g.*, if out of 100 military personnels 25 personnels use tank, 30 personnels use warship, 40 personnels use aircraft and rest of them use rifles. Then pie-chart of the above data is

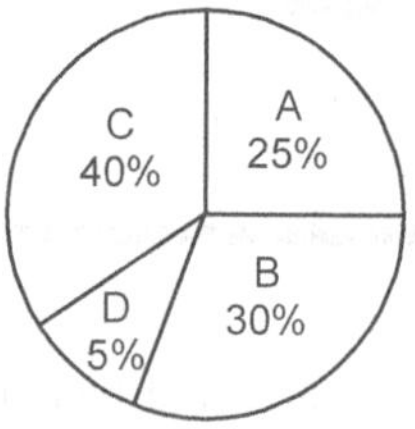

$$\text{A uses tank} = \frac{25}{100} \times 360 = 90^\circ$$

$$\text{B uses warship} = \frac{30}{100} \times 360 = 108^\circ$$

$$\text{C uses aircraft} = \frac{40}{100} \times 360 = 144^\circ$$

$$\text{D uses rifles} = \frac{5}{100} \times 360 = 18^\circ$$

EXAMPLE: Find out the marks obtained in different subjects from the following pie-diagram, if the total marks be 540.

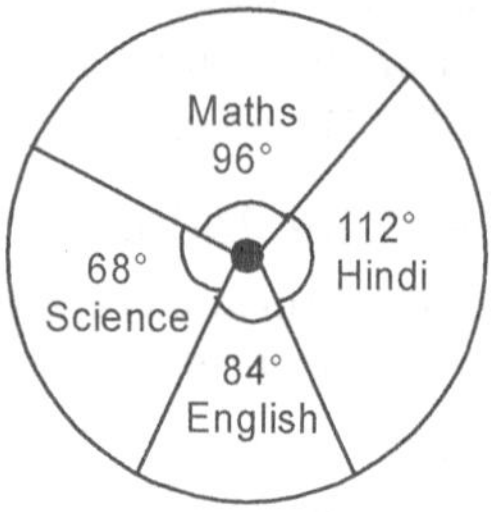

SOLUTION: Sum of the angles at the centre of circle = 360°

$$\text{Total marks} = 540$$

$$\therefore \text{ Marks obtained in Hindi} = \frac{112}{360} \times 540 = 168$$

$$\text{Marks obtained in English} = \frac{84}{360} \times 540 = 126$$

$$\text{Marks obtained in Science} = \frac{68}{360} \times 540 = 102$$

$$\text{Marks obtained in Maths} = \frac{96}{360} \times 540 = 144$$

MULTIPLE CHOICE QUESTIONS

Directions (Qs. 1 to 5): *Answers the questions on the basis of the following table:*

Assume all colleges sent equal number of candidates in all subjects for the examination.

Percentage of results for Subjects

College	Maths	Physics	Chemistry	Zoology	Botany
A	52	65	62	47	40
B	47	62	52	35	38
C	53	70	46	54	39
D	35	72	58	62	57

1. Taking all the colleges into account which subject has shown highest percentage result?
A. Chemistry
B. Maths
C. Zoology
D. Physics

2. Taking the performance in all the subjects into account which college has shown highest level of percentage results?
A. D B. A
C. B D. C

3. Seeing the performance of all the four colleges together which combination of groups has shown lowest level of percentage results?
A. Zoology and Botany
B. Physics and Chemistry
C. Maths and Physics
D. Chemistry and Botany

4. Taking all the colleges into account which subject has shown lowest percentage result?
A. Maths
B. Physics
C. Chemistry
D. Botany

5. Taking the performance in all subjects into account which college has shown lowest level?
A. A B. B
C. C D. D

Directions (Qs. 6 to 10): *These questions refer to the following circle graph showing the expenditure distribution of a certain family. The family spends ₹6500 per month.*

Expenditure Distribution of a Certain Family

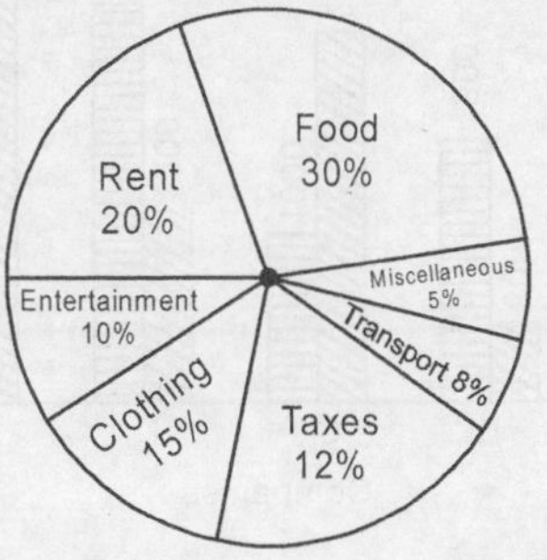

6. How much it spends on food per month?
A. ₹ 1950
B. ₹ 2950
C. ₹ 4850
D. ₹ 850

7. How much are its annual taxes?
A. ₹ 6500 B. ₹ 9360
C. ₹ 8900 D. ₹ 9500

8. How many degrees should there be in the central angle showing clothing, taxes and transportation combined?
A. 100 B. 115
C. 118 D. 126

9. How much more money per month is spent by the family on food as compared to the rent?
A. ₹ 650 B. ₹ 750
C. ₹ 550 D. ₹ 850

10. If the expenditure budget of the family is raised to ₹ 8000 per month and distribution on various items remain the same, then the monthly expenses on both, the entertainment and the transport, will be:
A. ₹ 1700
B. ₹ 1650
C. ₹ 1440
D. ₹ 1320

Directions (Qs. 11 to 15): *Study the following graph carefully and answer the following questions.*

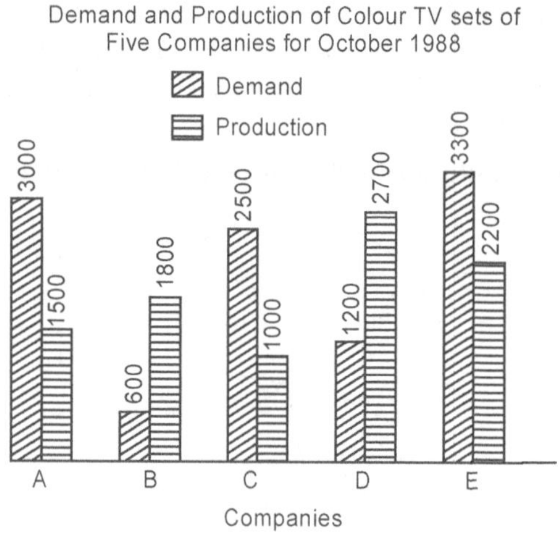

11. What is the ratio of companies having more demand than production of those having more production than demand?

A. 2 : 3 B. 4 : 1
C. 2 : 2 D. 3 : 2

12. What is the difference between average demand and average production of the five companies taken together?

A. 1400 B. 400
C. 280 D. 138

13. The production of Company 'D' is approximately how many times that of the production of the Company A?

A. 1.8 B. 4.5
C. 2.5 D. 4.9

14. The demand for Company 'B' is approximately what per cent of the demand for Company 'C'?

A. 4% B. 24%
C. 20% D. 60%

15. If Company A desires to meet the demand by purchasing surplus TV sets from a single company, which one of the following companies can meet the need adequately?

A. B B. C
C. D D. None of these

Directions (Qs. 16 to 20): *Study the following graph to answer the given questions.*

Per cent profit earned by two companies over the given years

$$\% \text{ Profit} = \frac{\text{Income} - \text{Expenditure}}{\text{Expenditure}} \times 100$$

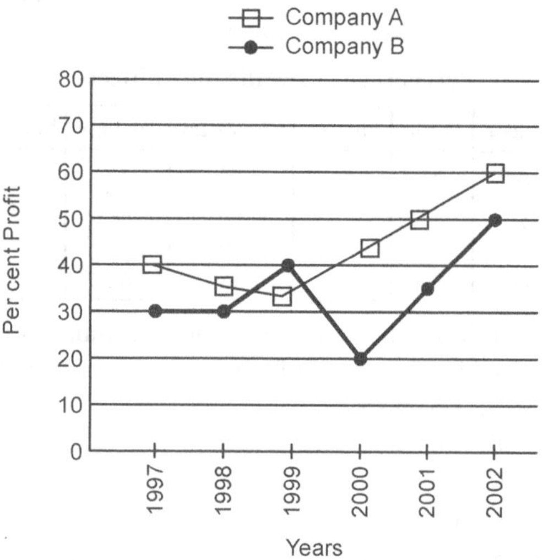

16. If the expenditure of Company B in 2000 was ₹ 200 crores, what was its income?

A. ₹ 240 crores B. ₹ 220 crores
C. ₹ 160 crores D. ₹ 180 crores

17. If the income of Company A in 2002 was ₹ 600 crores, what was its expenditure?

A. ₹ 360 crores B. ₹ 480 crores
C. ₹ 375 crores D. ₹ 320 crores

18. If the income of Company B in 1998 was ₹ 200 crores, what was its profit in 1999?

A. ₹ 21.5 crores
B. ₹ 153 crores
C. ₹ 46.15 crores
D. Cannot be determined

19. If the incomes of the two companies in 1998 were equal, what was the ratio of their expenditure?

A. 1 : 2 B. 26 : 27
C. 4 : 5 D. 100 : 67

20. What is the per cent increase in per cent profit for Company B from year 2000 to 2001?

A. 75 B. 175
C. 160 D. 150

Directions (Qs. 21 to 25): *Study the graph given below and answer the questions asked thereunder.*

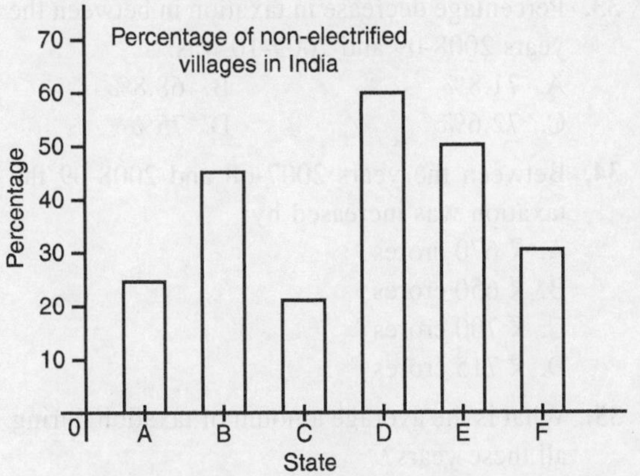

21. According to the table given above which state of India has the highest percentage of electrified villages?

A. A B. B
C. C D. D

22. If central govt. decides to extend financial assistance for prompt electrification and begins with the state having the least electrified villages, then in the order of preference which of the following states will be fourth?

A. C B. B
C. A D. F

23. How many states have at least 60% or more electrified villages?

A. Five B. Three
C. Four D. Two

24. In which of the following states percentage of electrified villages is double the percentage of electrified villages in state D?

A. C B. F
C. A D. B

25. What is the percentage of electrified villages in the state A?

A. 65% B. 25%
C. 35% D. 75%

Directions (Qs. 26 to 30): *The pie-chart given below shows the household expenditure of a family on different items. Study the chart carefully and answer the questions that follow:*

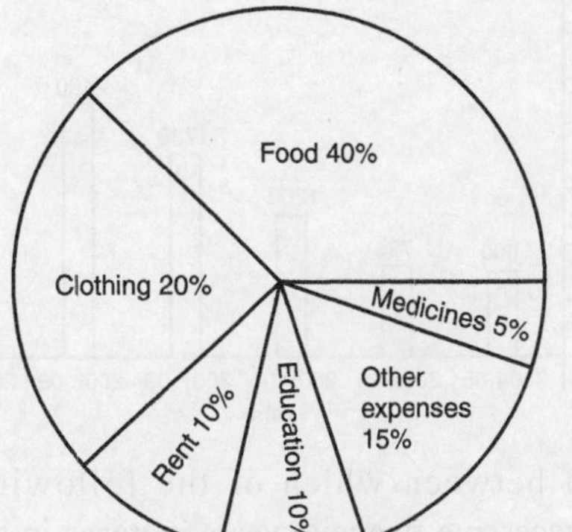

26. If the family's expenditure on education is ₹ 375 then the same amount is being expent by this famly on which of the following items?

A. Medicines
B. Other expenses
C. Rent
D. Clothing

27. If the family expends ₹ 750 per month on food, what is the annual expenditure of this family on education?

A. ₹ 2150 B. ₹ 1022.50
C. ₹ 2250 D. ₹ 1400

28. If total expenditure of this family is ₹ 4500, find the expenditure of this family on clothing?

A. ₹ 800 B. ₹ 900
C. ₹ 840 D. ₹ 950

29. What is the angle subtended on the centre by the segment representing other expenses?

A. 64° B. 54°
C. 36° D. 15°

30. What is the ratio of total expenses on rent and clothing to the total expenses on medicines and other expenses of this family?

A. 2 : 3 B. 3 : 4
C. 3 : 5 D. 3 : 2

Directions (Qs. 31 to 35): *The following bar chart shows the amount accrued from additional taxation by the government during certain successive years. Study the chart carefully and answer the questions that follow:*

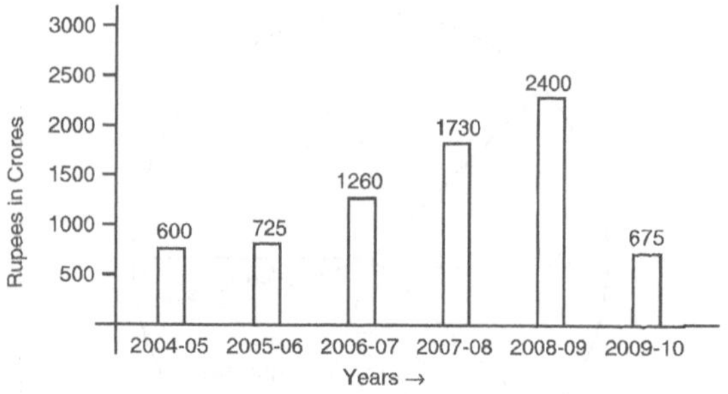

31. In between which of the following two successive financial years increase in taxation was at the highest level?
A. 2004-05 and 2005-06
B. 2007-08 and 2008-09
C. 2008-09 and 2009-10
D. 2006-07 and 2007-08

32. Total increase in taxation was how much percent between the years 2006-07 and 2007-08?
A. 37.3% B. 35.4%
C. 38.5% D. 36.6%

33. Percentage decrease in taxation in between the years 2008-09 and 2009-10 was:
A. 71.8% B. 68.8%
C. 72.6% D. 75%

34. Between the years 2007-08 and 2008-09 the taxation was increased by:
A. ₹ 670 crores
B. ₹ 650 crores
C. ₹ 700 crores
D. ₹ 715 crores

35. What is the average amount of taxation during all these years?
A. ₹ 1233.7 crores
B. ₹ 1433.5 crores
C. ₹ 1231.7 crores
D. ₹ 1400 crores

ANSWERS

1	2	3	4	5	6	7	8	9	10
D	A	A	D	B	A	B	D	A	C
11	**12**	**13**	**14**	**15**	**16**	**17**	**18**	**19**	**20**
D	C	A	B	C	A	C	D	B	A
21	**22**	**23**	**24**	**25**	**26**	**27**	**28**	**29**	**30**
C	D	B	A	B	C	C	B	B	D
31	**32**	**33**	**34**	**35**					
B	A	A	A	C					

EXPLANATORY ANSWERS

1. Maths : 52 + 47 + 53 + 35 = 187
Physics : 65 + 62 + 70 + 72 = 269
Chemistry : 62 + 52 + 46 + 58 = 218
Zoology : 47 + 35 + 54 + 62 = 198
Botany : 40 + 38 + 39 + 57 = 174
Clearly, Physics has shown highest percentage result.

2. A : 52 + 65 + 62 + 47 + 40 = 266
B : 47 + 62 + 52 + 35 + 38 = 234
C : 53 + 70 + 46 + 54 + 39 = 262
D : 35 + 72 + 58 + 62 + 57 = 284
Clearly, college D has shown highest level of percentage result.

3. Zoology and Botany of groups has shown lowest level of percentage result.

4. Total marks of Botany = 174 which shows lowest percentage result.

5. College B has shown lowest level because its total percentage result in all five subjects is 234 which is lowest.

6. Food 30% of ₹ 6500 = $\frac{30}{100} \times 6500$ = ₹ 1950

7. Taxes = 12% of ₹ 6500

$= \frac{12}{100} \times 6500$ = ₹ 780/month

= ₹ 780 × 12 = ₹ 9360/year

∴ Annual taxes = ₹ 9360

8. Clothing, taxes and transportation combined are 35%.

Now, $100\% = 360°$

$35\% = \frac{360°}{100} \times 35 = 126°$

9. 10% of ₹ 6500 = $\frac{10}{100} \times 6500$ = ₹ 650/month

10. 18% of ₹ 8000 = $\frac{18}{100} \times 8000$ = ₹ 1440

11. The companies having more demand than production are A, C and E *i.e.* their number is 3. The companies having more production than demand are B and D *i.e.* their number is 2. So, the required ratio is 3 : 2.

12. Average demand

$= \frac{1}{5}(3000 + 600 + 2500 + 1200 + 3300)$

$= \frac{10600}{5} = 2120$

Average production

$= \frac{1500 + 1800 + 1000 + 2700 + 2200}{5}$

$= \frac{9200}{5} = 1840$

∴ Difference between average demand and average production = 2120 – 1840 = 280

13. Let $K(1500) = 2700$

$\Rightarrow \quad K = \frac{2700}{1500} = \frac{9}{5} = 1.8.$

14. Let x% of (demand for C) = (demand for B)

$\Rightarrow \quad \frac{x}{100} \times 2500 = 600$

$\Rightarrow \quad x = \frac{600 \times 100}{2500} = 24\%$

15. Since Company D produces highest number of TV sets and Company A desires to meet the demand by purchasing surplus TV sets from a single Company.

Clearly, D can meet the demand of A.

∴ Correct answer is C.

16. Let the income be ₹ x crores

$\therefore \quad 20 = \frac{x - 200}{200} \times 100$

$\Rightarrow \quad 40 = x - 200$

$\Rightarrow \quad x = 240$

∴ Income = ₹ 240 crores

17. The income of Company A in 2002 = ₹ 600 crores

% Profit = 60

Let the expenditure be ₹ x crores.

$\therefore \quad 60 = \frac{600 - x}{x} \times 100$

$\Rightarrow \quad x = \frac{600 - x}{60} \times 100$

$\Rightarrow \quad x = \frac{(600 - x)5}{3}$

$\Rightarrow \quad 3x = 3000 - 5x$

$\Rightarrow \quad 8x = 3000$

$\Rightarrow \quad x = \frac{3000}{8} = 375$

Hence, expenditure = ₹ 375 crores.

18. It cannot be determined as Income and Expenditure of respective year is not known.

19. Let their equal incomes be ₹ 1 crore. Also, let expenditure of Company A be ₹ E_1 crores and that of Company B be ₹ E_2 crores.

Now, $35 = \frac{1 - E_1}{E_1} \times 100$

$35\,E_1 = 100 - 100\,E_1$

$135\,E_1 = 100 \quad ...(i)$

Similarly $30 = \frac{1 - E_2}{E_2} \times 100$

$130\,E_2 = 100 \quad ...(ii)$

From (*i*) and (*ii*)

$135\,E_1 = 130\,E_2$

$\Rightarrow \quad \frac{E_1}{E_2} = \frac{130}{135} = \frac{26}{27}$

$\therefore \quad E_1 : E_2 = 26 : 27$

20. Required percentage = $\frac{35-20}{20}\times 100$

$= \frac{15}{20}\times 100 = 75$

21. In the state C percentage of non-electrified villages is the least. It means the percentage of electrified villages for the state C is the highest.

22. The order of preference of the least electrified villages is given below:
D, E, B, F, A, C

23. In A, C and F states, percentage of non-electrified villages are 25, 20 and 30 percent respectively. Hence percentages of electrified villages for these three states are 75, 80 and 70 percent respectively.

24. Percentage of electrified villages in state D
$= 100 - 60 = 40$
Percentage of electrified villages in state C
$= 100 - 20 = 80$
Hence the percentage of electrified villages in the state C is double the percentage of electrified villages in state D.

25. Percentage of electrified villages in the state A $= 100 - 75 = 25\%$.

26. Both segments representing education and rent respectively are each subtending a central angle of 36°. Hence family's expenditure on these two items will be equal, *i.e.,* ₹ 375 will be expent on rent.

27. Expenditure on food = ₹ 750

$\therefore$ Total expenditure $= \frac{100\times 750}{40}$ = ₹ 1875

$\because$ Expenditure on education = 10%

$\therefore$ Amount spent on education $= \frac{1875\times 10}{100}$
= ₹ 187.50

$\therefore$ Annual expenditure of the family on education
$= 187.50 \times 12$ = ₹ 2250.00.

28. Expenditure on clothing = 20%

$\therefore$ Total expenditure on clothing $= \frac{20}{100}\times 4500$
= ₹ 900.

29. Central angle for 15% $= \frac{15}{100}\times 360° = 54°$.

30. Expenditure on rent and clothing
$= 10\% + 20\% = 30\%$
Expenditure on medicine and other expenses
$= 5\% + 15\% = 20\%$
$\therefore$ Ratio of the two $= 30\% : 20\% = 3 : 2$.

31. Between the financial years 2007-08 and 2008-09, maximum increase of ₹ 670 crores had been registered in taxation.

32. Percentage of total increase

$= \frac{(1730-1260)}{1260}\times 100$

$= \frac{470\times 100}{1260} = 37.3\%$.

33. Percentage of total decrease in taxation between the years 2008-09 and 2009-2010

$= \frac{(2400-675)}{2400}\times 100$

$= \frac{1725\times 100}{2400} = 71.8\%$.

34. Increase in taxation in between the financial years 2007-08 and 2008-09
= ₹ (2400 – 1730)
= ₹ 670 crores.

35. Average of the total taxation during these years

$= \frac{600+725+1260+1730+2400+625}{6}$

$= \frac{7390}{6}$ = ₹ 1231.7 crores.

English

1

COMPREHENSION PASSAGES

ENGLISH LANGUAGE COMPREHENSION

The objective of language comprehension test is to ascertain the ability of the candidates to understand the passage properly. Therefore candidates are required to take notice of the following points:

1. Read the full passage very attentively and intelligently.
2. Try to comprehend the gist of it.
3. Make a mental note of all the important details and points given in the passage.
4. Read the passage for the second time in case you have not been able to understand it satisfactorily.
5. Divide the time proportionately for all the passages.
6. Answer the questions on the basis of facts, as given in the paragraph.
7. Don't waste much time in answering the questions of any one passage.
8. Check all the answers once again, very carefully, to see whether any question is left unanswered by mistake.

MODEL QUESTIONS (FOR PRACTICE)

Directions: *Each of the following passages is followed by five questions. Read the passage carefully and then answer the questions that follow each. For each question, four probable answers A, B, C and D are given. Only one out of these is correct. Choose the correct answer.*

PASSAGE-1

The use of words like 'welcome', 'thank you', 'please', etc., at the right moment reflects a polite nature. The civic sense also lies within the scope of good manners. We should not shout or talk loudly in public places like hospitals and libraries and create disturbance. We should not cheat people or make fun of them. Cleanliness is also necessary. We must not throw the waste on roads and make use of dustbins. We should not harm the public property as it belongs to all of us. While in a queue, discipline should be maintained. We must give fair chance to others.

1. Expressions like 'welcome' 'thank you' and 'please' reflect
   A. happiness B. discipline
   C. civic sense D. polite nature
2. While in a library, we should
   A. respect others B. avoid arguments
   C. talk in low tone D. be courteous
3. A public property belongs to
   A. nobody
   B. all of us
   C. government
   D. one who maintains it

4. Discipline is
   A. the rule of proper conduct or action
   B. the rule of road sense
   C. making use of dustbins
   D. forming a queue
5. The most appropriate title for this passage would be
   A. Polite Nature
   B. Courtesy
   C. Good Manners
   D. Civic Sense

PASSAGE-2

There is an old proverb 'Early to bed and early to rise makes a man healthy and wise.' I am in the habit of getting up early in the morning and have formed the habit of taking long morning walks in the past two years. It is a light exercise and best for physical fitness. The morning air which is fresh and pure is beneficial for the lungs. The early rays of the rising sun are good for healthy skin. 'Health is wealth' and doctors also recommend morning walk to their patients for gaining sound health and freshness of energy.

1. What is good for lungs?
   A. Sunrays B. Fresh air
   C. Sound sleep D. Light exercise
2. What is a light exercise?
   A. Early to bed
   B. Early to rise
   C. Morning walk
   D. Gaining sound health
3. What is good for skin?
   A. Fresh air
   B. Morning air
   C. Morning walk
   D. Rising sun's rays
4. What is best for physical fitness?
   A. Light exercise
   B. Long morning walk
   C. Early to rise
   D. Fresh and pure air
5. Long morning walk
   A. bring sound sleep
   B. ensures physical fitness
   C. ensures healthy skin
   D. keeps healthy, wealthy and wise

PASSAGE-3

Mahatma Gandhi lived a splendid long life and has set great moral standards before us. He showed to the world the true way to peace. He wished to see India prosper but he became a martyr for the noble cause of Hindu-Muslim unity at the time of partition when a religious fanatic, Nathuram Godse, shot him dead on January 30, 1948. His last words were 'Hey Ram'. He lived and died for his country and countryman.

1. Mahatma Gandhi showed the world the true way to
   A. prosperity B. love
   C. truth D. peace
2. Mahatma Gandhi became a martyr for the noble cause of
   A. truth
   B. non-violence
   C. freedom of India
   D. Hindu-Muslim unity
3. Mahatma Gandhi was shot dead
   A. before India achieved independence
   B. by a mad man
   C. by an intolerant religious person
   D. by a non-religious person
4. Mahatma Gandhi set great moral standards. It means
   A. he was a great religious teacher
   B. he was a great moralist
   C. he made India morally stronger
   D. moral was everything to him
5. Gandhiji lived and died for his country and countryman. It means
   A. he was born in India and died in India
   B. he was a patriot
   C. he was a great moralist
   D. he sacrified his life for India and her people

PASSAGE-4

On one hot day a crow felt very thirsty. He flew from one place to another in search of water. After long hours of labour he found a pitcher. Eagerly, he perched on the mouth of the pitcher. He found that the water was at the bottom of the vessel. He tried his best to dip his beak but did not succeed. He did not know what to do. Suddenly some pebbles lying nearby gave him an idea. One by one he dropped the pebbles with his beak into the pitcher. The level of water slowly came up to the mouth of the pitcher. The crow then drank the water and quenched his thirst.

1. The crow found a pitcher
   A. as it flew
   B. after many hours of labour
   C. full of water
   D. which was empty
2. What is the moral of the passage?
   A. No pains, no gains
   B. God helps those who help themselves
   C. Necessity is the mother of invention
   D. Try and try again, you will succeed at last
3. The crow flew from place to place
   A. in search of pitcher
   B. in search of pebbles
   C. in search of water
   D. in search of a vessel
4. The pitcher, the crow found
   A. was full of water
   B. was dry
   C. had little water in the bottom
   D. had water up to its mouth
5. As the crow dropped pebbles into the pitcher, what happend?
   A. The pitcher broke down
   B. The water leaked one of the pitcher
   C. The level of water into the pitcher rose up slowly
   D. Water level immediately rose to the mouth of the pitcher

PASSAGE-5

Once upon a time a crane and a fox lived in a forest. They were good friend. One day the fox invited the crane to a feast. He made a tasty food and served it before the crane on a plate. The crane could not eat anything because of the long beak. But the fox licked all his food. The crane felt insulted. He decided to teach the fox a lesson. Next day he invited the fox. He prepared the same tasty food and placed it in front of the fox inside a narrow glass. The crane ate easily while the fox looked on. Now, it was the fox's turn to remain hungry.

1. What is the moral of the passage?
   A. Beware of the wicked
   B. One good turn deserves another
   C. Be contented with what you have
   D. Tit for tat
2. The crane could not eat tasty food because the
   A. food was served in a shallow plate
   B. food was very hot
   C. food was served in a long jar
   D. crane was not hungry
3. The fox had to remain hungry because
   A. the food served was not enough in quantity
   B. the food was served inside a narrow glass
   C. the food served was not tasty
   D. the food was all liquid
4. Why did the crane feel insulted?
   A. Because he was invited to feast but he could not eat anything
   B. Because the food was served in a shallow plate and he could not eat
   C. Because the food was too hot
   D. Because the fox gulped all the food quickly
5. The crane successfully taught a lesson to the fox when he invited the fox to a feast and served the food
   A. in a narrow glass
   B. in a large plate
   C. in a broken plate
   D. in a long jar

PASSAGE-6

The family set down at the table and began to talk about the summer holidays. They had to decide a place to visit during the vacation. Should they go to their village or to a hill station? The parents preferred the village while the children wished to go the hill station. After few moments of discussion the elders decided to visit both the places. First they shall go to the village for a week and then stay at the hill station for the remaining days. For the first time the family shall be together during the holidays. The children were happy with the holiday plan.

1. The purpose for which the family set down at the table was
   A. to decide a place to visit during the vacation
   B. to educate the children how to carry articles during a visit to a hill station
   C. to decide the date when they should start their journey
   D. to tell the children that they will visit a hill station during this vacation
2. The final plan was to visit
   A. their village
   B. a hill station
   C. their village as well as a hill station
   D. their home town
3. The final decision was made by
   A. the boys B. the girls
   C. the women D. the elders
4. They decided first to go to their village and stay there for
   A. a day B. a week
   C. ten days D. a fortnight
5. Why were children happy?
   A. Because a hill station was included in their holiday plan
   B. Because a visit to their village was excluded from their holiday plan
   C. Because their choice prevailed
   D. Because they were going all alone to the hill station

PASSAGE-7

Once Govind intended to go on pilgrimage with his family. He asked Mirind to accompany. But for his trade's reason, he did not go with him. So Govind thought it safe to leave the box of his jewellery with him, as it was dangerous to leave it in a lone house or take it on the journey. So he went to him with the box. He took him to a lonely place under a tree and handed it over to him. He told Mirind, "Keep it safe with you. I shall return from the journey after six month then I shall take it back from you." Mirind said, "Don't worry, I shall keep it as safe as own."

1. Govind intended to go
   A. for a business trip
   B. to a hill station
   C. on a long journey to a sacred place
   D. to his home town for a long period
2. Why did Govind leave his box of jewellery with Mirind?
   A. Because it was not safe to take the box with him on a long journey
   B. Because Mirind was his fast friend
   C. Because the box was very heavy
   D. Because his house was unsafe
3. Why did Govind take Mirind to a lonely place?
   A. To tell him that the box contained valuable jewellery
   B. So that no third person could see box
   C. To show him what was within the box
   D. To tell him that the box will remain with him
4. Where did Govind hand over the box of jewellery to Mirind?
   A. At Mirind's house
   B. At his own house
   C. In a lonely place
   D. In a lonely place under a tree
5. It was not safe to leave the box in a lone house. Here the word 'lone house' means
   A. a house in a deserted place
   B. a house where none lives
   C. a house without door and lock
   D. a house near the forest

PASSAGE-8

Zahir-ud-din Babar was the first Mughal emperor of India. A descendent of Timur on father's side and Changez Khan on his mother's side, Babar was a brave warrior. After defeating Ibrahim Lodhi in the First Battle of Panipat in 1526 he entered Delhi and soon gained control over Agra. After many more battles with Rajputs he extended his empire over Punjab, Uttar Pradesh and north Bihar. He died at a young age of 48 years in 1530 at his capital Agra without getting much time to consolidate his victories.

1. Zahir-ud-din Babar was the first
   A. Muslim ruler of India
   B. Mughal ruler of India
   C. Afghan ruler of India
   D. Turk ruler of India
2. Babar was born in the years
   A. 1480 B. 1482
   C. 1492 D. 1962
3. Babar first occupied
   A. Punjab B. Agra
   C. Delhi D. Panipat
4. Babar was a brave warrior. Here brave warrior means
   A. courageous soldier
   B. a kind hearted soldier
   C. a clever fighter
   D. a victorious general
5. Babar extended his empire over Punjab and Uttar Pradesh after many more battles with the
   A. Afghans B. Rajputs
   C. Mughals D. Lodhies

PASSAGE-9

Our National Flag is tricolour. It has three equal horizontal strips. The strip at the top is saffron, in the middle is white and at the bottom is green, The ratio of width to length of the flag is 2 : 3. In the centre of the white strip is a wheel in navy blue. The wheel represents the *chakra.* Its design is similar to the wheel which appears on the abacus of the Sarnath Lion Capital of Ashoka. Its diameter approximates to the width of the white strip. The wheel has 24 spokes. It was adopted by Constituent Assembly on July 22, 1947. We love our national flag. We respect it. We are ready to sacrifice our life to protect its honour. It represents the nation. So it is a symbol of national honour.

1. In our national flag the wheel is located in the centre of
   A. saffron strip B. white strip
   C. green strip D. blue strip
2. In our national flag which of the strips is at the bottom in our national flag
   A. blue C. saffron
   B. white D. green
3. Why do we love our national flag?
   A. Because it is tricolour
   B. Because it has three strips
   C. Because it has a wheel at the centre
   D. Because it is a symbol of national honour
4. Our national flag was approved by
   A. President
   B. Lok Sabha
   C. Parliament
   D. Constituent Assembly
5. The diameter approximates to the width of the white strip. Here the word 'approximates' means
   A. is more or less equal
   B. is exactly equal
   C. is not equal
   D. is related

PASSAGE-10

Distance in large cities are long. All the people do not have their own means of transport. They have to depend upon the state or private buses. The number of bus users is very large. Every bus stop is, therefore, crowded. The number of buses is not adequate. Thus people suffer the torture of long wait at the bus stop. Some bus stops are quite orderly. People form queues and get into the buses turn by turn. However, often this order is forgotten and confusion spreads when the bus comes and the law of jungle prevails.

1. Why are the bus stops crowded?
   A. Because they are small is size
   B. Because the number of passengers is very large
   C. Because they are situated at some busy centre
   D. Because people do not form queues
2. Long wait at the bus stop is the result of
   A. over-crowding in the buses
   B. late running of buses
   C. shortage of buses
   D. slow speed of buses
3. Some bus stops are quite orderly where
   A. there is no crowd
   B. the number of buses is adequate

C. people do not have to wait for long
D. people form queues and enter the buses one by one

4. Most of the people who travel by buses are
A. non-working
B. do not have their own vehicles
C. have to go a long distance
D. live in large cities

5. What happens when people do not have their own transport?
A. They have to wait for a bus at a bus stop
B. They have to depend upon the state or private buses
C. They have to travel long distances
D. They form queues and get into buses one by one

PASSAGE-11

A certain king once fell ill and doctors said that only a sudden fright would restore his health but the king was not a man for anyone to play tricks on, except his fool. One day, when the fool was with him in his boat he cleverly pushed the king into water but he was rescued and put to bed. The fright, the bath and bed cured the diseased king, but he was so angry with the fool that he turned him out of the country.

1. What did the doctor say about the king?
A. Only a sudden fright would restore the king's health
B. Only fool would cure the king
C. Only a boat trick could cure the king
D. The king had suffered a sudden fright

2. He cleverly pushed the king into water but *he* was rescued and put to bed. In this sentence *he* refers to
A. the king B. the fool
C. the doctor D. the river

3. When the fool pushed the king into water they were
A. in the palace B. in the bed
C. in the garden D. in a boat

4. Who played the trick on the king?
A. The doctor B. The boatman
C. The fool D. The fright

5. The fool who cured the king was
A. rewarded
B. thrown into water
C. turned out of the country
D. put into jail

ANSWERS

Passage	1	2	3	4	5
Passage 1.	D	C	B	A	C
Passage 2.	B	C	D	B	B
Passage 3.	D	D	C	B	D
Passage 4.	B	C	C	C	C
Passage 5.	D	A	B	B	A
Passage 6.	A	C	D	B	A
Passage 7.	C	A	B	D	B
Passage 8.	B	B	C	A	B
Passage 9.	B	D	D	D	A
Passage 10.	B	C	D	B	B
Passage 11.	A	A	D	C	C

2

ENGLISH GRAMMAR

PARTS OF SPEECH

Part of speech	Definition or Function	Examples
Noun	Name of a person, place, animal, quality or thing	Ram, boy, dog pen, sun, Delhi, truth, honesty
Pronoun	Used in place of a noun	I, you, he she, they
Articles & Determiners	Points out indefinite and definite nouns	a, an, the, few, some
Adjective	Describes a noun or pronoun	big, honest, wooden valuable, quiet, deep, soft, narrow
Adverb	Describes a verb, an adjective or another adverb	silently, widely, softly, quietly, very, carefully
Verb	Tells about action or state of something or someone	is, am, was, have, do, like, walk, work, make, throw, tell
Conjuction	Joins words, clauses or sentences	and, but, when, yet, while, else
Preposition	Links a noun or pronoun to another word	at, to, after, on for, under, over, with
Interjection	Expresses sudden feelings or emotions	Ah!, Alas!, oh!, ouch!, hi!, well!, Hurrah!

NOUNS

A word which denotes a person, a thing, an animal or a place is said to be a noun.

There are two noun numbers in English— the *Singular* and the *Plural.*

Singular Numbers : A noun that denotes one person or one thing, is said to be in the Singular number. For example — book, pencil, bird, dog, hen etc. are in singular number.

Plural Number : A noun that denotes more than one person or one thing is said to be in plural number. For example — boys, pens, lions, girls, men etc. are in plural number.

REMEMBER

Singular	*Plural*
Cat	Cats
Book	Books
Pen	Pens
Room	Rooms
Tree	Trees
Bus	Buses
Bush	Bushes
Box	Boxes
Glass	Glasses
Dish	Dishes
Judge	Judges
Tax	Taxes
Watch	Watches
Calf	Calves
Thief	Thieves
Knife	Knives

Singular	Plural
Scarf	Scarves
Wife	Wives
Leaf	Leaves
Wolf	Wolves
Half	Halves
Monarch	Monarchs
Roof	Roofs
Hoof	Hoofs
Gulf	Gulfs
Staff	Staffs
Radio	Radios
Bamboo	Bamboos
Folio	Folios
Hero	Heroes
Volcano	Volcanoes
Mango	Mangoes
Potato	Potatoes
Photo	Photos
Piano	Pianos
Baby	Babies
Fly	Flies
Country	Countries
Lady	Ladies
Boy	Boys
Monkey	Monkeys
Ox	Oxen
Child	Children
Man	Men
Woman	Women
Tooth	Teeth
Axis	Axes
Basis	Bases
Foot	Feet
Goose	Geese
Englishman	Englishmen
Radius	Radii
Vertex	Vertices
Stimulus	Stimuli

1. Note the plurals of the following nouns:

Singular	*Plural*	*Singular*	*Plural*
copy	copies	cry	cries
baby	babies	duty	duties
body	bodies	country	countries
family	families	diary	diaries
fly	flies	fairy	fairies
city	cities	spy	spies
army	armies	storey	storeys
bay	bays	monkey	monkeys

2. The following nouns do not undergo any change in plural form, in general.

Singular	*Plural*	*Singular*	*Plural*
deer	deer	sheep	sheep
thousand	thousand	pair	pair
hundred	hundred	score	score
dozen	dozen	gross	gross

Note: We can write—

(*a*) thousands of men; (*b*) two pairs of shoes; (*c*) dozens of mangoes; (*d*) scores of people etc.

But—

(*a*) two thousand rupees; (*b*) three hundred men; (*c*) five dozen eggs, etc.

3. The following nouns are usually used in plural forms. They take a plural verb after them—

eatables	fetters	surroundings
riches	alms	spectacles
trousers	pants	scissors
premises	thanks	annals
congratulations	goods	shorts
tongs	pains	arms
breeches	(for troubles)	

4. The following are the nouns which are plural in appearance but are usually used in singular number. They are followed by a singular verb—

news	politics	physics
mathematics	economics	ethics
politics	classics	gallows
statistics	athletics	innings
mechanics	summons	mumps

5. Collective nouns often used as plurals—

public	police	cattle
audience	clergy	folk
people	poultry	nation
elite	gentry	glitterati

6. The nouns that are usually used in singular forms—

advice	hair	rice
fuel	alphabet	machinery
offspring	issue	furniture
mischief	stationery	luggage
bedding	information	abuse

7. Material nouns are always used in singular number—

gold	copper	milk
water	silk	wool

Note: They may be used in plural with a different meaning.

copper coins (coppers), chains or fetters (irons), cans made of tin (tins).

GENDERS

The difference in sex is denoted by Gender in grammar. The various genders are as follows :

1. **Masculine Gender :** A noun that denotes a male is said to be of the masculine gender, as man, uncle, ox, boy etc.
2. **Feminine Gender :** A noun that denotes a female is said to be of feminine gender, as woman, aunt, princess, cow etc.
3. **Common Gender :** Nouns which denote both males and females are said to be of the common gender, as friend, cousin, person, parent, baby etc.
4. **Neuter Gender :** A noun that denotes the name of object without life is said to be of neuter gender, as file, table, pencil.

REMEMBER

Masculine	*Feminine*
Boy	Girl
Son	Daughter
Brother	Sister
Murderer	Murderess
Sorcerer	Sorceress
Son-in-law	Daughter-in-law
Father-in-law	Mother-in-law
Man-servant	Maid-servant
Land-lord	Land-lady
Bachelor	Maid
Gentleman	Lady
Monk	Nun
Earl	Countess
Lad	Lass
Sir	Madam
Duke	Dutchess
Emperor	Empress
Milk-man	Milk-maid
Pea-cock	Pea-hen
Step-father	Step-mother
Hero	Heroine
Viceroy	Vicerine
Mr.	Mrs.
Governor	Governess
Master	Mistress
Wizard	Witch
Heir	Heiress
Host	Hostess
Lion	Lioness
Mayor	Mayoress
Actor	Actress
Buck	Doe
Colt	Filly
Dog	Bitch
Horse	Mare
Count	Countess
Hunter	Huntress
Prince	Princess
Abbot	Abbess
God	Goddess
Author	Authoress
Ox	Cow
Widower	Widow
Grand-father	Grand-mother
He-goat	She-goat
Milk-man	Milk-woman
Bridegroom	Bride
Tiger	Tigress
Priest	Priestess
Poet	Poetess
Shepherd	Shepherdess
Nephew	Niece
Stag	Hind

PRONOUNS

The repetition of a noun in a sentence or a set of sentences is really boring. So, instead of repeating the noun, we can use a word (for that noun) called the pronoun.

"A pronoun is a word that we use instead of a noun".

Example:

This is *Sachin. He* plays cricket.

Note: *He* is the pronoun used in place of *Sachin.*

Kinds of Pronouns

1. **Personal pronouns :** A pronoun which is used instead of the name of a person is known as a 'Personal Pronoun'. A list of the 'Personal pronouns' is listed below :

   I, my, mine, me, we (First Person)

   You, your, yours (Second Person)

   He, his, him, she, her, hers, it, its, they, their, theirs, them (Third Person)

2. **Demonstrative, Indefinite and Distributive Pronouns :**

   (a) Demonstrative Pronouns : Pronouns used to point out the objects to which they refer are called Demonstrative Pronouns.

   Examples :

   (i) *This* is a present from my uncle.
   (ii) *These* are merely excuses.
   (iii) Bembay mangoes are better than *those* of Bangaluru.

   (b) Indefinite Pronouns : All pronouns which refer to persons or things in a general way and do not refer to any particular person or thing are called Indefinite Pronouns.

   Examples :

   (i) *Somebody* has stolen my watch.
   (ii) *Few* escaped unhurt.
   (iii) Did you ask *anybody* to come?

   (c) Distributive Pronouns : Each, either, neither are called distributive pronouns because they refer to persons or things one at a time. For this reason they are always singular and followed by the verb in singular.

   Examples :

   (i) *Each* of the men received a reward.
   (ii) *These* men received *each* a reward.
   (iii) *Either* of you can go.

3. **Relative Pronouns :** A relative pronoun refers or relates to some noun going before, which is called its Antecedent.

   Examples :

   (i) I met Hari *who* used to live here.
   (ii) I have found the pen *which* I had lost.
   (iii) Here is the book *that* you lent me.

4. **Interrogative Pronouns :** These pronouns, are used for asking questions.

   Examples :

   (i) *Whose* book is this?
   (ii) *What* will all the neighbours say?
   (iii) *Which* do you prefer, tea or coffee?

Note : Interrogative pronouns can also be used in asking indirect questions. Consider the following examples :

(i) I asked *who* was speaking.
(ii) Tell me *what* you have done.
(iii) Say *which* you would like best.

Behaviour of the Pronouns

1. If three pronouns are used together in the same sentence they are arranged in the following order :

2	+	3	+	1
↓		↓		↓
Second Person		Third Person		First Person

   Examples :

   I, you and he must help *that* poor man. (Incorrect)

   You, he and I must help *that* poor man. (Correct)

2. When two or more singular nouns are joined by and, the pronoun used for them should be plural.

   Examples :

   Mohan and Sohan are friends. *They* play football. *They* live at Lajpat Nagar.

3. But if these nouns joined by and refer to the same person or thing, the pronoun used should be singular.

   Examples :

   (i) Delhi, the beautiful city and the capital of India, is famous for *its* historical monuments.
   (ii) The manager and owner of the firm expressed *his* views on the demands of the workers.

4. When two nouns are used with as well as, the pronoun agrees with the first subject.

Examples :

(a) Mohan as well as his friends is doing *his* work.

(b) The students as well as their teachers are doing *their* work.

5. When two singular nouns joined by 'and' are preceded by *each* or *every,* the pronoun used must be singular and should agree in gender with the second noun.

Examples :

(a) Every man and every woman will do *her* best for the nation.

(b) Each boy and each girl went to *her* house.

6. When two nouns are joined by using 'with', the pronoun agrees with the noun coming before 'with'.

Examples :

(a) The boy with *his* parents has gone to see a movie.

(b) The children with *their* parents have gone to picnic.

7. When two different nouns are joined by either......... or; neither .... nor, the pronoun is used according to the number and gender of the second noun.

Examples :

(a) Either your sister or you have done *your* work.

(b) Neither the students nor the teacher was in *his* class.

8. The pronoun coming after '*than*' must be in the same case as that coming before '*than*'.

Examples :

(a) She plays better than *me*. (Incorrect)
She plays better than *I.* (Correct)

(b) His elder brother is more intelligent than *him*. (Incorrect)
His elder brother is more intelligent than *he*. (Correct)

9. 'Many a' always takes a singular pronoun and singular verb.

Example :

Many a soldier has met *his* death in the battle field.

10. 'Who', 'Whose', 'Whom' are used only for persons.

Examples :

(a) *Who* is knocking at the door?

(b) *Whose* pen is this?

(c) *What* do you want?

11. 'Which' is used for things.

Example :

Which game do you like?

MULTIPLE CHOICE QUESTIONS

Directions: *In the following questions choose the correct options to fill the blanks.*

1. The place was so dirty that ..... wished to run away from there.
A. everybody B. anybody
C. few D. some

2. ..... was there to help me.
A. Somebody B. Anything
C. Anybody D. Nobody

3. Is there .... to eat?
A. some B. something
C. any D. few

4. ..... of the students were making a great noise.
A. Anyone B. Somebody
C. Many D. Nobody

5. ..... of the students can solve this sum.
A. Someone B. Anybody
C. Somebody D. None

6. ...... of us should try our best to make India a heaven.
A. Any B. Somebody
C. Anybody D. All

7. ...... of us do not know the real meaning of our lives.
A. Any B. Something
C. Several D. Many

8. My .... black.
A. hairs are B. hair is
C. hairs shall D. hair will

9. She saw two .... on the last Sunday.
A. thiefs B. theifs
C. thieves D. theives

10. My sister is a ....
A. bacheloress B. bachelor
C. unmaried D. spinster

11. One is supposed to do ....
A. our duty B. their duty
C. one's duty D. his duty

12. Take anything .... you want.
A. that B. which
C. than D. then

13. I cannot tolerate ....
A. separated you
B. your separation
C. separation from you
D. you separated

14. He is .... faithful partner.
A. Yours B. You
C. Your D. Your's

15. Ajay is more smart than ....
A. her B. hers
C. herself D. she

16. Vivek works harder than ....
A. me B. I
C. her D. his

17. They should help ....
A. the poor people B. the poor
C. the poor persons D. the poor peoples

18. .... are mad.
A. All his sons B. His all sons
C. Sons all his D. All sons his

19. The poor fellow .... to fate.
A. resigned
B. resigned himself
C. resigned itself
D. resigned themselves

20. Nobody will help you but ....
A. I B. me
C. ours D. his

21. It is a good chance, You must avail .... this opportunity.
A. of B. yourself of
C. for D. from

22. The person who is elected .... my relative.
A. is B. he is
C. his D. him

23. He made ....
A. yours mention B. mention of you
C. mention for you D. mention about you

24. .... I know, he is quite faithful.
A. As far as B. So far as
C. So far this D. So far so

25. It is a duty of a person to take .... for his family.
A. pain B. pains
C. pain-killers D. pained

26. She does not love .... husband.
A. his B. her
C. its D. their

27. Let .... work together.
A. him and me B. he and I
C. he and him D. I and me

28. Copper, Silver and Gold ....
A. each will do B. either will do
C. any one will do D. any will do

29. Jessica and Roma are very irregular .... habits.
A. in her B. in their
C. in its D. in every

30. One likes to enjoy .... who was a great poet.
A. The sonnets of Shakespeare
B. Shakespeare's sonnets
C. Sonnets
D. Shakespeare

31. That is the boy .... everybody loves.
A. whom B. who
C. that D. whose

32. That is the girl .... won the first prize.
A. whom B. who
C. whose D. which

33. That is the man .... purse was lost.
A. who B. whom
C. whose D. their

ANSWERS

1	2	3	4	5	6	7	8	9	10
A	D	B	C	D	D	D	B	C	D
11	**12**	**13**	**14**	**15**	**16**	**17**	**18**	**19**	**20**
C	A	C	C	D	B	B	A	B	B
21	**22**	**23**	**24**	**25**	**26**	**27**	**28**	**29**	**30**
B	A	B	A	B	B	A	C	B	A
31	**32**	**33**							
A	B	C							

ARTICLES

The family of the articles has only three members. They are : A, An and The. However, they fall under two groups :

(a) Definite Article *(b)* Indefinite Article

'The' is known as definite article whereas 'a' and 'an' are known as indefinite articles.

Use of the Definite Article 'The'

'The' is used before

1. The superlative degree :
   He is the ablest man of the town.
   (ablest is a superlative degree)
2. The name of states, countries etc. having a descriptive name :
   (i) The J & K is a small state. (J & K is a descriptive name)
   (ii) He lives in the U.S.A. (U.S.A. is a descriptive name)
   (But the Delhi and the America are wrong because neither Delhi nor America is a descriptive name)
3. The names of the scriptures :
   The Gita is a holy book. (Gita is a scripture)
4. Name of newspapers :
   The Tribune is published from Chandigarh.
5. Name of rivers, canals, seas, oceans, bays, gulfs, groups of islands etc. :
   (i) The Ganga is a holy river.
   (ii) The Indian Ocean is the deepest ocean.
   (iii) The Persian Gulf is a narrow gulf.
6. The name of famous buildings :
   The Taj is one of the best buildings in India.
7. The names of nationals, sects and communities:
   (i) The English defeated the Germans in the World War.
   (ii) The rich should help the poor.
   (iii) The Hindus believe in the caste system.
8. Proper nouns used as common nouns :
   (i) Kalidas is the Shakespeare of India.
   (ii) Delhi is the London of India.
9. Famous historical events :
   The Industrial Revolution changed the face of England.
10. The directions and the celestial bodies:
    The sun rises in the east.
11. Titles :
    Akbar, the Great was loved by his subjects.

Do not use 'the'

1. Before languages :
   The English is an international language. (Incorrect)
   English is an international language. (Correct)
2. Before the names of games :
   The hockey is a popular game. (Incorrect)
   Hockey is a popular game. (Correct)

Use of the Indefinite Articles 'A' and 'An'

'A' is used before :

1. All singular common nouns beginning with a consonant :
   (i) A boy sings a song.

(ii) A black and a white cow were grazing in the field.

2. If a word begins with a vowel but gives the sound of a consonant, 'a' should be used before it :
   (i) He was helped in his work by a European.
   (ii) He is a one-eyed man.
   (iii) It is a useful work.

'An' is used as follows :

1. All singular common nouns beginning with a vowel (*i.e.*, a, e, i, o, u) :
   (i) He is an artist.
   (ii) He is an old man.
   (iii) I intend to buy an umbrella.
2. If a word starts with a consonant but gives the sound of a vowel, "an" should be used before it :
   (i) Brutus is an honourable man.
   (ii) He is an honour to his profession.
   (iii) He is an L.L.B.
   (iv) He is an M.A.
   (v) You will reach there in an hour.

Demonstratives, that, these and those

1. The demonstrative adjectives and pronouns are for objects nearby the speaker:
   this (singular) those (plural)
   and for objects far away from the speaker.
   That (singular) those (plural)
2. Demonstratives are the only adjectives that agree in number with their nouns.
   That hat is nice.
   Those hats are nice.
3. When there is the idea of selection, the pronoun "one" (or "ones") often follows the demonstrative.
   I want a book. I'll get this (one).
   If the demonstrative is followed by an adjective, "one"(or "ones") must be used.
   I want a book. I'll get this big one.

MULTIPLE CHOICE QUESTIONS

Directions: *In the following questions choose the correct options to fill the blanks.*

1. .... will have to be paid for this material.
A. Half rupee B. Half a rupee
C. A half rupee D. An half rupee

2. .... is taking keen interest in India.
A. The USA B. USA
C. An USA D. A USA

3. Only .... can save our country.
A. the Hitler B. a Hitler
C. Hitler D. an Hitler

4. I can run for ....
A. hundred miles B. the hundred miles
C. a hundred miles D. an hundred miles.

5. .... man-eater has been killed.
A. The B. A
C. An D. Either A or B

6. What .... fine idea!
A. the B. an
C. a D. No article

7. .... earth is moving around the sun.
A. An B. A
C. The D. No article

8. This is .... first example while I got.
A. the B. a
C. an D. No article

9. This is .... house which was built during earthquake.
A. a B. an
C. the D. No article

10. .... America is a rich country.
A. The B. An
C. A D. No article

11. .... U.S.A. is a developed country.
A. A B. An
C. The D. No article

12. .... Bible is a holy book.
A. A B. The
C. An D. No article

13. .... rich should help the poor.
A. The B. A
C. An D. No article

14. .... Gold is a costly metal.
A. The B. A
C. An D. No article

15. Kalidas is .... Shakespeare of India.
A. a B. an
C. the D. No article

16. I cannot do .... difficult work.
A. a such B. the such
C. such the D. such a

17. How foolish .... plan it is!
A. a B. an
C. the D. No article

18. An ink is .... useful article.
A. an B. a
C. the D. No article

19. There are .... husband and wife.
A. a B. an
C. the D. No article

20. He is learning .... French
A. the B. a
C. an D. No article

ANSWERS

1	2	3	4	5	6	7	8	9	10
B	A	B	C	D	C	C	A	C	D
11	**12**	**13**	**14**	**15**	**16**	**17**	**18**	**19**	**20**
C	B	A	D	C	D	A	B	D	D

ADJECTIVES & ADVERBS

An Adjective is a word which adds something to the meaning of a noun or a pronoun.

Mridula is an *intelligent* girl.
He has a *black* goat.
He is a *brilliant* student.
She is a *clever* girl.
It is a *beautiful* picture.

In the sentences given above, the words in italics are adjectives.

An Adverb is a word which qualifies the meaning of a Verb, an Adjective or another Adverb.

(*i*) He talks *slowly.*
(*ii*) He is a *very* good student.
(*iii*) He talks *very* slowly.

In sentence (*i*), *slowly* qualifies the verb *talks.*

In sentence (*ii*), *very* qualifies the adjective *good.*

In sentence (*iii*), *very* qualifies the adverb *slowly.*

Adjectives have three degrees of comparison :

1. **Positive Degree :** It expresses the common form of an adjective.
   Example :
   Ram is a *tall* boy.
   In the above sentence *tall* is an adjective and expresses the common form.
2. **Comparative Degree :** It expresses the more of the same form.
   Example :
   Ram is *taller* than Mahesh.
   In the above sentence *taller* is an adjective that expresses the more of the common form of the adjective *tall.*

"When and How to Use" Comparative Degree?

(a) Comparative Degree is used when two persons or two groups of persons or things are compared.

Examples :
(a) He is *wiser* than his younger brother.
(b) This glass is *cleaner* than the other.

(b) When two different qualities in the same person are compared, more is used instead of 'er' to form the comparative. The formula used in this case should be :

More + Positive Degree
She is *fairer* than polite. (Incorrect)
She is *more fair* than polite. (Correct)

(c) When selection of one out of two persons or things is meant, the degree of comparison is followed by of and *the* is used before it.

Example :
Zia is abler of *the* two sisters.

(d) If two comparatives are used in the same sentence to impress upon an idea, both should be preceded by the definite article.

Examples :

(i) The higher you go, the cooler it is.

(ii) The more we get, the more we desire.

(e) When one person or thing is compared with another of the same kind, other is used after the comparative degree. In such sentences other is normally preceded by any or all.

Examples :

(i) Kalidas is greater than any dramatist. (Incorrect)

Kalidas is greater than any other dramatist. (Correct)

(ii) Lead is heavier than all metals. (Incorrect)

Lead is heavier than all other metals. (Correct)

(f) Senior, junior, superior, inferior, prior, anterior (earlier than) and posterior (later than) are always followed by 'to'.

Examples :

(i) Ram is senior *to* Mohan by three years.

(ii) That pen is inferior *to* that.

(iii) He is junior *to* me in rank.

(iv) This event was posterior *to* that.

Note: Never use *than* after the above mentioned adjectives.

Important Information

(a) 'Preferable' is also used as an adjective of the comparative degree. As such, it is always followed by *to* and not *a*.

Death is preferable than dishonour. (Incorrect)

Death is preferable *to* dishonour. (Correct)

(b) To intensify the Degree of comparison, we use *far* or *much* before the comparative.

Examples :

(i) This book is *far* better than that.

(ii) His performance was *much* better than Mohan's.

Warning : Always avoid the use of double comparatives.

Don't say : Ram is more cleverer than his younger brother.

Say: Ram is cleverer than his younger brother.

3. Superlative Degree : It expresses the most of the common form of an adjective.

Example :

He is the ablest man of the town.

How and when to use the Superlative Degree?

(a) The Superlative Degree is used when more than two persons or things are compared.

(b) The Superlative Degree is generally preceded by 'the' and followed by 'of' in most of the cases or otherwise.

(c) When an adjective of the superlative degree is preceded by a Possessive Adjective or a Noun in the Possessive case, 'the' should not be used before it.

Example :

Which is Kalidas' best play?

It will be a blunder to use 'the' before the Superlative Degree in such cases.

Don't say : Which is Kalidas' the best play.

(d) To intensify the degree of comparison, *by far* is used before the superlative degree.

Example :

India is *by far* the most beautiful country of the world.

Note: Always avoid the use of double superlatives.

Don't say : He is the most strongest boy in the class.

Say : He is the strongest boy in the class.

Use of some Important Adjectives

1. (a) '**Some**' is used as follows :

(i) With countable nouns where it means— a little, a small quantity.

(ii) In a question which shows some request.

Examples :

(i) There is some water in the bottle.

(ii) Some of the students were absent yesterday.

(iii) Will you have some milk?

(iv) Will you buy some fruit for me?

(b) **'Any'** is used as follows :

(i) In negative sentences.

(ii) In interrogative sentences.

(iii) After 'Hardly', 'Scarcely' and 'Barely'.
(iv) After 'If'.

Examples :

(i) There is not any sugar in the pot.
(ii) We haven't any rice in the house.
(iii) I have hardly any money.
(iv) There are scarcely any plants in this field.
(v) If there is any danger, blow the whistle.

2. (a) **Older :** Older (and oldest) are used for persons animals and things. But 'Older' and 'Oldest' refer to the persons who do not belong to the same family.

Examples :

(i) Radha is older than Shyama.
(ii) John is the oldest member of the staff. 'Older' and 'Oldest' refer to the persons who do not belong to the same family.

(b) **Elder** (and **eldest**) are used in respect of the members of the same family like sons, daughters, brothers, sisters.

Examples :

(i) My elder sister is a lecturer.
(ii) Meenakshi is the eldest of the three sisters.

Note :

(i) 'Elder' is not followed by 'than'
(ii) 'Elder' and 'Eldest' cannot be used for things.

3. (a) **'Few'** is negative and is the opposite of 'Many'. It means 'not many'.
(b) **'A few'** is positive and means 'some at least'. It is the opposite of 'None'.
(c) **'The few'** means 'minority' and suggests 'whether there is'

Examples :

(i) We have few holidays in school.
(ii) Only a few boys will fail in the examination.
(iii) The few poems that he wrote are very popular.

4. (a) **Further** means 'something additional'.
(b) **Farther** means 'a greater distance'.

Examples :

(i) Further discussion will be held in the office of the principal.
(ii) Amritsar is farther from Delhi than Ambala.

5. (a) **Little** is negative. It means, 'not much', or 'hardly any'
(b) **A little** is positive. It means 'some quantity'.
(c) **The little** denotes quantity. It means, 'not much but all that is, or whatever quantity there is'.

Examples :

(i) There is little hope of his success.
(ii) He knows a little of everything.
(iii) I have spent the little money I had.
(iv) The little knowledge of shoe-making proved very useful to me.

6. (a) **'Much'** expresses 'quantity'.
(b) **'Many'** expresses 'number'.
(c) **'Many a'**—'Singular noun' and 'Singular verb' are used with 'many a'.

Examples :

(i) There is not *much* water in the jug.
(ii) *Many* boys are absent today.
(iii) *Many* a battle has been fought on the soil of India.

7. (a) **'Less'** denotes 'in a small degree'.
(b) **'Fewer'** denotes 'number'.

Examples :

(i) He devotes less time to his studies.
(ii) There are no fewer than ten chairs in this room.

8. (a) **'Each'** is used for a single number of 'two persons' or 'things'.
(b) **'Every'** is used for a single number of 'many persons' or 'things'.

Examples :

(i) Each boy must take part in games.
(ii) There are only two poets. Each poet recited his poem.
(iii) Every man dies in this world.
(iv) Every man is expected to do his duty.

9. (a) **'Either'** means one of the two or both.
(b) **'Neither'** is negative of the either.

Examples :

(i) You may buy either of these two chairs.
(ii) Neither of them could speak on the stage.

10.(a) '**Later**' expresses 'late in time'.

(b) '**Latter**' means 'second in position or order'.

Examples :

(i) My father reached later than I expected.

(ii) The latter position was better than the former.

Use of some Important Adverbs

1. (a) Also, too, enough:

(i) He taught English. Also, he edited the school magazine

(ii) He is a writer and also he is a painter.

(iii) He is too obstinate to listen to any reason.

(iv) This is too difficult a piece for the junior students.

(v) Sarla was kind enough to help the poor.

(vi) He is brave enough to help the truth.

Note: 'Too' is used in a negative sense, but enough is used in a positive sense.

(b) Fairly and rather: Both suggest the meaning 'moderately'. But, mainly 'fairly' is used with the words that denote a positive meaning and rather is used with the words that denote a negative meaning:

(i) Rita did fairly well in that competition, but her performance was rather poor in sports.

(ii) Mona is fairly rich, but she is rather stingy.

Note: 'Rather' can also be used in a positive sense.

(i) This is a rather interesting job.

(ii) That boy is rather smart.

(c) Hardly, barely, scarcely: These words mostly convey the negative suggestions and are almost similar.

(i) I have hardly any strength now.

(ii) There was barely any supply to the township,

(iii) There were scarcely a hundred guests present.

Note: With slight variance in the meaning, the words given above convey the idea of 'very little', 'not enough', 'lack of quantity and number'.

(d) Yet, Still: These adverbs can often be used to connect the sentence units:

(i) He has been defeated many times in the contest; still he wants to be a competitor.

(ii) Mona was sick; yet she went on doing her work.

(e) Alone:

(i) He alone (none else) is capable of handling that fire,

(ii) He hunted all alone in the forest. (not in any company)

Special Note:

(a) Apart from their conventional positions the adverbs might be used in different positions with different meanings and angles.

(i) He had only four books.

(ii) John only contacted his friend in need.

(iii) He greeted me only.

(iv) Only he greeted me there.

(b) Inversion: Some adverbs can be inverted *i.e.* placed in the beginning of the sentence and then be followed by an interrogative form. The most common of these adverb are: so, seldom, never, nowhere, under no circumstances, hardly, scarcely etc.

(i) So big was the bus that it could not enter the narrow lane.

(ii) Hardly had he reached the station when he received the message.

MULTIPLE CHOICE QUESTIONS

Directions: *In the following questions choose the correct options to fill the blanks.*

1. The girl whom you met is the .... sister of Ravi.

A. eldest B. elder
C. older D. oldest

2. The historical place is ....

A. seeing worth

B. worthy of seeing
C. worth seeing
D. worthy seeing

3. These flowers smell ....
A. sweet B. sweetly
C. more sweetly D. sweetest

4. .... aspirant cannot pass the entrance examination.
A. Each B. Every
C. All D. No

5. Harivansh Rai .... second Shakespeare.
A. is a B. is
C. is the D. is an

6. .... student in the class got prizes.
A. Each and every B. Every and each
C. Every D. Never

7. It is .... picture than the one we saw last Monday.
A. interesting B. much interesting
C. more interesting D. most interesting

8. She is clever ....
A. that her mother is
B. as her mother is
C. to her mother is
D. than her mother is

9. They will get ....
A. Red, green and black paper
B. Red, green black paper
C. Red and green and black paper
D. Red green black paper

10. Health is .... wealth.
A. preferable to
B. more preferable than
C. more preferable to
D. most preferable then

11. .... water that was in the jug evaporated.
A. Little B. The little
C. Small D. A small

12. He has not sung .... songs.
A. much B. most
C. more D. many

13. Srishti has searched .... office.
A. whole the B. the whole
C. a whole D. some whole

14. Premchand was .... best and .... famous writer.
A. a, the most B. the, a most
C. the, more D. the, the most

15. William Shakespeare is famous as ....
A. a poet and a dramatist
B. a poet and dramatist
C. the poet and the dramatist
D. a poet and the dramatist

16. What does .... leader suggest?
A. other B. another
C. others D. anothers

17. He .... money.
A. has few B. have few
C. has little D. have little

18. The .... boys are rewarded.
A. first two B. two first
C. firsts two D. two's first

19. He is .... brave.
A. stronger than
B. stronger then
C. more strong then
D. more strong than

20. No sooner said ....
A. so done B. and done
C. then done D. but done

21. She returned .... than I had thought.
A. quickly B. more quicker
C. more quickly D. quicker

22. He is .... foolish person.
A. rather the B. a rather
C. rather a D. rather

23. This pen .... rupees.
A. costs twenty
B. twenty costs only
C. costs only twenty
D. only costs twenty

24. It is .... pride.
A. nothing else but
B. nothing else than
C. else nothing than
D. but

25. This tea is .... to drink.
A. too hot B. very hot
C. enough hot D. much hot

ANSWERS

1	2	3	4	5	6	7	8	9	10
A	C	A	B	A	C	C	C	A	A
11	**12**	**13**	**14**	**15**	**16**	**17**	**18**	**19**	**20**
B	D	B	D	B	B	C	A	D	C
21	**22**	**23**	**24**	**25**					
C	C	C	A	A					

DETERMINERS

Determiners are actually Adjectives. They are always followed by nouns.

Determiners are of the following kinds:

1. Demonstrative Determiners

this, that, these, those

2. Possessive Determiners

my, our, your, his, her, its, their

3. Quantitative Determiners

some, any, much, enough, sufficient, whole, a little, the little, little, all, both

4. Numerical Determiners

a few, some, few, the few, any, several, many, no, etc.

One, two, three ... (Cardinals)

First, second, third ... (Ordinals)

5. Distributive Determiners

either, neither

6. Articles

Indefinite: a, an

Definite: the

MULTIPLE CHOICE QUESTIONS

Directions: *In the following questions choose the correct options to fill the blanks.*

1. Give me .... rice.
A. some B. few
C. a few D. any

2. .... sheep grazing on the slope of the hill had gone away.
A. Any B. The few
C. This D. Much

3. Have you got .... magazines to read?
A. all B. much
C. some D. little

4. I have .... money that I want to spend on shares.
A. any B. much
C. less D. some

5. There is .... owl on the branch of the tree.
A. a B. the
C. an D. some

6. My brother is .... MBA.
A. a B. an
C. the D. any

7. Have you got .... cheese?
A. some B. many
C. a few D. few

8. No, I have not got .... cheese.
A. many B. few
C. any D. some

9. There is only .... milk left in the bottle.
A. enough B. few
C. much D. a little

10. There is .... hope of his recovery.
A. any B. little
C. many D. few

11. .... dogs were barking at the strangers.
A. Some B. Any
C. Much D. Less

12. The girl bought her father .... juice.
A. few B. some
C. any D. many

13. You should take .... honey everyday.
A. any B. many
C. a little D. a few

14. .... boy was punished by the teacher.
A. Either B. All
C. Any D. Many

15. .... girl was asked to join the army.
A. None B. Neither
C. All D. Any

16. .... water in the jug has been drunk by Mohan.
A. The little B. The few
C. A few D. Few

17. I shall play .... piano at the party.
A. some B. any
C. the D. few

18. .... labourers were found dead in the mine.
A. Any B. Fewer
C. Many D. Less

19. Could I borrow .... umbrella?
A. our B. your
C. yours D. my

20. My brother is standing in the .... row.
A. any B. many
C. some D. first

ANSWERS

1	2	3	4	5	6	7	8	9	10
A	B	C	D	C	B	A	C	D	B
11	**12**	**13**	**14**	**15**	**16**	**17**	**18**	**19**	**20**
A	B	C	A	B	A	C	C	B	D

THE VERB

A Verb is a word that tells something about the action or state of or happenning to a person or thing.

A Verb tells the following:

1. What a person or thing does.
Sachin goes to school daily.
The bell *rang* loudly.
Many birds fly in the sky.
She *sang* a song.

2. What a person or thing is.
India *is* the biggest democracy in the world.
Ram Mehar *is* very rich.
They *are* happy.

3. What is done to a person or thing.
You *are liked* by all.
Two thieves *were arrested.*
Four students *were punished* by the teacher.

4. What happens to a person or thing.
His maternal uncle *died* last week.
Two ships *sank* yesterday.
Leaves *turn* yellow in autumn.

5. What a person or thing has, had, and so on.
I *have* a new car.
He *had* a scooter last year.
He *has* several cows and goats.

It goes without saying that a verb is the most important part of a sentence. No sentence is complete without a Verb.

Important Information

1. If two or more singular nouns are joined by 'and' the verb used will be plural.

   Example:
   (i) He and I were going to the market.
   (ii) Ram and Mohan are friends.

2. If two singular nouns joined by 'and' points out to the same thing or person, the verb used must be singular.

   Example:
   (i) Rice and curry is the favourite food of the Punjabis.
   (ii) The Collector and District Magistrate is away.

3. In case two subjects are joined by 'as well as' the verb agrees with the first subject.

   Example :
   (i) Kanta as well as her children is playing.
   (ii) Children as well as their mother are playing.

In the case of first sentence the verb (is) agrees with Kanta and in the case of second sentence the verb (are) agrees with the children.

4. 'Neither', 'Either', 'Every', 'Each', 'Everyone', and 'Many a' are followed by a singular verb.
   Example :
   (i) Either of the plans is to be adopted.
   (ii) Neither of the two brothers is sure to pass.
   (iii) Every student is expected to be obedient.
   (iv) Everyone of them desires this.
   (v) Many a person is drowned in the sea.
5. If two subjects are joined by 'Either .... or' / 'Neither .... nor', the verb agrees with the subject near to it.
   Example :
   (i) Either my brother or I am to do this work.
   (ii) Neither he nor they are prepared to do this work.
6. 'A great many' is always followed by a 'plural noun' and a 'plural verb'. For example :
   A great many students have been declared successful.
7. Similarly if two subjects are joined by 'with', 'together with', 'no less than', in addition to 'and not', etc. the verb agrees with the first subject.
   Example :
   (i) The boy with his parents has arrived.
   (ii) He, no less than I, is to blame.
8. Nouns, plural in form, but singular in meaning, take a singular verb.
   Example :
   This news was broadcast from television yesterday.

MULTIPLE CHOICE QUESTIONS

Directions: *In the following questions choose the correct options to fill the blanks.*

1. The bus with all its passengers .... lost.
A. were B. was
C. are D. would

2. You as well as I .... responsible for this work.
A. am B. are
C. was D. is

3. Raghava like all his companions .... a spoiled child.
A. are B. were
C. is D. will be

4. Pen and ink .... required for me.
A. are B. were
C. is D. has required

5. Every girl and every boy .... attended the seminar.
A. have B. has
C. is D. are

6. Not only she but all her sisters ...... been married.
A. has B. have
C. is D. are

7. There .... nothing but miseries in life.
A. is B. are
C. were D. will be

8. Neither prose nor poem .... given.
A. were B. was
C. has D. have

9. Either he or I .... wrong.
A. is B. are
C. am D. were

10. Either Sulekha or Rekha .... coming here.
A. are B. is
C. were D. have

11. .... the child or his parents to blame?
A. Is B. Are
C. Were D. Has

12. You and I .... neighbours.
A. am B. are
C. was D. has

13. The house with all its belongings ..... sold away.
A. were B. are
C. was D. must

14. Either water or juice .... required.
A. is B. are
C. were D. has

15. There were not as many tables as .... required.
A. was B. were
C. is D. are

16. They each .... a book.
A. have B. are
C. has D. is

17. He and I .... class friends.
A. is B. am
C. was D. are

18. She as well as I .... guilty.
A. is B. are
C. am D. must be

19. Purushottam .... not read more on this chapter.
A. needs B. has been need
C. need D. had been need

20. He came .... to his aunt.
A. run B. running
C. to run D. in run

21. She dislikes .... meat.
A. eat to B. to eat
C. eating D. to eating

22. He likes ....
A. sing to B. singing
C. to sing D. to singing

23. We are ready .... the match.
A. play to B. to playing
C. playing D. to play

24. .... is injurious to health.
A. Smoking B. To smoke
C. To smoking D. Smoke to

25. He loves .... raw vegetables.
A. eaten B. eating
C. to eating D. eat to

26. He seemed .... finished his homework.
A. have to B. to have
C. having D. to having

ANSWERS

1	2	3	4	5	6	7	8	9	10
B	B	C	C	B	B	A	B	C	B
11	**12**	**13**	**14**	**15**	**16**	**17**	**18**	**19**	**20**
A	B	C	A	B	A	D	A	C	B
21	**22**	**23**	**24**	**25**	**26**				
C	B	D	A	B	B				

CONJUNCTIONS

A conjunction is a word which connects words, clauses or sentences.

Look at the following sentences.

(i) He bought apples *and* mangoes.

(ii) God made the country *and* man made the town.

(iii) The door was open *but* there was no one in the house.

(iv) He knows that I am here *and* that I want to see him.

In the sentence (i), *and* connects two words—*apples* and *mangoes.*

In the sentence (ii), *and* connects two sentences—*God made the country* and *man made the town.*

In the sentence (iii), *but* connects two sentences—*The door was open* and *there was no one in the house.*

In the sentence (iv), *and* connects two clauses—*that I am here* and *that I want to see him.*

The main coordinating conjunctions are: and, but, for, or, nor, also, either ..... or, neither ..... nor.

There are some conjunctions which are used in pairs. They are:

either .... or, ... neither .... nor, both .... and, though .... yet, whether .... or, not only .... but also.

Example: *Either* take it *or* leave it.

It is *neither* useful *nor* ornamental.

They *both* like *and* respect me.

Though he is suffering from high fever, *yet* he does not cry.

He does not care *whether* you go *or* stay.

He is *not only* doltish, *but also* obstinate.

The conjunctions which are used in pairs in this way, are called correlative conjunctions, or merely correlatives.

Use of Important Conjunctions

1. **As soon as :** As soon as denotes simultaneous time.
   Example : As soon as he saw his enemy, he took to his heels.
2. **No sooner .... than :**
   (a) 'No sooner' is always followed by 'than'.
   (b) Please remember that 'No sooner' is always followed by do/does/did. As such only first form of the verb should be used after the subject.
   Example :
   No sooner did he see his enemy than he took to his heels.
3. **Hardly :** Hardly is followed by when.
   Examples :
   (i) Hardly had I left the house when it started raining.
   (ii) We had hardly come into the room when his father began chastising him.
   Note :
   A. Hardly is never followed by than.
   B. 'Scarcely' can also be used in the sense and manner of 'Hardly'.
4. **Lest :** Lest is used in the sense of so that .... not. It is always followed by should. Lest is negative in sense. Hence 'not' should never be used with it.
   Example :
   Work hard lest you should fail.
   Note : 'Lest' is always followed by 'should' and not 'may'.
5. **Unless :** Unless expresses condition. It is also used in the negative sense. Use of 'not' is not allowed with unless because unless is already in the negative sense.
   Example :
   Unless you labour hard you will not pass.
6. **Until :** 'Until' expresses time. It means 'till not'.
   Example :
   Wait here until I return.
   Note : Until is in the negative sense. So 'not' should not be used with it. Example :
   Wait here until I do not return. (Incorrect)
   Wait here until I return. (Correct)
7. **As well as :** When two subjects are joined by 'as well as', the verb always agrees with the first subject.
   Examples :
   (i) The teacher as well as students is playing.
   (ii) Students as well as the teacher are playing.
   Note : 'Both' and 'as well as' cannot be used together in the same sentence.
   Examples :
   Both Sita as well as Kanta are beautiful. (Incorrect)
   Sita as well as Kanta is beautiful. (Correct)
   Both Sita and Kanta are beautiful. (Correct)
8. **As if :** 'As if' is used in the sense of pretension. While using 'as if' in a sentence, we should see that even the third person singular subject gets 'were'.
   Example :
   He talks as if he were mad.
9. **Till :** Till expresses time. Till is always used in the affirmative.
   Example :
   We did not come back till sunset.
10. **Rather than :** 'Rather than' is used in the sense of 'preference'. 'Rather' is always followed by 'than'.
    Example :
    I would rather die than submit.
11. **As long as/so long as :** Both express time during which an action or event takes place.
    Example :
    As long as there is life, there is hope.
12. **However :** It is both a subordinate and co-ordinate clause.
    Examples :
    (a) Mala worked hard, she however, failed.
    (b) However hard he may work, he cannot pass.
13. **Such as :** 'Such as' gives us the sense of 'like'. Such is always followed by 'as'.
    Example :
    Life is such a puzzle as cannot be solved.

MULTIPLE CHOICE QUESTIONS

Directions: *In the following questions choose the correct options to fill the blanks.*

1. Neither he .... his friend is good.
A. or B. and
C. but D. nor

2. The officer asked the peon .... why he was late.
A. that B. if
C. but D. No word needed

3. Both Ajay .... Vijay are intelligent.
A. or B. nor
C. and D. No word needed

4. No Sooner did the thief see the public .... he ran away.
A. then B. and
C. but D. than

5. Abhinav .... his brothers was going to Mumbai.
A. but B. yet
C. No word needed D. together with

6. He behaves .... he were the captain of the team.
A. as if B. as
C. No word needed D. that

7. Either Rupali .... Sonali is going to attend the meeting.
A. and B. but
C. nor D. or

8. Neither Nirmal .... Ashwinee is going to listen the speech.
A. and B. but
C. nor D. or

9. Ravi .... Prakash are going to Kolkata.
A. or B. nor
C. but D. and

10. Rice .... curry is my usual breakfast.
A. and B. but
C. then D. than

11. Hardly had he left .... his brother came.
A. then B. than
C. when D. that

12. I would rather have a copy .... a book.
A. then B. than
C. when D. that

13. He is no other .... my friend.
A. then B. than
C. when D. but

14. He saw a snake ....he awoke.
A. then B. when
C. than D. No word needed

15. Ten years have passed .... my grandmother died.
A. since B. when
C. then D. than

16. She is .... good .... bad.
A. either, not B. neither, or
C. neither, nor D. neither, than

17. The cellphone is both cheap .... best.
A. than B. and
C. then D. or

18. No sooner did the rogue see the police .... he disappeared.
A. then B. than
C. so D. because

19. Srishti will go .... Sanju goes.
A. if B. than
C. then D. although

20. She is wise .... timid.
A. and B. yet
C. but D. however

21. Make hay .... the sun shines.
A. though B. while
C. after D. before

22. He is so weak .... he cannot walk.
A. but B. that
C. then D. so

23. Although he is rich, ... he is unhappy.
A. but B. yet
C. so D. still

24. Wait here .... I come back.
A. till B. until
C. before D. after

25. He is my friend .... I shall help him.
A. so
B. hence
C. that is why
D. therefore

26. He must go away .... he will be beaten.
A. otherwise B. and
C. or D. else

27. God loves good men .... good men love God.
A. and B. or
C. that D. those

28. He was late .... he was not punished.
A. but B. yet
C. still D. therefore

29. Walk slowly ...., you may fall.
A. and B. or
C. so D. otherwise

30. Work hard, ... you will fail.
A. and B. or
C. otherwise D. else

ANSWERS

1	2	3	4	5	6	7	8	9	10
D	D	C	D	D	A	D	C	D	A
11	**12**	**13**	**14**	**15**	**16**	**17**	**18**	**19**	**20**
C	B	B	B	A	C	B	B	A	C
21	**22**	**23**	**24**	**25**	**26**	**27**	**28**	**29**	**30**
B	B	B	A	B	C	A	C	D	D

PREPOSITIONS

A *Preposition* is a word which is placed before a noun or a pronoun to show its relation to some other word in the sentence.

1. I saw a goat *in* the field.
2. I am fond *of* hot coffee.

In sentence 1, the word *in* shows the relation between two things—*goat* and *field.*

In sentence 2, the word *of* shows the relation between the attribute expressed by the adjective *found* and *tea.*

The words *in* and *of* are here used as prepositions.

The noun or pronoun which is used with a preposition is called its object. The noun or pronoun is in the objective case. It is governed by the preposition. Now it is absolutely clear that in sentence 1, the noun *field* is in the objective case. The word *field* is governed by the preposition *in.*

A preposition may have two or more objects.

The road runs over *hill* and *plain.*

Here, the words *hill* and *plain* are used as objects.

Use of Important Prepositions

1. Among, Between

'**Among**' is used for more than two persons or things; '**Between**' is used only for two.

Examples :

(i) Distribute these sweets *among* the poor students of the class.

(ii) Distribute these books *between* Ram and Shyam.

2. Among, In

'**Among**' is used before collective plural nouns. '**In**' is used before collective singular nouns.

Examples :

(i) I found him standing *among* the crowd.

(ii) I saw him in the crowd.

3. Beside, Besides

'**Beside**' means 'by the side of'. '**Besides**' means 'in addition to'.

Examples :

(i) The daughter was sitting *beside* her mother.

(ii) *Besides* his relatives, he invited his friends also.

4. In, Within

'**In**' means at the expiry of a period of time in future, '**Within**' means before the expiry of a period of time in any tense.

Examples :

(i) She will return *in* a week.

(ii) I shall finish my work *within* a weak.

5. On, Upon

'**On**' is used for things at rest; '**Upon**' is used for things in motion.

Examples :

(i) He is sitting *on* the floor.

(ii) The dog sprang *upon* the table.

6. By, With

'**By**' denotes the agent or doer, '**With**' denotes the instrument with which anything is done.

Examples :

(i) The bird was killed *by* the hunter with an arrow.

(ii) He beat the dog *with* a stick.

(iii) I shall reach here *by* five o'clock.

7. After, In

'**After**' means at the end of a period of time in the past. '**In**' means at the end of a period of time in future.

Examples :

(i) I shall return your book *in* a week.

(ii) He returned the book *after* a week.

8. For, From, Since

'**For**' is used before a noun denoting a period of time with all the tenses. '**From**' is used before a noun or phrase denoting a point of time, it is used in all the tenses. '**Since**' is used before a noun or phrase denoting some point of time and is always produced by a verb in the perfect continuous tense or third form of a verb.

Examples :

(i) We have been playing cards *for* two hours.

(ii) She stayed with her uncle *from* the 15th of March to the 15th of May.

(iii) I have been reading this book *since* morning.

9. Above, Over

'**Above**' means 'higher from', **Over** is used in the following four senses :

(i) In the sense of 'above' :
At noon, the sun is *over* our heads.

(ii) In the sense of 'beyond' :
I cannot get *over* my disappointment.

(iii) In the sense of 'Superiority' :
God *over* all blesses for ever more.

(iv) In the sense of 'Conclusion' :
It is all *over* with me.

10. At, Towards

'**At**' denotes the idea of aim, '**Towards**' denotes the idea of destination.

Examples :

(i) He threw the stone *at* the cat.

(ii) He went *towards* the house.

11. At, In, On

'At' is used as follows :

(i) '**At**' is used with small towns and villages.

Examples :

(a) He was born *at* Sonepat.

(b) He lives *at* village Bangra. (Bangra is a village)

(ii) '**At**' is used before a noun denoting a definite point of time.

Example :

He called on me *at* 9 p.m. yesterday.

'In' is used as follows :

(iii) '**In**' is used with the names of big cities, provinces and countries.

Examples :

(a) His father lives *in* England.

(b) His younger brother lives *in* Calcutta.

(iv) '**In**' is used before the names of months and years.

Example :

His elder sister was born *in* 1972 *in* the month of May.

'**On**' is used with dates and names of days.

Examples :

(a) I joined college *on* the 26th April.

(b) He will leave for Kolkata *on* Wednesday next.

Important Information

1. '**In**' is also used in the following phrases :
In the morning; In the evening, In winter, In summer.

2. '**In**' also denotes a place inside anything. He travelled *in* a crowded bus.
3. '**At**' is used in the following phrases : *At* home, *At* the station, *At* work, *At* play.

12. Below, Beneath

Below means 'of lower level in position, dignity and expectation' etc. *Beneath* means 'under'.

Examples :

(i) It is *below* my dignity to talk to her.
(ii) They rested *beneath* the shade of a tree.

13. In, Into, To

'**In**' expresses Rest or Motion inside anything. '**Into**' expresses Motion towards the inside of anything or change from one medium to another. '**To**' denotes motion from one place to another.

Examples :

(i) The boys are *in* the room.
(ii) Translate this passage from English *into* Hindi.
(iii) Every morning he goes *to* the temple.

14. Till, By, Of, Off

- 'Till' means upto or not earlier than.
- 'By' means not later than.
- 'Of' shows cause, source, separation, quality, contents, possession, apposition, point of reference, space in time etc.
- 'Off' shows separation at a near distance, and detached condition.

Consider the following examples:

(i) I shall work *till* 5 a.m.
(ii) Madhu died *of* cancer.
(iii) The nib *of* the pen is made *of* gold.
(iv) He presented me a bottle *of* perfume.
(v) Our principal is a man *of* principle.
(vi) He lived in the house *of* his friend.
(vii) *By* this time tomorrow, I'll have finished my job.
(viii) My house is *off* the road.
(ix) The book fell *off* the table.

MULTIPLE CHOICE QUESTIONS

Directions: *Tick the correct preposition for the blank in each of the following sentences.*

1. He applied ...... the manager.
A. for B. to
C. with D. by

2. Trust ...... God and do the right.
A. in B. for
C. to D. with

3. She is worthy ...... a prize.
A. with B. for
C. to D. of

4. Mr. Gomes has no taste ...... music.
A. of B. for
C. with D. to

5. You are hard ...... hearing.
A. at B. of
C. with D. for

6. He is sure ...... his success
A. for B. with
C. on D. of

7. Preeti was warned ...... the danger ahead.
A. for B. at
C. of D. about

8. I am thankful ...... you for a good advice.
A. for B. with
C. to D. of

9. Deepak would not surrender ...... the police.
A. with B. to
C. for D. on

10. The small plant in your lawn is very sensitive ...... touch.
A. on B. with
C. to D. about

11. Divya was sure to succeed ..... the examination.
A. for B. in
C. to D. with

12. Geeta was jealous ...... Ravina's beauty.
A. to B. with
C. for D. of

13. He was ignorant ..... what was happening there.
A. for B. of
C. to D. with

14. Your pen is inferior ...... mine.
A. than B. with
C. from D. to

15. Reenu is no match ...... Meenu.
A. to B. for
C. with D. upon

16. It is necessary ...... you to apply for this job.
A. on B. with
C. for D. to

17. Be loyal ...... your country.
A. for B. to
C. on D. with

18. Mukesh is junior ...... me.
A. than B. to
C. from D. of

19. Deepika was innocent ...... the crime.
A. of B. with
C. from D. to

20. I am desirous.... joining the Indian cricket team.
A. for B. of
C. to D. on

ANSWERS

1	2	3	4	5	6	7	8	9	10
B	A	D	B	B	D	D	D	B	D
11	**12**	**13**	**14**	**15**	**16**	**17**	**18**	**19**	**20**
B	D	B	D	B	D	B	B	A	B

SYNONYMS

A synonym is a word which conveys a meaning similar to the given word.

REMEMBER

Words	*Synonyms*
Add	Increase
Adequate	Enough
Adjust	Adapt
All	Aggregate
Allow	Permit
Abode	Dwelling
Apt	Proper
Assess	Appraise
Accuse	Calumniate
Abashed	Timid
Annoy	Displease
Ample	Enough, Sufficient
Amplify	Increase
Apathetic	Unenthusiastic
Accost	Address
Authentic	True

Words	*Synonyms*
Adjust	Fit
Approve	Assent, Allow, Accept
Adapt	Conform
Adversary	Opponent, Rival, Competitor
Beat	Whack
Benign	Kind
Breeze	Zephyr
Baffle	Puzzle
Booty	Spoil
Beauty	Charm
Beast	Animal
Bandit	Robber
Blaze	Shine
Bond	Tie
Bend	Twist
Bate	Diminish
Beg	Plead
Barbaric	Wild, Savage
Bashful	Shy, Reserved

Words	Synonyms
Begin	Start
Blend	Mix, Mingle
Bizarre	Funny
Below	Under
Bedevil	Confuse
Bemoan	Lament
Babble	Nonsense
Blame	Fault
Behaviour	Demeanour
Call	Accost
Copy	Imitate
Close	Shut
Caress	Love
Camp	Stay
Connect	Attach
Cut	Injure, Curtail
Cling	Stick
Conical	Funny
Convey	Carry
Conspicuous	Prominent
Cheerful	Happy, Pleasant
Curtail	Decrease
Cheerless	Sad, Dejected
Curious	Strange
Circumstance	Factor, Situation, Condition
Competent	Capable
Congruent	Overlapping
Cope	Deal, Endure
Confident	Sure
Complex	Intricate
Cajole	Coax, Flatter
Cunning	Crafty
Delectable	Joyful, Delightful
Devilish	Diabolical
Delicate	Soft
Devil	Fiend
Delay	Postpone
Dislike	Repugnance
Destroy	Ruin

Words	Synonyms
Dwell	Live, Dilate
Declare	Pronounce
Drunk	Flushed
Deficient	Lacking
Damn	Condemn, Curse
Decrease	Diminish
Destruction	Devastation
Efficient	Competent
Ethnic	Racial
Enthral	Enslave
Earnest	Serious
Envious	Jealous
Ending	Final
Egg	Incite
Extempore	At once
Extensive	Far-ranging
Extra	Surplus
Existence	Life
Exceed	Overstep
Enormous	Vast
Excessive	Superfluous
Free	Unhindered
Frigid	Cold
Feed	Cater
Fame	Reputation
Frame	Make
First	Initial
Frighten	Terrorise, Intimidate
Fervent	Fervid
Fall	Decline
Feeble	Frail
Fickle	Changeable
Finish	Conclude
Fraud	Deception
Forgiving	Placable
Grow	Develop
Greed	Avidity
Greet	Welcome
Grave	Serious
Group	Constellation

Words	*Synonyms*
Given	Bestowed
Gratitude	Thankfulness
Have	Possess
Hire	Rent
Hit	Strike
Handsome	Beautiful
Hinder	Prevent
Heap	Pile
Hope	Expect
Hard	Harsh
Help	Aid
Hymn	Song
Henpecked	Enslaved
Hoodwink	Mystify, Cheat
Humble	Polite, Urbane, Modest
Harass	Vex, Trouble
Impart	Instil
Intact	Untouched
Instal	Establish
Indict	Impeach
Imitate	Ape
Instigate	Incite
Initiate	Start, Introduce
Inimical	Unfriendly
Insufferable	Intolerable
Impartiality	Justice
Jolly	Merry
Joyful	Delectable
Join	Conjoin
Kind	Benign
Kill	Murder
Kindred	Similar
Kinship	Relationship
Keen	Sharp
Knowledge	Scholarship
Lazy	Slothful
Large	Substantial, Gargantuan
Listless	Careless, Lackadaisical
Lax	Loose
Little	Small
Lifelike	Realistic

Words	*Synonyms*
Lofty	High
Lenient	Soft, Gentle
Lacking	Deficient, Wanting
Lessen	Decrease
Middleclass	Bourgeois
Mitigate	Lessen, Abate
Modesty	Humility, Lowliness
Mix	Mingle, Blend
Mixture	Mingling
Mixed	Assorted
Modify	Decrease
Mean	Imply
Multifarious	Varied
Miscarry	Abort
Note	Notice
Noble	Stately
Native	Indigenous
Needful	Necessary
Notify	Declare
Nervous	Shaky, Tremulous, Timid
Natural	Spontaneous
Near	Close
Normal	Natural
Offend	Displease
Oppress	Persecute, Tyrannize
Opponent	Adversary
Obstruct	Hinder, Check
Offence	Fault
Offender	Villain
Overstep	Exceed
Overlapping	Congruent
Occult	Mystic
Profane	Unholy
Patience	Forbearance
Pornographic	Obscene
Plenitude	Abundance
Prominent	Important
Prodigal	Spender
Procrastinate	Postpone
Promote	Develop, Honour
Persecute	Tyrannise

Words	*Synonyms*
Profess	Claim
Pliant	Flexible
Plebian	Common
Polished	Sophisticated
Quake	Shake
Quit	Leave
Queer	Eccentric
Quell	Suppress
Quantify	Allot
Reply	Answer
Relinquish	Retire
Read	Peruse
Relation	Reference
Render	Do
Remainder	Residuals
Repeat	Reiterate
Repentant	Contrite
Retaliative	Retaliatory
Rumour	Hearsay
Reveal	Divulge
Ritualistic	Ceremonious
Soft	Delicate
Sort	Kind, Choose, Select
Selfish	Egoistic
Sensual	Earthly
Suppress	Quell, Check
Stimulate	Provoke
Tasteless	Insipid
Travel	Journey
True	Authentic, Faithful, Truthful
Turbulence	Turmoil
Tragedy	Calamity
Tasteful	Tasty, Delicious
Touching	Painful
Thankful	Grateful
Tremendous	Great, Huge
Tough	Strong
Terminate	Conclude, End
Theory	Doctrine
Tell	Relate
Tremble	Shake, Shiver
Urge	Spur

Words	*Synonyms*
Unbeaten	Unsubdued
Use	Utilize, Practise
Underhand	Unfair, Undue
Unfair	Unjust
Unravel	Reveal, Divulge
Unimportant	Common
Unconcerned	Apathetic
Unimitated	Inimitable
Unfortunate	Unlucky
Understand	Perceive, Comprehend
Vain	Proud, Haughty, Conceited, Shameless
Vale	Valley, Dale, Dell
Vice	Fault
Virtue	Quality
Veracity	Reality
Value	Price, Prize
Vex	Tease
Vibrate	Quiver, Shake
Violent	Excessive
Vivid	Clear, Lucid
Victory	Triumph
Vulgar	Indecent
Virtuous	Honest
Variegated	Varied, Multifarious
Well	Good
Yell	Cry, Shout
Yonder	There
Yearn	Wish, Desire
Yoke	Slavery
Zest	Earnestness, Enthusiasm
Zealous	Earnest

ANTONYMS

A antonym is a word which conveys a meaning opposite to the given word.

REMEMBER

Words	*Antonyms*
Abhor	Love
Abnormal	Normal
Able	Unable
Acceptable	Unacceptable
Adequate	Inadequate
Amusing	Boring

Words	*Antonyms*
Angry	Calm
Apex	Bottom
Attract	Repel
Bad	Good
Barren	Fertile
Beautiful	Ugly
Bitter	Sweet
Brave	Cowardly
Brief	Lengthy
Bright	Dull
Calm	Violent
Careful	Careless
Clear	Vague, Cloudy
Cold	Hot
Cruel	Kind
Dear	Cheap
Deep	Shallow
Difficult	Easy
Direct	Indirect
Dishonest	Honest
Disobey	Obey
Encourage	Discourage
Enormous	Tiny
Excellent	Bad
Expensive	Cheap
Eat	Fast
Fair	Unfair
Fake	Authentic
False	True
Famous	Notorious
Fool	Genius
Generous	Miserly
Genius	Fool
Genuine	Unauthentic
Gigantic	Tiny
Glad	Depressed
Good	Bad
Great	Little
Happy	Sad

Words	*Antonyms*
Hard	Soft
Hate	Love
Honest	Dishonest
Idle	Busy
Immoral	Moral
Include	Exclude
Incorrect	Correct
Intelligent	Unintelligent
Kind	Cruel
Like	Dislike
Long	Short
Lucid	Vague
Major	Minor
Naive	Experienced
Nadir	Apex
Neat	Clumsy
Obedient	Disobedient
Obscure	Clear
Oppose	Support
Optimistic	Pessimistic
Out	In
Patience	Impatience
Peaceful	Belligerent
Pious	Impious
Polite	Impolite
Potent	Impotent
Prominent	Unimportant
Proper	Improper
Pure	Impure
Quick	Slow
Quiet	Disturbance
Real	False, Unreal
Reject	Select, Choose
Reliable	Unreliable
Respect	Disrespect
Right	Wrong
Robust	Feeble, Weak
Sad	Happy

Words	Antonyms
Secret	Open
Sensible	Insensible
Severe	Mild
Sharp	Blunt
Simple	Complex
Sociable	Unsociable
Tall	Short
Tidy	Untidy
Uncanny	Canny
Violent	Calm
Vivid	Vague

Words	Antonyms
Strong	Weak
Big	Small
Easy	Difficult
Fast	Slow
High	Low
Catchy	Unattractive
Ugly	Handsome, Beautiful, Tidy
Tasty	Insipid
Sonorous	Harsh

MULTIPLE CHOICE QUESTIONS

Directions (Qs. 1 to 20): *In the following questions choose the word which best expresses the meaning of the given word.*

1. ABSURD
A. Foolish B. Simple
C. Courageous D. Silly

2. ABANDON
A. Lose B. Profit
C. Vacate D. Foil

3. CAJOLE
A. Pause B. Lenient
C. Blast D. Lure

4. COMBAT
A. Fight B. Conflict
C. Shoot D. Quarrel

5. LAMENT
A. Condone B. Console
C. Complain D. Contribution

6. DEBACLE
A. Disgrace B. Defeat
C. Collapse D. Decline

7. SHIVER
A. Fear B. Tremble
C. Shake D. Ache

8. TORTURE
A. Terror B. Harassment
C. Torment D. Tranquility

9. LAUDABLE
A. Lovable B. Commendable
C. Profitable D. Oblivious

10. FIXED
A. Sterile B. Static
C. Stubborn D. Parennial

11. QUEER
A. Unfamiliar B. Cute
C. Curious D. Strange

12. SUFFICIENT
A. Fit B. Proper
C. Adequate D. Vast

13. GLOSS
A. Brightness B. Soothing
C. Rubbing D. Miracle

14. LONGING
A. Prune B. Apathy
C. Curtail D. Craving

15. JEER
A. Applaud B. Magnanimity
C. Avoid D. Scoff

16. ZENITH
A. Minimum B. Nadir
C. Plant D. Peak

17. GARB
A. Distort B. Dress
C. Trivial D. Rage

18. ABHOR
A. Rude B. Reconcile
C. Crave D. Detest

19. YIELD
A. Shum B. Incisive
C. Retain D. Surrender

20. YOKE
A. Twist B. Release
C. Link D. Extra

Directions (Qs. 21 to 38): *In the following questions choose the word which best expresses the opposite of the given word.*

21. TRAGIC
A. Dramatic B. Strong
C. Gentle D. Comic

22. ORAL
A. Verbal B. Sane
C. Minor D. Written

23. ADMIRE
A. Hate B. Unlike
C. Dislike D. Enough

24. VIOLENT
A. Gentle B. Savage
C. Haughty D. Decline

25. ADVERSITY
A. Windfall B. Inprosperity
C. Prosperity D. Slave

26. GENUINE
A. Spurious B. Obscure
C. Countless D. Apathetic

27. GRUDGE
A. Essence B. Guile
C. Goodwill D. Ill-will

28. STIFF
A. Soft B. Courteous
C. Lively D. Flexible

29. VANITY
A. Conceit B. Pride
C. Ostentious D. Humility

30. FRONT
A. Upper B. Unusual
C. Back D. Rear

31. ATTRACT
A. Lured B. Longing
C. Repel D. Disguise

32. COMFORT
A. Discomfort B. Discontent
C. Uncomfort D. Miscomfort

33. WELCOME
A. Repel B. Accept
C. Resist D. Fight

34. TACTFUL
A. Naive B. Loose
C. Strict D. Uncivilized

35. DUTIFUL
A. Harmful B. Watchful
C. Forgetful D. Remiss

36. RIGID
A. Flux B. Adoptable
C. Yielding D. Adaptable

37. RARE
A. Petty B. Poor
C. Small D. Common

38. ZEAL
A. Despair B. Calmness
C. Passiveness D. Indifference

ANSWERS

1	2	3	4	5	6	7	8	9	10
D	C	D	A	C	C	B	C	B	B
11	**12**	**13**	**14**	**15**	**16**	**17**	**18**	**19**	**20**
D	C	A	D	D	D	B	D	D	C
21	**22**	**23**	**24**	**25**	**26**	**27**	**28**	**29**	**30**
D	D	C	A	C	A	C	D	D	D
31	**32**	**33**	**34**	**35**	**36**	**37**	**38**		
C	A	C	A	D	D	D	D		

3

SENTENCE COMPLETION

It is such an exercise which starts with the primary schools and continues in the highest level of competitive examinations. One must practise it regularly to score well.

Directions (Qs. 1 to 15): *Pick out the most effective word(s) from the given words to fill in the blanks to make the sentence meaningfully complete.*

1. The student ...... that book from the library to study at home.
A. issued B. borrowed
C. hired D. lent

2. I wish I ...... a king.
A. was B. am
C. should be D. were

3. He ...... to listen to my arguments and walked away.
A. denied B. disliked
C. objected D. refused

4. The flow of blood was so ...... that the patient died.
A. intense B. adequate
C. profuse D. extensive

5. When I met her yesterday, it was the first time I ...... her since Christmas.
A. saw B. have seen
C. had seen D. have been seing

6. Can you pay ...... all these articles?
A. for B. of
C. off D. out

7. I ...... you to be at the party this evening.
A. expect B. hope
C. look forward to D. desire

8. ...... being a handicapped person, he is very cooperative and self-reliant.
A. Because B. Although
C. Since D. Despite

9. The child broke ...... from his mother and ran towards the painting.
A. away B. after
C. down D. with

10. With his ...... income, he finds it difficult to live a comfortable life.
A. brief B. sufficient
C. meagre D. huge

11. He could ...... a lot of money in such a short time by using his intelligence and working hard.
A. spend B. spoil
C. exchange D. accumulate

12. Though the brothers are twins, they look ......
A. alike B. handsome
C. indifferent D. different

13. Unfavourable weather conditions can ..... illness.
A. cure B. detect
C. treat D. enhance

14. No sooner did the bell ring, ... the actor started singing.
A. when B. than
C. after D. before

15. If I ...... realised it, I would not have acted on his advice.
A. was B. had
C. were D. have

Directions (Qs. 16 to 25): *In each question, an incomplete statement (Stem) followed by four fillers* *is given. Pick out the best one which can complete the incomplete stem correctly and meaningfully.*

16. Unless you work harder you will fail, means .....
A. if you fail you will work harder.
B. you must at least plan well than you will not fail.
C. hardly you will fail if you do not desire so.
D. if you do not put more efforts, then you will fail.

17. Even if it rains I shall come, means .....
A. if I come it will not rain.
B. if it rains I shall not come.
C. I will certainly come whether it rains or not.
D. whenever there is rain I shall come.

18. Dinesh is as stupid as he is lazy means .....
A. Dinesh is stupid because he is lazy.
B. Dinesh is lazy because he is stupid.
C. Dinesh is either stupid or lazy.
D. Dinesh is equally stupid and lazy.

19. He is so lazy that he .....
A. cannot depend on others for getting his work done.
B. cannot delay the schedule of completing the work.
C. can seldom complete his work on time.
D. dislike to postpone the work that he undertakes to do.

20. He always stammers in public meetings, but his today's speech .....
A. was fairly audible to everyone present in the hall.
B. was not received satisfactorily.
C. could not be understood properly.
D. was free from that defect.

21. In order to raise the company's profit, the employees .....
A. demanded two additional increments.
B. decided to go on paid holidays.
C. requested the management to implement new welfare schemes.
D. offered to work overtime without any compensation.

22. Although, he is reputed for making very candid statements, ...
A. his today's speech was not fairly audible.
B. his promises had always been realistic.
C. his speech was very interesting.
D. his today's statements were very ambiguous.

23. I felt somewhat more relaxed .....
A. but tense as compared to earlier.
B. and tense as compared to earlier.
C. as there was already no tension at all.
D. and tension-free as compared to earlier.

24. With great efforts his son succeeded in convincing him not to donate his entire wealth to an orphanage .....
A. and lead the life of a wealthy merchant.
B. but to a home for the forsaken children.
C. and make an orphan of himself.
D. as the orphanage needed a lot of donations.

25. Even though it is a very large house, ...
A. there is a lot of space available in it for children.
B. there is hardly any space available for children.
C. there is no dearth of space for children.
D. the servants take a long time to clean it.

ANSWERS

1	**2**	**3**	**4**	**5**	**6**	**7**	**8**	**9**	**10**
B	D	D	C	C	A	A	D	A	C
11	**12**	**13**	**14**	**15**	**16**	**17**	**18**	**19**	**20**
D	D	D	B	B	D	C	D	C	D
21	**22**	**23**	**24**	**25**					
D	D	D	C	B					

4

SPOTTING ERRORS

The most common errors in English are of spellings, grammar and usage of words. By regular practice, the errors can be easily spotted and minimised.

MULTIPLE CHOICE QUESTIONS

Directions: *In the following questions some of the sentences have errors and some are correct. Find out which part of a sentence has an error, the number of that part is your answer. If a sentence is free from errors, then your answer is D i.e., No error.*

1. (A) Either Ram or/(B) you is responsible/(C) for this action./(D) No error.

2. (A) The student flatly denied/(B) that he had copied/(C) in the examination hall./(D) No error.

3. (A) By the time you arrive tomorrow/(B) I have finished/(C) my work./(D) No error.

4. (A) The captain with the members of his team/ (B) are returning/(C) after a fortnight./(D) No error.

5. (A) After returning from/(B) an all-India tour/ (C) I had to describe about it./(D) No error.

6. (A) The teacher asked his students/(B) if they had gone through/(C) either of the three chapters included in the prescribed text./(D) No error.

7. (A) Do you know/(B) how old were you/(C) when you came here?/(D) No error.

8. (A) Beware of/(B) a fair-weather friend/(C) who is neither a friend in need nor a friend indeed./ (D) No error.

9. (A) Copernicus proved/(B) that Earth/(C) moves round the Sun./(D) No error.

10. (A) The property/(B) was divided/(C) among the two brothers./(D) No error.

11. (A) I am quite certain/(B) that the lady is not only greedy/(C) but miserly./(D) No error.

12. (A) The brilliant success in the examination/ (B) as well as his record in sports/(C) deserves high praise./(D) No error.

13. (A) I cannot find/(B) where has he gone/(C) though I have tried may best./(D) No error.

14. (A) If I was/(B) the Prime Minister of India/(C) I would work wonders/(D) No error.

15. (A) If it weren't/(B) for you,/(C) I wouldn't be alive today./(D) No error.

16. (A) He looked like a lion/(B) baulked from/ (C) its prey./(D) No error.

17. (A) Widespread flooding/(B) is affecting/(C) large areas of the villages./(D) No error.

18. (A) If we really set to/(B) we can get the whole house/(C) cleaned in an afternoon./(D) No error.

19. (A) It's arrogant for you/(B) to assume you'll/ (C)win every time./(D) No error.

20. (A) The two books are the same/(B) except for the fact that this/(C) has an answer in the back./(D) No error.

21. (A) Your husband doesn't/(B) believe that you are older/(C) than I./(D) No error.

22. (A) I could not/(B) answer to/(C) the question./(D) No error.

23. (A) Two years passed/(B) since/(C) my cousin died./(D) No error.

24. (A) I am learning English/(B) for ten years/(C) without much effect./(D) No error.

25. (A) Ramesh has agreed/(B) to marry with the girl/(C) of his parent's choice./ (D) No error.

26. (A) When he was arriving./(B) the party was/(C) in full swing./(D) No error.

27. (A) The most studious boy/(B) in the class/(C) was made as the captain./(D) No error.

28. (A) I am participating/(B) in the two-miles race/(C) tomorrow morning./(D) No error.

29. (A) When the boy committed a mistake/(B) the teacher made him to do/(C) the sum again./(D) No error.

30. (A) Whenever a person lost anything/(B) the poor folk around/(C) are suspected./(D) No error.

ANSWERS

1	2	3	4	5	6	7	8	9	10
B	D	B	B	C	C	D	D	B	C
11	12	13	14	15	16	17	18	19	20
C	D	B	A	C	C	C	A	A	C
21	22	23	24	25	26	27	28	29	30
C	B	A	A	B	A	C	B	B	A

EXPLANATORY ANSWERS

1. Replace 'is' by 'are'.
2. No error.
3. Replace 'have' by 'would have'.
4. Replace 'are' by 'is'.
5. Replace 'had to describe' by 'described'.
6. Replace 'either' by 'any'.
7. No error.
8. No error.
9. Omit 'that'.
10. Replace 'among' by 'between'.
11. Add 'also'.
12. No error.
13. Replace 'has he' by 'he has'.
14. Replace 'was' by 'were'.
15. Replace 'wouldn't be' by 'would not have been'.
16. Replace 'its' by 'his'.
17. Replace 'areas' by 'area'.
18. Replace 'set to' by 'set on'.
19. Replace 'for' by 'of'.
20. Replace 'in' by 'on'.
21. Replace 'I' by 'me'.
22. Omit 'to'.
23. Replace 'passed' by 'have passed'.
24. Replace 'am' by 'have been'.
25. Omit 'with'.
26. Replace 'was arriving' by 'arrived'.
27. Omit 'as'.
28. Replace 'in' by 'at'.
29. Omit 'to'.
30. Replace 'lost' by 'loses'.

5

ONE WORD SUBSTITUTION

There are many single words in English language which can be perfectly used for a number of words. These words help in expressing ideas in a short and correct manner for the right occasion. Such words not only increase the vocabulary but also enable you to economise in the use of words to a great extent.

Multiple Word Expression	*Substitution*
One who always looks towards the bright side of things	Optimist
One who always looks towards the dark side of things	Pessimist
The time when one develops from a child into an adult	Adolescence
The process of growing more plants in order to form a forest.	Afforestation
The science which deals with farming	Agriculture
From some other country or place etc.	Alien
A term, etc. giving more than one meaning	Ambiguous
A vehicle which is used to carry sick persons	Ambulance
An animal which can live both in water and on land	Amphibian
A lawless situation when there is no government	Anarchy
Belonging to the history of thousands of years old	Ancient
Once a year	Annual
A very old object but still valuable	Antique
Words of opposite meanings	Antonyms
Words of similar meanings	Synonyms
Signatures of a famous person	Autograph
A government led by one person with absolute authority	Autocracy
A written work of one's own life history	Autobiography
A person who has never been married	Bachelor
A person usually having no hair on his head	Bald
A place where one can deposit money and get interest	Bank
A person who cuts our hair	Barber
A building/group of buildings where soldiers live	Barracks
A person who makes buns and biscuits	Baker
A person who lives by asking people for food and money without doing any useful job	Beggar
The crime of having married to two persons at the same time	Bigamy
The branch of science which deals with the study of plants	Botany
Able to speak two languages	Bilingual

Multiple Word Expression	*Substitution*
Able to speak more than two languages	Polyglot
The branch of science which deals with the living organisms	Biology
A powerful snow storm	Blizzard
A great successful book or movie	Blockbuster
A short news on the radio or TV	Bulletin
A system in which the most important works are organised by the government officials	Bureaucracy
A person who has no vision in his eyes	Blind
A page or a series of pages on which the information of days, weeks, months, etc. is given	Calendar
A person who eats human flesh	Cannibal
A complete list of items often arranged alphabetically	Catalogue
A sudden disaster	Catastrophe
A period of 100 years	Century
A branch of science which deals with chemicals	Chemistry
A printed leaf usually issued by banks that we sign to carry certain financial deal	Cheque
A person who makes or mends shoes	Cobbler
A group of people who has been chosen by others to make decisions on their own	Committee
A building in which nuns live	Convent
An animal which feeds on other animals	Carnivorous
A person who does criticism	Critic
A person who cannot hear	Deaf
A condition in which one loses a lot of water from one's body because of vomiting, etc.	Dehydration
A system of government in which the people cast their votes to elect their leaders	Democracy
The study of skin problems	Dermatology
A long piece of land covered with sand	Desert
The art of managing relationships between countries	Diplomacy
A piece of information about the words in a book form	Dictionary
A piece of information about the telephone numbers of the people in a book from	Directory
A person in charge of a newspapers, magazine etc.	Editor
A person who thinks he is better than the others	Egoist
To leave your country and settle in some other country	Emigrate
A book or series of books giving almost all knowledge about an area or some persons etc.	Encyclopaedia
Study of insects	Entomology
Time when day and night are of the same duration	Equinox
To sell things out of the country	Export
To purchase things from some other country	Import
A plant or animal no longer in existence	Extinct
A situation when there is a shortage of food for a long period of time	Famine
An amount of money that we pay for some action or services	Fee
Related to women	Feminine
An animal strong and aggressive	Ferocious

Multiple Word Expression	*Substitution*
A piece of land where plants grow easily from the soil that is favourable to them	Fertile
A work of literature having some imaginary events	Fiction
A large amount of water covering certain area	Flood
A person who sells flowers	Florist
A religious ceremony for burying or cremating a dead person	Funeral
A substance which kills fungus	Fungicide
A person studying or having studied the diseases and the related things of female reproductory system	Gynaecologist
The murder of the person of the same group race or country	Genocide
A substance which kills germs	Germicide
A situation in which many people die because of fire during war	Holocaust
The act of killing a person deliberately	Homicide
A word having the pronunciation as the other one does but it differs in meaning	Homophone
A word having the same spelling as the other one does but it is pronounced in some other way	Homonym
A person who is attracted towards the person of the same sex	Homosexual
Go across and parallel to the ground	Horizontal
A substance which kills the insects	Insecticide
That cannot be corrected	Incorrigible
That cannot be defeated	Invincible
That cannot be eaten	Inedible
That cannot be seen	Invisible
A place in a school or college where books are kept for the benefit of students, teachers etc.	Library
A place in a school or college where scientific experiments are performed	Laboratory
An official who is a judge in the lowest court	Magistrate
A piece of music or a book before it is printed	Manuscript
Related to men	Masculine
One who believes in the existence of God	A theist
One who does not believe in the existence of good	An atheist
That can be believed	Credible
That cannot be believed	Incredible
That which dissolves in a solvent	Soluble
That which does not dissolves in a solvent	Insoluble
Hard writing that can be read	Legible
Hard writing that cannot be read	Illegible
A person who does jobs beneficial to mankind	Philanthropist
A person who goes on foot	Pedestrian
A person who fights for his own country	Patriot
An act of killing oneself	Suicide
A woman whose husband is dead	Widow
A man whose wife is dead	Widower
A person who eats vegetarian and non-vegetarian diets	Omnivorous

Multiple Word Expression	Substitution
Something which is everywhere at the same time	Omnipresent
One who knows everything	Omniscient
A child who does not have parents	Orphan
An award etc. given after the death of the person	Posthumous
The place where animals are kept for amusement and to increase the knowledge of the public	Zoo
The science which deals with the study of animals	Zoology

MULTIPLE CHOICE QUESTIONS

Directions: *In questions given below, out of the four alternatives, choose the one which can be substituted for the given words/sentences.*

1. Something that relates to everyone in the world
A. General B. Common
C. Usual D. Universal

2. An expression of mild disapproval
A. Warning B. Denigration
C. Impertinence D. Reproof

3. One who is not easily pleased by anything
A. Maiden B. Medieval
C. Precarious D. Fastidious

4. Murder of a king
A. Infanticide B. Matricide
C. Genocide D. Regicide

5. A remedy for all diseases
A. Stoic B. Marvel
C. Panacea D. Recompense

6. A dramatic performance
A. Mask B. Mosque
C. Masque D. Mascot

7. Study of birds
A. Orology B. Optology
C. Ophthalmology D. Ornithology

8. Ready to believe
A. Credulous B. Credible
C. Creditable D. Incredible

9. Incapable of being seen through
A. Ductile B. Opaque
C. Obsolete D. Potable

10. One who eats everything
A. Omnivorous B. Omniscient
C. Irresistible D. Insolvent

11. A place where bees are kept is called
A. An apiary B. A mole
C. A hive D. A sanctuary

12. One who cannot be corrected
A. Incurable B. Incorrigible
C. Hardened D. Invulnerable

13. One who is in charge of a museum
A. Curator B. Supervisor
C. Caretaker D. Warden

14. Continuing fight between parties, families, clans, etc.
A. Enmity B. Feud
C. Quarrel D. Skirmish

15. A voice loud enough to be heard
A. Audible B. Applaudable
C. Laudable D. Oral

16. A paper written by hand
A. Handicraft B. Manuscript
C. Handiwork D. Thesis

17. Habitually silent or talking little
A. Serville B. Unequivocal
C. Taciturn D. Synoptic

18. To slap with a flat object
A. Chop B. Hew
C. Gnaw D. Swat

19. A person who speaks many languages
A. Linguist B. Monolingual
C. Polyglot D. Bilingual

20. A light sailing-boat built specially for racing
A. Canoe B. Yacht
C. Frigate D. Dinghy

21. A fixed orbit in space in relation to earth
A. Geological B. Geo-synchronous
C. Geo-centric D. Geo-stationary

22. A style in which a writer makes a display of his knowledge
A. Pedantic B. Verbose
C. Pompous D. Ornate

23. A religious discourse
A. Preach B. Stanza
C. Sanctorum D. Sermon

24. A place that provides refuge
A. Asylum B. Sanatorium
C. Shelter D. Orphanage

25. Detailed plan of a journey
A. Travelogue B. Travelkit
C. Schedule D. Itinerary

26. A person who insists on something
A. Disciplinarian B. Stickler
C. Instantaneous D. Boaster

27. A drawing on transparent paper
A. Red print B. Blue print
C. Negative D. Transparency

28. One who believes that all things and events in life are predetermined is a
A. Fatalist B. Puritan
C. Egoist D. Tyrant

29. A school boy who cuts classes frequently is a
A. Defeatist B. Sycophant
C. Truant D. Martinet

30. The act of violating the sanctity of the church is
A. Blasphemy B. Heresy
C. Sacrilege D. Desecration

31. A place where monks live as a secluded community
A. Cathedral B. Diocese
C. Convent D. Monastery

32. One who is fond of fighting
A. Bellicose B. Aggressive
C. Belligerent D. Militant

33. Tending to move away from the centre or axis
A. Centrifugal B. Centripetal
C. Axiomatic D. Awry

34. Words inscribed on tomb
A. Epitome B. Epistle
C. Epilogue D. Epitaph

35. Leave or remove from a place considered dangerous
A. Evade B. Evacuate
C. Avoid D. Exterminate

36. Original inhabitants of a country
A. Abroge B. Aborger
C. Aborgory D. Aborigins

37. Government by the officials
A. Theocracy B. Plutocracy
C. Bureaucracy D. Democracy

38. Incapable of being exhausted
A. Inexhaustible B. Inaexhaustible
C. Exhaustable D. Non-tired

39. A person of good understanding, knowledge and reasoning power
A. Expert B. Intellectual
C. Snob D. Literate

40. One absorbed in his own thoughts and feelings rather than in things outside
A. Scholar B. Recluse
C. Introvert D. Intellectual

ANSWERS

1	2	3	4	5	6	7	8	9	10
D	D	D	D	C	C	D	A	B	A
11	**12**	**13**	**14**	**15**	**16**	**17**	**18**	**19**	**20**
A	B	A	B	A	B	C	D	A	B
21	**22**	**23**	**24**	**25**	**26**	**27**	**28**	**29**	**30**
D	A	D	A	D	B	D	A	C	C
31	**32**	**33**	**34**	**35**	**36**	**37**	**38**	**39**	**40**
D	A	A	D	B	B	C	A	B	C

6

SPELLING ERRORS

There are thousands of words in English language. It is difficult to remember the spellings and meanings of all at once. Try to learn as many as you can. Use a dictionary regularly.

Directions: *Find the correctly spelt words.*

1. A. Damage B. Dammage C. Damaige D. Dammege
2. A. Efficiant B. Effecient C. Efficient D. Eficient
3. A. Schedule B. Schdule C. Schedale D. Schedeule
4. A. Occurad B. Occurred C. Ocurred D. Occured
5. A. Grieff B. Grief C. Grieef D. Grrief
6. A. Guarantee B. Garuntee C. Guaruntee D. Gaurantee
7. A. Meddicine B. Medicine C. Medicene D. Medicinne
8. A. Benefeted B. Benefitted C. Benifited D. Benefited
9. A. Acommodation B. Acomodation C. Accomodation D. Accommodation
10. A. Querrelsome B. Quarrelsame C. Quarrelsome D. Querralsome
11. A. Sympathetic B. Smypathetic C. Sympothetic D. Sympethetic
12. A. Prograssive B. Progressive C. Progresive D. Prograsive
13. A. Uncivilized B. Uncevilized C. Uncivillized D. Uncevelized
14. A. Extravagant B. Extreragent C. Extreregant D. Extravegent
15. A. Missunderstood B. Miesunderstood C. Misunderstood D. Misunderstod
16. A. Belligerent B. Beligirent C. Belligarant D. Belligerrent
17. A. Astonished B. Astronished C. Astoneshed D. Asstonished
18. A. Sincerely B. Sencerely C. Sincerelly D. Sincerrely
19. A. Rigourous B. Rigerous C. Rigorous D. Regerous
20. A. Satellite B. Sattellite C. Satelite D. Sattelite
21. A. Pesanger B. Passenger C. Pessenger D. Pasanger
22. A. Humurous B. Humorous C. Humoreus D. Humorrous
23. A. Exeggerate B. Exaggerate C. Exadgerate D. Exagerate
24. A. Fariegn B. Forein C. Foriegn D. Foreign
25. A. Excesive B. Excessive C. Exccessive D. Exccesive
26. A. Forcaust B. Forcast C. Forecast D. Forecaste
27. A. Paralleted B. Paralelled C. Parralleled D. Parallelled

28. A. Ocasion B. Occassion
C. Occasion D. Ocassion

29. A. Boquet B. Bouquet
C. Bouquete D. Bouquette

30. A. Chettering B. Chaterring
C. Chattering D. Chatering

31. A. Discourage B. Disscourage
C. Discourege D. Discaurage

32. A. Curageous B. Courageous
C. Courrageous D. Couregeous

33. A. Abandon B. Abanddon
C. Abendon D. Abbandon

34. A. Embarassment
B. Emberrassement
C. Embarrassment
D. Embbaresment

35. A. Eccintric B. Eccentrie
C. Eccentric D. Eccintrie

36. A. Occasional B. Occassional
C. Occesional D. Occessional

37. A. Querrel B. Querral
C. Quarrel D. Quarel

38. A. Contrebution B. Contribution
C. Contributtion D. Conterbution

39. A. Desgrace B. Disgrece
C. Disgrice D. Disgrace

40. A. Harassment B. Herassment
C. Harasment D. Harassmient

41. A. Imaginative B. Imeginative
C. Imagenative D. Imaginetive

42. A. Suficient B. Suficiant
C. Sufficient D. Sufficiant

43. A. Adequate B. Edequate
C. Adaquete D. Edaquete

44. A. Exparienced B. Experianced
C. Experienced D. Experrienced

45. A. Flatering B. Fletering
C. Flattering D. Fletaring

46. A. Cuttiveted B. Culltrivated
C. Cultivated D. Caltivated

47. A. Praiceworthy B. Peiseworthy
C. Praiseworthy D. Praisaworthy

48. A. Profesional B. Professionel
C. Professional D. Profissional

49. A. Ameteur B. Amateur
C. Amataur D. Amateor

50. A. Unfevourable B. Unfevaurable
C. Unfavourable D. Unfivourable

ANSWERS

1	2	3	4	5	6	7	8	9	10
A	C	A	B	B	A	B	B	D	C
11	**12**	**13**	**14**	**15**	**16**	**17**	**18**	**19**	**20**
A	B	A	A	C	A	A	A	C	A
21	**22**	**23**	**24**	**25**	**26**	**27**	**28**	**29**	**30**
B	B	B	D	B	C	A	C	B	C
31	**32**	**33**	**34**	**35**	**36**	**37**	**38**	**39**	**40**
A	B	A	C	C	A	C	B	D	A
41	**42**	**43**	**44**	**45**	**46**	**47**	**48**	**49**	**50**
A	C	A	C	A	C	C	C	B	C

General Knowledge/Awareness

1 The Universe

The Solar System: Some Facts

Number of Planets: 8—Mercury, Venus, Earth, Mars, Jupiter, Saturn, Uranus and Neptune.

Largest most

Massive planet	Jupiter
Brightest planet	Venus
Brightest star	Sirius
Fastest orbiting planet	Mercury
Longest (Synodic) day	Mercury
Planet with largest natural satellite	Saturn
Greatest average density	Jupiter
Tallest mountain	Earth
Strongest magnetic fields	Jupiter
Most circular orbit	Venus
Shortest (synodic) day	Jupiter
Hottest planet	Venus
No natural satellite	Mercury, Venus
Planet with natural satellite with most eccentric orbit	Neptune
Lowest average density	Saturn
Greatest amount of liquid on the surface	Earth

The Earth: Facts and Data

Composition of the Earth: Aluminium (0.4%), Sulphur (2.7%), Silicon (13%), Oxygen (28%), Calcium (1.2%), Nickel (2.7%), Magnesium (17%), Iron (35%)

Surface area		510100500 sq km
Land Surface (29.1%)	:	148950800 sq km
Ocean Surface (70.9%)	:	361149700 sq km
Type of water	:	97% salt, 3% fresh
Total area of water	:	382672000 sq km
Equatorial diameter	:	12753 km
Equatorial Circumference	:	40066 km
Polar Circumference	:	39992 km
Polar diameter	:	12710 km
Equatorial radius	:	6376 km
Polar radius	:	6335 km
Mass (estimated weight)	:	594×10^{19} metric tons
Mean distance from the Sun	:	149407000 km
Earth's orbit speed (around sun)	:	107320 kmph
Period of Revolution (round the sun)	:	365 days 5 hrs 48 min. 45.51 seconds
Time of Rotation (on its axis)	:	23 hrs 56 min. 4.09 seconds
Inclination of the axis (to the plane of the ecliptic)	:	23º27'

Solar Statistics

Distance from the Earth	:	149.8 million km
Absolute Visual Magnitude	:	4.75
Diameter Core	:	13,84,000 km
Temperature	:	15000000 K
Photosphere Temperature	:	5770 K

Rotation as seen from the Earth (at the equator)	:	25.38 days
Rotation as seen from the Earth (near the poles)	:	33 days
Chemical Composition	:	Hydrogen 71% Helium 26.5% Other elements 2.5%
Age	:	About 4.5 billion years
Expected lifetime of a normal star	:	About 10 billion years

Oceans of the World

Pacific	16,62,41,000 sq km
Atlantic	8,65,57,000 sq km
Indian	7,34,27,000 sq km
Arctic	94,85,000 sq km

Longest Rivers

Name	*Country/ Continent*	*Length in Kilometres*
Nile	Africa	6650
Amazon	S. America	6437
Mississippi-Missouri	USA	6020
Yangtze-Kiang	China	5494
Ob-Irtysh	Russia	5410
Lena	Russia	4400
Hwang Ho	China	4344
Niger	Africa	4180
St. Lawrence	Canada (USA)	4023
Murray-Darling	Australia	3780
Volga	Russia	3690
Indus	Asia	2900
Danube	Europe	2850
Orinoco	S. America	2575

Major Riverside Cities

City	*River*	*Country*
Alexandria	Nile	Egypt
Amsterdam	Amsel	The Netherland
Ankara	Kizil	Turkiye
Baghdad	Tigris	Iraq
Bangkok	Menam	Thailand
Belgrade	Danube	Serbia
Berlin	Spree	Germany
Budapest	Danube	Hungary
Cairo	Nile	Egypt
Chittagong	Karnaphuli	Bangladesh
Karachi	Indus	Pakistan
Khartoum	Blue & White Nile	Sudan
Lahore	Ravi	Pakistan
Lisbon	Tagus	Portugal
Liverpool	Mersey	England
London	Thames	England
Moscow New	Moskva	Russia
Orleans	Missisipi	USA
New York	Hudson	USA
Paris	Seine	France
Yangon	Irawadi	Myanmar
Rome	Tiber	Italy

Major Gulfs of the World

Names	*Areas (Sq. Km.)*
Gulf of Mexico	15,44,000
Gulf of Hudson	12,33,000
Arabian Gulf	2,38,000
Gulf of St. Lawrence	2,37,000
Gulf of California	1,62,000
English Channel	89,900

Major Mountain Ranges of the World

Range	*Location*	*Length (km)*
Andes	South America	7,200
Himalayas-Karakoram-Hindukush	South Central Asia	5,000
Rockies	North America	4,800

Range	Location	Length (km)
Great Dividing Range	East Australia	3,600
Atlas	North West Africa	1,930
Western Ghats	Western India	1,610
Caucasus	Europe	1,200
Alaska	USA	1,130
Alps	Europe	1,050

Largest Deserts of the World

Subtropical

Sahara, North Africa	94,00,000 sq. km.
Kalahari, Southern Africa	9,00,000 sq. km.
Thar, India/Pakistan	2,00,000 sq. km.
Great Sandy, Australia	4,00,000 sq. km.

Cool Coastal

Atacama, Chile S.A.	1,40,000 sq. km

Cool Winter

Gobi, China	13,00,000 sq. km.
Colorado, Western USA (also called the painted desert)	3,37,000 sq. km.

Atmosphere

Composition of Gases in Atmosphere

Nitrogen	78.03%
Oxygen	20.99%
Argon	0.93%
Carbon dioxide	0.03%
Hydrogen	0.01%
Neon	0.0018%
Helium	0.0005%
Crypton	0.0001%
Xenon	0.000,005%
Ozone	0.000,0001%

World Important Local Winds

Chinoon: A warm day wind frequently experienced on the eastern side of the Rocky Mountains.

Fohn: A warm dry wind descending a mountain, as on the north side of the Alps.

Haboob: A sand storm or a dust storm in north and north-east Sudan near Khartoum.

Bagrrio: It is the tropical cyclone of the Philippine Island.

Loo: A hot wind which blows in summer season in Indian sub-continent.

Papasago: A cold northerly wind sometimes felt on the Mexico plateau.

Bora: It is the name given to the cold dry wind experienced particularly in winter along the eastern coast of the Atlantic Ocean and in northern Italy.

Black Toller: A hot dust wind which blows in the vast plain of North America.

Principal Mountain Peaks of the World

Mountains	Height in Metres	Range	Date of First Ascent
1. Mount Everest	8,848	Himalayas	May 29, 1953
2. K-2 (Godwin Austen)	8,611	Karakoram	July 31, 1954
3. Kanchenjunga	8,597	Himalayas	May 25, 1955
4. Lhotse	8,511	Himalayas	May 18, 1956
5. Makalu I	8,481	Himalayas	May 15, 1955
6. Dhaulagiri I	8,167	Himalayas	May 13, 1960
7. Mansalu I	8,156	Himalayas	May 9, 1956
8. Chollyo	8,153	Himalayas	Oct. 19, 1954
9. Nanga Parbat	8,124	Himalayas	July 3, 1953
10. Annapurna I	8,091	Himalayas	June 3, 1950

Mountains	Height in Metres	Range	Date of First Ascent
11. Gasherbrum I	8,068	Karakoram	July 5, 1958
12. Broad Peak I	8,047	Karakoram	June 9, 1957
13. Gasherbrum II	8,034	Karakoram	July 7, 1956
14. Shisha Pangma (Gosainthan)	8,014	Himalayas	May 2, 1964
15. Gasherbrum III	7,952	Karakoram	Aug. 11, 1975

Types of World Agriculture

Viticulture: The cultivation of the vine for production of grapes and wine.
Pisciculture: The breeding, rearing and transplantation of fish by artificial means.
Sericulture: The raising of silk worms for the production of raw silk.
Horticulture: To grow flower front, vegetables on small plots.
Apiculture: Bee keeping on a commercial scale for the sale of honey.
Floriculture: The cultivation of flowers or flowering plants.
Mariculture: Sea farming, or the cultivation of marine plants and animals for commercial purposes.
Olericulture: The cultivation of vegetables and kitchen herbs.

Famous Straits of the World

Strait	Between	Country
Malacca Strait	Andaman Sea and South China Sea	Indonesia
Palk Strait	Mannar and Bay of Bengal	India-Sri Lanka
Magellan Strait	Pacific and South Atlantic Ocean	Chile
Dover Strait	English Channel and North Sea	England-France
Berring Strait	Berring Sea and Chukasi Sea	Alaska-Russia
Sugaroo Strait	Japan Sea and Pacific Ocean	Japan
Sunda Strait	Java and Indian Ocean	Indonesia
Gibralter Strait	Mediterranean Sea and Atlantic Ocean	Spain
Harmuj Strait	Persia and Bay of Oman	Oman-Iran
Hudson Strait	Bay of Hudson and Atlantic Ocean	Canada

World's Famous Official Documents

White Paper: India; **Orange Book:** Netherlands; **Yellow Book:** France; **Green Book:** Italy and Iran; **White Book:** Portugal, China and Germany; **Grey Book:** Japan and Belgium.

Famous Newspapers of the World

Newspaper	Place of Publishing	Language
Daily News	New York (America)	English
Guardian	London (Britain)	English
Pravada	Moscow (Russia)	Russian
Al-Ahram	Cairo (Egypt)	Arabic
Merdeca	Jakarta (Indonesia)	Indonesian
Times	London (Britain)	English
People's Daily	Beijing (China)	Chinese
New Statesman	Britain	English
Daily Mirror	Britain	English
Hindu, Hindustan Times, Times of India, Tribune, Statesman, Indian Express, Economic Times	India	English
Hindustan, Nav Bharat Times, Rashtriya Sahara, Dainik Jagaran, Punjab Kesari	India	Hindi

Important Boundary Lines

Boundary Line	Countries
Hindenberg Line	Germany-Poland
Maginot Line	France and Germany
Mannerhein Line	Russia-Finland
Mc Mahon Line	India and China
Order Niesse Line	Germany-Poland
Radcliff Line	India-Pakistan
Seigfrid Line	Germany-France
Durand Line	Pakistan and Afghanistan
17th Parallel	The line which defined the boundary between North Vietnam and South Vietnam before the two were united.
38th Parallel	North Korea and South Korea
49th Parallel	U.S.A. and Canada

Areawise 10 Big and Small Countries

10 Big Countries

S. No.	Country	Sq. km (Total Portion) sq. km)	Area (Thousand)
1.	Russia (Europe-Asia)	17,098,242	16,889
2.	Canada (N. America)	99,84,670	9,221
3.	China (Asia)	95,96,961	9,327
4.	U.S.A. (N. America)	93,72,614	9,159
5.	Brazil (S. America)	85,14,877	8,457
6.	Australia (S. Pacific)	77,41,220	7,682
7.	India (Asia)	32,87,263	2,973
8.	Argentina (S. America)	27,80,400	2,737
9.	Kazakhstan (Europe-Asia)	27,24,900	2,671
10.	Algeria (Africa)	23,81,741	2,381

10 Small Countries

S. No.	Country	Area (Sq. km)
1.	Vatican City (Europe)	0.44
2.	Monaco (Europe)	1.95
3.	Nauru (Southern Pacific)	21.10
4.	Tuvalu	26.00
5.	San Marino (Europe)	61.00
6.	Liechtenstein (Europe)	160.00
7.	Marshall Island (Central Pacific)	181.00
8.	St. Kitts and Nevis (Eastern Caribbean)	261.00
9.	Grenada (Eastern Caribbean Sea)	344.00
10.	Seychelles (Indian Ocean)	455.00

Populationwise 10 Big and Small Countries

10 Big Countries

S. No.	Country	Population (2021) (In Million)
1.	China (Asia)	1,397.898
2.	India (Asia)	1,339.000
3.	U.S.A. (North America)	334.998
4.	Indonesia (Asia)	275.122
5.	Pakistan (Asia)	238.181
6.	Nigeria (Africa)	219.464
7.	Brazil (South America)	213.445
8.	Bangladesh (Asia)	164.099
9.	Russia (Europe-Asia)	142.321
10.	Japan (Asia)	124.687

10 Small Countries

S. No.	Country	Population (2021)
1.	Vatican City (Europe)	1000
2.	Tuvalu (Southern Pacific)	11,448
3.	Palau (Western Pacific)	21,613
4.	Monaco (Europe)	31,223
5.	San Marino (Europe)	34,467
6.	Liechstein (Europe)	39,425
7.	St. Kitts and Nevis (Eastern Caribbean)	54,149
8.	Marshall Island (Central Pacific)	78,831
9.	Seychelles	96,387
10.	St. Vincent and The Grenadines	1,01,145

Signals/Signs and Meaning

Signal/Sign	*Meaning*
Red Triangle	Family Planning
Red Cross	Medical Help
Red Light	Danger, 'Stop' for the movement of vehicles
Green Light	Go
Olive Branch	Peace
White Pigeon or Dove	Peace
Black Strip on Arm	(i) Opposition (ii) Sorrow
Black Flag	Opposition
Red Flag	(i) Danger (ii) Revolution
White Flag	Treaty or Surrender
Yellow Flag	Vehicles with patients of contagious diseases
Two Bones across with a Skull	Danger of electricity
Half mast flown Flag	National mourning
Lotus	Sign of civilization and culture
Wheel (Chakra)	Sign of Progress
A blind folded woman with scale in hand	Sign of Justice
Reversed flown	National calamity flag

National Emblems of Important Countries

Country	*National Emblem*
America	Golden Rod
Australia	Kangaroo
Ireland	Shamrock
Italy	White Lily
Israel	Candelabrum
Iran	Rose
Canada	White Lily
Great Britain	Rose
Chile	Candor and Huemul
Germany	Corn Flower
Japan	Chrysanthemum
Zimbabwe	Zimbabwe Bird
Denmark	Beach
Turkiye	Crescent and Star
The Netherlands	Lion
New Zealand	Kiwi, Fern Southern Cross
Norway	Lion
Nepal	Kukri
Pakistan	Crescent
Poland	Eagle
France	Lily
Belgium	Lion
Bangladesh	Water Lily
Mongolia	The Soyombo
Russia	Double headed eagle
Lebanon	Cedar Tree
Sudan	Secretary Bird
Syria	Eagle
India	Lioned Capital

Continents : Some Facts

Continent	*Biggest Counrty*	*Highest Peak*	*Longest River*
Asia	China	Mt. Everest (8848 m)	Yangtze Kiang
Africa	Algeria	Mt. Kilimanjaro (5895 m)	Nile
North America	Canada	Mt. Mckinley (6194 m)	Mississippi Missouri
South America	Brazil	Mt. Acancagua (6960 m)	Amazon
Europe	Russia	Mt. Elbrus (5642 m)	Ob
Australia	Australia	Mt. Coscuisco (2228 m)	Darling
Antarctica	—	Vinson Massif (5140 m)	—

International Date Line

It roughly corresponds to 180°E or W meridian of longitude which falls on the opposite side of the Greenwich meridian and the date changes by one day (i.e. 24 hours), as this line is crossed. On crossing this line from east to west a day is added, and a day is subtracted on crossing it from west to east.

✻ ✻ ✻ ✻ ✻

2 World Geography

Earth

The earth constitutes land, water and air. Land is made up of rocks and soil. It is distributed in continents and islands. The water found in oceans, seas, lakes, etc. occupies about 2/3 of the earth's surface. The earth is surrounded by a cover of air, called atmosphere, which extends up to several hundred kilometres above its surface.

Shape: In ancient times people believed that the earth was flat in shape. Greek philosopher Pythagoras (6th century BC) was the first person to declare that the earth was round. After careful measurement, the scientists have found that the earth is slightly oblate (flattened at poles) and not exactly round.

Motions: The earth has two motions: *(i) Rotation:* Earth makes a complete round on its axis once each 24 hours (more exactly 23 hours, 56 minutes and 4.09 seconds). It causes days and night on the earth. *(ii) Revolution:* The earth makes a complete round of the Sun in one year. This revolution of earth produces alternate seasons.

Some Facts:

1. Equal Day and Night — March 21 and September 23.

2. Longest Day — June 21.

3. Shortest Day — December 22.

4. The sunlight takes eight minutes in travelling from the Sun to the Earth.

5. Average speed of the earth in orbit ---- 66,600 miles (107,220 km) per hour.

6. Earth's equatorial diameter is about 7926 miles (12,756 km).

7. Water (oceans, seas, lakes and rivers) occupies nearly 75 per cent of the surface of the earth.

8. Earth's average distance from the Moon — 2,38,857 miles (3,84,400 km).

9. Earth's average distance from the Sun — 93 million miles (149.4 million km).

Greenwich Time: It is the local time of the Greenwich observatory in London on 0° meridian. Greenwich time is international standard time.

International Date Line: Half way round the earth from the Greenwich is International Date Line on 180° longitude. It runs down mid-Pacific. It is one day earlier on the east of this line than it is on the west of the line. When it is Monday east of the line, it is Tuesday west of the line.

Zones: On the basis of temperature and distribution of solar heat on the surface of the earth, the earth has been divided into five zones: 1. Torrid Zone; 2. North Temperate Zone; 3. South Temperate Zone; 4. Arctic Zone, and 5. Antarctic Zone.

Continents

Large land masses forming large geographical divisions are called continents. There are seven continents:

1. Asia (29.5%)
2. Africa (20%)
3. Europe (6.5%)
4. North America (16.3%)
5. South America (11.8%)
6. Australia (5.2%), and
7. Antarctica (9.6%).

Highest Mountain Peaks

1. Everest (Asia-8848 metres)
2. Aconcagua (South America-6960 metres)
3. Mckinley (North America-6194 metres)
4. Kilimanjaro (Africa-5895 metres)
5. Elbrus (Europe-5642 metres)
6. Vinson Massif (Antarctica-5140 metres)
7. Kosciusko (Australia-2228 metres).

Largest Oceans

1. Pacific Ocean (The largest, covers almost 1/3 of the earth's total area, and the deepest about 6.8 miles at Mariana Trench in western Pacific);
2. Atlantic Ocean, and
3. Indian Ocean.

Other seas and gulfs are — the Mediterranean Sea, South China Sea, Bering Sea, Caribbean Sea, East China Sea, Sea of Japan, North Sea, Baltic Sea, Hudson Bay and Gulf of Mexico.

Longest Rivers

1. Nile (6650 km-Africa),
2. Amazon (6570 km-South America)
3. Mississippi-Missouri (5970 km-North America)
4. Yangtze Kiang (5470 km-Asia)
5. Ob Irtysh (5150 km-Europe)
6. Congo (4666 km-Africa).

Great Deserts

1. Sahara (94 lakh sq km-North Africa)
2. Libyan (11.65 lakh sq km-North Africa)
3. Australian (16 lakh sq km-Australia)
4. Gobi (13 lakh sq km-Mongolia)
5. Great Victoria (6,47,000 sq km-Australia)
6. Syrian (5,20,000 sq. km. Arabia)
7. Arabian (23,30,000 sq km Arabia).

Largest Islands

1. Greenland (21,75,600 sq km)
2. New Guinea (7,77,000 sq km)
3. Borneo (7,25,545 sq km)
4. Malagasy (5,90,000 sq km)
5. Baffin Island (4,76,070 sq km).

Highest Waterfalls

1. Angel (807 m-Venezuela)
2. Mongefossen (774 m-Norway)
3. Kukenaam (610 m-Venezuela)
4. Ribbon (491 m-USA)
5. King George VI (487 m-Guyana)
6. Upper Yosemite (435 m-USA).

Major Producers of Crops, Minerals and Industrial goods

Coal : China, USA, UK, Germany, Russia, Australia and India

Cocoa : Ghana, South Africa, West Indies, Cote d'Ivaire, Indonesia, Nigeria

Coffee : Brazil, Columbia

Copper : Chile, USA, Canada, Peru, China

Cotton : China, India, USA, Russia, Egypt, Brazil, Argentina, Pakistan

Gold : China, South Africa, Australia, Canada, USA, India

Grapes : France, Italy, Portugal, California, USA

Iron : China, Australia, Brazil, Russia, USA, UK, France, Germany, India, Spain

Jute : India, Bangladesh

Manganese : China, South Africa, Australia, Brazil

Petroleum : USA, Saudi Arab, Venezuela, Russia, Iran, Myanmar, UAE

Rice : China, India, Indonesia, Bangladesh, Vietnam, Japan, Myanmar

Rubber : Thailand, Malaysia, Indonesia, Sri Lanka, Vietnam, India

Silk : Japan, USA, France, China, India

Silver : Mexico, USA, Russia, Peru, India, China

Steel : China, Japan, USA, Germany, Russia, UK

Tea : China, India, Sri Lanka, Kenya, Vietnam

Wheat : China, India, Russia, USA, Canada, Argentina, Australia

Wool : Australia, Argentina, New Zealand, South Africa

Tobacco : China, USA, India, Brazil, Russia, Indonesia

Dimond : Russia, Botswana, Australia, DR Congo

Uranium : Kazakhstan, Canada, Australia

Thorium : India, Australia

Tin : China, Indonesia, Peru

Platinum : South Africa, Russia, Zimbabwe

Bauxite : Australia, China, Guinea

Biggest, Largest, Tallest of the World

Largest Desert	Sahara (Africa)
Rainiest Place	Mowsynram near Cherrapunjee (Meghalaya, India)
Biggest Ocean	Pacific Ocean
Deepest Ocean	Pacific Ocean
Largest Mammal	Whale
Fastest Animal	Cheetah
Lightest Substance	Hydrogen gas
Longest River	Nile
Highest Waterfalls	Salto Angel Falls (Venezuela)
Tallest Animal	Giraffe
Largest Bird (Land)	Ostrich
Hardest Mineral	Diamond
Largest Delta	Sunderbans (W.B. India)
Largest Art Museum	The Louvre (France)
Longest Day	June, 21
Shortest Day	December, 22
Biggest Army	People's Liberation Army, China
Largest Salt Water Lake	Caspian Sea
Highest Mountain Peak	Everest (8848 metre high)
Longest Wall	Great Wall of China
Largest Peninsula	Arabia
Largest Planet	Jupiter
Smallest Continent	Australia
Largest Lake	Caspian Sea
Deepest Lake	Baikal, 3200 ft.
Finest Harbour	Sydney Harbour
Smallest Planet	Mercury
Largest Continent	Asia
Planet nearest to the Sun	Mercury
Highest Building	Burj Khalifa, Dubai
City largest (Area)	Jiuquan Gansu, China
City highest	Wen Chuan (China)
Country Biggest	Russia (17075000 sq. km.)
Electorate, Largest	India (over 90 crores)
Longest Epic	Mahabharat
Island, Biggest in the World	Greenland
Population, Largest	China
Longest Railway Platform	Shree Siddharoodha Swamiji Railway Station Hubballi, Karnataka (India)
Swimming Course	English Channel

Currencies of Different Countries

Country	Currency
Australia	Australian Dollar
Bangladesh	Taka
Belgium	Euro
Britain	Pound (Sterling)
Myanmar	Kyat
Canada	Canadian Dollar
Germany	Euro
Iran	Rial
India	Rupee
Sri Lanka	Sri Lankan Rupee
China	Yuan
Czech Republic	Koruna
Denmark	Krone
France	Euro
Pakistan	Rupee
Poland	Zloty
Spain	Euro
Indonesia	Rupiah
Iraq	Dinar
Italy	Euro
Japan	Yen
Mexico	Peso
The Netherland	Euro
European Union	Euro
Sweden	Krone
Switzerland	Swiss Franc
Turkiye	Turkish Lira
U.A.E.	Dirham
U.S.A.	Dollar
Russia	Rouble

Capital of Countries

Country	Capital	Country	Capital
Austria	Vienna	Indonesia	Jakarta
Afghanisatan	Kabul	Iraq	Baghdad
Albania	Tirana	Italy	Rome
Algeria	Algiers	Ireland	Dublin
Andorra	Andorra la Vella	Japan	Tokyo
Angola	Luanda	Combodia	Phnom Penh
Australia	Canberra	Korea (North)	Pyong Yang
Azerbaijan	Baku	Korea (South)	Seoul
Argentina	Buenos Aires	Kenya	Nairobi
Bahamas	Nassau	Kuwait	Kuwait
Bahrain	Manama	Laos	Vientiane
Bangladesh	Dhaka	Lebanon	Beirut
Barbados	Bridgetown	Mexico	Mexico City
Belarus	Minsk	Malaysia	Kualalumpur
Belgium	Brussels	Morocco	Rabat
Bolivia	Lapaz	Mozambique	Maputo
Bulgaria	Sofia	New Zealand	Welington
Bhutan	Thimpu	The Netherlands	Amsterdam
Brazil	Brasilla	Panama	Panama City
Combodia	Phnom Penh	Portugal	Lisbon
Cameroon	Yaounde	Poland	Warsaw
Canada	Ottawa	Sri Lanka	Colombo
Chad	N'djamena	Sweden	Stockholm
Chile	Santiago	Switzerland	Bern
China	Beijing	Sudan	Khartoum
Cyprus	Nicosia	Sierra Leone	Freetown
Columbia	Bagota	South Africa	Capetown
Croatia	Zagreb	Saudi Arabia	Riyadh
Cuba	Havana	Spain	Madrid
Denmark	Copenhegan	Thailand	Bangkok
Ethiopia	Addis Ababa	Turkiye	Ankara
Egypt	Cairo	Russia	Moscow
Finland	Helsinki	Azerbaijan	Baku
France	Paris	Armenia	Yerevan
Germany	Berlin	Latvia	Riga
Greece	Athens	Ukrain	Kiev
Guatemala	Guatemala City	U.S.A.	Washington
Hungary	Budapest	U.K.	London
Iran	Tehran	Vietnam	Hanoi
India	New Delhi	Zambia	Lusaka

Wonders of the World

Seven Wonders of the Ancient World:

1. the Pyramids of Egypt, built in approximately 2700 BC;
2. the Hanging Gardens at Babylon;
3. the temple of Artemis at Emphesus;
4. the statue of Zeus at Olympia;
5. the tomb of Mausolus at Halicarnassus, built in nearly 350 BC;
6. the Colossus of Rhodes, built in nearly 280 BC;
7. the Pharos Lighthouse at Alexandria.

Seven Wonders of the Medieval World:

1. the Colosseum of Rome;
2. the Great Wall of China;
3. the Porcelain Tower of Nanking;
4. the Mosque at St. Sophia (Constantinople);
5. Stonehenge;
6. the Catacombs of Rome;
7. the Leaning Tower of Pisa.

Seven New Wonders of the World:

1. Taj Mahal of Agra (India);
2. Pyramid at Chichen Itza (Mexico);
3. Machu Picchu (Peru);
4. Statue of Christ The Redeemer (Brazil);
5. Great Wall of China;
6. Roman Colosseum, Italy;
7. Ruins of Petra, Jordan.

First in the World

First Chinese visitor to India	Fahien
First foreign invader of India	Alexander, the Great (Greek)
First person to climb Mt. Everest	Tenzing Norgay (India) and Edmund Hillary (New Zealand) (1953)
First atom bomb dropped at	Hiroshima (Japan)
First man in the space	Yuri Gagarin (former USSR)
First woman in the space	Valentina Tereshkova (former USSR)
First person to walk in the space	Alexei Leonov (former USSR)
First person to land on the moon	Neil Armstrong (USA)
First and the only woman to have climbed Mt. Everest twice	Santosh Yadav (Indian; May 12, 1992; May 10, 1993)
First person on Mt. Everest without oxygen	Phu Dorjee (Indian; May 9, 1984)
First person to climb Mt. Everest twice	Nawang Gombu
First President of the USA	George Washington
First woman Prime Minister	Sirimavo Bandaranaike (Sri Lanka)
First person to swim across English Channel	Mathew Webb
First woman to swim across English Channel	Gertrude Caroline Ederle
First woman to climb Mt. Everest	Junko Tabei (Japan)
First woman to climb Mt. Everest alone and without oxygen supplies	Alison Hargreaves (Briton: May 13, 1995)
First Aeroplane to fly around the world without refuelling	Voyager (Dec. 1986)

First test-tube Baby	Louise Brown (UK; 1978)
First all-talking Film	Jaz Singer (1927)
First Secretary-General of the UN	Trygve Lie (Norway: 1946-53)
First woman President of the UN General Assembly	Vijayalakshmi Pandit (India: 1953)
First woman to reach North Pole	Ann Bancroft (1986)
First person to reach North Pole	Robert Peary
First person to reach South Pole	Amundsen (1911)
First woman to command Spacecraft in space	Ellin Collins

Popular Names

Popular Name	*Real Name*
Badshah Khan	Abdul Ghaffar Khan
Bapu, Father of Nation	M.K. Gandhi
Bard of Avon	William Shakespeare
Chachaji *or* Panditji	Jawaharlal Nehru
Desert Fox	Gen. Rommel (Germany)
Desh Bandhu	C.R. Das
Father of English Poetry	Geoffrey Chaucer
Fuhrer	Adolf Hitler
Grand Old Man of India	Dadabhai Naoroji
Grand Old Man of Britain	W.E. Gladstone
Gurudev	Rabindra Nath Tagore
Guruji	M.S. Golwalkar
Grand Commoner	Pitt, the younger
Iron Man of India	Sardar Patel
Lady with the Lamp	Florence Nightingale
Lal, Bal, Pal	Lala Lajpat Rai, Bal Gangadhar Tilak, Bipin Chandra Pal
Li-Kwan	Pearl Buck
Little Corporal *or* Man of Destiny	Napoleon Bonaparte
Lokmanya	Bal Gangadhar Tilak
Lok Nayak	Jayaprakash Narain
Mahamana	Pt. Madan Mohan Malaviya
Maid of Orleans	Joan of Arc
Maiden Queen	Queen Elizabeth I
Man of Blood and Iron	Prince Bismark
Netaji	Subhash Chandra Bose
Nightingale of India	Sarojini Naidu
Priyadarshini	Indira Gandhi
Punjab Kesari	Lala Lajpat Rai
Wizard of the North	Walter Scott

Geographical Surnames

Geographical Surname	*Real Name*
Bengal's Sorrow	Damodar River
Blue Mountains	Nilgiri Hills
China's Sorrow	Hwang-Ho
City of Palaces	Kolkata
City of Skyscrapers *or* Empire City	New York
City of Dreaming Spires	Oxford
Cockpit of Europe	Belgium
Dark Continent	Africa
Emerald Isle	Ireland
Eternal City	Rome
Forbidden City	Lhasa (Tibet)
Gateway of India	Mumbai
Gate of Tears	Strait of Bab-el-mandab
Gift of the Nile	Egypt
Granite City	Aberdeen (Scotland)
Hermit Kingdom	Korea
Holy Land	Jerusalem
Island of Pearls	Bahrain (Persian Gulf)
Island of Cloves	Zanzibar
Key to the Mediterranean	Gibraltar
Land of Five Rivers	Punjab
Land of Golden Pagoda	Myanmar (Burma)
Land of Kangaroo	Australia
Land of Maple Leaf/Lillies	Canada
Land of Midnight Sun	Norway
Land of Morning Calm	Korea
Land of the Rising Sun	Japan
Land of Thousand Lakes	Finland
Land of Thunderbolt	Bhutan
Land of the White Elephants	Thailand
Manchester of the Orient	Osaka (Japan)
Pearl of the Antilles *or* Sugar Bowl of the World	Cuba
Pink City	Jaipur
Playground of Europe	Switzerland
Queen of the Adriatic	Venice (Italy)
Roof of the World	Pamirs
Sick Man of Europe	Turkiye
Venice of the North	Stockholm (Sweden)
Windy City	Chicago
Whiteman's Grave	Guinea Coast of Africa
World's Loneliest Island	Tristan de Cunha

Countries'/Cities' Names—Old and New

Old Name	New Name
Abyssinia	Ethiopia
Basutoland	Lesotho
Bechuanaland	Botswana
British Honduras	Belize
Burma	Myanmar
Ceylon	Sri Lanka
Zaire	Democratic Republic of the Congo
Constantinople	Istanbul
Dahomey	Benin
Dutch East Indies	Indonesia
East Pakistan	Bangladesh
Formosa	Taiwan
Gold Coast	Ghana

Old Name	New Name
Leningrad	St. Petersburg
Leopoldville	Kinshasa
Mesopotamia	Iraq
North Rhodesia	Zambia
Nyasaland	Malawi
Peking	Beijing
Persia	Iran
Rangoon	Yangon
Salisbury	Harare
Siam	Thailand
South West Africa	Namibia
Southern Rhodesia	Zimbabwe
Turkey	Turkiye

IMPORTANT RESIDENCES

• **Buckingham Palace (London):** King/Queen of Britain • **10, Downing Street (London):** Prime Minister, Britain • **Elysee Palace (Paris):** President, France • **Rashtrapati Bhawan (New Delhi):** President, India • **White House (Washington):** President, USA • **Vatican (Rome):** Pope

Important towns situated on the River Banks

Town	River
Agra	Yamuna
Ahmedabad	Sabarmati
Ayodhya	Saryu
Baghdad	Tigris
Berlin	Spree
Cairo	Nile
Kolkata	Hooghly
Cuttack	Mahanadi
Delhi	Yamuna
Dibrugarh	Brahmaputra
Dublin	Liffey
Hardwar	Ganga
Hyderabad	Musi
Jabalpur	Narbada
Kanpur	Ganga
Karachi	Indus
Lahore	Ravi

Town	River
Leh	Indus
London	Thames
Lucknow	Gomati
Nasik	Godavari
New York	Hudson
Paris	Seine
Patna	Ganga
Prayagraj	Confluence of the Ganga and the Yamuna
Rome	Tiber
Srinagar	Jhelum
Surat	Tapti
Sydney	Murray-Darling
Varanasi	Ganga
Vienna	Danube
Washington	Potamac
Yangon	Irawadi

Books and Authors

FOREIGN

Book	Author	Book	Author
Aesop's Fables	Aesop	Moor's Last Sigh	Salman Rushdie
Adventure of Robinson Crusoe	Daniel Defoe	Mother	Maxim Gorky
Adventures of Sherlok Holmes	Arthur Conan Doyle	Mother India	Katherine Mayo
Alice in Wonderland	Lewis Carrol	Nana	Emile Zola
Apple Cart	G.B. Shaw	Ninteen Eighty Four	George Orwell
Arabian Nights	Sir Richard Burton	Odyssey	Homer
As You Like It	William Shakespeare	Origin of Species	Charles Darwin
A Tale of Two Cities	Charles Dickens	Othello	William Shakespeare
A Tale of Two Gardens	Octavio Paz	Paradise Lost	John Milton
A Thousand Suns	Dominique Lapierre	Paradise Regained	John Milton
August Coup	Mikhail S. Gorbachev	Path to Power	Margaret Thatcher
Ben Hur	Lewis Wallace	Pickwick Papers	Charles Dickens
Candida	G.B. Shaw	Pride and Prejudice	Jane Austen
Das Kapital	Karl Marx	Razor's Edge	Somerset Maugham
David Copperfield	Charles Dickens	Republic	Plato
Divine Comedy	A. Dante	Romeo and Juliet	William Shakespeare
Doctor's Dilemma	G.B. Shaw	Round the World in Eighty Days	Jules Verne
Famished Road	Ben Okri	Rubaiyat-i-Omar Khayyam	Edward Fitzgerald (Translator)
Freedom From Fear	Aung San Suu Kyi	Shape of Things to Come	H.G. Wells
Gulistan Bostan	Sheikh Saadi	The Satanic Verses	Salman Rushdie
Gulliver's Travels	Jonathan Swift	The Social Contract	Rousseau
Hamlet	William Shakespeare	The Tempest	William Shakespeare
Iliad	Homer	Time Machine	H.G. Wells
Inferno	A. Dante	Tom Sawyer	Mark Twain
In Memoriam	Lord Tennyson	Treasure Island	R.L. Stevenson
Ivanhoe	Walter Scott	Twelfth Night	William Shakespeare
Julius Caesar	William Shakespeare	Uncle Tom's Cabin	H.B. Stowe
Lady Chatterley's Lover	D.H. Lawrence	Unto This Last	John Ruskin
Lajja	Taslima Nasreen	Utopia	Thomas More
Les Miserable	Victor Hugo	Universe Around Us	James Jeans
Leviathan	Thomas Hobbes	Vicar of Wakefield	Oliver Goldsmith
Lolita	V. Nobokov	War and Peace	Leo Tolstoy
Lycidas	John Milton	Wealth of Nations	Adam Smith
Mein Kampf	Adolf Hitler	Wonder That was India	A.L. Basham
Merchant of Venice	William Shakespeare	Wuthering Heights	Emily Bronte
Midnight's Children	Salman Rushdie		

INDIAN

Book	Author	Book	Author
Abhigyan Shakuntalam	Kalidas	Anand Math	Bankim Chandra Chatterjee
Ain-i-Akbari	Abul Fazal		

Book	Author
Arthashastra	Kautilya
A Suitable Boy	Vikram Seth
Bhagwat Gita	Ved Vyas
Chidambara	Sumitranandan Pant
Devdas	Sarat Chandra Chatterjee
Diwan-i-Ghalib	Mirza Ghalib
Discovery of India	Jawaharlal Nehru
Essays on Gita	Aurobindo Ghosh
Eternal India	Indira Gandhi
Faces of Everest	Major H.P.S. Ahluwalia
Ganadevata	Tarashankar Bandopadhyaya
Geet Govind	Jaya Dev
Geetanjali	R.N. Tagore
Glimpses of World History	Jawaharlal Nehru
Godaan	Prem Chand
Gul-e-Nagma	Firaq Gorakhpuri
Gunahon ka Devta	Dharmveer Bharti
Harsh Charita	Bana Bhatta
Hindu View of Life	S. Radhakrishnan
Idols	Sunil Gavaskar
India Divided	Dr. Rajendra Prasad
The Judgement	Kuldip Nayyar
Juhi ki Kali	Surya Kant Tripathi 'Nirala'
Justice of Peace ke Aansu	Janardan Prasad Singh
Chand ka Munh Terha Hai	Muktibodh
Kapalkundala	Bankim Chandra Chatterjee
Kadambari	Bana Bhatta
Kagaz Te Kanwas	Amrita Pritam
Kamayani	Jai Shankar Prasad
Kitni Nawon Mein Kitni Bar	S.H. Vatsyayan
Kumar Sambhav	Kalidas
Mahabharata	Ved Vyas
Malgudi Days	R.K. Narayan
Manvini Bhavai	Pannalal Patel
Mati Matal	Gopi Nath Mohanty
Meghdoot	Kalidas
Meri Ekyavan Kavitain	Atal Bihari Vajpayee
Meri Sansadiya Yatra	Atal Bihari Vajpayee
Mritunjaya	B.K. Bhattacharya
Mudrarakshasa	Vishakhadatta
My Experiments with Truth	M.K. Gandhi
My Own Boswell	M. Hidayatullah
My Presidential Years	R. Venkataraman
Nisheeth	Uma Shankar Joshi
'No, Sir'	P.G. Mavlankar
One Day Wonders	Sunil Gavaskar
Panchtantra	Vishnu Sharma
Passage to England	Nirad C. Chaudhuri
Prison Diary	Jaya Prakash Narayan
Raghuvansha	Kalidas
Rajtarangini	Kalhana
Ramayana	Balmiki
Ramcharit Manas	Tulsidas
Rukh Te Rishi	Harbhajan Singh
Satyarth Prakash	Swami Dayanand
Sur Sagar	Surdas
The Guide	R.K. Narayan
The Insider	P.V. Narasimharao
The Post Office — *Dak Ghar*	Rabindra Nath Tagore
The God of Small Things	Arundhati Roy
Urvashi	Ram Dhari Singh 'Dinkar'
Yama	Mahadevi Verma
My Country : My Life (Autobiography)	L.K. Advani
The Test of My Life	Yuvraj Singh
Twenty Years in a Decade	Shah Rukh Khan

IMPORTANT BOOKS WRITTEN IN JAIL

Book	Author
My Experiments with Truth	Mahatma Gandhi
Glimpses of World History	Jawaharlal Nehru
Discovery of India	
Gita Rahasya	Lokmanya Bal Gangadhar Tilak
Pilgrim's Progress	John Bunyan
Bible (in German language)	Martin Luther
Les Miserables	Victor Hugo
Long Walk to Freedom	Nelson Mandela

* * * * *

3 Our India

INDIA : AT A GLANCE

Population (2011)	:	1,21,08,54,977
Capital	:	New Delhi
Area	:	32,87,263 sq km
Geographic Location	:	Between 8°4' and 37°6' north latitudes
	:	Between 68°7' and 97°25' east longitudes
Coastline Length	:	7,516.6 km including the coastline of Lakshadweep, Andaman & Nicobar Islands.
Major Languages	:	22
National Anthem	:	Jana Gana Mana
National Currency	:	Rupee (₹)
National Animal	:	Tiger
National Aquatic Animal	:	Dolphin
National Bird	:	Peacock
National River	:	Ganga
Characteristics of Indian Constitution	:	Socialist, Secular, Democratic, Republic
Legislature	:	Bicameral Legislature at the Centre Uni/Bicameral Legislatures in States
Executive	:	President, Vice-President and Council of Ministers at the Centre Governor and Council of Ministers in States
Judiciary	:	Independent from Executive with Supreme Court at the apex of the hierarchy
Total Road Length	:	63.45 lakh kilometres (December 2024)

India: States & Union Territories

States/Union Territories	*Capital*	*Area in (Sq. Km.)*	*Language*
Andhra Pradesh	Amravati	1,60,229	Telugu
Arunachal Pradesh	Itanagar	83,743	Nyishi, Miji, Wancho etc.
Assam	Dispur	78,438	Assamese
Bihar	Patna	94,163	Hindi, Maithili
Chhattisgarh	Raipur	136,034	Hindi
Goa	Panji	3,702	Marathi and Konkani
Gujarat	Gandhinagar	1,96,024	Gujarati
Haryana	Chandigarh	44,212	Hindi
Himachal Pradesh	Shimla	55,673	Hindi and Pahari
Jharkhand	Ranchi	79,714	Hindi, Santhali
Karnataka	Bengaluru	1,91,791	Kannada
Kerala	Thiruvananthapuram	38,863	Malayalam
Madhya Pradesh	Bhopal	308,000	Hindi
Maharashtra	Mumbai	307,713	Marathi
Manipur	Imphal	22,327	Manipuri
Meghalaya	Shillong	22,429	Khasi, Garo and English
Mizoram	Aizawl	21,081	Mizo and English
Nagaland	Kohima	16,579	Sema, English
Odisha	Bhubaneswar	155,707	Odiya
Punjab	Chandigarh	50,362	Punjabi
Rajasthan	Jaipur	3,42,239	Hindi and Rajasthani
Sikkim	Gangtok	7,096	Bhutia, Nepali, Lepcha and Limbu
Tamil Nadu	Chennai	1,30,058	Tamil
Telangana	Hyderabad	1,14,840	Telugu
Tripura	Agartala	10,491	Bengali, Kakborak, Manipuri
Uttar Pradesh	Lucknow	2,40,928	Hindi and Urdu
Uttarakhand	Dehradun	53,484	Hindi
West Bengal	Kolkata	88,752	Bengali
Jammu & Kashmir	Srinagar (Summer) Jammu (Winter)	2,22,236*	Kashmiri, Urdu, Dogri
Andaman & Nicobar Island	Sri Vijaya Puram	8,249	Bengali, Hindi, Nicobarese, Tamil, Telugu, and Malayalam
Chandigarh	Chandigarh	114	Hindi, Punjabi
Dadara & Nagar Haveli and Daman & Diu	Daman	603	Gujarati and Hindi
Delhi	Delhi	1483	Hindi, Punjabi and Urdu
Lakshadweep	Kavaratti	32	Malayalam
Puducherry	Puducherry	492	Tamil, Telugu, Malayalam, English and French
Ladakh	Leh	—	Ladakhi

* including areas of Ladakh and illegally occupied by China and Pakistan.

POPULATION

Second Largest Nation : In terms of the size of population, India is the second largest country in the world, next only to China. China tops the list with 1398 million people. India's population constitutes nearly 17.5 per cent of the total world population while her geographical area is only 2.42 per cent of the world area. With such a huge population to support on so small an area, the country finds herself in great difficulty in making any significant dent on its poverty and economic backwardness. India's national income, which is barely 2 per cent of the total global income, clearly shows the tremendous strain of population on her economy.

2011 Census Highlights

Population of India–Total Indian population is 17.7% of total world population	:	1,21,08,54,977 (Male: 62,32,70,258; Female: 58,75,84,719)
Decadal Growth (2001-2011)	:	17.7 per cent (Males: 17.19 per cent; Females: 18.12 per cent)
Hightest Decadal Growth (State-wise)	:	Meghalaya (27.9 per cent)
Lowest Decadal Growth (State-wise)	:	Manipur (–18.6 per cent)
Most populous State	:	Uttar Pradesh (16.51 per cent of National Population)
Density of population	:	382 persons per sq. km.
Most densly populated State	:	Bihar : 1106 per sq. km
Sex Ratio	:	943 females per 1000 males
Total Literacy Rate	:	73% (Males – 80.9%), (Females – 64.6%)
Highest Literacy (State-wise)	:	Kerala (94%)
Lowest Literacy (State-wise)	:	Bihar (61.8)

OTHER DETAILS

POPULATION OF INDIA

1951	36,10,88,090	1961	43,92,34,771
1971	54,81,59,652	1981	68,33,29,097
1991	84,64,21,039	2001	102,87,37,436
2011	1,21,08,54,977		

DENSITY OF POPULATION (Persons per square kilometre)

1951	113	1961	138
1971	177	1981	216
1991	267	2001	324
2011	382		

ANNUAL COMPOUND RATE OF GROWTH

1941-1951	1.25 per cent	1951-1961	1.96 per cent
1961-1971	2.22 per cent	1971-1981	2.20 per cent
1981-1991	2.14 per cent	1991-2001	1.95 per cent
2001-2011	1.64 per cent		

2011 CENSUS OF INDIA : POPULATION DISTRIBUTION, POPULATION DENSITY AND LITERACY RATE

S. No.	State/ Union Territories*	Population 2011			Population Density (per sq. km.)	Literacy Rate 2011		
		Persons	Males	Females	2011	Persons	Males	Females
	INDIA	**1,21,08,54,977**	**62,32,70,258**	**58,75,84,719**	**382**	**73.0**	**80.9**	**64.6**
1.	Jammu and Kashmir	1,25,41,302	66,40,662	59,00,640	124	67.2	76.8	56.4
2.	Himachal Pradesh	68,64,602	34,81,873	33,82,729	123	82.8	89.5	75.9
3.	Punjab	2,77,43,338	1,46,39,465	1,31,03,873	551	75.8	80.4	70.7
4.	Chandigarh	10,55,450	5,80,663	4,74,787	9,258	86.0	90.0	81.2
5.	Uttarakhand	1,00,86,292	51,37,773	49,48,519	189	78.8	87.4	70.0
6.	Haryana	2,53,51,462	1,34,94,734	1,18,56,728	573	75.6	84.1	65.9
7.	Delhi	1,67,87,941	89,87,326	78,00,615	11,320	86.2	90.9	80.8
8.	Rajasthan	6,85,48,437	3,55,50,997	3,29,97,440	200	66.1	79.2	52.1
9.	Uttar Pradesh	19,98,12,341	10,44,80,510	9,53,31,831	829	67.7	77.3	57.2
10.	Bihar	10,40,99,452	5,42,78,157	4,98,21,295	1,106	61.8	71.2	51.5
11.	Sikkim	6,10,577	3,23,070	2,87,507	86	81.4	86.6	75.6
12.	Arunachal Pradesh	13,83,727	7,13,912	6,69,815	17	65.4	72.6	57.7
13.	Nagaland	19,78,502	10,24,649	9,53,853	119	79.6	82.8	76.1
14.	Manipur	28,55,794	14,38,586	14,17,208	128	76.94	83.58	70.26
15.	Mizoram	10,97,206	5,55,339	5,41,867	52	91.3	93.3	89.3
16.	Tripura	36,73,917	18,74,376	17,99,541	350	87.2	91.5	82.7
17.	Meghalya	29,66,889	14,91,832	14,75,057	132	74.4	76.0	72.9
18.	Assam	3,12,05,576	1,59,39,443	1,52,66,133	398	72.2	77.8	66.3
19.	West Bengal	9,12,76,115	4,68,09,027	4,44,67,088	1,028	76.3	81.7	70.5
20.	Jharkhand	3,29,88,134	1,69,30,315	1,60,57,819	414	66.4	76.8	55.4
21.	Odisha	4,19,74,218	2,12,12,136	2,07,62,082	270	72.9	81.6	64.0
22.	Chhattisgarh	2,55,45,198	1,28,32,895	1,27,12,303	189	70.3	80.3	60.2
23.	Madhya Pradesh	7,26,26,809	3,76,12,306	3,50,14,503	236	69.3	78.7	59.2
24.	Gujarat	6,04,39,692	3,14,91,260	2,89,48,432	308	78.0	85.8	69.7
25.	Daman and Diu	2,43,247	1,50,301	92,946	2,191	87.1	91.5	79.5
26.	Dadra & Nagar Haweli	3,43,709	1,93,760	1,49,949	700	76.2	85.2	64.3
27.	Maharashtra	11,23,74,333	5,82,43,056	5,41,31,277	365	82.3	88.4	75.9
28.	Andhra Pradesh	4,93,86,799	2,47,38,068	2,46,48,731	308	67.4	74.8	60.0
29.	Karnataka	6,10,95,297	3,09,66,657	3,01,28,640	319	75.4	82.5	68.1
30.	Goa	14,58,545	7,39,140	7,19,405	394	88.7	92.6	84.7
31.	Lakshadweep	64,473	33,123	31,350	2,149	91.8	95.6	87.9
32.	Kerala	3,34,06,061	1,60,27,412	1,73,78,649	860	94.0	96.1	92.1
33.	Tamil Nadu	7,21,47,030	3,61,37,975	3,60,09,055	555	80.1	86.8	73.4
34.	Puducherry	12,47,953	6,12,511	6,35,442	2,547	85.8	91.3	80.7
35.	Andaman & Nicobar Island	3,80,581	2,02,871	1,77,710	46	86.6	90.3	82.4
36.	Telangana	3,51,93,978	17,704,078	17,489,900	308	66.5	75.0	57.9

* * * * *

4 Indian History

Famous Sites of Indus Valley Civilization

Name of Site	*Year of Excavation*	*River/ Sea coast*	*Discoverer*
Harappa (Montgomery–Pakistan)	1921	Ravi River	Dayaram Sahney
Mohanjodaro (Larkana–Pakistan)	1922	Indus River	Rakhal Das Banerjee
Chanhudaro (Sindh–Pakistan)	1931	Indus River	N.G. Mazumdar
Alamgir pur (Meerut - U.P.)	1952-55	Hindan River	Yagyadatta Sharma
Ropar (Punjab)	1953	Sutlej River	Yagyadatta Sharma
Rangpur (Kathiabar–Gujarat)	1953	Bhabar River	Madho Swaroop Vatsa, Rang Nath Rao
Kotdigi (Sindh–Pakistan)	1953	Indus River	Fazal Ahmed Khan
Lothal (Ahmedabad–Gujarat)	1954	Bhogwa River	Rang Nath Rao
Kalibanga (Ganganagar–Rajasthan)	1961	Ghaggar	Brajwasi Lal
Surkotara (Kutch–Gujarat)	1967	Ghaggar River	Ravindra Singh Vishta
Banawali (Hissar–Haryana)	1973	Ghaggar River	Ravindra Singh Vishta
Balakote	1979	Arabian Sea	George F. Dales
Dhaulavira (Gujarat)	1963-68	—	J.P. Joshi
	1990-91	—	Dr. R.S. Vishta

Well known Quotations

"Swarajya is My Birthright"	— Bal Gangadhar Tilak
"Give me blood, I shall give you freedom"	— Netajee Subhash Chandra Bose
"Inqalab Zindabad"	— Bhagat Singh
"Saare Jahan Se Achcha, Hindustan Hamara"	— Dr. Mohammed Iqbal
"Dilli Chalo"	— Subhash Chandra Bose
"Sarfaroshi ki tamanna, Ab Hamare Dil Mein Hai."	— Ram Prasad Bismil
"I am socialist by nature".	— Jawahar Lal Nehru
"Go to Vedas"	— Swami Dayanand
"Aaram Haram Hai"	— Jawahar Lal Nehru
"Jai Jawan, Jai Kisan"	— Lal Bahadur Shastri
"Jai Jawan, Jai Kisan, Jai Vigyan"	— Atal Bihari Vajpayee
"Speak less, work more"	— Sanjay Gandhi
"Vijayee Vishwa Tiranga Pyara"	— Shyam Lal Gupta

"Quit India"	— Mahatma Gandhi
"Hindi, Hindu, Hindustan"	— Bhartendu Harishchandra
"Purna Swarajya"	— Jawahar Lal Nehru
"Every lathi blow inflicted on my body will prove a nail in British coffin"	— Lala Lajpat Rai
"Jai Hind"	— Subhash Chandra Bose
"Do or die"	— Mahatma Gandhi
"Who lives if India dies"	— Jawahar Lal Nehru
"Vande Mataram"	— Bankim Chandra Chatterjee
"Jana Gana Mana Adhinayaka Jai Hai"	—Rabindranath Tagore
"Hate sin, not the sinner."	— Mahatma Gandhi
"Service of the people is the service of God"	— Swami Vivekananda
"Truth and non-violence are my God."	— Mahatma Gandhi

Battles and Wars In India

War	Year	Result
Battle of Kalinga	(261 B.C.)	Ashoka defeated the king of Kalinga
Second battle of Tarain	(1192 A.D.)	Muhammad Gori defeated Prithviraj Chauhan
First battle of Panipat	(1526 A.D.)	Babar defeated Ibrahim Lodi
Battle of Khanwa	(1527 A.D.)	Babar defeated Rana Sanga
Battle of Chausa	(1539 A.D.)	Shershah Suri defeated Humayun and became ruler of Delhi
Second Battle of Panipat	(1556 A.D.)	Akbar defeated Hemu
Battle of Talikota	(1565 A.D.)	Allied forces of Bijapur, Bidar, Golkunda and Ahamadnagar defeated the King of Vijay Nagar
Battle of Haldighati	(1576 A.D.)	Some historian say that this battle was indecisive but some say that Rana Pratap was defeated by Akbar
Battle of Palasey	(1757 A.D.)	British forces defeated Nawab of Bengal Sirajudoulla
Battle of Wandiwash	(1760 A.D.)	British forces defeated the French
Third battle of Panipat	(1761 A.D.)	Maratha were defeated by Ahmad Shah Abadali
Battle of Buxar	(1764 A.D.)	British forces defeated the combined forces of Mir Quasim, Shah Alam Mughal empire and Awadh's Nawab
Third Anglo-Maratha War	(1792 A.D.)	Maratha were conclusively defeated
Fourth Anglo-Mysore War	(1799 A.D.)	Tipu Sultan died fighting the British forces
Second Anglo-Sikh War	(1848 A.D.)	British forces annexed Punjab from Sikh rulers
Indo-China War	(1962 A.D.)	China attacked India unilaterally and annexed some area
Indo-Pak War	(1965 A.D.)	Pakistan attacked India but had to suffer severe setbacks
Indo-Pak War	(1971 A.D.)	Pak declare war against India.

* * * * *

5 Indian Constitution & Polity

Indian Constitution is a comprehensive document and it is the lengthiest written Constitution in the World.

The Preamble of the Constitution: "We the people of India, having solemnly resolved to Constitute India into a Sovereign, Socialist, Secular Democratic Republic and to secure to all its citizen.

Justice: Social, economic and political.

Liberty: Of thought, expression, belief, faith and worship.

Equality: Of status and of opportunity, and to promote among them all.

Fraternity: Assuring the dignity of the individual and the unity and integrity of the nation.

In Our Constituent Assembly this twenty-sixth day of November, 1949, do Hereby Adopt, Enact and Give to Ourselves This Constitution."

The preamble of the Constitution is the basic philosophy of the Constitution on which it is based. It is the Key of the Constitution. Though it has a limited role legally, whenever there is an ambiguity, the courts refer to the Preamble to get insight into various clauses of the Constitution. The words SECULAR and SOCIALIST were not there in the original Constitution but were incorporated subsequently in 1976 after the 42nd constitutional amendment. The preamble clearly outlines the essential features of our Constitution:

1. The final power lies in the hands of the people.
2. India is a sovereign, socialist, secular, democratic republic.
3. Efforts will be made to give social, economic and political justice.
4. Every citizen of India will have liberty of thought, expression, belief, faith and worship.
5. There will be equality of status and opportunity.
6. The feeling of fraternity among the people will be encouraged.
7. The Unity and Integrity of the nation is of paramount importance.

SALIENT FEATURES OF THE INDIAN CONSTITUTION

1. The Indian Constitution is a written and detailed one. The framers, considering the political inexperience of the countrymen and complicated situation, deemed it fit to explain the provisions and not leave anything to chance.
2. India is a Sovereign, Socialist, Secular, Democratic republic. The real power vests with the people. They elect their representatives who, in turn, take decisions on their behalf. The country does not encourage any religion and does not interfere in religious affairs. The country is trying to bridge differences between people, varying in social or economic grounds. The country does not have a monarch. We have a President, who is the head of the nation.
3. Indian Constitution has provided a Federal Government. Our Constitution is written and rigid. There is a clear division of powers between the Centre and States. The Supreme Court has been established to give judgements in case of differences between the Centre and States.
4. Indian Constitution has a unitary bias. The Centre has been made powerful than States with more powers in the executive, legislative and financial fields. The entity of States can be dissolved but the Centre will always exist.

5. Parliamentary form of Government has been provided. The head of the nation is President and he is indirectly elected. To advise the President, a Council of Ministers exists. The Council is responsible to the Parliament. The members of Parliament are elected by adult universal suffrage.
6. India has been made a secular country, with no interference in religious affairs.
7. Unlike America, India has single citizenship. People, living in any State, will be citizens of India only.
8. The Indian Constitution has a combination of flexibility and rigidity. Some provisions can be altered by a simple majority in the parliament while a few need ratification by States. Already, over 100 amendments in the Constitution have been made.
9. The Indian Constitution provided for seven fundamental rights, which are essential for all-round development of an individual. These are written and can get remedy from the courts, in case of violation. After 44th amendment, one fundamental right—Right to Property has been deleted.
10. The Indian Constitution envisages fundamental duties for all citizens. All these duties make people aware of their responsibilities towards the nation.
11. The Directive Principles of State Policy are the guidelines and objectives which every state and Central government should aspire. These principles cannot be enforced legally but have the moral backing of people.
12. Independent judiciary is an important achievement of the Constitution. The judiciary has been kept away from executive control. Moreover, rule of law has been applied. The criminal law is same all over the country but personal laws, as per religion and caste, have been allowed.
13. Judicial review has been allowed. So, the legislature and the executive are kept in check. Any transgression on the basic feature of the Constitution is declared null and void by the courts.

TERRITORY OF THE UNION

India is a Union of States and Union Territories. Parliament has the power to create any State, increase the area of any State, reduce it, change the name or boundaries of any State. However, the President's prior approval is required before the introduction of a bill in the Parliament. The President can consult the concerned State but the view of the latter are not binding.

CITIZENSHIP

The Constitution provides for a single citizenship. Following categories of persons became citizens of India at the commencement of the Constitution:

1. Persons born and domiciled in India.
2. Persons domiciled in India and either of whose parents was born in India.
3. Persons domiciled in India and residing in India ordinarily for a period of at least five years.
4. Certain categories of people, who had migrated from Pakistan to India.
5. Indians residing abroad but who make an application to acquire Indian citizenship.

The Parliament passed Citizenship Act in 1955, providing for following methods for acquiring Indian citizenship:

1. Citizenship by birth
2. Citizenship by descent
3. Citizenship by registration
4. Citizenship by naturalisation
5. Citizenship by incorporation of territory

The Central Government has the discretion to waive off any or all the conditions of citizenship if it thinks that the applicant has rendered distinguished service to the cause of science, art, philosophy, literature, world peace or human progress in general.

Indian citizenship can be lost by:

(*a*) renunciation;

(*b*) termination — it takes place if a citizen of India voluntary acquires the citizenship of another country; and

(*c*) deprivation — if the Government terminates the citizenship.

Some of the Fundamental Rights belong only to the citizens. They only can contest for the public offices in the country like President, Prime Minister, Chief Minister etc. Indian citizens also get the right to vote.

SCHEDULES TO THE CONSTITUTION

The Constitution of India originally contained only eight schedules. Presently there are 12 schedules in the constitution.

First Schedule: It consists the list of the States and Union territories. ***Second Schedule:*** This Schedule is related to salary and allowances of the President, Governors, Speaker, Supreme Court and High Court Judges etc. ***Third Schedule:*** Contains forms of oath and affirmation. ***Fourth Schedule:*** Contains allocation of seats to each State and Union territory in the Council of States. ***Fifth Schedule:*** Provides for administration and control of scheduled areas and scheduled tribes. ***Sixth Schedule:*** Provides for administration of Tribal Areas in Assam, Meghalaya and Mizoram. ***Seventh Schedule:*** Distribution of powers and functions between the centre and state governments under three lists. ***Eighth Schedule:*** The languages recognised by Parliament. ***Ninth Schedule:*** It contains laws passed by the Union or States which cannot be taken to courts. ***Tenth Schedule:*** Provisions as to disqualification on the ground of political defection. ***Eleventh Schedule:*** Provisions regarding powers, authority etc. of Panchayati Raj institutions. ***Twelfth Schedule:*** Provisions regarding powers, authority etc. of Municipalities etc.

Foreign Sources of Indian Constitution

Foreign Sources	*Subject*
Britain	Parliamentary system, collective responsibilities of Cabinet
America	Fundamental right, Citizenship, Independent Judiciary, Judicial review
Canada	Division of powers
Ireland	Directive principles
Germany	Emergency provisions
Russia	Fundamental duties
Australia	Concurrent list

THE SUPREME COURT

Supreme Court of India, the highest Court of the country, consists of a Chief Justice and not more than 33 Judges appointed by the President. The Judges hold office till the age of 65. For appointment as a Judge of the Supreme Court, a person must be a citizen of India and must have been for at least five years as Judge of a High Court or Advocate of a High Court for at least ten years or he must be, in the opinion of the President, a distinguished jurist. The Supreme Court normally sits in New Delhi.

PARLIAMENT

Parliament is the national legislature of the Indian Union. It consists of two Houses known as the Council of States or the Rajya Sabha and the House of People or Lok Sabha. The President is an integral part of Parliament.

Rajya Sabha: The Rajya Sabha is the Upper House of the Parliament and it is constituted of representatives from the States or the Constituent units of the Indian Union. It is a permanent body, one third of its members retiring after every two years. Its maximum strength is 250. Out of these, twelve members are nominated by the President from well-known personalities in the realm of Science, Art, Literature and Social Service. Rest of 238 representatives of the States and Union Territories are elected. Rajya Sabha at present consists of 245 members.

Lok Sabha: The Lok Sabha whose life is five years, is the Lower House of Parliament and comprises of members directly elected by the people. The House of the people (Lok Sabha) at present consists of 543 members directly elected from the states and Union Territories. By the 104th amendment of the constitution the reservation for two members of Anglo Indian Community nominated by President have been abolished. The House of the People shall continue for five years (unless sooner dissolved) from the date of its meeting and no longer and the expiry of the said period of 5 years shall operate as dissolution of the House.

Parliamentary Committees: There are several Parliamentary Committees to assist the Parliament in its deliberations. These are appointed or elected by the respective Houses of Lok Sabha and Rajya

Sabha on a motion made or are nominated by their presiding officers, *i.e.,* the Speaker of Lok Sabha and the Chairman of Rajya Sabha respectively. Broadly, Parliamentary Committees are of two kinds–standing committees and ad-hoc committees. Among the Standing Committees, three are financial Committees:

(*i*) Public Account Committee; (*ii*) Estimate Committee; (*iii*) Public undertaking Committee.

Ad-hoc Committees are appointed as the need arises and cease to exist when the work is over.

Speaker of Lok Sabha: Speaker is elected by the Lok Sabha from among its members. The Speaker will have the final power to maintain order within the House of the People and to interpret its rules of procedure. Speaker decides whether a bill is a money bill or a non-money bill.

Indian States & Union Territories: Allocation of Seats

S. No.	*State/UT*	*Seats of Lok Sabha*	*Seats of Rajya Sabha*	*Legislative Assembly*	*Legislative Council*
1.	Andhra Pradesh	25	11	175	58
2.	Arunachal Pradesh	2	1	60	
3.	Assam	14	7	126	
4.	Bihar	40	16	243	75
5.	Chhattisgarh	11	5	90	
6.	Goa	2	1	40	
7.	Gujarat	26	11	182	
8.	Haryana	10	5	90	
9.	Himachal Pradesh	4	3	68	
10.	Jharkhand	14	6	81	
11.	Karnataka	28	12	224	75
12.	Kerala	20	9	140	
13.	Madhya Pradesh	29	11	230	
14.	Maharashtra	48	19	288	78
15.	Manipur	2	1	60	
16.	Meghalaya	2	1	60	
17.	Mizoram	1	1	40	
18.	Nagaland	1	1	60	
19.	Odisha	21	10	147	
20.	Punjab	13	7	117	
21.	Rajasthan	25	10	200	
22.	Sikkim	1	1	32	
23.	Tamil Nadu	39	18	235	
24.	Telangana	17	7	119	40
25.	Tripura	2	1	60	
26.	Uttar Pradesh	80	31	403	100
27.	Uttarakhand	5	3	70	
28.	West Bengal	42	16	294	

S. No.	State/UT	Seats of Lok Sabha	Seats of Rajya Sabha	Legislative Assembly	Legislative Council
29.	Jammu & Kashmir	5	4	—	—
30.	Andaman & Nicobar Islands	1	—	—	—
31.	Chandigarh	1	—	—	—
32.	Dadra & Nagar Haveli and Daman & Diu	2	—	—	—
33.	Delhi	7	3	70	—
34.	Lakshadweep	1	—	—	—
35.	Puduchery	1	1	30	—
36.	Ladakh	1	—	—	—

Table of Precedence

1. President
2. Vice-President
3. Prime Minister
4. Governors of States within their respective states
5. Former Presidents

5A. Deputy Prime Minister

6. Chief Justice of India, Speaker of Lok Sabha
7. Cabinet Ministers of the Union, Chief Ministers of States within their respective States, Deputy Chairman NITI Aayog.
   Leaders of opposition in Rajya Sabha and Lok Sabha

7A. Holders of the Bharat Ratna Decoration

8. Ambassadors Extraordinary and Plenipotentiary and High Commissioners of Commonwealth Countries accredited to India
   Chief Ministers of States outside their respective States
9. Judges of the Supreme Court
10. Deputy Chairman Rajya Sabha, Deputy Chief Minister of States
    Deputy Speaker Lok Sabha, Members of the NITI Aayog, Minister of State of the Union and Other Minister in the Ministry of Defence.

PRESIDENT

The President is the Constitutional head of the Republic of India. He is more or less the titular head of the executive. Really speaking, he is the constitutional head but not the real executive. The real power is vested in the hands of the Council of Ministers.

Qualifications: (*i*) Indian citizen, (*ii*) age not less than 35 years, (*iii*) should have qualification for election to Lok Sabha, (*iv*) should not hold any office of profit, (*v*) should not be a Member of Parliament or State Legislature.

Powers: He makes appointments to all the constitutional posts. He can address either House of Parliament and dissolve Lok Sabha. All Bills passed by Parliament must receive his assent to become an Act. He issues ordinances when Parliament is not in session. No Money Bill can be introduced in Lok Sabha without his recommendation. He can grant pardon, reprieve or remit punishment and he can commute death sentences, can declare national emergency, state emergency and financial emergency.

Term and Emolument: The President holds the office for a period of five years. He is eligible for re-election. He draws a fixed salary per month with various allowances. He is also entitled to rent free official residence called Rashtrapati Bhawan.

VICE-PRESIDENT

The Vice-President acts as the ex-officio Chairman of the Council of States (Rajya Sabha). He is elected by an electoral college consisting of the members of both Houses of Parliament in accordance with the system of proportional representation by means of the single transferable vote. He must be a citizen of India, not less than 35 years of age, and should be eligible for election as a member of the Council of States. Disputes in connection with election of a president or a vice-president are to be a dealt with in accordance with Article-71. Such disputes shall be decided by the Supreme Court.

PRIME MINISTER

The Constitution lays down that there shall be a Council of Ministers headed by the Prime Minister to aid and advise the President in the exercise of his functions. The Prime Minister is the head of the Cabinet. Other Ministers are appointed by the President on his advice. He is the leader of the majority party in the Lok Sabha.

FUNDAMENTAL RIGHTS

Following fundamental rights are enjoyed by every Indian citizen, irrespective of caste, colour, creed and sex:

1. Right to Equality: No special privileges, no distinction on grounds of religion, caste, creed and sex.

2. Right to Freedom: The right to freedom of expression and speech, the right to choose one's own profession, the right to reside in any part of the Indian Union.

3. Right to Freedom to Religion: Except when it is in the interest of public order, morality, health or other conditions, everybody has the right to profess, practice and propagate his religion freely.

4. Cultural and Educational Rights: The Constitution provides that every community can run its own institutions to preserve its own culture and language.

5. Right against Exploitation: Traffic in human beings and forced labour and the employment of children under 14 years in factories or mines, are punishable offences.

6. Rights to Constitutional Remedies: When a citizen finds that any of his fundamental rights has been encroached upon, he can move the Supreme Court, which has been empowered to safeguard the fundamental rights of a citizen (Article 32).

Jurisdiction and Seat of High Courts

Name	*Year*	*Territorial Jurisdiction*	*Seat*
Allahabad	1866	Uttar Pradesh	Prayagraj (Bench at Lucknow)
Andhra Pradesh	2019	Andhra Pradesh	Amaravati
Bombay	1862	Maharashtra, Goa, Dadar and Nagar Haveli and Daman and Diu	Mumbai (Benches at Nagpur, Panaji and Sambhajinagar)
Calcutta	1862	West Bengal and Andaman & Nicobar	Kolkata (Circuit Benches at Sri Vijaya Puram and Jalpaiguri)
Chhattisgarh	2000	Chhattisgarh	Bilaspur
Delhi	1966	Delhi	Delhi
Gauhati	1948	Assam, Nagaland, Mizoram and Arunachal Pradesh	Guwahati (Benches at Kohima, Aizawl and Itanagar)
Gujarat	1960	Gujarat	Ahmedabad
Himachal Pradesh	1971	Himachal Pradesh	Shimla
Jammu & Kashmir and Ladakh	1928	Jammu & Kashmir, Ladakh	Srinagar and Jammu
Jharkhand	2000	Jharkhand	Ranchi
Karnataka	1884	Karnataka	Bengaluru (Circuit Benches at Dharwar and Gulbarga)
Kerala	1958	Kerala & Lakshadweep	Ernakulam
Madhya Pradesh	1956	Madhya Pradesh	Jabalpur (Benches at Gwalior and Indore)

Name	Year	Territorial Jurisdiction	Seat
Madras	1862	Tamil Nadu & Puducherry	Chennai (Bench at Madurai)
Orissa	1948	Odisha	Cuttack
Patna	1916	Bihar	Patna
Punjab and Haryana	1966	Punjab, Haryana and Chandigarh	Chandigarh
Rajasthan	1949	Rajasthan	Jodhpur (Bench at Jaipur)
Sikkim	1975	Sikkim	Gangtok
Uttarakhand	2000	Uttarakhand	Nainital
Tripura	2013	Tripura	Agartala
Meghalaya	2013	Meghalaya	Shillong
Manipur	2013	Manipur	Imphal
Telangana	2019	Telangana	Hyderabad

FUNDAMENTAL DUTIES

The fundamental duties for the Indian citizens have been incorporated in the Constitution through the Constitution (42nd) Amendment Act, 1976. These duties are:

(*i*) to abide by the Constitution and respect its ideals and institutions, the National Flag and the National Anthem;

(*ii*) to cherish and follow the noble deeds which inspired our national struggle for freedom;

(*iii*) to uphold and protect the sovereignty, unity and integrity of India;

(*iv*) to defend the country and render national service when called upon to do so;

(*v*) to promote harmony and the spirit of common brotherhood amongst all the people transcending religious, regional or sectional diversities and to renounce practices derogatory to the dignity of women;

(*vi*) to value and preserve the rich heritage of our composite culture;

(*vii*) to protect and improve natural environment including forests, lakes, rivers and wildlife, and to have compassion for living creatures;

(*viii*) to develop the scientific temper, humanism and the spirit of inquiry and reform;

(*ix*) to safeguard public property and to abjure violence;

(*x*) to strive towards excellence in all spheres of individual and collective activity so that the nation constantly rises to higher levels of endeavour and achievement.

(*xi*) who is parent or guardian to provide opportunities for education to his child or, as the case may be, ward between age of six and fourteen years.

DIRECTIVE PRINCIPLES OF STATE POLICY

The Directive Principles of State Policy are contained in Article 36 to 51 in Part IV of the constitutions. Directive principles are not enforceable through courts. Main aim of Directive principles is to provide social and economic base of a genuine democracy.

Some Important Directive Principles:

- Provisions for adequate means of livelihood for all citizens (Art. 39).
- Right to work (Art. 41).
- Right to human condition of work and maternity relief (Art. 42).
- Right to a living wage and condition of work ensuring decent standard of life of worker (Art. 43).
- Common Civil Code (Art. 44).
- Prohibit consumption of liquor (Art. 47).

- Prevent slaughter of useful cattle (Art. 48).
- Organise Panchayati Raj (Art. 40).
- Separate the judiciary from the executive (Art. 50).
- Protect and maintain places of historic monuments (Art. 49).
- International peace (Art. 51).

Voting Age: The voting age in the election to the Lok Sabha and State Legislative Assemblies has been reduced from 21 to 18 years by the Constitution (61st) Amendment Act, 1989.

GOVERNOR

The Governor is appointed by the President and holds office during the pleasure of the President. Apart from the power to appoint the council of ministers, if the governor finds that the government of state cannot be carried on in accordance with the provisions of the constitution (Art. 356), he may send his report to the President who may assume to himself the functions of the government of the state. (This is popularly known as 'President's Rule').

COUNCIL OF MINISTERS

As in the Centre, there is a Council of Ministers at the State level. It is appointed by the Governor but is responsible to Vidhan Sabha, the lower house of State legislature. The leader of the majority party/group is appointed Chief Minister and other ministers are appointed on his recommendation. The Chief Minister allocates work among the ministers. He can recommend their dismissal, or can bring about changes in the portfolios of the ministers. All the ministers are individually as well as collectively responsible to Vidhan Sabha.

The Chief Minister is first among the equals. Besides appointing his other ministers and allocating work to them, he takes all the major policy decisions. He presides over the Cabinet meetings and all the ministers consult him on important matters. The Chief Minister suggests names for the posts for which the Governor makes appointments in the State. He is the Chief spokesman of the Government and is the communication link between the Government and the Governor.

STATE LEGISLATURE

For every State there is a legislature comprising the Governor and two houses. However, some legislatures do not have the upper house — the legislative council. The legislative assemblies have the right to pass a resolution to abolish or create the legislative council. It must be passed by a majority of the total membership of the assembly and a two-third majority of the members of the assembly present and voting. The resolution is then sent to the Parliament which makes law, creating or abolishing the Council.

The legislative council cannot have less than forty members and not more than one-third of the strength of the assembly. One-third of the council members are elected by an electoral college, consisting of members of municipalities, district boards and other local bodies. One-third of the council members are elected by assembly members. One-twelfth members are elected by graduates of the State who have been qualified for at least three years. One-twelfth of the members are elected by persons who have been for at least three years engaged in teaching in educational institutions, not lower in standard than that of a secondary school, in the State. The remaining number is filled through Governor's nomination.

The legislative council elections are held on the basis of proportional representation with a single transferable votes. The candidates have to be above 30 years of age, voter in any assembly constituency of the State and is not an employee of the Government. It is a permanent house, with one-third members retiring every two years. The legislative council of a State is not subject to dissolution.

The legislative assembly is the lower house and in each State, its members are directly elected by the residents of the State. Legislative Assembly (Vidhan Sabha) of a state consists of not more than 500 and not less than 60 members (Legislative Assembly of Sikkim has 32 members vide Article 371F of the Constitution) chosen by direct election from territorial constituencies in the state. The candidate for assembly seats have to be 25 years of age, citizens of India, not disqualified by any court, have his name in the voter list and does not hold any office of profit in the Government. If a member of assembly abstains for 60 days without informing the house, he stands disqualified. If a person is elected from two assembly seats or from one assembly seat and a parliamentary seat, he can retain only one seat.

The tenure of the assembly is five years, but it can be dissolved earlier also. The Governor summons the house regularly, but not more than six months gap can be there between the last meeting of a session and the first meeting of the forthcoming session. Each assembly has a speaker and a deputy speaker who preside over the meetings. One-tenth of the total members or ten members form the quorum, without which the meeting cannot begin.

The State legislatures can make laws on subjects given in the State or Concurrent List. However, some laws have to be approved by the President while some need prior approval of the President, even before introduction in the legislature. During emergency all subjects, and, in case of Rajya Sabha passing a resolution, a particular subject comes under the Parliament's jurisdiction. The legislature passes all financial bills, without which the State Government cannot spend a single paisa. The legislature controls the executive, through no-Confidence motion, adjournment motion, rejecting the budget, proposing changes in the budget or asking questions. Among the two houses, the lower house or legislative assembly is mere powerful as it can even recommend abolition of the upper house. The State Government is also responsible to the assembly and in the field of legislations, its role is paramount.

THE ATTORNEY GENERAL OF INDIA

The Attorney General of India is the first law officer of the Government of India. Though he is not a member of cabinet he has the right to speak in the House of Parliament, but he has no right to vote. The Attorney General of India shall be appointed by the President and shall hold office during his pleasure. His duty shall be to give advice on such legal matter from time to time as may be referred to him by the President.

COMPTROLLER & AUDITOR GENERAL OF INDIA (CAG)

The Comptroller and Auditor General of India is guardian of the public purse and it is his duty to see that not a *paisa* is spent out of consolidated fund of India or of a state without the authority of the appropriate legislature. He is appointed by President of India.

Status

- Appointed by the President.
- A person with long administrative experience & knowledge of accounts is appointed.
- Holds office for 6 yrs or till 65 yrs of age.
- The President can remove him only on the recommendation of the 2 houses of Parliament (as in case of judge of Supreme Court).

INTER-STATE COUNCILS

Article 263 provides for inter-state councils. The power of the President to set up Inter-State Councils not only for advising upon disputes but also for investigating and discussing subjects in which some or all of the states, or the Union and one or more of the states have common interest.

UNION PUBLIC SERVICE COMMISSION (U.P.S.C.)

This Commission is responsible for (i) recruitment to all civil services and posts, under the Union Government by written examinations, interviews and promotions, and (ii) advising the Government on all matters relating to methods of recruitment, principles to be followed in making promotions and transfers. Its Chairman is appointed by the President.

STAFF SELECTION COMMISSION

The Union Government has constituted the Staff Selection Commission for recruitment to non-technical Group C and some of Group B posts in the central departments and in subordinate offices. The administrative Reforms Commission had recommended the setting up of such a Commission.

* * * * *

6 Planning In India

The need for planning was felt in India even before independence. A National Planning Committee was set up by the Indian National Congress as early as 1938. The Planning Commission was set up in 1950. It is an advisory body engaged in the task of meaningful national planning. The main objectives of India's Economic Planning are as follows : (*i*) securing an increase in National Income; (*ii*) achieving a planned rate of investment within a given period to bring the actual investment as a proportion of national income to a higher level; (*iii*) reducing inequality in the distribution of income and wealth; (*iv*) providing additional employment; (*v*) adopting measures to increase agricultural production, manufacturing capacity for producers and a favourable balance of payments.

Five Year Plans in India

Plans	Period	Investment (₹ Crore)	Objectives
First Plan	April 1, 1951–March 31, 1956	1,960	Priority to agriculture, electricity and irrigation.
Second Plan	April 1, 1956–March 31, 1961	4,672	Development of basic and heavy industries.
Third Plan	April 1, 1961–March 31, 1966	8,577	Long term development of India's economy.
Annual Plan	April 1, 1966–March 31, 1967	2,137	
Annual Plan	April 1, 1967–March 31, 1968	2,205	
Annual Plan	April 1, 1968–March 31, 1969	2,283	
Fourth Plan	April 1, 1969–March 31, 1974	15,779	Enlarge the income of rural population and supply of goods of mass consumption.
Fifth Plan	April 1, 1974–March 31, 1979	39,426	Attain increased self reliance and employment avenues.
Annual Plan	April 1, 1979–March 31, 1980	12,176	
Sixth Plan	April 1, 1980–March 31, 1985	1,09,292	Removal of unemployment
Seventh Plan	April 1, 1985–March 31, 1990	2,18,730	Food work and productivity were the basic priorities.
Eighth Plan	April, 1992–March 31, 1997	4,95,670	Raising employment
Ninth Plan	April 1, 1997–March 31, 2002	9,41,041	Agriculture and rural development
Tenth Plan	April 1, 2002–March 31, 2007	14,91,610	Growth rate 7.8 percent per annum.
Eleventh Plan	April 1, 2007–March 31, 2012	36,44,718	Literacy, Employment, Rural development & Transport development.
Twelfth Plan	April 1, 2012–March 31, 2017	43,33,739	Long term development of India's economy.

INDIA'S AMBITIOUS 15-YEAR VISION PLAN

NITI Aayog has come forward with a draft 15-year vision plan to catapult the country's economy to more than three times as compared to the present day. The new plan is set to replace the centralised five-year plans the country has been following for decades. The new plan is accompanied by shorter sub-plans—a seven-year strategy for 2017-24, and a three-year 'Action Agenda' from 2017-18 to 2019-20. No less than 300 specific action points covering a wide range of sectors have been drawn up as part of the 15 year vision.

The salient features of 15-year vision plan are :

- India aims to more than triple the size of its economy in 15 years with gross domestic product (GDP) expected to rise to ₹ 469 lakh crores from ₹ 137 lakh crore in 2015-16. Per capita GDP is expected to rise by three times to ₹ 3,14,667 in 2015-2016.
- NITI Aayog plans to work closely with staes to boost infrastructure and services, including regions that require special attention. The government made a big push for Goods and Services Tax (GST), urging the state governments to speed up the legislation of state GST bills.
- India's urban population is expected to increase by 22 crores by 2031. The plan is likely to lay emphasis on urban development, taking a note from China's elaborate long-term development agenda.
- The plan envisages a central body for overseeing the implemention of sustainable development goals. Specific goals will cover clean water, removing hunger, climate efforts, responsible consumption, clean energy, quality educaiton, reduced inequality and gender equality, among others.

NITI AAYOG

The National Institution for transforming India Aayog (NITI Aayog) is a Government of India Policy. NITI Aayog seeks to facilities and empower the critical requirement of good governance, which is people-centric, participative, collaborative, transparent and policy-driven.

The started aim for NITI Aayog's creation is to foster involvement and participation in the economic policy-making process by the state Governments of India. It has adopted a "bottom-up" approach in planning which is remarkable contrast to the planning commission's tradition of "top-down" decision-making. The prime minister will serve as chairperson for NITI Aayog.

NITI Aayog was established on 1 January 2015.

Members of NITI Aayog

The NITI Aayog comprises the following:

1. Prime Minister of India as the Chairperson
2. Governing Council comprising the Chief Ministers of all the States and Union territories with Legislatures and lieutenant governors of other Union territories.
3. Regional Councils will be formed to address specific issues and contingencies impacting more than one state or a region. These will be formed for a specified tenure.
4. Experts, specialists and practitioners with relevant domain knowledge as special invitees nominated by the Prime Minister
5. Full-time organizational framework (in addition to Prime Minister as the Chairperson) comprising
   - (*i*) *Vice-Chairperson*
   - (*ii*) *Members:* Three (3) Full-time
   - (*iii*) *Part-time members:* Maximum of two from leading universities research organizations and other relevant institutions in an ex-officio capacity. Part-time members will be on a rotational basis.
   - (*iv*) *Ex Officio members:* Maximum of four members of the Union Council of Ministers to be nominated by the Prime Minister.
   - (*v*) *Chief Executive Officer:* To be appointed by the Prime Minister for a fixed tenure, in the rank of Secretary to the Government of India.
   - (*vi*) Secretariat as deemed necessary.

FINANCE COMMISSION

Article 280 of the Constitution provides for the appointment of a finance commission every five year. President appoints chairman and members of this commission. Finance commission are to recommend to President the basis for the distribution of the net proceeds of taxes between the centre and the states and the principles which should govern the grants-in-aid to be given to the states out of the consolidated funds of India.

NATIONAL DEVELOPMENT COUNCIL

The National Development Council, set-up in 1952, consists of representatives of the Central Government as well as the State governments. It is the supreme body insofar as planning is concerned and it determines policies, issues guidelines, reviews working of the plan and finally approves the plan. The Council consists of the Prime Minister (Chairman), all Union Cabinet Ministers, Chief Ministers of all States and Union Territories and the Chairman and members of the NITI Aayog. For matters relating to Plans and planning, the Union Minister of Planning is responsible to the Parliament.

RESERVE BANK OF INDIA

- It is the Central Bank of the country.
- It was established on April 1, 1935 with a capital of ₹ 5 crore. This capital of ₹ 5 crore was divided into 5 lakh equity shares of ₹ 100 each. In the beginning, the ownership of almost all the share capital was with the non-government share-holders.
- It was nationalized on Jan 1, 1949 as govt. acquired the private share holdings.
- **Governors:** Ist Governor - Sir Smith (1935-37) Ist Indian Governor - C.D. Deshmukh (1948-49)

Other Financial Institutions

- **Industrial Credit & Investment Corporation of India Bank (ICICI Bank) :** Established in 1955 as a public limited company to encourage and assist industrial units of the nation. It has been converted into a bank with effect from May 3, 2002.
- **Small Industries Development Bank of India (SIDBI) :** Established in 1990; promotes small scale sector.
- **National Bank of Agriculture & Rural Development (NABARD) :** Established on Nov 5, 1982; gives credit facilities to farmers.
- **Export-Import Bank of India (EXIM) :** Set-up on Jan 1, 1982; grants deferred credit to Indian exporters in order to operate in the International market.
- **Industrial Development Bank of India (IDBI) :** Established in 1964; to provide financial assistance to industrial enterprises.
- **Industrial Reconstruction Bank of India (IRBI) :** Set-up in 1971 with the objective of reviving and revitalizing sick industrial units in public and private sectors.

* * * * *

7 National Symbols

State Emblem: State Emblem of India is an adaptation from the Sarnath Lion Capital of Ashoka. It was adopted by the Government of India on January 26, 1950. In the adapted form, only three lions are visible, the fourth being hidden from the view. The wheel (Dharma Chakra) appears in relief in the centre of the abacus with a bull on the right and a horse on the left. The bell-shaped lotus has been omitted. The words ''Satyameva Jayate'' meaning ''Truth alone triumphs'' are inscribed below the Emblem in Devanagari script.

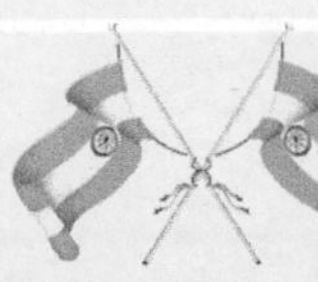

National Flag: The National Flag of India is a horizontal tricolour of deep saffron (Kesari), white and dark green in equal proportion. In the centre of the white band there is a wheel in navy blue colour. It has 24 spokes. The ratio of the length and the breadth of the flag is 3 : 2. Its design was adopted by the Constituent Assembly of India on July 22, 1947.

National Anthem: Rabindranath Tagore's song 'Jana-gana-mana' was adopted by the Constituent Assembly as the National Anthem of India on January 24, 1950.

Jana-gan-mana-adhinayaka jaya he,
Bharata-bhagya-vidhata
Punjab-Sindh-Gujarat-Maratha-Dravida-Utkala-Banga
Vindhya-Himachala-Yamuna-Ganga Uchhala-jaladhi-taranga.
Tava subha name jage, Tava subha asisa mange,
Gahe tava jaya gatha,
Jana-gana-mangala-dayak, jaya he Bharata bhagya vidhata,
Jaya he, jaya he, jaya he, Jaya jaya jaya, jaya he.

National Song: Bankim Chandra Chatterji's 'Vande Mataram' which was a source of inspiration to the people in their struggle for freedom, has been adopted as National Song. It has an equal status with the National Anthem.

Vande Mataram
Sujalam, suphalam, malayaja-shitalam,
Shasya shyamalam, Mataram
Shubhrajyotsna,pulkita yaminim,
Phulla kusumita drumadalashobhinim,
Subhasinim sumadhura—bhashinim,
Sukhadam, Varadam, Mataram.

National Bird and Animal of India: Peacock and Tiger; **National Aquatic Animal:** Dolphin; **National Flower:** Lotus; **National Calendar:** It was adopted on March 22, 1957. It has 365 days in the year and the first month of the year is Chaitra.

Months of the National Calendar

(1) Chaitra, (2) Vaishakha, (3) Jaishtha, (4) Ashadha, (5) Shravan, (6) Bhadra, (7) Ashvina, (8) Kartika, (9) Marga-Shirsha, (10) Pausha, (11) Magha, (12) Phalguna.

* * * * *

8 General Science

INVENTIONS AND DISCOVERIES

Important Inventions

Name of Invention	*Inventor*	*Nationality*	*Year*
Aeroplane	Orville & Wilbur Wright	U.S.A.	1903
Ball-Point Pen	John J. Loud	U.S.A.	1888
Barometer	Evangelista Torricelli	Italy	1644
Bicycle	Kirkpatrick Macmillan	Britain	1839-40
Bifocal Lens	Benjamin Franklin	U.S.A.	1780
Car (Petrol)	Karl Benz	Germany	1888
Celluloid	Alexander Parkes	Britain	1861
Cinema	Nicolas & Jean Lumiere	France	1895
Clock (mechanical)	I-Hsing & Liang Ling-Tsan	China	725
Diesel Engine	Rudolf Diesel	Germany	1895
Dynamo	Hypolite Pixii	France	1832
Electric Lamp	Thomas Alva Edison	U.S.A.	1879
Electric Motor (DC)	Zenobe Gramme	Belgium	1873
Electric Motor (AC)	Nikola Tesla	U.S.A.	1888
Electro-magnet	William Sturgeon	Britain	1824
Electronic Computer	Dr. Alan M. Turing	Britain	1943
Film (moving outlines)	Louis Prince	France	1885
Film (musical sound)	Dr. Le de Forest	U.S.A.	1923
Fountain Pen	Lewis E. Waterman	U.S.A.	1884
Gramophone	Thomas Alva Edison	U.S.A.	1878
Helicopter	Etienne Oehmichen	France	1924
Jet Engine	Sir Frank Whittle	Britain	1937
Laser	Charles H. Townes	U.S.A.	1960
Lift (Mechanical)	Elisha G. Otis	U.S.A.	1852
Locomotive	Richard Trevithick	Britain	1804
Machine Gun	James Puckle	Britain	1718
Microphone	Alexander Graham Bell	U.S.A.	1876
Microscope	Z. Janssen	Netherlands	1590
Motor Cycle	G. Daimler	Germany	1885
Photography (on film)	John Carbutt	U.S.A.	1888
Printing Press	Johann Gutenberg	Germany	c.1455
Razor (safety)	King C. Gillette	U.S.A.	1895
Refrigerator	James Harrison & Alexander Catlin	U.S.A.	1850

Name of Invention	*Inventor*	*Nationality*	*Year*
Safety Pin	Walter Hunt	U.S.A.	1849
Sewing machine	Barthelemy Thimmonnier	France	1829
Ship (steam)	J.C. Perier	France	1775
Ship (turbine)	Hon. Sir C. Parsons	Britain	1894
Skyscraper	W. Le Baron Jenny	U.S.A.	1882
Slide Rule	William Oughtred	Britain	1621
Steam Engine (condenser)	James Watt	Britain	1765
Steel Production	Henry Bessemer	Britain	1855
Steel (stainless)	Harry Brearley	Britain	1913
Submarine	David Bushnell	U.S.A.	1776
Tank	Sir Ernest Swinton	Britain	1914
Telegraph	M. Lammond	France	1787
Telegraph Code	Samuel F.B. Morse	U.S.A.	1837
Telephone (perfected)	Alexander Graham Bell	U.S.A.	1876
Television (mechanical)	John Logie Baird	Britain	1926
Television (electronic)	P.T. Farnsworth	U.S.A.	1927
Thermometer	Galileo Galilei	Italy	1593
Transformer	Michael Faraday	Britain	1831
Transistor	Bardeen, Shockley & Brattain	U.S.A.	1948
Washing Machine (elec.)	Hurley Machine Co.	U.S.A.	1907
Zip-Fastener	W.L. Judson	U.S.A.	1891

Important Discoveries

Discovery	*Discoverer*	*Nationality*	*Year*
Aluminium	Hans Christian Oerstedt	Denmark	1827
Atomic number	Henry Moseley	England	1913
Atomic structure of matter	John Dalton	England	1803
Chlorine	C.W. Scheele	Sweden	1774
Electromagnetic induction	Michael Faraday	England	1831
Electromagnetic waves	Heinrich Hertz	Germany	1886
Electromagnetism	Hans Christian Oersted	Denmark	1920
Electron	Sir Joseph Thomson	England	1897
General theory of relativity	Albert Einstein	Switzerland	1915
Hydrogen	Henry Cavendish	England	1766
Law of electric conduction	Georg Ohm	Germany	1827
Law of electromagnetism	Andre Ampere	France	1826
Law of falling bodies	Galileo	Italy	1590
Laws of gravitation & motion	Isaac Newton	England	1687
Laws of planetary motion	Johannes Kepler	Germany	1609-19
Magnesium	Sir Humphry Davy	England	1808
Neptune (Planet)	Johann Galle	Germany	1846
Neutron	James Chadwick	England	1932
Nickel	Axel Cronstedt	Sweden	1751
Nitrogen	Daniel Rutherford	England	1772

Discovery	Discoverer	Nationality	Year
Oxygen	Joseph Priestly C.W. Scheele	England Sweden	1772
Ozone	Christian Schonbein	Germany	1839
Pluto (Planet)	Clyde Tombaugh	U.S.A	1930
Plutonium	G.T. Seaborg	U.S.A	1940
Proton	Ernest Rutherford	England	1919
Quantum Theory	Max Planck	Germany	1900
Radioactivity	Antoine Bacquerel	France	1896
Radium	Pierre & Marie Curie	France	1898
Silicon	Jons Berzelius	Sweden	1824
Special theory of relativity	Albert Einstein	Switzerland	1905
Sun as centre of solar system	Copernicus	Poland	1543
Uranium	Martin Klaproth	Germany	1789
Uranus (Planet)	William Herschel	England	1781
X-rays	Wilhelm Roentgen	Germany	1895

Geographical Explorations/Discoveries

Place	Explorer/Discoverer	Nationality	Year
America	Christopher Columbus	Italy	1492
Hawaii Islands (Sandwich Islands)	Captain James Cook	England	1778
Newfoundland	John Cabot	England	1497
New Zealand	Abel Janszoon Tasman	Holland	1642
North Pole	Robert Peary	USA	1909
Sea Route to India (via Cape of Good Hope)	Vasco da Gama	Portugal	1498
South Pole	Roald Amundsen	Norway	1911

Scientific Instruments

Name of Instrument	Used for
Altimeter	measuring altitude
Ammeter	measuring strength of an electric current
Anemometer	measuring the velocity of wind
Audiometer	measuring level of hearing
Barometer	measuring atmospheric pressure
Callipers	measuring the internal and external diameters of tubes
Calorimeter	measuring quantity of heat
Compass	finding out direction
Dynamo	converting mechanical energy into electrical energy
Eudiometer	measuring volume changes during chemical reactions between gases
Galvanometer	detecting and determining the strength of small electric currents
Hydrometer	measuring specific gravity of a liquid
Hygrometer	measuring the humidity in the atmosphere
Lactometer	measuring the purity of milk
Manometer	measuring the gaseous pressure
Micrometer	measuring minute distances, angles, etc.

Name of Instrument	*Used for*
Microscope	seeing magnified view of very small objects
Periscope	with the help of this instrument an observer in a submarine can see what is going on the surface of the sea
Photometer	measuring intensity of light from distant stars
Pyrometer	measuring high temperatures
Radar	detecting and finding the presence and location of moving objects like aircraft, missile, etc.
Radiometer	measuring the emission of radiant energy
Rain Gauge	measuring the amount of rainfall
Seismograph	measuring and recording the intensity and origin of earthquake shocks
Sextant	measuring altitude and angular distances between two objects or heavenly bodies
Spectrometer	measuring the refractive indices
Spherometer	measuring the curvature of spherical objects/surface
Sphygmomanometer	measuring blood pressure
Stethoscope	ascertaining the condition of heart and lungs by listening to their function
Stroboscope	viewing objects that are moving rapidly with a periodic motion as if they were at rest
Tachometer	measuring the rate of revolution or angular speed of a revolving shaft
Telescope	viewing magnified images of distant objects
Theodolite	measuring the horizontal and vertical angles
Thermocouple	measuring the temperature inside furnaces and jet engines
Thermometer	measuring human body temperature
Thermostat	regulating constant temperature
Ultrasonoscope	measuring utrasonic sounds
Viscometer	measuring the viscosity of a fluid
Voltmeter	measuring potential difference between two points.

Diseases and the Parts of Body they Affect

Disease	*Part of body affected*
AIDS	Immune system of body
Arthritis	Inflammation of joints
Asthma	Lungs
Cataract	Eyes
Conjunctivitis	Eyes
Diabetes	Pancreas
Diphtheria	Throat
Glaucoma	Eyes
Eczema	Skin
Goitre	Front of the neck (due to enlargement of thyroid gland)
Gout	Joints of bone

Disease	*Part of body affected*
Jaundice	Liver
Meningitis	Brain or spinal cord
Pleurisy	Pleura (inflammation of)
Polio	motor neurons
Pneumonia	Lungs
Pyorrhoea	Sockets of teeth
Tuberculosis	Lungs
Typhoid	Intestine
Malaria	Spleen
Leukaemia	Blood
Rickets	Bones

✱ ✱ ✱ ✱ ✱

9 Space Research

First in Space

First creator of rules regarding space research	— Isaac Newton
First artificial satellite launched in space	— Sputnik-1 (1957)
First living being sent in space	— Louika (a dog)
Firstever manned spacecraft	— Vostok-I
First man in space	— Yuri Gagarin, U.S.S.R. (1961)
First woman in space	— Valentina Tereshkova, U.S.S.R. (June 1963)
First man who moved in space out of the spacecraft	— Alexi Livonov, U.S.S.R. (June 1965)
First person to land on moon	— Neil Armstrong, America (21st July, 1969)
First fourwheeled carriage without human being on moon	— Leunokhev-I, U.S.S.R. (1970)
First space lab in orbit	— Skylab (America, 1973)
First space shuttle	— Columbia (America, 1981)
First Indian (man) in space	— Sq. led. Rakesh Sharma (13th April, 1984)
First Indian (Woman) in space	— Kalpana Chawla (19th Nov., 1997)
First American woman in space	— Sailyride (1983)
First spacecraft on Mars	— Pathfinder (6 July, 1997)
First woman who lead spacecraft	— Allin Collis (America)
First spacecraft without man	— Shenzoo, China (20th Nov. 1999)
First country in the world to succeed in an inter-planetary mission on mars in the maiden attempt	— India (MOM Spacecraft)
First country to Land on Moon's South Pole	— India (Chandrayaan-3)

INDIAN SPACE RESEARCH PROGRAMME

Indian space programme is directed towards self-reliance in the usage of space science and technology for national development. Main thrust is in the areas of:

(*i*) satellite communications for various national applications including telecommunication, TV broadcast and radio networking;

(*ii*) resources survey and management, environmental monitoring and meteorological services through remote sensing; and

(*iii*) development of indigenous satellites and launching of vehicles to achieve the above objectives.

Space Commission

For promoting a unified development and application of space science and technology for national development, Space Commission and Department of Space were created in 1972 to evolve policies and guidelines to achieve envisaged objectives. Policies framed by Space Commission are implemented through Department of Space (DoS) and Indian Space Research Organisation (ISRO). DoS is also the nodal agency charged with the responsibility of establishing National Natural Resources Management System (NNRMS). The activities of ISRO are carried out by following centres/units.

1. Vikram Sarabhai Space Centre (VSSC), Thiruvananthapuram.
2. Indian Satellite Application Centre (ISAC), Bengaluru.
3. SHAR Centre, Sriharikota (Andhra Pradesh).
4. Space Applications Centre (SAC), Ahmedabad.
5. Liquid Propulsion Systems Centre (LPSC) with its facilities at Bengaluru, Thiruvananthapuram and Mahendragiri.
6. ISRO Telemetry Tracking and Command Network (ISTRAC) with its network of ground stations and Development and Educational Communication Unit (DECU), Ahmedabad.
7. Master Control Facility (MCF), Hassan (Karnataka).
8. National Remote Sensing Agency (NRSA), Secundrabad.

The headquarters of Department of Space and ISRO are located at Bengaluru.

Background

Indian participation in the field of space research dates back to 1962 when an Indian National Committee for Space Research was set up under the chairmanship of Dr. Vikram A. Sarabhai.

India's practical space activity began with the establishment of the Thumba Equatorial Rocket Launching Station (TERLS) at the Vikram Sarabhai Space Centre (VSSC) in 1963. VSSC had been established a year earlier.

Progress

Between July 14, 1964 and the end of 1968, India launched over 500 sounding rockets from the TERLS. Scientists from the (erstwhile) U.S.S.R., France, Germany, the United Kingdom and the United States participated in the projects involving these rockets launched for meteorological, ionospheric, serenomic and astronomical studies. Ariane Passenger Payload Experiment (APPLE) satellite was launched at 4.43 PM on June 19, 1981. The 673 kg. satellite was put into orbit by ESAs Ariane launch vehicle under ESA-ISRO joint venture along with two other satellites Meteorite - 2 (European Weather Satellite) and CAT (Ariane Technology Capsule) from Kourou in French Guyana.

Aryabhatta

India began its experimental satellite missions during the seventies and it ultimately led to the establishment of operational space systems. Aryabhatta, the first Indian satellite was launched in April 1975 by an Intercosmos Rocket of the former U.S.S.R. Aryabhatta had carried on board three scientific payloads.

Bhaskara

Aryabhatta was followed by two remote sensing satellites, Bhaskara-1 and Bhaskara-2 launched in 1979 and 1981 respectively. The Bhaskaras paved the way for further space programmes.

Rohini

India's indigenous Satellite Launch Vehicle SLV-3 blasted off from the Sriharikota range (SHAR) on May 31, 1981, on its first development flight. It lifted into orbit the 40 kg Rohini satellite 12 minutes later, travelling at a speed of 28,000 km an hour.

INSAT SYSTEM

The Indian National Satellite (INSAT) System is a great gift, the Government and the brilliant Indian scientists have given to the people of India, during last two decades of the previous century. India has achieved a lot in its endeavours in space, in these two decades. Through 1980s, India succeeded in establishing operational space system. INSAT was commissioned in 1983 by way of multipurpose satellites. In fact INSAT system is a multipurpose operational satellite system, involving a multi-agency system for inland telecommunications, direct telecasting broadcasting, through satellites, relaying data and meteorological observations.

Impact of INSAT System

This system has brought about a revolutionary change in the field of telecommunications, weather forecasting and television expansion. In other words, it has had a tremendous impact on the above said three areas and indirectly on all other related areas, benefitting the Indian people, as whole.

*****

10 Computers

Introduction

The term computer is derived from the Latin word compute, which means to calculate. A computer is an electronic machine, devised for performing calculations and controlling operations that can be expressed either in logical or numerical terms. In simple terms, a computer is an electronic device that performs diverse operations with the help of instructions to process the information in order to achieve the desired results. A Computer application extends to cover huge area including education, industries, government, medicine, scientific research etc.

A computer is one of the most influential forces available in modern times. Due to its memory, high speed and perfection, its application can be extended to almost infinite levels. Millions of complex calculations can be done in mere fraction of time. Difficult decisions can be made with accuracy for comparatively little cost. Computers are widely seen as instruments for future progress and as tools to achieve substantiality by way of improved access to information by means of video conferencing and e-mail. Indeed computers have left such on impression on modern civilization that we call this era as the information age.

Computer System

A computer system is a combination of various components. It performs the system functions such as input, processing, output, storage and control. A computer system consists of the following components: 1. Hardware; 2. Software

Hardware

The physical components of the computer, such as electrical, electronics and mechanical unit are known as the hardware of the computer. That is, the input units, output units and CPU are called hardware. Thus hardware is the equipment involved in the function of a computer. It consists of the components that can be physically handled.

Software

The computer performs operations like addition, subtraction, multiplication and division only when the user instructs it to do so. The user issues instructions and the CPU acts in accordance with the instructions. The sets of instructions, which control the sequence of operations, are known as programs, and collectively programs are called software. The software can be broadly classified into two types. They are: (a) System Software (b) Application Software.

Difference between Hardware & Software

Hardware

1. It is the physical unit of the computer
2. Hardware understands only machine language, lower level language or binary
3. It works with binary code, the presence or absence of Pulses as 1's or 0's.

Software

1. It is a collection of programs to bring the hardware system into operation
2. It is written by a well versed programmer and generally in higher level language which is readable by human being.
3. It is represented by the Higher Level Languages such as BASIC, COBOL, *etc.*,

System Software

System software consists of several Programs, which are directly responsible for controlling, integrating and managing the individual hardware components of a computer system. They provide basic functionality like file management, visual display and keyboard input which are used by application software. Some examples of system software are operating system, device drivers, language translators, system utilities.

Application Software

A computer program used to perform a specific task, rather than just managing a computer system. Some examples of application software are word processing, spread sheets, database management systems.

Two Types of Computer Systems

Analog Computers : The analog computers operate by measuring instead of counting. The analog computer works on the supply of continuous electrical signals. The display is also continuous. Its output is in the form of graphs.

Digital Computers : These computers work with quantities represented as digits. They operate on discrete quantities. In digital computer, both numeric and non-numeric information are represented as strings of digits. These computers use binary codes, 0's and 1's, to represent the information. The information is given to the computer in the form of discrete electrical signals.

Input/Output Devices

Input Devices : An input device is any machine that feeds data into a computer. For example, a keyboard is an input device. Input devices other than the keyboard are sometimes called alternate devices. Trackballs, mouse and light pens are all alternate input devices.

Output Devices : Output is anything that comes out of a computer. Output can be meaningful information or gibberish, and it can appear in a variety of forms - as binary numbers, as characters, as pictures, and as printed pages. Output devices include display screens, loudspeakers, printers, plotters, etc.

Computer Memory

There are two kinds of computer memory: primary and secondary. Primary memory is accessible directly by the processing unit. RAM is an example of primary memory. As soon as the computer is switched off the contents of the primary memory is lost. You can store and retrieve data much faster with primary memory compared to secondary memory. Secondary memory such as floppy disks, magnetic disk, etc., is located outside the computer. Primary memory is more expensive than secondary memory. Because of this the size of primary memory is less than that of secondary memory.

Types of Primary Memory

- Random Access Memory (RAM)
- Read Only Memory (ROM)
- Programmable Read Only Memory (PROM)
- Erasable Programmable Read Only Memory (EPROM)

Cache Memory

To decrease the mismatch in operating speed, a small memory chip is attached between CPU and Main memory whose access time is very close to the processing speed of CPU. It is called CACHE memory. CACHE memories are accessed much faster than conventional RAM. It is used to store programs or data currently being executed or temporary data frequently used by the CPU.

Types of Secondary Memory

- Magnetic Tape • Magnetic Disk • Floppy Disk
- Optical Disk–1. Compact Disk/ Read Only Memory (CD-ROM), 2. Erasable Optical Disk.

The memory is measured by the following units:

(*a*) **BIT (Binary digit):** It is the smallest possible unit of information. It can be either 0 or 1.

(*b*) **NIBBLE:** Four bits form one nibble.

(*c*) **BYTE:** It is a unit of information consisting of fixed number of bits. It is a combination of 8 bits.

(*d*) **CHARACTER:** It is represented by one byte. It can be a letter, digit, punctuation mark or special characters.

(*e*) **WORD:** The combination of 2 bytes or 4 bytes or 8 bytes is a word.

The data measurement is as follows:

8 bits - 1 byte

1024 bytes - 1 Kilo Byte (KB)

1024 KB - 1 Mega Byte (MB)

1024 MB - 1 Giga Byte (GB)

1024 GB - 1 Tera Byte (TB)

Word keyboard shortcuts

Action	*Key Stroke*
Open a file	Ctrl + O
New file	Ctrl + N
Close a file	Ctrl + W
Save As	F12
Save	Ctrl+S or Shift+F12
Print Preview	Ctrl + F2
Print	Ctrl + P
Show/Hide paragraph symbols	Ctrl + *
Spelling and grammar	F7
Help	F1
Find	Ctrl + F
Replace	Ctrl + H
Go To	Ctrl + G
Select all - entire document	Ctrl + A
Select from cursor to beginning of line	Shift + Home
Select from cursor to end of line	Shift + End
Go to beginning of line	Home
Go to end of line	End
Go to beginning of document	Ctrl + Home
Go to end of document	Ctrl + End
Cut	Ctrl + X
Copy	Ctrl + C
Paste	Ctrl + V
Undo	Ctrl + Z
Redo	Ctrl + Y
Format painter	Ctrl + Shift + C
Left alignment	Ctrl + L
Center alignment	Ctrl + E
Right alignment	Ctrl + R
Justified	Ctrl + J
Delete previous word	Ctrl + Backspace
Apply bulleted list	Ctrl + Shift + L
Indent	Ctrl + M
Page break	Ctrl + Enter
Font face	Ctrl + Shift + F
Font size	Ctrl + Shift + P
Bold	Ctrl + B
Italics	Ctrl + I
Underline	Ctrl + U
Double underline	Ctrl + Shift + D
Word underline	Ctrl + Shift + A
Change case	Shift + F3
Subscript	Ctrl + =
Superscript	Ctrl + Shift + =
Make web hyperlink	Ctrl + K
Go to next cell	Tab
Go to previous cell	Shift + Tab
Go to beginning of column	Alt + PageUp
Highlight to beginning of column	Alt + Shift + PageUp
Go to end of column	Alt + PageDown
Highlight to end of column	Alt + Shift + PageDown
Go to beginning of row	Alt + Home
Highlight to beginning of row	Alt+Shift+Home
Go to end of row	Alt + End
Highlight to end of row	Alt+Shift+End
Column break	Ctrl+Shift+Enter
Copyright ©	Alt + Ctrl + C
Date field	Alt + Shift + D
Go to footnotes	Alt + Ctrl + F
Show/Hide ¶	Ctrl + Shift + 8
Theasaurus	Shift + F7

Operating System

It is the first layer of software loaded into computer memory when it starts up. As the first software layer, all other software that gets loaded after it depends on it for various common core services. In simple words, the operating system organizes and controls the hardware. Examples of operating systems are Windows XP, UNIX, and Linux.

Programming Languages

Computers are machines. Unfortunately they cannot understand natural languages, such as Hindi, English, Tamil, etc. that human beings speak and understand. Therefore, to give instructions to computers, different languages have been developed. These languages are called computer languages. It is a general purpose language that is designed to combine business and scientific processing features and that can easily learned by novice programmers, yet contains advanced features for experienced programmers.

Computer languages are classified into three categories: 1. Low Level Language; 2. Machine language; 3. High level languages.

Compiler

A compiler is a kind of translator that translates a program into another program, known as target language. Usually, the term compiler is used for language translator of high-level language into machine language. The compiler replaces single high-level statement with a series of machine language instruction.

Interpreter

Unlike compilers, an interpreter translates a statement in a program and executes the statement immediately, before translating the next source language statement. Similar to compilers, every interpreted language such as BASIC and LISP has its own interpreters.

Computer Networks

A **computer network**, often simply referred to as a **network**, is a collection of computers and devices connected by communications channels that facilitates communications among users and allows users to share resources with other users.

Categories of Network

(*i*) **LAN :** LAN stands for Local Area Network. These networks evolved around the PC revolution. LANs enabled multiple users in a relatively small geographical area to exchange files and messages, as well as access shared resources such as file servers.

(*ii*) **WAN :** WAN stands for Wide Area Network. The interconnection of various LAN's through telephone network, which unites geographically distributed users, is achieved through WAN. In short when we log on to the internet, we become a part of a WAN.

(*iii*) **MAN :** MAN stands for Metropolitan Area Network. It is usually the interconnection between various LAN's in a particular geographical area like a metropolitan city like Bombay.

Internet

Internet is a communication network which bridges all the small computer networks worldwide as a whole. Internet is based upon Internet technology, in particular World Wide Web (WWW), to build Information System within organization or enterprise to accomplish standardization and automation. Fundamentally, it means network computing environments which let the users share the information through the Internet and Web browsers.

Characteristics of Intranet

The following are the important characteristics of the Intranet.

(*a*) It is an extended internet-private business networks located outside of the corporate firewall.

(*b*) It can be referred to an intranet that is partially accessible to authorized outsiders.

(*c*) It is a network that uses the internet to link businesses with others that share the common goals.

E-MAIL

E-mail is an electronic message sent from one computer to another. We can send or receive personal and business-related messages with attachments, such as pictures or formatted documents. We can even send songs and computer programs.

* * * * *

11 United Nations

- **Origin:** UN Charter was signed by 50 members on June 26, 1945. It officially came into existence on October 24, 1945.
- **UN Charter:** The Charter is the Constitution of the UN and contains its aims and objectives and rules and regulations for its functioning.
- **Aims and Objectives:** They are security, welfare and human rights.
- **Headquarters:** New York.
- **Flag:** The flag is light blue in colour, and emblazoned in white, in its centre is the UN symbol—a polar map of world embraced by twin olive branches open at the top.
- **Official Languages:** The official languages of the UN are: English, French, Chinese, Russian, Arabic and Spanish. However, working languages are English & French only.
- **Main Organs of the UN:** There are six main organs:
  1. General Assembly
  2. Security Council
  3. Economic and Social Council
  4. Trusteeship Council
  5. International Court of Justice, and
  6. Secretariat.

  1. **General Assembly:** It consists of representative of all members of the UN. Each member country has only one vote. It meets once a year and passes UN Budget.
  2. **Security Council:** It is the Executive body of the UN and is mainly responsible for maintaining international peace and security. It has 15 members, 5 of which (USA, UK, France, Russia and China) are permanent members. The 10 non-permanent members are elected by General Assembly for two-year term and are not eligible for immediate re-election.
  3. **Economic and Social Council:** It has 54 members elected by General Assembly.
  4. **Trusteeship Council:** It looks after interest of the people in areas not yet independent and leads them towards self-government.
  5. **International Court of Justice:** It has 15 judges, no two of whom may be nationals of the same state. They are elected by General Assembly and Security Council for a term of 9 years. The Court elects its President and Vice-President for a 3-year term.
  6. **Secretariat:** It is the Secretariat of the UN and is headed by the Secretary General.

Years Observed by United Nations

1967: International Tourism Year
1968: Human Rights Year
1970: International Education Year
1972: International Book Year
1973: Copernicus Year
1974: World Population Year
1975: International Women's Year
1979: International Year of the Child
1981: International Year of Disabled
1983: World Communication Year
1985: International Youth Year
1986: International Year of Peace
1987: International Year of Shelter for the Homeless

1990 : International Literacy Year
1992 : International Space Year
1993 : International Year for World's Indigenous People
1994 : International Year of Family
1995 : International Year of Tolerance
1996 : International Year for Eradication of Poverty
1998 : Human Rights Year
1999 : Year of Older Persons
2000 : Year of the Culture of Peace
2001 : International Year of Volunteer
2002 : International Year of Eco-tourism
2003 : International Year of Fresh Water
2004 : International Rice Year
2005 : International Year of Sports and Physical Education
2006 : International Year of Deserts and Desertification
2008 : International Year of Potato
2009 : International Year of Astronomy
2010 : International Year of Bio-diversity
2011 : International Year of Forest
2012 : International Year of Cooperatives
2013 : International Year of Water Cooperation
2014 : International Year of Family Farming
2015 : International Year of Soils
2016 : International Year of Pulses
2017 : International Year of Sustainable Tourism for Development
2019 : International Year of Indigenous Languages.
2020 : International Year of Plant Health
2021 : International Year of Peace and Trust
2022 : International Year of Artisanal Fisheries and Aquaculture.
2023 : International Year of Millets
2024 : International Year of Camelids
2025 : International Year of Glaciers Preservation; International Year of Quantum Science and Technology; International Year of Coopera-tives; International Year of Peace and Trust.

- **Present Membership:** At present 193 countries are members of the UNO. South Sudan is the latest entrant to this world organisation.

Famous International Organisations, Headquarters and Year of Establishment

International Organisations	*Headquarters*	*Year of Establishment*
United Nations (U.N.)	New York	1945
International Monetary Fund (I.M.F.)	Washington D.C.	1945
World Health Organisation (W.H.O.)	Geneva	1948
Food & Agricultural Organisation (FAO)	Rome	1945
International Labour Organisation (ILO)	Geneva	1919
UNESCO	Paris	1946
International Court of Justice	The Hague	1945
Universal Postal Union (UPU)	Berne	1874
International Civil Aviation Organisation (ICAO)	Montreal	1947
UNIDO	Vienna	1966
International Atomic Energy Agency (IAEA)	Vienna	1957
International Finance Corporation (IFC)	Washington D.C.	1956
United Nations Development Programme (UNDP)	New York	1965
UNICEF	New York	1946
International Maritime Organisation (IMO)	London	1948
World Meteorological Organisation (WMO)	Geneva	1950
International Telecommunication Union (ITU)	Geneva	1865
Arab League	Cairo	1945
Commonwealth of Nations	London	1931
World Trade Organisation (WTO)	Geneva	1995

International Organisations	*Headquarters*	*Year of Establishment*
International Development Association (IDA)	Washington D.C.	1960
International Bank for Reconstruction and Development (IBRD)	Washington D.C.	1944
World Intellectual Property Organisation (WIPO)	Geneva	1967
Organisation of Islamic Conference (OIC)	Jeddah (Saudi Arabia)	1969
Red Cross	Geneva	1863
Interpol	Lyons	1923
Asian Development Bank (ADB)	Manila	1966
North Atlantic Treaty Organisation (NATO)	Brussels	1949
Association of South East Asian Nations (ASEAN)	Jakarta	1967
South Asian Association for Regional Cooperation (SAARC)	Kathmandu	1985
Asia-Pacific Economic Cooperation (APEC)	–	1989
Organisation for Economic Cooperation and Development (OECD)	Paris	1961
Organisation of Petroleum Exporting Countries (OPEC)	Vienna	1960
Common Wealth of Independent States (CIS)	Minsk	1991
International Olympic Committee (IOC)	Switzerland	1894
European Union (EU)	Brussels	Changed form of EEC Established in 1958
Amnesty International (AI)	London	1961
Shanghai Cooperation Organisation (SCO)	Beijing	2002
BRICS Bank	Shanghai	2014

* * * * *

12 First in India

First in India

Nobel Prize for Literature (1913)	Rabindra Nath Tagore
Nobel Prize for Physics (1929)	C.V. Raman
Nobel Prize for Peace (1979)	Mother Teresa
Nobel Prize for Economics (1998)	Amartya Sen
Special Oscar award winner (1992)	Satyajit Ray
Governor-General of free India (Last also)	C. Rajagopalachari
Woman Governor of the State	Smt. Sarojini Naidu
Indian Commanders-in-Chief	General K.M. Cariappa
Woman Chief Minister of a State	Smt. Sucheta Kripalani
Woman President of United Nations General Assembly (1954)	Smt. Vijaylakshmi Pandit
President of International Court of Justice	Dr. Nagendra Singh
Woman to swim across the English Channel	Ms. Aarti Saha
Miss Universe	Miss Sushmita Sen
Miss World	Reita Faria
Indian to swim across the English Channel	Mihir Sen
Field Marshal	S.H.F.J. Manekshaw
Indian recipient of Victoria Cross	Khudadad Khan
Indian to conquer Mt. Everest	Sherpa Tenzing, May 29, 1953
Indian male cosmonaut (1984)	Rakesh Sharma
Indian female cosmonaut	Kalpana Chawla (19 Nov., 1997)
Woman to climb Mt. Everest	Miss Bachendri Pal, May 23, 1984
Woman to get Olympic Medal	Karnam Malleswari
Indian to address the UN General Assembly in Hindi	Atal Bihari Vajpayee
Newspaper	Bengal Gazette, Jan 27, 1780
Postage Stamp issued	In 1852
Telegraph line laid	In 1851, Kolkata; Diamond Harbour
Railways run	April 16, 1853; Bombay-Thana
Electric Train run	1925: Bombay-Kurla
Atomic Power Station	Tarapore (Maharashtra)
Passenger-cum-cargo ship made in India	Harshavardhan
Satellite	Aryabhatta (1975)
Rocket	Rohini (1967)
Atomic Reactor	Apsara (1956)
Climb Everest without oxygen	Phu Dorjee (1987)
First film (movie)	Raja Harishchandra (1913)
First film (talkie)	Alam Ara (1931)
Metro Railway	Kolkata Metro Railway

Test-tube baby, scientifically documented	Born on August 6, 1986 at K.E.M. Hospital, Mumbai
TV Centre	At Delhi
Indian to get an Oscar	Bhanu Athaiya
Woman pilot in IAF	Ms Harita Kaur Deol
Cellular Phone	Kolkata, August 1, 1995
Women president of Indian National Congress	Smt. Annie Besant
President of Indian National Congress	W.C. Banerjee (1885)
Indian who passed in I.C.S. Examination	Satendra Nath Tagore
Woman chief justice of High Court	Lila Saith (Himachal Pradesh)
Woman Foreign Secretary	Chokila Iyyar

First Important Officials of India

The Governor-General of free India	Lord Mountbatten
President	Dr. Rajendra Prasad
President (Female)	Pratibha Patil
Vice-President	Dr. S. Radhakrishnan
Prime Minister	Jawahar Lal Nehru
Prime Minister (Female)	Indira Gandhi
Deputy Prime Minister	Sardar Vallabhbhai Patel
Chief Justice	Harilal J. Kania
First Female Judge in Supreme Court	Smt. Meera Sahib Fatima Bibi
Speaker, Lok Sabha	Ganesh Vasudeo Mawlankar
Woman Speaker of Lok Sabha	Meira Kumar
Chief Election Commissioner	Sukumar Sen
Indian Commander-in-Chief	General K.M. Cariappa
Indian Chief of Army Staff	General Maharaj Rajendra Sinhji
Indian Chief of Air Staff	Air Marshal S. Mukherjee
Indian Chief of Naval Staff	Vice Admiral Ramdas Katari
Chief of Defence Staff (CDS)	General Bipin Rawat
Female Minister	Raj Kumari Amrit Kaur (Health Minister)
Female Governor	Sarojini Naidu (U.P.)
Female Chief Minister	Sucheta Kripalani (U.P. 1963)
Finance Commissioner	K.C. Niyogi
Leader of Opposition in Lok Sabha (Recognised)	Y.V. Chavan (Congress)
Leader of Opposition in Rajya Sabha (Recognised)	Kamalapati Tripathi (Congress)

Highest, Biggest, Largest & Longest in India

Award for Gallantry, Highest	Param Vir Chakra
Award, highest civilian	Bharat Ratna
Bank with largest number of branches	State Bank of India
River bridge, Longest	Bhupen Hazarika (across Lohit River : Assam 9.15 km)
Cantilever Span Bridge, Largest	Howrah Bridge (Kolkata)
Cattle Fair, Largest	Sonepur Fair (Bihar)
City, Most Populous	Mumbai
Corridor, Longest	Ramanathaswamy Corridor, Tamil Nadu (1,220 mt.)
Desert, Largest	Thar (Rajasthan)
Dam, Longest	Hirakud Dam (Odisha)
Dam, Highest	Tehri Dam on Bhagirathi river in Uttarakhand (855 ft.)

Delta, Largest	Sunderban (12,872 Sq. km.)
Dome, Largest	Gol Gumbaz (Bijapur)
Gateway, Highest	Buland Darwaja at Fatehpur Sikri (54 m.)
Lake, Largest (Fresh water)	Wular Lake (Kashmir)
Literacy, Highest	Kerala
Museum, Largest	Indian Museum (Kolkata)
Mosque, Biggest	Jama Masjid (Delhi)
Peak, Highest	K-2 (8,611 mt.)
Railway Platform, Longest	Shree Siddharoodha Swamiji Railway Station Hubballi, Karnataka (1507 mt.)
Railway Bridge, Largest	Vembanad Bridge, Kerala (4.6 km)
River, Longest	The Ganga river (2,525 km.)
Rainfall, Highest (annual mean)	Mowsynram near Cherrapunji (Meghalaya)
Road, Longest	NH-44 (3,745 km)
Rock-cut Temple, Largest	Kailash Temples, Ellora (Maharashtra)
State, maximum forest cover	Madhya Pradesh
State, Largest (area)	Rajasthan (3,42,239 sq. km.)
State, Most Populous	Uttar Pradesh (19,98,12,341)
State with Maximum density of population	Bihar (1106 persons per sq. km.)
Tunnel, Longest (Road)	Dr. Shyama Prasad Mukherjee Tunnel (J & K—9.28 km)
Tunnel, Longest (Railway)	T-50 Tunnel (Khari-Sumber section) (12.77 kms) (J&K)
Waterfall, Highest	Kunchikal Waterfall, Karnataka (455 m.)
Zoo, Largest	Arignar Anna Zoological Park, Chennai, Tamil Nadu
Man-made Lake, Largest	Govind Sagar (Bhakra)

Indian Banks

- **Reserve Bank of India:** It was established in 1935 and nationalised in 1949. It is the Central Bank of the country and issues all currency notes except one rupee note. It acts as a banker to the Government and exercises control over other commercial banks in the country. Headquarters of Reserve Bank of India is in Mumbai.
- **The State Bank of India:** Largest commercial bank was nationalised in 1955. Till September 2025, State Bank of India has 22,500 branches in India and world.
- **Nationalisation of Banks:** The Government of India on July 19, 1969, took over 14 biggest commercial banks incorporated in the country. On April 15, 1980, six more banks were nationalised. In March 1994, the Parliament passed the Banking Regulation (Amendment) Bill, 1994 which inter alia provided for establishment of private sector banks. Till June 2025 there were 12 public sector banks including SBI in India.

Insurance

- **Life Insurance Corporation of India:** Since September 1, 1956, when the L.I.C. of India was established, life insurance business in India is transacted by the Corporation and, in a restricted sphere by the Posts and Telegraphs Department of the Government of India and by some State Governments.
- **General Insurance Corporation of India:** It was established in November, 1972 and with effect from January, 1974 the erstwhile 107 Indian and Foreign insurers were grouped by this corporation into four operation companies, namely National Insurance, New India Assurance, Oriental Insurance and United India Insurance.

✱ ✱ ✱ ✱ ✱

13 Cultural Activities

AKADEMIES

There are three akademies for promotion of creative art.

1. **Lalit Kala Akademi, New Delhi:** Established in 1954, the Lalit Kala Akademi strives for the popularisation of Indian art within the country and in various countries of the world through exhibitions, publications, workshops and camps. Every three year it organises the Triennale India, an international exhibition. It publishes research papers on Indian arts. Besides organising seminars, it honours eminent artists. The Akademi has set up regional centres called Rashtriya Lalit Kala Kendras at Lucknow, Kolkata, Chennai and Bhubaneswar and a small office at Mumbai.
2. **Sangeet Natak Akademi, New Delhi:** The Sangeet Natak Akademi, set-up in 1953, aims at the promotion and development of dance, drama and music. It holds seminars and festivals, presents awards to the eminent artists and extends financial assistance to traditional teachers and scholarships to students. It also operates a scheme of exchange of troupes.
3. **Sahitya Akademi, New Delhi:** The Sahitya Akademi, established in 1954, has the main functions of development of Indian letters, setting up high literary standards, translation of literary works of one Indian language into other Indian languages, publication of books on history of literature and criticism, bibliographies and reference books. The Akademy has regional offices at Mumbai, Kolkata, Bengaluru and Chennai.
4. **National School of Drama:** It is one of the top theatre training institutes in the world and only one of its kind in India. It was set up in 1959 under Sangeet Natak Akademi but was later made autonomous organisation in 1975.

SCULPTURE

Archaeological Survey of India, set up in 1861, is responsible for preservation and maintenance of sculptures and historical monuments and manages a number of archaeological museums.

National Archives of India, established in 1891, it is the official custodian of all non-current records of permanent value of the Government of India and its predecessor bodies.

MUSEUMS

They are repositories of the cultural heritage and conserve and preserve historical technical and other materials against decay and transmit them to posterity as records of history.

MUSIC

Main Schools of Classical Music: There are two main schools of classical music, namely, the Hindustani and the Carnatic. The Hindustani school of classical music is in vogue in north-western India, eastern India and northern parts of the South India.

Musical Instruments: They are: Tabla, Mridangam, Pakhawaj, Chandai, Dholak, Veena, Sitar, Sarod, Gootuvadhyam, Sarangi, Flute, Nadaswaram, Shehnai, Shringi and Turahi.

DANCE

India has a very rich tradition of tribal, folk and classical dances.

Classical Dance

Dance	State	Famous Artists
Bharat Natyam	Tamil Nadu	Yamini Krishnamurthy, Rukmini Devi Arundale, Swapna Sundari, Sonal Mansingh, Vaijanti Mala, Mrinalini Sarabhai, Chandralekha, Indrani, Ram Gopal, Bal Saraswati
Kathakali	Kerala	Gopinath, K.K. Nayar, Kunju-Kurup, T.K. Chandu
Kuchipudi	Andhra Pradesh	Sapna Sundari, Raja Reddy, Shobha Nayar, Radha Reddy, Vedantam Satyanarayan, Vimpanti Chinna Satyam.
Kathak	North India	Birju Maharaj, Gopi Krishna, Shambhu Maharaj, Sitara Devi, Vishnu Sharma, Durga Lal, Shobhana Narayan
Odissi	Odisha	Kelucharan Mahapatra, Indrani Rehman, Madhavi Mudgal, Protima Bedi, Samyukta Panigrahi, Sonal Mansingh, Debudas
Manipuri	Manipur	Uday Shankar, Bipin Singh, Suryamukhi, Darohra Jhaveri

Famous Folk-Dance

State	Folk Dance
Andhra Pradesh	Dandari, Banjara
Asom	Bihu, Keli Gopal, Sataria
Bihar	Chhau, Magahi, Durga dance
W. Bengal	Kirtan, Kalatri, Asweabadh, Brita, Kalidance
Chhattisgarh	Saila, Karama, Bhagoria
Gujarat	Garba, Rasalila, Tippani, Dandia,
Haryana	Damyal, Lahoor
Himachal Pradesh	Dussehra dance, Hikat, Notio
Jammu & Kashmir	Dumhal
Jharkhand	Jhau, Ghumakudia, Jadur, Sarhul, Soharai, Karama, Vaima, Loojhari, Jat-Jatin, Vidayat
Karnataka	Yakshagan, Dolu Kunitha
Kerala	Mohini Attam, Padayuni
Madhya Pradesh	Lota Nritya, Jawara
Maharashtra	Tamasha, Dahi Handi, Gof, Deepak Dindi
Manipur	Dhol Cholam
Meghalaya	Nongakarem
Nagaland	Bamboo dance
Odisha	Chhau, Maya Shabari, Dalachai
Punjab	Gidda, Bhangra, Panihari
Rajasthan	Thumar, Kathaputali, Tera Tali
Tamil Nadu	Terukalathu, Kabalatam, Kargam, Pulivesham
Tripura	Hazagiri
Uttar Pradesh	Rasalila, Nautanki, Thali, Dhurang, Jhumela, Huraka, Bol.
Uttarakhand	Kajari, Karan
Goa	Dhode Modini

Musical Instruments and Artists

Musical Instrument	*Artists*	*Musical Instrument*	*Artists*
Flute	Hari Prasad Chaurasia, Panna Lal Ghosh, T.R. Mahalingam, N. Ramani, Vijaya Raghava Rao	Sitar	Pandit Ravishankar, Vilayat Khan
		Santur	Shiv Kumar Sharma
		Rudraveena	Zia Mohiuddin Dagar
Tabla	Allah Rakha, Gudai Maharaj, Latif Khan, Zakir Hussain	Pakhawaj	Govind Rao, Anokhe Lal, Kanthi Maharaj
		Mridanga	Palghat R. Raghu, U.S. Burman
Violin	Lalgudi Jayaraman, L. Subramaniam, M.S. Gopal Krishnan, S. Subrahmaniam, V.G. Jog, N. Rajan	Harmonium	Purushottam Walawakar, M. Dhaulpuri
		Guitar	Pt. Vishnu Mohan Bhatt, Brij Bhushan Kalra
Shehnai	Bismilla Khan, Imrat Khan Ali Akbar	Ghatam	T.H. Vinayakaram
Sarod	Khan, Amjad Ali Khan, Alauddin Khan, Saren Rani, Brij Narayan	Janjira	V. Nagarajan
		Symphony	Jubin Mehta

Wild Life Sanctuary in India

India is rich in flora and fauna. However, due to increasing population and industrial and commercial activities, there has been acute pressure on forests. The Government has taken several steps to check the sharp fall in the number of these species. Among the measures are declaration of certain habitats as national parks and sanctuaries. 106 national parks and 573 sanctuaries have been established till June 2025, important ones being given below:

Assam: Kaziranga National Park (know for one-horn Rhinoceroses); Manas Sanctuary.
Jharkhand: Hazaribagh National Park; Betla Tiger Reserve Palamau.
Gujarat: Valvadar National Park, Bhavnagar; Marine National Park, Gir Forests.
Himachal Pradesh: Rohla National Park; Motichur Sanctuary.
Jammu & Kashmir: Dachigam Sanctuary.
Karnataka: Bandipur National Park; Bannargheta National Park, Bangalore; Nagorhole National Park, Coorg; Ranganthitto Bird Sanctuary.
Kerala: Eravikulam Rajmallay National Park, Idduki; Periyar Game Sanctuary.
Madhya Pradesh: Kanha National Park; Bandhavgarh National Park, Shahdol; Shivpuri National Park.
Maharashtra: Taloba National Park, Chandrapur; Panch National Park, Nagpur; Borivali National Park, Mumbai; Nawagaon National Park, Bandara; Melghat National Park.
Manipur: Reibul Lamjao National Park.
Odisha: Simlipal, Tiger Sanctuary.
Rajasthan: Sariska Sanctuary; Ghana Bird Sanctuary, Ranthambhor Sanctuary.
Sikkim: Khangchandzenda National Park, Gangtok.
Tamil Nadu: Vedanthangal Bird Sanctuary; Guindy National Park, Chennai; Mudumalai Sanctuary; Kalakad-Munden Thurai Reserve.
Uttar Pradesh: Chandraprabha Sanctuary; Dudhwa National Park, Lakhimpur.
West Bengal: Jaldapara Sanctuary; Sunderbans.
Uttarakhand: Corbett National Park; Nainital.

✵ ✵ ✵ ✵ ✵

14 Awards

NATIONAL AWARDS

★ **Bharat Ratna:** This is India's highest civilian award. It is given for exceptional work on art, literature, science and recognition of public service of the highest order. Government servants are not eligible for it.

★ **Padma Vibhushan:** This award is given for exceptional and distinguished service in any field, including service rendered by Govt. servants.

★ **Padma Bhushan:** This award is given for distinguished service of a high order in any field, including service rendered by Govt. servants.

★ **Padma Shri:** This award is given for distinguished service in any field, including service rendered by Government servants.

GALLANTRY AWARDS

★ **Param Vir Chakra:** The highest award for bravery or some daring and pre-eminent act of valour or self-sacrifice in the presence of the enemy, whether on land, at sea or in the air.

★ **Mahavir Chakra:** It is the second highest decoration and is awarded for acts of conspicuous gallantry in the presence of the enemy, whether on land, at sea or in the air.

★ **Vir Chakra:** It is the third in order of awards given for acts of gallantry in the presence of enemy, whether on land, at sea or in the air.

★ **Ashok Chakra:** This medal is awarded for the most conspicuous bravery or some daring or pre-eminent act of valour or self-sacrifice on land, at sea or in the air but not in the presence of enemy.

★ **Vishishta Sewa Medal:** It is awarded to personnel of all the three Services in class I, II and III in recognition of distinguished service of the "most exceptional" and "exceptional" and a "high" order respectively. Prefixes *Parma* and *Ati* are added before first two categories of medals respectively.

★ **Jeewan Raksha Padak:** Awarded for meritorious acts or a series of acts of a human nature displayed in saving life from drowning, fire and rescue operations in mines etc.

National Sports Awards

★ **Major Dhyan Chand Khel Ratna Award:** The scheme was launched in the year 1991-92 with the objective of honouring sportspersons to enhance their general status and to give them greater dignity and place of honour in society. Under this scheme, an amount of ₹ 25 lakh is given as award for the most spectacular and outstanding performance by a sportsperson over a period of four years immediately preceding the year in which award is to be given.

★ **Dronacharya Award:** Dronacharya Award is an award presented by ministry of youth Affairs and Sports, Government of India for excellence in sports coaching. The Dronacharya (Lifetime) awardees gets ₹ 15 lakh and Dronacharya (Regular) awardees gets ₹ 10 lakh a bronze statuette of Dronacharya and scroll of honour. The award was instituted in 1985.

★ **Arjuna Award:** The Arjuna Awards are given by the ministry of youth Affairs and sports, government of India to recognize outstanding achievement in National sports. Instituted in 1961 the award carries a cash prize of 15,00,000 a bronze statue of Arjuna and a scroll.

★ **Arjuna Award (Lifetime):** Arjuna Award (Lifetime) is India's highest award for lifetime achievement in sports and games, given by the ministry of youth Affairs and sports, government of India. The award is initiated in 2002. The award carries a cash prize of ₹ 10,00,000 a plaque and a scroll of honour.

★ **Maulana Abul Kalam Azad Trophy:** This trophy was instituted in 1956-57. The top overall performing university in the inter-university tournaments is given the Maulana Abul Kalam Azad (MAKA) Trophy, which is a rolling trophy. A small replica of the MAKA Trophy is also awarded for retention by the university. In addition, the university also gets a cash prize of ₹ 15 lakh. The second and third best universities also receive cash awards amounting to ₹ 5 lakh and ₹ 3 lakh respectively.

Other Awards

★ **Jnanpith Award:** Awarded to outstanding authors of creative literature in any of the Indian languages recognised by the Constitution of India. It was sponsored by the Bharatiya Jnanpith a culturo-literary society founded in 1944 by Shanti Prasad Jain, an eminent industrialist.

★ **Sahitya Akademi Award:** It is awarded for outstanding literary works and comprises a cash prize of ₹ 1,00,000 in each of the 22 languages mentioned in the Eighth schedule of the Constitution and Rajasthani and English that it supports and a copper plaque.

★ **Saraswati Samman:** The award is given by K.K. Birla Foundation to an outstanding author for his literary work in any Indian language mentioned in the Eighth Schedule of the Constitution and published during the last 10 years.

★ **Dada Saheb Phalke Award:** The prestigious Dada Saheb Phalke Award is given to the persons for outstanding contribution to the growth and development of Indian cinema. First presented in 1969, the award was introduced by the government of India to commemorate Dadasaheb Phalke's contribution to Indian Cinema. Phalke, who is popularly known as and often regarded as a the Father of Indian Cinema was an Indian film-maker who directed India's first-length feature film, Raja Harishchandra. The first recipient of the award was actress Devika Rani, who was honoured at the 17th National film Awards.

★ **Indira Gandhi Award:** The award has been instituted for promoting national integration and understanding amongst the religious groups, communities and ethnic groups of India.

★ **Bhartendu Harishchandra Awards:** The Bhartendu Harishchandra Awards were instituted in 1983, by the Ministry of Information and Broadcasting for original Hindi writing on any subject in mass communications like journalism, publication, advertising, broadcasting films, etc.

INTERNATIONAL AWARDS

★ **Nobel Prizes:** The most prestigious award in the world is supported by the Nobel Foundation of US. This award was set up in 1900 under the will to Alfred Bernhard Nobel (1833-96). Alfred Nobel was an unmarried, Swedish scientist and chemical engineer who discovered Nitroglycerin ($C_3H_5N_3O_9$) and its use in the manufacture of dynamite in 1966. The interest accrued on the fortune left by him is divided annually among the persons who have made outstanding contribution in science, literature, peace and economics. Swedes found out about the prizes only after his death in 1896. When they read his will in which he had donated the annual income from his fortune to support the awards. In his will he ordered that 'the most worthy shall receive the prize, whether he is Scandinavian or not. This led to his criticism as being unpatriotic for not reserving the prizes only for Swedes.

Nobel Foundation's Prize Awarding Bodies

(*i*) The Royal Swedish Academy of Sciences, awards the Nobel prize in Physics and Chemistry.

(*ii*) The Nobel Assembly of Karolinska Chirugical Institute. Sweden, awards the Nobel Prize in Medicine and Physiology.

(*iii*) The Swedish Academy awards the Prize in Literature.

(*iv*) The Committee of the Norwegian Parliament awards the Prize for Peace.

(*v*) The Bank of Sweden awards the Nobel Prize in Economics.

★ **Ramon Magsaysay Award:** The Raman Magsaysay Award, named after a Philippines President, who died in an air crash in 1957, is given annually to Asian nationals or institutions who have made worthy contributions to public service, community leadership, journalism, literature and the creative arts and international understanding. It carries a gold medal, a certificate and US$ 50,000.

★ **Pulitzer Prize:** Instituted in 1970 and named after the US publisher Joseph Pulitzer (1847-1911). It is conferred annually in the United States for accomplishment in journalism, literature and music under the management to the Pulitzer Prize Board at Columbia University.

★ **Man Booker Prize:** Instituted in 1968, it is the highest literary award set up by the Booker Company and the British Publishers Association along the lines of the Pultizer Prize, of USA, worth £ 20,000 (1992). Since 2002, it has been known as the **'Man Booker Prize'**, reflecting the sponsorship by an investment company, the Man Group plc. The winner receives £ 50,000 and both the winner and the shorlisted authors are guaranteed a world wide readership plus a dramatic increase in book sales.

★ **Oscar Awards:** The annual Oscar presentation has been held since 1929. After three-quarters of a century of recognizing excellence in cinema achievement, the annual presentation of the Oscars has become the Academy of Motion Picture Arts and Sciences' most famous activity.

★ **Kalinga Award:** The award given for popularisation of science is an international award conferred annually by the United Nations Educational, Scientific and Cultural Organisation (UNESCO) to a person with a distinguished career of service in the interpretation of science and research to the public. The award was instituted in 1952 at the initiative of Mr Biju Patnaik the founder of the Kalinga Foundation Trust in Odisha.

★ **Grammy Award:** The Grammy Foundation was established in 1989 to cultivate an awareness, appreciation and advancement of the contribution of recorded music American culture from the and technical legends of the past to the still unimagined musical breakthroughs of the future generations of the music professionals. The Grammy Foundation works in partnership with its founder, the Recording Academy, to bring national attention to important issues such as the value and impact of music and arts education and the urgency of preserving our rich cultural legacy.

Highest Honours of Some Countries

Country	*Highest Honour*
India	Bharat Ratna
Pakistan	Nishan-e-Pakistan
Kuwait	Mubarak-Al-kabir Medal
Saudi Arabia	Shah Abdul Aziz Medal
Argentina	The Order of Sona Martin
Nicaragua	Augusto-Caesar Sandino Order
Vietnam	The order of the Golden Star
Hungary	The Order of Banner
Britain	Member of British Empire, Victoria Cross
Japan	Order of Moulovenice Sun
Denmark	Order of Diana Brog
France	Legend of Honour
America	Presidential Medal of Freedom
Germany	Pore Lee Merit Iron Cross
The Netherlands	Netherlands Lion

✱ ✱ ✱ ✱ ✱

15 Sports

Important Cups & Trophies

International

• *American Cup*	:	Yacht Racing	• *Walker Cup*	:	Golf
• *Ashes*	:	Cricket	• *Westchester Cup*	:	Polo
• *Benson and Hedges*	:	Cricket	• *Wightman Cup*	:	Lawn Tennis
• *Canada Cup*	:	Golf	• *World Cup*	:	Cricket
• *Colombo Cup*	:	Football	• *World Cup*	:	Hockey
• *Corbitton Cup*	:	Table Tennis (Women)	• *Reliance Cup*	:	Cricket
• *Davis Cup*	:	Lawn Tennis	• *Rothman's Trophy*	:	Cricket
• *Derby*	:	Horse Race	• *William's Cup*	:	Basketball
• *Grand National*	:	Horse Streple Chase Race	• *European Champions Cup*	:	Football
• *Jules Rimet Trophy*	:	World Soccer Cup	• *Eisenhower Cup*	:	Golf
• *King's Cup*	:	Air Races	• *Essande Champions Cup*	:	Hockey
• *Merdeka Cup*	:	Football	• *Rene Frank Trophy*	:	Hockey
• *Ryder Cup*	:	Golf	• *Grand Prix*	:	Table Tennis
• *Swaythling Cup*	:	Table Tennis (Men)	• *Edgbaston Cup*	:	Lawn Tennis
• *Thomas Cup*	:	Badminton	• *Grand Prix*	:	Lawn Tennis
• *Uber Cup*	:	Badminton (Women)	• *World Cup*	:	Weightlifting
• *U. Thant Cup*	:	Tennis			

National

• *Agarwal Cup*	:	Badminton	• *C.K. Naidu Trophy*	:	Cricket
• *Agha Khan Cup*	:	Hockey	• *Chakola Gold Trophy*	:	Football
• *All India Women's Guru Nanak Championship*	:	Hockey	• *Divan Cup*	:	Badminton
• *Bandodkar Trophy*	:	Football	• *Deodhar Trophy*	:	Cricket
• *Bangalore Blues Challenge Cup*	:	Basketball	• *Duleep Trophy*	:	Cricket
• *Barna-Bellack Cup*	:	Table Tennis	• *D.C.M. Cup*	:	Football
• *Beighton Cup*	:	Hockey	• *Durand Cup*	:	Football
• *Bombay Gold Cup*	:	Hockey	• *Dhyan Chand Trophy*	:	Hockey
• *Burdwan Trophy*	:	Weightlifting	• *Dr. B.C. Roy Trophy*	:	Football (Junior)
• *Charminar Trophy*	:	Atheletics	• *Ezra Cup*	:	Polo
• *Chadha Cup*	:	Badminton	• *F.A. Cup*	:	Football
			• *G.D. Birla Trophy*	:	Cricket
			• *Ghulam Ahmed Trophy*	:	Cricket
			• *Gurmeet Trophy*	:	Hockey

- *Guru Nanak Cup* : Hockey
- *Gyanvati Devi Trophy* : Hockey
- *Holkar Trophy* : Bridge
- *Irani Trophy* : Cricket
- *I.F.A. Shield* : Football
- *Indira Gold Cup* : Hockey
- *Jawaharlal Challenge* : Air Racing
- *Jaswant Singh Trophy* : Best Services Sportsman
- *Kuppuswamy Naidu Trophy* : Hockey
- *Lady Rattan Tata Trophy* : Hockey
- *MCC Trophy* : Hockey
- *Moinuddaula Gold Cup* : Cricket
- *Murugappa Gold Cup* : Hockey
- *Modi Gold Cup* : Hockey
- *Narang Cup* : Badminton
- *Nehru Trophy* : Hockey
- *Nixan Gold Cup* : Football
- *Obaidullah Gold Cup* : Hockey
- *Prithi Singh Cup* : Polo
- *Rani Jhansi Trophy* : Cricket
- *Ranji Trophy* : Cricket
- *Rangaswami Cup* : Hockey
- *Ranjit Singh Gold Cup* : Hockey
- *Rajendra Prasad Cup* : Tennis
- *Ramanujan Trophy* : Table Tennis
- *Rene Frank Trophy* : Hockey
- *Radha Mohan Cup* : Polo
- *Raghbir Singh Memorial* : Football
- *Rohinton Baria Trophy* : Cricket
- *Rovers Cup* : Football
- *Sanjay Gold Cup* : Football
- *Santosh Trophy* : Football
- *Sir Ashutosh Mukherjee* : Football
- *Subroto Cup* : Football
- *Scindia Gold Cup* : Hockey
- *Sahni Trophy* : Hockey
- *Sheesh Mahal Trophy* : Cricket
- *Todd Memorial Trophy* : Football
- *Tommy Eman Gold Cup* : Hockey
- *Vittal Trophy* : Football
- *Vizzy Trophy* : Cricket
- *Vijay Merchant Trophy* : Cricket
- *Wellington Trophy* : Rowing
- *Wills Trophy* : Cricket

Sports Measurements

- *Badminton Courts:* 44 ft. by 20 ft. (doubles) 44 ft. by 17 ft. (singles)
- *Boxing Ring:* 12 ft. by 28 ft. Sq.
- *Cricket Pitch:* 22 yards (distance)
- *Derby Course:* 1½ miles. (2.4 km)
- *Football Field:*
  (a) Length : 100 – 120 yards.
  Breadth: 50 – 56 yards.
  (b) Rugby : 100 yards by 75 yards
- *Hockey Ground:* 100 yards by 55 to 60 yards
- *Lawn Tennis Court:* 78 ft. by 36 ft. (double), 78 ft. by 28 ft. (single)
- *Marathon Race:* 26 miles, 385 yards
- *Polo Ground:* 300 yards by 200 yards (if boarded)
- *Golf:* Hole 4½ inches in diameter.

Sports Terms

- **Badminton:** Mixed doubles; Deuce; Drop; Smash; Let; Foot work; Setting.
- **Base Ball:** Pitcher; Put out, Strike; Home; Bunt.
- **Billiards:** Cue; Jigger; Pot; Break; In Baulk; In Off; Cannons.
- **Boxing:** Upper cut; Round; Punch; Bout; Knock down; Hitting below the belt; Ring.
- **Bridge:** Finesse; Dummy; Revoke; Grand Slam; Little Slam; No Trump; Rubber.
- **Chess:** Bishop, Gambit; Checkmate; Stalemate.
- **Cricket:** L.B.W. *(leg before wicket)*; Creases, Popping-creases; Stumped; Bye; Leg-Bye; Googly; Hattrick; Maiden over; Drive; Bowling; Duck; Follow-on; No ball; Leg Break; Silly point; Cover point; Hit-wicket; Late-cut; Slip; Off-spinner.
- **Football:** Off Side; Block; Drop-kick; Penalty-kick (or *goal kick*); Corner-kick; Free-kick; Dribble; Thrown-in; Foul.
- **Golf:** Boggy; Foursome; Stymic; Tee; Put; Hole; Niblic; Caddie; Links; The green; Bunker.
- **Hockey:** Carried; Short Corner; Bully; Sticks; Off side; Roll in; Striking Circle; Under-cutting.
- **Horse racing:** Jockey; Punter.
- **Polo:** Bunker; Chukker; Mallet.
- **Tennis:** Back hand drive; Volley; Smash; Half-volley; Deuce; Service; Let; Grand Slam.

Name of Playing Compound of Different Games

Name of Compound	*Related Sports*	*Name of Compound*	*Related Sports*
Court	Lawn Tennis, Badminton, Netball, Hand ball, Volleyball, Squash, Kho-Kho, Kabaddi	Pool	Swimming
		Alley	Bowling
		Mat	Judo, Karate II
Diamond	Baseball	Arena	Horse Riding
Ring	Boxing, Skating, Wrestling, Circus, Riding display	Vellodrum	Cycling
		Field	Polo, Football, Hockey
		Track	Athletics
Course	Golf	Pitch	Cricket, Rugby
Board	Table Tennis	Rink	Ice Hockey

National Sports and Games of Some Countries

Australia	Cricket	Spain	Bull Fighting
Canada	Ice Hockey	USA	Baseball
England	Cricket and Rugby Football	China	Table Tennis
Russia	Chess	Malaysia	Badminton
Scotland	Rugby Football	Pakistan	Hockey

OLYMPIC GAMES

First of all these games were held by the Greeks in 776 B.C. on Mount Olympus in honour of the Greek God Zeus. In this way, the history of Olympic Games is about twenty eight hundred years old. These games continued to be held every four years until 394 A.D. When these games were stopped by a royal order of the emperor of Rome. The modern Olympic Games which started in Athens in 1896, are the result of the devotion and dedication of a French educator Baron Pierre de Coubertin and the first Olympic meet in the modern series was held in 1896 in Athens, the Capital of Greece. Since then, they are being held every four years except for breaks during world wars. The Olympic flag is white in colour with five coloured rings, each ring symbolic of a continent. Summer as well as winter Olympics are held in the same year.

COMMONWEALTH GAMES

The Commonwealth Games are held every four years, in the year in which Asian Games are held. All the Commonwealth Countries (former colonies of Britain) can take part in it. The first Commonwealth Games were held in 1930 at Hamilton (Canada).

ASIAN GAMES

After the Second World War, most of the Asian Countries gained independence. On the lines of Olympic Games, Asian Games were planned every four years. India hosted the first Asian Games in 1951.

CRICKET WORLD CUP

The first Cricket World Cup was organised in England in 1975. A separate women's Cricket World Cup has been held every 4 years since 1973. Australia is the winner of 2023 Cricket World Cup.

HOCKEY WORLD CUP

The first Hockey World Cup was organised in Barcelona (Spain) in 1971. Women's Hockey World Cup has been held since 1974.

FOOTBALL WORLD CUP

The Football World Cup is organised by FIFA (Federation of International Football Association). The World Cup is called 'Jules Rimet Cup' named after the name of FIFA President Jules Rimet. The first Football World Cup was organised in Uruguay in 1930.

Personalities Associated with Sports

- **Athletics:** Carl Lewis, Linford Christy, Ben Johnson, Calvin Smith, Edwin Moses, Sergei Bubka, Sebestian Coe, Rosa Mota, Harold Schmidt, Milkha Singh, P.T. Usha, Shiny Abraham, Jesse Owens, Jyotirmoy Sikdar.
- **Boxing:** Cassius Clay (Mohammad Ali), Joe Frazier, Mike Tyson, Larry Holmes, Frank Bruno, Henry Cooper, Archie Moore, Evander Holyfield, George Foreman.
- **Badminton:** Prakash Padukone, Syed Modi, Dinesh Khanna, Jamie Paulson, Nandu Natekar, Liem Swie King, Saina Nehwal, P.V. Sindhu.
- **Billiards:** Wilson Jones, Geet Sethi, Michael Ferreira, Pankaj Advani.
- **Chess:** Boris Spausky, Gary Kasparov, Anatoly Karpov, Victor Korchonoi, Vishwanathan Anand, Konern Humpy, Parveen Thipsay.
- **Cricket:** Sunil Gavaskar, Bishen Singh Bedi, Kapil Dev, Mohd. Azharuddin, Sachin Tendulkar, G.R. Vishwanath, Lala Amarnath, Ajit Wadekar, B.S. Chandrashekhar, E.A.S. Prasanna, S. Venkatraghvan, Don Bradman, Richard Hadlee, Gary Sobers, Ian Botham, Vivian Richards, Clive Llyod, Dilip Sardesai, Charles Griffith, Imran Khan, Mushtaq Mohammad, Geoff Boycott, Tony Greg, Wasim Akram, Richie Benaud, Michael Holding, Greg Chappell, Javed Miandad, Vijay Manjrekar, M.A.K. Pataudi, S.M.H. Kirmani, Bill Lawry, Clive Rice, Mark Taylor, Joel Garner, Arjuna Ranatunga, Arvinda De'Silva, Saurav Ganguly, Virat Kohli, M.S. Dhoni, Ajit Agarkar, Jacques Kallis, John Traicos, W.R. Hammond, Sanath Jaisurya.
- **Hockey:** Dhyan Chand, Ashok Kumar, Ajit Singh, Pargat Singh, Pritpal Singh, Zafar Iqbal, Shankar Laxman, Mervyn Fernandes, Mohammad Shahid, R. Charlesworth, Balbir Singh, Terry Walsh, Kishan Lal, Udlam Singh, Dhanraj Pillai.
- **Football:** Pele, Diego Maradona, Franz Beckenbour, Socrates, Raud Gullit, Garry Linekar, Emilo Butraguino, Coreca, P.C. Bannerji, Arunlal Ghosh, Chuni Goswami, Davor Suker, Ronaldo, Rivaldo, Deschamps.
- **Tennis (Lawn):** Bjorn Borg, Jimmy Connors, John Mcenroe, Ivan Lendl, Pete Sampras, Billie Jean Kings, Chris Evert Lloyd, Martina Navratilova, Steffi Graf, Stefan Edberg, Andre Agassi, Michael Chang, Boris Becker, Leander Paes, Vijay Amritraj, Anand Amritraj, Jaideep Mukherjee, Rod Laver, Roy Emerson, Naresh Kumar, Premjit Lall, Martina Hingis, Mary Pierce, Jana Novotna, Rozer Federer.
- **Golf:** Greg Norman, Jack Nikalus, Sandy Lyle, Seve Bellestros, Nick Faldo, Nick Price, Sher Ali, Jeeve Milkha Singh, S. Choudhary, R.K. Pitamber, Vikramjit Singh.
- **Gymnastics:** Nadia Comaneci, L. Latynina, V. Kaslavska, E. Szebo, W. Kim. Y. Ma, Y. Shrusunova, Daniela Silivas, A. Braglia, V. Chukarin, N. Andrianov, Sergi Kharkhov.
- **Swimming:** Arti Gupta, Arun Kumar Shaw, Baidyanath, Mihir Sen, Aarti Saha, Mark Spitz.
- **Wrestling:** Dara Singh, Bhim Sen, Mukhtiar Singh, Sudesh Kumar, Chandagi Ram.

Stadia in Various Cities of India

- **Delhi:** Ambedkar Stadium, Arun Jaitley Stadium, Jawaharlal Nehru Stadium, Indira Gandhi Indoor Stadium, Shivaji Stadium, National Stadium.
- **Mumbai:** Brabourne Stadium, Wankhede Stadium.
- **Kolkata:** Eden Gardens, Salt Lake Stadium, Ranjit Stadium, Subhas Sarovar.
- **Chennai:** Nehru Stadium, Chidambaram Stadium, Chepauk.
- **Cuttack:** Barabati Stadium.
- **Kanpur:** Green Park.
- **Jamshedpur:** Keenan Stadium.
- **Nagpur:** Vidarbha CA Ground
- **Jaipur:** Swai Mansingh Stadium
- **Gwalior:** Roop Singh Stadium
- **Vadodara:** Moti Bagh Stadium
- **Patna:** Moin-ul-Haq Stadium
- **Hyderabad:** Lal Bahadur Stadium
- **Patiala:** Yaduvindra Stadium.
- **Bengaluru:** Chinnaswami Stadium.
- **Siliguri:** Kanchenjunga Stadium.
- **Vishakhapatnam:** Indira Priyadarshini Stadium.

* * * * *

16 National/International Days

JANUARY

Infant Protection Day	: January 7
African National Congress Foundation Day	: January 8
NRI Day (India)	: January 9
World Laughter Day	: January 10
National Youth Day (India)	: January 12
Army Day (India)	: January 15
Indian Tourism Day	: January 25
Republic Day (India); International Customs Day	: January 26
Martyrs' Day (India); World Leprosy Eradication Day	: January 30

FEBRUARY

World Wetlands Day	: February 2
World Marriage Day	: Second Sunday of February
Valentine Day (World)	: February 14
Mother Tongue Day (World)	: February 21
National Science Day (India)	: February 28

MARCH

International Women's Day;	: March 8
World Disabled Day : World Consumer Rights Day	: March 15
World Forestry Day; International Day for Elimination of Racial Discrimination	: March 21
World Day for Water	: March 22
World Meteorological Day	: March 23
World TB Day	: March 24

APRIL

National Maritime Day (India)	: April 5
World Health Day	: April 7
World Aviation and Cosmonautics Day	: April 12
World Haemophilia Day	: April 17
World Heritage Day,	: April 18
Earth Day (World)	: April 22
World Book and Copyright Day	: April 23

MAY

Workers' Day (International Labour Day)	: May 1
Press Freedom Day; World Asthma Day	: May 3
World Red Cross Day	: May 8
World Mother's Day (2nd Sunday of May)	: May 8
World Thalassaemia Day	: May 9
National Technology Day	: May 11
International Nurses Day	: May 12
International Day of the Family	: May 15
World Telecommunication Day	: May 17
Anti-Terrorism Day	: May 21
Commonwealth Day	: May 24
Anti-Tobacco Day	: May 31

JUNE

International Day of Innocent Children Victims of Aggression	: June 4
World Environment Day	: June 5
Father's Day (3rd Sunday of June)	: June 19
International Yoga Day	: June 21
International Day Against Drug Abuse & Illicit Trafficking	: June 26

JULY

Doctors' Day	: July 1
American Independence Day	: July 4
World Zoonosis Day	: July 6
World Population Day	: July 11

AUGUST

World Breast Feeding Week	: August 1-7
International Friendship Day	: August 3
Hiroshima Day	: August 6
World Senior Citizen's Day	: August 8
Quit India Day; Nagasaki Day	: August 9
Indian Independence Day	: August 15
International Day of the World's Indigenous People	: August 18
Sadbhavna Divas (India)	: August 20
National Sports Day (India)	: August 29

SEPTEMBER

World Yoga Day	: September 2
Teachers' Day	: September 5
World (International) Literacy Day	: September 8
Hindi Day (India)	: September 14
All India Flag Day	: September 15
World Ozone Day	: September 16
Alzheimer's Day (World)	: September 21
Day for Peace & Non-Violence (UN)	: September 21
Rose Day (Welfare of Cancer Patients) World Heart Day	: September 22
International Tiger Day	: September 25
World Tourism Day	: September 27

OCTOBER

International Day for the Elderly People	: October 1
Gandhi Jayanti, International Day of Non-Violence	: October 2
World Animal Day	: October 2
World Vegetarian Day	: October 2
World Habitat Day	: October 3
World Animal Welfare Day	: October 4
World Post Office Day	: October 9
National Post Day (India)	: October 10
World Allergy Awareness Day	: October 11
UN International Day for Natural Disaster Reduction	: October 13
World Standards Day	: October 14
World Food Day	: October 16
International Day for the Eradication of Poverty	: October 17
UN Day	: October 24
World Development Information Day	: October 24
Infants Day	: October 27
World Thrift Day	: October 30
National Integration Day (India)	: October 31

NOVEMBER

Legal Services Day	: November 9
Children's Day (India)	: November 14
Diabetes Day	: November 14
National Epilepsy Day	: November 17

DECEMBER

World AIDS Day	: December 1
World Disabled Day	: December 3
International Volunteer Develompent Day	: December 5
Armed Forces Flag Day (India)	: December 7
Human Rights Day (World)	: December 10
National Energy Conservation Day	: December 14
Farmer's Day	: December 23

* * * * *

17 Multiple Choice Questions

1. The part of the Sun, which is visible during eclipses only, is known as
   A. photosphere
   B. chromosphere
   C. corona
   D. all the parts are visible with naked eye
2. Sphygmomanometer is used for
   A. measuring the brain pulse of a patient
   B. measuring the systolic and diastolic blood pressures of man
   C. measuring the amount of blood in a human body
   D. measuring the haemoglobin count in a human body
3. The most abundant gas in air is
   A. nitrogen B. hydrogen
   C. oxygen D. ozone
4. The most commonly found acid in nature is
   A. hydrochloric acid
   B. sulphuric acid
   C. lactic acid
   D. acetic acid
5. This bomb is used to destroy living beings but would not damage the buildings and other property
   A. napalm bomb
   B. neutron bomb
   C. hydrogen bomb
   D. None of the above
6. Electrical energy is measured in terms of units which are also termed as
   A. KW B. KWH
   C. WH D. KVAR
7. In cold countries, the radiator water of cars is mixed with glycerol. This is done to
   A. increase the specific heat of water
   B. reduce the freezing point of water
   C. improve the engine efficiency
   D. glycerol is not added in radiator water
8. If the Richter scale shows a value of 7.2, then the seismograph indicates
   A. an earthquake of low intensity
   B. an earthquake of very high intensity
   C. an earthquake of moderate intensity
   D. either A or C
9. The theory of origin of species is based primarily on
   A. the process of biological evolution
   B. the process of natural selection
   C. the evolution of life from the oceans
   D. the evolution of man from apes
10. Common coal used in our households is
    A. Anthracite B. Bituminous coal
    C. Lignite D. All of the above
11. Some recent findings on moon, which point out towards the possibility of settlement of man on moon, include
    A. nil atmospheric gases
    B. ice reserves on the poles
    C. micro-organisms
    D. None of the above
12. Viagra is a medicine for
    A. treatment of AIDS
    B. treatment of female fertility
    C. treatment of male impotency
    D. treatment of Lukaemia
13. Rickets is a disease which is caused by the deficiency of
    A. Vitamin A B. Riboflavin
    C. Vitamin C D. Vitamin D
14. When a ship enters waters of the sea from a river, then its level
    A. rises as the sea water is saline and hence bouyancy force is more

B. decreases as ocean is a large mass of water
C. remains the same as water is the same for the river and the sea
D. None of the above

15. The major constituent of pearl is
A. calcium carbonate
B. calcium oxide and ammonium chloride
C. organic mass
D. calcium carbonate and silica

16. A healthy person needs ..... calories per day.
A. 2200 B. 2400
C. 2500 D. 1800

17. The value of one (marine) Naut is
A. 1951 metre per hour
B. 1852 metre per hour
C. 2305 metre per hour
D. 1860 metre per hour

18. Acid and base combine to form
A. salt and nitrogen
B. nitrogen and oxygen
C. salt and water
D. acid and alkali

19. Cellulose could be obtained from
A. wood and cotton B. silk and cotton
C. paper and silk D. wood and silk

20. ELISA test is done for the detection of
A. cancer B. AIDS
C. diabetes D. None of the above

21. Triple Antigen, prevents
A. small pox, malaria, whooping cough
B. tetanus, diphtheria, small pox
C. whooping cough, tetanus, polio
D. diphtheria, tetanus, whooping cough

22. A freely falling body
A. would fall towards the surface of the earth
B. would have no weight
C. would have one half of its original weight
D. None of the above

23. If the motor neurons of the spinal cord of a child are damaged, then he would develop the following disease.
A. Rickets B. Polio
C. Diphtheria D. Jaundice

24. Which one of the following is not a part of the balanced diet?
A. Vitamins B. Carbohydrate
C. Proteins D. Alcohol

25. Which statement is not correct in connection with human physiology?
A. The length of the small intestine is 7 metres and its diameter is 2.5 cm.
B. There are 639 muscles in a human body
C. An infant breathes 45 times per minute whereas a six year old child breathes 25 times per minute
D. The weight of the adult human brain is nearly 700 gms

26. The bottles of beer are not kept in the deep freezer because
A. beer is an alcohol which could burst under conditions of low temperature
B. alcohol could damage the deep freezer due to its corrosive action if the bottles break accidently
C. water content in beer gets converted into ice which expends (after change of state from water to ice) and this could lead to bursting of beer bottles
D. the low temperature could degrade the beer and hence, it may not good remain for consumption

27. Rocket works on the basis of
A. principle of conservation of momentum
B. principle of relativity
C. principle of conservation of mass
D. principle of conservation of energy

28. Which one of the following groups is more closely related from the viewpoint of taxonomy?
A. silverfish, starfish, cuttlefish
B. earthworm, seahorse, hookworm
C. housefly, dragonfly, butterfly
D. None of the above

29. Red blood corpuscles are produced in
A. liver B. spleen
C. bone marrow D. kidneys

30. The disease for which the first oral drug has been developed for treatment.
A. Cancer B. Pneumonid
C. Small pox D. Plauge

31. E-comm is a short form of
A. Engineering Commercial
B. Electronic Commercial
C. Electronic Commerce
D. None of the above

32. High AC voltages are used for transmitting electric power because
A. at high voltages, current is low and hence, losses are low
B. the transmission of power is quicker
C. the high voltages a consume lesser materials for transmission
D. None of the above

33. There is a hole in the boat through which, water is seeping into the boat. Just before the boat capsizes
A. water level would decrease
B. water level would increase
C. water level would remain the same
D. None of the above

34. During which month, the rate of rotation of the earth on its axis is the fastest?
A. December
B. May
C. the rate of rotation is fixed
D. It is fastest when the earth is closest to the Sun.

35. The time taken by the Sun rays to reach the earth is
A. 9 minutes B. 10 minutes
C. 7 minutes D. 8 minutes

36. The outer planets are
A. Moon, Earth, Mercury, Venus
B. Jupiter, Saturn, Uranus, Earth, Mars
C. Jupiter, Uranus, Saturn, Neptune
D. None of the above

37. According to the astrophysicists
A. the universe is mobile and expanding
B. the universe is heading for a collision with another universe
C. the universe is stationary
D. the doomsday of universe is near due to the formation of many new black holes

38. Which is popular as the White City?
A. New York B. Belgrade
C. Bangalore D. Bab-el-mandab

39. The national currency of Haiti is
A. Rupiah B. Gourde
C. Quetzal D. Dong

40. Which one is not a news agency of India?
A. UNI
B. PTI
C. Hindustan Samachar
D. Reuters

41. The abundant element of the earth's atmosphere is:
A. Oxygen B. nitrogen
C. hydrogen D. CO_2

42. The first talking movie of India was ..... and the first silent movie of India was .....
A. Aan, Aawara
B. Raja Harish Chandra, Alamara
C. Alamara, Raja Harish Chandra
D. Purana Mandir, Raja Harish Chandra

43. Hair becomes grey because
A. rays of the Sun force it to become grey
B. the quantity of melanin is reduced in human body with growing age
C. there is a lack of vitamins in the body due to growing age
D. None of the above

44. Salaries of Supreme Court judges are drawn from:
A. Law Ministry Grants
B. Consolidated Fund of India
C. Home Ministry Grants
D. Parliamentary Grants

45. The term "Paper-gold" is associated with
A. deficit budgeting
B. loans from the World Bank
C. Special Drawing Rights (SDRs) from the IMF
D. None of the above

46. TRAI refers to
A. Terresteral Remote Sensing Authority of India
B. Telecommunication Research Authority of India
C. Transport Regulatory Authority of India
D. Telecom Regulatory Authority of India

47. NSDL is an organisation in India which
A. provides security to depositors
B. accepts deposits from recognised bodies

C. provides data security for on-line computer systems
D. None of the above

48. The enzyme pepsin converts
A. proteins into peptones
B. fats to amino acids
C. carbohydrates to sugars
D. proteins to amino acids

49. Who among the following is not a winner of the PVC?
A. Bana Singh
B. Nirmal Jeet Singh Sekhon
C. Somnath Sharma
D. Shanti Swaroop Rana

50. Which one of the following pairs is not correct?
A. Narmada – Betul district
B. Krishna – near Mahabaleshwar
C. Chambal – near Mhow
D. Godavari – Nashik district

51. The Japanese art of flower arrangement is known as
A. Bonsai
B. Ongami
C. Ikebota
D. None of the above

52. The meaning of the Latin word *Vive Rex* is
A. Long live the king!
B. Let the Nation Live
C. A middle course
D. Nothing wrong here

53. The permanent station of India in Antarctica is known as
A. *Vikalp*
B. Antarctica India Station
C. *Maitri*
D. *Dakshin Yamunotri*

54. A man dies due to electrocution because
A. electric current passes through his body to earth which leads to sudden contraction and expansion of muscles (including heart muscles) and this, alongwith development of heat in the body, leads to heart failure.
B. there is no resistance offered by the body
C. the body allows the current to flow through the blood which cannot circulate any longer
D. None of the above

55. "Blue Dwarfs" are
A. members of the Russian circus
B. warriors of Mongolia
C. young stars of the universe
D. naval officers in the high seas

56. What is a fly leaf?
A. thin paper sheet for making packaging material
B. a blank page at the beginning or end of a book
C. a marker in a book
D. a sheet of paper next to the main title of the book

57. Who is associated with the theory of inheritance of acquired characters?
A. Spencer B. Mandeleev
C. Lamarck D. All of the above

58. Ligaments and tendons in the body are made up of
A. skeletal tissue
B. muscular tissue
C. connective tissue
D. epithelial tissue

59. A cell membrane is
A. completely permeable
B. impermeable
C. semi-permeable
D. None of the above

60. The tenure of the non-permanent members of the UN Security Council is
A. one year
B. three years
C. two years
D. there is no fixed tenure

61. Why proper earthing is necessary?
A. It reduces the consumption of electricity
B. It allows the current to flow through the earth wire and into the earth, thus protecting the person
C. It allows the appliance to operate efficiently
D. None of the above

62. Which one of the following items has not been included in the minimum needs programme?
A. unemployment allowance
B. rural water supply
C. rural electrification
D. adult education

63. This is not the principle organ of digestion and absorption in the human body.
A. small intestine B. stomach
C. large intestine D. Both A and B

64. Which are the two stars which appear as morning stars in the Eastern sky and evening stars in the Western sky?
A. Jupiter and Mars
B. Mars and Venus
C. Saturn and Mercury
D. Mercury and Venus

65. Which planet rotates on its axis from East to West?
A. Mercury B. Jupiter
C. Earth D. Venus

66. The chemical compound present in the stone of human kidney is
A. calcium phosphate
B. calcium carbonate
C. silica
D. calcium oxalate

67. Which one of the following diseases would be caused by bacterial infection?
A. tetanus B. rabies
C. cancer D. malaria

68. India On-line Limited is
A. an advertising agency
B. a reservation office
C. an information service
D. an internet services provider

69. CTBT is related to
A. economic sanctions imposed by the USA on India
B. the codename of Pokharan-II blasts
C. the nuclear test ban treaty which India is being forced to adhere to
D. codename of Pakistani nuclear arsenal

70. The disagreement between Lok Sabha and Rajya Sabha is solved by:
A. setting up Joint Select Committee
B. dissolving Lok Sabha
C. setting up adjudication committee
D. calling a joint session

71. The national anthem was written by ..... and was translated into English by .....
A. Bankim Chandra Chatterji, Aurobindo Ghosh
B. Rabindra Nath Tagore, Aurobindo Ghosh
C. Bankim Chandra Chatterji, Rabindra Nath Tagore
D. the national anthem was originally written in English and was translated later

72. The tear in human body is a solution of :
A. Sodium hydroxide and sodium chloride
B. Calcium bicarbonate and sodium chloride
C. Magnesium bicarbonate and sodium hydroxide
D. Sodium bicarbonate and Magnesium chloride

73. The drug seroxat is
A. a new medicine for treating the lepers.
B. a new medicine developed by British scientists and is used for the treatment of shyness and social phobia
C. is anti-AIDS therapy developed by France
D. is an antacid developed in India under guidance of WHO

74. What is "Bermuda Triangle" sometimes referred to as the "Grakeyard of ships", located?
A. in the South Pacific ocean
B. in the North Atlantic ocean
C. in the Indian ocean
D. in the Arctic ocean

75. The theory propounded by Nobel laurate Professor Amartya Sen–is commonly known as
A. The Famine Economics
B. The Theory of Economic Divide
C. The Amartya Sen Shift
D. The Amartya Sen Divide

76. Which is known as the Electronics City of India?
A. Tumkoor B. Secunderabad
C. Bhopal D. None of the above

77. The main objective behind the creation of concept of *Navratnas* in the public sector was

A. to increase the control of the PSUs over economy
B. to boost local manufacturing and exports in the core sectors
C. to improve the functional autonomy
D. to improve their image and efficiency by giving them high status

78. The North American seaport on the Pacific side is
A. Baltimore B. Boston
C. New York D. Seattle

79. The old name of Harare was
A. Sam B. Rhodesia
C. Salisbury D. Batavia

80. The famous Prince of Wales Museum is located in
A. Mumbai B. Kolkata
C. Vadodara D. Bangalore

81. Who invented Atom Bomb (Uranium Fission)?
A. A W Haffmann
B. Otto Hahn
C. A Einstein
D. None of the above

82. The first ever woman to go into space was
A. Kalpana Chawla
B. Valentina Tereshkova
C. Mary Pierce
D. None of the above

83. The highest mountain peak in India is
A. K-2 B. Everest
C. Kanchanjunga D. Makalu-I

84. The "Garden City" of England is
A. Portsmouth B. Manchester
C. Kent D. Warwickshire

85. *Habeas Corpus* is
A. an order of the International Court of Justice
B. a type of writ issued by a High Court or Supreme Court against illegal detention of a person.
C. the petition of a lawyer in the Supreme Court on behalf of his client for bail against the orders of any other court in India
D. None of the above

86. If impeachment motion is passed by the American Senate against the US President, he would have to
A. leave office and all his assets created by him during Presidency
B. leave office, lose his pensions, security cover and all those benefits that are accorded to a retired US President
C. jailed for five years and will not get any benefits.
D. retire honourably with all his benefits, compensations, assets and pensions remaining intact

87. Who appoints the non-permanent members of the UN Security Council?
A. the permanent members
B. the General Assembly
C. the International Court of Justice
D. None of the above

88. The Preamble of the Constitution was amended by:
A. 1st amendment B. 26th amendment
C. 42nd amendment D. 44th amendment

89. NNP is equal to
A. GNP + Depreciation
B. GNP – Depreciation
C. GNP + Exports
D. GNP – Exports

90. The official airline of Australia is
A. SIA B. Lufthansa
C. Modiluft D. None of the above

91. Which one of the following types of coal contains a higher percentage of carbon than the rest?
A. Bituminous Coal B. Lignite
C. Anthracite D. Peat

92. Ten Commandments were revealed by God to:
A. Abraham B. Moses
C. Jesus D. Peter

93. Kalinga in older days, is now known as:
A. Odisha B. Kohima
C. Karnataka D. Maharashtra

94. Bihu festival is celebrated in:
A. Gujarat B. Assam
C. Bihar D. West Bengal

95. Milk is an example of
A. gel B. emulsion
C. suspension D. mixture

96. The President can dissolve the Lok Sabha before expiry of its term, on the advice of:
A. Prime Minister
B. Speaker
C. Vice-President
D. Election Commissioner

97. The State Emblem of India is taken from:
A. Patna
B. Sarnath
C. Bodh Gaya
D. Kolkata

98. Tughlaq dynasty occupied Delhi throne after decline of:
A. Suri dynasty
B. Slave dynasty
C. Lodhi dynasty
D. Khilji dynasty

99. Governors of states are:
A. appointed by Chief Ministers
B. appointed by the President
C. elected by members of Legislative Assembly
D. elected by people

100. The partition of Bengal was carried out by:
A. Lord Curzon
B. Lord Minto
C. Lord Canning
D. Lord Ripon

101. The Air Force Day falls on
A. October 10 B. October 9
C. September 5 D. October 8

102. MAD stands for
A. Most Active Disease
B. Mica Aluminium Duo
C. Mutually Assured Death
D. Mutually Assured Destruction

103. "Disguised Unemployment" means
A. more persons employed for a job that only a few could accomplish
B. people without any technical jobs
C. woman without jobs in rural areas
D. employment of children in factories

104. In India, an active volcano is situated at
A. Lakshadweep
B. Chhotanagpur Plateau
C. Andaman and Nicobar
D. Malawa Plateau

105. The first country to establish trade relationships with India was
A. England B. France
C. Holland D. Portugal

106. Which has the highest share of electrical power generation in India?
A. thermal power
B. nuclear power
C. hydro-power
D. naphtha-based and gas-based power

107. The great ocean liner, known to be the best and luxurious during her times, sank in the year
A. 1902 B. 1912
C. 1908 D. 1889

108. Who among the following is known as the Indian Napoleon?
A. Chandra Gupta Maurya
B. Bindusar
C. Samudra Gupta
D. Harshvardhana

109. Time gap between two sessions of Parliament cannot exceed:
A. 3 months B. 6 months
C. 1 year D. no fixed gap

110. In which state, Panchayati Raj was introduced for the first time?
A. Bihar
B. Punjab
C. Rajasthan
D. Andhra Pradesh

111. Which one is not a national duty?
A. Respect the Constitution
B. Respect the President
C. Defend the country
D. Protect natural environment

112. Treaty of Seringapatam was signed between:
A. Tipu Sultan and Nawab of Hyderabad
B. Tipu Sultan and English
C. Tipu Sultan & Rani of Jhansi
D. Tipu Sultan and French

113. NHRC stands for
A. National Hydro Research Committee
B. National Handicapped Rahabilitation Council
C. National Human Rights Commission
D. None of the above

114. "Water water everywhere but not a drop to drink" who stated these lines in a poem?
A. John Milton
B. Samuel Taylor Coleridge
C. Lord Byron
D. P.B. Shelley

115. Rabindranath Tagore gave up his knighthood after:
A. Jallianwala Bagh Tragedy
B. Introduction of separate electorates
C. Bengal faminine
D. Bengal Partition

116. Which country is known as the land of golden wool?
A. India B. Turkiye
C. Australia D. Myanmar

117. BIFR stands for
A. Bilateral and International Foreign Regulation
B. Board of Industrial Financial Resurrection
C. Board of Industrial and Financial Reconstruction
D. None of the above

118. Pinaca is a
A. drug for curing AIDS
B. multi-barrel rocket system
C. fighter aircraft developed by HAL
D. codename of the nuclear test operation carried out on May 11, 1998

119. Vice-President is ex-officio:
A. Member of Rajya Sabha
B. Chairman of Rajya Sabha
C. Member of Lok Sabha
D. Speaker of Lok Sabha

120. Vitamin C is not available in this food in sufficiently large quantities.
A. lemon B. tomato
C. cod liver oil D. fresh fruits

121. This book was not written in a jail
A. *Glimpses of World History* – J L Nehru
B. *The Bible* (German) – Martin Luther
C. *Les Miserables* – Victor Hugo
D. *Yama* – Mahadevi Verma

122. Who among the following can be removed from office through impeachment by Parliament?
A. Speaker of Lok Sabha
B. Prime Minister
C. President of India
D. Vice-President of India

123. The following is not the function of the liver.
A. to store excesssive sugar in the form of glycogen
B. the produce an antidote for neutralising poison
C. to manufacture red blood corpuscles
D. to purify the blood through bile

124. A fascist is a person whose views are extremely
A. left-winged B. rational
C. right-winged D. liberal

125. The famous mathematician and a professor of Astronomy designed this building in London
A. Westminister Abbey
B. St Paul's Cathedral
C. Stock Exchange
D. Tower of London

126. Which one of the following sounds cannot be heard by a human ear?
A. 30,000 vibrations per second
B. 10,000 vibrations per second
C. 1,000 vibrations per second
D. 300 vibrations per second

127. A weather balloon may not be inflated completely on the ground because
A. it cannot withstand the atmospheric pressure if inflated fully
B. if the balloon is inflated fully on ground, fuel consumption would be higher
C. the air inside the balloon expands as it rises and hence, the balloon could get burst
D. None of the above

128. Which one of the following vitamins is stored in the liver?
A. Vitamin C

B. Vitamin B_{12}
C. Vitamin A
D. Vitamin K and Vitamin A

129. All of the following are plant products except
A. silk B. cork
C. hemp D. linen

130. Which one of the following organs in the human body is known as "Adam's Apple"?
A. thyroid B. liver
C. thymus D. adrenal

131. Insecticides or medicines could be harmful
A. to the insects and weeds as they kill them instantaneously upon consumption
B. to the habitat as the environment could become polluted due to excessive usage of chemicals in our crop management processes
C. to the human beings and animals who consume the food adulterated by the insecticides and weedicides
D. to the transporters and movers of the crops who could inhale noxious fumes of insecticides and weedicides

132. Name the assassin of John Lennon
A. Art Buchwald
B. Lee Oswald
C. Mark David Chapman
D. None of the above

133. Which one of the following is not a sprinter?
A. Marion Jones
B. Florence Griffith Joyner
C. Ben Johnson
D. Susie O' Neill

134. Which of the following is called the "Gateway to the Pacific"?
A. Suez Canal
B. Bering Sea
C. Panama Canal
D. Gulf of Alaska

135. Which one of the following statements is true regarding the treaty on banning the landmines?
A. the USA does not want to sign the CTBT
B. the treaty was kept open for signatures in Ottawa in December, 1997.
C. India has already signed it
D. A and B are true

136. Disease that affects many people of different countries is termed as:
A. Sporadic B. Epidemic
C. Endemic D. Pandemic

137. The famous Gandhian, who was also known as the "Frontier Gandhi," is
A. Liaqat Ali Khan
B. Yusuf Khan
C. Khan Abdul Ghaffar Khan
D. Abdul Wali Khan

138. Which one of the following is an alloy?
A. copper B. lanthanum
C. bronze D. uranium

139. World Environment Day is celebrated on
A. June 4 B. June 5
C. June 7 D. March 5

140. This country is the largest producer of cotton in the world.
A. India B. China
C. Egypt D. the USA

141. International Youth Day is observed on ____.
A. August 11th B. August 10th
C. August 12th D. August 9th

142. The temples of Khajuraho were built by
A. Chalukyas B. Pallavas
C. Rashtrakutas D. Chandelas

143. National Remote Sensing Agency (NRSA) is located at:
A. Hyderabad
B. Bengluru
C. Thiruvananthapuram
D. Gadanki, near Tirupati

144. The clones for .... and .... have been developed.
A. man, cow B. crow, sheep
C. rat, cat D. sheep, rat

145. AWWA stands for
A. All Women Welfare Association
B. Army Wives Welfare Association
C. Airport Weather and Welfare Authority
D. None of the above

146. The popular book *The Gift of Time* by Jonathan Schell, deals with

A. the lewid affair of Bill Clinton and Monica Lewinsky
B. the elimination of nuclear weapons from the world
C. Indo-US relationships
D. the deteriorating environment in industrial America

147. How can a person move on a hard icy surface?
A. he should use roller skates
B. he should hop, sneeze, jump and step in the direction which is opposite to the direction of his required movement
C. he should hop, sneeze, jump and step in the direction in which the movement is required
D. he should skid on his knees and hands

148. Which states are deriving benefits from the Tungbhadra project?
A. Tamil Nadu, Karnataka, Kerala
B. Tamil Nadu only
C. Andhra Pradesh and Tamil Nadu
D. Tamil Nadu, Andhra Pradesh, Karnataka

149. The famous 'Lucknow Pact' was signed between the Congress and the Muslim League in:
A. 1913 B. 1916
C. 1914 D. 1915

150. Pyroclastics are
A. non-toxic gases
B. lava flows
C. fragments of hot rock and spattering lava
D. pollutant chemicals from a leather factory

151. Which one of the following is not a sedimentary rock?
A. slate B. limestone
C. clay D. sandstone

152. Oketa is
A. used to define human-induced climatic changes
B. used to describe increasing drought periods of high magnitudes
C. a unit to describe the prevailing cloudiness
D. None of the above

153. The following state produces the maximum quantities (85 percent) of raw silk in India
A. Kerala B. Jammu and Kashmir
C. Karnataka D. Tamil Nadu

154. Salal Hydro Electric Project is situated on the river
A. Beas B. Jhelum
C. Chenab D. Sutlej

155. Which of the following cities is located along the side of river Seine?
A. Belgrade B. Paris
C. Lisbon D. Budapest

156. What is the name of the bell used at the Lloyds in London?
A. The Great Bell B. The Charmer
C. The Tower Bell D. Lutine

157. What are "The Hagiographs?"
A. These are the poems written by Lord Byron
B. These are the holy writings of Jewish scriptures
C. These are the geographical lines representing same rainfall levels
D. None of the above

158. Which one of the following forms would provide the lowest protection?
A. Patent B. Trademark
C. Copyright D. Logo

159. The twenty-fifth State of India is
A. Goa B. Nagaland
C. Mizoram D. Delhi

160. What does the 17th Parallel line separate?
A. South and North America
B. North and South Korea
C. South and North Yemen
D. South and North Vietnam

161. Operation Flood-II, the prestigious milk products revolution of India, was initiated on
A. October 1, 1979 B. October 2, 1979
C. January 26, 1979 D. October 2, 1978

162. After World War I, the peace treaty was signed in:
A. Geneva B. Versailles
C. Paris D. Venice

163. Potassium chloride is given to the patient for
A. curing his bleeding gums
B. reducing his cholestrol level
C. reducing his blood pressure
D. alleviating his arthiritis pain

164. What is notation?
A. It is another word for “Mutually Assured Destruction”
B. It is the Latin deformation of the phrase “to swim”
C. It is a term used to denote the growth of illeterate masses
D. None of the above

165. The hideout of Adolf Hitler in the mountains was
A. Stuttgart B. Heidelberg
C. Berchtesgaden D. Both A and C

166. Who stated, “Where wealth accumulates decay?”
A. J M Keynes B. Adam Smith
C. Frederic Engels D. Oliver Goldsmith

167. Who was the national leader who wrote History of India on the walls of the Andaman Cellular Jail?
A. Ambedkar B. Vir Savarkar
C. Nandlal Bose D. Jyotiba Phule

168. The USA does not possess the following space shuttle
A. Columbia B. Atlantis
C. Challenger D. Discovery

169. The term “White Elephant” is used to denote
A. very bright and white item
B. very costly and expensive item
C. an item or a head that is very costly to maintain
D. an item or a head that is a part of the national economic budget of a country

170. Kolar Gold Mines are in this state.
A. Karnataka B. Bihar
C. Odisha D. Madhya Pradesh

171. Which is the morning star?
A. Pluto
B. Venus
C. Neptune
D. None of the above

172. Which one of the following is not an alkali?
A. sodium hydroxide
B. calcium carbonate
C. magnesium hydroxide
D. sodium sulphate

173. Polar ice is melting due to greenhouse effect. This would lead to
A. more melting of the polar glaciers and hence, subsequent submerging of land areas of earth
B. increasing temperatures on polar caps
C. reduction in temperature of ocean waters and rise in temperature of the Arctic circle waters as well as those of the Antartic circle waters
D. no impact

174. *India 2020* is a book written by
A. Trilok Gurtu
B. Khushwant Singh
C. P Chidambaram
D. A P J Abdul Kalaam

175. The Panama Canal connects:
A. The Pacific and Atlantic Oceans
B. The Pacific and Arctic Oceans
C. The Atlantic and Arctic Oceans
D. The Atlantic and Indian Oceans

176. The following are single cell structures
A. Paramaecium B. Amoebia
C. Both A and B D. None of A or B

177. ‘The Last Supper’ was painted by:
A. Picasso B. Francis Bacon
C. Michaelangelo D. Raphael

178. The plants, which can resist high temperatures, are known as
A. thermophilic B. thermophobic
C. thermoduric D. Both A and B

179. Which one of the following vaccines is used for controlling tuberculosis among the cattle?
A. Cell Culture Vaccine
B. Goat Tissue Adapted Vaccine
C. Adjuvant Vaccine
D. BCG Vaccine

180. Which one of the following chemicals is carcinogenic if inhaled?
A. carbon dioxide
B. suspended particulate matter
C. lead oxide
D. sulphur dioxide

181. What is a “Tenurial System?”
A. It is a system that identifies the ownership of land and the relationship of the land owner with the actual cultivator

B. It identities the land size and the *modus-operandi* of its usage
C. It identifies the ownership of the land
D. None of the above

182. Pulses are deficient in
A. methionine B. lysine
C. leusine D. iso-leusine

183. Which types of roses are grown in India for industrial applications?
A. R Centripetala and Bushra Rose
B. R Damascena Var Bifera
C. Rosa Damascena
D. A, B and C

184. Why sprinkler irrigation is preferred over other methods of irrigation?
A. It is a cheap method and does not require canal-digging and canal maintenance
B. It uses water effectively and water resolves are optimally utilised
C. It does not require well-digging measures which are costly
D. It supplies water only to those fields where the same is required

185. The size of clay particles is
A. greater than 0.2 mm
B. 0.02 mm – 0.2 mm
C. 0.002 mm – 0.02 mm
D. less than 0.002 mm

186. Which one of the following plants is of great medicinal value?
A. Ranwolfia Serpentiana
B. Thea Sinesis
C. Coffea Robusta
D. Ficus Religiosa

187. Biological control agents of soil borne plant pathogens act by
A. rapidly repleting nutrients and thereby, causing starvation and death of the pathogen
B. secreting toxic metabolitics
C. direct parastism or predation on the pathogens
D. All of the above

188. Nearly 80 percent of sugarcane in India is planted during
A. July – December B. May – August
C. June – August D. December – April

189. Soluble salt content of soil is determined by measuring its
A. pH Value
B. organic matter content
C. Sulphur content
D. electrical conductivity

190. Operation Flood is related to ..... whereas development of fisheries is related to .....
A. white revolution, black revolution
B. white revolution, blue revolution
C. green revolution, blue revolution
D. blue revolution, green revolution

191. An upper air wind system with very high velocities in certain parts of the atmosphere is called
A. Cyclone B. Anticyclone
C. Jet stream D. Tsunami

192. "Mixed Farming" refers to
A. farming by traditional and modern methods
B. agriculture and dairy farming clubbed together
C. farming without synthetic fertilisers but with traditional manure
D. farming with synthetic fertilisers and with traditional manure

193. The main constituent of *Gobar Gas* is
A. butane B. carbon monoxide
C. methane D. octane

194. Speed of sound waves is maximum in
A. solids B. liquids
C. gases D. vacuum

195. When a body gets positively charged, it actually
A. gains electrons
B. loses electrons
C. becomes a donor of ions
D. becomes a receptor of ions

196. Which type of nerves carries impulses from the sense organs in response to the stimulus?
A. sensory B. motor
C. secretory D. None of the above

197. Which gas does not pollute air (for human and animal consumption)?
A. carbon monoxide B. nitrogen dioxide
C. sulphur dioxide D. carbon dioxide

198. The human brain sends and receives signals as
A. electrical impulses
B. chemical impulses
C. motor movements
D. either A or B

199. "Foot and Mouth" disease attacks
A. cattle
B. pigs and cattle
C. sheep and pigs
D. cattle, sheep and pigs

200. While returning to earth, the spacecraft has a total communication blackout. The reason is
A. during the re-entry period, the density of the plasma generated by the intense functional heat is so high that the operational frequencies used for communication become much lesser than the plasma cut-off frequency, thus resulting in a total blackout
B. the electromagnetic waves present in the space above the earth temporarily over-power the communication system of the aircraft, thus completely crippling its operation and transmission
C. the force of gravity counters the radiowaves emitted by the aircraft
D. None of the above

201. The first winning stroke in Lawn Tennis gives the player:
A. 2 points B. 1 point
C. 10 points D. 15 points

202. Which of the following game is played for stipulated period of 70 minutes?
A. Hockey B. Football
C. Rugby D. Basketball

203. Who is the winner of World Cup Football-2022?
A. Brazil B. Argentina
C. Germany D. France

204. Arjuna Award has been instituted for outstanding contribution in the field of
A. Social Service
B. Games and Sports
C. Literature
D. Art and Music

205. Murugappa Gold Cup is associated with:
A. Football B. Polo
C. Hockey D. Bridge

206. Jimmy Connors and Geoff Boycott are related with following games respectively:
A. Tennis, Football B. Tennis, Cricket
C. Chess, Cricket D. Football, Hockey

207. What is the ratio of the width to the length of the National Flag of India?
A. 2 : 4
B. 3 : 5
C. 2 : 3
D. 3 : 4

208. Surat is located on the banks of:
A. Narmada B. Tapti
C. Godavari D. Yamuna

209. The term 'Steeple Chase' is associated with which of the following games
A. Polo B. Tennis
C. Horse Racing D. Cricket

210. Who is known as Father of India's "White Revolution" and "Operation Flood"?
A. Dr. Verghese Kurien
B. J.B. Kripalani
C. Baba Amte
D. Har Gobind Khorana

211. The first Olympic games were revived by ..... in 1896 at Athens
A. Lord Welsley
B. Queen Elizabeth-I
C. Baron Piere de Cubertin
D. None of the above

212. The national game of the USA is
A. swimming B. baseball
C. athletics D. None of the above

213. Jules Rimmet Cup is associated with
A. hockey B. archery
C. football D. table tennis

214. The approximate weight of a cricket ball is
A. 5.25 Oz B. 6.30 Oz
C. 7.20 Oz D. 8.25 Oz

215. The number of players on each side in a basketball match is
A. 10 B. 6
C. 5 D. 8

216. The first woman in the history of US open Championship to have played 100 matches, is:
A. Martina Navaratilova
B. Chris Evert
C. Steffi Graf
D. Helena Sukova

217. Swaythling Cup is associated with
A. World Table Tennis Tournament (men)
B. World Table Tennis Tournament (university)
C. World Table Tennis tournament (women)
D. World Hockey Tournament (university)

218. Which one of the following is not a cricket - playing nation?
A. West Indies B. Zimbabwe
C. Kenya D. Columbia

219. The first recipient of Major Dhyanchand Khel Ratna Award was
A. Geet Sethi B. N Kunjurani Devi
C. V Anand D. P K Garg

220. The first Olympic Games were held at Olympia (Greece) in the year:
A. 300 BC B. 776 BC
C. 500 BC D. 394 AD

221. Which of the following is the National Game of Spain?
A. Bull fighting B. Baseball
C. Rugby D. Golf

222. 'Ashes' is the name of a series between ..... and ..... and it relates to .....
A. Pakistan, Australia, Hockey
B. India, England, Cricket
C. England, Australia, Cricket
D. New Zealand, Australia, Cricket

223. The term "Butterfly Stroke" is associated with
A. Kabaddi B. Wrestling
C. Polo D. Swimming

224. The Australian Open Tennis Women's Championship (2025) was won by
A. C. Martinez
B. Garbine Muguruza
C. Madison Keys
D. Serena Williams

225. 'Gambit' is a term normally associated with
A. Bridge B. Chess
C. Billiards D. Polo

226. 'Bunker' and 'Chukker' are the two terms associated with
A. Polo B. Rowing
C. Bungey Jumping D. Ice Hockey

227. A Lawn Tennis court measures
A. 78 feet by 28 feet
B. 79 feet by 29 feet
C. 76 feet by 26 feet
D. 70 feet by 24 feet

228. 'Breast stroke' is related with:
A. Polo
B. Tennis
C. Golf
D. Swimming

229. Which one of the following has been entrusted with the responsibility of training coaches in various disciplines of sports?
A. Tata Football Academy
B. Ministry of Human Resource Development
C. Netaji Subhash Institute of Sports
D. Lakshmibai National College of Physical Education

230. ICC Champions Trophy-2025 was won by
A. Australia
B. Pakistan
C. India
D. New Zealand

231. Governor will act on the advice of Council of Ministers while
A. Dissolving the Legislative Assembly
B. Appointing the Chairman of the State Public Service Commission
C. Recommending for President's Rule in the State
D. Returning a bill for reconsideration

232. Who was the first deaf & dumb swimmer in the world to swim 30 km Gibralter strait?
A. Des Renford
B. Mihir Sen
C. Arti Pradhan
D. Taranath Shenoy

233. The height of the net in the centre of the tennis court is
A. 3 feet, 5 inches
B. 3 feet, 2 inches
C. 2 feet, 8 inches
D. 2 feet, 6 inches

234. 'Canon' is a sports term associated with the following game.
A. Billiards B. Volleyball
C. Shot-Put D. Table Tennis

235. The Himalayan Mountaineering Institute is located in
A. Leh B. Darjeeling
C. Kohima D. Dispur

236. The diameter of a golf hole is
A. 4.36 inches B. 4.50 inches
C. 5.63 inches D. 4.75 inches

237. The total distance of a Marathon Race is ..... miles and ..... yards.
A. 29, 388 B. 26, 380
C. 26, 385 D. 25, 372

238. The first woman, who won six gold medals in a single Olympics tournament, was
A. Evelyn Ashford
B. Florence Griffth Joyner
C. Kristin Otto
D. Susi Susanti

239. In which year on account of a decree issued by Roman Emperor the Olympic Games were ceased to be played?
A. 350 AD B. 394 AD
C. 300 BC D. 384 AD

240. Putney (UK) is a place most frequently associated with
A. swimming B. horse racing
C. boat rowing D. polo

241. Dipa Karmakar is associated with which sports?
A. Gymnastics
B. Boxing
C. Badminton
D. Cricket

242. The term 'Finesse' is normally associated with this game.
A. Chess B. Bridge
C. Snooker D. Rowing

243. The following trophy is not associated with cricket.
A. Ranji Trophy
B. Rohintan Baria Trophy
C. C.K. Naydu Trophy
D. Jules Rimet Trophy

244. Who is the first Indian to take a Hat-trick in an International Test Match?
A. Kapil Dev
B. Jasu Patel
C. Harbhajan Singh
D. B.S. Chandrashekhar

245. When and where the first Asian Games were held?
A. 1955, Seoul B. 1951, New Delhi
C. 1954, Manila D. 1970, Bangkok

246. Ryder Cup is famous trophy of:
A. Badminton B. Golf
C. Lawn Tennis D. Shooting

247. What is the measurement of a Golf Hole?
A. 3½ inch in diameter
B. 4½ inch in diameter
C. 7½ centimeter in diameter
D. 10 inch in diameter

248. The Supreme Court of India was set up by the
A. Regulating Act, 1773
B. Pitts India Act, 1784
C. Charter Act, 1813
D. Charter Act, 1833

249. K Sasikaran is well known as a
A. table tennis player
B. swimmer
C. chess player
D. football player

250. Where is the Head Quarter of Asian Development Bank?
A. Washington B. Paris
C. Manila D. Canberra

251. In which of the following years 'Nobel Prizes' were instituted?
A. 1910 B. 1905
C. 1901 D. 1911

252. The writer who refused the Nobel Prize for Literature was:
A. Winston Churchill
B. Prem Chand
C. Jean Paul Sartre
D. None of the above

253. Which country awards the Noble Prize?
A. USA B. India
C. Russia D. Sweden

254. In which of the following years Arjuna Awards were instituted

A. 1951 B. 1971
C. 1961 D. 1965

255. National Awards for Popularising Science was instituted in the year

A. 1981 B. 1985
C. 1987 D. 1988

256. The Government of which state has instituted the 'Tansen Samman'?

A. Madhya Pradesh B. Uttar Pradesh
C. Gujarat D. Maharashtra

257. Who among the following has not been awarded the Bharat Ratna?

A. Indira Gandhi
B. Mahatma Gandhi
C. Sardar Patel
D. Dr. Radha Krishnan

258. Who returned the award of 'Sir' given by the British government in protest against the "Jallianwala Bagh Massacre" on April 13, 1919?

A. Prem Chand
B. Thomas Roe
C. Rabindra Nath Tagore
D. Dada Bhai Nauroji

259. Nobel Prize is not awarded in the following disciplines

A. Chemistry and Physics
B. Literature and Peace
C. Economics and Medicine
D. Geography and Space Research

260. In which year Nehru Award for International Understanding instituted

A. 1965 B. 1969
C. 1974 D. 1964

261. Dada Saheb Phalke Award is given for:

A. Drama B. Films
C. Social Welfare D. Literature

262. 'Pulitzer' prizes are awarded to Americans for excellence in

A. Films B. Journalism
C. Medicine D. Social Work

263. C.V. Raman received Nobel Prize in the year

A. 1934 B. 1931
C. 1932 D. 1930

264. Saraswati Samman is awarded by

A. Government of India
B. Sahitya Academy
C. K.K. Birla Foundation
D. Lalit Kala Akademi

265. On which day every year National Awards for Teachers are announced?

A. August 15 B. September 5
C. November 19 D. November 14

266. The National Award given to the distinguished sportsmen/women in India is known as

A. Dronacharya Award
B. Param Vir Chakra
C. Arjun Award
D. Nehru Award

267. The prestigious Ramon Magsaysay Award was instituted in the memory of Mr Ramon Magsaysay who was

A. the Secretary – General of UN
B. the Commander of NATO in Europe
C. the President of the Philippines
D. the President of Cambodia

268. The Kalinga Prize is awarded by UNESCO but it was founded by an Indian. His name is

A. Biju Patnaik
B. Sharad Pawar
C. C V Raman
D. Piloo Modi

269. Who was the first Indian to receive the World Food Prize

A. Dr. M.S. Swaminathan
B. Dr. Amrita Patel
C. Dr. Verghese Kurien
D. None of these

270. Jesse Owens Global award is given in the field of:

A. Literature B. Sports
C. Science D. Journalism

271. Nobel Alfred Bernhard after whom Nobel Prizes are given was:

A. Engineer B. Doctor
C. Chemist D. Pilot

272. Grammy Awards are given in the field of

A. painting B. architecture
C. music D. rock dance

273. The highest civilian award of India is
A. *Padma Vibhushan*
B. *Padma Shri*
C. *Bharat Ratna*
D. *Param Vir Chakra*

274. The highest military award of India is
A. Shaurya Chakra
B. Param Vishisht Sewa Medal
C. Param Vir Chakra
D. Kirti Chakra

275. The first ever B R Ambedkar National Award was given to
A. Baba Amte
B. T Shiv Shankar Pillai
C. International Red Cross
D. National Institute for Social Work and Social Sciences

276. 'Victory Medal' is awarded in:
A. UK B. USA
C. Russia D. France

277. Which one of the following is not a Shram Award
A. Shram Bhushan
B. Shram Dev
C. Shram Devi
D. Shram Vir

278. The Rashtriya Vigyan Puraskar is awarded in how many Categories?
A. 2 B. 3
C. 4 D. 5

279. Neeraj Chopra is associated with which game?
A. Badminton
B. Javelin Throw
C. Hockey
D. Wrestling

280. First Miss World Competition was established by 'Miss World Incorporation' in the year
A. 1941 B. 1950
C. 1951 D. 1957

281. The size of an Olympic medal is ..... mm and thickness is ..... mm.
A. 50, 2.5 B. 60, 3.0
C. 60.5, 3.5 D. 55.2, 2.5

282. "Dhanwantari Award" is given in the field of
A. swimming
B. Bharata Natyam
C. cinema
D. medicine

283. Which is the most ancient musical instrument of India?
A. Tabla B. Veena
C. Flute D. Sitar

284. Which is the second Highest Civilian award in India?
A. Padma Vibushan
B. Padma Shri
C. Bharat Ratna
D. Ashok Chakra

285. Gandhiji started the Dandi March for
A. Poorna Swaraj
B. Home-rule
C. Protest against the imposition of Salt Tax
D. Responsible Government

286. The second highest gallantry award in India is:
A. Padma Bhushan
B. Vir Chakra
C. Mahavir Chakra
D. Ashok Chakra

287. 'Mubarak-Al-Kabir' medal is the highest honour of
A. Kuwait B. Iran
C. Afghanistan D. Iraq

288. Bharatendu Harish Chandra awards are given annually for:
A. best local self administration
B. showing kindness and generosity of unusual kind
C. promoting original writing in Hindi
D. None of the above

289. Rigveda is divided into how many Mandals?
A. 10 mandals B. 7 mandals
C. 15 mandals D. 20 mandals

290. GST has been implemented from:
A. January 1, 2017
B. July 1, 2017
C. January 1, 2018
D. April 1, 2018

291. Which tax can be levied by Gram Panchayat?
A. Sales Tax
B. Land Revenue
C. Custom Duty
D. Tax on local fairs

292. Oscar award is related to
A. books
B. politics
C. European Community
D. films

293. USB stands for
A. Unique Serial Bus
B. Universal Serial Bus
C. Unary Serial Bus
D. Universal Secondary Bus

294. Out of the Gallantry awards — PVSM, AVSM and VSM — the most exceptional medal is
A. PVSM
B. AVSM
C. VSM
D. All have equal recognition status

295. *Jeewan Raksha Padak* is awarded for
A. bravery in the battle front
B. fine display of vocal music skills
C. saving the life of human beings
D. None of the above

296. Who is not eligible for Bharat Ratna?
A. A government official
B. A sportsperson
C. A film actress
D. A Prime Minister

297. Jamnalal Bajaj award is given in the field of
I. Social Work
II. Fine Arts
III. Application of Science and Technology
IV. Literature
A. I and II B. I, II and III
C. II and IV D. I and III

298. In which year Indira Gandhi Peace Prize was instituted?
A. 1985 B. 1984
C. 1986 D. 1987

299. Borlaug Award was instituted for recognising outstanding contribution in the field of:
A. Ecology B. Medicine
C. Agriculture D. Journalism

300. Except Dr. Nelson Mandela, who is the other non-Indian so far honoured with Bharat Ratna
A. Dr. Julius Nyerere
B. Helen Hint
C. Hideki Yuka
D. Khan Abdul Ghaffar Khan

301. The book "*The Insider*" is written by
A. Madhav Rao Scindia
B. Nana Patekar
C. Shobha De
D. P V Narasimha Rao

302. *India Wins Freedom* was written by
A. Dadabhai Nauroji
B. Ashfaqulla Khan
C. Sarojini Naidu
D. Maulana Abul Kalam Azad

303. *A Tale of Two Cities* is, in fact, the story of two famous cities. Those cities are
A. Paris and New York
B. London and New York
C. London and Paris
D. Stockholm and New York

304. *Ben Hur* was penned by
A. Lewis Wallace
B. Lord Byron
C. William Shakespeare
D. None of the above

305. *Panchatantra* was written by
A. R K Narayan B. R K Laxman
C. Vishnu Sharma D. None of the above

306. Arundhati Roy has been awarded the prestigious
A. Booker's Prize – 1997
B. Jnanpeeth Award – 1997
C. Sahitya Akademi Award – 1998
D. None of the above

307. Who wrote *Odyssey?*
A. George Orwell B. Homer
C. Dom Moraes D. None of the above

308. Which one of the following was not written by Shakespeare?
A. *As You Like It*
B. *Mcbeth*

C. *Hamlet*
D. *A Farewell to Arms*

309. Lewis Carol wrote a masterpiece. What is its name?
A. *Don Quixote*
B. *Alice in Wonderland*
C. *Adventures of Robinson Crusoe*
D. *Great Expectations*

310. The *Tamil Ramayana* is the work of
A. Tulsidas B. Jayangondar
C. Kambar D. Veda Vyas

311. In *Shrimad Bhagwat Geeta,* Lord Krishna teaches his disciple Arjuna to
A. rise to the occasion and fight with his near and dear ones
B. withdraw from the battlefield
C. do his duty and not to expect anything in return
D. attack the enemy in a planned and meticulous approach

312. Who wrote *Origin of Species?*
A. Charles Darwin
B. Alexander Flaming
C. G.B. Shaw
D. D.H. Lawrence

313. The poet and the well-known friend of Prithvi Raj Chauhan, who wrote *Prithvi Raj Raso,* was
A. Harisena B. Vishnu Datt
C. Chand Bardai D. None of the above

314. The first book was printed in India in the year 1561. Its name was
A. *The spiritual Compendium of the Christian Life*
B. *Aain-e-Akbari*
C. *Babur Nama*
D. *Ram Charit Manas*

315. The famous book *Runs and Ruins* was written by
A. Sir Donald Bradman
B. Sunil Gavaskar
C. Kapil Dev
D. Richard Hadlee

316. Adam Smith wrote the following famous book
A. The Wreck
B. Dr Zhivago
C. The Wealth of Nations
D. Tarzan of the Apes

317. H G Wells is known as a
A. poet
B. science-fiction writer
C. thriller-fiction writer
D. essay writer and critic

318. Tukaram wrote his devotional songs in this language
A. Urdu B. Gujarati
C. Hindi D. Marathi

319. Our ancient scholars and writers used this language for their social, religious and political books and works
A. Tamil
B. Sanskrit
C. Urdu
D. Hindi *(Devanagari)*

320. *Gora* is the hero of a book written by Rabindra Nath Tagore. What is the name of the book?
A. *Geetanjali* B. *Patanjali*
C. *Gora* D. *Twelfth Night*

321. Shylock is
A. the villain *in A Pound of Flesh* by William Shakespeare
B. an old Jew who is a famous hero of the Israeli nation
C. the hero of *Miranda,* written by William Shakespeare
D. the comic character of *Alice In the Wonderland* by Lewis Caroll

322. The following was a famous Hindi author and story-writer
A. Shobha De B. Aruna Asaf Ali
C. Mahadevi Verma D. Amrita Pritam

323. *Mudrarakshasa* was composed by
A. Vishakhadatta B. Bhavabhuti
C. Sivananda D. Jayadeva

324. *Razor's Edge* was written by
A. Toni Morrison
B. Saul Bellow
C. W Somerset Maugham
D. None of the above

325. *Sakharam Binder* is a famous play written by
A. Anil Barve B. Vijay Tendulkar
C. V S Naipaul D. Tasleema Nasreen

326. The major work of Sir Isaac Newton is
A. *Principia*
B. *Heritage*
C. *Human knowledge*
D. *I Dare*

327. The hero of *The Jungle Book,* written by Rudyard Kipling, is
A. the lion
B. Mowghuli
C. the father of Mowghuli
D. there is no hero

328. Who stated, "Peace hath her victories, no less renowned than war?"
A. Alfred Lord Tennyson
B. William Shakespeare
C. John Milton
D. None of the above

329. Macawber is a character who was created by
A. Thomas Hardy
B. P G Wodehouse
C. Charles Dickens
D. J W Von Goethe

330. *Pride and Prejudice* was written by
A. Anton Chekhov B. Maxim Gorky
C. Jane Austen D. Anthony West

331. *In the Afternoon Time* is the English translation of the autobiography of the famous poet, Harivansh Rai Bachchan. The autobiography was translated into English by
A. Vikram Seth
B. Dr Rupert Snell
C. William Faulkner
D. P D Tandon

332. Who is the author of the book *The Celestine Vision?*
A. Paul Hockins B. Salman Rushdie
C. Joseph Conrad D. James Redfield

333. The author of the famous book *Blue Mountain Revisited* is
A. Charles Kingsley B. Virginia Woolf
C. Arthur Koestler D. Peter Topkins

334. Homer was the great poet of the following language
A. Italian B. Greek
C. Arabic D. French

335. When is the Human Rights Day observed every year?
A. 10th April
B. 10th September
C. 10th December
D. 12th December

336. *Godaan* was written by Munshi Prem Chand and it depicts
A. the methodology for taking adequate care of the cows
B. exploitation of simple rural folk by the rich landlords of rural India
C. the mutiny of 1857 in which, Indians refused to bite the *Kartoos* made with cow beef
D. None of the above

337. Manu wrote a book during ancient times in which, he divided the Aryan society into four distinct classes. What was the name of the book?
A. *Arthashastra* B. *Manusmriti*
C. *Moti Mahal* D. *My Truth*

338. R. Venkataraman wrote *My Presidential Years.* What was the main theme of the book?
A. It described the aristocratic procedures being followed in the *Rashtrapati Bhawan* during his tenure as President
B. It described the power equations and ploys in the centre and in the states during his term
C. It described how he felt caged while he was President due to a load of procedures and formalities
D. It explained the machinations of the political party which was in power during his tenure as President

339. The hero of the play cried in the end, "Et Tu, Brute!" and died. Which is the play and who is the author?
A. The Wealth of Nations — Adam Smith
B. Mein Kempf — Adolf Hitler
C. Julius Caesar — William Shakespeare
D. None of the above

340. Don Veto Corleone was the undisputed king of the underworld in this novel. This masterpiece was also converted into a film in which Al Pacino played the role of the Don. What is the name of the novel and that of the author?
A. *A Farewell to Arms* — E Hemingway
B. *The Godfather* — Mario Puzo
C. *From Here to Eternity* — James Jones
D. *Dialogue with Death* — Arthur Koestler

341. *Gypsy Camp Vanishes Into the Blue* was a famous blockbuster movie made by the erstwhile USSR. The original story was written by a famous author. His name is
A. Leo Tolstoy
B. Anton Chekhov
C. Maxim Gorky
D. Leon Uris

342. The total number of *Puranas* written during the Vedic age is
A. 22
B. 9
C. 18
D. 25

343. In computer network terminology. WAN stands for
A. World area network
B. Wide area network
C. Wide array net
D. Wireless area network

344. The first woman in the world to have climbed Mt. Everest twice is
A. Bachendri Pal
B. Molly Chacko
C. Santosh Yadav
D. Theresia Kiesl

345. According to *The Ramayana,* who received the last teaching lessons from the knowledge-able Ravana while he was on his death-bed?
A. Rama
B. Sugreeva
C. Laxmana
D. Both A and C

346. He was a German but he saved many a Jew from the cruel hands of the Nazis. A movie was made on this theme which won the coveted Oscar Prize. The book and the author are
A. *Operation Shylock* — Philip Roth
B. *Schindler's List* — Thomas Keneally
C. *The Rescue* — Joseph Conrad
D. *The Slave* — Isaac Bashevis Singer

347. He was the favourite assistant of Sherlock Holmes, the famous character created by Arthur Conan Doyle. His name is
A. Zhivago
B. Watson
C. Hawkins
D. Hector

348. 'New Silk Route' is a rail route which links China with the European Country ______.
A. Germany
B. France
C. Italy
D. None of the above

349. He wrote *Sharmili*, *Gaylord* and *Kati Patang*. His novels were written in Hindi and some of them have been converted into films also. His name is
A. Gita Mehta
B. B N Mullick
C. Nirad C Chaudhary
D. Gulshan Nanda

350. Pt. Shiv Kumar Sharma is an exponent of
A. Mandolin B. Santoor
C. Sitar D. Veena

ANSWERS

1	2	3	4	5	6	7	8	9	10
C	B	A	D	B	B	B	B	B	A
11	**12**	**13**	**14**	**15**	**16**	**17**	**18**	**19**	**20**
B	C	D	A	A	C	B	C	A	B

21	**22**	**23**	**24**	**25**	**26**	**27**	**28**	**29**	**30**
D	B	B	D	D	C	A	C	C	C
31	**32**	**33**	**34**	**35**	**36**	**37**	**38**	**39**	**40**
C	A	A	C	D	C	A	B	B	D
41	**42**	**43**	**44**	**45**	**46**	**47**	**48**	**49**	**50**
B	C	B	B	C	D	A	A	D	A
51	**52**	**53**	**54**	**55**	**56**	**57**	**58**	**59**	**60**
D	A	C	A	C	B	C	A	C	C
61	**62**	**63**	**64**	**65**	**66**	**67**	**68**	**69**	**70**
B	A	C	B	D	D	A	C	C	D
71	**72**	**73**	**74**	**75**	**76**	**77**	**78**	**79**	**80**
B	B	B	B	C	D	C	D	C	A
81	**82**	**83**	**84**	**85**	**86**	**87**	**88**	**89**	**90**
B	B	A	C	B	B	B	C	B	D
91	**92**	**93**	**94**	**95**	**96**	**97**	**98**	**99**	**100**
C	B	A	B	B	A	B	D	B	A
101	**102**	**103**	**104**	**105**	**106**	**107**	**108**	**109**	**110**
D	D	A	C	D	A	B	C	B	C
111	**112**	**113**	**114**	**115**	**116**	**117**	**118**	**119**	**120**
B	B	C	B	A	C	C	B	B	C
121	**122**	**123**	**124**	**125**	**126**	**127**	**128**	**129**	**130**
D	C	D	C	B	A	C	C	A	A
131	**132**	**133**	**134**	**135**	**136**	**137**	**138**	**139**	**140**
C	C	D	C	D	D	C	C	B	B
141	**142**	**143**	**144**	**145**	**146**	**147**	**148**	**149**	**150**
C	D	A	D	B	B	B	D	B	C
151	**152**	**153**	**154**	**155**	**156**	**157**	**158**	**159**	**160**
A	C	C	C	B	D	B	A	A	D
161	**162**	**163**	**164**	**165**	**166**	**167**	**168**	**169**	**170**
B	B	C	B	C	D	B	C	C	A
171	**172**	**173**	**174**	**175**	**176**	**177**	**178**	**179**	**180**
B	D	A	D	A	C	C	C	D	C
181	**182**	**183**	**184**	**185**	**186**	**187**	**188**	**189**	**190**
A	A	D	B	D	A	D	D	D	B
191	**192**	**193**	**194**	**195**	**196**	**197**	**198**	**199**	**200**
C	B	C	A	B	A	D	B	D	A
201	**202**	**203**	**204**	**205**	**206**	**207**	**208**	**209**	**210**
D	A	B	B	C	B	C	B	C	A
211	**212**	**213**	**214**	**215**	**216**	**217**	**218**	**219**	**220**
C	B	C	A	C	B	A	D	C	B
221	**222**	**223**	**224**	**225**	**226**	**227**	**228**	**229**	**230**
A	C	D	C	B	A	A	D	C	C
231	**232**	**233**	**234**	**235**	**236**	**237**	**238**	**239**	**240**
A	D	B	A	B	B	C	C	B	C
241	**242**	**243**	**244**	**245**	**246**	**247**	**248**	**249**	**250**
A	B	D	C	B	B	B	A	C	C

251	252	253	254	255	256	257	258	259	260
C	C	D	C	C	A	B	C	D	D
261	**262**	**263**	**264**	**265**	**266**	**267**	**268**	**269**	**270**
B	B	D	C	B	C	C	A	C	B
271	**272**	**273**	**274**	**275**	**276**	**277**	**278**	**279**	**280**
C	C	C	C	D	B	B	C	B	C
281	**282**	**283**	**284**	**285**	**286**	**287**	**288**	**289**	**290**
B	D	C	A	C	C	A	C	A	B
291	**292**	**293**	**294**	**295**	**296**	**297**	**298**	**299**	**300**
D	D	B	A	C	A	D	C	C	D
301	**302**	**303**	**304**	**305**	**306**	**307**	**308**	**309**	**310**
D	D	C	A	C	A	B	D	B	C
311	**312**	**313**	**314**	**315**	**316**	**317**	**318**	**319**	**320**
C	A	C	A	B	C	B	D	B	C
321	**322**	**323**	**324**	**325**	**326**	**327**	**328**	**329**	**330**
A	C	A	C	B	A	B	C	C	C
331	**332**	**333**	**334**	**335**	**336**	**337**	**338**	**339**	**340**
B	D	D	B	C	B	B	C	C	B
341	**342**	**343**	**344**	**345**	**346**	**347**	**348**	**349**	**350**
C	C	B	C	C	B	B	A	D	B

* * * * *